Criminal Investigation
The Art and the Science

Michael D. Lyman
Columbia College of Missouri

edition

6

Prentice Hall
Boston   Columbus   Indianapolis   New York   San Francisco   Upper Saddle River
Amsterdam   Cape Town   Dubai   London   Madrid   Milan   Munich   Paris   Montreal   Toronto
Delhi   Mexico City   São Paulo   Sydney   Hong Kong   Seoul   Singapore   Taipei   Tokyo

Editor in Chief: Vernon Anthony
Acquisitions Editor: Eric Krassow
Development Editor: Elisa Rogers
Editorial Assistant: Lynda Cramer
Director of Marketing: David Gesell
Marketing Manager: Adam Kloza
Senior Marketing Coordinator: Alicia Wozniak
Senior Managing Editor: JoEllen Gohr
Project Manager: Jessica H. Sykes
Senior Operations Supervisor: Pat Tonneman
Operations Specialist: Deidra Skahill
Senior Art Director: Diane Ernsberger
Text and Cover Designer: Rokusek Design
Manager, Visual Research: Beth Brenzel

Photo Researcher: Jerry Marshall
Manager, Rights and Permissions: Zina Arabia
Image Permission Coordinator: Debbie Hewitson
Manager, Cover Visual Research & Permissions: Karen Sanatar
Cover Art: Rokusek Design
Media Editor: Michelle Churma
Lead Media Project Manager: Karen Bretz
Full-Service Project Management: Karpagam Jagadeesan
Composition: GGS Higher Education Resources, A Division of Premedia Global, Inc.
Printer/Binder: Quebecor World Color/Versailles
Cover Printer: Coral Graphics
Text Font: Sabon

Library of Congress Cataloging-in-Publication Data

Lyman, Michael D.
    Criminal investigation : the art and the science / Michael D. Lyman. — 6th ed.
        p. cm.
    Includes bibliographical references and index.
    ISBN-13: 978-0-13-506057-5 (alk. paper)
    ISBN-10: 0-13-506057-5 (alk. paper)
    1. Criminal investigation.   I. Title
    HV8073.L94 2011
    363.25–dc22

                                        2009044103

10 9 8 7 6 5 4 3 2 1

Prentice Hall
is an imprint of

www.pearsonhighered.com

ISBN 13: 978-0-13-506057-5
ISBN 10:   0-13-506057-5

dedication

This book is dedicated to the most important people in my life, my wife Julie and my daughter Kelsey, who have offered their continual support of me in the painstaking preparation of this book. Their understanding of this huge undertaking played no small role in this book's successful completion.
Thanks, guys.

brief contents

contents

PART I

Fundamentals of Criminal Investigation   1

chapter 1

chapter 2

PART II

Follow-Up Investigative Processes   99

PART III

Obtaining Information   191

chapter 7

chapter 8

PART IV

Crimes Against Persons   283

PART V

Crimes Against Property   453

PART VI

Vice and Profit-Related Crime   541

PART VII

preface

Criminal investigation represents a timeless and dynamic field of scientific study. This book, evolving now into its sixth edition, was written with the perception that crime detection is a field that relies heavily on the past experiences of investigators as well as recent practical, forensic, and technological innovations. The investigator's success in crime detection can be influenced by several external variables. For example, increased pressure by public interest groups and courts of law has caused police supervisors to place greater emphasis on case management and officer accountability. In addition, because of increased social problems associated with drug abuse, criminal violence, and the use of computers, the public spotlight has focused more than ever before on methods of crime detection and the successful prosecution of offenders. Finally, because of the ongoing incidence of mass and serial murders, the public is now more insistent that criminal investigations are conducted quickly and with thoroughness.

This book is intended to meet the needs of students and others interested in criminal justice by presenting information in a logical flow, paralleling the steps and considerations observed in an actual criminal investigation. Additionally, it is designed to fulfill an ongoing need for a book that explains clearly and thoughtfully the fundamentals of criminal investigation as practiced by police investigators on the job in communities across the nation.

The book is written with several observations in mind. First, as its title indicates, it is designed to blend scientific theories of crime detection with a practical approach to criminal investigation. Its underlying assumption is that sound criminal investigations depend on an understanding of the science of crime detection procedures and the art of anticipating human behavior. There is yet another critical observation made in the book: It recognizes that both the uniformed officer and the criminal investigator play important roles in the field of criminal investigation. The duties of each are outlined throughout the book, recognizing that there is a fundamental need for both to work in tandem throughout many aspects of the criminal investigation process.

One underlying theme of the book is that as with all police endeavors, criminal investigation is a law enforcement responsibility that must be conducted within the framework of the U.S. Constitution and the practices of a democratic society. Consequently, court decisions and case studies have been quoted extensively for clarification of issues and general reader information.

New to This Edition

- The sixth edition represents a major revision, resulting in a total of 18 chapters (opposed to 23 from the last edition). The guiding philosophy behind the revision of this text is to make it easier for instructors to align their coverage of the text's material with the class schedule and academic term.
- Features of the sixth edition include new and improved pedagogical aids such as the MyCrimeKit companion website (www.mycrimekit.com), which includes numerous media and tools to assist the student in understanding career choices in forensics and criminal investigation, reviewing material

contained in the chapters, and observing simulations relating to the duties of a criminal investigator in the field.

- Margin notes throughout the chapters mark videos, simulations, and other media on MyCrimeKit that relates to the chapter material. A box at the end of each chapter lists the study tools and resources available for that chapter on MyCrimeKit.

The updates in this edition are considerable. These include:

- police lineups and misidentifications
- new research on eyewitness testimony
- updated statistical crime data and new material on identity theft investigations and computer crimes
- new sections on terrorism, gangs, white-collar crime, and organized crime
- new discussions of cognitive interview techniques
- a newly incorporated piece on the SAFE exam as it relates to victims of assault
- new research on the hazards of undercover work and advances in forensic science
- updated case studies as well as photos and graphics
- each chapter ends with a newly designed "Summary Checklist" section, which serves as a chapter review

SUPPLEMENTS

Supplements include an Instructor's Manual with Test Item File, TestGen test generator, PowerPoint presentations, and a CourseSmart electronic version of the text.

To access supplementary materials online, instructors need to request an instructor access code. Go to **www.pearsonhighered.com/irc**, where you can register for an instructor access code. Within 48 hours after registering, you will receive a confirming e-mail, including an instructor access code. Once you have received your code, go to the site and log on for full instructions on downloading the materials you wish to use.

In summary, I am hopeful that this will prove to be an engaging textbook that is descriptive of the duties of modern-day crime detection and police professionalism. For more efficient use, this book has been designed to follow closely to a standard curriculum format. Accordingly, each chapter contains key terms and discussion questions that also aid in the instructional process. Finally, as a learning aid, this text is accompanied by a companion website that offers videos and test items as well as many other learning tools. I know this book will provide you with what you need to understand the art of criminal investigation as well as the many new forms of scientific innovations that modern investigators now use to catch perpetrators of some of the nation's most heinous crimes. Read and enjoy!

Michael D. Lyman

acknowledgments

No book can be written entirely as a solo effort, and this project was no exception. The preparation of this book represents hundreds of painstaking hours maintaining continuous contact with criminal justice agencies, federal information clearinghouses, police practitioners, and colleagues in the field of criminal justice. In addition, to offer the reader the most up-to-date and relevant information, it was important to consult libraries, police journals, periodicals, newspapers, government publications, and other sources of literature germane to the field of crime detection on an ongoing basis.

Many persons were helpful in the preparation of this book, including practitioners in the field as well as experts in academe. Among these, the contributions of certain persons deserve special recognition. Included are the men and women of the Columbia Police Department, the Missouri State Highway Patrol, agents from the Federal Bureau of Investigation and Drug Enforcement Administration, contributors from the Department of Homeland Security, and the International Association of Chiefs of Police.

A special debt of gratitude goes to Detective Michael Himmel of the Columbia Police Department (ret.) and Brian Hoey of the Missouri State Highway Patrol Crime Laboratory, who both provided a number of crime scene and laboratory photos for this new edition. Without the cooperation and guidance of these persons and organizations, this book would not have been possible.

A special thank you is also well deserved for Associate Editor Elisa Rogers and Senior Acquisitions Editor Tim Peyton, along with the many other dedicated publishing professionals at Pearson for their hard work and support for the sixth edition of this text. Finally, I would like to extend special thanks to those criminal justice academics and practitioners who painstakingly reviewed the manuscript of this book. These persons include James T. Burnett, Rockland County Community College, Suffern, NY; David Graff, Kent State University—Tuscarawas Campus, New Philadelphia, OH; Harold Frossard, Moraine Valley Community College, Palos Hills, IL; Mark McCoy, University of Central Oklahoma, Edmond, OK; Elvage Murphy, Edinboro University, Erie, PA; and Gary Yoshonis, Grossmont Community College, San Diego, CA.

Thanks also to the following reviewers: James M. Adcock, University of New Haven; John M. Beal, University of Akron; Aric Steven Frazier, Vincennes University; Maurice Godwin, North Carolina Central University; Lisa McBride, Tallahassee Community College; and Robert NeVille, College of the Siskiyous.

Without the support and assistance of all these people and many more, this book would not have become a reality. Thank you all.

Michael D. Lyman

Michael D. Lyman is a Professor of Criminal Justice at Columbia College of Missouri, located in Columbia, MO. In addition to being a teaching faculty member, he serves as the program liaison for the Master of Science of Criminal Justice Program and the founder and program director of the college's Forensic Science Program. Before entering the field of college teaching, he was employed as a criminal investigator for state police organizations in Kansas and Oklahoma and has taught literally thousands of law enforcement officers in the proper police techniques and methods of professional criminal investigation. Dr. Lyman has authored numerous textbooks in criminal justice dealing with the areas of criminal investigation, policing, organized crime, drug enforcement, and drug trafficking. He received both his bachelor's and master's degrees from Wichita State University and his Ph.D. from the University of Missouri–Columbia. He has been called upon on an estimated 200 occasions by law enforcement and the legal communities to review criminal investigations and render the results of his evaluations and his opinions in federal court proceedings nationwide.

Textbooks such as this are an ongoing work in progress, and the author welcomes communication and correspondence about his work. Dr. Lyman can be contacted at Columbia College, 1001 Rogers Street, Columbia, MO 65216 or at mlyman@ccis.edu. Thank you for using this textbook.

Michael D. Lyman

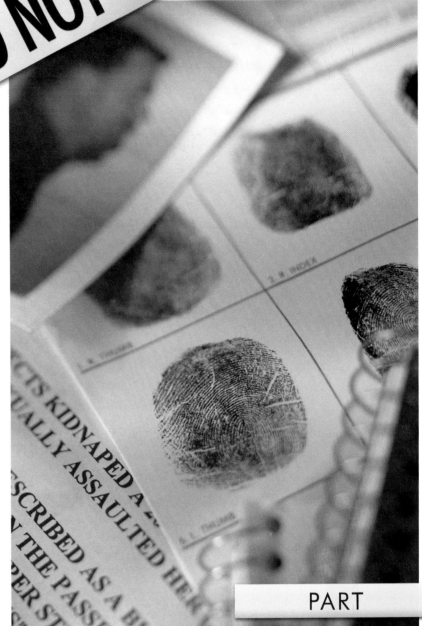

Fundamentals of Criminal Investigation

PART

1

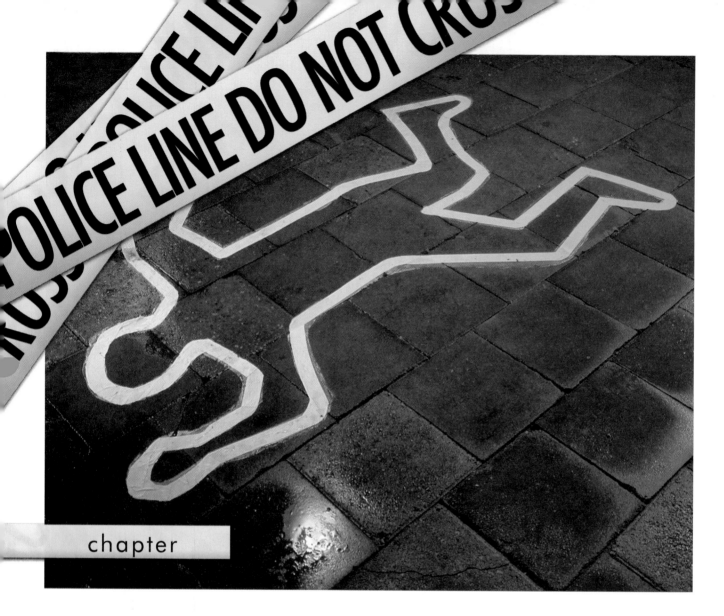

1 Foundations of Criminal Investigation

This chapter will enable you to:

- Understand the myths of crime solving and the criminal investigation process.
- Explain the ways in which our English roots have influenced current methods of criminal investigation.
- Understand the modern developments in science and crime detection.
- Consider recent research in criminal investigation.
- Compare and contrast deductive and inductive reasoning.
- Understand the various types of investigations, investigators, and modes of investigation.
- Explain the role of the patrol officer in the preliminary investigation.

Introduction

The study of criminal investigation involves probing several different fields at once, and is therefore a difficult task about which to write. For example, it is important for an investigator to understand basic techniques of collection and preservation of evidence, but to do so, a fundamental understanding of criminalistics or forensic science is often required. In addition to technical competence, modern-day investigators must be well versed in the law. Legal skills include a working knowledge of criminal law, constitutional law, and rules of evidence, all of which are essential for successful prosecution of a criminal case. This chapter is designed to give the reader the underlying essentials of this field of policing, which is both rewarding and challenging.

The Romance and Reality of Crime Solving

Throughout modern history, people have harbored a fascination with cops and criminals—crime and crime fighting. Whenever there is a public crime scene, large groups of people gather to watch crime scene investigators in action. For the average citizen, police cars and emergency units with their screaming sirens and flashing lights spark an insatiable curiosity. Fueling people's interest and imagination are newspapers and periodicals that sensationalize criminal investigations, which often involve both heinous and interesting aspects. Recent examples are the 2008 and 2009 Bernard Madoff and Caylee Anthony cases, both of which illustrate the importance of sound investigative principles.

For example, in 2008, Bernard Madoff was arrested and accused of masterminding history's largest investor fraud scheme committed by a single person. Madoff headed the Wall Street firm Bernard L. Madoff Investment Securities LLC, from 1960 until his arrest on December 11, 2008. His sons Andrew and Mark had tipped off authorities, saying that their father had confided in them that his investment fund was a colossal Ponzi scheme. Since Madoff's arrest, his assets and those of his firm were frozen, affecting many businesses and charity organizations that had trusted money to him, forcing several of them to close. One client of Madoff's, René-Thierry Magon de la Villehuchet, a prominent French businessman whose firm, Access International Advisors LLC, had invested $1.4 billion with Madoff's firm, was found dead in an apparent suicide on December 23, 2008. According to the U.S. Securities and Exchange Commission, Madoff has admitted that his firm's liabilities amount to "approximately $50 billion." (Read more about Bernard Madoff in Chapter 17.)

In another case, 22-year-old Casey Anthony waited at least a month before reporting that her daughter Caylee, 2, was missing. And even then, it wasn't Casey who called the Sheriff's Office to report that the toddler had been abducted; it was Casey's mother, Cynthia Anthony. In July 2008, Cindy Anthony, Casey's mother, called Orange County Florida's 911 line. After initially reporting that she wanted her daughter arrested for stealing her car, Cindy told the dispatcher, "I have a 3-year-old that's missing for a month." An hour later, Cindy called 911 again. This time she reported, "There's something wrong," she told the dispatcher. "I found my daughter's car today. It smells like there's been a dead body in the . . . car."

On July 17, two days after Casey reported Caylee missing, a police cadaver dog alerted to the odor of a decomposing human body coming from the trunk of Casey's Pontiac. Investigators also found human hair in the trunk, similar, they said, to Caylee's hair. And they found what they described as a "questionable" stain, meaning it was possibly caused by blood or other human bodily fluids.

FIGURE 1.1 Photo of Caylee Anthony.

Lab results showed air samples taken from the trunk of Casey's car indicated it had once held a decomposing human body.

Preliminary FBI lab reports also showed the presence of chloroform in the trunk, a chemical compound that can be used to render a person unconscious. Investigators discovered that someone using a computer in Casey Anthony's home had searched Web sites for information on how to make chloroform three months before Caylee was last seen.

On October 14, 2008, a Florida grand jury indicted Casey Anthony for first-degree murder, aggravated manslaughter, aggravated child abuse, and four counts of lying to investigators. Over the following few weeks, Casey bounced in and out of jail on various charges, but Caylee's body had not yet been found. On December 11, 2008, a utility worker found the remains of Caylee Anthony in a black plastic trash bag. The case is ongoing as of the writing of this book. (Read more about the Caylee Anthony abduction and investigation in Chapter 12.)

These cases illustrate the complexities of the investigative process and show the great extent that the public shows interest in such cases.

Adults aren't the only ones who show an interest in crime detection; children too visualize the clashing forces of good and evil in vividly illustrated children's books, comic books, and early morning television cartoons. Examples are Hollywood movies *Batman: The Dark Knight* (2008) and *X-Men Origins* (2009) that portray the clash between good and evil. Even television shows watched by young children portray fictional crime fighters such as Kim Possible, Ben 10, and the Power Puff Girls who, with each episode, confront evil foes. Indeed, American pop culture typically portrays the conflict between the forces of good and evil in movies, novels, and television cartoons.

Notorious outlaw gangs of the Old West have also interested people for decades. Gangs active on the western frontier, such as the Younger brothers and the Dalton gang, represent the colorful heritage of the antihero. Another outlaw, Jesse James, was one of the most famous of the American West. During his time, he acquired a Robin Hood reputation. With brother Frank and several other men, the James gang gained national notoriety by robbing banks, trains, and stagecoaches.

Detective magazines, books, and movies pitting the shrewd criminal against his or her persevering police counterpart have also perpetuated the detective mystique. For generations, fabled yarns featuring sleuths such as Sherlock

Holmes and Hercule Poirot have presented readers with a menagerie of far-fetched tales filled with unlikely clues and colorful suspects. In fact, part of the allure of the classic detective novels of the early twentieth century was the introduction of the private eye. Mickey Spillane's Mike Hammer, for example, had a remorseless desire to punish wrongdoers who managed to escape an impotent criminal justice system while walking a fine legal line himself.

As with the private eye, the spy of the 1960s enlivened espionage stories featuring such heroes as James Bond, whose popularity rivaled even that of Sherlock Holmes. In reading the material, however, readers would gain little practical insight into the mind of the criminal, the nature of crime, the science of detection, the techniques of law enforcement officers, or courtroom procedures where one is found either guilty or innocent. Although entertaining, such stories bear little resemblance to the real world of criminal investigation.

FIGURE 1.2 During the settlement of the western frontier, wanted posters were used to identify persons wanted by law enforcement.
Courtesy of the State Historical Society of Missouri.

The Historical Context of Criminal Investigation

The history of criminal investigation is vast, and over the years many writers have attempted to engage the topic. In this section, we focus on the roots of our criminal justice heritage in Great Britain as it pertains to the field of criminal investigation.

Criminal Investigation and Our English Heritage

We begin our story during the era of Europe's Industrial Revolution, which attracted the peasant class from the countryside into the towns and cities. The ensuing crime wave forced law enforcement officials to take drastic measures. As a result, **thief catchers** were recruited from the riffraff of the streets to aid law-enforcement officials in locating criminals. Two classes of thief catchers were identified: (1) hirelings, whose motivations were mercenary in nature; and (2) social climbers, who would implicate their accomplices in order to move up the social ladder.

One hireling, Jonathan Wild, gained fame in eighteenth-century England for operating a London brothel that also served as headquarters for thieves and thugs, with whom he was well acquainted. Coining the phrase "set a thief to catch a thief," Wild operated simultaneously as an undercover operative for London's authorities and as a criminal in London's underworld. It soon became clear, however, that he could profit more from arranging the return of stolen goods to the police than from selling the goods at outrageous discounts to the local fence. So while he acted as the receiver of stolen goods masquerading as the "recoverer" of lost property, he also served as the middleman, taking his cut for finding stolen goods while hiding and protecting thieves in his employ.

In England, the first police worked only at night and were originally called the Watch of London. They soon developed into the Old Charleys, who were paid by the residents they served. These parish constables originated in London in 1253 and lasted until 1829. Soon after the hanging of Jonathan Wild, Henry Fielding was appointed magistrate in Westminster, a city adjacent to central London. Fielding, a writer known for his novel *Tom Jones,* located himself in a house on Bow Street that served as both home and office and soon began what is credited as England's first police force.

The Bow Street Runners. During the 1750s, crimes such as burglary and street robbery were rampant in England. Fielding took on the challenge of reducing the profits realized by criminals. Working relationships were established with local business owners, in particular pawnbrokers, who were provided with lists of stolen property. Fielding encouraged them to contact him if any stolen property came to their attention. Fielding took seriously his new duty as crime fighter and promptly employed new crime-fighting methods. One such method was the appointment of a handful of parish constables acclimated to night watchman duties. These trackers soon began performing criminal investigation functions and became well known as successful thief takers by using their ties with London's criminal underworld. Originally called "Mr. Fielding's People," they soon became known as the **Bow Street Runners,** the first well-known investigative body in England. Fielding's runners were not paid as police officers but rather, in terms of thief-taker rewards, a percentage of all fines resulting from successful prosecution of thieves. Shortly after his appointment as magistrate, Fielding's health deteriorated, and he started to use a wheelchair. As a result, his half-brother, John Fielding, was appointed to share his magistracy. Because of his blindness, John Fielding was soon dubbed the "blind beak" (*beak* meaning magistrate) to the criminal underworld in London.

The Bow Street Runners were forerunners of a trend in policing for specialization within the police force. In fact, by 1800, the Bow Street Police Office was considered by many to be the leading law enforcement organization in the area. Johnson adds: "Even if the evils of the justice/constable system had been eliminated from Bow Street Office operations, no local jurisdiction could combat the rising crime wave throughout London."[1] Between 1760 and 1800, Fielding was given authority to organize a horse patrol, which was later followed by a permanent foot patrol. The patrol officers, smartly outfitted in red vests and blue jackets and trousers, became the pioneers of England's uniformed police.

The London Metropolitan Police. The great watershed in British police development occurred in 1829 with the establishment of the London Metropolitan Police Department. Officers of the department were dubbed **bobbies** after the department's founder, Home Secretary Sir Robert Peel. The "new" police were England's first paid, full-time police force, consisting of about 1,000 uniformed officers. In addition, they replaced the old constables, such as the Bow Street Runners, who had ultimately gained a reputation of incompetency and inefficiency. Indeed, the bobbies were required to meet rigid standards of professionalism. Minimum standards included minimum weight and height requirements and standards of literacy and character. A detective bureau was created in the police force in 1842 but was not publicly acknowledged until some 35 years, later for fear that the specter of French-style repression would be remembered.

Technology in crime detection began to flourish during the nineteenth century with the creation of a personal identification system by Alphonse Bertillon, the director of the criminal identification section of the Paris Police Department. The **Bertillon system** was based on the idea that certain aspects of the human body, such as skeletal size, ear shaping, and eye color, remained the same after a person had reached full physical maturity. It used a combination of photographs with standardized physical measurements. In the mid-1840s, the study of fingerprint patterns became a popular means to identify suspects in crime. Although the use of fingerprints is a commonplace today, it wasn't until the late nineteenth century that it was learned that a person's fingerprints could act as a unique, unchangeable method of personal identification. Such discoveries have been credited to the Englishmen William J. Herschel and Henry Faulds, who were working in Asia at the time. The use of fingerprints was refined by Sir Francis Galton and was adopted by Scotland Yard in 1901.

The Creation of Scotland Yard. For many people, much misunderstanding has existed about the function and role of **Scotland Yard**. Some believe that it represents a single police authority in Great Britain. In fact, it is the headquarters of London's Metropolitan Police and has never exerted any authority over other police organizations in Great Britain. Although London's Metropolitan Police was founded in 1829, it took more than 10 years to organize a detective branch. Even then, however, "the Yard" was only a small division within the department. The strength of the force was increased in 1867 after an incident in which an explosion occurred when a small group of Irishmen were trying to free a prisoner from the Clerkenwell House of Detention. Several citizens were killed. A decade later, another reorganization occurred when several senior detectives of Scotland Yard were convicted of corruption charges.

A strengthened Criminal Investigation Division (CID) was then set up and has endured to the present. In fact, the phrase "Call in Scotland Yard" refers entirely to the investigative section of the force. The CID officers of the Yard are selected from candidates who have served as uniformed constables. To avoid the problem of complacency within the force, officers are regularly rotated from the uniformed division to the detective division and back again.

Criminal Investigation in America

As the American frontier moved westward during the nineteenth century, outlaws posed serious problems in newly settled areas. Mining camps and cattle towns seemed to experience more violence than other areas. The movement west had moved men and women far from the institutions that had served them previously. Law enforcement agencies and criminal courts, if present at all, made only minor strides in protecting the vast areas under their jurisdictions. Indeed, it was in these areas that criminals could easily hide and witnesses would often move away, making detection and apprehension of criminals a discouraging task.

Following the lead of London's police force, the first professional police forces were established in the United States at Boston in 1837, New York in 1844, and Philadelphia in 1854. By the 1870s, almost all major U.S. cities had municipal police departments. As in England, criminal investigation by public law enforcement was viewed as politically hazardous because it favored only those who could pay. But the rapid growth of cities produced violence, crime, and vice activities that demonstrated a breakdown of social order in small communities. Growing incidents of mob violence between Protestants and Catholics, immigrants and Native Americans, and abolitionists and pro-slavery groups were probably the most crucial catalysts for expanded police functions. During the middle of the nineteenth century, three significant elements emerged that had an impact on criminal investigation:

1. Municipal police were supplemented by the county sheriff in rural areas.
2. Establishment of the Texas Rangers (established before Texas became a state).
3. Expansion of police functions with establishment of the U.S. Marshal's Service and the Secret Service, formed during the Civil War to investigate counterfeiters.

In the 1890s, criminal investigators became an important part of the U.S. Post Office and the Bureau of Immigration and Naturalization. Because of the lack of effective law enforcement in rural areas, however, people banded together on their own to investigate crimes and apprehend perpetrators. Vigilantes in the mining camps would conduct trials and even execute some of the most dangerous offenders. Cattle ranchers would often hire range detectives to capture rustlers. As a result, some business firms emerged, such as the famed Pinkerton's Detective Agency, which offered to protect property and pursue offenders for a fee.

The Pinkerton National Detective Agency. Pinkerton's National Detective Agency, founded in 1850 by Scottish immigrant Allan Pinkerton, was the first organization of its type in the United States. In fact, its organizational structure was later adopted by the Federal Bureau of Investigation (FBI). The Pinkerton Agency was called on by communities to handle cases that local law enforcement officers were unable to investigate due to incompetency or limited resources. Pinkerton offered the field of criminal investigation several innovations in crime detection. For example, he was the first to devise a **rogues' gallery**, which was a compilation of descriptions, methods of operation, hiding places, and names of associates of known criminals.

Pinkerton gained national fame when he uncovered a plot to kill Abraham Lincoln during the 1860s. The plot was designed to kill Lincoln on a train while en route to give his first inaugural speech in Washington. Pinkerton outwitted the assassins by putting Lincoln on an earlier train. Soon after, Pinkerton was placed in charge of the secret service operations during the Civil War. After Pinkerton's death in 1884, agency detectives gained a reputation for the use of violence to undermine unions as well as to frame and convict their leaders. Among the more notable Pinkerton cases were those in which dozens of union spies were used by the infamous Jay Gould to break a strike against the Texas and Pacific Railroads and when Pinkerton detectives were used in 1905 to involve labor leaders in the murder of ex-Governor Frank Steunenberg of Idaho. After Congress declared labor spying unconstitutional in 1937, the industrial division of the Pinkerton agency was officially dissolved.

FIGURE 1.4 Allan Pinkerton, President Abraham Lincoln, and General McClellan at Antietam, Maryland, circa 1866. Courtesy of the Library of Congress.

Prohibition. Prohibition (1920–1933) represented another significant period in which criminal investigation underwent change. Unlike the drug trade of later years, the Volstead Act of the Prohibition period failed to criminalize the purchase or consumption of alcohol—only its manufacture, transportation, and sale. Because liquor was legal in other countries, smuggling (bootlegging) was a major criminal enterprise. Prohibition criminals avoided the federal law against alcohol by creating a cottage industry manufacturing beer and wine at home. By 1924, rival gangs organized themselves for control of "speakeasy" operations, prostitution rings, and virtually any other source of illegal income. Police corruption flourished as many law enforcement officers accepted bribes from mobsters. During this time, the FBI had no jurisdiction in enforcing the Volstead Act. Instead, enforcement responsibility was given to the Treasury Department.

The Creation of the FBI. Probably the single most significant development in criminal investigation in the United States was the establishment of the FBI in 1924. Originating as the Justice Department's Bureau of Investigation in 1907, the FBI originally had very few responsibilities. When new federal laws governing interstate transportation of stolen automobiles were passed, however, the bureau gained much notoriety. John Edgar Hoover, the bureau's newly named director, announced in 1924 that he would strive to eliminate corruption and get the agency out of politics. In doing so, he raised the qualifications of agent personnel, reduced the number of agents nationwide, and closed some field offices. It was

FIGURE 1.5 "We Never Sleep." The famous Pinkerton "private eye" became the logo of Allan Pinkerton's National Detective Agency. Printed with permission of Pinkerton's, Inc.

only after Hoover's death in 1972 that many of his abuses of power surfaced. For example, it became widely known that the FBI kept files on certain persons, such as politicians and adversaries of the FBI. Today, the FBI is one of many federal investigative agencies that has made great strides in professionalizing the field of criminal investigation.

The Increase of Research and Science in Crime Detection

mycrimekit

Review: History of criminal investigation.

The seeds of modern forensic science were sown in the last quarter of the nineteenth century. Progress from that time has been slow but steady. The American Academy of Forensic Sciences (AAFS), a professional organization of forensic scientists in America, was established in 1948. Specific areas of expertise of AAFS members include pathology and biology, toxicology, criminalistics, questioned documents, and forensic odontology and anthropology.

In addition to the development of fingerprinting as an aid to criminal detection, several other forensic advances were either being developed or had already been placed into service by the late nineteenth century. Historic strides in criminal investigation included study in serology, forensic dentistry, and ballistics. For example, research into human blood was vastly expanded during the early twentieth century by Paul Uhlenhuth, a German physician. Uhlenhuth's work created serums that enabled one to distinguish one species of animal blood from another. Consequently, **serology** was a procedure that was established to study human blood stains and distinguish them from the blood of most other animals.

A CLOSER LOOK

Modern Fields of Forensic Science

Today, a number of fields have surfaced relating to forensics and crime detection. Some of these are widely accepted, and others have drawn criticism. Modern fields of forensics include:

- *Computational forensics* concerns the development of algorithms and software to assist forensic examination.

- *Criminalistics* is the application of various sciences to answer questions relating to examination and comparison of biological evidence, trace evidence, impression evidence (such as fingerprints, footwear impressions, and tire tracks), controlled substances, ballistics, firearm and toolmark examination, and other evidence in criminal investigations. Typically, evidence is processed in a crime lab.

- *Digital forensics (computer forensics)* is the application of proven scientific methods and techniques used to recover data from electronic and digital media. Digital Forensic specialists work in the field as well as in the lab (see Data Recovery).

- *Forensic anthropology* is the application of physical anthropology in a legal setting, usually for the recovery and identification of skeletonized human remains.

- *Forensic archaeology* is the application of a combination of archaeological techniques and forensic science, typically in law enforcement.

- *Forensic DNA* analysis takes advantage of the uniqueness of an individual's DNA to answer forensic questions such as determining paternity or maternity or placing a suspect at a crime scene.

- *Forensic entomology* deals with the examination of insects in, on, and around human remains to

A CLOSER LOOK CONTINUED

assist in determination of the time or location of death. It is also possible to determine if the body was moved after death.

- *Forensic geology* deals with trace evidence in the form of soils, minerals, and petroleums.

- *Forensic interviewing* is a method of communicating designed to elicit information and evidence.

- *Forensic meteorology* is a site-specific analysis of past weather conditions.

- *Forensic odontology* is the study of the uniqueness of dentition better known as the study of teeth.

- *Forensic pathology* is a field in which the principles of medicine and pathology are applied to determine a cause of death or injury in the context of a legal inquiry.

- *Forensic psychology* is the study of the mind of an individual using forensic methods. Usually, it determines the circumstances behind a criminal's behavior.

- *Forensic toxicology* is the study of the effect of drugs and poisons on or in the human body.

- *Forensic document examination* or *questioned document examination* answers questions about a disputed document using a variety of scientific processes and methods. Many examinations involve a comparison of the questioned document or components of the document to a set of known standards. The most common type of examination involves handwriting wherein the examiner tries to address concerns about potential authorship.

- *Veterinary forensics* is forensics applied to crimes involving animals.

Thematic Question

If you are interested in any of the above-listed career fields, is your interest more in field investigative processes as a criminal investigator or those that take place in a laboratory as a criminalist? To what extent have you given thought to the fields of biology and chemistry to further a career in forensic science?

In what other ways do you foresee the fields of science and crime detection becoming more infused as time goes by?

Sources: Kind S., and M. Overman. (1972). *Science against crime*. New York: Doubleday, pp. 12–13; McRoberts, F. From the start, a faulty science. *Chicago Tribune*, October 19, 2004. Available at http://www.baltimoresun.com/news/specials/chi-041019forensics,0,4915311.story; Raloff, J. (2008). Judging science. *Science News* 173(3):42. Available at http://www.sciencenews.org/articles/20080119/bob10.asp.

Forensic dentistry was widely studied during the mid-nineteenth century as a means of identifying teeth marks in victims. Because bite marks are so distinctive, they are now commonly used as evidence. Whether on the body of a suspect or victim, such evidence can implicate suspects in crimes such as assault, rape, and murder. **Ballistics** is yet another critical area of investigative detection. In 1835, the use of ballistics to solve a murder was first conducted by Bow Street Runner Henry Goddard. Since then, evidence such as powder burns and markings on bullets and casings is accepted as valuable evidence to connect suspects with both victims and weapons used.

Today, increases in the demand for scientific techniques by investigators have created special financial burdens on law enforcement agencies. Techniques such as these call for people with a high degree of formal education in areas such as chemistry, forensic science, and physiology.

Criminal Investigation Research

As with other aspects of criminal justice, research plays an important role in helping us to understand how criminal investigations can be more effective. Early studies by both the RAND Corporation and the Police Executive Research Forum challenged long-held opinions about criminal investigation and made some practical recommendations.

mycrimekit

Video: Job profile: FBI Agent

The RAND Corporation Study

In the late 1970s, the National Institute of Law Enforcement and Criminal Justice awarded a grant to the RAND Corporation to undertake a nationwide study of criminal investigations by police agencies in major U.S. cities. The goals of the study were to determine how police investigations were organized and managed, as well as to assess various activities as they relate to the effectiveness of overall police functioning. Until this study, police investigators had not been placed under as much scrutiny as those in patrol functions or other areas of policing.

Design of the Study. The focus of the RAND study was the investigation of "index" offenses: serious crimes such as murder, robbery, and rape. Other less serious crimes, such as drug violations, gambling, and prostitution, were not considered in the study. A national survey was conducted that assessed investigative practices of all municipal and county police agencies employing more than 150 sworn personnel or serving a jurisdiction with a population over 100,000. Observations and interviews were conducted in more than 25 departments, which were chosen to represent various investigative methods.

The *Uniform Crime Reports* (UCRs), administered by the FBI, were used to determine the outcome of investigations. Data on the allocation of investigative endeavors were obtained from a computerized network operated by the Kansas City Police Department. In addition, information from the National Crime Victimization Survey and the UCRs were linked to identify the effectiveness of arrest and the overall relationships between departments. Finally, the study analyzed case samples to determine how specific cases were solved.

Recommendations of the Study. A number of policy recommendations were made as a result of the study. First, it was recommended that post-arrest activities be coordinated more closely with the prosecutor's office. This could be accomplished by assigning an investigator to the prosecutor's office or by permitting prosecutors discretionary guidance over the practices of investigators, thus increasing the number of prosecutable cases. The second recommendation was that patrol officers be afforded greater responsibilities in conducting preliminary investigations, providing greater case-screening capabilities for investigators while eliminating redundancy. The study suggests that many cases can be closed at the preliminary investigation stage. Therefore, patrol officers should be trained to perform such duties. The third recommendation was to increase forensic resources for processing latent prints and to develop a system to organize and search fingerprint files more effectively. Finally, the study recommended that with regard to investigations of cases that the agency chose to pursue, a distinction should be made between cases that require routine clerical skills and those that require special investigative abilities. Investigations falling into the second category should be handled through a specialized investigation section.

In addition to the RAND Corporation's study, several others have offered support for its findings. Block and Weidman's study of the New York Police Department and Greenberg et al.'s decision-making model for felony investigations both support the idea that patrol officers make the majority of arrests during preliminary investigations and can provide excellent case-screening benefits for investigations.[2]

The PERF Study

In one important study, the Police Executive Research Forum (PERF) considered the roles played by detectives and patrol officers in the course of burglary and robbery investigations. The study examined three areas: DeKalb County, Georgia; St. Petersburg, Florida; and Wichita, Kansas. Of the major findings of the study,

Recommendations of the RAND Study

☑ Coordinate police investigations more closely with prosecutors.

☑ Expand the investigative role of patrol officers.

☑ Provide additional resources to process, organize, and search for latent prints.

☑ Distinguish between cases that can be handled clerically and those that require specially trained investigators.

several observations were made.[3] For example, PERF concluded that detectives and patrol officers contributed equally to the resolution of burglary and robbery cases. However, it was determined that in most cases, a period of four hours (stretched over several days) was sufficient to close cases and that 75 percent of burglary and robbery cases were suspended in less than two days due to a lack of leads. In the remainder of cases, detectives played a major role in follow-up work conducted to identify and arrest suspects. It was determined, however, that both detectives and patrol personnel are too reliant on victim information for identification purposes, as opposed to checking leads from sources such as informants, witnesses, and other information sources in the police department.

The implications of the PERF study suggest that there is not as much waste or mismanagement in investigations as earlier thought as a result of similar studies. The value of follow-up investigations by detectives in identifying and arresting suspects is also thought to be much greater than indicated by earlier studies.

Other Recommendations. The PERF study also recommended that greater emphasis be placed on the collection and use of physical evidence when applicable. Although physical evidence is seldom used in identifying suspects, it can be effective in corroborating other evidence of suspect identification, indicating that although not all police departments use extensive training of evidence technicians, many have established policies regulating situations in which they should be used. In the past, many departments overused the services of evidence technicians in cases in which physical evidence was minimal, resulting in the collection of more evidence than required. As a result, another recommendation by the PERF study is that police departments develop policies and guidelines regulating the use of evidence technicians in routine cases such as burglary and robbery when there has been no physical injury to victims. This policy should be based on the assumption that if the suspects can be found through other means of identification, physical evidence is not likely to be useful.

Yet another recommendation of the PERF study is that officers dedicate greater effort to locating witnesses through the use of a neighborhood canvass. This was not found to be common practice by patrol officers in the cities studied because initial information was commonly learned via interviews with witnesses and victims. It was suggested that to expand the scope of their investigations, patrol officers seek additional witnesses and victims through a neighborhood canvass. Finally, PERF recommended that patrol officers make more extensive use of department records and informants to develop and identify suspects. Although checking department records would be a relatively easy task, the skills needed to develop and interview informants are not common among patrol officers. Supervisors in the patrol area could make a greater effort to provide such training to street officers to help them develop informants.

Computer-Aided Investigations

One example of how science and technology has changed crime and criminal investigation is the personal computer. Discussed in greater detail in Chapter 17, modern-day criminals make regular use of computers to communicate, share, and store information. However, the law enforcement community has also taken advantage of the computer age. For example, many police departments use large computer databases that can cross-reference specific information about crimes to determine patterns and to identify suspects. One of the earliest of these programs was HITMAN, developed by the Hollywood, California, Police Department in 1985. HITMAN has since evolved into a department-wide database that assists detectives in the Los Angeles Police Department (LAPD) in solving violent crimes. The LAPD uses a similar computer program to track a target population of approximately 60,000 gang members.[4]

Computers use artificial intelligence to make inferences based on available information and to draw conclusions or make recommendations to the systems operators. **Expert systems**, as these computer models are often called, depend on three components:

1. The user interface or terminal
2. A knowledge base containing information already known in the area of investigation
3. A computer program, known as an inference engine, that compares user input and stores information according to established decision-making rules

Numerous expert systems exist today. For example, one is used by the FBI's National Center for the Analysis of Violent Crime (NCAVC) in a project designed to profile violent serial criminals. The NCAVC PC system depends on computer models of criminal profiling to provide a theoretical basis for the development of investigative strategies. A number of other systems have been developed that specifically focus on serological (blood serum) analysis, narcotics interdiction, serial murder and rape, and counterterrorism.[5]

Similar to expert systems are **relational databases**, which permit fast and easy sorting of large records. Perhaps the best-known early criminal justice database was called Big Floyd. It was developed in the 1980s by the FBI in conjunction with the Institute for Defense Analyses. Big Floyd was designed to access more than 3 million records in the FBI's organized crime information system and to allow investigators to decide which federal statutes apply in a given situation and whether investigators have enough evidence for a successful prosecution. In the years since Big Floyd was developed, other relational databases targeting offenders of various types have been created, including computer systems to track deadbeat parents and quack physicians. In 1996, President Bill Clinton ordered the Department of Justice to create a computerized national registry of sex offenders. The national sex offender registry, developed as part of an overhaul of the FBI's computer systems, went online in 1999.

Some systems are even more problem specific. For example, ImAger, a product of Face Software, Inc., uses computer technology to artificially age photographs of missing children. The program has been used successfully to identify and recover a number of children. In one case, an abducted six-month-old child was found after ImAger depicted what the child would look like at age five. The child was recognized by viewers who called the police.[6] Another composite imaging program, by Visatex Corp., is used by police artists to create simulated photographs of criminal suspects.

The most advanced computer-aided investigation systems are being touted by agencies such as NASA and the Defense Advanced Research Projects Agency (DARPA) as having the ability to prevent crime. DARPA, for example, announced its new Total Information Awareness (TIA) program in 2003.[7] The five-year development project uses information-sorting and pattern-matching software to sift through vast numbers of business and government databases in an effort to identify possible terrorist threats. The software attempts to detect suspicious patterns of activity, identify the people involved, and locate them so that investigations can be conducted.

Suspected insurgents might be identified when the software detects a series of credit card and official transactions that form a pattern that resembles preparation for an insurgency attack. The process, known as **data mining**, will generate computer models in an attempt to predict terrorists' actions. Privacy advocates have raised concerns about DARPA's initiatives, but the agency has tried to defuse concerns by assuring the public that the project is not an attempt to build a supercomputer to snoop into the private lives or track the everyday activities of American citizens. The agency claims that all TIA research complies with all privacy laws, without exception.

Another DARPA project that could aid law enforcement but is currently being developed for military use overseas is called Combat Zones That See (CZTS).[8] The CZTS program will build a huge surveillance system by networking existing cameras from department stores, subway platforms, parking lots, and other points of surveillance and feeding images to supercomputer-like processors capable of recognizing suspects by face, gait, and mannerisms as they move from one place to another. The data can be fed via satellite to remote locations across the globe, allowing the agency to track suspects on the move—either within cities or between countries. A CZTS is being introduced gradually in selected locations beginning in areas in and around American military bases. Future uses of CZTS include nano-cameras equipped with micro-miniaturized transmitters that can be spread over a city like particles of dust that communicate relatively detailed information to local cellular-like installations for entry into the CZTS network. (See more on computer crime and investigative processes in Chapter 17.)

The Objectives of Criminal Investigation

Because of the changing nature of criminal activity and the role of the investigator, the objectives of the criminal investigation may be more complex than people imagine. The objectives of criminal investigations are to:

- Detect crime
- Locate and identify suspects in crimes
- Locate, document, and preserve evidence in crimes
- Arrest suspects in crimes
- Recover stolen property
- Prepare sound criminal cases for prosecution

The premise behind the criminal investigation field is that people make mistakes while committing crimes. For example, a burglar may leave behind broken glass or clothing fibers; a rapist may leave fingerprints, skin tissue, semen, or blood. As a result of these oversights, evidence of who they are is also left behind. It is the job of the criminal investigator to know how, when, and where to look for such evidence. In doing so, he or she must be able to draw on various resources, such as:

- Witnesses and informants, for firsthand information about the crime
- Technological advances in evidence collection and preservation
- Their own training and experience in investigative techniques

In summary, almost all crimes require some degree of investigation. The extent to which any particular violation is investigated depends largely on resources available to the department and how the department prioritizes it.

Inductive and Deductive Reasoning

After an initial evaluation of evidence in a case, the criminal investigator draws conclusions through a process of reasoning. This process is typically achieved through inductive or deductive reasoning. The distinctions are as follows:

Inductive Reasoning. Induction or **inductive reasoning**, sometimes called inductive logic, is reasoning that takes us beyond what we know (our current evidence or information) to conclusions about what we don't know. Induction is used, for example, in using "specific" propositions such as:

> "All of John Wayne Gacy's victims found to date were male—so Gacy did not kill females."
> Or:
> "This ice is cold. (Or, all ice I have ever touched was cold.)...to infer general propositions such as: 'All ice is cold.'"

The calculus of inductive reasoning can also be broken down into conclusions that are strong versus those that are not so strong or even weak. For example, the following are examples of strong and weak induction.

Strong Induction

> "All observed crows are black; therefore, all crows are black."

This exemplifies the nature of induction: inducing the universal from the particular. However, the conclusion is not certain. Unless one can systematically falsify the possibility of crows being another color, the conclusion that all crows are all black may actually be false.

Technically speaking, one could examine a crow's genome and learn whether it's capable of producing a differently colored bird. In doing so, we could discover that, in fact, colored crows are genetically possible. Consequently, a strong induction is an argument in which the truth of the premises would make the truth of the conclusion probable but not necessary.

Weak Induction

> "I always hang pictures on nails; therefore, all pictures hang from nails."

Assuming the first statement to be true, this example is built on the certainty that "I always hang pictures on nails" leading to the generalization that "All pictures hang from nails." However, the link between the premise and the inductive conclusion is weak. In other words, there is no reason to believe that just because one person hangs pictures on nails that there are no other ways for pictures to be hung or that other people cannot do other things with pictures.

Of course, not all pictures are hung from nails, and for that matter; many pictures aren't hung at all. So the conclusion cannot be strongly inductively made from the premise. Using other knowledge, we can easily see that this example of induction would lead us to a clearly false conclusion. Conclusions drawn in this manner are usually overgeneralizations that are in need of further investigation. Consider another example of weak induction:

"Many speeding tickets are given to teenagers; therefore, all teenagers drive fast."

In this example, although the premise is built upon a certainty, it is not one that leads to a reasonable conclusion. Not every teenager observed has been given a speeding ticket. In other words, unlike "The sun rises every morning," there are already plenty of examples of teenagers who have not received speeding tickets. Therefore, the conclusion drawn can easily be true or false, and the inductive logic does not give us a strong conclusion. In both of these examples of weak induction, the logical means of connecting the premise and conclusion (with the word "therefore") are faulty and do not give us a strong inductively reasoned statement.

Deductive Reasoning. Sometimes called deductive logic, **deductive reasoning** is reasoning based on specific pieces of evidence to establish proof that a suspect is guilty of an offense—for example, identifying muddy footprints outside a window where a burglary has occurred. An issue would be whether the footprints belonged to an occupant of the house, to the burglar, or to someone else.

Deductive reasoning is often contrasted with inductive reasoning. For example, by thinking about phenomena such as how apples fall and how the planets move, Isaac Newton induced his theory of gravity. In the nineteenth century, Adams and LeVerrier applied Newton's theory (general principle) to deduce the existence, mass, position, and orbit of Neptune (specific conclusions) from perturbations in the observed orbit of Uranus (specific data).

In the context of criminal investigation, investigators must anticipate all possible scenarios and know what evidence is needed to support prosecution of the case because each issue in dispute must be supported by evidence. The more evidence an investigator collects, the stronger the case and the stronger the proof of guilt. Conversely, the criminal investigator must also consider what evidence is available to exonerate innocent parties.

Challenging Inductive and Deductive Reasoning. In 2002, Jon J. Nordby questioned the processes of inductive and deductive reasoning in his book *Dead Reckoning: The Art of Forensic Detection.* Nordby suggested that it's not enough to just collect and analyze evidence; investigators also need a guiding theory that's flexible enough to accommodate new information and sufficiently logical to show a clear pattern of cause and effect.[9]

For example, Nordby states that a homicide investigation could show that the killer did not need to break in to a residence because he had a key. This theory would significantly narrow the possibilities. It is important for investigators to not only have a theory that guides the investigation but also that any theory that is contradicted be discarded. In other words, it is important for investigators to understand how logic and science work together.

Abduction is the process, therefore, of proposing a likely explanation for an event that must then be tested. For example, the killer had a key to the victim's home. Nordby suggests:

Induction is the wrong way of looking at science...because the classic problem of induction is the contrary instance [something that contradicts the claim].

Let us consider the notion that once a crime scene investigator observes a hair or piece of fiber, he or she now has their evidence. The reality is that many if not most crime scenes exist in dirty, debris-filled rooms. Such places are abundant with hair and fibers. So what is the investigator actually looking for? Which of all of those hairs and fibers is actually evidence? Unless the criminal investigator has an idea or theory that will make one object relevant and another irrelevant, the evidence-collection process will be overwhelming. In order to have purpose in what is being done, the investigator must have something in mind. That comes from abduction.

Developing an explanation that can be tested moves the investigation forward and guides the accumulation of knowledge, giving way only when contradicted. Abduction helps to make links among events, and the development of the overall theory of a crime depends on adding new links. Nordby suggests that abduction keeps guessing to a minimum.

Critical Thinking and Scientific Methodology

In addition to the use of deductive and inductive logic in interpreting evidence, the criminal investigator must incorporate skills of critical thinking with known scientific methods in their investigations. Let's look at how these two approaches to criminal investigation compare. In a most basic sense, critical thinking is the use of rational skills, worldviews, and values to get as close as possible to the truth. It is judgment about what to believe or what to do in response to observations or experiences. Fisher and Scriven define critical thinking as: "Skilled, active, interpretation and evaluation of observations, communications, information, and argumentation."[10] Critical thinking can also involve determining the meaning and significance of what is observed to determine whether there is adequate justification to accept whether a conclusion is true.

In contemporary usage, "critical" has the connotation of expressing disapproval, which is not always true of critical thinking. A critical evaluation of an argument, for example, might conclude that it is good.

Whereas thinking is often *casual* or routine, critical thinking deliberately evaluates the *quality* of thinking. In an early study on critical thinking in 1941, Edward Glaser wrote that the ability to think critically involves three things:[11]

1. An attitude of being disposed to consider in a thoughtful way the problems and subjects that come within the range of one's experiences
2. Knowledge of the methods of logical inquiry and reasoning
3. Some skill in applying those methods

Critical thinking calls for a persistent effort to examine any belief or supposed form of knowledge in the light of the evidence that supports it and the further conclusions to which it tends. It also generally requires ability to recognize problems and to find workable means for meeting those problems. Critical thinking may occur whenever one judges, decides, or solves a problem; in general, critical thinking may be used whenever one must figure out what to believe or what to do and do so in a reasonable and reflective way.

Critical thinking is an important element of all professional fields, including criminal investigation. It is important because it enables one to analyze, evaluate, explain, and restructure one's thinking, thereby decreasing the risk of adopting, acting on, or thinking with a false belief.

In contrast with critical thinking, the scientific method refers to techniques for investigating phenomena, acquiring new knowledge, or correcting and integrating previous knowledge. To be termed scientific, a method of inquiry must be based on gathering empirical and measurable evidence.[12] A scientific method consists of the collection of data through observation and experimentation and the formulation and testing of hypotheses. Each element of a scientific method is subject to peer review for possible mistakes.

The processes of critical thinking and scientific method need not be mutually exclusive. Rather, reasonable and informed investigators consider both as tools in their investigative arsenal, allowing for critical thinking in determining the direction of the investigation and scientific methods in evaluating the value of and usefulness of evidence.

The Emergence of the Police Specialist

The process of investigating criminals in the United States is structured very differently from the process followed in England. In the U.S., typically, a division exists within law enforcement agencies between officers whose responsibility it is to maintain order and those who investigate crimes. In larger departments, specialized squads typically perform the investigative function in law enforcement agencies. In fact, many such departments have several detective divisions within, each dealing with different categories of crime, such as crimes against persons (e.g., rape, assault, robbery), crimes against property (e.g., burglary, larceny, auto theft), and vice (e.g., drug violations, gambling, prostitution). Smaller rural departments often lack financial resources to specialize, so patrol officers often conduct criminal investigations in addition to their patrol duties.

In some types of crime, such as homicide, investigators must develop leads through interviews with friends, family, and associates of the victim as well as witnesses to the crime. In other cases, investigative leads are developed by sifting through files and prior police records and establishing the suspect's mode of operation (MO). In all cases, the investigative process uses traditional and historical methods of detection through the use of official records, photographs, fingerprints, and so on, as opposed to daily face-to-face contacts with the citizenry, such as with the patrol division. The investigative specialist is generally an older person who has had considerable experience in police work. Most detectives are former patrol personnel who have worked up through the ranks due to the common practice of promoting from within.

Types of Investigations

The mission of law enforcement is complex and demanding but contains some fundamental components, including the maintenance of peace in our communities and the protection of lives and property. When people choose to violate laws that provide for these essentials, the perpetrators must be identified and brought before a court. It is the task of identifying such offenders that is the quintessence of criminal investigation. Criminal investigators confront investigations in several areas in the regular course of their duties:

- Personal background, to determine a person's suitability for appointment to sensitive public trust positions
- Suspected violations of criminal law
- Infractions of civil law
- Vice (drug and organized crime activity)

Crime Scene Investigators

The popular television show *CSI* (Crime Scene Investigation) has brought the role of the crime scene investigator to the public, creating considerable interest in forensic science. Of course, crime scene investigators require very specific training with

FIGURE 1.6 The television show *CSI* (*Crime Scene Investigation*) has led the general public to hold certain beliefs about criminal investigation, which may be exaggerated or outright inaccurate. Here actors Marg Helgenberger and William Petersen search for evidence in CBS TV series *CSI*. In what ways have you observed inaccuracies in the television show and your understanding of the investigative process in the real world? With permission of Picture Desk, Inc./Kobal Collection.

regard to crime scene protection and the identification and preservation of evidence, and not every law enforcement agency is able to support a dedicated CSI unit. A description of the crime scene unit (CSU) is provided by Michael Weisberg (2001):[13]

> The CSU provides support services in the form of crime processing, fingerprint identification, and forensic photography. The CSU responds to major crime scenes to detect, preserve, document, impound and collect physical evidence. The unit assists in the identification of unknown subjects, witnesses and victims involved in criminal investigations.... The CSU will work closely in conjunction with the Detective Bureau in providing assistance in follow-up investigations, as well as subject apprehension and arrest. Members of the CSU may be either sworn or non-sworn.

Major Task Forces

A multidisciplinary approach to case investigation uses specialists in various fields from within a particular jurisdiction. A multi-jurisdictional investigation, in contrast, uses personnel from different police agencies. Many larger municipalities consist of 20 or more municipalities that surround a core city. In many metropolitan areas, multi-jurisdictional **major case squads**, or metro crime teams have organized, drawing the most talented investigative personnel from all jurisdictions. In addition, federal, state, or county police personnel may be used.

In some major cases—for example, homicides involving multi-jurisdictional problems, serial killers and rapists, police officer killings, or multiple sex offenses—it is advisable to form a major case squad from the jurisdictions that has a vested interest in the case. Evidence located from the joint investigation is sent to the same laboratory for continuity and consistency.

Modes of Investigation

Criminal investigations are conducted through the use of three different responses: reactive, proactive, and preventive. The **reactive response** addresses crimes that have already occurred, such as murder, robbery, and burglary. In this case, investigators typically respond to a crime, collect evidence, locate and interview witnesses, and identify and arrest a suspected perpetrator. Investigations are also conducted as a **proactive response** to anticipated criminal activity, as with many vice and organized crime investigations. Proactive investigations differ from reactive investigations in two major regards: (1) the investigation is conducted before the crime is committed (rather than after) and (2) the suspect is identified before he or she commits the crime. Finally, investigations are sometimes conducted as a **preventive response**. Prevention through deterrence is sometimes achieved by arresting the criminal and by aggressive prosecution.

The Role of the Criminal Investigator

As indicated earlier, many myths exist regarding the role of criminal investigators. Perhaps these were best summarized by Herman Goldstein, who wrote:[14]

> Part of the mystique of detective operations is the impression that a detective has difficult-to-come-by qualifications and skills; that investigating crime is a real science; that a detective does much more important work than other police officers; that all detective work is exciting; and that a good detective can solve any crime. It borders on heresy to point out that, in fact, much of what detectives do consists of very routine and very elementary chores, including much paper processing; that a good deal of their work is not only not exciting but downright boring; that the situations they confront are often less demanding and challenging than those handled by patrol officers; that it is arguable whether special skills and knowledge are required for detective work; that a considerable amount of detective work is usually undertaken on a hit-or-miss basis; and that the capacity of detectives to solve crimes is greatly exaggerated.

Indeed, some studies have suggested that the role played by investigators is overrated and that their time could probably be spent more productively by focusing on crimes with the best likelihood of clearance.[15] Other researchers suggest that the investigative process is a valid utility in crime detection but should be augmented by the use of proactive patrol programs.

Characteristics of the Investigator

What characteristics best define a professional criminal investigator? Certainly, standards vary from one law enforcement agency to the next, but certain commonalities can be identified. To recognize these qualities, many police agencies implement a supervisory performance appraisal system to evaluate suitability for appointment to investigator. Once taken, the police manager can choose from candidates who possess the most sought-after qualities. According to a study by the National Institute of Justice (NIJ), investigative traits most commonly desired include:[16]

- Motivation
- Intuition
- Stability
- Judgment
- Street knowledge
- Teamwork
- Persistence
- Reliability
- Intelligence
- Dedication
- Integrity

FIGURE 1.7 Police academy recruits train in crime scene investigation by assisting the search of an actual outdoor crime scene. *Courtesy of Mark Ide.*

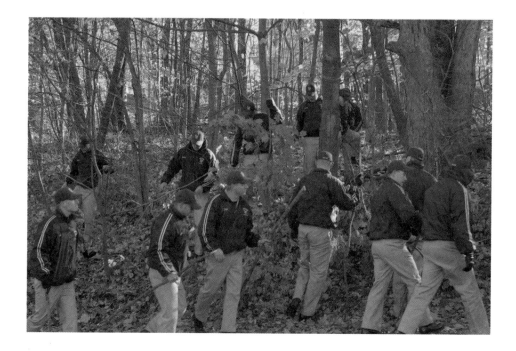

Investigators are specialists. They undertake activities related primarily to law enforcement; patrol officers, on the other hand, routinely spends their time in order maintenance and the provision of general services (e.g., emergency aid, finding lost children, traffic control). Despite the diversity of tasks performed by patrol officers, investigators also assume many substantial duties. For example, detectives gather crime information, effect arrests, and prepare cases for prosecution and trial.

Gathering Information

Many criminal investigations are initiated with a call to the police dispatcher during which a crime is reported. Some of the most critical tasks performed by detectives include rapid arrival at crime scenes; searching the area; and identifying, collecting, and preserving evidence. In addition, investigators must be familiar with the department's computer and manual records, which contain such information as mug shots, fingerprints, intelligence, and stolen property files. Depending on the assignment, detectives must be able to follow up on leads through the use of various methods and procedures. These include visits to pawn shops, suspected fencing locations, taverns, and other places thought to be frequented by criminals.

Field Operations

The best investigators have a demonstrated ability to function in field operations such as patrol and surveillance functions (stakeouts). At times, an investigator may even be required to perform in an undercover capacity to procure information on illegal activities such as drug trafficking, fencing operations, prostitution, or corruption. In addition, such investigations require the investigator to know how to operate technical and complicated electronic surveillance equipment, such as hidden-body transmitters, night-viewing devices, and photography equipment. Along with these skills, stamina and a willingness to work long hours are prerequisites.

Arrests

One of the basic functions of law enforcement is to arrest violators of the law. Accordingly, making arrests is a significant objective for investigators because they spend so much time collecting and evaluating information on criminal

mycrimekit

Video: Career profile: Police detective

Qualities Involved in Investigative Performance

Gathering Information	Intelligence	**Prosecutions**
Crime scene management	Perseverance	Quantity
Communication skills	Initiative	Presentation of testimony
Field Operations	Judgment	Percent of convictions
Stakeouts	Teamwork	**Personnel Performance**
Patrol	Involvement	Absenteeism
Crime pattern analysis	Dedication	Complaints
Developing informants	**Arrests**	Awards
Street knowledge	Quantity	Dedication
Personal Traits	Quality	**Qualifications**
Motivation	**Public–Victim Satisfaction**	Education
Stability	Crime reduction	Training
Persistence	Diminution of fear	Previous assignments in department

FIGURE 1.8 Qualities involved in investigative performance.

activity. The quality of arrests is also an important variable because an officer who has a reputation for making many poor-quality arrests will probably not be considered for the position of detective. Because a major purpose of an arrest is to secure a conviction, the quality and number of prosecutions and convictions are critical elements in assessing the performance of investigators.

The Patrol Officer as an Investigator

Traditionally, the responsibility of patrol officers in criminal investigations has been limited. Patrol officers have been required only to collect and record the most basic information by asking simple questions of the victims and witnesses and recording their answers on a report form. While in the past, patrol officers have studied crime scenes for physical evidence, usually the time spent on any one incident has been minimal. As a rule, reports have been reviewed by a supervisor and then sent to the detective division or an investigative unit for follow up. In many cases, this process has resulted in duplication of efforts by investigators.

Over the past decade, many police departments have expanded the role of the patrol officer to responsibilities which are traditionally assigned to investigators. These new responsibilities include the following:

- The patrol officer provides immediate assistance to victims, locates witnesses, interviews both victims and witnesses, and records information about the crime scene. Depending on the seriousness of the crime or the presence of physical evidence, the patrol officer may call for a more specialized search by evidence technicians. To a great extent, this procedure initiates the case.

- The patrol officer has the authority to initiate and complete investigation of certain classifications of crime, such as all misdemeanors, cases that involve property value up to $1,500, and auto larceny cases. Investigations of more serious crimes continue to be referred to specialized investigative units. The practical effect of this "sorting out" of responsibilities for different types of investigations is that patrol officers investigate high-volume crimes that can be investigated as effectively by patrol as by criminal investigators. Conversely, investigations that require more time, specialized skill, and effort are handled by trained criminal investigators.

- In rare cases, the police officer may be given responsibility for the entire investigative process. In these situations, the patrol officer carries out all investigative functions. Investigators, if there are any, perform as consultants to the patrol officers.

For the most part, police administrators agree that these changes in the patrol officers' role have produced a number of benefits, including:

- The cases are handled completely and expeditiously.
- Relationships and communications between patrol officers and investigators have improved.
- The frequency of morale problems among patrol officers has decreased, and the decrease is attributable to the officers' belief that their skills are being better used in the investigative process.
- An increase in investigator productivity has resulted from a light caseload, which produced more time to focus investigative resources on specific high-profile cases.
- There is better management of the entire investigative effort by the police administrator.

Solvability Factors

A police department's reporting system and the investigative role of patrol car are inextricably bound. The redefining of the role of patrol officer is intended to ensure that evidence supporting the continual investigation or case closure is collected at the earliest possible point in the investigative process. This reporting system serves as the foundation for the criminal investigation.

The reporting system is defined by two basic components, which in combination form the basis for an initial investigation. The first is a format that logically guides the identification leads, or **solvability factors**, that experience and research of demonstrated are most likely to result in case solution. The second provides an opportunity for details of the investigation thus far expended so the follow-up plans do not unnecessarily duplicate tasks already completed.

A police department's reporting system should indicate not only that solvability factors are present but it should also identify the investigative effort expended in searching for leads. For example, if witnesses have been sought in a number of locations, the report should indicate where the search was conducted, who was contacted, and what was found. Without this description, the follow-up investigator will not have a clear idea of where the patrol officer has located the existing solvability factors and will end up duplicating his or her efforts.

Unless the patrol officer is able to make an immediate, on-scene arrest, 12 essential questions need direct answers. These solvability factors are logically based on existing police practices. All agencies may have different capabilities and procedures that result in slightly different solvability factors. The primary factors are as follows:

1. Immediate availability of witnesses
2. Name(s) of the suspect
3. Information about the suspect's location
4. Information about the suspect's description
5. Information about the suspect's identification

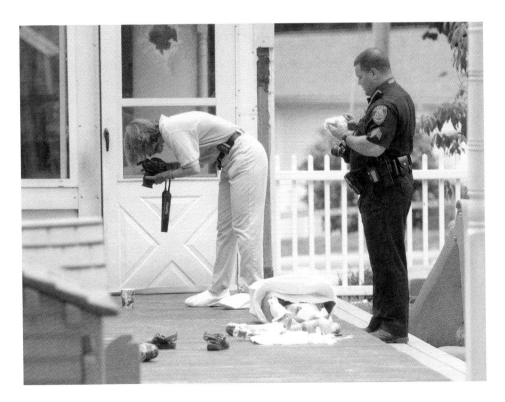

FIGURE 1.9 Patrol officers often conduct their own investigations or assist criminal investigators when requested. Here a patrol officer is assisting in the investigation of a domestic violence case.
Courtesy of Mark Ide.

6. Information about the suspect's vehicle and vehicle movement

7. Information about traceable property

8. Information about significant MO

9. Information about significant physical evidence

10. Discovery of useful physical evidence

11. Judgment by the patrol officer that there is sufficient information available to conclude that anyone other than the suspect could not have committed the crime

12. Judgment by the patrol officer on case disposition. If the officer believes there is enough information available and with a reasonable and investment of investigative effort that the probability of the case solution is high, then the investigation should be continued.

From an investigative standpoint, these 12 structured questions serve to define what the patrol officer should accomplish. By directing his or her activities to areas of inquiry that are the most promising for a successful case solution, the role of the patrol officers not only broadened at the same time given effective limitations to resolve the dilemma regarding just where the patrol officer should terminate in an investigation. Furthermore, utilization of the solvability factors emphasizes the importance of a thorough initial investigation even when it is being turned over for a continuing investigation. The patrol officer has provided the direction of the investigation, up to this point.

In summary, the expanded role of patrol officers in recent years has meant increased efficiency and effectiveness in policing in general and criminal investigation specifically. It has also served to enlighten those who serve the community in the capacity as patrol officers and to make them more aware of their important role as first responders to crime scenes and as the police department's eyes and ears on the street. In their role as first responders to crime scenes, patrol officers have many specific duties. These duties are encompassed in a process known as the preliminary investigation.

The Preliminary Investigation

Although the primary purpose of a patrol force is to prevent crime, patrol officers have assumed many other responsibilities, including the investigation of crimes (discussed earlier). In modern police departments, the patrol force participates fully in the preliminary investigation of crimes.

The preliminary investigation is the responsibility of the first officer at the crime scene. His or her actions at the scene can greatly influence the ultimate success or failure of the investigation. In other words, a job well done during a preliminary investigation should provide the information or evidence needed to build a solid case. Conversely, errors made during the preliminary investigation, especially those that involve a failure to properly safeguard or identify physical evidence, cannot be rectified at a later time.

From the time the officer receives information to proceed to a crime scene, his or her preliminary investigation objectives are the following:

- Determine what has happened
- Locate witnesses and sources of evidence that aid in determining what has occurred
- Locate and preserve physical evidence
- Determine what further investigative steps should be taken
- Obtain and evaluate the accuracy of witnesses' statements
- Determine whether to act on the statements and evidence found at the scene
- Record what has been done, what has been learned, and what is left to be done
- Complete the investigation and make an apprehension if appropriate

One of the primary objectives of the preliminary investigation is to establish whether the necessary elements of a crime exist. All information obtainable at the scene of a crime should be gathered and reported at the time of the initial police response. The follow-up investigation by specialists is a second step, when a postponement of the work of investigation will not necessarily jeopardize the successful completion of the investigation.

The preliminary investigation should begin when an officer is assigned to proceed to a crime scene and only terminate when he or she has completed the task to the point at which a delay in further action does not substantially affect successful outcome of the investigation. For the most part, the nature of the crime and the relationship between a time of occurrence and the time of arresting the perpetrator determine whether or not the offense is investigated to conclusion by the patrol officer. When a suspect is arrested at or near the scene of a crime or during or shortly after the crime, the limits of a preliminary investigation need to be extended. If an extensive search of the crime scene for physical evidence is necessary, the preliminary and follow-up investigations overlap into a single operation. An example of this is homicide investigations.

Typically, patrol officers proceed to crime scenes with sketchy information that must first be verified and then expanded to be of investigative use. However, as far as crime scene response only is concerned, the patrol officer usually has two facts that shape his or her preliminary plans: the type of crime and the location of the crime. These facts usually indicate the urgency of a call and thus the degree to which a patrol officer can conduct the culinary investigation.

The Crime Scene Response

While approaching the crime scene, the responding officer must remain observant for potential suspects fleeing the area. The officer should note descriptions of people and vehicles leaving the crime area. A critical decision needs to be made by the responding officer when he or she observes a suspect. The officer must decide whether to stop his or her approach to the crime scene and investigate a suspicious person who may be fleeing or to proceed directly to the crime scene. The decision to stop must be based on the likelihood that the suspicious person is the offender fleeing the crime scene.

If it is necessary to stop a suspicious person, the officer should notify the dispatcher immediately so that other units are aware of the situation. The dispatcher should assign a backup unit to assist the officer and then send another officer to the crime scene.

Aid to the Injured. The first duties of police officers at the scene of the crime are to administer first aid and obtain medical assistance for injured parties when required. All considerations are secondary to the well-being of injured parties. Even the capture of suspects and the integrity of valuable clues or evidence may need to be sacrificed to aid a victim. Obviously, if other apparently qualified persons are at the crime scene to provide first aid, an officer can then pursue fleeing suspects.

While rendering aid, officers should disturb the scene as little as possible. They should not unnecessarily move furniture, use facilities, or litter the area. For example, first aid supplies should be collected after use. Ambulance personnel should be directed how to enter and work within the crime scene so as not to needlessly disturb it.

Evaluate the Situation. After caring for any injured people, the officer should make an evaluation of the crime scene before proceeding with the preliminary investigation. Evaluation of the scene at this time often prevents false moves and mistakes. By observing the overall crime scene, a police officer can gain a reasonably accurate mental image of how the crime occurred and where it was committed. Of course, if additional assistance is needed at the crime scene, the officer should request it immediately.

After arriving at the scene, the officer must exercise extreme caution. He or she should concentrate on identifying potential evidence and avoid disturbing the likely locations of fingerprints and other evidence. For example, the swinging double doors common to many commercial establishments should be pushed open at a point lower than normally touched by a person. After the doors are identified as possible sources of fingerprints, they can be protected from contamination by locking them or tying them open.

The officer should observe and record the details of the scene. This is done by beginning to take notes as soon as possible. The longer the officer waits, the greater the danger becomes of omitting small but often important facts. The type of small details include whether a door was closed or locked, the lights were all on or off, or the blinds were open or closed.

Obtain Basic Information. For the most part, the preliminary sources of immediate information at a crime scene are victims and witnesses. From them, the officer can obtain the essential facts of the case. Although a lengthy inquiry cannot be conducted when the officer first arrives, he or she should establish the following points:

- The identities of victims, witnesses, and others present at the scene when the officer arrived

- A brief account from each witness or victim of what occurred, including descriptions of any suspects

After basic information has been obtained, the officer should broadcast a lookout alert or BOLO ("be on the lookout"). Alerting other field units about the nature of the offense and the details about the suspect, mode and direction of travel, description of the vehicle, proceeds of the crime, and type of weapon used may lead to an immediate arrest of a fleeing suspect.

Interview Witnesses. The first officer at the scene must detain witnesses. The officer should quickly remove all persons from the crime scene and should not allow them to return until all of the necessary crime scene work is completed. The witnesses should be separated so they cannot discuss the case with each other. Such discussions among witnesses about the crime can adversely influence the witnesses' memories and statements.

The officer must obtain adequate information to identify and locate witnesses. Some witnesses may volunteer and offer to provide information to the officer. However, witnesses are not always easy to find. Many persons are reluctant to accept the role of witness, and they avoid becoming involved with the investigation in any manner.

One technique for identifying witnesses is watching the crowd for persons who are describing what they observed. Also, the officer should ask each witness to point out anyone else who was present at the time of the crime. In major crimes, the license numbers of vehicles parked near the crime scene and in the immediate neighborhood should be documented.

The officer should determine which witnesses have the most helpful information and obtain full details from them. Other witnesses who have not observed a significant part of the crime should be permitted to give a brief statement. When possible, witnesses and others should be interviewed in the following order:

- Victim
- Eyewitnesses
- Persons observing the suspect entering or leaving the crime scene
- Persons having knowledge or events leading up to the crime
- Persons in the neighborhood

When a crime is committed within a residential building, the number of possible witnesses may be few. On the other hand, when a crime is committed in a store or on the street, a large number of persons may typically have witnessed the offense. The officer may need to visit adjoining places of business, apartments, or homes to determine if other persons might have knowledge of the crime.

The officer's inquiries must go beyond simply taking statements. He or she cannot accept without question anything stated by a witness. The officer must be observant and quick to recognize discrepancies or unusual behavior on the part of witnesses. Furthermore, the officer must examine the interrelationships between the accounts of witnesses and other evidence in the case. This involves more than establishing that the witness has personal knowledge of the circumstances of the crime; it also involves an examination of the statements of witnesses in relation to their physical ability, geographic layout of the crime scene, weather, and degree of visibility. Other factors include reasons for the witness being present at the scene.

Summary Checklist

This chapter essentially gives you, the reader, a look at the foundations of modern criminal investigation. See how well you are able to answer the following questions in your checklist.

1. **Why are the lines sometimes blurred between the romance and reality of crime solving?**

The criminal investigative process has intrigued people for generations. Sensational and historic cases of murder, fraud, and betrayal have long been the focus of books, movies, and television shows. Such popular portrayals of the investigative process often misstate or distort the realities of the investigative process. Forces of good and evil appear in vividly illustrated children's books and have been a traditional theme in Hollywood. Notorious outlaw gangs of the Old West have also fascinated people for decades. Gangs active on the Western frontier. These include:

- The Younger brothers
- The Dalton gang
- Jesse James

Detective magazines, books, and movies pitting the shrewd criminal against his or her persevering police counterpart have also perpetuated the detective mystique. These include fabled sleuths such as:

- Sherlock Holmes
- Hercule Poirot
- Mickey Spillane's Mike Hammer

2. **To what extent have our historical roots impacted our current system of criminal investigation?**

As with other aspects of American culture, the police criminal investigative process originated in England. It began with the Bow Street Runners, the London Metropolitan Police, and Scotland Yard.

- The Bow Street Runners were founded by Henry Fielding, the magistrate in Westminster.

- The Bow Street Runners were forerunners of a trend in policing for specialization within the police force.
- By 1800, the Bow Street Police Office was considered to be the leading law enforcement organization in London.
- The London Metropolitan Police Department was established in 1829.
- Officers were called bobbies after the department's founder, Home Secretary Sir Robert Peel.
- The London Metropolitan Police Department was England's first paid, full-time police force, consisting of about 1,000 uniformed officers. They replaced the Bow Street Runners.
- Bobbies were required to meet rigid standards of professionalism, including minimum weight and height requirements and standards of literacy and character.
- A detective bureau was created in the Metropolitan Police Department in 1842.
- Scotland Yard was created over 10 years after the establishment of the Metropolitan Police Department.

The early beginnings of criminal investigation in the United States can also be linked to:

- Alan Pinkerton, founder of the Pinkerton National Detective Agency
- The creation of the Federal Bureau of Investigation (FBI) in 1924

During the middle of the nineteenth century, three significant elements emerged that had an impact on criminal investigation:

1. Municipal police were supplemented by the county sheriff in rural areas.
2. The Texas Rangers were established (before Texas became a state).
3. Police functions were expanded with the establishment of the U.S. Marshal's Service and the Secret Service, formed during the Civil War to investigate counterfeiters

3. **What were some of the early advancements in forensic science in crime detection?**

Advances in science and research have furthered the professionalizing of criminal investigation and have made it possible for investigators to more accurately identify persons suspected of committing crimes. This has been aided with the use of computers to analyze data and store evidence. Newly discovered techniques included:

- Serology
- Forensic dentistry
- Ballistics

The practice of considering evidence and drawing conclusions is typically accomplished through the process of inductive and deductive reasoning. These methods allow the investigator to make inferences regarding what is known about the crime and evidence connected to the crime.

4. **Explain the contributions research had offered to criminal investigation research.**

In many law enforcement organizations, the crime scene technician is the person trained to respond to the scene of a crime and identify, collect, and preserve evidence. The investigation is then taken over by the criminal investigator, who responds in a reactive or preventive manner. Investigations can also be of a proactive nature. Research in criminal investigation includes:

- The RAND study found (1) post-arrest activities be coordinated more closely with the prosecutor's office ; (2) the investigative role of patrol officers should be expanded; (3) additional resources should be established to process, organize, and search for latent prints; and (4) investigators should distinguish between cases that can be handled clerically and those that require specially trained investigators.
- The PERF study found: (1) detectives and patrol officers contribute equally to the resolution of burglary and robbery cases; (2) in most cases, a period of four hours (stretched over several days) is sufficient to

close cases; (3) 75 percent of burglary and robbery cases are suspended in less than two days due to a lack of leads; (4) detectives play a major role in follow-up work conducted to identify and arrest suspects; and (5) both detectives and patrol personnel are too reliant on victim information for identification purposes.

5. **What is the role of the criminal investigator?**

Successful criminal investigators assume a number of responsibilities. These include the following:

- Determine whether a crime has been committed.
- Gather information.
- Identify an offender's MO.
- Make an arrest if necessary.
- Follow up on the case afterwards

In some cases, depending on the nature of the case and available resources of the law enforcement agency, the patrol officer conducts the investigation.

6. **What is the patrol officer's role in the investigative process?**

Patrol officers are assuming a greater role in the investigation of criminal offenses.

- The patrol officer may initiate the case by calling for a more specialized search by evidence technicians.
- The patrol officer has the authority to initiate and complete investigation of certain classifications of crime, such as all misdemeanors.
- Patrol officers investigate high-volume crimes that can be investigated as effectively by patrol as by criminal investigators.
- Patrol officers are "first responders" to crime scenes and assume the initial responsibility for aiding possible injured persons, identifying witnesses and suspects, identifying physical evidence, and protecting the crime scene.

A police officer can be given responsibility for the entire investigative process by carrying out all investigative functions.

Key Terms

abduction
ballistics
Bertillon system
bobbies
Bow Street Runners
data mining
deductive reasoning

expert systems
forensic dentistry
inductive reasoning
major case squads
preventive response
proactive response
Prohibition

reactive response
relational databases
rogues' gallery
Scotland Yard
serology
solvability factors
thief catchers

Discussion Questions

1. Discuss ways in which the media have affected our perceptions of the reality of criminal investigation.
2. Compare and contrast criminal investigation and our English heritage and how that affected the beginnings of criminal investigation in America.
3. Compare and contrast the processes of deductive and inductive reasoning.
4. Discuss the ways in which increases in science have influenced modern methods of criminal investigation.
5. Explain the differences between proactive and reactive investigations.
6. Discuss the various types of criminal investigations.
7. The role of the patrol officer in criminal investigation has changed in recent years. Explain the ways in which criminal investigation can become more efficient and effective by utilizing the patrol officer.

mycrimekit

Go to MyCrimeKit.com to explore the following study tools and resources specific to this chapter:

- *Practice Quiz:* Multiple-choice, true/false, short-answer, and essay questions.
- *Flashcards:* There are 21 key terms in this chapter. Flashcards test your knowledge of the chapter's key terms.
- *Web Links:* Check out the hotlink to *The New York Times* criminology articles.
- *Career Center:* Check out the hot links to interesting careers in criminal justice, criminology, and juvenile justice.
- *The Research Center:* Check out the Cybrary and research navigator for even more resources.

Notes

1. JOHNSON, H. A. (1988). *History of criminal justice*. Cincinnati, OH: Anderson.
2. BLOCK, P., and D. WEIDMAN (1975). *Managing criminal investigations: Perspective package*. Washington, DC: U.S. Government Printing Office. GREENBERG, B., C. V. ELLION, L. P. KRAFT, and H. S. PROCTOR (1977). *Felony decision model: An analysis of investigative elements of information*. Washington, DC: U.S. Government Printing Office.
3. ECK, J. (1983). *Solving crimes: The investigation of burglary and robbery*. Washington, DC: Police Executive Research Forum.
4. SESSIONS, W. S. (2003). Criminal justice information services: Gearing up for the future. *FBI Law Enforcement Bulletin* 181–188.
5. OFFICE OF TECHNOLOGY ASSESSMENT. (1988). *Criminal justice: New technologies and the constitution—A special report*. Washington DC: U.S. Government Printing Office.
6. Saving face. (1998). *PC Computing* 60.
7. Security or Privacy/DARPA's Total Information and Awareness Program Tests the Boundaries. InformationWeek.com.
8. Information in this paragraph comes from U.S. Sensors Could Track Any Car. All Passengers in Foreign Cities. Worldtribune.com, July 30, 2003.
9. NORDBY, J. J. (2002). *Dead reckoning: The art of forensic detection*. Boca Raton, FL: CRC Press.

10. FISHER, A. AND M. SCRIVEN. (1997) *Critical thinking: Its definition and assessment.* Center for Research in Critical Thinking (UK)/Edgepress (US).

11. GLASER, E. M. (1941). *An experiment in the development of critical thinking.* Teacher's College, Columbia University.

12. NEWTON. (1999). Rules for the study of natural philosophy. From the General Scholium, which follows Book 3, *The system of the world* 794–796.

13. WEISBERG, M. W. (2001). Recent directions in crime scene investigations. *The Law Enforcement Trainer* March/April:44–48.

14. GOLDSTEIN, H. (1977). *Policing a free society.* Cambridge, MA: Ballinger, p. 1.

15. MORE, H. (1988). *Critical issues in law enforcement*, 4th ed. Cincinnati, OH: Anderson.

16. NATIONAL INSTITUTE OF JUSTICE (1987). *Investigators who perform well.* Washington, DC: U.S. Department of Justice, September.

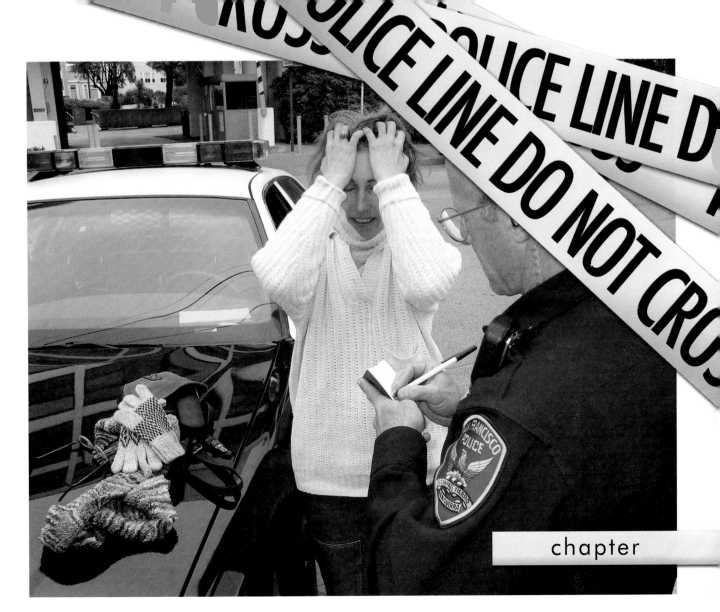

The Crime Scene: Field Notes, Documenting, and Reporting

2

This chapter will enable you to:

- Explain the ways that field notes can be used to assist the investigator in the preparation of his or her report.
- Learn the proper structure of the report.
- Explain the proper methods of crime scene photography and preservation of photographic evidence.
- Understand how to properly capture the crime scene on digital video.
- Understand the usefulness of the rough and finaling the crime scene sketch.

Introduction

A fundamental premise of criminal investigation is that investigators have the ability to reconstruct the facts and circumstances surrounding each case. This is generally accomplished through well-written reports, photographs, and crime scene sketches. Accompanying such evidence are the ever-important laboratory testing of objects seized from the scene and supportive testimony by investigators and laboratory technicians. With the exception of unusual circumstances, such as the removal of injured parties or inclement weather at a crime scene, all evidence at the scene is properly recorded before any objects are collected or removed.

Field Notes and Reports

Many law enforcement organizations place a high value on an officer's ability to document information through note taking and report writing. Indeed, good report writing skills are one consideration in both an officer's qualifications for promotion and in his or her ability to present a thoroughly investigated and understandable case to a prosecutor. The practice of taking notes is one that is common in many professions. For example, physicians take notes regarding the physical and psychological condition of their patients; attorneys commonly interview witnesses in criminal and civil cases as well as victims and suspects in crimes; and police officers are certainly in need of accurate notes to record conversations, events, and observations. A good investigator should develop the ability to write down information as it is learned, not later. Failure to do this could result in information being forgotten or confused. In many cases, it will be difficult or even impossible to locate witnesses or victims of crimes for a second interview because they may relocate or even die. Most departments furnish officers with a notebook in which field notes can be made. It is usually up to the officer what type of notebook he or she carries. Most typically, a small spiral-bound notebook is used. In any case, it should be accessible to the officer at all times.

The Role of Field Notes

When one thinks of a police officer taking field notes, the Hollywood portrayal of an officer writing down bits and pieces of information on the inside of a match-book cover may come to mind. Unfortunately, in some cases, this is a reality, but it is not the prescribed method of note taking. **Field notes** have many benefits for both the officer and the department. Most notes result from interviews, but there are other uses as well. For example, notes may be the most important step in documenting a crime scene initially. An investigator's field notes are his or her most personal and readily available record of the crime scene search. It is difficult, if not impossible, to recommend a particular form of field note taking because most officers usually adopt their own style. However, one objective of this process remains clear: The notes taken at a crime scene must adequately reflect the condition and state of the location at the time of the crime scene search.

When to Take Notes

The investigative process begins as soon as an officer gets a call to the scene of a crime. Accordingly, the note-taking process also begins at this time. Officers should remember that note taking is a continual process that occurs throughout the duration of an officer's involvement in an investigation. Some victims or witnesses may be intimidated by an officer taking down what is said during an

	4-16-10
◯	Case # 1122-07
	Time of violation: 2015 hours
	Burglary – 1210 Watson Place, St. Louis, MO
	Victim – Thomas Thompson
	Phone – (314) 234-1212
	Mr. Thompson stated that he arrived home at 1930 hours.
◯	He stated that his front door was ajar and a window was broken
	and opened.
	Mr. Thompson stated the following items were missing from the
	residence:
	1. RCA 32" stereo television – serial number not known, black in
	color, value $900
	2. Gold watch with brown leather band. Wittinauer Longlife
	brand, no serial numbers
◯	

FIGURE 2.1 Sample crime scene field notes.

interview. If it appears that this is the case, the investigator should take the time to explain the importance of brief notes and how they will benefit the overall investigation. If a subject simply refuses to talk while comments are being recorded, the officer can wait and make the required notes immediately after the interview.

What to Write Down

It would be ideal if investigative notes could begin with the assignment of the officer to the case and follow through in a logical flow of events to the culmination of the investigation. In reality, however, notes most probably are written in the order in which information is learned, resulting in fragmented bits of information being logged. This is not unusual and should not pose a problem for the investigator provided that notes are complete and well organized. Remember to get the specifics.

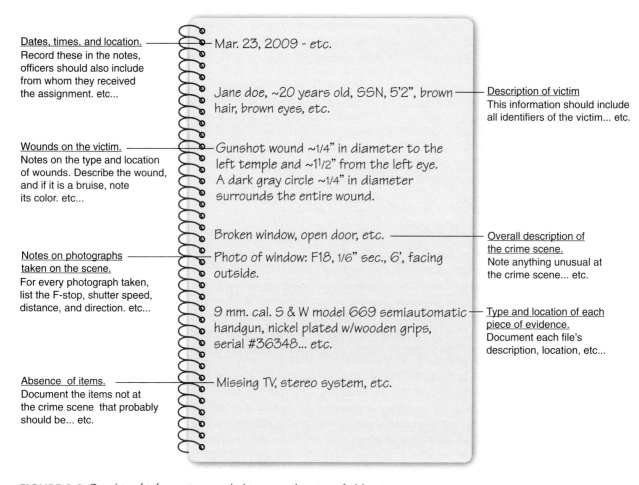

FIGURE 2.2 Graphic of information needed in properly written field notes.

When first encountering a witness or victim, it is important for the investigator to allow the person to state in his or her own words what occurred. This is best accomplished by asking the simple question, "What happened?" It is likely that much of the desired information will be communicated to the investigator at that point. After the subject provides his or her initial explanation, then more specific questions should be asked to pinpoint exactly what occurred. Most information can be learned with answers to who, what, when, where, why and how. For example:

Certain specifics should be included in the note-taking process. The following are some examples of essential topics of information:

- *Dates, times, and locations.* To begin, the date and time of the investigator's assignment to the case should be well recorded in his or her notes. Additionally, officers should include from whom they received the assignment. Supplementary information should include the exact time of arrival at the crime scene, the location of the scene, lighting and weather conditions, and the names of other officers contacted and other persons present at the scene.

- *Description of victim.* This information should include all identifiers of the victim, including name, age, social security number, height, weight, color of hair and eyes, and so on. In addition, clothing should be noted as to style (if possible) and color of garment. Special attention should be given to extemporaneous identifiers such as complexion, tattoos, and scars.

- *Wounds on the victim.* Notes regarding the type and location of wounds should be documented carefully. It is important to emphasize descriptions of the wound, and if it is a bruise, its color should be noted. For example, notes of a gunshot wound might read: "Gunshot wound approximately 1/4 inch in diameter to the left temple and approximately 1-1/2 inches from the left eye. A dark gray circle about 1/4 inch in diameter surrounds the entire wound."

- *Overall description of the crime scene.* Investigators must note anything unusual at the crime scene. This includes items damaged or in disarray, items that seem misplaced or that don't seem to belong in the scene, open (or closed) doors or windows, and so on.

- *Notes on photographs taken on the scene.* For every photograph taken of the scene (and there should be many), the F-stop, shutter speed, distance, and direction of the photo should be logged in an officer's notes. Also included should be the time and location of each photograph. In the event that a video camera is used to document the scene, an officer's notes should include the type of camera and any special attachments that may have been used.

- *Type and location of each piece of evidence.* An investigator should be careful to document adequately the location of each piece of evidence found at the crime scene. This includes its description, location, the time it was discovered and by whom, the type of container in which it was placed, how the container was sealed and marked, and the disposition of the item after it was collected. For example:

  > 9mm cal. S & W model 669 semiautomatic handgun, nickel plated with wooden grips, Serial #36348. 71 inches from the S.W. corner of the master bedroom, 16 inches E. of S. edge of W. door. Marked "WT" on evidence tag placed on trigger guard. Placed in manila evidence envelope, sealed with tape, and marked #11 WT 7-21-01 at 03:25 hrs. Released to Officer Mary Schultz, laboratory firearms examiner, 09:35 hrs. 7-21-09 WT.

- *Absence of items.* This notation includes the documentation of items not at the crime scene that probably should be such as certain articles of clothing missing from the deceased or certain home furnishings absent from the scene.

Developing a Note-Taking System

It is advisable for a system of note taking to be developed to allow an officer greater swiftness in his or her interviews. For example, initials can be used in place of complete names. This can be illustrated by using "S" for suspect, "V" for victim, "W-1" for witness number 1, "C" for complainant, and so on. When adopting this system, officers should be careful not to move into "shorthand," making it difficult for others to interpret what the notes are trying to say. Remember that field notes may be required later as evidence in court.

Field Interview Cards

One unique and successful method of documenting information on the street is through the use of **field interview cards** (FI cards). These are used when patrol officers happen on people or circumstances that appear suspicious but there is not sufficient cause for arrest. The FI card is used to document the name(s), address(es), and other pertinent information. At the end of the officer's watch, he or she turns in the FI cards, and they are filed for future reference.

Putting Field Notes to Work

As much as we have emphasized the importance of field notes on the crime scene, it should be stressed that notes are only a means to aid an investigator's recall at the time that he or she prepares the official detailed investigative report. The officer should be prepared to testify in court as to the findings of the investigation. The notes taken on the crime scene as well as the investigative report will be needed for review by the officer before testifying. The officer must also turn his or her notes over to defense counsel if required to do so.

Storage of Field Notes

After crime scene notes have been compiled, they must be stored in a safe place to avoid loss and tampering. This should remain the rule of thumb even after the suspect is convicted and the case is subsequently closed. This is performed in anticipation of a future appeal of the case, retrial, or possible civil action brought against the department or officer by the defendant.

Using a Tape Recorder

In many cases, investigators choose to use a small tape recorder in lieu of a notebook pad for note taking. Aside from the convenience of using a small tape recorder, investigators can also make more detailed memos about the scene. A drawback to the use of such a device is the difficulty on the part of the officer to review his or her notes on short notice. In the event that a tape recorder is used, however, transcripts should be made of the information contained on the tape, and great effort must be made to protect the tapes as evidence and to ensure that they do not become inadvertently erased or damaged during transportation or storage.

Using Field Notes in the Courtroom

As with many other types of evidence, notes are an important item of evidence in the case and can be required by the court. It is acceptable for a person who did not prepare the field notes to testify about their reliability provided that the person was present at the time the notes were written. It is also acceptable for officers to use their notes to refresh their memory before testifying in court. Doing so, however, enables the defense council to take possession of them and examine them if he or she wishes. Typically, the defense will attack the validity of the notes based on the conditions under which they were taken or attack the notes on their face value (e.g., poor weather conditions, poor lighting conditions, spelling errors).

Recalling the matchbook example cited at the beginning of this chapter, at times the type of notebook used by investigators has become an issue in a courtroom. Because the notes taken at a crime scene may be designated as evidence by the court, officers should be careful not to use one notebook for more than one investigation. This eliminates the embarrassment of disclosure of sensitive information regarding a case different from the one at hand. Therefore, officers should either use a different notebook for every investigation or a loose-leaf notebook so the pages can easily be removed and filed.

As a provision of the best evidence rule (*Cheadle* v. *Barwell*, 1933), the original notes must be provided in court whenever possible. In a legal sense, original notes are the archetype from which other documents are copied or duplicated (*Arenson* v. *Jackson*, 1916). In the event that the original notes cannot be located, photocopies may be used pursuant to a reasonable explanation to the court. In any case, however, it is important for the officer to protect his or her original notes by storing or filing them where they can easily be retrieved for court.

Writing the Official Police Report

A criminal investigator's written report represents the final product of his or her investigative efforts. The report informs others of what events have occurred and provides a permanent record useful in numerous ways as evidentiary matter at trial, intelligence information, and crime analysis data. To many readers, the report represents their only opportunity to learn about the background of the investigation. Consequently, it is essential the report be written so it can be understood, and more importantly, so it is not misunderstood.

Many police officers write mediocre reports. A poorly prepared report can easily become evident when one officer tries to read another officer's reports and tries to interpret what is being said. If an official report is difficult to understand, the complaint-issuing process will be bogged down, and it will be difficult for the prosecutor to decipher the facts and circumstances of the case. In addition, a poorly written report gives the defense attorney a tool to use during trial to confuse the officer's testimony and to muddle the issue.

Investigators should remember that the official police report is the backbone of the criminal prosecution process. It is a permanent record of the complaint and of the facts and events leading up to the arrest of the suspect. An important three-pronged rule of thumb to remember is that official reports should be factual, thorough, and to the point because they will be under close scrutiny when the case goes to court.

mycrimekit

Review field notes.

Factuality

The police report must be prepared carefully so that it accurately reflects all pertinent facts learned by investigators. Special attention should be given to dates, times, and other details of the investigation. In addition, these facts must be written in such a manner that the reader of the report easily understands them. It is important that the police report be factual and not contain hearsay information, speculation, or opinions of the investigator. Facts are generally defined as information learned personally by the investigator and not conclusions presumed by him or her. For example, if an informant tells the investigator that a suspect is a heroin addict, this information should be verified before stating it as fact in the official report.

After the information has been verified, the investigator should include in the report how the information was validated. For example, were undercover officers used to converse with the suspect, or were court orders obtained for disclosure of medical records? In the event that verification is not possible, the investigator should mention that the information was "alleged" to be true by the source (e.g., confidential informant, witness, newspaper article).

Steps in Report Writing

1. Collect information about the crime scene, informants, and witnesses.
2. Take complete notes.
3. Organize the information.
4. Prepare the report.
5. Proofread and evaluate the report.

Thoroughness

All facts learned pertaining to the investigation should be included in the official report. This practice is necessary for completeness of the report and for the credibility of the investigation. For example, if an undercover officer was offered illegal drugs and declined to purchase them, the offer should be documented in the event that the dealer later claims to have sold the drugs to the officer. In addition to the narrative aspect of the report, copies of related documentation should be attached with every report. For example, if investigators are looking at a check-kiting ring, copies of the suspect's checks should be attached to the report. Additionally, if surveillance photos are taken, they become part of the official report.

The report should also reflect the **chain of custody** of all evidence in the case. For example, in a drug case, the report should reflect how the drugs were collected, who handled them after seizure, where and how they were stored, and who now has possession of them (e.g., the crime laboratory).

Getting to the Point

The best investigative report is one that is not only thorough but is concise as well. In preparing such a report, the investigator must be aware that although details and completeness are important, excess information can bog down the report and possibly confuse the reader. For example, if the investigation involves an informant with the assigned number CI-10-28, this should be referred to the first time the informant is mentioned in the report but not every time thereafter. Subsequent references to the informant should simply be "CI," which will result in a more readable document.

Accuracy and Objectivity

An investigator's ability to report accurately is highly dependent on both the ability to conduct an objective and thorough investigation and to express the results of this inquiry and writing. In order to report objectively, investigator must distinguish between facts and hearsay accounts and be able to relay exactly a factual accounting of the incident.

It is essential that all relevant facts and details should be presented in an unbiased manner without any indication of the officer's feelings or opinions about the case. Writing the report should be considered as an extension of the investigation in which the officer is basically an inquirer whose purpose is to gather information. Even when conclusions or opinions are called for in the report summary, the officer must make sure that such judgments reflect his/her thinking and not his/her feelings. The officer must be sure to clearly indicate when a statement is his/her opinion.

Word Choice

The narrative portion of the report, in which the reporting officer brings the facts together in a story form, requires the effective use of language. In writing the narrative section of the report, the officer should be concerned with two basic items: presentation and diction (choice and use of words). As a rule, the most effective report presentation is a chronological narrative, in which events are described as they occurred from the officer's perspective. Accordingly, the narrative should unfold from the point when the officer received a service call or otherwise became involved in the case.

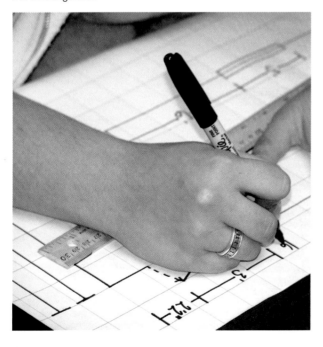

FIGURE 2.3 Careful preparation of the police report and related documents are an essential part of documenting the investigation.

One of the most difficult aspects of writing well is the proper choice and use of words. This is especially true with police reports because accuracy and brevity are all important. The following are suggestions in writing effective police reports:

1. Avoid the use of unnecessary words; for example, in "the aforementioned suspect," the word "aforementioned" is not needed. If more than one suspect is involved, they should be identified in some other way.

2. Avoid the use of elaborate or unfamiliar words when a small or commonly used term will do; for example, "the victim is cognizant of" should be written as "the victim knows."

3. Use specific words rather than vague terms; for example, "the victim said she proceeded to the living room" should be written as, "the victim said she (walked, ran, limped, hurried, etc.) to the living room."

4. Try to use the active voice; for example, "The message was received from the dispatcher at 10:40 a.m." can be improved by stating, "I received a message from the dispatcher at 10:40 a.m."

5. Use standard abbreviations; other persons will not necessarily understand individual abbreviations.

6. Write short, simple sentences whose meanings are clear and direct. Do not try to crowd many ideas into one sentence.

7. Avoid the use of double negatives such as, "No evidence could not be found at the crime scene." At the least, such expressions are confusing and, in some cases, the double negative can be misunderstood as a positive statement.

8. Be sure modifiers, adjectives, and adverbs are used sparingly because these words usually do not contribute much to a fact-finding report.

9. Use standard English rather than jargon or slang except when quoting witnesses, victims, and suspects.

The Structure of the Report

The report should be structured so that the reader is able to learn pertinent information quickly and succinctly. To best accomplish this, the effective organization of information on the report is critical.

Elements of the Report

- ☑ Who the officer was met by at the crime scene
- ☑ What the officer found at the scene
- ☑ What the officer did at the scene (e.g., administered first aid, notified immediate supervisor)
- ☑ Description of injuries to victim or suspect
- ☑ Type of weapon used
- ☑ Description of all evidence
- ☑ Names and identifiers of all suspects arrested
- ☑ Names of all witnesses
- ☑ Copies of written statements given by witnesses

Documenting Interviews

In forming questions for taking reports, the criminal investigator is much like a newspaper reporter. The investigator needs to know the answers to questions who, what, when, where, and how. More specifically, the following items are considered as an essential information.

- *Preliminary information.* This category of data includes the time and manner in which the complaint was received; identification of the location, time, and nature of the crime; and full identification of the victim.
- *Witnesses.* This grouping refers to information provided by victims, witnesses, or other persons at the crime scene.
- *Physical evidence.* The search for a discovery of evidentiary items must be included in the officer's records.
- *Modus operandi.* This is an extremely important category because in many cases, the method of operation is a clue to determining the suspect.

Obtaining information from victims, witnesses, or bystanders is more demanding than recording conversations at a crime scene. Interviews involve a variety of skills, both communicative and investigative, that require the investigator's full attention.

The use of basic interviewing techniques opens up communication between the investigator and the person being interviewed. However, the investigator must be skilled at forming questions and "digging" for information either temporarily forgotten or considered unimportant by the person being interviewed. At the same time, the investigator should guide the interview so that information flows sequentially and logically. This makes the investigator's job as recorder a much simpler task.

When recording the interview, the investigator must distinguish between items that are known and verified and those that are based on judgment of others or him- or herself. For example: "The suspect was described as 5'6" and 140 pounds by the victim" indicates the source of the information and the fact that it is not verified. In comparison, the phrase: "The suspect is 5' 6" inches and 140 pounds" is an absolute and overly positive. If untrue, such a statement could mislead the investigation.

Conclusions that are unsubstantiated by fact should be presented as opinion. For example, "The witness heard gunfire in the vicinity of its home" should be stated as "The witness heard a loud noise that he believes was gunfire in the vicinity of its home."

As a rule, investigations are documented by the initial complaint (the face sheet) and supplemental reports (describing new findings). Formats for these reports are considered next.

The Initial Complaint

Also called the *face sheet* or *initial page*, the complaint depicts an "at-a-glance" summary of the investigation. This information includes the suspect's name and related identifiers as well as a brief summary of the facts and circumstances surrounding the case (e.g., times, dates, locations, who did what, who saw what, what evidence was collected). The initial complaint is the first report seen by anyone examining the file of the investigation, so it is important to keep it direct and to the point. Although individual departmental policies dictate the precise manner in which the reports are organized, the following sections are usually included:

- *Type of crime.* Depending on the department, crimes are generally designated as crimes against property, crimes against persons, or vice crimes. In addition, they are indexed according to the specific act that is being alleged, such as robbery, burglary, or drug distribution.

- *Date.* This is the date of the offense.
- *Case number.* Before any paperwork is filed at the department, it must have a case number assigned by the records division. This number will be used on all subsequent reports in the investigation.
- *Officer's name.* This is the investigator's full legal name (no nicknames), rank, and badge number.
- *Suspect's name and address.* This includes the suspect's full legal name, monikers, addresses, date of birth, social security number, and any other pertinent information known about the suspect.
- *Victim.* The name of the victim(s) and address(es). No additional identifiers are required. For vice cases, the victim part of the report will either remain blank or reflect the jurisdiction in which the offense occurred (e.g., the state of Washington).
- *Witnesses.* This includes the names and addresses of witnesses of the crime.
- *Synopsis of crime and investigation.* This section should be no longer than one paragraph and should contain all general details of the case.
- *Details of crime and investigation.* This section is much longer than the synopsis because it encompasses all pertinent details of the investigation in a logical progression.
- *Attachments.* This section includes a list of all evidence relating to the case. Included are drugs, weapons, statements by victims and witnesses, references to videotapes used by investigators, photos, and so on.

Supplemental Reports

As the case progresses, investigators will undoubtedly develop new sources of information, such as new witnesses, physical evidence, and documents. As this information is gathered, a supplemental report is generated to update the case. The supplemental report is considerably longer than the initial complaint because it goes into much greater detail on pertinent aspects of the case. In fact, it is the supplemental report that incorporates the who, what, when, where, how, and (sometimes) why of the case.

The report begins with a brief synopsis of the subject of the report, which gives the reader an overall view of the body of the report. The main portion is the details section. As the investigator formulates this section, events are prepared in paragraphs and in chronological order. For example, a report of a drug purchase by an undercover agent should contain the following information in the details section of the report:

- Type of offense (e.g., possession, distribution)
- Date and time of offense
- Location of violation (e.g., suspect's residence, parking lot)
- Description of suspect's vehicle
- Description of weapons possessed by suspect
- Description of how the violation was discovered (e.g., through informant information, undercover agents, search warrants)
- Who (undercover agent or informant) was wearing concealed transmitters and names of officers monitoring the conversation, if relevant
- Description of evidence in the case (e.g., drugs, weapons, videotape of transaction, statement of informant)
- Field test results of drugs seized

FIGURE 2.4 Sample complaint form.

COMPLAINT FORM

Note: Hand print names legibly: handwriting satisfactory for remainder.

Subject's name and aliases	Address of subject	Character of case
Baker, Shawn Willis	1234 Cutter Ct. St. Louis, MO 65203	Burglary

Complainant	Complainant's address and telephone number	Complaint received
Officer William O'Shay	City Police Department (555) 456-7899	☒ Personal ☐ Telephonic Date April 14, 2010 Time 7:35 pm

Race W	Sex ☒ Male	Birth date and birthplace 9/18/85	Hair Brn.	Build Avg.	Height 6' 0"
Age 25	☐ Female		Eyes Blu.	Complexion Med.	Weight 190

Scars, marks, or other data

Tattoo on left forearm: "Ride to Live — Live to Ride"

Facts of complaint

Advised by radio at 1930 hours that a prowler was in the vicinity of 309 Watson Place in the city limits. Proceeded to the area and observed a white, older model Ford van parked on Watson Place in front of the residence at 309. Summoned backup and proceeded on foot to inspect the residence and discovered an open window on the north side. Paint chips and pry marks were visible on the window and on the ground.

Standing to the side of the house, suspect Baker exited the dwelling at approx. 1935 hrs. as he was apprehended. In his possession were two bags, one a canvas bag containing a screwdriver, slim jim, and pry bar. In the second bag, which was a brown paper bag, a gold watch and three gold and diamond rings were found.

Suspect was read his rights under *Miranda* in the presence of officers Larry White and Sandra Winslow. Baker then admitted illegally entering the residence and stealing the jewelry. Baker was transported by this officer to the city police department for processing and field notes were turned over to Detective Samuel Ramone for follow-up investigation.

Baker's van, which was registered to him, was towed to the city impound lot.

Action recommended

William O'Shay
(Agent)

Each report must also reflect additional details of the case, such as:

- Chain of custody of evidence
- Statements made by suspects (before and after arrest)
- How the suspect was identified
- Names of all witnesses in the case (e.g., officers, informant [identify by number, not name])
- List of property seized (e.g., cars, guns)

FIGURE 2.5 Investigators must carefully document every piece of evidence.

Copies of legal documents (e.g., search warrants, search warrant returns, vehicle seizure forms, informant statements) should be attached.

In summary, because reports are the tangible in product of an investigator's effort, his or her competency is often linked to the ability to write accurate and complete records of work performed. In other words, a criminal investigator's career is closely associated with his or her success, or failure, to report in writing what has been done.

Photographing the Crime Scene

As with the use of crime scene sketches (discussed later), the use of photographs in crime scene investigations has been fundamental for decades. It is important to note that both photos and sketches are necessary in criminal investigations because photos may distort distance, color, and so on. Today, the practice of crime scene photography has been extended to digital recorders to depict crime scenes. In this section, the term *photograph* (or *photo*) will allude to either or both forms of audiovisual reproduction.

Although the adage "a picture is worth a thousand words" might seem unrealistic, a visual portrayal of the crime scene clearly adds a dimension to both the investigation and prosecution of the case that no other medium can emulate. In fact, without the benefit of pictures, a witness or juror may be influenced by past experiences, preconceptions, stereotypes, and biases in making decisions about a crime scene. Indeed, photos and videotapes may convey information to the court more accurately than verbal descriptions of the crime.

The New Age of Digital Imaging

A key challenge today in law enforcement is the switch from film to digital imaging technology for criminal investigations. On a global basis, digital technology is becoming state of the art. Not only are many law enforcement agencies going digital, but many camera manufacturers are also abandoning their 35-mm lines in favor of digital technology. Some police administrators are resisting the digital trend, arguing that silver-based film (35 mm) is still the best because it cannot be manipulated and or changed. However, with today's low-cost computer software, even photos taken with the older 35-mm film are subject to some manipulation.

Although some departments continue to resist the switch, many have gone totally digital. For example, in 2004, the Miami-Dade Police Department adopted digital imaging and had begun to phase out instant-film technology (e.g., Polaroids), initially as a cost-cutting measure.[1] Other departments have been more reluctant to move away from 35-mm film but have adopted some form of digital imaging technology. For example, some departments have almost completely stopped using 35-mm film in capturing latent fingerprint evidence in the laboratory. This is now accomplished through digital imaging. Laboratory technicians are using software packages that enable them to make enhancements to fingerprints. Such enhancements can make identification easier and in some cases make identification possible when before it was not.

Making the switch to digital photography is not an easy commitment for a department. Much thought must be given to what must be done before the transition is made. This includes consideration of legal, technical, training, and hardware and software issues, to name only a few. Proper planning helps law enforcement organizations avoid unnecessary expenses and duplication of efforts.

Photographs as Evidence

The principal requirements to admit a photograph into evidence are relevance and authentication. In general, a photograph is admitted into evidence at the discretion of the trial judge. In rare cases, a chain of custody is required, or the best evidence rule may be invoked if the photograph is offered for its truth and is the basis of a controlling issue in the case.

The most important requirement is authentication. Specifically, the party seeking to introduce the photograph into evidence must be prepared to present testimony that the photograph is accurate and correct. In most cases, the testimony need not be from the photographer; a qualified witness who has knowledge of the scene and can testify that the photograph accurately portrays the scene will suffice. Some courts will rule that a photograph is self-authenticating or presumptively authentic. If the authenticity of the photograph is challenged, it is usually a question for the trier of fact (e.g., the jury).[2]

An inquiry into relevancy assures the trial court will at least consider whether a photograph, even if probative, might unduly confuse or deceive the trier of fact. The authentication requirement serves as a check against outright fraud, and a chain of custody requirement applied in particular instances provides additional insurance. Last, although federal laws allow the introduction of a print made from a negative as an original (rather than a duplicate), in the few cases involving the best evidence rule, even this relaxed application provides some protection. At a minimum, it indicates official recognition that there is (or was) a negative—a "super original," which, in accordance with the laws of physics, must bear some logical relationship to any duplicates.

Due to the recent advances in digital imaging technology, it has become necessary for police organizations to develop procedures that support the use of digital images as evidence in criminal investigations.

Preserving Digital Images

From an evidentiary standpoint, digital images must be handled with special care and consideration to preserve their integrity as evidence. As a rule, digital images are stored on removable media such as Secure Digital (SD) cards, CompactFlash (CF) cards, and Memory Sticks. Images saved to these storage media must be stored immediately, or as soon as reasonable, on a compact disc (CD) or other protected medium to create the "master disc." Digital images contained on this master disc must not be altered or manipulated in any way. Of course, the master disc must then be properly stored and protected so images can be viewed in the future. After the master disc is successfully made, the original medium contained in the camera may be erased and reused for subsequent investigations.

A "working copy" of the master disc can then be made for investigative purposes while protecting original images contained on the master disc. Images contained on the working copy can be manipulated for investigative purposes. However, any changes or adjustments must be properly documented. Finally, the master disc must be safely maintained until such time as there is an official determination that there will be no future need for the images.[3]

What to Photograph

Extensive expertise in photography and audio electronics is always a clear benefit to a crime scene investigator, but such training is not always required for good pictures of the scene. Any camera is better than no camera at all, and many relatively low-cost cameras come equipped with auto focus and rewind features. In any case, one important point to remember is that when photographing a crime scene, there can never be too many pictures. Depending on the crime scene, 100 to 200 photos may be typical for proper documentation. When using digital technology, it is vital for the investigator to back up crime scene photos and digital video (as discussed above).

Because digital media are relatively inexpensive, most departments can afford to take numerous photographs. In doing so, mistakes or problems encountered with one photo can usually be circumvented through the choice of others depicting the same scene or item. Photographs of the crime scene are usually taken in three stages: from the general view to the medium-range view to the close-up view. This approach enables a picture of all circumstances to be painted for jurors while leading up to the most critical part of the crime scene.

General Views. The general photograph is a sweeping view of the crime scene area (i.e., an overall scene, such as the neighborhood, including angles from all streets leading up to the crime scene). It demonstrates what the scene looks like in its own environment. Examples are:

- Photo of a bank that was robbed
- Photo of a house that was burglarized
- Abandoned "getaway" car in a wooded area

Photos depicting such scenes should be taken at a distance to reveal the natural surroundings of the location. In the case of a bank robbery, the bank should be photographed from across the street and from both sides of the building. This will give jurors a perspective of where the structure was situated and the location of possible escape routes.

Medium-Range Views. As we move in closer to the subject of the crime scene, additional photos should be taken. These photos should be taken at a distance no greater than 20 feet away from the subject or item being photographed. The intent of the medium-range photo is to depict specific items or objects in the crime scene. Some examples are blood splatters on the walls or an open window that served as the entry point for an intruder. Different lenses can be used to accomplish this phase of photography. For example, a wide-angle digital lens should be considered for a broad panoramic view of the scene. The purpose of the medium-range photography process is to allow jurors to link each print with the general crime scene photos.

Crime Scene Photographs

Benefits

- ☑ Provide easy storage and retrieval of data on the crime scene.
- ☑ Remove many inferences by practically placing the judge and jury at the crime scene.
- ☑ Give the investigator a source of reference as to the location of evidence at the scene.

Disadvantages

- ☑ Do not show true or actual distances.
- ☑ Can distort color and perceptions.
- ☑ Can be ruined by mechanical errors in processing.

Close-up Views. Moving from the broad to the specific, the last phase in photographing the crime scene is the close-up. These photos are taken at a distance of less than 5 feet using the zoom feature on the digital camera, and they should focus on small segments of a larger surface or on specific objects in the scene. Examples are bullet holes in the walls, weapons, blood-splatter stains, latent fingerprints, and so on. As with medium-range photos, these photographs should include some identifiable item from the medium-range photos to link object(s) being photographed with the general crime scene. It is also important to note that close-up photos should be taken with and without a small ruler or other item, such as a coin, to provide perspective.

Other Hints

Because many types of evidence undergo significant changes at the crime scene, it is important for investigators to photograph the crime scene in a timely fashion. This should typically precede most other tasks of the crime scene processing because objects cannot be examined adequately until after they are photographed from every angle. Accordingly, it is important that all camera angles and settings be recorded on the crime scene sketch.

Photos of the interior scenes should be conducted to depict the entire area. This is accomplished by overlapping photos from one scene to the next and working in one direction around the room. In the use of video, a slow panorama of the crime scene is necessary. It is usually advisable to either use a tripod or attempt to keep the camera at eye level for all the photos. Fox and Cunningham offer several other considerations that crime scene photographers should consider:[4]

- Approaches to and from the scene
- Surrounding areas (e.g., the yard of a house in which the homicide occurred, the general area surrounding an outdoor crime scene)
- Close-up photographs of the entrance and exit to the scene, or if these are not obvious, those most likely to have been used
- A general scenario shot showing the location of the body and its position in relation to the room or area in which it was found
- At least two photographs of the dead body at 90-degree angles to each other, with the camera placed as high as possible, pointing downward toward the body

As many close-ups of the dead body should be taken as needed to show wounds or injuries, weapons lying near the body, and the immediate surroundings. After the body is removed and after the removal of each item of evidence, the area underneath should be photographed if there is any mark, stain, or other apparent change. All fingerprints that do not need further development or that cannot be lifted should be photographed. Areas in which fingerprints were discovered are photographed to show the locations if these areas were not included in other photographs. Bloodstains should always be photographed, including their locations. Today, color digital images are considered the norm and, almost without exception, are accepted by courts as the best photographic evidence.

Perspective. It is important that the crime scene photographer show the relationship between one item of evidence and another. This is accomplished by showing the location of the articles in accordance with recognizable backgrounds. In the event that an item to be photographed is smaller than 6 inches, two photos should be taken. The first should be taken at close range, and the second should be taken from at least 6 feet away. This portrays the object in proper perspective.

Suitable Lighting. As a rule, the crime scene photographer will find that natural light at the scene is inadequate for good-quality photos and that artificial lighting is required. Investigators must therefore select the proper equipment for this task. Whether a flash or a more elaborate lighting system is used, it is of utmost importance to avoid unnecessary shadows. Shadows tend to hide details, some of which might be of grave significance to the investigation. In addition, the part of the photo that is closest to the flash may become washed out, and details might be lost. A good solution to this problem is the strategic use of floodlights to ensure consistent illumination.

Use of Markers. A generally accepted practice in crime scene photography is the use of measuring or other identifying devices in photos. These include rulers, tapes, coins, and so on. **Markers** such as these are included in the finished photograph and call attention to specific objects or enable the viewer of the photo to get a sense of the size of the object or the distance between objects. Some markings can be made with chalk to show specific locations of objects such as dead bodies, footprints, or weapons. Other markers include ink markings made on the surface of photographs after they have been printed.

Because the use of a marker introduces something foreign into the crime scene, investigators should take a photo of the area before placement of the marker and then take a second photo of the same setting after the marker is in place. Another marking technique is to place over the photo a transparent overlay containing all necessary arrows, circles, and so on to depict relevant information. This technique preserves the original photo and allows for comparison between the two.

Admissibility of Photographic Evidence

Trial courts bear the responsibility of admissibility of photographs as evidence in court. Such determinations have been based on several legal precedents:

1. *Materiality.* The object portrayed in the photo must be material and relevant to the case at hand. All photographs, provided that they serve to prove a particular point in the issue, should be admitted into evidence.

   a. A *material photograph* is one that relates to and makes a substantive contribution to the specific case in question.

FIGURE 2.6 A bloody shoeprint is photographed using a marker to show perspective. *Courtesy of Mike Himmel and the Missouri State Highway Patrol.*

b. A *relevant photograph* also applies to the matter in question and is used to support testimony. It is representative of the evidence that relates it to the matter in question to determine the truth of the circumstances (*Barnett* v. *State*, 1922).

2. *Prejudicial images.* Any photograph or image admitted must not prejudice, or appeal unfairly, to the emotions of the jury. Some judges have suppressed photos depicting unusually gruesome crime scenes. In one recent case, photos were taken of a defendant immediately after his arrest, showing him as dirty and unkempt. The photos were offered as evidence to contrast the defendant's clean and polished image in the courtroom. The judge refused to admit the image into evidence on the basis that it was prejudicial.

3. *Distorted photos.* Photographs must be kept free of distortion. Three types of distortion have generally been common in crime scene photographs: incorrect point of view, perspective, and misrepresentation of tone or color. These problems commonly occur through improper use of angles of the photo. For example, a handgun lying next to a dead body may be photographed to appear much larger in size than it actually is, thus distorting the perception of the scene. Another example is bruises on a body, which might indicate the extent of the wound or even the time it was inflicted. Therefore, if the tone of a bruise is shown in a photo as greenish in color rather than bluish, a different conclusion may be made as to the extent of the injuries. Because of this, the photographer or laboratory technician may be subjected to rigorous cross-examination regarding his or her expertise in the processing of digital images. Such distortions must be avoided because they will taint the case and will probably cause the images to be excluded as evidence.

Additionally, photos and physical evidence have different requirements regarding the chain of custody. For example, it is not necessary for the person taking the photograph to be the one to testify about it in court. In *State* v. *Fournier* (1963), however, the court held that evidence must be offered to show that the photograph is an accurate representation of the object(s) portrayed (as mentioned above). Such evidence is usually given by an officer who was present on the crime scene and who can vouch for the validity of the photo.

Since the late 1960s, an avalanche of cases have regarded the admissibility of videotape recordings in criminal trials. Generally, the courts have held that such evidence is admissible on the same basis as motion picture films with sound and is subject to the same rules of evidence as motion pictures and photographic evidence. Many courts have even admitted videotapes that had inferior-quality sound but permitted the sound track to be "cleaned up" electronically.

Identification of Photographs

It is of critical importance for investigators to log their photos carefully as to date, time, and sequence number. Also included should be the following:

- Type of case
- Description of subject of photo
- Location
- Names of persons handling evidence
- Assigned case number
- Any other relevant information

Using this technique will reduce hours of sorting out finished photos and trying to determine what picture goes where.

PHOTOGRAPHIC LOG   PAGE __1__ of __1__

LOCATION ___Living Room___   CAMERA ___#31___

DATE ___4-16-10___   CAMERA TYPE ___Nikon Coolpix___

CASE # ___0211-10___   ___P-1 digital___

OFFICERS ___Lt. Johnson, Officer Watson, Officer Smith___   COMMENTS ___SD Disk #14___

Photo #	Description of Subject Photographed	Scale	Misc. Comments	Sketch (if required)
1	Long-range shot — living room		Photos from top	
2	Close-up — defense wound			
3	Medium-range shot — knife			
4	Close-up — powder burns			
5	Long-range shot — hallway		From left side	
6	Medium-range shot — handgun		From right side	
7	Close-up — handgun			
8	Close-up — knife			

FIGURE 2.7 Sample photographic log.

Surveillance Photographs

Surveillance photography is used covertly in establishing identities or in document-ing criminal behavior. Photography of this nature is selective and may have many benefits. For example, it may aid officers in identifying the physical locations of criminal activity or in formulating a raid plan for serving a search warrant. The covert use of **surveillance** is now used commonly in banks and convenience stores as a deterrent for would-be robbers and as an aid in prosecution. Some systems use single-reflex cameras with telephoto lenses, and others use infrared film.

Most investigations using surveillance photography are vice and organized crime operations, and a specially outfitted van or truck is usually used by investi-gators. In these operations, illegal transactions are made discreetly among crimi-nals, and thorough documentation is necessary to establish proof beyond a reasonable doubt. Such photography can be problematic, however, in that proper lighting is sometimes difficult to come by. In response, many police agencies have purchased night-vision devices that affix to surveillance cameras. These devices use natural light emitted by stars or the moon and usually produce identifiable images.

Capturing the Crime Scene on Digital Video

In addition to the use of digital photography at crime scenes, the use of digital video of crime scenes is becoming commonplace. There are many benefits to the use of digital video cameras at the crime scene. They are easy to use; relatively inexpensive; faster than photographs; and, in many ways, offer jurors a more complete reproduction of the crime scene.

Several distinct advantages exist in using digital video at crime scenes. For example, officers are able to begin recording at the extreme perimeters of the crime scene (i.e., point of entry) and walk closer and closer to the specific objects in question. Such evidence lends great perspective to photographs, which can depict minute details of the same objects. For example, a panoramic video view of a dead body lying near a handgun can show proportional distance between the two. In conjunction with the video, a close-up photograph can further depict details of bloodstains, possible powder burns, and wounds on the victim.

Another advantage is that digital video can easily be used in the courtroom because many players can play back digital tapes. In addition, because digital media are "developed" instantly, prosecutors can view the evidence moments after recording. Another benefit of digital video recording at the crime scene is the use of the freeze-frame feature in most video systems. This enables the viewer to stop the tape at any critical point for a closer view of the subject being recorded. Many photo and video stores also have the capability to make indi-vidual photographs directly from digital video, which can be useful in the inves-tigation or prosecution of the case.

The Crime Scene Sketch

The crime scene sketch complements photographs and videos taken of the scene. With increased use of video and digital cameras at crime scenes, one might argue that preparation of the sketch is no longer needed. In actuality, because videos and photos may tend to distort the dimensions of the crime scene, a properly prepared crime scene sketch is all the more important to a properly documented crime scene. In other words, whereas a photograph represents the scene as it is perceived by the viewer, the diagram represents the scene as it actually is.

In many ways, the crime scene sketch can show certain details better than a photograph. For example, photographs are two-dimensional and may fail to show the distance between objects. Also, a photograph cannot show the entire crime scene; whereas, a sketch can.

A crime scene sketch is a scale drawing that locates evidence in relation to other factors. As a rule, the sketch will not identify such items as the color of a wall, the type of floor, the general condition of the area, and non-evidential matter.

Whereas a sketch that is properly prepared can virtually always be used in court,; photographs may not be permitted under certain circumstances. In cases in which photographs may inflame the jury, courts often refuse to admit them into evidence. When this occurs, the diagram is of major importance. Additionally, a crime scene sketch can supplement the verbal description to present spatial relationships of the evidence.

A properly prepared sketch is an important tool for the prosecutor as well. The sketch can become the focus point of courtroom testimony. Witnesses can show on the diagram their relationship to observations of the crime, and each item of evidence can be pinpointed.

Putting It Together

Several methods have been developed over the years to best conduct a detailed sketch of the scene. One should remember that the objective of the crime scene sketch is to portray the scene accurately, not artistically. Too much detail in a crime scene sketch will remove the advantage of a sketch over a photograph. Thus, most officers can be expected to produce a sketch successfully.

In each crime scene sketch, some items are considered essential. As with note taking, however, such items should not be considered the only items needed for complete documentation of the scene. The crime scene sketch should include the following information:

- The investigator's complete name and rank
- The date, time, type of crime, and assigned case number
- The complete names of other officers assisting in the making of the sketch
- The address of the crime scene, its position in a building, landmarks, and so on
- The scale of the drawing (if no scale, indicate by printing "not to scale")
- The primary items of physical evidence and other critical features of the crime scene, located by detailed measurements from at least two fixed points of reference
- A key or legend identifying the symbols or points of reference used in the sketch

Measurement

One general rule of sketching is that the sketch should reflect as accurately as possible the important details of the scene. Such information must be recorded uniformly. For example, if the dimensions of a dead body in a field are recorded accurately but the location of a handgun found near the body is estimated only roughly, the sketch is virtually useless. Accordingly, all measures of distance must be conducted by using the same method. Specifically, one part of the scene should not be paced off and another area of the scene measured with a tape measure.

After the case goes to court and a measurement error is discovered, the explanation of such an error may prove embarrassing and difficult. Use of a tape measure is therefore considered the most effective method of measuring the scene. Other tools for crime scene sketching include:

- Paper for the sketch (preferably graph paper)
- Clipboard
- Colored pencils (if necessary)
- Fifty-foot steel tape
- Thumbtacks to hold down one end of the tape if the investigator is alone
- Straight-edge ruler
- Eight- to 12-foot tape for measuring from the baseline

Rough and Finished Sketches

There are generally two sketches for every crime scene: a rough sketch and a finished sketch. The **rough sketch** is the one drawn by officers on the crime scene. Generally, it is not drawn to scale but should reflect accurate dimensions and distances between objects of importance. At times, it might be necessary to draw more than one rough crime scene sketch. For example, one sketch might portray the overall scene, and a second sketch could show only the body and its immediate surroundings. Alterations to the rough sketch should not be made after the investigator leaves the scene.

The **finished sketch** is simply a completed sketch drawn to scale. This is drawn from information contained on the rough sketch and should accurately reflect all measurements indicated on the rough sketch. With the finished sketch being drawn to scale, however, it is not necessary to include the specific measurements on the sketch itself. If the finished sketch is not drawn to scale, measurements are required. Finished sketches need not be prepared by the crime scene investigator, although in court, the investigator will be required to affirm that the finished sketch is an accurate portrayal of the scene. In many cases, the finished sketch is prepared by a professional draftsperson or is made with the use of specially designed computerized programs.

FIGURE 2.8 Final sketches much depict precise measurements and can be accomplished using computerized programs such as shown here.

FIGURE 2.9 In the absence of a computerized program, investigators can rely on a handwritten diagram of the scene. Finalized sketches must be drawn to scale, as depicted here.

Choosing the Best Method

Different crime scenes present different sketching problems. Let's now consider three of the most widely used sketching methods:

1. *Coordinate method.* The **coordinate method** uses the practice of measuring an object from two fixed points of reference. One such procedure is the **baseline technique,** in which a line is drawn between two known points. The baseline could also be a wall or a mathematically derived point along a designated area where exact measurements can be determined. The measurements of a particular item are then taken from left to right along the baseline to a point at right angles to the object that is to be plotted. This distance is noted in the legend with a circled number after the name of the object.

2. *Triangulation method.* The **triangulation method** is a bird's-eye view of the scene that uses fixed objects from which to measure. This is particularly useful for sketching outdoor crime scenes where there are no easily identifiable points of reference. In this procedure, two or more widely separated points of reference are required. The item of interest is then located by measuring along a straight line from the reference points.

3. *Cross-projection method.* The **cross-projection method** is used in indoor crime scenes. It is basically a top-down view of the crime scene, with the walls of the room "folded" down to reveal locations of bullet holes, blood-spatter evidence, and so on, which would not be apparent otherwise. Measurements are then made from a designated point on the floor to the area on the wall in question.

On completion of the sketch, the investigator should be prepared to do two things: (1) photocopy the sketch and attach the copy to the officer's report and (2) file the original sketch in a secure location so it is ready for presentation in court at a later date. The officer should remember that both the rough and finished sketches are admissible in court if they are prepared or witnessed by the investigator, provided that they both portray the crime scene accurately.

In summary, the crime scene sketch is an integral part of the crime scene investigation because it gives perspective to what happened at the time of the crime. Jurors, typically, can relate to a well-drafted sketch depicting all-important areas of the crime scene location; thus, investigators must take appropriate measures to ensure an accurate and meaningful crime scene sketch.

FIGURE 2.10 Handwritten rough sketch of a burglary crime scene. The rough sketch is the basis for the finalized or formal sketch. *Courtesy of John Mitchell.*

FIGURE 2.11 Baseline or coordinate method.

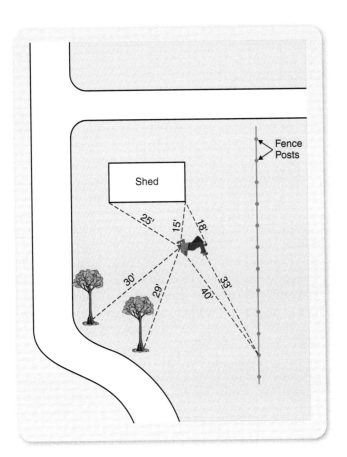

FIGURE 2.12 Triangulation sketching method.

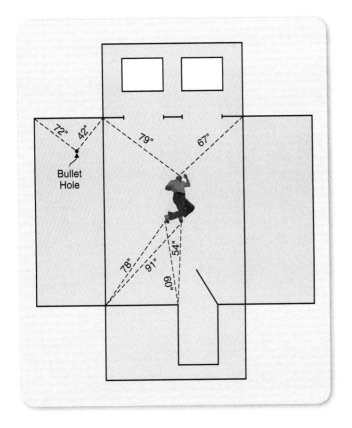

FIGURE 2.13 Cross-projection sketching method. Note that in this type of sketch, the walls are drawn as if folded flat.

CASE IN POINT:

Investigative "Tunnel Vision"—The Duke Lacrosse Rape Case

In May 2007, North Carolina Attorney General Roy A. Cooper dismissed rape charges that were been brought against three former members of the Duke University lacrosse team, saying that the players were innocent of all charges. Those charges were brought by Durham County Prosecutor Michael B. Nifong after an exotic dancer who had performed at a house party in 2006 told police she had been raped, sodomized, strangled, and beaten by the partygoers. Contradictions in the accuser's statements, however, along with a lack of DNA and other evidence, convinced Cooper that the attack never occurred. Cooper stated publicly that Nifong should have seen the contradictions himself. Calling Nifong "a rogue prosecutor," Cooper said "When you have a prosecutor who takes advantage of his enormous power and overreaches like this, then yes, it's offensive."

Durham County Prosecutor Michael Nifong, along with the Durham Police Department relentlessly pursued criminal charges against three Duke University students for the alleged rape of an exotic dancer. The North Carolina Attorney General determined that no such crime ever occurred and charges against the students were dismissed.

Public accusations against investigators with the Durham Police Department also resulted from the Duke rape case. Specifically, the methods of the photo identification process were placed into question, and accusations surfaced that police have been known to use intimidation tactics on witnesses and that the police supervisor in the case, Sergeant Mark Gottlieb, has unfairly targeted Duke students in the past.

The majority of criticism came from the police lineup whereby the exotic dancer identified the Duke University students. Lawyers and media reports alike suggested that the photo identification process was severely flawed. For example, during the photo identifications, Mangum was told that she would be viewing Duke University lacrosse players who attended the party, and she was asked if she remembered seeing them at the party and in what capacity. Defense attorneys suggested that this was essentially a "multiple-choice test in which there were no wrong answers." U.S. Department of Justice guidelines suggest including at least five non-suspect filler photos for each suspect included.

At least two photo lineups were reported by the media. In the March identification process, Mangum

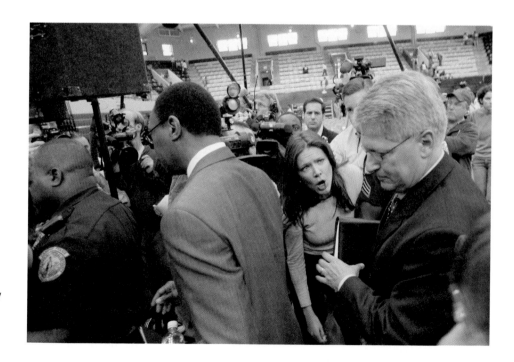

FIGURE 2.14 Photograph of former Prosecutor Mike Nifong being scorned by members of the public after evidence was made public that he improperly charged members of the Duke University Lacrosse Team.
Courtesy of AP Wide World Photos.

selected at least five different individuals, one of whom was Reade Seligmann (whom she identified with 70% certainty). During the April identification process, Mangum identified at least 16 lacrosse players. She identified Seligmann and Finnerty with 100% certainty and Dave Evans with 90% certainty during the April identification procedure. In the disclosed report, there were only two individuals that she identified during both the March and April lineups—Brad Ross and Reade Seligmann.

Ross (the only player she identified as attending the party with 100% certainty during both procedures) provided to police investigators indisputable evidence through cell phone records and a sworn affidavit from a witness that he was with his girlfriend at North Carolina State University before, during, and after the party. Another person Mangum identified in April also provided police with evidence that he did not attend the party at all. In regards to Seligmann's identification, Mangum's confidence increased from 70% in March to 100% in April.

Gary Wells, an Iowa State University professor and expert on police identification procedures, replied that memory does not get better with time. According to the transcript of the photo identification released on The Abrams Report, Mangum also stated that Dave Evans had a mustache on the night of the attack. Dave Evans' lawyer stated that his client has never had a mustache and that photos as well as eyewitness testimony would reveal that Dave Evans has never had a mustache.

These examples of how investigators conducted their investigation shows how police can be blinded and mistakenly led by a prosecutor whose "tunnel vision" blinds them to all available evidence.

One day later, Cooper dismissed the criminal charges Nifong apologized to the students, saying, "To the extent that I made judgments that ultimately prove to be incorrect, I apologize to the three students that were wrongly accused." He added, "I also understand that when someone has been wrongly accused, the harm caused by the accusations might not be immediately undone by merely dismissing them...." Calls for further action against Nifong led to his being disbarred in 2007 after an ethics hearing by the North Carolina Bar Association. He was later found guilty of criminal contempt of court and spent only one day in jail.

Thematic questions:

1. Given what we know about the Duke Lacrosse investigation, in what ways should criminal investigators have changed their tactics to ensure a fair and partial investigation?

2. How does the investigative process in this case contribute to the wrongful prosecution of Duke Lacrosse defendants?

3. Given the discretion of a prosecutor to file criminal charges, to what extent is it proper for a criminal investigator to speak up whenever he or she feels that the prosecutor is abusing their authority?

Sources: "As Duke rape case unravels, D.A.'s judgment questioned: Defense describes him as willing to skirt law for conviction." *San Francisco Chronicle,* December 24, 2006; Benjamin, N., A. Blythe. "Easley awaiting Nifong resignation". *News and Observer,* June 16, 2007. Available at http://www.newsobserver.com/news/story/607879.html; Biesecker, M., B, Niolet, and J. Neff. "DA on the spot for comments." *The News & Observer,* April 22, 2006; Digital image of 33 page Amended Complaint, as filed; Graham, D. "State Bar finds Nifong guilty on 27 counts of misconduct." *The Duke Chronicle,* June 16, 2007. Available at http://media.www.dukechronicle.com/media/storage/paper884/news/2007/06/14/News/State.Bar.Finds.Nifong.Guilty.On.27.Counts.Of.Misconduct-2915504.shtml; Neff, J. "Quest to convict hid a lack of evidence." *The News and Observer,* March 14, 2007. Available at http://www.newsobserver.com/1537/story/564100.html; "Nifong will be disbarred for ethics violations." *Associated Press,* June 18, 2007. Available at http://www.msnbc.msn.com/id/19264396/; Parker, L. "Disbarment may not be end for Nifong." *USA Today,* June 19, 2007. Available at http://www.usatoday.com/news/nation/2007-06-17; Pressure on Nifong in Duke case: Misstatements may cost him his career, *The News & Observer.* December 24, 2006; Available at http://news.findlaw.com/hdocs/docs/duke/ncbnifong12407cmp.html.

Summary Checklist

In this chapter, we consider the ways that information about crimes is documented by the criminal investigator. A properly documented case is one that is more likely to succeed in court. See how well you are able to answer the following questions in your checklist.

1. Describe the usefullness of field notes.

An investigator's field notes are his or her most personal and readily available record of the crime scene search. Allow victims and witnesses to state in their own words what occurred. Be sure they answer the who, what, when, where, why, and how of what occurred.

A shorthand system should be devised for use in the field. This can include using "S" for suspect, "V" for victim, "W-1" for witness number 1, "C" for complainant, and so on. An investigator's notes might be required later on for court purposes.

- Notes taken at a crime scene must adequately reflect the condition and state of the location at the time of the crime scene search.
- Field notes should be written in the order in which information is learned.
- When first encountering a witness or victim, it is important for the investigator to allow the person to state in his or her own words what occurred.

2. Identify the proper information to be contained in the police report.

The police report is the formal record of the offense and a record of investigative steps taken to solve the crime. As with field notes, the rule of thumb is to seek answers to the questions who, what, when, why, how, and where. The police report should also be prepared chronologically and factual (i.e., contain no personal observations). The police report must also be thorough and to the point.

3. In what ways do photographs assist in documenting the crime scene?

Photographs are excellent sources of evidence to document the crime scene. They can be either film or digital format, but digital photography is rapidly becoming the standard in crime scene documentation.

- Photos of the scene should include general, medium-range, and close-up views.

Photos must be taken and preserved so as to be admissible in court. The principal requirements to admit a photograph into evidence are relevance and authentication. From the investigator's standpoint, the most important requirement is authentication (i.e., the photo must be accurate and correct).

- Police organizations must develop a procedure that supports the use of digital images as evidence in criminal investigations.

In addition to being material and relevant, crime scene photos must not be prejudicial or distorted in any fashion. Doing so will risk the possibility that the photo might not being admitted into evidence. Photos and physical evidence have different requirements regarding the chain of custody; as a rule, it is not necessary for the person taking the photograph to be the one to testify about it in court.

Surveillance photography can have many benefits:

- It can aid officers in identifying the physical locations of criminals.
- It can help in formulating a raid plan for serving a search warrant.
- It can record illegal transactions.

Most investigations using surveillance photography are vice and organized crime operations.

4. How has the video camera become such an important piece of equipment in documenting crime scenes?

The use of digital video of
the crime scene is becoming
commonplace. It is easy to
use; relatively inexpensive;
faster than photographs; and
in many ways, offers jurors a
more complete reproduction of the crime scene.

Other advantages of digital video include:

- Officers are able to begin recording at the
extreme perimeters of the crime scene and
walk closer and closer to the specific
objects in question.

- A panoramic video view of certain evidence can show proportional distance
between the two.

- A close-up photograph can show details of
bloodstains, powder burns, and wounds
on the victim.

- Digital video can easily be used in the
courtroom.

- The use of the freeze-frame feature is
useful in court.

**5. What important point should you remember
when preparing a crime scene sketch?**

The crime scene sketch can
show certain details better
than a photograph. It is a
scale drawing that locates
evidence in relation to other
factors. Items such as the
color of a wall, the type of
floor, the general condition of the area, and non-
evidential matter are normally not depicted.

A sketch that is properly prepared can virtually always be used in court, but photographs
that inflame the jury might be excluded in court.

- A crime scene sketch can supplement the
verbal description to present spatial relationships of the evidence.

- The objective of the crime scene sketch is to
portray the scene accurately, not artistically.

In each crime scene sketch, some items are
considered essential. As with note taking,
however, such items should not be considered

the only items needed for complete documentation of the scene. The crime scene sketch
should include:

- All relevant information regarding the
incident

- The person drawing the sketch

- Primary items of evidence

One general rule of sketching is that the
sketch should reflect as accurately as possible
the important details of the scene. Such information must be recorded uniformly. For example, if the dimensions of a dead body in a field
are recorded accurately but the location of a
handgun found near the body is estimated
only roughly, the sketch is virtually useless.
Accordingly, all measures of distance must be
conducted by using the same method. Specifically, one part of the scene should not be
paced off and another area of the scene measured with a tape measure.

Two sketches are generally made for every
crime scene: a rough sketch and a finished sketch.

- The rough sketch is the one drawn by officers on the crime scene and is typically not
drawn to scale. The finished sketch is simply
a completed sketch drawn to scale. This is
drawn from information contained on the
rough sketch and should accurately reflect all
measurements indicated on the rough sketch.

Different crime scenes call for the use of
different sketching methods:

- The coordinate method uses the practice
of measuring an object from two fixed
points of reference. One such procedure is
the baseline technique, in which a line is
drawn between two known points.

- The triangulation method is a bird's-eye
view of the scene, utilizing fixed objects
from which to measure. This is particularly
useful for sketching outdoor crime scenes.

- The cross-projection method is used in
indoor crime scenes. It is basically a top-
down view of the crime scene, with the
walls of the room "folded" down.

Key Terms

baseline technique

chain of custody

coordinate method

cross-projection method

field interview cards

field notes

finished sketch

markers

rough sketch

surveillance

triangulation method

Discussion Questions

1. Discuss the types of information that should be included in the note-taking process at a crime scene.

2. Explain the primary purpose of the official police report and how the three-pronged rule of thumb applies in writing official reports.

3. In what ways can the perspective of a crime scene be distorted through photography?

4. With the exception of any unusual circumstances, explain why evidence at a crime scene should be recorded before objects are collected or removed.

mycrimekit™

Go to mycrimekit.com to explore the following study tools and resources specific to this chapter:

- *Practice Quiz:* Multiple-choice, true/false, short-answer, and essay questions.
- *Flashcards:* There are 11 key terms in this chapter. Flashcards test your knowledge of the chapter's key terms.

- *Web Links:* Check out the hotlink to *The New York Times* articles on criminology and criminal law.
- *Career Center:* Check out the hot links to interesting careers in criminal justice, criminology, and juvenile justice.
- *The Research Center:* Check out the Cybrary and research navigator for even more resources.

Notes

1. Sanfilippo, P. J. (2004). Tips on managing the switch from conventional film to digital *Evidence Technology Magazine* 2(5):18–21.
2. Tyler, P. B. (1995). The Kelly-Frye "general acceptance" standard remains the rule for admissibility of novel scientific evidence: *People* v. *Leahy.*
3. Scientific Working Group Imaging Technology (SWGIT). *Definitions and guidelines for the use of imaging technologies in the criminal justice system.* Federal Bureau of Investigation; June 8, 1999; International Association of Identification (1997), 1997 *Resolution and legislative committee, Resolution 97–9.*
4. Fox, R. H. and C. L. Cunningham (1989). *Crime scene search and physical evidence handbook.* Washington, DC: U.S. Department of Justice.

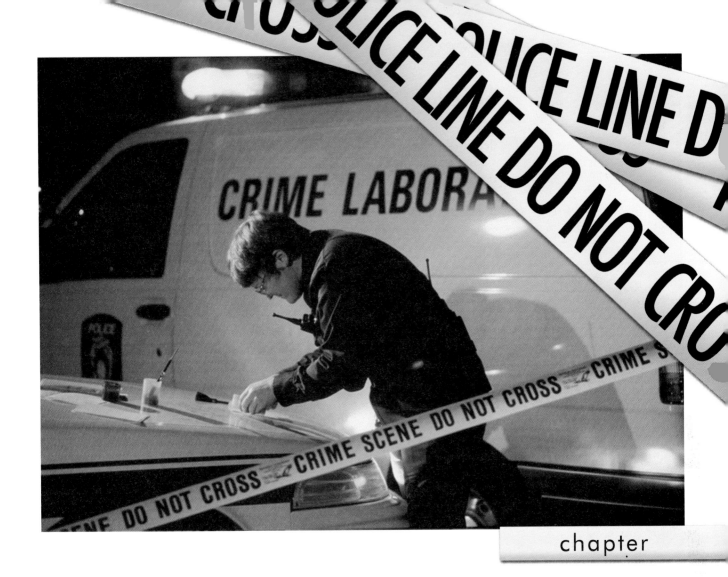

Processing the Crime Scene

This chapter will enable you to:

- Understand the stage of the preliminary investigation and the role of the first officer.
- Understand the various methods for handling special situations at the scene.
- Explain the importance of interviewing witnesses at a crime scene and proper ways of conducting a neighborhood canvass.
- Describe how to properly prepare crime scene reports.
- Explain how to properly perform a follow-up investigation.

Introduction

The actions taken by patrol and investigative personnel at a crime scene often determine the success or failure of a criminal investigation. The survival of victims, the apprehension of the perpetrator, and the ultimate outcome of any resulting criminal prosecution may depend entirely upon prompt and proper responses by the officers at the scene. All personnel must understand, and be prepared to carry out correctly, the operational procedures established by the department for the management of crime scenes. Police officers responding to a crime scene have several very important responsibilities. They must:

- Be prepared to inform superiors of their findings
- Assist victims
- Secure and protect the crime scene
- Apprehend the perpetrator
- Collect and preserve evidence
- Interview witnesses
- Perform other necessary operational functions

Even though some of these tasks may be the responsibility of departmental specialists, every officer in the department should be able to conduct all of these functions properly if called upon to do so. Above all, the patrol officers initially responding to the scene must understand that they have a heavy responsibility to ensure that the appropriate actions are taken to protect life and property, preserve evidence, and make it possible for subsequent investigative work to be successful.

Any officer responding to a crime scene must understand that the proper management of a crime scene has at least three distinct aspects: administrative, operational, and legal. The officer must comply with the administrative requirements of the officer's department as to procedures to be followed en route to the scene, while at the scene, and after departure from the scene (e.g., investigative follow-up and submission of reports). From an operational standpoint, the officer must be aware of all applicable departmental policies (e.g., assisting victims, securing the crime scene, collecting evidence, or preserving it in place for collection by others) and must be able to carry out these functions effectively. Furthermore, the officer must be aware of the legal constraints applicable to the conduct of officers regarding crime scenes (e.g., authority to enter a suspected scene, authority to search the scene, authority to arrest or otherwise detain persons found there). This three-fold responsibility can be carried out properly only if the department provides adequate guidance through well-crafted crime scene policies and the necessary training to ensure that all officers understand what is expected of them and what they are and are not permitted to do.

The Preliminary Investigation

Evidence of one type or another exists in all crimes. A logical procedure for identifying, collecting, and preserving evidence is therefore essential. The practice of following prescribed steps in the identification and collection of evidence is critical in making an arrest and in subsequent prosecution of the offender. The evidence collection process begins immediately after the discovery of a crime. In most situations, this precursory investigative phase is known as the **preliminary investigation**. Generally, the term *preliminary investigation* is defined as an initial inquiry by officers to establish facts and circumstances of a suspected crime and to preserve any evidence related to that crime. Preliminary investigation includes:

- Securing the crime scene
- Considering the possible arrest of a suspect
- Locating and questioning witnesses and victims
- Documenting the crime scene
- Identifying and collecting evidence

The function of the preliminary investigation is closely linked with the duties of the first officer to arrive at the crime scene (discussed later), who, in most cases, is a respondent from the patrol division. As with any crime scene, the first officer and investigators should consider the scene itself as evidence. This is because much valuable information can be learned from items left on the scene, provided that it has not been tampered with or altered in any way.

The crime scene represents the ultimate situation that places many responsibilities on the first officer arriving at the scene. These include making an arrest, rendering first aid to injured parties, and protecting evidence at the scene. The latter responsibility includes preservation of trace evidence, firearms, and blood or other bodily fluids.

Investigators must remember that a crime scene is a location where evidence of a crime may be found. It is not necessarily where the crime was committed. Consequently, there are primary, secondary, and sometimes tertiary crime scenes. For example, investigators may use a warrant to search a suspect's home. Even though the suspect did not commit the crime at that location, evidence of the crime may be found there. In another instance, an offender might kidnap someone at one location (primary crime scene), transport the victim (the car being a secondary crime scene), commit another crime at a distant location (murder, for instance) and then dispose of the body at a fourth scene.

Crime Scene Evidence

Crime scene evidence is dynamic. Protection and preservation of the scene are therefore crucial because both avert the possibility of contamination, loss, or unnecessary movement of physical evidence. In the evidence-collection process, contamination of evidence occurs most commonly when evidence is not properly secured, is wrongfully mixed with other types of evidence, or is altered significantly from its original condition at the **crime scene**. When this occurs, the evidence is usually rendered inadmissible or "incompetent" by the court.

The preliminary investigation involves the identification and preservation of evidence, much of which is minute or "trace" evidence. Trace evidence is any type of material left at—or taken from—a crime scene or the result of contact between two surfaces, such as shoes and the floor covering or soil or fibers from where someone sat on an upholstered chair.

When a crime is committed, fragmentary (or trace) evidence needs to be collected from the scene. A team of specialized police technicians go to the scene of the crime and seal it off. They both record video and take photographs of the crime scene, victim (if there is one), and items of evidence. If applicable, they undertake a firearms and ballistics examination. They also check for shoe and tire mark impressions, examine any vehicles, and check for fingerprints.

Each item found as evidence is put into a sterilized container (contrary to popular belief, this is almost never a plastic bag but is actually a paper bag or envelope, which prevents further decomposition of evidence) and labeled for later analysis at the laboratory.

The **Locard exchange principle**, also known as Locard's theory or the transfer of evidence theory, was first put forward by twentieth-century forensic scientist, Edmond Locard. Locard was the director of the first known crime laboratory, located in Lyon, France. Locard's exchange principle states, "With contact between two items, there will be an exchange."[1]

For the most part, Locard's principle is applied to crime scenes where the perpetrator(s) of a crime comes into contact with the scene, so he or she will both bring something into the scene and leave with something from the scene. Every contact leaves a trace. For example, Locard stated:

> Wherever he steps, whatever he touches, whatever he leaves, even unconsciously, will serve as a silent witness against him. Not only his fingerprints or his footprints, but his hair, the fibers from his clothes, the glass he breaks, the tool mark he leaves, the paint he scratches, the blood or semen he deposits or collects. All of these and more, bear mute witness against him. This is evidence that does not forget. It is not confused by the excitement of the moment. It is not absent because human witnesses are. It is factual evidence. Physical evidence cannot be wrong, it cannot perjure itself, it cannot be wholly absent. Only human failure to find it, study and understand it, can diminish its value (Edmond Locard).

An easier way to remember this is: "Every contact leaves a trace."

Material transferred in this fashion is usually referred to as **trace evidence**, which generally refers to minute or even microscopic bits of matter that are not immediately apparent to the naked eye. Consequently, such evidence is extremely difficult to locate at the crime scene. Because of its microscopic nature, the criminal may be far less likely to eliminate it purposely than with more telltale evidence such as blood splattering or fingerprints. As a reminder of the significance of trace evidence, one should remember that serial killers such as Wayne Williams, John Gacy, and Gary Ridgeway (the "Green River Killer") were apprehended as a result of trace evidence or implements of their crimes being found in their possession.[2] Hence, the first officer at the scene bears the critical responsibility of protecting such evidence from contamination.

In criminal investigations, the utility of physical evidence should be clearly understood. Some types of physical evidence are more obvious in nature than others. For example:

- Physical evidence can prove the elements of a crime or reveal that a crime has been committed. *Case example:* A search warrant served on the residence of a suspected drug dealer revealed a quantity of cocaine, scales, paraphernalia, business records showing drug dealing, and large amounts of cash concealed in shoeboxes.
- Physical evidence may be used to place the suspect at the scene. *Case example:* Shoe impressions found in the mud outside a burglary victim's residence were found to match those of a known burglar in the community.
- Physical evidence can be used to eliminate innocent persons. *Case example:* A murderer was careful not to leave fingerprints at the crime scene. However, blood samples taken from the scene later revealed, through DNA typing, the true identity of the perpetrator.
- Suspects confronted with physical evidence may confess to a crime. *Case example:* Although a convenience store robbery suspect was wearing a ski mask at the time of the robbery, he admitted his role in the crime when a hidden-camera shot of him during the crime revealed a recognizable torn edge on the corner of his jacket.
- Witness testimony can be supported with physical evidence. *Case example:* A neighbor told the police that she heard glass breaking at about 1:30 A.M.

Investigators later located a broken pane of glass in a nearby house and, through use of the witness's statement, were able to determine the time of the offense.

- Physical evidence can have a powerful positive impact on juries in criminal cases. *Case example:* As the nickel-plated .38-caliber handgun was handed to the first jury member for inspection, fellow jurists leaned forward and watched while anticipating their chance to touch and hold the weapon that the prosecutor claimed was used in the crime.

Types of Evidence

Evidence can also be classified in several distinct ways. Classifications can be considered either individually or in combination with other classes of evidence. In general, there are two commonly used classifications: corpus delicti and associative evidence. The term **corpus delicti** simply refers to evidence that establishes that a crime has been committed, such as pry marks on a doorjamb. Conversely, **associative evidence** links a suspect with a crime, such as fingerprints, footprints, bloodstains, and fibers. Examples of evidence are:

- *Physical evidence.* As a practical matter, physical evidence could be considered as a classification of its own. Physical evidence is self-explanatory in nature and generally speaks for itself in a court of law. Examples are weapons, fingerprints, blood, and drugs. (See Appendix A for a list of types of physical evidence.)

- *Direct or prima facie evidence.* Prima facie evidence is evidence established by law that at face value proves a fact in dispute. For example, states establish the minimum blood alcohol content to show that a person is under the influence.

- *Indirect or circumstantial evidence.* Circumstantial evidence merely tends to incriminate a person without offering conclusive proof. For example, although a person's footprint located outside a burglary victim's residence doesn't show that the person who left the print was the burglar, it does suggest that he or she could be.

- *Testimonial evidence.* As the term implies, testimonial evidence consists of a verbal statement offered by a witness while under oath or affirmation. It may also be evidence offered by way of a sworn pretrial deposition. Although many people define testimony in the same way as evidence, they are clearly distinct. Simply, testimony is evidence offered in an oral manner and is used most commonly to explain some form of physical evidence (e.g., gunpowder residue, fingerprints).

- *Trace evidence.* Trace evidence consists of extremely small items of evidence, such as hair or clothing fibers. With the aid of modern forensic analysis, trace evidence plays a greater role today than ever before in solving capital cases.

- *Demonstrative evidence.* Demonstrative evidence is evidence used to demonstrate or clarify an issue rather than to prove something. An example is the use of anatomical dolls to aid in the testimony of children in a sexual molestation case.

Legal Considerations

Officers collecting evidence, or "evidence custodians," must have a good working knowledge of state and federal laws governing the handling and disposition of evidence under their control. As custodians of evidence, they are often called upon to testify concerning their evidence management practices in general and

FIGURE 3.1 Investigators wearing protective biohazard suits while documenting a homicide crime scene. Courtesy of Mike Himmel.

their control over specific items of evidence in particular. As such, evidence custodians should be familiar with the following general federal restrictions on the gathering, preserving, and disposing of evidence, as well as state law and court rulings that may affect their responsibilities.

Search Warrants. The Fourth Amendment to the U.S. Constitution is the primary constraint on the seizure of property by government agents. A search warrant designating the specific premises to be searched and the specific items to be seized is the basic requirement for law enforcement officers to seize property. The types of property subject to seizure include stolen property, property unlawfully possessed or contraband, property used or possessed for the purpose of being used to commit or conceal the commission of an offense, and property constituting evidence or tending to demonstrate that an offense was committed.

Under certain circumstances, a warrant to search or seize property need not be obtained. Included are searches conducted incident to arrest and those conducted with consent of the individual having authority over the premises, property in "plain view" of the officer making a lawful search even though the property was not named on the search warrant, property uncovered during the lawful "stop and frisk" of a subject, property seized in hot pursuit of a criminal in order to safeguard the officer, and property seized under exigent circumstances in which there is likelihood that it will be destroyed or removed if time is taken to obtain a search warrant.

Continuity of Evidence. A fundamental rule to remember is that evidence in support of an arrest must be preserved untainted by the passage of time. This requirement mandates that the "chain of custody" of the evidence be documented during custody and storage. Innumerable criminal cases have been lost or their prosecution inhibited by failure to observe commonly accepted procedures for the preservation of evidence and maintenance of records regarding personal custody. Because of the singular importance of this aspect of evidence control, it is examined in depth.

Custody and Disposition. Normally, evidence must be held in custody of the law enforcement agency until a prosecutor or similar authority formally issues a release allowing it to be returned to its owner or otherwise disposed of. In certain jurisdictions, release of evidence is guided by statute or case law.

Under other circumstances, however, the custody and release of evidence may be guided by other regulations. Even when no longer needed as evidence in a criminal proceeding, items may be held pursuant to civil forfeiture proceedings under state or federal law. Under the federal Comprehensive Drug Abuse Prevention and Control Act of 1970, Section 511 (a)(6), as amended, 21 U.S.C.A. Section 881 (a)(6), the federal government may seize property for forfeiture as long as there is a substantial connection between the property and illegal drug transactions. Most state forfeiture laws are more restrictive than their federal counterparts.

Evidence in custody may also be subject to other federal or state laws. For example, reacting to public health concerns over the dumping of potentially harmful biological wastes, Congress enacted the 1988 Medical Waste Tracking Act. Although this act addresses the management and tracking of medical wastes in particular, in certain states it also has present and future implications for the disposal of certain biologically contaminated wastes under law enforcement control. This is particularly the case with regard to blood, blood products, and other bodily secretions in vitro; materials contaminated by such fluids; and sharp implements such as knives and IV needles that may also have been contaminated. Law enforcement officers, laboratory technicians, and evidence custodians should be aware of the risks of exposure to HIV and hepatitis B infections through these and related sources and should take the steps necessary to protect themselves and others from exposure. Disposal of these and related waste products should conform to state and federal laws and to procedures set forth by the Centers for Disease Control and Prevention (CDC).[3]

Evidence custodians should also be familiar with federal and any state regulations relating to the handling, storage, transportation, and disposal of chemical wastes. Chemicals seized during drug raids, particularly with regard to clandestine laboratories, can individually or in combination be explosive, toxic, or carcinogenic. At the federal level, the handling of these materials from an employee health and safety standpoint is regulated by provisions of standards

FIGURE 3.2 Photo of an outdoor crime scene and the painstaking search for evidence. *Courtesy of Mike Himmel.*

CFR 1910.1200 of the Occupational Safety and Health Administration (OSHA). Included in these provisions are requirements that employees be trained in the recognition of chemical health hazards, safe chemical-handling techniques, and first aid. OSHA has also set standards for clothing, equipment, and working conditions in clandestine laboratory-dismantling operations.

The Department of Transportation (DOT), under CFR 49, regulates the carriers of hazardous materials, and the Environmental Protection Agency (EPA), pursuant to CFR Title 40, controls the handling and destruction of hazardous wastes. Law enforcement agencies that are inexperienced with handling these types of chemical wastes should consult their regional office of the Drug Enforcement Administration (DEA) or appropriate state or federal agencies for guidance.

Records Maintenance. A variety of records are related to the control and management of evidence in custody, many of which vary by state law or local custom. In all cases, however, evidence custodians must take the steps necessary to ensure that these records are properly compiled, organized, and preserved. In so doing, the fulfillment of legally prescribed procedures can be fully documented and referenced as necessary, potential questions concerning the chain of custody and related matters can be readily answered, and cumulative information can be compiled concerning the volume and flow of evidence through the agency's evidence control operation.

The First Officer's Responsibilities

The initial response to a call by the responding officer is a critical phase of any criminal investigation. This response is usually made by patrol officers, who must be prepared to initiate a preliminary investigation and carry out the functions discussed below until they are relieved by superior officers or specialists (e.g., detectives or crime scene specialists) who then assume responsibility for their specific functions at the scene. Unfortunately, improper actions by responding patrol officers can cause a loss of evidence or otherwise so prejudice an investigation that a subsequent successful criminal prosecution becomes impossible. Furthermore, in some instances, improper initial actions may result in aggravation of injuries to victims, endangerment of other officers, and even loss of life. Therefore, the responding officers must be prepared to carry out the following initial actions promptly and correctly.

In certain situations, it may not be possible to perform the actions described below in the order in which they are listed. However, all of the actions discussed below, when appropriate, should be taken as soon as circumstances permit.

1. *Actions while en route to the crime scene.* While en route to the location, officers must be alert to the possible presence of perpetrators or perpetrators' vehicles fleeing from the scene. Although actions taken to detain suspicious vehicles or persons must comply with legal requirements for investigative detention and arrest, the information furnished to the responding units by the dispatcher or by other officers normally provides sufficient "reasonable suspicion" to justify detention of persons or vehicles found in or leaving the crime scene area. In addition, the suspects' own conduct (e.g., suspicious appearance or behavior, traffic violations) may provide grounds for an investigatory stop. Although the opportunity to apprehend a perpetrator while en route to the crime scene may not arise in a large percentage of cases, officers while en route to the location of a crime should always be alert for such possibilities.

2. *Initial actions upon arrival.* Upon arrival at the location, officers should, if possible, first verify that a crime has been committed. In many instances, it will be obvious that a crime has been committed or that, at the very

least, there is sufficient evidence to justify further investigation. However, officers should be aware that, unless the circumstances are sufficient to justify a reasonable belief that a major crime has occurred or is occurring within a dwelling or that some other exigent situation exists, they may not enter that dwelling without a warrant. To do so risks subsequent suppression of evidence and possible civil liability. Even when circumstances do not justify an immediate entry, officers may remain outside to protect the premises while additional information or a warrant is obtained. Reasonable belief that a crime has been or is being committed may be based on such various factors as information from dispatchers, statements provided by neighbors upon arrival, physical aspects of the scene (e.g., broken windows or doors), or sounds from the premises indicating that a crime is in progress within (e.g., screams, gun shots).

Deciding whether or not to enter premises where a crime may have been committed is often difficult. Such entries are considered "searches," and often the police on the scene must make an on-the-spot decision under borderline circumstances. Although each case is different and state or local law may vary, in general it may be said that under "exigent" (i.e., emergency) circumstances, officers are permitted to enter any premises, even using force if necessary, without a warrant and conduct a "protective" search of the premises when the officers have reasonable grounds to believe that a person within the premises is in immediate need of assistance or a perpetrator is present.[4]

Officers entering premises under these circumstances are not permitted to search the premises for evidence. The "protective search" is limited by law to a "sweep" of the premises to discover victims or perpetrators. Any search beyond the scope of a protective sweep requires a search warrant. However, if in the course of the protective sweep, evidence is discovered in plain view, it may be seized without a warrant or noted for later removal after a warrant has been obtained.

Whenever possible, verification of a crime at the location, or the responding officers' reasonable suspicion thereof, should be communicated immediately to the dispatcher or superiors so that decisions can be made regarding backup, entry into the structure, dispatch of medical assistance or crime scene specialists to the location, and so on. Failing to communicate promptly may endanger victims, the responding officers, and all subsequent aspects of the investigation.[5]

In many instances, circumstances do not permit transmission of complete information at the time of the initial arrival at the scene. In that event, follow-up communications should be made to provide the necessary additional information. See "Follow-up Communications."

3. *Assistance to victims and protection of witnesses and bystanders.* Administering first aid to and summoning medical assistance for any victims present must be a top priority of responding officers. If the victim(s) is still in danger, either from the perpetrator or from other circumstances (e.g., fire), immediate steps must be taken to ensure the victim's safety. Similar protection must be rendered to witnesses and other bystanders. However, unless the bystanders are in danger or circumstances otherwise make it necessary, the officers should avoid ordering bystanders from the scene until it has been determined which, if any, of the bystanders is also a witness or potential witness to some aspect of the crime.

4. *Arrest of the perpetrator.* If the perpetrator is at the scene and probable cause for arrest exists or an arrest warrant has been issued, the perpetrator should be arrested in accordance with departmental policy and local law.

If officers need to leave the scene to effect the arrest (e.g., the perpetrator is fleeing from the scene and must be pursued by officers), the officers must determine whether it is appropriate to leave the crime scene at that time. Conflicting considerations are often present in such circumstances. For example, the officers must balance the need to remain on the scene to render assistance to victims or to protect others from harm against the risk to the public if the perpetrator escapes. Ideally, sufficient personnel will be available to perform both functions simultaneously; if not, the officers present must decide where the priorities lie. Circumstances will dictate the decision, but in general, protecting the crime scene, any victims present, and the witnesses and bystanders will be the first consideration. Other units may then be alerted to pursue the fleeing perpetrator.

5. *Follow-up communications.* As noted above, initial communication at the time of the officers' arrival at the crime scene is essential. However, circumstances may not permit the responding officers to furnish complete information to their headquarters at that point. Further communications should be made to provide, at a minimum, the following information:

Superiors must be informed of the apparent nature of the offense discovered by the officers. When possible, reports should be factual in nature. When it is necessary to state opinions or conclusions in such transmissions, these opinions or conclusions should be supported by the known facts. Approved departmental codes may be used when appropriate.[6] If the exact nature or seriousness of the crime cannot yet be determined, the possibility of the more serious offense should be made clear in the transmission.

If the perpetrator has fled the scene, a full description of the perpetrator, together with any information regarding the perpetrator's mode and direction of flight, should be communicated as soon as possible. If there were accomplices, similar information about them should be included. Likewise, if a vehicle was involved either in the commission of the crime or in the flight of the perpetrators from the scene, this information should also be communicated.

If the perpetrators are known or believed to be armed, it is especially important that this information be transmitted as soon as possible. Any information available regarding the number and nature of the weapons possessed by the perpetrators should be provided. This permits other officers who may encounter the perpetrators to assess the threat level and proceed appropriately.

If not already requested during the initial transmission, support units may be requested during follow-up communications.

6. *Identification of witnesses and vehicles.* The identification and preliminary interviewing of witnesses are extremely important considerations for officers arriving at a crime scene. These functions are discussed in detail below.

License numbers and descriptions of vehicles parked in the area should be noted. In addition, the license number and description of any vehicle moving through the area in a slow, repeated, or otherwise suspicious manner should be recorded.

Officers should also be alert for suspicious persons who, although not present in the immediate vicinity of the crime scene, are observed in the general area. Such persons should be approached; identified; and, if circumstances justify it, detained for further investigation.

7. *Briefing investigators and superiors.* Officers should be prepared to brief investigators and other authorized personnel when they arrive on the scene. All information gathered, together with a summary of the actions taken by the responding officers up to that time, should be provided. Unfortunately,

experience shows that in many instances, valuable information known to the officers making the initial response is not communicated to detectives, superiors, or other personnel. Responding officers should therefore make it a point to communicate all known facts accurately and completely to investigators or other authorized persons arriving on the scene.

Broadcasting a Flash Description

Additional preliminary duties may include the broadcasting of a **flash description** of the suspect and the suspect's vehicle (also called a BOLO—"be on the lookout"). If able to determine certain facts about possible suspects, weapons, and vehicles, the responding officer should put out a flash description to other officers in case the suspects are still in the vicinity. Flash descriptions vary in nature, depending on the specific law enforcement agency. Generally, they should be precise and to the point. The flash description consists of the following information:

1. The type of crime, location of crime, and time of occurrence
2. The number of suspects involved in the crime
3. The physical description of those involved:
   - Gender
   - Race
   - Age
   - Height
   - Weight
   - Eye color
   - Hair color
   - Style or type of hair
   - Length of hair
   - Facial hair, if any
   - Clothing description
   - Other outstanding physical characteristics (e.g., tattoos, scars)
4. Weapons used
5. Direction in which the suspect was last observed proceeding and how long ago
6. Means of escape (mention any possible route that suspects may take)
7. If anyone was wounded.
8. Any vehicle used. When broadcasting flash descriptions of vehicles, remember the CYMBL rule:
   C: color
   Y: year
   M: make, model
   B: body style
   L: license number

Managing Emergency Situations

Unless a life-threatening situation or other exigent circumstances exist, the responding officer must attend to any injured party. Because the preservation of human life is a fundamental premise of public safety, this responsibility should take priority over apprehension of the suspect. If the situation calls for summoning emergency personnel, it should be done immediately. As soon as emergency personnel arrive on the scene, the officer should instruct them carefully on how to enter the scene without causing damage to the evidence at the scene. This must be done in a manner that does not impede the responsibilities of emergency personnel.

Securing the Scene

One of the more important functions of responding officers is to ensure that neither their actions nor the actions of others will disturb the crime scene unnecessarily. Much too often, criminal evidence and many criminal cases have been lost because the crime scene was not adequately secured and protected. Protecting the crime scene has always been essential to good police work, and this is doubly true today because scientific evidence analysis techniques are becoming an increasingly important part of criminal investigations. Unnecessary or improper entry into the crime scene may:

- Destroy or contaminate important evidence.
- Introduce items or substances into the crime scene that may mislead investigators.
- Provide defense attorneys with a basis for discrediting the investigators or the findings of a crime laboratory.

For these reasons, the following principles should be observed. The responding officers should enter the crime scene only for the limited purposes of:

- Determining that a crime has been committed
- Aiding victims
- Apprehending perpetrators
- Securing the area

Unless circumstances or departmental policies dictate otherwise, after these initial functions have been performed, the responding officers should thereafter avoid entering the crime scene and prevent others from doing so until superiors, detectives, or crime scene specialists relieve the responding officers of that responsibility.

Although, as mentioned above, responding officers must often enter the crime scene to perform their essential preliminary functions, every entry into a crime scene area has the potential to destroy evidence and introduce irrelevant substances into the scene. Therefore, even when entering the crime scene to perform necessary actions as described above, responding officers should, to the greatest extent possible, avoid touching or moving objects at the scene or entering areas where entry is unnecessary to accomplish the above-stated purposes. In addition, whenever possible, the crime scene should be entered only by one narrowly defined route to avoid the destruction of evidence, the contamination of possible scent trails, and so on.

In addition to keeping their encroachment upon the crime scene to a minimum, officers should also carefully note the portions of the scene through which they have passed, the routes taken, the objects they have touched, and any other actions they have taken that may have altered or tainted the scene. This information will assist investigators in determining the original state of the crime scene and will enable them to disregard matters that are not relevant to the crime itself.

After the responding officers have completed their preliminary examination of the scene, the scene should be secured to protect it from encroachment by unauthorized persons. This is not always a simple task, and circumstances may dictate what can and cannot be done. However, in general, the following actions should be taken:

1. *The area to be declared a crime scene must be defined.* This includes any portion of the premises that may reasonably be anticipated to contain useful evidence. Although it is often impossible to cordon off all of the surrounding areas that might conceivably hold such evidence, the area designated as a crime scene should be as large as the circumstances require or permit. Remember that it is always a better practice to secure a larger area and narrow it down than to identify a small scene and attempt to expand it at a later time.

   The seriousness of the crime, the location of the crime, the nature of the surrounding environment, the amount of manpower available to maintain a perimeter, and similar factors determine the definition and extent of the crime scene in a given case. The specific nature of the suspected crime may also dictate the definition of the crime scene. For example, in a homicide case, the place where the body is found is obviously considered the crime scene, even though the actual death may later be determined to have occurred elsewhere; in the case of a suspected kidnapping, the place where the victim was last seen should be regarded as a crime scene and treated accordingly. If the perpetrator has fled or a victim or other significant person is believed to be missing from the scene, the widest possible area should be protected to preserve any evidence present, including any possible scent trails leading away from the immediate scene.

2. *Backup should be requested to help restrict access to the defined crime scene and to control onlookers.* Only rarely will one or two responding officers be able to maintain complete control of a crime scene by themselves. Assistance should be obtained quickly before others encroach upon the scene and evidence is lost.

3. *The interior of the crime scene area should be cleared.* Persons other than law enforcement officers or other officials actively engaged in crime scene duties should be removed from the premises.[7] The crime scene should be secured by the use of tape, rope, barricades, locks, or other appropriate measures. After the crime scene has been secured, access to the scene should be restricted to authorized personnel.

4. *Record actions previously taken at the scene.* Responding officers should note and record any alterations that may have occurred to the crime scene due to their own activities or the activities of personnel rendering emergency assistance to victims. In addition, officers should determine if any actions of the persons reporting the crime or of other persons present on the scene before the arrival of the officers may have altered or tainted the crime scene in any way. In particular, actions involving moving or otherwise disturbing the victim's body should be noted. All of this information should be communicated to investigators, superiors, or both at the earliest possible opportunity.

5. *Restrict access to the scene.* After the crime scene has been defined, cleared, and secured, access to the scene should be limited to authorized personnel directly involved in the investigation. In the case of major crimes, the identities of all persons entering the perimeter should be recorded, and, if possible, the times at which they entered and left the scene should be noted.

Attempts by news media personnel, nonessential city or county officials, and others to gain access to the scene should be referred to the supervisor in charge of the scene or other officer designated to handle requests for entry.[8] When a decision is made to allow any such persons to have access to the scene, they should be escorted by an officer during the period of their entry to prevent their taking any action that might result in the loss of evidence or otherwise endanger the investigation. In this regard, a "contamination log" should also be kept to document all persons entering the scene.[9]

Handling Special Situations at the Scene

Myriad situations may present themselves to officers at a crime scene, so they should be able to adapt to different circumstances. The key in the preliminary investigation is for the responding officer to maintain control. Examples include the following:

Dead Body

In the event that a body is located on the scene, the officer must make a precursory determination of the cause of death or injury. In an obvious cause of death, certain signs may be evident. Such indications may include odor or early stages of decomposition of the body. Other signs include postmortem lividity or rigor mortis. In any case, the body should not be touched, moved, or tampered with until investigators arrive. On discovery of a dead body, supervisors should be notified immediately as to the nature of the scene.

Hanging Victim

In the case of a person found hanging, the body should generally not be moved at all (also see Chapter 9 on wrongful death). Careful attention to protect the knot on the noose is important because many investigative leads may be developed from rope or other materials used as a ligature. If, however, the responding officer finds it necessary to cut down the deceased, the rope should be cut far above the knot so the knot can be preserved for examination. In this case, care should be taken to support the body as best as possible so that there is no additional damage to the body upon impact with the floor or ground. Critical attention should be given to all evidence in hanging cases because the appearance of suicide may actually be a cover-up for a murder.

Firearms

Generally speaking, all objects at the crime scene should remain untouched, particularly firearms, bullets, and shell casings. Additionally, the first officer at the scene must remember that he or she, too, can be a valuable source of physical evidence. For example, ballistics experts commonly testify that shells found at the scene of a homicide match the corresponding markings on a shell test fired from the defendant's revolver.

Accordingly, experts may also testify that an empty shotgun shell casing found at the scene of a homicide was fired from the defendant's shotgun. Such a statement can be made based on breech-face markings on the shell developed through macrophotography. In many cases, however, such evidence is difficult to find and may not be discovered until after the body or other evidence has been removed. Officers searching for firearms should remember that shell casings should be nearby. Both types of evidence are extremely valuable. Fingerprints, for example, may exist on a weapon in the oils present on the weapon. Great care should be exercised in this case to preserve such evidence.

When seizing a handgun as evidence, officers should never attempt to pick up the weapon by inserting a pen or pencil into the barrel. This could damage or destroy valuable evidence such as blood or fibers deposited inside the barrel, which could later be retrieved by specialists. Generally, the prescribed way for officers to move a handgun is to pick it up using two fingers on the textured part of the grip where no fingerprints can be removed.

Other considerations are that officers must never adjust the safety catch, unload, or alter the condition of the weapon in any fashion until a complete examination has been performed. Only after investigators inspect and properly mark the position of the cylinder can the weapon be unloaded. Officers should remember that the weapon and all related objects must remain in exactly the same condition as they were found. Weapons, of course, should always be properly documented through photos and sketching before they are moved.

Collecting Electronic Evidence

The Internet, computer networks, and automated data systems present many new opportunities for committing criminal activity.[10] Computers and other electronic devices are increasingly used to commit, enable, or support crimes perpetrated against people, organizations, money, and property. Whether the crime involves attacks against computer systems—or the information they contain—or more traditional offenses such as murder, laundering, drug trafficking, or fraud, **electronic evidence** is increasingly important.

It could be said that electronic evidence is information and data of investigative value that is stored in or transmitted by an electronic device. Such evidence is often required when physical items such as computers, removable disks, CDs, DVDs, magnetic tape, flash memory chips, cellular telephones, personal digital assistants, and other electronic devices are collected from a crime scene or are obtained from a suspect.

Electronic evidence has special characteristics: (1) it is latent; (2) it can transcend national and state borders quickly and easily; (3) it is fragile and can easily be altered, damaged, compromised, or destroyed by improper handling or improper examination; and (4) it *may not be* time sensitive. Similar to DNA and fingerprints, electronic surveillance is **latent evidence** because it is not readily visible to the human eye under normal conditions. Special equipment and software are required to "see" and evaluate electronic evidence. In the courtroom, expert testimony may be needed to explain the acquisition of electronic evidence and the examination process used to interpret it.

In 2002, in recognition of the special challenges posed by electronic evidence, the Computer Crime and Intellectual Property section of the Criminal Division of the U.S. Department of Justice released a how-to manual for law enforcement officers called *Searching and Seizing Computers and Obtaining Electronic Evidence in Criminal Investigations*.

About the same time, the Technical Working Group for Electronic Crime Scene Investigation (TWGECSI) released a detailed guide for law enforcement officers to use in gathering electronic evidence. The manual, *Electronic Crime Scene Investigation: A Guide for First Responders*, grew out of a partnership formed in 1998 between the National Cybercrime Training Partnership, the Office of Law Enforcement Standards, and the National Institute of Justice. The working group was asked to identify, define, and establish basic criteria to assist federal and state agencies in handling electronic investigations and related prosecutions.

TWGECSI guidelines specify that law enforcement must take special precautions when documenting, collecting, preserving, and examining electronic evidence to maintain its integrity. The guidelines also note that the first law enforcement

Investigator's Checklist: Crime Scene Equipment

☑ *Surveillance equipment.* Night vision equipment, listening devices.

☑ *Cameras.* The digital camera has surpassed the 35-mm camera as the photographic tool of choice for crime scene documentation. Both cameras and editing software have now become affordable for even the smallest departments. Digital video cameras are another recent innovation in crime scene documentation, offering the best evidence of crimes in progress and fresh crime scene evidence. Camera accessories such as lenses, tripods, and lighting attachments may be required for unusual crime scenes.

☑ *Lights.* Handheld flashlight (e.g., Streamlight), emergency flashing strobes instead of vehicle fog lights, handheld floodlights for crime scenes.

☑ *Notebook.* Sketching material for producing rough sketches while on the scene. Writing utensils such as pencils, pens, and markers must be available.

☑ *Other materials.* Tape measures (both cloth and metal), evidence tape, a carpenter-type ruler, eraser, chalk, tweezers, scissors, labels, tongue depressors, a clipboard, and outdoor and indoor templates.

☑ *Containers.* Envelopes, boxes, plastic and paper bags, and glass bottles of all sizes and shapes.

☑ *First aid kit.* To treat injured parties at the scene.

☑ *Casting material.* Plaster or dental stone to make casts (e.g., pry marks, footprints).

officer on the scene should take steps to ensure the safety of everyone at the scene and to protect the integrity of all evidence, both traditional and electronic.

Biohazardous Materials

All crime evidence rooms must be equipped to maintain evidence from crimes contaminated by bodily secretions such as blood, semen, urine, and feces. In addition, evidence rooms are generally required to secure laboratory samples and similar items that have been or will be tested. Wherever blood is apparent, there is the potential for infection by HIV (AIDS) and hepatitis B virus as well as other blood-borne diseases. To ensure the highest degree of safety, one should assume that all items contaminated with human or other animal secretions are potential sources of infection and should take steps necessary to protect themselves and others who may come into contact with the items.

Under normal circumstances, evidence custodians should not allow contaminated materials to be brought into the evidence room unless they have been adequately packaged beforehand. Evidence custodians should retain the prerogative of refusing to accept materials that are not properly packaged. Any biohazardous materials should be double bagged in secure plastic bags, taped or secured by adhesives (never stapled), and labeled as a biohazardous material. In To avoid reducing its evidentiary value, soaked clothing should be air dried before being bagged. As noted, however, organic matter containing moisture to any degree may be subject to decay if sealed in a nonporous container. Such items should be packaged in porous containers so they can breathe.

In cases in which items must be inventoried at or after intake at the evidence room, "universal precautions"—as prescribed by the CDC for prevention of exposure to HIV and hepatitis B viruses should be closely followed.[11] At a minimum, during inventories, disposable rubber gloves should be worn; cuts or abrasions should be covered by bandages or dressing; hand contact with the mouth, eyes, or nose should be avoided; and smoking, eating, drinking, and applying makeup should not be permitted. The handling of needles and other sharp objects should require the wearing of leather gloves over disposable rubber gloves. Cleanup of any areas, such as counters, tabletops, or equipment that may have come in contact with contaminated items, should be performed using a diluted chlorine bleach solution of one part chlorine to 10 parts water. In all cases after dealing with such materials, one should thoroughly wash any exposed skin surfaces with hot running water and soap for at least 15 seconds before drying. Any contaminated clothing should be carefully removed as soon as practicable, separated from noncontaminated linens, and laundered in water at least 160°F for 25 minutes. Latex gloves should be rinsed before removal, and hands and arms should then be cleansed in the prescribed manner. All sharp instruments, such as knives, razors, scissors, and broken glass, should be encased before being enclosed in the evidence envelope, and the exterior of the envelope should indicate that a sharp object is enclosed. In most cases, contaminated samples that may require laboratory analysis should not be encased directly in plastic because of the possibility of contaminating the evidence. Other packaging material is often required, and laboratory technicians should be consulted for instructions.

Evidence samples that may be subject to DNA testing must be kept in a frozen state to avoid deterioration, and samples destined for blood typing and certain other forensic tests should be refrigerated. A freezer and a refrigerator are required in nearly all evidence rooms for this type of evidence as well as for any perishable products that must be stored for evidentiary purposes.

The handling and packaging of hypodermic needles and syringes have become common tasks for many officers and evidence custodians in the wake of increased narcotics use on the street. Most plastic or paper evidence containers are not puncture-proof, so particular care must be taken to avoid needle sticks. Some agencies use flexible plastic tubes with screw-on or pressure tops for this purpose, although some of these have been subject to leakage. Puncture-resistant containers for used syringes and needles can be purchased from medical supply distributors or local hospitals. A special device has recently been introduced into the market that is a tube constructed of seamless, heavy-gauge transparent polypropylene in two parts with a mechanical seal joining the two halves. It is long enough to accommodate most syringes, even with the plungers extended; comes in a small plastic bag with instructions for use; and is affixed with a label for recording the officer's name, assignment, and case number.

Chemical and Other Hazardous Wastes

Most chemical agents are seized by law enforcement officers in connection with clandestine drug manufacturing operations. Enforcement actions against these operations require specialized training and equipment to avoid the dangers of fire; explosions; and contact with caustic, corrosive, toxic, or carcinogenic substances. As discussed earlier, the occupational and environmental dangers associated with these chemicals have caused federal and state regulatory agencies to impose strict standards for the handling, transportation, storage, and disposal of these substances. The DEA requires that all its agents, chemists, and task force officers who deal with clandestine laboratories be certified by a special safety school. State and local law enforcement officers should not conduct raids on or make arrests within suspected clandestine laboratories without proper training and equipment. Before conducting any such raid, officers without this training and equipment should consult the regional office of the DEA or a properly trained and outfitted enforcement unit of their state or local government.

A chemist or other qualified individual should always be available when conducting enforcement operations on clandestine laboratories. These are the appropriate individuals for making decisions on the packaging, transportation, and storage of all chemical substances. Normally, chemicals should not be housed in evidence storage rooms and require specialized offsite storage facilities. Chemicals seized during the investigation of environmental crimes or under other circumstances should also not be moved or otherwise handled until assistance can be obtained from a hazardous materials (HAZMAT) or similarly qualified unit. The same precautions should be followed for the handling, transportation, or storage of potentially explosive and other dangerous substances.

Assessing the Crime Scene

To the extent practical, the investigator in charge should develop a plan for processing the crime scene. The plan should include information learned from any responding officers as well as observations and information known to the investigator. Crime scene assessment includes the following steps:

1. Evaluate measures and steps that have been taken to include safety procedures, perimeter security and access control, the adequacy of investigative resources, whether witnesses and suspects have been identified, and the degree to which preliminary documentation of the crime scene has been made.

2. Conduct a crime scene walk-through in cooperation with the first responder and individuals responsible for processing the crime scene to identify any threats to crime scene integrity and begin an initial identification of evidence.

3. Determine the need for a search warrant before collection of evidence.

4. Assess the overall crime scene before evidence collection to develop a plan for working within the crime scene without unnecessarily destroying or contaminating evidence.

5. Identify evidence collection and document team members, including specialists such as odontologists, bomb technicians, arson investigators, entomologists, fingerprint technicians, and others.

6. Identify protective equipment and clothing that are required to safely process the crime scene.

7. Identify a separate area, if necessary, for equipment and personnel staging and for gathering and sanitizing tools, equipment, and personal protective gear between evidence collections.

8. Assign one officer whose primary responsibility is recording and collecting items of evidence. This will increase efficiency, establish the chain of custody, help prevent loss, and reduce the number of officers who must appear in court.

9. Determine the evidence search method to be used and the point(s) at which the search will begin and establish a working route around the scene to minimize disruption and contamination.

10. Develop, in cooperation with crime scene technician(s) or other trained personnel, a collection plan for identified items of evidence detailing the process and the order of collection.

- Focus initially on easily accessible areas in open view and work outward.
- Select a systematic search pattern.
- Select the best progression of processing and collection so as not to compromise subsequent processing and evidence collection efforts.

Beginning the Search

After an investigator has documented a crime scene, the actual search must begin. Generally speaking, evidence discovered at the crime scene will serve four objectives: (1) to determine the facts of the crime, (2) to identify the lawbreaker, (3) to aid in the arrest of the perpetrator, and (4) to aid in the criminal prosecution of the perpetrator. History has shown that there are many different ways to search a crime scene for evidence. Indeed, methods for crime scene searching vary according to the types of crime scenes and evidence at hand. Varieties of crime scene evidence include firearm evidence, trace material collection, tool mark evidence, collection of bodily fluids, standards of evidence, fire and explosion evidence, outdoor crime scenes, vehicle searches, and interior and victim searches. The search of the crime scene consists of several distinct phases:

- Surveying the crime scene
- Documenting the crime scene through sketches and photographs
- Recording all physical evidence
- Searching for fingerprints

Search Patterns

Regardless of the method used, the search of the scene should be conducted in a systematic way. Of the most often used methods of searching, several have been most commonly used over time. The most common search patterns include the spiral search method, grid search method, strip- or line-search method, and quadrant- or zone-search method. Some methods of searching are best suited for indoor scenes, and others are more applicable to outdoor crime scenes. Other scenes present unique problems and are discussed next. Whichever method is adopted, the rule to remember is that the search must be thorough.

Indoor Crime Scene Searches. It is generally recommended that at least two officers search an indoor crime scene. This may best be accomplished by dividing the room in half and having each investigator search half of the room (also known as the quadrant or zone-search method). At the conclusion of the search, the investigators switch halves. In this fashion, each half of the room is searched twice.

Outdoor Crime Scene Searches. In most cases, the outdoor crime scene covers a broader area than those that are indoor. If this is the case, more investigators are required. Accordingly, with the increased size of the scene, a more systematic searching method must be used. One way is to rope off the scene into a grid. Each square, averaging about 6 square feet, represents a specific search area that is a manageable size for each investigator (also known as the grid search method).

FIGURE 3.3 Search patterns.

Nighttime Crime Scene Searches. If possible, investigators should wait until daylight to search a crime scene. Obviously, circumstances may require investigators to proceed with the search at night. These may include inclement weather or other emergency circumstances. In the event that such a search is to be conducted, lighting generators should be used to provide sufficient illumination for the search.

Vehicle Searches. The search of a vehicle requires the same degree of attention as indoor and outdoor searches. Obviously, the nature of the crime dictates the area of the vehicle to be searched. For example, whereas a drug smuggling or murder case requires closer examination of the interior of the vehicle, a hit-and-run investigation necessitates examination of the exterior of the vehicle. Similar to an interior search, a vehicle should also be searched for fingerprints. This should be done after other trace evidence has been sought.

Strip Searches

A strip search must be conducted in a private and controlled environment. This technique requires the suspect to undress completely, and all clothing is searched. In some cases, the suspect's body cavities may need to be searched. Officers are allowed to search the ears, mouth, and nose visually, but the vaginal and rectal areas may be searched only by authorized medical personnel. It is also recommended that investigators communicate with the prosecutor before conducting a strip search of any suspect to safeguard against possible procedural errors.

Body Cavity Searches

In early 2005, officers of the Suffolk County (New York) Police Department arrested 36-year-old Terrance Haynes and charged him with marijuana possession. After placing him in the back of a patrol car, officers noted that Haynes appeared to choke and have difficulty breathing. Soon his breathing stopped, prompting officers to use the Heimlich maneuver, which dislodged a plastic bag from Haynes' windpipe. The bag contained 11 packets of cocaine. Although Haynes survived the ordeal, he now faces up to 25 years in prison.

Although some suspects may literally "cough up" evidence, some are more successful at hiding it in their bodies. Body cavity searches are among the most problematic types of searches for police today. "Strip" searches of convicts in prison, including the search of body cavities, have generally been held to be permissible.

The 1985 Supreme Court case of *U.S. v. Montoya de Hernandez* focused on the issue of "alimentary canal smuggling," in which the offender typically swallows condoms filled with cocaine or heroin and waits for nature to take its course to recover the substance.[12] In the *Montoya* case, a woman known to be a "balloon swallower" arrived in the United States on a flight from Colombia. She was detained by customs officials and given a pat-down search by a female agent. The agent reported that the woman's abdomen was firm and suggested that x-rays be taken. The suspect refused and was given a choice of submitting to further tests or taking the next flight back to Columbia. No flight was immediately available, however, and the suspect was placed in a room for 16 hours, where she refused all food and drink. Finally, a court order for an x-ray was obtained. The procedure revealed "balloons," and the woman was detained another four days, during which time she passed numerous cocaine-filled plastic condoms. The Court ruled that the woman's confinement was not unreasonable, based as it was on the supportable suspicion that she was **"body-packing"** cocaine. Any discomfort she experienced, the court ruled, "resulted solely from the method that she chose to smuggle illicit drugs."

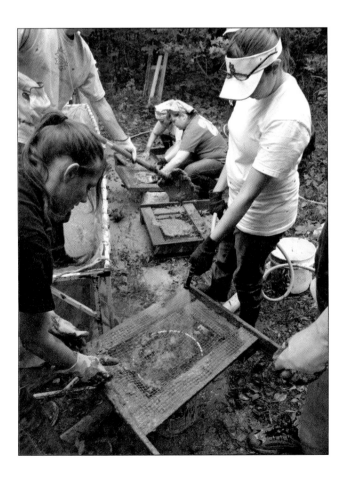

FIGURE 3.4 A crime scene search in a rural area. Courtesy of Mike Himmel.

The Crime Scene Search

Evidence of crimes is dynamic. That is, it is unique, often fragile, and may constantly be undergoing change. Experience indicates that there is usually only one chance to search a crime scene properly, so for this reason, it is a good idea to survey the scene carefully before embarking on the search process itself.

There are two approaches to crime scene searches. As a first step, the investigator should consider all information provided to him or her by officers who arrived earlier on the scene. Such information includes the officers' perceptions of what occurred and the nature of the evidence. Next, investigators should rationalize which evidence items seem to play the greatest role in the alleged crime. In brief, the principal concern at this point is to observe and document the scene rather than take action.

Of specific importance in the observation phase is the relative distance of any object to the victim. The distance between an object and a victim may play a greater role in the evidence collection phase than the item itself. For example, if the crime scene consists of a dead person who has apparently been shot and a 9mm handgun, the locations of spent shell casings could indicate the angle of the weapon or the position of the victim at the time the gun was

Proper Sealing of Evidence

The method shown below permits access to the invoice letter without breaking the inner seal. This allows the person entitled to receive the evidence to receive it in a sealed condition just as it was packed by the sender.

1 Pack bulk evidence securely in box.

2 Seal box and mark as evidence.

5 Wrap sealed box in outside wrapper and seal with gummed paper.

6 Address to: Director
Federal Bureau of Investigation
10th & Pennsylvania, N.W.
Washington, DC 20535

and mark: Attention: FBI Laboratory

FIGURE 3.5 Method for the proper sealing of crime scene evidence.

discharged. Such a determination could point to either suicide or homicide and may subsequently alter the character of the investigation. As indicated, while observations are being carried out, notes should be taken to organize the sequence of events. Witnesses' statements should be taken as well, regarding the victim(s) or related information. Additionally, videotapes and photographs should be made during this phase to document the scene adequately for future reference. Both of these considerations are discussed in greater detail later in the book.

Collecting Evidence

There is a tendency on the part of many investigators to rush the evidence collection process and focus attention on the obvious. Understandably, the task of observing firsthand the scene of another's misfortune is a difficult one for many, and one might appreciate the desire for expeditiousness on the part of the investigator. It is a fact, however, that much critical evidence, often seemingly unimportant, can be located in and around the scene of almost every crime. As discussed in the earlier section on crime scene searches, investigators must choose which method of searching is best suited for the crime in question.

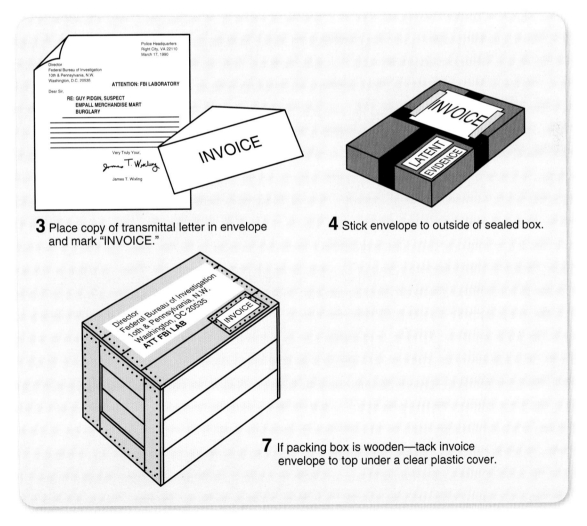

3 Place copy of transmittal letter in envelope and mark "INVOICE."

4 Stick envelope to outside of sealed box.

7 If packing box is wooden—tack invoice envelope to top under a clear plastic cover.

FIGURE 3.5 (Continued)

Regardless of the method used, evidence must be collected in a comprehensive, nondestructive manner; within a reasonable period; and with a minimum of unnecessary movement about the scene. Although every criminal case is unique and should be evaluated on an individual basis, experience has shown that the following general recommendations are beneficial in organizing the search and preventing errors.

Gathering and Preserving Evidence. After the initial crime scene search has been completed and the sketching and photographing of the scene have been done, evidence should be collected. The manner in which evidence is collected must be consistent with each law enforcement agency's policies and procedures and should be in keeping with accepted rules of evidence. The evidence collected first is usually that which is most fragile. Therefore, fingerprints should be lifted as a priority. Next, other fragile evidence, such as blood and other trace evidence, should be collected. It is important for officers to search the crime scene a second time after the evidence has been collected. This should uncover any evidence overlooked accidentally. When possible, one investigator should serve as the evidence collector. This designation ensures that all evidence gets recorded and processed at the scene in a uniform and correct manner. It also ensures that evidence will be moved only when the collector decides that it can be moved.

When the case goes to court, both the investigator who discovered the evidence and the collector are usually required to testify. The greatest advantage to using this system is that all evidence is collected in a uniform manner, and one officer is responsible for packaging and marking the evidence and filling out the necessary paperwork. This reduces the need to tie up additional officers back at the office for such a task.

Chain of Custody. Evidence that has been collected must be safeguarded until the case goes to court. During the trial, if it is determined that labels are missing and evidence is not properly initialed or is otherwise missing or altered, the evidence may be considered inadmissible and the case thrown out. The total accounting of evidence is known as the **chain of custody**. This is made up of all persons (usually, law enforcement personnel) who have taken custody of the evidence since its collection and who are therefore responsible for its protection and storage. The chain of custody is established by adhering to certain guidelines:

- The number of persons handling evidence from the time that it is safely stored should be limited. If the evidence leaves the possession of an officer, he or she should record to whom the evidence was given, the date and time, and the reason it was turned over.
- Anyone who handles evidence should affix his or her name and badge number to the package containing evidence.
- A signed receipt should be obtained from the person accepting the evidence. In turn, the investigator should sign a receipt or log when the item is returned.
- When a piece of evidence is turned in, the investigator should check his or her identification mark on it to ensure that it is the same item.
- After an item is returned to the investigator, he or she should determine if the item is in the same condition as when it was discovered. Any change in the physical appearance of the evidence should be called to the attention of the court.

Evidence can be stored in vehicle trunks, strongboxes, property rooms, locked file cabinets, evidence lockers, or vaults. The only stipulation is that it be marked properly and protected from tampering and destruction. Most evidence is turned over to an evidence custodian, who is usually an employee of the crime lab. This person signs off on an evidence form as the recipient of the evidence. The seizing officer then indicates in his or her investigative report the person to whom the evidence was given.

Marking the Evidence.   Another important rule to remember during the evidence collection process is that all evidence must be marked immediately upon seizure to ensure proper identification later because it is common for the officer who seizes evidence to identify it at trial. Such testimony ensures the integrity of the chain of custody. Proper marking of each piece of evidence also ensures organization of all items of evidence for restructuring the events of the crime and the questioning of witnesses. Generally, it does not matter how the officer marks evidence as long as the initials of the seizing officer and the date of the seizure are clearly indicated on the seized item and on any container used to enclose the object, such as an envelope or cardboard box.

In many cases, the officer's department will require additional information. Such information includes the assigned case number; the type of crime; and the victim's name as well as the defendant's name, address, and date of birth. After physical evidence has been marked, sealed, counted, weighed (if necessary), and placed within a sealed container, a label is affixed containing identifying information. The following details should be included on the evidence label:

- Case number
- Exhibit number (when numerous items are seized)
- Date and time of seizure
- Name and description of articles
- Location at time of discovery
- Signature or initials of officer making the discovery
- Name or initials of others witnessing the discovery

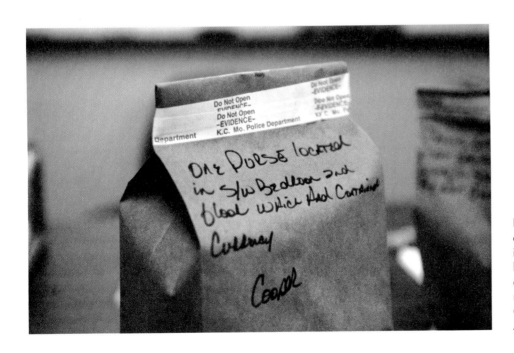

FIGURE 3.6 Proper marking of evidence is vital to protect its integrity for court. Here a brown paper bag containing evidence has been sealed and marked "Do Not Open." Courtesy of Mikael Karlsson, Arresting Images.

Special Cases in Evidence Handling

Just as evidence can be damaged or destroyed in the mishandling of a crime scene, improperly collected and managed evidence can sabotage an otherwise successful investigation. For example, improperly handled evidence, if contaminated, may either result in investigators reaching inaccurate conclusions or wasting time trying to correct the problem. The question commonly arises as to whether or not an object is or is not evidence. The decision is based on the officer's ability to consider the facts and circumstances at the crime scene, as well as his or her good judgment, common sense, and past experience. When any doubt exists, the object should be collected and processed as evidence; the object can be reevaluated later. Let's now examine some ways that certain types of critical evidence should be dealt with at the crime scene.

Infected Evidence

Among the many dangers encountered by law enforcement officers in the performance of their duties is the threat of street violence and even death. The rising specter of AIDS has created a health concern for criminal investigators charged with collection and preservation of crime scene evidence. Problems in collection of suspected infected evidence arise out of the fact that unlike many health care professionals, crime scene investigators are operating in an uncontrolled environment and often under extremely adverse conditions. Even the use of protective devices such as gloves and masks may not provide the investigator with adequate protection from communicable diseases such as HIV, tuberculosis, and hepatitis B.

This is partly due to the fact that such protective measures often fail to protect against cutting or puncturing, allowing the transmission of disease and infection through blood or other bodily fluids. Implements such as weapons, drug paraphernalia, razor blades, and hypodermic needles, which can be secreted in pockets, drawers, and in automobiles, all pose threats to crime scene technicians.

An unfortunate side effect of the AIDS epidemic is that it is likely that officers who either lack adequate protective equipment, who are uneasy about the prospect of contracting certain diseases, or who lack training on how best to deal with such problems might tend to limit their searches, intentionally or inadvertently, for fear of contracting an infectious organism. This could result in the attitude "it's just not worth it," which could have many negative side effects for the overall investigative process, including inadequately seized evidence, resulting in a poorly investigated case, which would, in turn, result in weak prosecution of the defendant. The National Institute of Justice has offered a list of recommendations on how best to deal with the problem of infected evidence.[13]

Firearms

Extreme care should be taken when handling firearms because of the types of trace evidence typically found on such evidence. The guidelines are as follows:

- The firearm should be handled carefully by the grip or the sides of the trigger guard.
- Never stick anything, such as a pencil, into the barrel of a firearm; this could destroy valuable trace evidence.
- No attempt should be made to fire the gun, dismantle it, or interfere with the mechanism in any way.

If the weapon is a revolver, mark empty cases or live cartridges and the rear edge of the cylinder with a code to show the chambers in which each empty case or live cartridge rested at the time of its removal.

Bullets, Cartridges, and Empty Cases

Bullets, cartridges, and empty cases should be handled with particular attention paid to the portions used in identification. Such evidence can be beneficial in determining the type of weapon used by a criminal. A more exact laboratory analysis may also determine the exact caliber of the weapon. Investigations have revealed instances in which criminals have purposely used one gun for the commission of a crime and a second gun to fire rounds into walls or the floor to confuse investigators. Certain areas of cartridges are typically used for identification: (1) the base and (2) the rim or cannelure (just above the base of the case).

The exact location of spent cases should be noted. Bullets must be removed carefully from their points of impact, and the locations they were found must be recorded accurately. In many cases, it is not advisable for a crime scene investigator to attempt to remove spent bullets. If possible, try to remove the material encasing a spent bullet (e.g., part of a door, wall) and transport it to the laboratory to be examined there. A spent bullet can be ruined by attempting to dig it out of an enclosure with a pocketknife. Care must be taken so that a drill, saw, or other cutting instrument does not damage the bullet. Bullets should be handled minimally and packaged to prevent movement and protect the side portions used in ballistic comparison and identification. Rather than attempting to mark a bullet directly, it should be packaged individually and the container marked appropriately.

Stains

Many crimes result in some type of characteristic stain being left at the crime scene. Blood is the stain most commonly found and can provide an investigator with much valuable evidence. Investigators should remember that not all bloodstains found at a crime scene belong to the victim. Indeed, a bloodstain may belong to the perpetrator, who might have been injured while committing the crime. It is usually a good idea in any case to adhere to the following guidelines when considering the collection of blood:

- Good photos and videos should be taken of bloodstains.
- Samples should be taken from all locations where blood is found.
- Blood samples can easily rot, so they should be swabbed and air dried before storage.

Glass

Glass fragments can result from many circumstances. For example, a bullet can shatter glass by passing through it; glass purposely broken will leave behind fragments in the crime scene and on the perpetrator. When collected, glass could be used to:

- Show the direction of travel of a projectile.
- Show the sequence of impact of a projectile.
- Match other broken glass.

Impressions

Many crimes result in the formation of impression marks. Such crimes include burglary and rape, but almost any crime could produce such evidence. In all cases, impression evidence should be regarded as valuable and must be protected. Examples of impression evidence include:

- Tool marks (usually found on metal doors or window frames and on locked metal desks, cabinets, and safes)
- Tire impressions
- Foot impressions
- Teeth impressions (sometimes located on partly eaten food at crime scenes)

Investigators should locate the object that made the impression so a comparison can be made in court.

Drugs

Studies have revealed that drug abuse is the greatest contributor to the commission of crime. Many illicit drugs exist and may appear quite different from one another in form. Therefore, great care must be practiced by evidence collectors to (1) preserve such substances for court, (2) transport the substances, and (3) protect themselves from the possible harmful effects of certain drugs. Most illicit drugs come in one of several forms: plant, powder, liquid, and tablet or capsule. Each requires specific attention from the evidence officer to avoid danger. For example, some drugs, such as liquid PCP and liquid LSD, may be absorbed accidentally through the skin. Others, such as marijuana, are more benign in nature and don't pose such a notable physical threat from handling. However, certain general considerations apply in any collection process.

Collecting Evidence

1. *Collection of evidence by responding officers: Limitations.* The collection of evidence at a crime has always involved significant operational and legal considerations. Today, because scientific analysis techniques (e.g., DNA testing) have become such a major part of criminal investigations, it is vital that trained specialists collect, preserve, and transmit evidence. Therefore, officers initially responding to a crime scene should not collect evidence unless (1) exigent circumstances exist that make it necessary to collect the evidence immediately to prevent its contamination or destruction or (2) authorization has been received from a supervisor to engage in collection activities.

2. Unless one or both of the foregoing circumstances exist, responding officers should limit their activities to securing the scene and preventing unauthorized persons from taking any action that might cause the alteration, loss, or destruction of evidence.

3. *Collection of evidence by responding officers under exigent circumstances.* If it appears that evidence will be altered, lost, or destroyed unless the responding officers secure the evidence, the evidence may be collected. However, such emergency actions should be taken in accordance with proper procedures, and even in an emergency, the authorization of a supervisor should be obtained whenever possible. Even when undertaken, emergency collection of evidence should be limited to the least interference needed to preserve the evidence from loss. Supervisory or specialized assistance should be obtained as soon as possible to minimize any adverse effects on the evidence or its admissibility due to the emergency collection.

4. *Collection of evidence by responding officers under direction of the officer in charge (OIC) of the crime scene.* When so directed by the crime scene OIC, officers may search the crime scene for the purpose of finding and collecting items that may establish how and by whom the crime was committed. This may include, but is not limited to, the following:

- Weapons, tools, clothing, stains, blood spatters, fingerprints, footprints, tire or tool marks, broken glass, hair, fibers, soil
- Any unusual objects or objects found in unexpected or unusual locations
- Any other object or substance that the police officer believes may be relevant to the investigation

In conducting the search, officers must comply with the directions of the crime scene OIC and all applicable departmental directives. In particular, the officers must comply with the department's policies and procedures regarding evidence control; photographing evidence before and after collection; and preserving, packaging, and labeling criminal evidence. Officers should be aware that failure to follow these procedures may result in the loss of the evidentiary value of the item or substance collected or suppression of the evidence at trial. (For example, the incorrect collection and packaging of a wet blood sample or stain may result in the deterioration of the sample to the point that its unique characteristics can no longer be identified by a crime laboratory, or the failure to mark or label any item of evidence correctly may lead the criminal defense to seek its subsequent suppression at a trial on the grounds that it cannot be adequately identified.)

Officers collecting evidence must preserve the chain of possession or chain of custody of all evidence collected. Departmental directives regarding initial collection, packaging, labeling, transporting, and maintaining custody of such evidence shall be scrupulously observed. Normally, this involves a series of written receipts that document the location of and access to the evidence at all times after its initial discovery by police. Any inability to present written documentation covering any period after this initial discovery of the evidence may result in suppression of the evidence at trial.

mycrimekit™

Virtual Lab: Blood spatter evidence

Interviewing Witnesses

As noted earlier, persons at the crime scene who are or may be witnesses to the crime or who may have information that may be relevant to the crime should be identified, and preliminary interviews of these persons should be conducted as soon as possible. Promptness is vital in this regard. Often, the arrival of police leads persons who have witnessed the crime or have information about it to leave the scene to avoid becoming involved. Therefore, potential witnesses must be identified before this occurs.

Witnesses' full identities, including addresses and phone numbers, should be obtained immediately. Witnesses who have been identified as such should be requested to remain on the scene until they can be interviewed more fully. Even persons who are present but who deny having witnessed the crime or having any information about it should be identified for further reference. Officers should also attempt to obtain information from those present about other persons who may have been witnesses but who have left the scene.

In addition, those present on the scene should be asked to provide the names of persons who are not present at the scene but who are known to live in the vicinity or who are known to be present in the area on a regular basis.

When circumstances permit, the neighborhood surrounding the crime scene should be canvassed to identify additional witnesses and other persons who may have information bearing upon the crime.[14] Even though detectives or other investigative personnel may conduct the follow-up on the information taken above, the officers who make the initial response must gather as much of this data as possible because crowds may disperse quickly, vehicles may be removed from the area, and so on before investigators arrive. Quick action by responding officers may preserve information that would otherwise be lost.

Contacting the Medical Examiner

The official determination regarding the death of the victim and circumstances surrounding the death is typically made by the **medical examiner** (or, in small jurisdictions, county coroner). The responding law enforcement agency's standard operating procedure (SOP) should set forth the circumstances regarding when these persons are contacted. For example, some police organizations wait to call the medical examiner until after the crime scene technicians have conducted preliminary investigations on the crime scene. Investigators must realize that in almost all jurisdictions, the medical examiner will have jurisdiction over the body, so police without proper authorization may not move it.

In the event that the responding officer must move the body, its position should be documented through the use of both photographs and sketching. Additionally, tape or chalk should be placed on the floor to indicate to crime scene investigators how the head, arms, and legs of the body were positioned. If possible, officers must take care to see that the body remains in exactly the same position in which it was found. Specifically, limbs that are bent should not be straightened; if the body was discovered lying face down, it should be returned to the same position to avoid any shifting of the blood and subsequent altering of lividity.

Conducting a Neighborhood Canvass

A **neighborhood canvass** may also be in order during the early phases of an investigation. Although investigators may perform this function, the first officer on the scene might be directed to conduct a neighborhood or door-to-door canvass of the area to identify witnesses. This could focus not only on residents but also on employees of stores, delivery personnel, utility personnel, bus and taxi drivers, and so on.

The neighborhood canvass is also important because it identifies material witnesses (those who have specific knowledge of the crime or parts of the crime) and general witnesses who can provide important background information about the victim and possible suspects.

Preparing Crime Scene Reports

Both responding officers and those conducting follow-up investigations should prepare reports in accordance with departmental policy. At a minimum, crime scene reports should include the following information:

- The date and time at which the officers arrived on the scene
- Relevant conditions at the time of arrival at the crime scene, including the weather and other observations

- The manner in which the crime was discovered and reported and the identity of the reporting individuals, if known, including their relationships to the victim or other persons involved

- Identity of any police officers or emergency personnel who were present at the time of arrival of the reporting officer or who arrived thereafter

- Physical evidence collected and the identities of those who collected it (special note should be made of any valuables discovered or collected, such as currency or jewelry)

- Full identification information, including name, address, telephone number, and other identifying data, regarding witnesses to the crime

- The results of interviews with victims and witnesses, including the identities and descriptions of suspects, the methods of operation and other actions of the suspects, the means and route of escape used by the suspects, and so on

- Diagrams, sketches, photographs, videotapes, and other information prepared at the scene or afterward, including the identity of the persons, whether officers or civilians, who recorded or prepared these items

- Recommendations that may be helpful to the follow-up investigation (e.g., the names of witnesses or other persons who may be able to provide additional information)

FIGURE 3.7 Detective conducting a follow-up investigation by interviewing a woman about a crime occurring in the area.
Courtesy of H. Huntly Hersch, Inc.

Performing the Follow-up Investigation

The investigator's duties don't end at the crime scene. Indeed, they may very well extend into the community to virtually any source of information that may be of value in the investigation. Accordingly, officers should not construe the **follow-up investigation** as a negative reflection on their investigative abilities. Conversely, it demonstrates that officers are conscientious enough to follow up on leads even after the preliminary investigation has long been concluded. The investigator should remember that the follow-up investigation should build on what has been learned in the preliminary investigation. Double checking addresses, possible escape routes, and other leads may provide the investigator with priceless new information. Tasks required of the follow-up investigator include:

- Analyzing reports of officers conducting the preliminary phases of the investigation
- Reviewing official departmental records and mode of operation (MO) files
- Gathering information on friends and associates of suspects
- Examining the victim's background
- Checking police intelligence files to develop potential suspects
- Organizing police actions, such as neighborhood canvassing, raids, and search warrants

In summary, investigators must possess organizational skills that enable them to sift through detailed and fragmented pieces of information. As with organizational skills, personality traits can aid in communicating with people in the community who may possess valuable information.

CASE IN POINT:

General Rules of Crime Scene Searching[15]

If there is an indication that evidence is deteriorating significantly with time or by the elements, these have first priority. Crime scene investigators should always wear protective clothing to protect evidence from contamination and to safeguard themselves as well.

All major items are examined, photographed, recorded, and collected, as appropriate, taking them in the order that is most logical, considering the requirement to conserve movement. Making casts and lifting latent prints from objects to be moved from the scene are done as necessary. Items should not be moved until they have been examined for trace evidence. Fingerprints should be taken, or at least developed and covered with tape, before the object is moved. When an (obviously) deceased person is involved, the evidence items lying between the point of entry to the scene and point of exit from the scene and the body are processed; then the detailed search of the deceased person is conducted. After the search, the body should be removed and the processing of obvious evidence continued as noted earlier.

After processing the obvious evidence, the search for and collection of additional trace material is begun. Trace evidence should be searched for and collected before dusting for fingerprints. After the trace materials have been collected, other latent prints are lifted. When sweeping or vacuuming, surface areas should be segmented, the sweepings from each area packaged separately, and the locations of their point of recovery noted. Normally, elimination fingerprints and physical evidence standards are collected after the preceding actions have been completed.

CASE IN POINT:

Recommendations for Dealing with Infected Evidence

- *Human bites.* Viral transmission through saliva is unlikely; however, if bitten, after milking the wound, rinse well and seek medical attention.
- *Saliva, urine, and feces.* Viral transmission through saliva is unlikely. In urine, the virus is isolated in very low concentrations and nonexistent in feces. No AIDS cases have been associated with urine or feces.
- *Cuts and puncture wounds.* When searching areas hidden from view, use extreme caution to avoid sharp objects. Cases involving needle sticks are very rare.
- *Cardiopulmonary resuscitation (CPR) and first aid.* Minimal risk is associated with CPR, but it is a good idea to use masks or airways and gloves when in contact with bleeding wounds.

- *Body removal.* As with all crime scenes, when in contact with a dead body, always wear protective gloves.
- *Casual contact.* No AIDS cases or infections have been associated with casual contact.
- *Any contact with bodily fluids or blood.* Wear protective gloves if contact with blood or bodily fluids is likely. If contact is made, wash the area thoroughly with soap and water. Clean up spills with one part water and 10 parts household bleach.
- *Contact with dried blood.* No cases of infection have been traced to exposure to dried blood. The drying process itself seems to deactivate any viruses in blood. However, it is still a good idea to wear protective clothing such as gloves.

Summary Checklist

1. What important points should you remember when conducting a preliminary investigation?

Generally, the term *preliminary investigation* is defined as an initial inquiry by officers to establish facts and circumstances of a suspected crime and to preserve any evidence related to that crime. Preliminary investigation includes:

- Securing the crime scene
- Considering the possible arrest of a suspect
- Locating and questioning witnesses and victims
- Documenting the crime scene
- Identifying and collecting evidence

Remember "Locard's principle." This principle, also known as the "transfer of evidence theory," is applied to crime scenes where the perpetrator(s) of a crime comes into contact with the scene, so he or she both brings something into the scene and leaves with something from the scene. Every contact leaves a trace.

2. Can you describe the duties of the first officer on the scene?

Remember that the initial response to a call by the responding officer is a critical phase of any criminal investigation. This response is typically made by patrol officers who must be prepared to initiate a preliminary investigation and

(continued)

Summary Checklist (Continued)

carry out important and timely functions until they are relieved by supervisors or investigators.

- While en route to the location, officers must be alert to the possible presence of perpetrators or perpetrators' vehicles fleeing from the scene.
- If possible, verify that a crime has been committed.
- Administer first aid to and summon medical assistance for any victims.
- If the perpetrator is at the scene and probable cause for arrest exists or an arrest warrant has been issued, arrest the suspect.
- Inform superiors of the nature of the offense.

3. **What must an investigator remember when searching a crime scene?**

It is important to remember that after an investigator has properly documented a crime scene, the actual search must begin. Generally speaking, evidence discovered at the crime
scene serves four objectives: (1) to determine the facts of the crime, (2) to identify the lawbreaker, (3) to aid in the perpetrator's arrest, and (4) to aid in the criminal prosecution of the perpetrator. Search patterns include:

- The spiral search method
- The grid method

- The strip- or line-search method
- The quadrant- or zone-search method

Evidence that has been collected must be safeguarded until the case goes to court. The total accounting of evidence is known as the chain of custody.

4. **Describe how to properly prepare crime scene reports.**

The crime scene report is the record of what was done to identify evidence of the crime and reconstruct what occurred at the time of the offense. At the very minimum, the crime scene report must include:

- The date and time at which the officers arrived on the scene
- Conditions at the time of arrival at the crime scene
- The manner in which the crime was discovered and reported
- The identities of police officers and emergency personnel who were present at the scene
- Physical evidence collected and the identities of those who collected it
- Identification of witnesses to the crime
- The results of interviews with victims and witnesses
- Diagrams, sketches, photographs, videotapes, and other information prepared

Key Terms

associative evidence

chain of custody

corpus delicti

crime scene

electronic evidence

flash description

follow-up investigation

latent evidence

Locard exchange principle

medical examiner

neighborhood canvass

preliminary investigation

trace evidence

Discussion Questions

1. Define the term *preliminary investigation* and discuss how it applies to a crime scene.

2. What is meant by the term *contamination of evidence*?

3. List and discuss the preliminary duties of the responding officer at a crime scene and measures that must be taken to ensure that a crime scene is secured.

4. With the exception of any unusual circumstances, explain why evidence at a crime scene should be recorded before any objects are collected or removed.

5. Discuss the ways that witnesses to a suspected crime can be identified.

6. Discuss the goals of a follow-up investigation.

mycrimekit™

Go to MyCrimeKit.com to explore the following study tools and resources specific to this chapter:

- *Practice Quiz:* Multiple-choice, true/false, short-answer, and essay questions.
- *Flashcards:* There are 13 key terms in this chapter. Flashcards test your knowledge of the chapter's key terms.

- *Web Links:* Check out the hotlink to *The New York Times* articles on criminology and criminal law.
- *Career Center:* Check out the hot links to interesting careers in criminal justice, criminology, and juvenile justice
- *The Research Center:* Check out the Cybrary and research navigator for even more resources.

Notes

1. Thornton, J. I. (1997). The general assumptions and rationale of forensic identification, in Faigman D. L., D. H. Kaye, M. J. Saks, and J. Sanders (Eds.), *Modern scientific evidence: The law and science of expert testimony*, vol 2. Cincinnati: West Publishing Co.

2. Keppel, R. D., and J. G. Weis (1993). HITS: Catching criminals in the Northwest. *FBI Law Enforcement Bulletin*, April:14–19.

3. Hammett T. M. (1989). 1988 update: AIDS in correctional facilities. Washington, DC: U.S. Department of Justice, National Institute of Justice. *Issues and Practices.*

4. The purpose of the entry by the officers affects the courts' views as to whether or not the entry was lawful. Courts have typically upheld an entry and protective sweep if the officers had any substantial reason to believe that there were victims within the premises who might be in need of help. In contrast, courts are much more likely to hold a warrantless entry unlawful when the entry was made primarily or solely for the purpose of apprehending a perpetrator thought to be inside.

5. In emergencies, entry to protect victims may have to take priority over communication with superiors. Even in emergency circumstances, however, whenever possible, communication should be simultaneous with emergency entries or the taking of other emergency measures, or if sufficient personnel is on the scene, one officer should communicate while other officers are performing emergency functions.

6. Note that police frequencies are often monitored by persons other than law enforcement officers and agencies. News media, curious citizens, and even the perpetrators themselves may be listening. This may require the use of discretion as to what is said on the radio. However, even when transmissions are subject to such monitoring, sufficient information must be provided by the responding officers to enable superiors to take appropriate action. The codes used must not be so cryptic that they fail to convey the information necessary to ensure an appropriate response from headquarters or other officers.

7. Persons who are or may be witnesses or have relevant information should not be allowed to leave the scene completely. They should, however, be moved out of areas in which their presence may result in loss or destruction of evidence. If the persons present at the scene include relatives of a victim or other persons who have a legal right to be on the premises, the clearing of the area must be accomplished with tact and, in some cases, may be subject to considerations of the welfare of the persons involved.

8. Local officials may, for various reasons not directly connected with the investigation of the crime, come to the scene of a major crime. Dealing with such persons requires tact. The officer in charge or some other experienced person should be designated to handle such situations.

9. The entry of any nonessential person into the crime scene area threatens the integrity of the case. In any subsequent legal proceeding, the criminal defense may claim that the entry of such persons into the area compromised the scene and cast doubt upon the validity of the prosecution's case.

10. Adapted from Technical Working Group for Electronic Crime Scene Investigation. (2001). *Electronic crime scene investigation: A guide for first responders.* Washington, DC: National Institute of Justice, from which much of the information in this section is taken.

11. Hammett T. M.(1989). 1988 update: AIDS in correctional facilities. U.S. Department of Justice, National Institute of Justice. *Issues and Practices.*

12. *U.S. V. Montoya de Hernandez*, 473 U.S. 531, 105 S. Ct. 3304 (1985).

13. National Institute of Justice (1987). *Investigators who perform well.* Washington, DC: U.S. Department of Justice, September.

14. Some departments prefer that development of this type of information be left to detectives or other investigators.

15. Fox, R. H and C. L. Cunningham (1985). *Crime scene search and physical evidence handbook.* Washington, DC: U.S. Department of Justice.

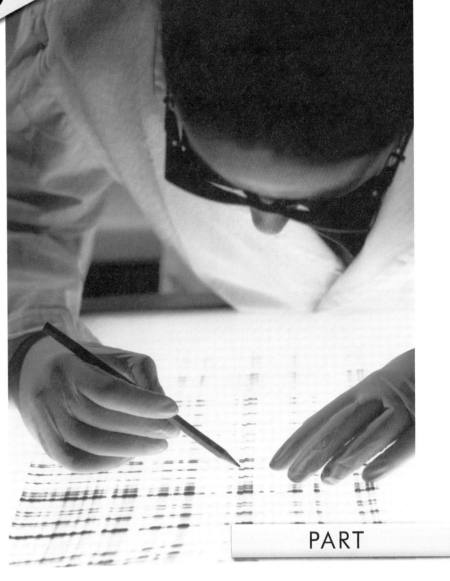

Follow-Up Investigative Processes

PART

2

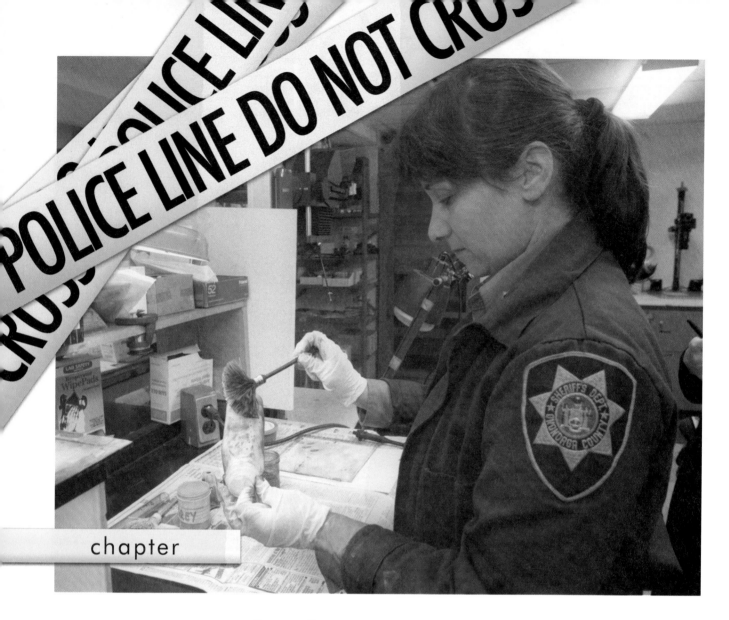

chapter

4

Identification of Criminal Suspects: Field and Laboratory Processes

This chapter will enable you to:

- Understand the fundamentals of fingerprint science.
- Identify the different types of fingerprint patterns.
- Comprehend the various techniques of developing fingerprints.
- Understand the significance of DNA analysis in the criminal investigation process.
- Understand the importance of handwriting analysis in suspect development.
- Learn the legalities of police lineups in suspect identification.

Introduction

Although many investigative techniques used in suspect identification involve forensic procedures, forensics is not the primary focus of this book. Rather, the intent is to provide the reader with a basic understanding of some of the technological advances in suspect identification through brief offerings of some of the most innovative and effective techniques in this area.

Of paramount importance to any criminal investigation is establishment of the identity of the perpetrator or victim. This can be accomplished through numerous investigative techniques. *Fact:* When criminals are at work, they cannot avoid leaving behind clues as to their true identity. Such clues include fingerprints, bloodstains, and handwriting specimens. Today, such evidence may be a clear indicator of the identity of the criminal and can help expedite criminal prosecutions. In this chapter, we will examine the role of the crime laboratory as well as some of the most critical techniques used in criminal investigation.

The Role of the Crime Laboratory

The crime laboratory plays a pivotal role in criminal investigation. Thus, criminalists are major contributors to the investigative process. The duties and qualifications of criminalists vary greatly from one position to the next. For example, positions in crime labs include specialists in DNA (blood), trace evidence, handwriting analysis, toxicology, and ballistics, to name only a few. Students interested in becoming criminalists must be mindful of the very different job requirements and specific college coursework required to successfully compete. Let's now look at a few of the investigative functions performed by the crime laboratory.

FIGURE 4.1 Criminalist working on DNA results. DNA blood typing in the laboratory is meticulous, and all steps must be thoroughly documented.
Courtesy of Mike Himmel and the Missouri State Highway Patrol.

Trace Evidence

The Trace Evidence Unit identifies and compares specific types of trace materials that could be transferred during the commission of a violent crime. These trace materials include human hair, animal hair, textile fibers and fabric, ropes, and wood. Physical contact between a suspect and a victim may result in the transfer of trace materials such as hairs and fibers. The identification and comparison of these materials may often link a suspect to a crime scene or to physical contact with another individual. Torn pieces of fabric may be positively associated with a damaged garment, and broken pieces of wood can be fit together. Odontology (forensic dentistry) and physical anthropology (skeletal remains) examinations assist in the identification of human remains.

Questioned Documents

The Questioned Documents Unit examines and compares data appearing on paper and other evidentiary materials. These surface data include handwriting, hand printing, typewriting, printing, erasures, alterations, and obliterations. Impressions in the surface of paper, such as those from indented writing or use of a check writer or dry seal, are also routinely evaluated by unit examiners, as are shoeprint and tire tread impressions.

In addition to data contained on the surface of documentary evidence, data *within* paper or other surfaces—watermarks, safety fibers, and other integral features—may be components of document examinations. Unit examiners also match the torn or perforated edges of items such as paper, stamps, or matches.

Other unit examinations include analyses of typewriter ribbons, photocopiers, facsimiles, graphic arts, and plastic bags.

Forensic Chemistry

A crime laboratory's chemistry section is typically divided into three subunits whose analyses and functions include the following:

GENERAL CHEMISTRY SUBUNIT

- Identifies specific dyes and chemicals used in bank security devices; analyzes items such as clothing or currency for the presence of these dyes and chemicals
- Analyzes controlled substances to determine identity and quantity
- Compares stains or markings with suspected sources. Detects the presence of lubricants and compares them with suspected sources
- Compares the formulations of known and questioned ink (e.g., pens, typewriters, stamp pads)
- Conducts chemical analysis of unknown solids or liquids
- Performs pharmaceutical identification of constituent composition, active ingredients, quantity, and weight

TOXICOLOGY SUBUNIT

- Conducts toxicological analyses of biological specimens or food products for drugs, drug metabolites, and poisons
- Investigates claims of product tampering

PAINTS AND POLYMERS SUBUNIT

- Analyzes paint chips for comparison with suspected sources
- Conducts automotive make, model, and year determinations from suspected paint samples

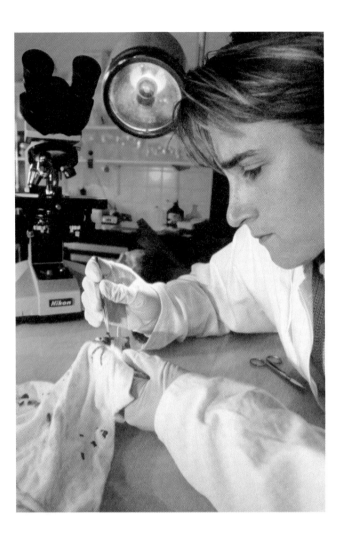

FIGURE 4.2 Working in the crime laboratory requires considerable focus to detail. Here a forensic scientist carefully removes a fragment of material from a bloodstained garment recovered from a crime scene. Courtesy of Dr. Jurgen Scriba/Photo Researchers, Inc.

- Compares plastics with suspected sources
- Determines tape composition, construction, and color for comparison to suspected sources; determines manufacturer of suspected duct tape; performs tape identifications with the torn or cut end of the tape and a roll of suspected tape
- Compares caulks, sealants, and adhesives by color and composition with suspected sources.

DNA Analysis

A crime laboratory's DNA Analysis Unit analyzes bodily fluids and bodily fluid stains recovered as evidence in violent crimes. Examinations include the identification and characterization of blood, semen, saliva, and other bodily fluids using traditional serological techniques and related biochemical analysis. After the stain has been identified, it is characterized by DNA analysis using the restriction fragment length polymorphism (RFLP) or polymerase chain reaction (PCR) techniques. The results of the analyses are compared with results obtained from known blood or saliva samples submitted from the victims or suspects.

In 1996, a number of DNA crime laboratory analysis units began using mitochondrial DNA (mtDNA) analysis, which is applied to evidence containing small or degraded quantities of DNA from hair, bones, teeth, and bodily fluids. The results of mtDNA analysis are compared with blood, saliva, or both submitted from victims or suspects. The unit examines evidence that may not have been suitable for significant comparison purposes before the development of this technique.

FIGURE 4.3 Blood evidence such as the one shown here tells a story as to its origin, point of impact, direction of trajectory, and other points of evidentiary information.
Courtesy of Mike Himmel and the Missouri State Highway Patrol.

The Mitochondrial DNA Population Database is composed of complete nucleotide sequences of the first and second hypervariable segments of the control region of the human mitochondrial genome and consists of two main data sets. The first data set contains individuals from populations of forensic relevance and is contributed mostly by the Scientific Working Group on DNA Analysis Methods and forensic laboratories. The second data set, based on mtDNA concordance, contains nucleotide sequences from ethnic groups around the world.

Mitochondrial DNA Analysis. Both data sets are bundled in MitoSearch, a software package specifically designed for the compilation and analysis of mtDNA databases. MitoSearch estimates the relative frequency of specific sequences for the various populations represented within the database and assesses the relative relatedness of each population with reference to the size of each database.

Ballistics

The Forensic Ballistics Unit receives and examines evidence related to firearms, firearm components, ammunition, ammunition components, tools, and tool marks. Evidence in a typical case may include a number of recovered rifles, pistols, shotguns, silencers and other muzzle attachments, magazines, holsters, and a variety of fired and unfired cartridges. Lead and other metal fragments, shot wads, shot cups, and bullets removed from bodies during an autopsy are also frequently received items in firearms-related casework. Evidence submitted in tool mark cases may include screwdrivers, scissors, knives, pliers, wrenches, crowbars, hammers, saws, wire, sections of sheet metal, chains, safety deposit boxes, human bone or cartilage, plates, locks, doorknobs, bolts, and screens.

Forensic firearms examinations are based on firearms identification, which involves the identification of a bullet, cartridge case, or other ammunition component as having been fired by or in a particular firearm. Firearms examiners microscopically compare bullets and ammunition components with each other as well as to any number of firearms to determine whether an association exists between or among items submitted as evidence and items whose origins are known. Similarly, forensic tool mark identifications involve the identification of a tool mark as having been produced by a particular tool to the exclusion of all others. Examiners compare the micro- and macroscopic features of tool-marked items with known and questioned tools that may have produced them.

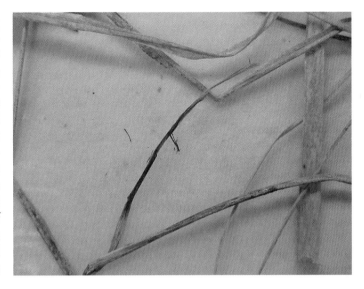

FIGURE 4.4 Straw (grass) close-up—dried grass on the roadside had blood on it. The blood trail on the grass led investigators to a body deposited several feet away from the roadside. The DNA matched the body. This evidence helped investigators theorize that the body had been dragged to its location. Courtesy of the Missouri State Highway Patrol Crime Laboratory.

Tests and examinations routinely performed by laboratory ballistic criminalists include:

- Trigger-pull tests
- Function tests
- Full-auto conversion tests
- Accidental discharge tests
- Shot pattern examinations
- Gunshot residue examinations
- Ejection pattern testing
- Trajectory analysis examinations
- Silencer (flash suppressor) testing
- Serial number restorations

FIGURE 4.5 Ballistics test. The gun is fired into the tank that is filled with water. The bullet is stopped by the water and can be fished out unharmed and compared with bullets found at a crime scene. Courtesy of the Nebraska State Crime Lab.

Latent Prints

The Latent Print Unit conducts all work pertaining to the examination of latent prints on evidence submitted to the FBI laboratory. Latent prints are impressions produced by the ridged skin on human fingers, palms, and soles of the feet. Unit examiners analyze and compare latent prints with known prints of individuals in an effort to make identifications or exclusions. The uniqueness, permanence, and arrangement of the friction ridges allow unit examiners to positively match two prints and determine whether an area of a friction ridge impression originated from one source to the exclusion of all others.

A variety of techniques, including use of chemicals, powders, lasers, alternate light sources, and other physical means, are used in the detection and development of latent prints. In instances in which a latent print has limited quality and quantity of detail, unit personnel may perform microscopic examinations o effect conclusive comparisons.

One technique for the development of fingerprints is **Amido black protein**. This is an amino acid–staining diazo dye used in biochemical research to stain for total protein on transferred membrane blots. It is used in criminal investigations to detect blood present with latent fingerprints by staining proteins in blood a blue-black color.

In 1999, the FBI developed and implemented a new automated fingerprint system known as the Automated Fingerprint Identification System (AFIS), which has since been adopted by most state crime laboratories as well. Although AFIS is primarily a 10-print system for searching an individual's fingerprints to determine whether a prior arrest record exists and then maintaining a criminal arrest record history for each individual, the system also offers significant latent print capabilities. Using AFIS, a latent print specialist can digitally capture latent print and 10-print images and perform several functions with each. These include:

- Enhancement to improve image quality
- Comparison of latent fingerprints against suspect 10-print records retrieved from the criminal fingerprint repository
- Searches of latent fingerprints against the 10-print fingerprint repository when no suspects have been developed
- Automatic searches of new arrest 10-print records against an unsolved latent fingerprint repository
- Creation of special files of 10-print records in support of major criminal investigations

Using the AFIS fingerprint search capability against data from the FBI Criminal Justice Information Services (CJIS) Division, which maintains one of the largest repositories of fingerprint records, identifications are made in cases for which no known suspects have been named for comparison purposes and in cases in which latent prints on crime scene-related evidence were not identified with suspects named in the investigation.

Personnel from a crime laboratory's Latent Print Unit may also form the nucleus of the local or state disaster squad, which renders assistance in identifying victims at disaster scenes.

Forensic Photography

A crime lab's Forensic Photography Unit is responsible for imaging operations. This unit captures, processes, produces, analyzes, archives, and disseminates

FIGURE 4.6 Pistols commonly encountered in shooting cases. In such cases, it is important to locate bullets and match spent shell casings to specific handguns to identify the weapon used in the crime. Doing makes it easier to identify the shooter. Pistols are as follows:
(1) 9mm caliber Smith & Wesson model 5906
(2) 9mm caliber Taurus model PT 99
(3) .40 caliber Glock model 22
(4) .45 auto caliber Colt model M1911A1
(5) 9mm caliber Sturm & Ruger model P89DC
(6) .25 auto caliber Beretta model 21A
(7) .22 caliber Beretta model 21A
(8) .380 auto caliber Walther model PPK/S

images using traditional silver-based photographic processes and digital imaging technologies. The unit is typically responsible for the following:

- Crime scene and evidentiary photography
- Forensic photography
- Surveillance photography
- Aerial photography
- Venue photography
- Tactical imaging
- Photographic scanners
- Field photographic equipment
- Regional color photographic processing mini-laboratories
- Silver-based and digital darkrooms
- Digital imaging technologies
- Courtroom presentations and exhibits

Specialized Laboratory Equipment

The use of specialized laboratory equipment is one of the hallmarks of the modern crime lab. For example, the spectrograph is used to identify minute samples of a substance by burning the material and interpreting the light emitted from the burning process. Another device, the spectrophotometer, is used to analyze coloring agents in small samples such as those found in paint and cloth. The gas chromatograph is most commonly used for isolating gases or liquids from complex solutions or mixtures, generally in the analysis of illicit drugs, plastics, and explosives. Another crucial instrument, the mass spectrometer, is used to separate and record ions according to their characteristic masses. It is most commonly used in the detection of trace elements in glass, ashes, and

FIGURE 4.7 DNA analysis—search for bloodstains. Special lighting is often required to cause bloodstains to show up on surfaces that would otherwise hide its presence. Courtesy of Mike Himmel and the Missouri State Highway Patrol.

other inorganic material. Throughout the remainder of this chapter, other important instruments used by the crime lab will be featured and discussed according to their particular purposes.

Fingerprinting

mycrimekit

Review: Function of a crime lab

Identifying criminal suspects through the use of fingerprinting has proven to be one of the most effective methods for apprehending persons who might otherwise go undetected and continue their criminal activities. In addition to identifying criminal suspects, the use of fingerprinting also makes it possible to learn accurately the suspect's number (and type) of previous arrests and convictions. This, of course, often results in more appropriate sentences being handed down to repeat or career criminals. Early on, fingerprinting, because of its peculiar adaptability to the field, has been associated in the layperson's mind almost exclusively with criminal identification. Interestingly, the civil fingerprint file of the FBI contains three times as many fingerprints as the criminal file. Such files also provide a humanitarian benefit to society in general by identifying missing persons, amnesia victims, and unknown deceased people.

In the latter case, victims of major disasters can be identified quickly and positively if their fingerprints are on file. The background and history of the science of fingerprints constitute an eloquent drama of human lives of good versus evil. Few developments in crime solving have played a more exciting role than that dramatized by the fascinating loops, whorls, and arches etched on the fingers and palms of a human being. Although faults have been found with earlier identification systems, to date no two fingerprints have been found to be identical.

The History of Fingerprinting

In earlier times, branding, maiming, distinctive clothing, and photography were used to distinguish the criminal for the crime that he or she committed. Thieves, for example, were sometimes deprived of the hand that committed a criminal act. Romans used the tattoo needle for identifying and preventing desertion of military soldiers. In more recent times, law enforcement officers relied heavily

FIGURE 4.8 DNA analysis equipment. *Courtesy of Mike Himmel and the Missouri State Highway Patrol.*

on identification of criminals by sight, or what was known as the "camera eye." In using this system, photography lessened the burden on memory but was not the answer to the criminal identification problem because personal appearances change. Throughout history, people have been aware of the friction ridges on the tips of fingers and palms. Although the precise origin of the science of personal identification is somewhat unclear, records show its application extending back to ancient civilizations.

For example, on the face of a cliff in Nova Scotia, a prehistoric Indian picture writing exists of a hand with ridge patterns crudely marked. Other examples include references to fingerprinting in clay tablets of recorded business transactions in ancient Babylon and to ancient Chinese documents identified with the eighth-century A.D. T'ang Dynasty, which refers to fingerprints being impressed on business contracts.

The first official use of fingerprinting was in 1858 by Sir William Herschel, British chief administrative officer for the Hooghly district, Bengal, India. He required natives to affix their fingerprints as well as their signatures to contracts. Although there is no evidence to suggest that Herschel was aware that fingerprints were individualized, he believed that to the native mind, this procedure would be impressive enough to discourage dishonesty.

Herschel continued his study of fingerprinting and in 1877 submitted a report to his superiors asking permission to identify prisoners through fingerprinting. Also around 1870, the French anthropologist Alphonse Bertillon developed a system to measure and record the dimensions of certain bony parts of the body. These measurements were reduced to a formula that, theoretically, would apply to only one person and would not change during his or her adult life. This system, called the Bertillon system, was generally accepted for more than 30 years but was pronounced as fallible as a result of the Will West case of 1903.

The value of fingerprints as a means of detecting the fallibility of the Bertillon system and establishing the value and reliability of individualized identification for criminal suspects was therefore established.

Between 1875 and the turn of the century, several new developments were documented regarding fingerprinting. For example, an article published in 1880 by Henry Faulds of the Tsukiji Hospital in Tokyo, Japan, discussed future possibilities of fingerprint science. He recommended the use of a thin film of printer's ink as a transfer medium, as is generally used today. He also discussed the potentialities of identification of criminals by their fingerprints left at the scenes of crimes. The first documented use of fingerprinting in the United States was in 1882. Gilbert Thompson of the U.S. Geological Survey, while in charge of a field project in New Mexico, used his own fingerprint on commissary orders to prevent their forgery. Later that year, Sir Francis Galton, a noted British anthropologist, published his book *Fingerprints*. He also contributed to the field by devising the first scientific method of classifying fingerprint patterns.

In 1891, the first files for fingerprint identification were installed as a means of identifying criminals. Juan Vuchetich, an Argentinean police official, based this system on pattern types by Sir Francis Galton. The Vuchetich system is the basis of systems presently used in many Spanish-speaking countries. Between 1890 and 1924, the official use of fingerprinting escalated in the United States. The New York Civil Service Commission implemented the use of fingerprints to prevent applicants from having better qualified persons take their tests for them (1902). The New York State prison system also adopted the first practical use of fingerprints in the United States for the identification of criminals (1903).

As the use of fingerprints became more accepted throughout the United States, the penitentiary in Leavenworth, Kansas, and the St. Louis, Missouri, Police Department both implemented fingerprint bureaus. The St. Louis system was activated through the assistance of a sergeant associated with London's Scotland Yard. As more and more police departments established identification bureaus, many sent copies of their files to the National Bureau of Criminal Identification, established by the International Association of Chiefs of Police. In 1924, the fingerprint records of both the National Bureau of Criminal Identification and the Leavenworth Penitentiary, totaling 810,188, were consolidated to form the nucleus of the FBI Identification Division. Between 1924 and 1954 alone, more than 130 million fingerprint cards had been received by the FBI. It has since become renowned as the world's largest repository of fingerprints.

Types of Prints

Among the most valuable clues for the investigator at the crime scene are fingerprints and palm prints. After such prints have been collected by investigators and evaluated by classification experts, a definitive determination can be made as to the exact identity of the suspect(s). Generally, fingerprints can be divided into three main groups: latent, plastic, and visible.

A **latent fingerprint** (also called a *patent fingerprint*) is one that occurs when the entire pattern of whorls on the finger, which contain small amounts of grease, oil, perspiration, or dirt, for example, is transferred to an object when it is touched. The grease and oil are usually natural and are transferred to the fingers when the person touches other areas of his or her body containing various bodily excretions. Latent prints include those not only visible to the naked eye but also those that can be examined properly only after development. Those are usually found on paper and smooth surfaces.

A **plastic fingerprint** results when a finger presses against plastic material and leaves a negative impression of friction ridges. Typically, these are found on recently painted surfaces; in wax, grease, tar, and putty; in the gum on stamps or envelopes; and on adhesive tape.

A **visible fingerprint** (also called a *dust print*) is a print that has been adulterated with foreign matter. If a finger is placed in a thin layer of dust, for example, the dust may cover the friction ridges. If the finger subsequently touches a clean surface, a visible fingerprint may result. A visible fingerprint may also develop as a result of touching other substances such as blood, flour, ink, or oil.

Types of Patterns

The use of fingerprints for identification purposes is based on distinctive ridge outlines that appear on the bulbs on the inside of the end joints of the fingers and thumbs. These ridges have definite contours and appear in several general pattern types. Each type has general and specific variations of the pattern, depending on the shape and relationship of the ridges. The ridge outlines appear most clearly when inked impressions are taken on paper, so that the ridges are black against a white background. This results from the ink adhering to the friction ridges. Impressions can be made by a variety of substances, including blood, dirt, grease, or any other foreign matter present on the ridges or the saline substance emitted by the glands through the ducts or pores that constitute their outlets. The background or medium may be paper, glass, porcelain, wood, cloth, wax, putty, silverware, or any smooth, nonporous material.

Fingerprints may be resolved into three large general groups of patterns: the arch, the loop, and the whorl. Each group bears the same general characteristics. Patterns can be further subdivided by means of the smaller differences existing between patterns in the same general group. Patterns are divided as follows:

- Arch loop
- Whorl
- Plain radial
- Plain tented
- Ulnar
- Accidental double
- Central pocket

FIGURE 4.9 Characteristics of a basic fingerprint showing characteristics such as arches, loops, deltas, and whorls.

Before pattern definition can be understood, it is necessary to understand the meaning of a few technical terms used in fingerprint work. As far as classification is concerned, the pattern area is the only part of the finger impression worth focusing on. It is present in all patterns, of course, but in many arches and tented arches, it is impossible to define. This is not important, however, because the only patterns in which one needs to define pattern areas for classification purposes are loops and whorls. The U.S. Department of Justice defines the pattern area as follows: the part of a loop or whorl in which appear the cores, deltas, and ridges with which we are concerned when classifying.[1] Type lines enclose the pattern areas of loops and whorls. *Type lines* may be defined as the two innermost ridges, which start parallel, diverge, and surround or tend to surround the pattern area. Fingerprint impressions can be made from blood, dirt, grease, or the saline substance emitted by the glands through ducts or pores in the skin.

Searching for Prints

Investigators must be judicious in their search for fingerprints, as such evidence may be located in not-so-obvious places at the crime scene. In a burglary case, for example, the search for prints should begin at the place of entry by the criminal. Investigators should be able, at that point, to determine whether or not the burglar's hands were protected. If a door has been forced open, prints may be located on the lock or its immediate surroundings or in the general area of entry. When entry is gained through windows, broken glass should be searched for and documented. Generally, this method of entry involves the criminal breaking a piece of glass just large enough for a hand to reach through and open the latch.

Broken pieces of glass don't always fall inside a residence. Indeed, they may or may not be in the structure at all, or the burglar might pick up the pieces and throw them outside, out of the way. When attempting to climb through the window, the burglar may leave fingerprints on a window jamb, frame, or sill. The search for fingerprints should begin at the place of entry by the criminal.

FIGURE 4.10 A side-by-side comparison of a latent print found on a crime scene against a file fingerprint. Courtesy of Sirchie Finger Print Laboratories, Inc.

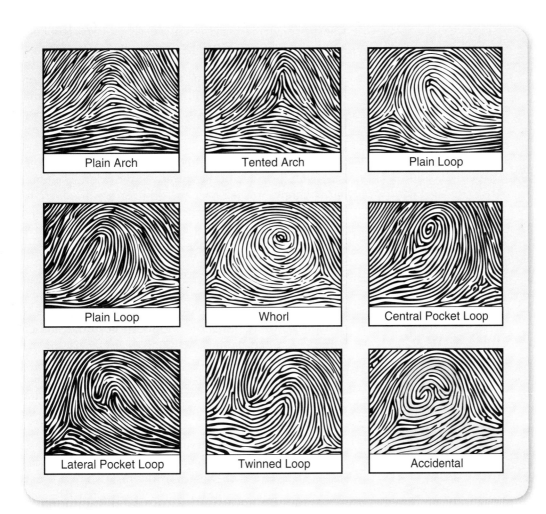

FIGURE 4.11 Basic fingerprint patterns. Having a general understanding of such patterns gives the investigator knowledge of what to look for once fingerprint evidence has been discovered at a crime scene.

Some burglars have been known to eat food or drink something while in a residence. The investigator must anticipate this and take care to preserve any fingerprints left on glassware (including liquor bottles) and even on some types of food (detectable by superglue fuming, discussed later). Electric light switches, circuit breakers, and light bulbs should also be examined closely for prints. If it has been determined that the burglar was wearing gloves, places where gloves would be awkward to wear should be examined because the burglar may have removed the gloves to accomplish a particular task. Experience shows that this is common and that it typically occurs early in the commission of a crime. Many police officers have grown accustomed to wearing gloves during their crime scene search. Today, this has become a recommended practice for the investigator's safety as well as to safeguard against contaminating the evidence.

Another technique used for recognizing fingerprints on a crime scene is shining a flashlight at an oblique angle at the suspected area. Although using this technique on some porous surfaces does not work well, it is effective on surfaces such as tile floors, glass surfaces, and countertops.

Developing Latent Fingerprints

The sole purpose of developing, or lifting, a latent fingerprint impression is to make it visible so that it can be preserved and compared. Several powders and chemicals are used for this purpose in addition to several techniques designed to develop such evidence.

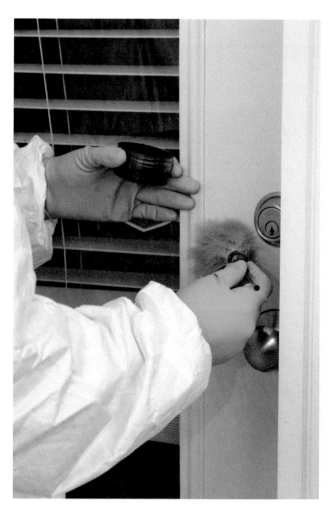

FIGURE 4.12 Great care must go into searching and dusting for fingerprints. Courtesy of Mike Himmel.

Powders. When a latent print is clearly visible, it should be photographed before attempts are made to develop it. Accordingly, wet fingerprints should be allowed to dry before any attempt is made to develop them. Failure to do so will probably result in the print being destroyed. The powder method is used to develop fingerprints by making them show up on a surface where they would otherwise go unnoticed. To develop a latent fingerprint with powder, the powder used should contrast with the color of the surface of the print. The powder is lightly brushed over the print so it will adhere to the oils on the surface of the print pattern. Generally, gray and black powder are best for latent fingerprint development: gray for dark backgrounds and black for light backgrounds.

Usually, a small camel hair, fiberglass, or nylon brush is used in dusting for latent prints. The brush must be kept dry to be effective. A small amount of powder is first placed on the brush for application to the surface being powdered. Some investigators prefer use of the Magna-Brush®, a magnetic brush that is used with magnetic powder. When the particles of the magnetic powder come into contact with the latent surface, the print becomes apparent. The sole purpose of developing, or lifting, a latent fingerprint impression is to make it visible so that it can be preserved and compared.

When brushing, the investigator should try to identify the contour of the ridges of the print so that brush strokes can go the same direction. Powder particles will then affix themselves to the oily ridges of the fingerprint, and the print will become visible. Typically, beginners tend to use too much powder and too little brushing, thus making the print unidentifiable.

Many investigators have adopted the use of fluorescent powders as an investigative alternative. Available in both powder and aerosol form, these are typically used to dust currency or other documents that may be handled by criminals. This technique differs from traditional fingerprinting in that these powders are used "before" the fingerprint is deposited. After the criminal touches the dusted object, the area is examined by the use of an ultraviolet light, which will display any fingerprints clearly. These are then photographed and classified.

Attempting to develop fingerprints on absorbent surfaces such as paper, cardboard, unpainted wood, and so on requires the use of more complicated procedures than the simple use of fingerprint powder, but positive results are worth the effort. Often, because powders cannot be removed from paper surfaces, it is best not to use them because the powder may interfere with writings on the document. In the next few paragraphs, we discuss the use of chemical developers. The first three, iodine, ninhydrin, and silver nitrate, are the most commonly used.

Iodine. Iodine is used on the premise that it attacks the object and changes its color. The grease and oils naturally produced by the skin discolor very easily and naturally become good candidates for development with iodine. Iodine prints, generally used on paper and wood, are temporary and begin to fade after the fuming has stopped. It is therefore necessary for the investigator to be prepared to photograph the prints immediately.

Iodine fumes are controlled through the use of an iodine gun for smaller specimens or a fuming cabinet for larger objects. The gun consists essentially of two parts: one tube (through which the breath is blown) containing a drying agent such as calcium chloride to remove moisture from the breath and a second tube containing a small number of iodine crystals that are vaporized by the heat of breath and the warm hand cupped around the tube containing the iodine. The vapor is blown on the specimen.

When an iodine cabinet is used, several pieces can be developed at a time, and the investigator can observe the process. The cabinet is constructed of wood or plastic with glass sides. Fumes are generated by placing a small glass dish containing the iodine crystals in a hole cut in the bottom of the cabinet. As soon as the fumes begin to appear in sufficient amounts, the burner is removed. Specimens can be hung in the cabinet by wooden clothespins fastened to a removable strip. The top of the cabinet is hinged to permit access.

Iodine fumes can be removed by placing the specimen in a current of air from a fan, blow-dryer, or other device. The process should be carried out in a well-ventilated area because fumes can cause respiratory damage if inhaled in large amounts.

Ninhydrin. A second process, involving the development of prints using amino acids present as a result of perspiration, is generally the most common method of fingerprint development for latent prints. Solutions of ninhydrin in powder or aerosol form can be acquired from fingerprint supply companies. Similar to chlorides, amino acids permeate the friction ridges of the fingerprint and remain unchanged for an extremely long time. In some cases, prints have been developed on paper 30 or 40 years after they were deposited. One fundamental requirement is that the paper must have been stored under dry conditions from the time deposited to the time developed.

A ninhydrin solution can be applied to the surface of an object by spraying, dipping, or brushing, with spraying being the method preferred. After treatment, prints should develop

FIGURE 4.13 Photo of a ceramic vase being "dusted" for fingerprints with zephyr brush. Courtesy of Dorling Kindersley Media Library.

FIGURE 4.14 Latent fingerprints developed on a doorknob. Courtesy of Mike Himmel.

A CLOSER LOOK

The FBI's National DNA Database: CODIS

When scientists James Watson and Francis Crick first mapped the structure of the DNA double helix a half century ago, little did they know that they were also unleashing a powerful weapon in the fight against crime and terrorism. DNA can uniquely identify an individual in ways that even fingerprints can't. DNA is found in virtually every human cell. It can be extracted from hair, teeth, bones, and body fluids (blood, saliva, semen, even sweat!). It leaves traces on everything from cigarette butts to postage stamps, from shirt collars to napkins. And it lasts for years—even in harsh conditions, even when there's little left of human remains. For example, after the September 11, 2001, attacks, investigators were able to find traces of DNA in the rubble of the World Trade Center that identified victims and brought some measure of closure and relief to their devastated families.

In 1990, the FBI began a pilot project called the Combined DNA Index System, or CODIS—which became fully operational in 1998. CODIS is a three-hitter:

1. Computer technology (a database program and software)

2. Forensic science (DNA profiles rigorously measured and maintained)

3. Telecommunications (the ability of local, state, and federal labs to share information and communicate electronically) all rolled into one system

Simply put, CODIS stores DNA profiles from across the country in a series of local, state, and national databases, all linked via computers, enabling crime labs at every level to share and compare DNA profiles electronically. Lightning fast searches using CODIS can link DNA found at one crime to other crime scenes and to convicted criminals whose DNA is already on file.

The overwhelming majority—more than 1.5 million DNA profiles—come from convicted felons. Depending on the state, the felons include those serving time for rape, murder, crimes against children, robbery, burglary, kidnapping, and

assault and battery. The National DNA Index System (NDIS) also includes more than 78,000 DNA samples collected from crime scenes, more than 100 from missing persons and another 300 from relatives of missing persons, and some 150 from unidentified human remains. DNA samples from suspected terrorists are also collected today, but they are not uploaded to NDIS. When you add it all up, there are more than 1.6 million DNA profiles in the national system.

CODIS is used by a total of 175 crime labs in all 50 states and Puerto Rico, as well as the FBI Lab

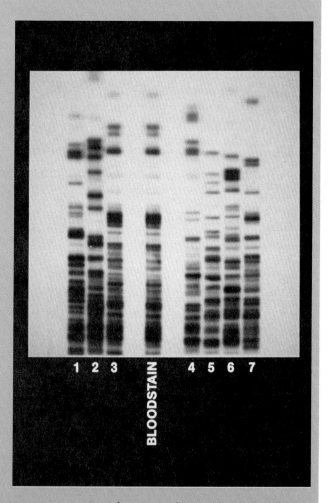

FIGURE 4.15 DNA fingerprints from a bloodstain left at the scene of a crime and from the blood of seven suspects. Courtesy of Orchid Cellmark, Inc.

A CLOSER LOOK CONTINUED

and the U.S. Army Crime Lab. And, in a sign of how effective the system is, 31 labs in 18 nations worldwide also use CODIS, but they are not connected to any DNA databases here in the United States. They simply borrow the FBI's technology to help investigations in their own countries, much as we do here.

The success of CODIS is measured primarily by keeping tabs on the number of investigations helped by CODIS through a hit or match that wouldn't have otherwise been developed. In December 2003, that total passed the 10,000 threshold. As of 2005, it stands at 10,770. "Forensic hits" are also measured when two or more DNA samples from a crime scene are linked in local, state, or national databases. "Offender hits" are measured when one or more DNA profiles from a crime scene are linked to a convicted felon. Between 1998 and 2005, there were more than 3,000 forensic hits and more than 7,000 offender hits.

Thematic question

The investigative uses of the CODIS system are apparent, but explain how the system could possibly be misused and how innocent persons could be wrongfully targeted for investigation.

Source: FBI, 2009. Available at http://www.fbi.gov/hq/lab/html/codis1.htm.

within 24 hours but will probably appear within an hour or two. Development can be expedited through the use of heat. Generally, a blow-dryer can accomplish this, but investigators should take care not to scorch the material being printed.

Silver Nitrate. Latent impressions developed by the use of silver nitrate are caused by the reaction of sodium chloride present in perspiration. When a person touches a surface with a sweaty finger, sodium chloride remains (almost indefinitely) while the other chemical compounds decompose. If a solution of silver nitrate is used on the impression, a chemical reaction occurs between the sodium chloride and the silver nitrate, resulting in the appearance of two new chemicals: sodium nitrate and silver chloride. Through the use of ultraviolet radiation or sunlight, the silver chloride is reduced to metallic silver, bringing out a brownish print. One commonly used procedure is to prepare a 5 percent silver nitrate solution in distilled water. The solution is either brushed on the paper or the paper is dipped in the solution. After it dries, the paper is exposed to sunlight or ultraviolet light to bring out the latent prints. Because the entire paper will soon darken, prints must be photographed immediately.

Superglue Fuming. Cyanoacrylate resin, or superglue, was developed in the late 1950s as a bonding adhesive for metals and plastics. The substance was first used in fingerprinting, however, by the Japanese national police in 1978. Since then, the process has been refined and accepted as valuable for developing latent fingerprints on various types of surfaces. The use of superglue fuming is a relatively simple procedure and is particularly valuable in developing prints on plastic bags, metal foil, waxed paper, lacquered wood, leather, and almost all hard surfaces. Even fruits, vegetables, and dinner rolls have been processed successfully with this procedure. The process occurs as the fumes adhere to the friction ridges and then harden as ridge detail is built up on the print.

The vapor is controlled through the use of an airtight container such as a tropical fish aquarium or other glass or plastic container. To begin, a small amount of glue is recommended, usually a 1- to 2-inch-diameter pool for approximately 8 cubic feet of container space. The glue can be placed on a disposable receptacle

FIGURE 4.16 Photo showing portable Cyanow and cyanoacrylate ("superglue") fuming device from Sirchie Finger Print Laboratories inserted in a hole in a cylindrical "superglue fuming chamber" containing a metal stand holding a handgun upright and an alligator clip holding a photo identification card. Superglue fuming is one of the easiest and most effective methods of developing latent fingerprints.
Courtesy of Sirchie Finger Print Laboratories, Inc.

made of aluminum foil. The glue is then heated to emit the fumes. This can be accomplished easily by placing a hot plate or light bulb under the receptacle. Objects to be printed are placed in the container, usually by suspending them with wooden clothespins or spring-loaded clips, allowing maximum exposure to fumes. Exposure time may vary, so periodic inspection of the objects is necessary to check progress. The investigator must remember that because the flashpoint of the glue may vary, great care should be given to maintain a desired temperature level. After the procedure, all prints are photographed, and the specimens should be powdered.

Lasers. The detection and development of latent fingerprints left at crime scenes have taken a quantum leap forward with the use of laser technology. Since its development in 1976, this technique has been used to develop prints that could not have been developed through the use of powders, iodine, ninhydrin, silver nitrate, or superglue fuming. The laser procedure is a clean, relatively easy method to develop prints, and pretreatment of the specimen is not required.

As with the ninhydrin method, the age of the print is of no importance. Additionally, there is no alteration of the evidence; therefore, it is generally used before other methods. In this process, an expanded laser beam is used to luminesce certain properties of perspiration, body oils, or other foreign substances found on a latent print. Three types of lasers are currently operational in the development of fingerprints: the argon ion laser, the copper vapor laser, and the neodymium:YAG laser. Because laser light is extremely bright, eye protection must be worn by equipment operators. Special light-filtering goggles can be worn to illuminate latent prints with greater clarity.

Preservation of Fingerprints

Because of the importance of latent fingerprints in any criminal investigation, great care must be taken to preserve them for later examination and use in court. Fingerprints remain on affected areas for varying amounts of time, depending on whether they are plastic, visible, or latent. Generally, plastic and latent prints may remain for years, depending on the type of surface on which they are located. Methods of fingerprint preservation include photography of the print and lifting techniques.

Often, fingerprints are left on a surface that can be transported to the crime laboratory for examination. Undoubtedly, this is the preferred way to facilitate classification of the print. Unfortunately, however, many prints must be processed on the crime scene because they are found on surfaces too large to transport. In general, plastic and latent prints can remain for years, depending on the type of surface on which they are located.

Fingerprint lifters are used to remove the print from surfaces that are curved or otherwise difficult to photograph. For surfaces such as these, rubber lifters are recommended. Rubber lifters are available at fingerprint supply houses and consist of a thin black or white flexible material coated with an adhesive. The adhesive side is guarded by a thin cover that is removed just before it is placed on the print and then replaced just after use. As a general rule, the latent fingerprint is dusted with print powder. The adhesive side of the lifter is then placed against the print and slowly pulled away. The print is preserved by the fingerprint powder being pressed against the lifter. After the print is lifted, the lifter cover is replaced.

Lifting tape is also a commonly used medium for fingerprint preservation. This is a special transparent tape supplied in rolls 1 to 2 inches wide. The procedure is to dust the print with fingerprint powder and then place the tape over the print, thus removing it. The investigator must take care to avoid air pockets in the tape while it is being applied because these will show up as void areas on the print impression. After it has been applied, the tape will adhere to the powder particles and transfer the fingerprint impression.

Prints from Gloves

The notoriety of the success of fingerprinting has resulted in the use of gloves by many criminals as a protective measure. Investigators may discover "smearing" from gloves on a crime scene but may give the matter little consideration. Indeed, such gloves, if located, may produce valuable evidence in locating the perpetrator. The glove itself may have a unique, identifiable pattern, as with a fingerprint.

Leather gloves, for example, may contain fatty material, and fabric gloves are often contaminated with soil or other foreign matter. In both cases, ridge patterns may be left behind. A leather glove may possess certain pattern characteristics that make it distinguishable. This is because animal hide possesses friction ridge skin similar to that of human beings, and its characteristics can readily be identified. Fabric gloves don't offer as identifiable a pattern as that of leather gloves, but certain features may still be identifiable. After wearing gloves for a period, certain wrinkles or cracks in the material may create distinguishable markings. Sometimes a fingerprint can be recovered from a glove, particularly if it is made of latex material.

The Integrated Automated Fingerprint Identification System

The Integrated Automated Fingerprint Identification System, more commonly known as IAFIS, is a national fingerprint and criminal history database maintained by the FBI's CJIS Division. The IAFIS provides automated fingerprint search capabilities, latent searching capability, electronic image storage, and electronic exchange of fingerprints and responses, 24 hours a day, 365 days a year. It combines with criminal histories, mugshots, scar and tattoo photos, height, weight, hair and eye color, and aliases to help match evidence with identities. As a result of submitting fingerprints electronically, agencies receive electronic responses to criminal 10-print fingerprint submissions within two hours and within 24 hours for civil fingerprint submissions.

The IAFIS maintains the largest biometric database in the world, containing the fingerprints and corresponding criminal history information for more than 47 million subjects in the Criminal Master File. The fingerprints and corresponding criminal history information are submitted voluntarily by state, local, and federal law enforcement agencies.

Just a few years ago, substantial delays were a normal part of the fingerprint identification process because fingerprint cards had to be physically transported and processed. A fingerprint check could often take three months to complete. The FBI formed a partnership with the law enforcement community to revitalize the fingerprint identification process, leading to the development of the IAFIS. The IAFIS became operational in July 1999.

FIGURE 4.17 The IAFIS fingerprint identification has revolutionized suspect identification. Here, an analyst examines identifiable points in a suspect print for comparison with the computerized fingerprint database. *Courtesy of Mike Himmel and the Missouri State Highway Patrol.*

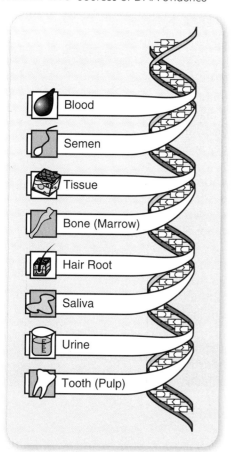

FIGURE 4.18 Sources of DNA evidence

Blood

Semen

Tissue

Bone (Marrow)

Hair Root

Saliva

Urine

Tooth (Pulp)

Since its implementation, the IAFIS has been responsible for the successful identification of suspects in hundreds of cases. Examples are as follows:

1. *The case of the cocaine murderer.* In April 2004, a man was arrested in Connecticut by a drug task force for possession of cocaine. He was fingerprinted, and his electronic prints were sent to IAFIS. Ten minutes later, there was a match. Turns out he'd been wanted in Miami since September 2002 for fleeing the state to avoid being prosecuted for homicide . . . and he'd been wanted in Fort Lauderdale since October 2003 on homicide charges. In no time, he was picked up and extradited to Florida for prosecution.

2. *The case of the vicious rapist.* In June 2004, a man was arrested by police in New Jersey for simple assault and endangering the welfare of children. That turned out to be the tip of the iceberg. When officers fingerprinted the man and sent his prints to IAFIS . . . 13 minutes later, a match! Turns out he'd been wanted in Norfolk, Virginia, since October 2000 for rape and sexual abduction . . . and he'd been wanted in Yorktown, Virginia, since May 2001 for kidnapping and sexual assault. In no time, he was facing charges in New Jersey before being shipped off to Virginia to face charges there.

3. *The case of the Christmas murderer.* In September 2004, a 57-year-old man was arrested in Massachusetts for slashing another man with a pocket knife. They'd been on a public bus, words were exchanged, and out came the knife. Fingerprints were taken at the booking station and sent to IAFIS. Turns out he was the man accused of a horrific crime in Baltimore in 1974. It was Christmas Eve 30 years earlier when police

department employee McKinley Johnson was helping to put together food baskets for the poor. Suddenly a young man approached and stole a can of lunch meat from one of the baskets. Johnson ran after him—and the thief shot him point blank. Before dying, Johnson identified his alleged assailant from photographs...and the hunt had been on ever since.

Since that time, the suspect had lived in different places, assumed 10 different identities, and was arrested five times in Boston in the 1980s for charges from shoplifting to weapon possession. In the meantime, though, IAFIS was created, allowing matches of fingerprints nationwide. And so, with the slash of a pocket knife, 30 years on the run came to an end.[2]

The Genetic Fingerprint: DNA

Because of its success in identifying suspects, fingerprinting has proven to be one of the most effective methods in law enforcement. However, a dramatic advance in forensic science may now overshadow the technique of fingerprinting: **DNA technology**. DNA has given scientists the means with which to detect the remarkable variability existing between individuals. The results of this technology hold great promise in aiding the criminal justice system in making positive determinations of criminal identity.

What Is DNA?

In all life forms, from viruses to human beings, the basis for difference lies in the genetic material known as deoxyribonucleic acid (DNA). In every living organism, with the exception of certain viruses that possess ribonucleic acid (RNA), DNA represents a genetic facsimile, or "blueprint," of that organism. Additionally, in every cell within each human body, the DNA is identical. This applies whether the cell is a white or a red blood cell, a piece of skin, spermatozoa, or even a follicle of hair.

Although DNA is extremely complex chemically, it consists of only five basic elements: carbon, hydrogen, oxygen, nitrogen, and phosphorus. These five elements combine to form certain molecules known as nucleotides. The four bases that code genetic information in the polynucleotide chain of DNA are thymine, cytosine, adenine, and guanine (T, C, A, and G, respectively). Although just four letters exist in this short alphabet, a variety of different sequences of nucleotides exist. A single strand of DNA can be millions of nucleotides long. For example, 6 billion nucleotides constitute the DNA in one human being.

In human beings, 23 pairs of chromosomes originate from each parent: one of each pair from the mother and one from the father at the time of conception. Therefore, when a person is born, his or her genes are made up of a combination of maternal and paternal genes. Because of this, no two persons are exactly alike except identical twins.

The History of DNA

Since it was introduced in the mid-1980s, DNA fingerprinting has revolutionized forensic science and the ability of law enforcement to match offenders with crime scenes. Literally thousands of cases have been closed and innocent suspects freed with guilty ones punished because of the power of a silent biological witness, DNA, at the crime scene.

DNA "fingerprinting" or DNA typing (profiling) as it is now known, was first described in 1985 by an English geneticist named Alec Jeffreys. Dr. Jeffreys discovered that certain regions of DNA contain DNA sequences that are repeated over and over again next to each other. He also discovered that the number of repeated sections present in a sample could differ from individual to individual. By developing a technique to examine the length variation of these DNA repeat sequences, Dr. Jeffreys created the ability to perform human identity tests.

These DNA repeat regions became known as VNTRs, which stands for variable number of tandem repeats. The technique used by Dr. Jeffreys to examine the VNTRs was called restriction fragment length polymorphism (RFLP) because it involved the use of a restriction enzyme to cut the regions of DNA surrounding the VNTRs. This RFLP method was first used to help in an English immigration case and shortly thereafter to solve a double homicide case. Since that time, human identity testing using DNA typing methods has been widespread.

The past 15 years have seen tremendous growth in the use of DNA evidence in crime scene investigations. Today, more than 150 public forensic laboratories and several dozen private paternity testing laboratories conduct hundreds of thousands of DNA tests annually in the United States.[3] In addition, most countries in Europe and Asia have forensic DNA programs. The number of laboratories around the world conducting DNA testing will continue to grow as the technique gains in popularity within law enforcement.

Let's go back to the early 1980s and review a murder case in England that was the first to use DNA technology in criminal investigation. Since the Narborough murders (discussed later in this chapter), the DNA technique has often been used successfully in the United States, beginning in 1987 in the *Florida* v. *Andrews* case, involving a sexual assault. Although it has been used successfully in many criminal trials, future issues will probably focus on the admissibility of DNA test results.

FIGURE 4.19 Graphic showing the steps typically followed by criminalists in DNA profiling.

In the *Florida* v. *Andrews* case, police in Orlando, Florida, suspected that one man was involved in more than 20 cases of prowling, breaking and entering, and attempted sexual assault. In every case, the modus operandi (MO) was similar: The man would stalk his victim for weeks, prowling around her house and peeping through windows. When attacked, the victim had little or no opportunity to make a visual identification. Until Tommie Lee Andrews was arrested, all police had to go on were composite drawings and several calls about a prowler. After his arrest, one rape victim (who had seen her assailant for only about six seconds while being attacked) picked Andrews out of a photo lineup.

When attorney Hal Uhrig was appointed to be the defense attorney for Tommie Lee Andrews, his concern was not about DNA evidence. Instead, he was worried about the amount of time and effort that would be required for him and his small law firm to defend Andrews against multiple rape charges. It was not until later, after prosecutor Jeffrey Ashton read an advertisement in a legal publication about DNA testing and employed the services of Lifecodes, Inc., that Uhrig discovered he was involved in the first-known DNA criminal case in the United States.

At Andrews's first trial, prosecutors successfully introduced results from the test by Lifecodes. The defense, however, successfully challenged the introduction of any testimony regarding the statistical probabilities resulting from the test. The trial ended in a hung jury. At the retrial, DNA evidence was again admitted. This time, the prosecution was prepared to argue that the statistical probabilities of the test be introduced. Using a relevance standard similar to that in the federal rules of evidence, the court admitted the statistical data. Andrews was subsequently convicted.

Prosecutor Ashton said that he was unaware at the outset that this was the first case to use DNA testing in the United States but that he believed it would be a powerful tool in future cases, especially when the suspect is a serial rapist who is careful not to leave much evidence. Defense attorney Uhrig said that he came away from his experience in defending against DNA evidence most concerned about the use of statistical data, which he believed carries inordinate weight in the minds of the jury. As more population data are collected, the numbers could become much smaller and lose "real-world meaning" to juries.

Hypothetically, said Uhrig, odds of 10 billion to one could be introduced into court. But if the defendant in such a case had an identical twin (and hence identical DNA patterns), the odds of a random match would be 5 billion to one but still a 50 percent probability that the DNA in question would not belong to the defendant. DNA typing, Uhrig said, might well result in more rape defenses that center on consent rather than on alibi or denial defenses.

Analyzing DNA

Genetic patterns found in blood or semen can be just as distinctive as fingerprints. Traditional serology tests on bodily fluids often do not discriminate enough to either exclude or include a suspect in a crime. DNA analysis provides much more conclusive analysis. The unique genetic patterns found in each person's DNA make it possible, with a high degree of accuracy, to associate a suspect with (or exclude a suspect from) a crime. Except in the case of identical twins, every person's DNA and resulting DNA pattern are different. The process of analyzing, or "typing," DNA begins with DNA source material such as blood or semen. After the DNA is removed from the sample chemically, restriction enzymes known as endonucleases are added that cut the DNA into particles or fragments. The particles are then mixed with a sieving gel and sorted out according to size by a process called electrophoresis. In this process, the DNA moves along the gel-coated plate, some faster than others. At the completion of the process, the double-stranded fragments of DNA are treated so that the strands separate from each other.

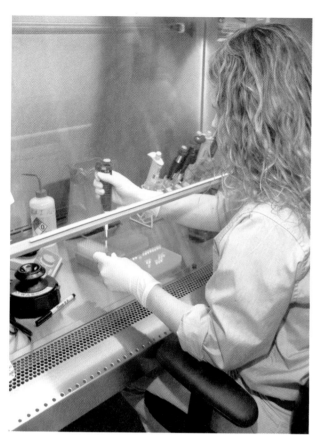

FIGURE 4.20 Crime lab biologist working with blood samples on the analysis of DNA. *Courtesy of Mike Himmel and the Missouri State Highway Patrol.*

Next, a transfer method developed by Edward Southern, called Southern blotting, is used. In this process, the DNA is transferred to a nylon membrane in much the same way that ink is transferred to a blotter. The nylon sheet is then treated with radioactively labeled DNA probes, single-stranded pieces of DNA that can bind through complementary base pairing with target DNA. Whereas a single-locus probe "looks" for only one field, a multilocus probe looks for numerous fields simultaneously. The radioactive probe then merges with the specific DNA sequences found on the membrane fragments. The images that result from x-ray film placed in contact with the membrane to detect the probe configuration look like the price bar codes used on supermarket products.

These images are analyzed visually or by computer. Although not yet considered a routine procedure for all police agencies, it is clear that DNA will prove to be one of the most exciting and valuable investigative tools developed in recent decades, possibly even more significant than that of fingerprinting technology. As time goes on, there will undoubtedly be significant legal and scientific challenges to the application of DNA technology in crime solving. Certainly, however, as the "bugs" are worked out, society as a whole will be the beneficiary of this captivating science, which enables virtually positive identification of both criminal suspects and their victims.

Because of the importance of biological evidence, investigators and laboratory personnel should work together to determine which pieces of evidence are more significant. As such, every officer should be aware of important issues involved in the identification, collection, transportation, and storage of DNA evidence. These issues are as important for the first responding patrol officer as they are for the experienced detective and the crime scene specialist. This is because biological material may contain hazardous pathogens such as the human immunodeficiency virus (HIV) and the hepatitis B virus that can cause potentially lethal diseases.

Biohazardous materials should be housed in a segregated area within the evidence room that is clearly marked "Biohazardous Material Only." Care must be taken to package items separately to avoid cross-contamination of other evidence.

Transportation and Storage

When transporting and storing evidence that may contain DNA, it is important to keep the evidence dry and at room temperature. After the evidence has been secured in paper bags or envelopes, it should be sealed, labeled, and transported in a way that ensures proper identification of where it was found and the proper chain of custody. DNA evidence should never be placed in plastic bags because plastic bags retain damaging moisture.[4] Direct sunlight and warmer conditions can also be harmful to DNA. Consequently, investigators should avoid keeping evidence in places that may get hot, such as a room or police car without air conditioning.

Elimination Samples

As with fingerprints, the effective use of DNA may require the collection and analysis of elimination samples.[5] Elimination samples can be used to determine whether the evidence comes from the suspect or from someone else. It is important for the investigator, while still on the crime scene, to think ahead to the time of trial and possible defenses. For example, in the case of a residential burglary in which the suspect may have drunk a glass of water at the crime scene, an officer should identify appropriate people, such as household members, for future elimination sample testing.

These samples may be needed for comparison with the saliva found on the glass to determine whether the saliva is valuable evidence. In homicide cases, be sure to collect the victim's DNA from the medical examiner at the autopsy, even if the body is badly decomposed. This may serve to identify an unknown victim or distinguish between the victim's DNA and other DNA found at the crime scene.

When investigating rape cases, it may be necessary to collect and analyze the DNA of the victim's recent consensual partners, if any, to eliminate them as potential contributors of DNA suspected to be from the perpetrator. If this is necessary, it is important to approach the victim with extreme sensitivity and provide a full explanation of why the request is being made. When possible, the help of a qualified victim advocate should be enlisted for assistance.

All contaminated evidence that is ready for disposal, as well as all disposable equipment or cleaning materials contaminated with bodily fluids, should be bagged in accordance with state and federal laws. The Centers for Disease Control and Prevention recommends that, in general, infective waste should be either incinerated or decontaminated before disposal in a sanitary landfill.[6] Bulk blood or other bodily fluids may be carefully poured down a drain connected to a sanitary sewer. Sanitary sewers may also be used to dispose of other infectious wastes capable of being ground and flushed into the sewer. In all cases, departments should be familiar with state and local laws governing such disposal.

Admissibility of DNA as Evidence

For evidence to be accepted into court, it must be offered by one of the parties and be admitted by the court. Questions regarding the admissibility of evidence have generally been handled at a pretrial hearing. Two standards have been used to govern the admission of scientific evidence: the relevancy test and the Frye test.

The relevancy test, which is based on the federal rules of evidence, permits the admission of relevant evidence that is helpful to the trier of fact. The second pretrial hearing, the Frye test, or Frye standard, involves the admission of scientific evidence. This test, named after the defendant in a 1923 murder case, is the oldest test and the one used most often for determining the admissibility of scientific evidence. Under the Frye standard, courts admit evidence based on novel scientific techniques only when the technique has gained general acceptance in the scientific community to which it belongs. General acceptance under the Frye test appears to require a two-step analysis:

1. Identifying the field in which the underlying theory falls (i.e., in determining whether the technique meets the test of acceptance in the scientific community, defining what community is relevant)
2. Determining whether the principle has been accepted by most members of the field identified

The Frye test has several perceived advantages and disadvantages. Its proponents note that the test guarantees a minimal amount of support by experts for a scientific test or procedure in its introduction in a court of law. As noted by one court, the experts "form a kind of technical jury, which must first pass on the scientific status of a procedure before the lay jury utilizes it in making its findings of fact." After the pretrial Frye or evidentiary hearing, a court rules whether DNA testing will be admitted into evidence and, if so, under what conditions. At trial,

FIGURE 4.21 The composite sketch can be an important component in the identification process. Here an investigator discusses a suspect's physical characteristics with a witness.

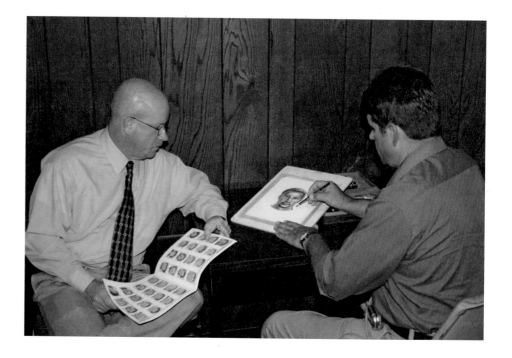

any party may offer expert testimony. It is the obligation of the party calling expert witnesses to lay the foundation for such testimony. The foundation includes the qualifications and experience of the witness, details on how DNA testing works, what procedures were followed, the results of the test, and facts and opinions that can be drawn from the test results.

The Daubert Standard

The Daubert standard is a legal precedent set in 1993 by the Supreme Court of the United States regarding the admissibility of expert witnesses' testimony during federal legal proceedings. The citation is Daubert v. Merrell Dow Pharmaceuticals, 509 U.S. 579 (1993). A Daubert motion, raised before or sometimes during trial, attempts to exclude the presentation of unqualified evidence to the jury. This is a special case of "motion in limine," which is typically used to exclude the testimony of an expert witness who has no such expertise or used questionable methods to obtain the information.

In the Daubert case, the Supreme Court held that federal trial judges are the "gatekeepers" of scientific evidence. Under the Daubert standard, therefore, trial judges must evaluate proffered expert witnesses to determine whether their testimony is both "relevant" and "reliable," a two-pronged test of admissibility. For example:

1. *The relevancy prong.* The relevancy of a testimony refers to whether or not the expert's evidence "fits" the facts of the case. For example, you may invite an astronomer to tell the jury if there was a full moon on the night of a crime. However, the astronomer would not be allowed to testify if the fact that the moon was full was not relevant to the issue at hand in the trial.

2. *The reliability prong.* The Supreme Court explained that for expert testimony to be considered reliable, the expert must have derived his or her conclusions from the scientific method. The Court offered "general observations" of whether proffered evidence was based on the scientific method, although the list was not intended to be used as an exhaustive checklist:

   • Empirical testing: the theory or technique must be falsifiable, refutable, and testable

- Subjected to peer review and publication
- Known or potential error rate and the existence and maintenance of standards concerning its operation
- Whether the theory and technique is generally accepted by a relevant scientific community

Although trial judges have always had the authority to exclude inappropriate testimony, before the Daubert trial, courts often preferred to let juries hear evidence proffered by both sides. After certain evidence has been excluded by a Daubert motion because it fails to meet the relevancy and reliability standard, it will likely be challenged when introduced again in another trial. Even though a Daubert motion is not binding to other courts of law, if something was found not trustworthy, other judges may choose to follow that precedent. Of course, a decision by the Court of Appeals that a piece of evidence is inadmissible under Daubert would be binding on district courts within that court's geographic jurisdiction.

Other Uses of DNA

In addition to its utility in criminal investigations, DNA blood typing can be put to use in other ways. For example, with the use of a new process called PCR, cells producing billions of DNA strips can be reproduced rapidly in a test tube, a feat that would take a dividing cancer cell at least a month to perform. The PCR technique has recently been used to perform the following examinations:

- Comparing the DNA of extinct animals with that of their closest living relatives
- Assisting the military in identifying the remains of soldiers who fought in wars such as Operation Desert Storm
- Helping physicians detect small numbers of cancer cells circulating in the bloodstream and to make prenatal diagnosis of genetic diseases such as sickle-cell anemia
- Ensuring better matches between organ donors and transplant recipients

In January 1992, the Defense Department announced that it would establish a repository of genetic information on all U.S. service members as a way of identifying future war casualties. The Armed Forces Institute of Pathology now collects t samples of DNA from blood and oral swabs and adds the information to fingerprint, dental, and other records.

DNA profiling may be the most significant breakthrough in forensic science since the development of fingerprinting. Federal, state, and local crime laboratories are currently working to enhance profiling techniques and to establish a national DNA index. In addition, a uniform approach to DNA testing is being sought to ensure an effective and secure system.

Handwriting Analysis

Similar to skills acquired in piloting an aircraft or interpreting a polygraph, accurate handwriting analysis requires many years of study and practice. From our earliest years in elementary school, we are taught how to sculpt letters of the alphabet meticulously to form words and sentences. People often adopt unique styles of their own, frequently characteristic only of that person. Such characteristics are identifiable to handwriting experts, who must be knowledgeable in both photography and microscopy.

Writings may occur in many forms, including that on personal correspondence, desks, walls, and even dead bodies. In all cases, they may offer the investigator valuable evidence in identifying suspects. To understand how best to proceed with the handwriting analysis process, we should first consider that the average handwriting specimen has 500 to 1,000 characters, including elements such as form, movement, connections, alignment, punctuation, slant, spacings, and embellishments. Any object containing handwritten or typewritten markings and whose source or authenticity is in doubt may be referred to as a questioned document.[7]

Collection of Exemplars

Cases involving questioned documents require a comparison between the suspect document and a sample or exemplar (also known as a *standard*). Two types of **exemplars** exist: the requested and the collected. In both cases, its origin must be well documented before analysis to ensure genuineness.

Requested Exemplars. A requested handwriting standard is obtained from a suspect at the formal request of a law enforcement officer and is performed solely as a means to acquire a comparison document. It is logical to assume that no two samples of a suspect's handwriting are identical. Therefore, a sufficient number of exemplars must be collected to demonstrate to the examiner the range of natural variations in a suspect's writing peculiarities. In the event that investigators might not be successful in obtaining exemplars of a suspect's handwriting, an exemplar may be obtained directly from the suspect.

In a 1967 case, *Gilbert v. California*, the court held that requiring a suspect to give a handwriting sample does not violate a person's Fifth Amendment protection against self-incrimination. Therefore, he or she cannot refuse. Exemplars requested by the police are a means to acquire a comparison document from a suspect.

Collected Exemplars. A collected handwriting exemplar is a sample of the suspect's handwriting that was not written for the purpose of examination and is not evidence in the crime under investigation. The obvious reason for this is that the sample document must be one that the suspect has not prepared or altered deliberately to match a suspect document.

The most valuable collected document is one that has been acquired close to the time the suspect document was produced. For example, if the document questioned was produced on a typewriter, an exemplar of the suspected typewriter would be collected. Accordingly, if the suspect's signature is in question, a standard of his or her handwriting must be collected. Typically, collected exemplars can be acquired from such documents as insurance policies, credit card receipts, canceled checks, and personal letters. Collected exemplars are samples of the suspect's handwriting that were not specially written for the purpose of examination that are used as comparison documents.

The Writing Medium

The process of collecting handwriting exemplars includes being sure that the writing instruments (e.g., paper, pencils) used in the sample are the same as those used in the suspect document. Things to look for in selection of paper include its size, thickness, color, and condition. In short, the sample paper should match, as closely as possible, that used by the suspect.

If more than one sample document is being acquired from the suspect, they should not be stacked on top of each other. This is because writing impressions might press through one page to another and hinder the examination of them.

Additionally, each handwriting sample should be taken from the suspect's sight as soon as it is obtained. This prevents the suspect from attempting to compare his writing from one exemplar to another.

The same type of instrument used for the document questioned should be furnished to the suspect for the control exemplar. This includes the pencil, pen, felt-tip marker, and so on. Special attention should also be given to matching the lead number of a pencil, the color of an ink pen, and the width of a felt-tip marker to that used on the questioned document.

The Writing Area

The suspect should be afforded a comfortable writing area. The backseat of a police car, for example, will prove to be a waste of time. The investigator must make sure that the suspect is writing in the same general style as in the suspect document: block letters for block letters, cursive writing for cursive writing, and so on. It might also be advisable to obtain a sample of writing in the suspect's opposite hand in the event that the suspect used this technique as a deception. In addition, the investigator will have to observe as the suspect writes the sample document because his or her testimony will be required in court. The investigator must make sure that the suspect is writing in the same general style as in the suspect document.

Facial Composites

One method of developing an idea of the suspect's general description is to have the witness provide information to a police artist so that a *facial composite* can be generated. In previous years, construction of the **composite** was done by a trained artist through drawing sketching or painting in consultation with a witness or crime victim. In the 1960s, techniques were devised for use by those who are less artistic, using interchangeable templates of separate facial features, such as Smith & Wesson's **Identi-Kit**. More recently, computer-generated imaging systems have been developed, such as Smith & Wesson's "Identi-Kit 2000." Today the FBI maintains that hand-drawing is still the correct method for constructing a facial composite. Many police agencies, however, use software because developed artistic talent is often not available. Technologically, the most popular software in the U.S. is FACES, although other popular products are "CompuSketch," "Mac-a-Mug," and "SuspectID."[8]

Although the classic use of the facial composite is the citizen recognizing the face as an acquaintance, there are other ways that a facial composite can prove useful. The facial composite can assist law enforcement in a number of ways. These include:

- Identifying the suspect in a wanted poster
- Additional evidence against a suspect
- Assisting investigation in checking leads
- Warning the public against serial offenders[9]

Facial composites have been used successfully to identify suspects in numerous cases. Included are the Oklahoma "Murrah Building" bomber Timothy McVeigh and Baton Rouge serial killer Derrick Todd Lee.[10] They have also been used extensively in television programs, such as *America's Most Wanted*,[11] that aim to reconstruct major unsolved crimes with a view to gaining information from the members of the public.

mycrimekit

Video: Career profile: Criminalist

Criminal Investigative Analysis

For years, the means of identifying the type of person responsible for a particular crime was known as personality profiling. Today, the process, known as **criminal investigative analysis,** is accomplished by identifying psychological and social characteristics surrounding the crime as well as the manner in which it was committed. An example is the Unabomber case, in which mail bombs killed four people in a period spanning 15 years. Forensic investigators subsequently determined that the bomber chose his postage carefully, using Frederick Douglass stamps when he wanted to injure his targets and stamps of playwright Eugene O'Neill when he intended to kill. O'Neill's plays were known for their dark themes.

One of O'Neill's plays, *Dynamo,* was highly critical of America's growing reliance on machinery and industrialization, a theme echoed in the Unabomber's manifesto. The profiling technique can be advantageous in illuminating certain clues at the crime scene that may not be apparent upon first examination. For example, hate, passion, fear, and confusion may all have certain indicators somewhere at the scene, such as postmortem slashing or cutting, rapes, lust and mutilation murders, and so on.

The practice of profiling was developed during World War II by government psychologist William Langer to predict Adolph Hitler's future actions. As it relates to criminal investigation, profiling is based on the notion that crime is, directly or indirectly, based on the personality of the person committing it. Profilers typically scrutinize evidence found on the crime scene and attempt to re-create the circumstances surrounding the crime and to predict the offender's frame of mind. The profile is then used to narrow down the list of suspects as it develops. From a practical standpoint, profiling can be helpful in investigating any crime in which the evidence suggests that the suspect is irrational or mentally or emotionally unstable.

Profiling gained popularity during the 1980s, when the FBI became heavily involved in the profiling of violent sex offenders and arsonists. More recently, caregivers with a disorder called Munchhausen syndrome by proxy (MSBP) have become the subject of profilers. The disorder involves offenders who injure or cause illnesses in their children to gain attention and sympathy for themselves. Past cases have revealed that most suspects are women who victimize their children so as to become the center of attention by police, doctors, family members, and others. MSBP is thought to be a serial offense usually affecting families with more than one child. Characteristics of offenders include a history of self-inflicted wounds, past psychiatric treatment, past attempted suicides, a middle- to upper-class background, a better-than-average education, and knowledge of the medical field and related procedures.

The field of psychological profiling continues to grow as new areas are developed. Two of the newest areas include hostage negotiation and terrorism.[12] The psychological profiling technique was used successfully by the FBI in the investigation of Theodore (Ted) Bundy, the serial murderer responsible for the murders of 30 young women in the northwestern United States between 1973 and 1978.

According to John Douglas and Robert Ressler of the FBI, most (normal) persons have personality traits that are more or less identifiable. However, an abnormal person tends to become more ritualized and tends to display a "pattern" to his or her behavior. Often, the suspect's

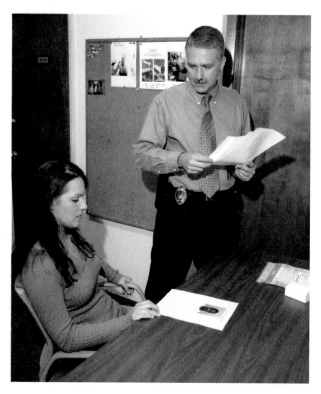

FIGURE 4.22 One method of conducting a "photo "lineup." It is important for the investigator to remember to avoid any suggestiveness.

personality is reflected in both the crime scene and in the furnishings of his or her home. Because of the nature of such evidence, the profiling procedure has limitations and should be used in conjunction with other investigative techniques. The profiling technique requires the collection of certain types of information:

- *Photographs* focused on the extent and depth of wounds
- *Neighborhood information*, including racial, ethnic, and social data
- *Medical examiner's report*, including photos of damage to body, such as stabs, gunshots, bruises, and lividity, and information regarding toxicology, postmortem wounds, and personal observations of the medical examiner
- *Map of the victim's travel before death*, including residence and employment information, where last seen, and crime scene location
- *Complete investigation report of the incident*, such as date, time, location, type of weapon used, and detailed interviews of witnesses
- *Background of victim*, including age, race, gender, physical description, marital status, lifestyle, sexual preference, medical history (physical and mental), personal habits, use of alcohol or drugs, and friends or enemies

The psychological profiling technique recognizes that hate, passion, fear, and confusion may all have certain indicators somewhere at the scene. These can include postmortem slashing or cutting, rapes, lust and mutilation murders, and so on.

After the information has been collected, the investigator analyzes the information and attempts to reconstruct the event. Techniques used are brainstorming to critique the case, use of intuition to follow hunches, and educated guessing. Profiling factors do not consist of clinical observations solely but rather a collection of investigative data from which to draw inferences about the suspect, victim, and motive of the crime.

Investigative Psychology

Another relative newcomer to the investigative process is investigative psychology. This technique essentially brings together the retrieval of investigative information and draws inferences about that information in as far as the ways that police decision making can be supported through scientific research. This area is different from investigative analysis or "profiling," which grew out of the experience of police officers offering opinions about the possible characteristics of unknown offenders.

Investigative psychology is grounded in empirical research and logical inference to cover the full range of investigative activities in addition to the preparation of "profiles." The inference processes at the heart of investigative psychology differ from the approach used by the FBI, which emphasizes a subjective processes such as "thinking like the criminal." Rather, investigative psychology stresses that the results of scientific psychology can contribute to many aspects of civilian and criminal investigation, including the full range of crimes from burglary to terrorism, not just the extreme crimes of violence that have an obvious psychopathic component.

The contribution to investigations draws on the extent to which an offender displays various tested characteristics[13] as well as procedures for enhancing the processes by which interviews are carried out or information is put before the courts. One goal of investigative psychology research is determining behaviorally important information regarding the consistency of the behavior of many different types of offenders. Although to date most studies have been of violent crimes, there is a growing body of research on burglary and arson. It is also important to establish valid and reliable methods of distinguishing between offenders and between offenses.[14]

Geographical Profiling

Geographic profiling is a criminal investigative technique that analyzes the locations of a connected series of crimes to determine where the offender most likely resides. The technique is typically used in cases of serial murder or rape (but also arson, bombing, robbery, and other crimes), but it also helps police investigators prioritize information in large-scale major crime investigations that can involve hundreds or thousands of suspects and tips.[15]

Although the use of spatial analysis methods in police investigations goes back many years (think of detectives gathered around a large city map with pins stuck in it), the formalized process known today as geographic profiling originated out of research conducted at Simon Fraser University's School of Criminology in British Columbia, Canada, in 1989. The theoretical foundation is in environmental criminology, particularly crime pattern theory, routine activity theory, and rational choice theory.[16] The Vancouver Police Department instituted the world's first geographic profiling capability in 1995, but the technique has now spread to several U.S., Canadian, British, and European law enforcement agencies. Originally designed for violent crime investigations, it is increasingly being used on property crime.

Tools used by geographic profilers include specialized software systems, such as Rigel or CrimeStat. System inputs are crime location addresses or coordinates, often entered through a geographic information system (GIS). The output is a jeopardy surface (three-dimensional probability surface) or color **geoprofile**, which depicts the most likely areas of the offender's residence or search base.[17]

Geographic profiling is a subtype of offender or criminal profiling (the inference of offender characteristics from offence characteristics). It is therefore related to psychological or behavioral profiling. If psychological profiling is the "who," geographic profiling is the "where."[18] All certified geographic profilers are members of the International Criminal Investigative Analysis Fellowship (ICIAF), a professional profiling organization first begun by investigators trained by the FBI in the mid-1980s.[19]

Safeguarding Against Misidentifications

One recurring problem in criminal investigation is the overreliance by criminal investigators on eyewitness accounts of crimes. This is especially a concern when the identification of a criminal suspect relies heavily on the word of eyewitnesses or victims. The problem is pervasive. For example, in 2009 the Innocence Project reported: "Eyewitness misidentification is the single greatest cause of wrongful convictions nationwide, playing a role in more than 75% of convictions overturned through DNA testing."[20] For more than 30 years, research has proven the unreliability of eyewitnesses testimony.[21] For example, (1) criminal suspects have been identified by eyewitnesses seated in the back of a patrol vehicle, a long distance away on a dimly lit street; (2) witnesses have been shown photo arrays in which only one photo is clearly marked with an "R"; (3) witnesses have changed their physical description of a criminal suspect after speaking with police and learning additional information about the suspect; (4) eyewitnesses and victims have been reluctant in identifying a suspect, but at trial prosecutors inform the jury that witnesses did not waiver in their identification.[22] Many such cases have resulted in innocent persons being wrongfully accused and convicted of crimes they did not commit.

It is common in criminal investigations for investigators to rely on eyewitness identifications. Experience and research have shown that civilian eyewitnesses frequently prove to be unreliable observers, and erroneous identifications are often the result. A number of factors contribute to misidentifications by eyewitnesses. For example, human perception tends to be inaccurate, especially under stress. The average citizen, untrained in observation and subjected to the stress of being a victim of or witness to a crime, is seldom able to describe a perpetrator accurately even in some cases after coming face to face with the individual. Also, a witness, especially one who is unsure what the perpetrator actually looked like, may be easily influenced by suggestions conveyed to him or her during the identification process. This fact was recognized in *United States v. Wade*, in which the Supreme Court of the United States stated:

> The influence of improper suggestions upon identifying witnesses probably accounts for more miscarriages of justice than any other single factor. Perhaps it is responsible for more such errors than all other factors combined.[23]

Law enforcement officers can also cause misidentifications by suggestive words or conduct. The average witness, anxious to make an identification and influenced by the police officer's image as an authority figure, tends to be very sensitive to any suggestion made by the police regarding the identity of the perpetrator. Officers may, intentionally or unintentionally, convey to the witness by words or conduct that a particular person being viewed is the perpetrator.

As a result, great care must be taken by officers conducting identification sessions of any type to avoid any action that might lead to an erroneous identification. Carefully adhering to the proper identification procedures will help avoid misidentifications that may lead to unjust accusations or even erroneous convictions of innocent persons and divert the investigation away from the actual offender. In addition, even if the actual offender is caught and brought to trial, using improper identification procedures during the investigation often causes the suppression of identification evidence at trial, resulting in dismissal of the charges or otherwise making it difficult or even impossible to convict the guilty party.

If a court determines that an identification procedure was excessively suggestive, the court may prohibit introduction of the evidence in question. It may rule that any in-court identification of the accused by the victim is inadmissible, suppress other evidence that was obtained as a result of an improper pretrial identification procedure, or both. Of course, any of these actions may result in prosecution being thwarted.

Today, in evaluating proper identification procedure, the courts are generally concerned with whether it was suggestive. If the court finds that the procedure was suggestive, the court will then proceed to determine whether, despite the suggestiveness, the identification was reliable when considering the "totality of the circumstances.[24] The court will consider the following six factors:

1. The opportunity of the witness to view the criminal at the time of the crime
2. The witness's degree of attention
3. The accuracy of the witness's prior description of the criminal
4. The level of certainty demonstrated by the witness at the confrontation
5. The length of time between the crime and the confrontation
6. Whether the witness was a "casual observer" or the victim of the crime

If in view of these various factors, it appears that the identification was reliable despite the suggestiveness of the procedure, evidence of the identification will be admissible to bolster a subsequent in-court identification.

Identification Procedures

For purposes of this chapter, identification procedures may be categorized as photo identifications, lineups, or show-ups. Photo identification procedures may involve the showing of one or several photographs to a witness for the purpose of obtaining an identification. In a **lineup**, eyewitnesses are presented simultaneously with a number of individuals.

Types of Lineups. For the most part, the function of a police lineup is to identify a suspect. Lineups are typically shown to victims of crime or eyewitnesses to a crime. From a procedural standpoint, a police lineup involves placing a suspect among people not suspected of committing the crime (fillers) and asking the victim or eyewitness if he or she can identify the perpetrator. This can be done using a live lineup of people or, as more commonly done in the nation's police departments, a lineup of photographs. Live lineups typically use five or six people (a suspect plus four or five fillers) and photo lineups six or more photographs.[25] There are two common types of lineups: simultaneous and sequential.

The type of lineup used by most police departments across the nation is the **simultaneous lineup**.[26] In this lineup, the eyewitness views all the people or photos at the same time. In comparison, a **sequential lineup** involves people or photographs that are presented to the witness one at a time.

In either model, the lineup administrator can be blind, meaning he or she does not know the identity of the suspect, or non-blind, meaning the administrator knows the identity of the suspect. Most police departments in the United States use photo lineups.

Historically, the investigator knows who the suspect is.[27] Critics suggest that in these cases, lineup administrators might either knowingly or unintentionally give the witness verbal or nonverbal cues as to the identity of the suspect. For example, if the eyewitness identifies a filler, the investigator might say to the witness, "Take your time. . . . Make sure you look at all the photos."

Such a statement may effectively lead the witness away from the filler.[28] However, in a "double-blind" lineup, neither the officer administering the lineup nor the witness knows the identity of the suspect, so there is no way the officer administering the lineup can influence the witness in any way.[29] In 2008, the National Institute of Justice reported that other variables that can affect the outcome of police lineups include:[30]

- *Pre-lineup instructions given to the witness.* This includes explaining that the suspect may or may not be present in the lineup. Research on pre-lineup instructions by Nancy Steblay, Ph.D., professor of psychology at Augsburg College in Minneapolis, Minnesota, revealed that a "might or might not be present" instruction reduced mistaken identification rates in lineups where the suspect was absent.[31]

- *The physical characteristics of fillers.* Fillers who do not resemble the witness's description of the perpetrator may cause a suspect to stand out.[32]

- *Similarities and differences between witness and suspect's age, race, or ethnicity.* Research suggests that when the offender is present in a lineup, young children and elderly people perform nearly as well as young adults in identifying the perpetrator. When the lineup does not contain the offender, however, young children and elderly people commit mistaken identifications at a rate higher than young adults. Research has also indicated that people are better able to recognize faces of their own race or ethnic group than faces of another race or ethnic group.[33]

- *Incident characteristics, such as the use of force or weapons.* The presence of a weapon during an incident can draw visual attention away from other things, such as the perpetrator's face, and thus affect an eyewitness's ability to identify the holder of the weapon.[34]

In summary, the most common lineup procedure in use by law enforcement is the simultaneous lineup.[35] Researcher Gary Wells argues however, that during simultaneous lineups, witnesses use **relative judgment**. This means that they compare lineup photographs or members with each other rather than to their memory of the offender. This is a problem when the perpetrator is not present in the lineup because the witness will often choose the lineup member who most closely resembles the perpetrator.[36]

On the other hand, during sequential lineups, witnesses must make a decision about each photograph or member before moving on to the next, prompting them to use **absolute judgment**. In other words, witnesses compare each photograph or person only with their memory of what the offender looked like.[37]

Research shows that the double-blind sequential method, in which the officer conducting the lineup does not know the identity of the suspect, produces fewer false identifications than the traditional simultaneous method.[38]

Photo Lineups   The photo lineup is a commonly used investigative technique to identify suspects. When used improperly, however, innocent persons can be singled out for prosecution. This very thing occurred in the case of Calvin Willis.

One night in 1982, three young girls were sleeping alone in a Shreveport, Louisiana home when a man in cowboy boots made entry into the house and raped the oldest girl, who was 10 years old. When police started to investigate the rape, the three girls all remembered the attack differently. One police report said the 10-year-old victim didn't see her attacker's face. Another report—which wasn't introduced at trial—said she identified Calvin Willis, who lived in the neighborhood. The girl's mother testified at the trial that neighbors had mentioned Willis' name when discussing who might have committed the crime. The victim testified that she was shown photos and told to pick the man without a full beard. She testified that she didn't pick anyone; police said she picked Willis. Willis was convicted by a jury and sentenced to life in prison. In 2003, DNA testing proved Willis's innocence and he was released. He had served 22 years.[39]

Photo identifications may take a number of forms. If a single photo is shown to the witness, the photo identification has all of the shortcomings of the show-up (discussed below) and is generally regarded by the courts as improper and suggestive. Consequently, multiple-photo procedures are preferable. In such procedures, the photos may be shown individually, one at a time, or displayed simultaneously in a book or array. This procedure is similar to a lineup (discussed below), and virtually all of the cautions set forth for lineups in the preceding discussion apply to multiple-photo identification procedures as well.

Specifically, the following recommendations are made regarding photo identifications in whatever fashion they are presented:

1. There should be at least six photographs.
2. The photographs should be of people who are reasonably uniform in age, height, weight, and general appearance and of the same gender and race.

3. The photographs themselves should be similar. For example, color photographs and black-and-white photographs should not be mixed; the photographs should also be of approximately the same size and composition.

4. Mug shots should not be mixed with snapshots because they are generally recognizable as such and have an immediate tendency to "brand" an individual.

5. If mug shots are used or if the photographs otherwise include any identifying information regarding the subject of the photograph, this information should be covered so it cannot be seen by the witness. If only some of the photos have such information, the corresponding portions of photos should be covered so that none of the photos will look different.

6. The array should not include more than one photo of the same suspect.

7. The photo array should be shown to only one witness at a time.

8. As with show-ups and lineups, no suggestive statements should be made. For example, witnesses should not be told that the suspect's photo is in the group or that someone else has already picked out one of the photos as being the criminal. Similarly, nothing should be said or done to direct the witness's attention to any particular photograph. For example, pointing to a particular photo and asking, "Is this the guy?" is improper and may lead to the identification being excluded.

9. If possible, the photo array should be preserved for future reference. In fact, in some states, failure to preserve the array will lead to suppression of the identification process. Additionally, full details about the identification process should be recorded and preserved. Assuming that the photo identification has been properly conducted and that the array itself was not in any way suggestive, preserving this information helps the prosecution refute any claims by the defense to the contrary.

The proper use of photographs to obtain identification of a perpetrator has been approved by the courts.[40] However, the courts appear to prefer that photo identification procedures be used only to develop investigative leads. Some courts have criticized the practice of using photo identifications after the suspect has been arrested, preferring that after the suspect is in custody and therefore readily available, a lineup be used for eyewitness identification.[41]

Physical Lineups   The lineup, if properly conducted, is significantly less suggestive than the show-up and hence is generally far preferable. Nevertheless, police officers conducting a lineup must use caution to avoid suggestive influences. Studies of witness psychology reveal that lineup witnesses tend to believe that the guilty party must be one of the individuals in the lineup. Consequently, witnesses tend to pick out the person in the lineup who most closely resembles their perception of the perpetrator, even though the perpetrator is not in fact present.

In addition, it is possible that witnesses, in an effort to please the police officers conducting the lineup, feel obligated to pick out someone from the lineup rather than "disappoint" the officers.[42] Such witnesses are often sensitive to, and strongly influenced by, clever clues conveyed by the officers that may indicate to the witness that the officer believes a particular individual in the lineup is the perpetrator. This makes it even more important that officers conduct the lineup—and their own behavior—in a nonsuggestive manner.

Preparing for a lineup may be as important to the validity of the procedure as actually conducting it. Selecting individuals for the lineup is a particularly

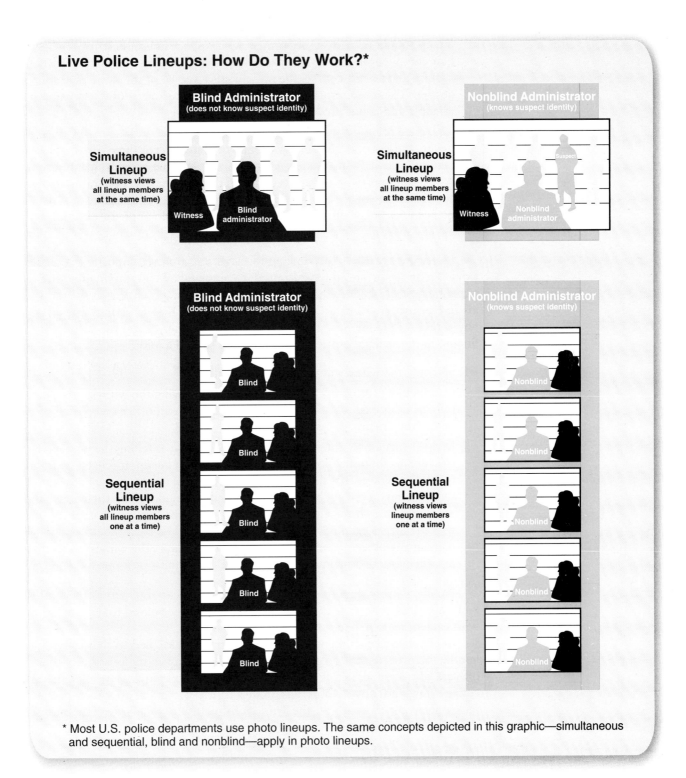

FIGURE 4.23 Most U.S. Police departments use photo lineups. The same concepts depicted in this graphic—simultaneous and sequential, blind and non-blind—apply in photo lineups. From Schuster, B. (2008). Police lineups, making eyewitness identification more reliable. National Institute of Justice, Issue No. 258.

important issue. In determining which individuals are to be presented to the witnesses in a lineup, the following principles should be observed:

1. *The lineup should consist of individuals of similar physical characteristics.*
   Witnesses tend to pick out anyone who stands out from the rest of the

group in any significant way. Therefore, the individuals who appear in the lineup should be reasonably similar with respect to age; height; weight; hair color, length and style; facial hair; clothing; and other characteristics such as glasses. Of course, the individuals must be of the same race and gender. Absolute uniformity of the lineup participants is obviously unattainable and is not procedurally necessary.[43]

2. *The lineup should consist of at least five or six persons.* The smaller the lineup, the less objective it is. A lineup with only two or three persons is little better than a show-up, and suggestive factors become excessively influential. As a result, most authorities recommend that at least five, preferably six, persons be in the lineup. In addition, some authorities caution against the use of plainclothes police officers in lineups because they do not naturally look or act like suspects, a factor that causes witnesses to reject them as possibilities.

Preparing a witness for viewing the lineup is another important consideration. Preparation should be limited to nonsuggestive statements, such as explaining the procedure that will be used and making it clear that the individuals in the lineup will be unable to see him or her. Officers should avoid taking any action or making any statement that will adversely affect the validity of the lineup. In particular, before a lineup, officers should avoid:

1. Showing the witness any photos of the suspect[44]

2. Conducting a show-up with the suspect or allowing the witness—accidentally or otherwise—to see the suspect, such as in an office or holding cell, before the lineup

3. Making suggestive statements to the witness, such as telling the witness that the person whom the police suspect will be in the lineup. It is even desirable to tell the witness that the perpetrator may not be among those in the lineup. Other common errors that should be avoided include telling the witness that another witness has identified someone in the same lineup, advising the witness to take special notice of some particular individual in the lineup, or making any other statement or action that may cause the witness to focus on a particular individual or to think that he or she must pick out somebody.

Finally, if more than one witness is to view a lineup, the witnesses should be kept separated before the lineup and should not be permitted to discuss the case with each other, compare descriptions, and so forth.

In conducting the lineup, officers who are not assigned to that case should handle the procedure if possible. This helps to minimize the possibility that the officers who are conducting the investigation will, in their zeal to solve the case, convey (inadvertently or otherwise) clues to the witness as to which person to pick out or put pressure on the witness to pick out somebody. The following should also be observed in conducting lineups:

1. *Statements that put pressure on the witness to make an identification should be avoided.* Witnesses are anxious to please the officers conducting the lineup, so they should not be made to feel that they are expected to pick out someone. For example, telling a witness that the person the police suspect is in the lineup or urging a hesitant witness to make an identification or to "try harder" would be improper.

2. *Statements that may cause the witness to focus on a particular individual should be avoided.* The same sort of statements discussed in regard to witness preparation should be avoided during the actual conduct of the lineup. Officers are often tempted to prompt a witness when someone in

the lineup is a prime suspect and the witness is hesitant to make an identification. Statements such as: "What about the second guy from the right?" or "Take another look at the one in the middle" are so suggestive that they will, if challenged by the defense attorney, almost certainly result in any subsequent identification being suppressed by the court.

3. *The lineup should be presented to one witness at a time.* The common practice of having a group of witnesses view a lineup simultaneously should not be permitted. Courts, including the U.S. Supreme Court,[45] have disapproved multiple-witness lineups. If for some reason, more than one witness must be present simultaneously, witnesses should be required to make their identifications silently in writing and should not be permitted to discuss the identification aloud with each other or with the officers present.

4. *If possible, conduct a "blank" lineup.* Conducting two or more lineups, where one lineup includes the suspect and the others do not, assists the prosecution in later refuting any claim by the defense that the lineup was too small or was suggestive.

5. *If multiple lineups are to be conducted for the same witnesses, do not put the suspect in more than one.* Seeing the same face in a second lineup may cause the witness to erroneously "recognize" the person as the perpetrator, merely because the face is familiar from the first lineup. Because of this, the courts have disapproved this practice.[46]

In another context, the U.S. Supreme Court has held that requiring a suspect participating in a lineup to speak, even to the extent of uttering the same words used by the criminal, does not violate the Fifth Amendment because it is not "testimonial self-incrimination." Other actions, such as standing, walking, gesturing, and the like, are similarly not self-incrimination within the meaning of the Fifth Amendment. Similarly, requiring the suspect to wear certain clothing has been held to be outside of the coverage of the Fifth Amendment.

After the lineup, certain precautions should be taken. For example, when more than one witness has viewed a lineup, witnesses should be kept separate after the lineup procedure has been completed. Although discussions between witnesses following a lineup will presumably not render any previously made identification invalid, it may affect the admissibility of a subsequent in-court identification of the defendant by these witnesses during the trial itself.

Additionally, witnesses should not be praised or congratulated for picking out the suspect. This may serve to reinforce a shaky identification, convincing the witness that he or she has picked out the actual perpetrator when the witness is in some doubt. In addition to increasing the chances of a miscarriage of justice, this may lead to suppression of a later in-court identification of the perpetrator by the same witness.

Show-ups. The show-up has been widely condemned by the courts and by experts in law, law enforcement, and law enforcement identification procedures.[47] Whereas the courts have not held show-ups to be categorically improper, they have ruled that the determination of whether a specific show-up was excessively suggestive will be made based on the "totality of the circumstances" attending that particular show-up. In practice, evidence deriving from show-ups is frequently suppressed because the show-up is so inherently suggestive that it is virtually impossible to eliminate suggestion from the procedure.

Consequently, the use of show-ups should be avoided whenever possible. Only when exigent circumstances make it absolutely necessary should this technique be used. When it must be used, certain guidelines should be followed to minimize the **suggestiveness** of the procedure and the risk of suppression of any resultant identification evidence.

Show-ups conducted in the station house or jail are the most unreliable and hence the most objectionable. When used, station house show-ups should, at a minimum, be subject to the following guidelines:

1. Show-ups should not be conducted when the suspect is in a cell, manacled, or dressed in jail clothing.

2. Show-ups should not be conducted at a late hour.

3. Show-ups should not be conducted with more than one witness present at a time. If show-ups are conducted separately for multiple witnesses, the witnesses should not be permitted to communicate before or after the show-up regarding the identification of the suspect.

4. The same suspect should not be presented to the same witness more than once.

5. Show-up suspects should not be required to put on clothing worn by the perpetrator, to speak words uttered by the perpetrator, or to perform other actions mimicking those performed by the actual perpetrator.[48]

6. Words or conduct by the police that may suggest to the witness that the individual is or may be the perpetrator should be scrupulously avoided. For example, one should never tell the witness that the individual was apprehended near the crime scene, that the evidence points to the individual as the perpetrator, or that other witnesses have identified the individual as the perpetrator. Unfortunately, the mere fact that the individual has been presented to the witness for identification strongly suggests that the officers believe him or her to be the guilty party.

Even when these guidelines are followed, it is entirely possible that a court may suppress the resulting evidence on the grounds that no amount of care can eliminate suggestion, and hence unreliability, from the procedure.

Yet exigent circumstances may justify the use of show-ups in certain instances. For example, in certain instances, a station house show-up may be tolerated by the courts if it can be demonstrated that time or other factors prevented the police from arranging a proper lineup. However, the reasons for not taking the time to prepare and conduct a lineup must be substantial and reasonably explained. Even then, they may not be accepted by the courts.

Exigent circumstances may also justify a show-up in the field. A show-up conducted shortly after the commission of the offense and in reasonable proximity to the crime scene may be tolerated by courts. The court may recognize that the realities of the situation often make it vital that a witness view a suspect immediately at or near the scene. Courts have noted that this procedure has potential advantages both for the suspect and the police. If the identification is negative, it will result in the freeing of the suspect and permit the officers to devote their time and attention to other leads. If the identification is positive, the police can focus their attention on the identified suspect. Consequently, some courts are more willing to tolerate this type of show-up.

The Right to Counsel at Eyewitness Identifications

In 1967, the Supreme Court of the United States held that a suspect has a right to counsel at a postindictment lineup.[49] Subsequently, the Court expanded this ruling to provide for a right to counsel at any lineup conducted after formal adversary proceedings have been initiated against the suspect, whether by way of formal charge, preliminary hearing, indictment, information, or arraignment.[50] There is, however, no right to have counsel present at a lineup conducted before such adversary proceedings have been initiated. These same rules apply to show-ups. However, there is no right to counsel at photo identification sessions.[51] The purpose of having counsel present at the identification is to enable counsel to detect any suggestiveness or other irregularities in the procedure. It should be recognized, however, that the presence-of-counsel requirement may actually help the police in certain instances. First, the department's goal should be to avoid any possibility of an erroneous identification and a resultant miscarriage of justice. Therefore, the presence of counsel may be regarded as a positive step in preventing any such occurrence. In addition, if counsel is present and acquiesces in the procedure being used, this may preclude any subsequent defense contention that suggestiveness or other impropriety occurred. This will strengthen the prosecution's case. Therefore, to the extent that defense counsel is responsible and objective, cooperation with counsel in constructing and conducting a nonsuggestive and otherwise proper identification procedure may benefit all concerned.

Of all investigative procedures used by police in criminal cases, probably none is less reliable than the eyewitness identification. Erroneous identifications create more injustice and cause more suffering to innocent persons than perhaps any other aspect of police work. Proper precautions must be followed by officers if they are to use eyewitness identifications effectively and accurately.

CASE IN POINT:

The Will West Case

When William (Will) West was received at Leavenworth Penitentiary, he denied previous imprisonment there. The record clerk, however, ran the Bertillon (body measurements) instruments over him anyway because he was aware of the reluctance of many criminals to admit previous crimes. Sure enough, when the clerk referred to the formula derived from West's Bertillon measurements, he located the file of one William West, whose measurements were almost identical and whose photograph appeared to be that of the new prisoner. Indeed, Will West was not being coy about a previous visit to Leavenworth; another William West was already at the prison and serving a life sentence for murder. Subsequently, the fingerprints of both William Wests were compared, and it was found that they bore no resemblance.

CASE IN POINT:

DNA's First Case: The Narborough Murders

The November 1983 discovery of a murdered 15-year-old girl in the English village of Narborough ultimately had an enormous impact on international criminal investigation. Before the four-year murder investigation was completed, a scientific discovery was applied that not only solved a double criminal homicide but also completely revolutionized forensic identification: the mapping of DNA fragments. At first, the murder of Lynda Mann was barely noticed outside the area known as Leicestershire, but it soon launched one of the biggest homicide investigations in English history. A squad of more than 150 detectives was formed and exhausted every lead in the case. So thorough was the investigation that every male between the ages of 13 and 34 living in the area of the murder was noted and in many cases questioned. Nonetheless, no murder suspect was apprehended.

CASE IN POINT continued

Then, in July 1986, 15-year-old Dawn Ashworth, also of Leicestershire, was found brutally raped and strangled. The MO indicated the same killer and alerted authorities to the possibility of a serial killer. This time, more than 200 investigators from all across the country were placed on the case. Word of the killings began to be cause for concern in almost all of England, but investigators were still unable to develop significant indicators as to who the killer might be. At last, a case against one suspect was developed. A 17-year-old hospital kitchen porter linked to the murder through circumstantial evidence was arrested. After interrogation, the suspect admitted the second killing but denied the first, despite the belief by the police that both victims were murdered by the same person.

The ultimate solution to the problem was found only a short distance away, at Leicester University. Alec J. Jeffreys, a university scientist working in the field of genetic research since the early 1980s, had recently discovered a process of human identification based on the DNA molecule. Whether the suspect's father or the British police first initiated contact with Jeffreys is still under dispute, but the scientist was well known for his work in a paternity lawsuit in which DNA technology established the identity of the father. In the Narborough murders, Jeffreys analyzed a semen sample from the body of Lynda Mann and then analyzed a sample from the Dawn Ashworth crime scene. The technique yielded a DNA image that was identical for both murders. Then, from the suspect's blood sample, Jeffreys obtained a comparison DNA fingerprint. Alarmingly, the suspect's DNA failed to match up with either murder, including the murder in which the suspect already confessed. The suspect was then released from custody.

Certain of one fact—that the same person had killed both teenagers—investigators decided to single out the perpetrator through genetic fingerprinting. Accordingly, in January 1987, all males 17 to 40 years of age living in the village were asked to submit blood samples. More than 4,500 samples were examined before the police, in September 1987, arrested a local baker, Colin Pitchfork, and charged him with the murders. Pitchfork had a long history of sexual assault and indecent exposure, and an informant had alerted police that he had cheated on his blood examination by persuading a coworker to submit a blood sample for him. When a legitimate test of the suspect's blood was conducted, an identical match was made with fingerprints found at both murder scenes. Based solely on DNA fingerprinting and the resulting confession, Pitchfork was convicted of both murders.

Thematic question: Absent blood and DNA evidence used to solve the Narborough murders, identify how other investigative methods could have possibly been used to solve this crime.

Sources: Batt, E. (1999) DNA fingerprinting: The capture of a murder. April. Available at http://www.suite101.com/article.cfm/leicestershire/17877; Leicestersound. Available at http://www.leicestersound.co.uk/Article.asp?id=1283518; Wambaugh, J. (1990). *The blooding: True story of the Narborough murders.* New York: Bantam Books.

CASE IN POINT:

DNA Evidence

Evidence suitable for DNA analysis can be found at many crime scenes and is a powerful investigative tool for linking suspects to crimes, eliminating suspects, and identifying victims. All officers must be aware of common sources of DNA evidence, ways to protect against contamination of samples, and basic collection and packaging guidelines, including:

1. Wear a mask to avoid contamination through talking, sneezing, or coughing over evidence.

2. Blood and semen are the two most common sources of DNA evidence. However, other body tissues and fluids can be used for analysis even in microscopic quantities.

3. DNA is particularly sensitive and subject to contamination. Therefore, first responders in particular must be familiar with situations that will degrade, destroy, or contaminate DNA evidence and must observe the following precautions:
   - Wear gloves and change them often.
   - Use disposable instruments or clean them thoroughly before and after handling each sample.
   - Avoid touching the area where DNA may exist.
   - Avoid talking, sneezing, and coughing over evidence.

CASE IN POINT continued

- Avoid touching your face, nose, and mouth when collecting and packaging evidence.
- Air dry evidence thoroughly before packaging.
- Put evidence into new paper bags or envelopes, not into plastic bags. Do not use staples.

4. If exigent circumstances dictate immediate action to prevent destruction of evidence, wet bloodstained materials may be rolled or folded in paper or placed in a brown paper bag or box, sealed, and labeled. Avoid folding garments through stains.

5. Bloodstained articles and blood samples must be transported as soon as possible and should never be stored in patrol vehicles or otherwise exposed to heat.

6. Use a cotton Q-Tip or swab lightly moistened with saline solution to collect dried bloodstains on fixed objects that are too large to transport or are on porous surfaces. If saline is not available, tap water may be used as long as a control standard of the water is collected for comparison.

7. As in the case of blood samples, clothing and bedding that may retain semen evidence must be air dried if wet, packaged separately in paper containers, and labeled.

CASE IN POINT:

DNA Evidence

Advantages

DNA can be used to test any DNA-containing biological trace evidence. The composition of the DNA molecule does not vary essentially from cell to cell; therefore, the DNA in blood is identical to that found in other biological material, such as hair, skin, and bone marrow. Because DNA testing is so sensitive, only a trace amount of biological material is needed for identification purposes. DNA evidence can identify probative physical evidence in some cases. For example, semen left at the scene of a rape is more closely related to the commission of the crime of rape than is the presence of a fingerprint. DNA is especially useful in crimes of violence that yield little useful evidence. Testing is potentially very helpful in identifying perpetrators of sexual assault in cases in which, although biological evidence is found, witnesses are often lacking and identification of the assailant by the victim is unreliable or nonexistent.

Using DNA test results, a crime laboratory can establish data banks that could identify serial criminals. For example, law enforcement agencies could determine that the same rapist is responsible for a series of assaults in several different jurisdictions. As suspects are identified by investigators through DNA data banks, investigators could redirect and narrow their search for the perpetrator. DNA testing provides crime labs and forensic scientists with a new tool that can be used for investigatory purposes (e.g., identifying remains), which in coordination with other types of evidence, could lead to more arrests and convictions.

Criticisms and Limitations

Some critics argue that the development of DNA data banking poses an invasion of civil liberties, particularly due process (the taking of a sample without establishing a foundation of probable cause) and privacy (because DNA can reveal more information than identity alone). Testing may involve the use of expert witnesses from private companies whose primary goal is to get into court first to achieve a judicial imprimatur of acceptability. DNA has been rushed into court without agreement being reached in the scientific community regarding standards that ensure the reliability of the evidence and guidelines for the interpretation of the results. The probability of a sample having come from someone other than the defendant can be so infinitesimal, according to statistical data, as to hold inordinate weight with a jury, thus obscuring other evidence.

Many defendants are not able to afford the cost of rebutting state-induced DNA evidence. Additional costs incurred in cases involving DNA evidence include testing, the cost of expert witnesses, and legal fees. If defendants cannot afford these costs, the difference between defense and prosecutorial resources—already large—could increase further.[52]

CASE IN POINT:

DNA at Work[53]

- In one amazing success, investigators linked the DNA in the saliva used to lick an envelope to one of the World Trade Center bombers.

- DNA matches have kept families united by allowing immigrants to stay in the United States legally when the genetic study proved they were related to a resident.

- DNA studies have freed persons wrongfully convicted of murder and rape. The Innocence Project at Yeshiva University in New York, founded in 1992 by Barry Scheck, has helped release 144 prisoners (as of July 2, 2004) when DNA tests proved they were innocent.

- Paternity suits are commonly settled by DNA testing. Former mayor Coleman Young of Detroit agreed to child support payments in 1992 after testing resolved a dispute.

CASE IN POINT:

The Case Against O.J. Simpson

In the early morning on June 13, 1994, two dead bodies were discovered at a West Los Angeles home. Dead was the attractive wife of football great O.J. Simpson, Nicole, and an aspiring young actor and waiter, Ronald Goldman. The murders were discovered at 875 South Bundy Drive in the exclusive Brentwood area of the city. Police discovered sufficient physical evidence along with a history of spousal abuse to charge Simpson with the murders. In a CBS television interview, lead detective Philip Vannatter commented that he had never, in 30 years of investigating crimes, seen so much conclusive evidence in a case.

But this case was unlike others seen by prosecutors and police. Both victims were white, and the defendant, Simpson, was black. In addition, he was a wealthy and famous sports hero with considerable public recognition and a nationwide base of adoring fans. To mount a defense, Simpson quickly hired a team of the best-known trial lawyers in the country. Included on this "dream team" were attorneys F. Lee Bailey, Johnnie Cochran, Alan Dershowitz, and Robert Shapiro. Each attorney brought with him special expertise in different aspects of the case, and all were well known for their considerable success in defending celebrities. The prosecution team was headed by veteran prosecutors Marcia Clark, Christopher Darden, and William Hodgman, and at their disposal were more than 800 deputy district attorneys available to help, including experts on DNA evidence. Long before the trial began, the case was receiving considerable media attention. As the case came to its conclusion, media analysts declared that the Simpson trial received more coverage than any other event in the history of television, with literally thousands of hours of television coverage of the proceedings being offered by network television and cable channels, accompanied by expert commentary from key legal personnel.

Evidence presented at the trial, which lasted nearly a year, was examined closely in detail by defense lawyers, and prosecution witnesses were all rigorously cross-examined. The trial ended in late 1995 with a "not guilty" verdict and cost California taxpayers in excess of $7 million.

Evidence in the Case

- Bloodstains were found on a pair of socks in Simpson's bedroom; one spot of blood matched Simpson's blood, and another matched Nicole Simpson's.

- A total of 11 bloodstains were found in Simpson's Ford Bronco: four were Simpson's blood, one matched Nicole Simpson's, and two were a mixture of Simpson, Nicole Brown Simpson, and Ronald Goldman's blood.

- The glove found on the grounds of Simpson's estate contained a mixture of blood consistent with the mixture of blood of Simpson, Nicole Brown Simpson, and Ronald Goldman. The glove also contained hair matching Nicole Brown Simpson and Ronald Goldman, fibers

CASE IN POINT continued

similar to those found in the Bronco carpeting, and fibers from Goldman's shirt.

- Blood drops were found at the crime scene leading away from the bodies; five drops matched O.J. Simpson's blood.
- The ski cap found at the crime scene contained "unusual" fibers similar to those from the carpet of the Bronco and contained 12 hairs similar to those of O.J. Simpsons.
- Goldman's shirt contained hairs similar to those of O.J. Simpsons.
- Two bloodstains in O.J. Simpson's driveway matched his blood.
- Bloodstains found in O.J. Simpson's house matched O.J. Simpson's own blood, and these were seen by Kato Kaelin and several police officers while O.J. Simpson was in Chicago before the police had a sample of O.J. Simpson's blood.

Blood Drops

- *Prosecution:* Argued that DNA tests on blood at the scene and in Simpson's Bronco and estate positively identified Simpson as the killer.
- *Defense:* Attacked DNA tests as unreliable, tried to cast doubt about DNA science, and argued that Simpson's blood at the scene and estate could be old.

Bloody Gloves

- *Prosecution:* Called Detective Mark Furman to testify that he found the bloody glove at Simpson's estate that matched a glove found at the crime scene.
- *Defense:* Attempted to impeach Furman's testimony, arguing that he was a racist who set up Simpson.

Hair Samples

- *Prosecution:* Argued that hair found on Goldman's body and a knit cap at Simpson's estate were those of a black man, and placed Simpson at the scene.
- *Defense:* Argued that hair could belong to any black man, including investigating officers.

Opportunity

- *Prosecution:* Argued that Simpson had more than enough time between 9:45 and 10:56 P.M. to kill the victims, get rid of the knife, and return to his estate about a mile away.
- *Defense:* Insisted that Simpson did not have enough time to kill two people and get back home.

Motive

- *Prosecution:* Introduced evidence that Simpson abused his ex-wife at least 19 times and argued that escalating violence led to murder.
- *Defense:* Argued that all of the abuse allegations were isolated incidents and irrelevant to the murder charges.

Summary Checklist

In this chapter, we consider the ways that information about crimes is documented by criminal investigators. A properly documented case is one that is more likely to succeed in court. See how well you are able to answer the following questions in your checklist.

1. **What important points should you remember when considering the role of the crime laboratory?**

   Crime labs include the analysis of DNA (blood), trace evidence, handwriting analysis, toxicology, and ballistics.

- The Trace Evidence Unit identifies and compares specific types of trace materials that could be transferred during the commission of a violent crime. These trace materials include human hair, animal hair, textile fibers and fabric, ropes, and wood.

(continued)

Summary Checklist (Continued)

- The Questioned Documents Unit examines and compares data appearing on paper and other evidentiary materials. These surface data include handwriting, hand printing, typewriting, printing, erasures, alterations, and obliterations.
- Forensic chemistry includes identifying chemicals, controlled substances, and questioned ink.
- Toxicology is the analysis of biological specimens.
- Paints and polymers analysis examines paint chips and compares them with suspected sources.
- DNA analyzes bodily fluids and bodily fluid stains recovered as evidence in violent crimes.
- The Forensic Ballistics Unit receives and examines evidence related to firearms, firearm components, ammunition, ammunition components, tools, and tool marks.
- Latent print analysis examines fingerprints on evidence. Latent prints are impressions produced by the ridged skin on human fingers, palms, and soles of the feet.

2. **Do you know in what ways fingerprinting remains an important investigative tool?**

Identifying criminal suspects through the use of fingerprinting is one of the most effective methods for apprehending criminal suspects. The use of fingerprinting also makes it possible to learn accurately the number (and type) of previous arrests and convictions.

1. Fingerprinting has been used for hundreds of years in crime solving.
2. Fingerprints can be divided into three main groups: latent, plastic, and visible
   - A latent fingerprint is one that occurs when the entire pattern of whorls on the finger, which contain small amounts of grease, oil, perspiration, or dirt.

- A plastic fingerprint results when a finger presses against plastic material and leaves a negative impression of friction ridges.
  - A visible fingerprint (also called a *dust print*) is a print that has been adulterated with foreign matter.

3. Fingerprints may be resolved into three large general groups of patterns: arches, loops, and whorls.
4. Prints can be identified a number of ways, including the use of powders, iodine, ninhydrin, silver nitrate, superglue fuming, and lasers.
5. Fingerprints can also be computerized in data banks for comparison and lasers

3. **Can you explain the uses of dna evidence and how it is obtained?**

DNA is a genetic "blueprint" of an organism. In every cell within each human body, the DNA is identical. This applies whether the cell is a white or a red blood cell, a piece of skin, spermatozoa, or a follicle of hair.

- DNA was first discovered by scientists in the 1980s.
- Genetic patterns found in blood or semen can be just as distinctive as fingerprints.
- For evidence to be accepted into court, it must be offered by one of the parties and be admitted by the court.
- Using DNA test results, a crime laboratory can establish data banks that could identify serial criminals. For example, law enforcement agencies could determine that the same rapist is responsible for a series of assaults in several different jurisdictions.

4. **Are you able to explain how handwriting analysis can be used in criminal investigation?**

People often adopt unique styles of their own, frequently characteristic only of that person.

Such characteristics are identifiable to the handwriting expert.

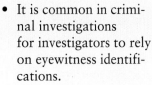

- Writings may occur in many forms, including that on personal correspondence, desks, walls, and even dead bodies.
- Cases involving questioned documents require a comparison between the suspect document and a sample or exemplar or standard.
- Exemplars can be acquired by request or collected from numerous sources.

5. **The problem of misidentifications by eyewitnesses has been known for decades. How can an investigator avoid such problems?**

   One recurring problem in criminal investigation is the overreliance by criminal investigators on eyewitness accounts of crimes. This is especially

a concern when the identification of a criminal suspect relies heavily on the word of eyewitnesses or victims.

- It is common in criminal investigations for investigators to rely on eyewitness identifications.
- A witness may be easily influenced by suggestions conveyed to him or her during the identification process.
- Police officers may also cause misidentifications by suggestive words or conduct.
- In evaluating proper identification procedure, the courts will consider whether it was suggestive.
- Identification procedures may be categorized as photo identifications, lineups, or show-ups.

Key Terms

absolute judgment	geoprofile	relative judgment
Amido black protein	Frye test	relevancy test
composite	Identi-Kit	sequential lineup
criminal investigative analysis	latent fingerprint	simultaneous lineup
DNA technology	lineup	suggestiveness
exemplars	plastic fingerprint	visible fingerprint

Discussion Questions

1. Discuss the three types of fingerprints and how they differ.
2. Review the various ways of locating and identifying fingerprints at a crime scene.
3. Discuss the new role that IAFIS fingerprinting technology offers the field of criminal investigation and identification.
4. To what extent has DNA technology improved methods of criminal identification?
5. Discuss the significance of recent court rulings addressing the admissibility of DNA evidence in the courtroom.
6. Discuss the value of the composite sketch in identifying a criminal suspect.
7. Discuss the proper method of conducting a photo lineup.

mycrimekit

Go to MyCrimeKit.com to explore the following study tools and resources specific to this chapter:

- *Practice Quiz:* Multiple-choice, true/false, short-answer, and essay questions.
- *Flashcards:* There are 18 key terms in this chapter. Flashcards test your knowledge of the chapter's key terms.

- *Web Links:* Check out the hotlink to *The New York Times* criminology articles.
- *Career Center:* Check out the hot links to interesting careers in criminal justice, criminology, and juvenile justice.
- *The Research Center:* Check out the Cybrary and research navigator for even more resources.

Notes

1. U.S. DEPARTMENT OF JUSTICE DRUG ENFORCEMENT ADMINISTRATION (1987). *Intelligence collection and analytical methods. Training manual.* Washington, DC: U.S. Government Printing Office.
2. Source: FBI.gov (2006).
3. DNA INITIATIVE. Available at http://www.dna.gov/audiences/investigators/know/collection.
4. IBID.
5. IBID.
6. IBID.
7. SAFERSTEIN, R. (1990). *Criminalistics: An introduction to forensic science.* Upper Saddle River, NJ: Prentice Hall.
8. DAVIES, G.M. AND T. VALENTINE. (2006). Facial composites: Forensic utility and psychological research, in *Handbook of eyewitness psychology.* Lindsay R. C. L., D. F. Ross, J. D. Read, and M. P. Toglia (Eds.), vol 2, pp. 59–96, Mahwah, NJ: Erlbaum.
9. BRACE, N., G. PIKE, AND R. KEMP. (2000). Investigating E-FIT using famous faces, in *Forensic psychology and law.* Czerederecka A., T. Jaskiewicz-Obydzinska, and J. Wojcikiewicz (Eds.), pp. 272–276. Krakow Institute of Forensic Research Publishers, Krakow, Poland.
10. BRUCE, V., H. HANNA, P. J. B. HANCOCK, C. NEWMAN, AND J. RARIRTY. (2002). Four heads are better than one: Combining face composites yields improvements in face likeness. *Journal of Applied Psychology* 87:894–902.
11. IBID.
12. STRENTZ, T. (1988). A terrorist psychological profile: Past and present. *FBI Law Enforcement Bulletin* April:13–19.
13. CANTER, D. (2004). Offender profiling and investigative psychology. *Journal of Investigative Psychology and Offender Profiling* 1:1–15.
14. IBID.
15. BRANTINGHAM, P. J. AND P.L. BRANTINGHAM. (1984). *Patterns in crime.* New York: Macmillan.
16. CANTER, D. (2003). *Mapping murder: The secrets of geographic profiling.* London: Virgin Publishing.
17. MACKAY, R. E. (1999, December). Geographic profiling: A new tool for law enforcement. *The Police Chief* 51–59.
18. ROSSMO, D. K. (2000). *Geographic profiling.* Boca Raton, FL: CRC Press.
19. IBID.
20. Innocence Project website (2009). Available at http://www.innocenceproject.org/understand/Eyewitness-Misidentification.php.
21. IBID.
22. IBID.
23. *United States v. Wade,* 388 U.S. 218, 229 (1967).
24. *Neil v. Biggers,* 409 U.S. 188 (1972). See also *Manson v. Brathwaite,* 432 U.S. 98 (1977) (*Biggers* test applied to photo identifications).
25. WELLS, G. L., A. MEMON, AND S. D. PENROD. (2006). Eyewitness evidence: Improving its probative value. *Psychological Science in the Public Interest* 7(2):45–75.
26. WELLS, G. L. AND E. OLSON. (2003). Eyewitness testimony. *Annual Review of Psychology* 54:277–295.
27. WELLS, G. L., A. MEMON, AND S. D. PENROD. (2006). Eyewitness evidence: Improving its probative value. *Psychological Science in the Public Interest* 7(2):45–75.
28. GARY L. WELLS' comments on the Mecklenburg Report (see note 8). Available at http://www.psychology.iastate.edu/faculty/gwells/Illinois_Project_Wells_comments.pdf.
29. MECKLENBURGH, S.H. *Report to the Legislature of the State of Illinois: The Illinois Pilot Program on Sequential Double-Blind Identification Procedures,* March 17, 2006. Available at www.chicagopolice.org/IL%20Pilot%20on%20Eyewitness%20ID.pdf.
30. SCHUSTER, B. (2008). Police lineups: Making eyewitness identification more reliable. *NIJ Journal.*
31. STEBLAY, N.M. (1997). Social influence in eyewitness recall: A meta-analytic review of lineup instruction effects. *Law and Human Behavior* 21:283–297.
32. WELLS, G. L., M. SMALL, S. PENROD, R. MALPASS, S. M. FULERO, AND C. A. E. BRIMACOMBE. (1998). Eyewitness identification procedures: Recommendations for lineups and photospreads. *Law and Human Behavior* Vol. II; 22(6).
33. WELLS, G. L. AND E. OLSON. (2003). Eyewitness testimony. *Annual Review of Psychology* 54:277–295.
34. IBID.
35. IBID.
36. WELLS, G. L. AND E. SEELAU. (1995). Eyewitness identification: Psychological research and legal policy on lineups. *Psychology, Public Policy and Law* 1:765–791.
37. MECKLENBURGH, S. H. *Report to the Legislature of the State of Illinois: The Illinois Pilot Program on Sequential Double-Blind Identification Procedures,* March 17, 2006. Available at www.chicagopolice.org/IL%20Pilot%20on%20Eyewitness%20ID.pdf.
38. IBID.
39. Innocence Project website (2009). Available at http://www.innocenceproject.org/understand/Eyewitness-Misidentification.php.
40. *Simmons v. United States,* 390 U.S. 377 (1968).

41. After a witness has identified a photo, subsequent identifications may be influenced. The contention is that the witness thereafter is really only recognizing the previously seen photograph, not the actual criminal. For this reason, the practice of showing a witness a photograph of the defendant just before trial to "refresh the witness's memory" should be avoided.

42. Although it may surprise many officers to hear it, the average citizen still sees the police officer as a benevolent "father figure" (or perhaps, in the case of a female officer, a "mother figure"), with the result that the lineup witness is often extremely anxious to please the officer by making an identification—even though the citizen is not at all certain that the person chosen is the guilty party.

43. *U.S.* v. *Lewis*, 547 F.2d 1030, 1035 (8th Cir. 1976).

44. Even a photo array should be avoided. This is especially true if the suspect is the only person in the photo array who is also in the lineup.

45. See *Gilbert* v. *California*, 388 U.S. 263 (1967).

46. See *Foster* v. *California*, 394 U.S. 440 (1969).

47. See *Stovall* v. *Denno*, 388 U.S. 293 (1967).

48. Although such requirements may sometimes be properly imposed during a lineup, the show-up is so inherently suggestive that the same court that would approve its use in a lineup may find it excessively suggestive when used during a show-up.

49. *United States* v. *Wade*, 388 U.S. 218 (1967) and *Gilbert* v. *California*, 388 U.S. 263 (1967).

50. *Kirby* v. *Illinois*, 406 U.S. 682, 688-89 (1972).

51. *U.S.* v. *Ask*, 413 U.S. 300 (1973). At least one state supreme court has held that when simulated lineups are filmed or videotaped for later exhibition, there is no right to have counsel present when the film or videotape is subsequently shown to witnesses, *People* v. *Lawrence*, 481 P.2d 212 (1971). Showing witnesses a film or tape of a previously recorded simulated lineup has become known as a "Lawrence lineup."

52. U.S. OFFICE OF TECHNOLOGY ASSESSMENT (1990). *Genetic witness: Forensic use of DNA tests*. Washington, DC: U.S. Congress.

53. SCHEFTER, J. (1994). DNA fingerprints on trial. *Popular Science* November:64.

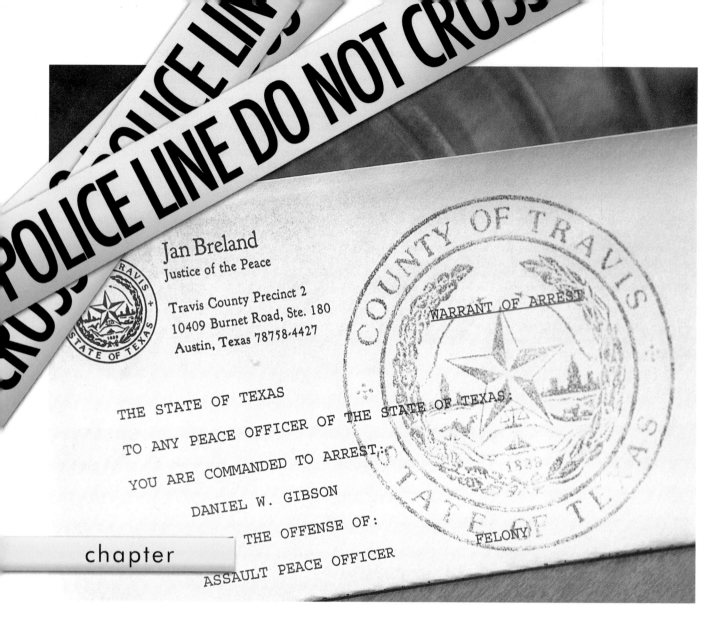

Jan Breland
Justice of the Peace

Travis County Precinct 2
10409 Burnet Road, Ste. 180
Austin, Texas 78758-4427

THE STATE OF TEXAS

TO ANY PEACE OFFICER OF THE STATE OF TEXAS

YOU ARE COMMANDED TO ARREST:

DANIEL W. GIBSON

THE OFFENSE OF:

ASSAULT PEACE OFFICER

chapter

5

Legal Issues in Criminal Investigation

This chapter will enable you to:

- Discuss relevant U.S. Supreme Court precedents relating to police searches.
- Understand the requirements of warrantless searches.
- Explain how to properly structure a search warrant.
- Describe the various methods of executing a search warrant.
- Explain the importance of marking and preserving physical evidence.
- Understand the process of using reasonable force in effecting an arrest.
- Define the term *arrest* and how that differs from an investigative detention.
- Understand the reasonable application of use of force.

Introduction

The body of constitutional law addressing searches and seizures by police is immense and includes thousands of case decisions from courts in virtually all levels of government. Of paramount importance in criminal investigations is the officer's ability to be aware of and work within constitutional (and departmental) guidelines. Issues such as what to search, when to search, and how to conduct a search play a vital role in determining what is fair in the eyes of the U.S. Supreme Court. In this chapter, we will examine some of the more crucial principles of searches and seizures and how officers must conduct themselves to present a legally sound criminal case.

Due Process and the Constitution

In addition to affording protection by ensuring a separation of powers within the government, the U.S. Constitution safeguards operations of the criminal justice system. One means of power was granting individual freedoms in what is called the Bill of Rights, which was added to the Constitution in 1791. Initially, the **Bill of Rights** applied only to the manner in which the federal government operated within the justice system. However, in 1868, the Fourteenth Amendment was passed extending **due process** to each of the states as well. Under this amendment, citizens are basically guaranteed three classes of rights:

1. Privileges and immunities of citizens of the United States
2. Due process of law
3. Equal protection under the law

For more than 30 years, the U.S. Supreme Court's interpretation of the Constitution has served as the basis for the establishment of legal rights of the accused. The fundamental principles that govern criminal procedure are required by the Bill of Rights. Therefore, it is here that we consider the implications of the Fourth, Fifth, and Sixth Amendments, which limit and control the manner in which government officials operate in our justice system.

1. *Fourth Amendment.* Two clauses of this amendment are significant in the realm of criminal investigation:
   - *Unreasonable searches and seizures clause.* "The right of the people to be secure in their persons, houses, papers, and effects, against unreasonable searches and seizures, shall not be violated."
   - *Warrants clause.* "No warrants shall issue, but upon probable cause, supported by oath or affirmation, and particularly describing the place to be searched and the persons or things to be seized."
2. *Fifth Amendment.* The principal component of this amendment is the self-incrimination clause:
   - *Privilege against self-incrimination clause.* "No person . . . shall be compelled in any criminal case to be a witness against himself."
3. *Sixth Amendment.* This amendment guarantees people the right to confront their accuser and to have legal representation.
   - *Right of confrontation clause.* "In all criminal prosecutions, the accused shall enjoy the right . . . to be confronted with the witness against him."

- *Right to counsel clause.* ". . . to have the assistance of counsel for his defense."

The Fourth, Fifth, and Sixth Amendments limit and control the manner in which government officials operate in the justice system.

Legal Guidelines for Searches

Investigators must remember that they not only should have legal grounds to begin a search but that while conducting the search, they must not contaminate any evidence. Doing so will result in the dismissal of such evidence in the courtroom. Additionally, searches must first be justified under law. In the past, officers have not always followed the rules, as the case histories discussed in this chapter show.

The Probable Cause Requirement

For the past three decades, courts have scrutinized virtually every aspect of the Fourth Amendment. The probable cause requirement is one of the most important components of the Fourth Amendment because it lies at the heart of police officers' authority to search, seize, and make arrests. Simply put, **probable cause** is the minimum amount of information necessary to warrant a reasonable person to believe that a crime has been or is being committed by a person who is about to be arrested. Officers generally establish probable cause through their own observations. For example:

- Did the suspect attempt to run away when approached by the officer?
- Did the suspect admit to any part of the alleged crime?
- Did the suspect behave furtively, as if he or she were trying to hide something?

It is unlikely that a single fact or circumstance will establish probable cause, but several such facts put together might. Probable cause is the minimum amount of information necessary to cause a reasonable person to believe that a crime has been or is being committed by a person who is about to be arrested.

It is also common for probable cause to be established through hearsay information provided by third-party sources, typically informants. Here officers must be careful that the information is reliable and verifiable and is not based on rumor or suspicion because such information is not sufficient to establish probable cause.

The Exclusionary Rule

The **exclusionary rule** relates primarily to cases involving issues of search and seizure, arrests, interrogations, and stop-and-frisk violations. In addition, it pertains to any evidence obtained illegally even though it may be both relevant and material. The exclusionary rule states that courts will exclude any evidence that was illegally obtained even though it may be relevant and material.

The exclusionary rule originated with the 1914 case of *Weeks* v. *United States* but was geared to apply to federal, not state, governments. Although the *Weeks* case was virtually ignored by the courts, the subsequent *Mapp* decision (*Mapp* v. *Ohio*, 1961) expanded the scope of the exclusionary rule by applying it to both federal and state courts. In 1957, Cleveland police officers went to the residence of Dolree Mapp while acting on information that a fugitive was in hiding there. Mapp refused to admit officers to the residence without a search warrant. The officers left but maintained surveillance on the residence. Three hours later, more officers arrived and forced their way into the Mapp residence. By this time, Mapp's attorney had arrived, but officers ignored him. Mapp then demanded to see a search warrant, at which time one of the officers held up a piece of paper, claiming that it was a search warrant. Mapp grabbed the piece of paper and stashed it in her blouse. A struggle ensued, and the officers retrieved the paper and arrested Mapp for being "belligerent." The officers then began to search the entire home. Although they never located the fugitive they were looking for, they ran across some obscene material for which Mapp was subsequently arrested and convicted. The U.S. Supreme Court overturned the conviction, stating that the methods used by officers to obtain the evidence were a violation of her constitutional rights.

The question in the *Mapp* case was whether or not the illegally seized evidence was in violation of the Fourth Amendment's search and seizure provisions, which would render it inadmissible in the state trial, in which Ms. Mapp was found guilty. Although the state supreme court in Ohio upheld the conviction, the U.S. Supreme Court overturned it. In addition to imposing federal constitutional standards on state law enforcement personnel, the Court pointed out that there was a relationship between the Fourth and Fifth Amendments that makes up the legal basis for the exclusionary rule.

Since the early days of the exclusionary rule, other decisions have highlighted the fact that the Fourth Amendment protects people, not places. Stated differently, although the old saying "a person's home is his castle" has a great deal of validity within the context of constitutional law, people have a reasonable expectation to privacy in "homes" of many descriptions, including apartments, duplexes, motel rooms, and even cardboard boxes or otherwise makeshift dwellings of the homeless. Indeed, all of these places can become protected under the Fourth Amendment. For example, in *Minnesota* v. *Olson* (1990), the U.S. Supreme Court extended the protection against warrantless searches to overnight guests residing in the home of another. The deciding factor

FIGURE 5.1 Justices of the Supreme Court of the United States pose for a 2006 "class photo" inside the Supreme Court in Washington, March 3, 2006. Standing from left to right are Justice Stephen Breyer, Justice Clarence Thomas, Justice Ruth Bader Ginsburg, and Justice Samuel Alito. Seated from left to right are Justice Anthony Kennedy, Justice John Paul Stevens, Chief Justice John Roberts Jr., Justice Antonio Scalia, and Justice David Souter. Larry Dowing, Landov LLC.

in one's capacity to claim the protection of the Fourth Amendment depends on whether the person who makes that claim has a legitimate expectation of privacy in the place searched.

Search Incident to Lawful Arrest

The legal considerations of what constitutes an arrest are discussed in Chapter 7, but because this chapter deals with search and seizure, we will now consider a search immediately after an arrest. *Chimel* v. *California* (1969) dealt with areas that are not in plain view that are searched without a warrant. The case also addresses arrest activities by police. Ted Chimel was approached in his home by police officers who possessed a valid arrest warrant for him. The officers then advised Chimel that they wanted to "look around" and proceeded to search the premises without Chimel's permission. After a one-hour search, some coins were located and seized as evidence in a crime. Although initially convicted, Chimel later appealed the case, which was reversed by the U.S. Supreme Court because the coins were not found lawfully. Although the coins were found "incident to a lawful arrest," the evidence was excluded because it was not in plain view and the officers did not have a search warrant to search Chimel's residence, only an arrest warrant. The *Chimel* decision established that a search made incidental to a lawful arrest must be confined to the area around the suspect's immediate control.

The point in the *Chimel* case is that the officers who searched Chimel's house went far beyond any area where he might have either hidden a weapon or been able to destroy any evidence. Therefore, there was no constitutional basis for an extended search of the house. The *Chimel* case is important, as it relates to criminal investigation, because it changed the policy with regard to the **scope of the search** as it relates to an officer's authority to search incident to an arrest. Before the *Chimel* case, officers had more leeway to search the area around an arrested suspect. Since the case, officers can search only the arrested person and the immediate physical surroundings under the defendant's control (i.e., within arm's length of the defendant). Such searches are for weapons or to safeguard against the destruction of evidence. To search further, officers must obtain a search warrant.

In 1990, the U.S. Supreme Court further defined the circumstances under which officers may conduct a limited search in the home of an arrested person. In *Maryland* v. *Buie* (1990), the Court held that a protective sweep during an arrest in a home is allowed if justified. Of course, this case authorized only a "protective" warrantless sweep for additional suspects who might be located in the residence.

In 1989, the U.S. Supreme Court clarified the basis on which law enforcement, lacking probable cause to believe that a crime has occurred, may stop and detain a person for investigative purposes. In *United States* v. *Sokolow* (1989), the Court ruled that the legitimacy of such a stop must be evaluated according to a "totality of the circumstances" criterion, in which the defendant's entire behavior is taken collectively to provide the basis for a legitimate stop. In this case, the defendant, Sokolow, appeared to be suspicious to police because while traveling under an alias from Honolulu, he paid $2,100 in $20 bills (taken from a larger sum of money) for a round-trip airline ticket to Miami, where he spent a very short period. Sokolow was noticeably nervous and had checked no luggage. A warrantless airport investigation by Drug Enforcement Administration (DEA) agents revealed more than 1,000 grams of cocaine on the defendant. Upon appeal, the Court ruled that although no single activity was proof of illegal activity, taken together they created circumstances under which suspicion of illegal activity was justified.

Exceptions to the Exclusionary Rule

Since the *Mapp* and *Chimel* cases, the U.S. Supreme Court has developed several exceptions to the exclusionary rule. These play a considerable role in shaping the manner in which police officers are allowed to behave before, during, and after a search and seizure of evidence.

The Good Faith Exception

In the years since the *Weeks* and *Silverthorne* cases, some people have criticized the U.S. Supreme Court for a "chipping away" of the exclusionary rule. One such case emerged in the summer of 1984 when the laws dealing with search and seizure changed dramatically in *United States* v. *Leon* (1984), when the first good faith exception to the exclusionary rule was decided. During the course of a drug trafficking investigation by the Burbank, California Police Department, officers secured a search warrant for the residence of Alberto Leon. The warrant was reviewed by three prosecutors before its being issued by a state court judge. The subsequent search netted large quantities of drugs, and Leon was arrested and charged with drug trafficking. The defense challenged the validity of the warrant based on the unreliability of the informant and moved to suppress the evidence. The district court and the U.S. Court of Appeals both held that the affidavit was insufficient, but the U.S. Supreme Court supported the prosecution, holding that the exclusionary rule was designed only as a deterrent for the abuse of police authority. The Court specified that evidence might be excluded if (1) police officers were dishonest in preparing the affidavit and (2) the warrant was deficient on its face (e.g., a wrong or missing description of the place to be searched) such that no officer could reasonably serve it or (3) if the magistrate was not found to be neutral.

The practical effect of the *Leon* case is that any evidence seized through a search warrant is immune from suppression even if the judge signing the warrant was wrong and there was not probable cause to believe that contraband or other evidence would be discovered under the warrant. The *Leon* case allows the use of evidence obtained by officers acting in reasonable reliance on a search warrant issued by a neutral magistrate but that is ultimately found invalid.

Another case decided by the U.S. Supreme Court that same year was *Massachusetts* v. *Sheppard* (1984), which reinforced the concept of good faith. In the *Sheppard* case, officers served a search warrant that failed to describe accurately the property to be seized. Although they were aware of the error, they were assured by the magistrate that the warrant was valid. After conviction of the defendant, the Massachusetts Supreme Court reversed the conviction of the trial court. But upon review, the U.S. Supreme Court supported the good faith exception and allowed the original conviction to stand. The scope of the exclusionary rule was diminished further in yet another case, *Illinois* v. *Rodriguez* (1990). In the *Rodriguez* case, Gail Fischer, who was badly beaten, complained that she had been assaulted in a Chicago apartment. She led police to the apartment, which she claimed she was sharing with the defendant, and produced a key and opened the door. The defendant, Edward Rodriguez, was found inside asleep on a bed with cocaine and drug paraphernalia spread around him. Rodriguez was arrested and charged with assault and possession of drug paraphernalia and cocaine.

After his conviction, Rodriguez demonstrated that Fischer had not lived with him for at least one month and argued that she no longer had legal control over the apartment. So the defense claimed that Fischer had no authority to give police warrantless access to the apartment. But the U.S. Supreme Court disagreed by stating that there was no Fourth Amendment violation because the police "reasonably believed" at the time of their entry that Fisher had authority for consent.

The Inevitable Discovery Doctrine

The inevitable discovery exception to the exclusionary rule was developed in the 1984 *Nix* v. *Williams* case. This exception states that evidence that has been seized illegally or evidence stemming from illegally seized evidence (e.g., fruit of the poisonous tree) (*Wong Sun* v. *United States*, 1963) is admissible if the police can prove that they would have inevitably discovered it anyway by lawful means. On Christmas Eve, a 10-year-old girl disappeared from the YMCA in Des Moines, Iowa. Shortly thereafter, Williams was seen leaving the YMCA carrying a large bundle wrapped in a blanket. A young boy who had helped Williams carry the bundle reported that he saw skinny white legs in it.

The next day Williams' car was located near Davenport, some 160 miles away. The police assumed that the girl's body would be located somewhere between the YMCA and Williams' car and began conducting a massive search. In the meantime, Williams was located and arrested in the town where the car was located. Williams' lawyer was told that Williams would be transported back to Des Moines without being interrogated. During the trip back, however, the officer had a conversation with Williams in which he suggested that it would be nice if the girl could be located before a predicted snowstorm and have a Christian burial. As Williams and the officer neared the town where the body was hidden, Williams directed the officer to the body, a location about two miles from one of the search teams.

During the trial, the motion to suppress the evidence was denied, and Williams was convicted of first-degree murder. On appeal, the U.S. District Court declared that the evidence was wrongfully admitted at Williams' trial. At his second trial, the prosecution did not offer Williams' statements into evidence and did not attempt to show that Williams led officers to the body. The trial court held that if Williams had not led police to the body, it would have been found by searchers anyway. Williams was convicted of murder a second time.

So, because the *Miranda* warnings were not read to the defendant before he confessed, evidence that was seized was excluded at the first trial. However, because the evidence would have been discovered anyway as a result of the police search, the court admitted the evidence.

The Computer Errors Exception

In the 1995 *Arizona* v. *Evans* case, the Court created a computer errors exception to the exclusionary rule. The exception held that a traffic stop, which led to the seizure of marijuana, was legal even though officers conducted the stop based on an arrest warrant stored improperly in their computer. The case was initiated in 1991 when Issac Evans was stopped in Phoenix, Arizona, for driving the wrong way on a one-way street in front of a police station. A routine computer check revealed an outstanding warrant for Evans, who was taken into custody. Police then found marijuana in Evans' car, and he was later convicted on drug charges. After the arrest, however, police learned that the arrest warrant reported to them by their computer had actually been quashed a few weeks earlier but had not been removed from the computer. The court upheld Evans' conviction by reasoning that officers should not be held responsible for a clerical error made by a court worker and concluded that the arresting officers were acting in good faith based on the information available to them at the time of the arrest.

Searches with a Warrant

Over the years, the **search warrant** has proven to be one of the most valuable tools in criminal investigation. It authorizes the search of homes, businesses, and vehicles of suspects; typically results in the arrest of multiple suspects; and expedites investigation and subsequent case closure.

mycrimekit

Review: Fourth amendment

When Are Search Warrants Necessary?

If the warrant specifies a certain person to be searched, the police can search only that person unless they have independent probable cause to search other persons who happen to be present at the scene of a search. However, if an officer has a reasonable suspicion that an onlooker is engaged in criminal activity, the officer can question the onlooker and, if necessary for the officer's safety, can frisk for weapons.

Technically, a person may require the police to produce a warrant before admitting them into his or her home for a search. However, people sometimes run into trouble when they "stand on their rights" in this way. A warrant is not always legally necessary, and a police officer may have information of which a person is unaware that allows the officer to make a warrantless entry. If an officer announces an intention to enter without a warrant, a person should not risk injury or a separate charge of "interfering with a police officer." Rather, the person should stand aside, let the officer proceed, and allow a court to decide later whether the officer's actions were proper. At the same time, the person should make it clear that he or she does not consent to the search.

When Search Warrants Aren't Required

Most searches occur without warrants being issued. Over the years, the courts have defined a number of situations in which a search warrant is not necessary, either because the search is per se reasonable under the circumstances or because, because of a lack of a reasonable expectation of privacy, the Fourth Amendment doesn't apply at all. Later on in this chapter, we will discuss some circumstances under which a search warrant is not required under law.

FIGURE 5.2 One of the most important aspects to serving search warrants is the briefing, as shown here. A thorough and properly conducted briefing helps avoid casualties by officers and civilians alike. Courtesy of Mike Himmel.

Advantages of Searching with a Search Warrant

Among the many tools afforded the criminal investigator, the search warrant has proven to be of substantial worth. It represents an authorization by the court for officers to enter a designated location or structure and search for specific items. It can be useful to a criminal investigator in many situations. The search warrant can be used to:

- Recover stolen property
- Seize drugs or other contraband
- Seize any other type of property used in the commission of a crime

The search warrant must contain specifics about the location to be searched, the objects being sought, the probable cause that indicates that there is property to seize, and a signature of the judge authorizing the search. Evidence obtained through the use of a search warrant may also be more readily accepted by courts than the evidence it was seized without a warrant or incident to arrest. In addition, the officer is protected from civil liability when a warrant is obtained. A search warrant also benefits the prosecutor by shifting the legal burden to the defendant. Instead of the prosecutor having to justify a presumably unreasonable search, it becomes the burden of the defendant to show that the evidence was seized illegally. This factor alone has encouraged officers to obtain search warrants when possible.

Structuring the Warrant

A search warrant cannot be issued unless it meets with constitutional guidelines. In addition, for the warrant to be legal, it must meet specific legal requirements. The legal requirements for a search warrant are:

- It must be authorized by the proper official
- It must be issued only for specifically authorized objects
- It must be issued on probable cause

FIGURE 5.3 Tactical unit being utilized to serve search warrant while approaching the suspect residence in a tactical "stack." Courtesy of Mike Himmel.

The search warrant **affidavit** presents facts that the officer believes constitute probable cause to justify the issuance of a warrant. Authorization of the warrant is through the judicial branch of government. If a magistrate agrees that probable cause exists, he or she signs the affidavit and issues the warrant. The warrant must contain the following information:

- Reasons to request the search
- Name of the officer requesting the warrant
- Items to be seized
- Specific place to be searched
- Signature of the issuing judge

IN THE DISTRICT COURT OF THE FIFTH JUDICIAL DISTRICT
IN AND FOR:
JACKSON COUNTY, MISSOURI

Before _____ Judge, District Court of
Jackson County, Missouri

State of Missouri ⎫ ss.
Jackson County ⎭

Affidavit for Search Warrant

On this ____ day of _____, 10, *Agent Brian Johnson* being first sworn, upon oath deposes and says:

That a certain *Residence* within said County and State, located and described as follows, to wit:

2304 N.W. 38th Place, Kansas City, Missouri located in Jackson County being a single family wood frame dwelling facing South, and under the control of Lance T. Anderson, and wife Chelsea. The garage area of the house is to the West end of the South side. The house is on the North side of the street with tan colored brick along the lower third of the front, while being fenced in, with a chain link fence, around the back yard area.

the same being the *residence* of *Lance and Chelsea Anderson* whose more full, true and correct name is unknown to the affiant, there is located certain property particularly described as follows, to-wit:

Controlled substances to include marijuana, Schedule I, LSD, Schedule I, Cocaine, Schedule II, and one fifty dollar bill ($50.00) U.S. currency bearing serial number JO3744496B, and any other records or documents showing illicit business dealings in controlled drugs.

which said property is subject to search and seizure as set out by the laws of Missouri for the following grounds, to-wit:

Violation of the state criminal code controlled substances section RsMo 195.233.

and that the probable cause of the affiant believing such facts exist as follows, to-wit:

1) Your affiant is a sworn police officer with the Kansas City Police Department, who has been a full time narcotics investigator for three years and seven months. 2) On April 30, 2010 at approximately 1630 hours, Officer Johnson purchased one (1) kilo of marijuana for $2500 from Chelsea Anderson which was contained in a black trunk located in the hallway of the residence. 3) On April 30, 2010 at approx. 1945 hours Officer Johnson purchased 100 units of LSD for $4350 from Lance Anderson which he acquired from the freezer area of the kitchen. 4) On April 30, 2010 Lance Anderson also displayed approx. one (1) ounce of white powder claiming it to be cocaine which was also kept in the refrigerator area of the kitchen.

_____
Affiant

Subscribed and sworn before me this ____ day of ____ 20*10*

_____
Judge, District Court of
Jackson County, Missouri

FIGURE 5.4 Sample search warrant affidavit.

After a warrant has been issued, it should be executed promptly. During the course of a search, other items of contraband should not be sought unless they are specified in the search warrant. The seizure of items other than those listed in the warrant is not considered "within the scope of the search" and will probably be excluded from the trial as evidence obtained illegally. The search warrant process consists basically of three stages: the affidavit, the search warrant, and the search warrant return.

The Affidavit. A search warrant affidavit must be prepared before obtaining a search warrant. The affidavit tells the judge three things:

1. What is being searched for
   - Contraband
   - Instrumentation of crime
   - Weapons
   - Fruits of crime
2. Where the search is to occur
   - Residence
   - Business
   - Vehicle
3. Why the search is to be conducted
   - Probable cause is adequately outlined
   - Facts establishing probable cause

The Search Warrant. Basically, the search warrant sets forth the same facts as outlined in the affidavit. Prior to signing the affidavit, the affiant (the officer) must be certain that he or she is first sworn in by a judge. The judge must then sign and date all pages of the affidavit and warrant.

The Search Warrant Return. The **search warrant return** is an itemized inventory of all property and material seized by officers at the location of the search. A copy is left with the defendant, and the return itself is returned to the issuing judge. In most cases, the officer who executes the warrant is the one to return it, and this must be accomplished within 24 hours after the search. The search warrant return should include the following information:

- The name of the officer serving the warrant
- The date the warrant was served
- An itemized list of all property seized
- The name of the owner of the place searched
- The signature of the officer who served the warrant (usually signed in the presence of the judge)
- The signature of the issuing judge and the date of the return

Execution of the Warrant

After it has been issued, the search warrant is basically an order by the court to execute it. The officer has no choice but to do so. If the warrant is valid on its face, has been authorized by the proper official, and is executed correctly, the officer is protected from both civil liability and criminal prosecution. Certain

FIGURE 5.5 Sample search warrant.

**IN THE DISTRICT COURT OF THE FIFTH JUDICIAL DISTRICT
IN AND FOR:
JACKSON COUNTY, MISSOURI**

BEFORE _____ JUDGE, DISTRICT COURT OF
JACKSON COUNTY, MISSOURI

State of Missouri ⎱ ss. **SEARCH WARRANT**
Jackson County ⎰

In the name of the State of Missouri, to any sheriff, constable, marshal, policeman, or peace officer in the County of Jackson, State of Missouri.

Proof by affidavit having been this day made before me, by _Agent Brian Johnson_ that there is probable cause for believing that in the herein described _residence_ is located the following property particularly described as follows, to-wit:

Controlled substances to include marijuana, Schedule I, LSD, Schedule I, and Cocaine, Schedule II, and one fifty dollar bill U.S. currency bearing serial number: JO3744496B

and that the herein described _residence_ should be searched by reason of the following grounds to-wit:

Possession of the above described controlled dangerous substances and currency is evidence of violation of the state criminal code controlled substances section RsMo 195.233.

YOU ARE THEREFORE COMMANDED at any time of day or night to make immediate search of the _residence_ of _2304 N.W. 38th Place, Kansas City, Missouri_ whose more full, true and correct name is unknown, located and described as follows, to-wit:

a single family wood frame dwelling facing South, and under the control of Lance Thomas Anderson, and wife Chelsea. The garage area of the house is to the West end of the south side. The house is on the north side of the street with tan colored brick along the lower third front, while being fenced in, with a chain link fence, around the back yard area.

for the said property above described, and, if you find the same or any part thereof to bring it forthwith before me at my office in Kansas City, Jackson County, Missouri.

Dated this _1st_ day of _May_, 2010.

_____
Judge, District Court of
Jackson County, Missouri

procedures should be adhered to carefully when executing the search warrant. Search warrant execution guidelines include:

- _A search warrant may authorize a specific officer (the affiant) to execute it._ Typically, however, a class of officers will be authorized to execute the warrant, so that anyone within that class may do so.

- _Time limitations must be adhered to._ Although the word _reasonable_ has not been defined by the courts, execution of a warrant must be within what a rational person would consider reasonable. To deal with this issue, many states have outlined a specific period in which the warrant must be issued. Periods may range from 48 to 96 hours. If the warrant cannot be executed within that designated period, it is invalid.

FIGURE 5.6 Photo of search warrant. Investigators must make certain that the search warrant contains specific details of where to be searched and what is to be searched for to avoid credibility problems in court. Here the address of a residence to be searched is compared with a suspect's driver's license for possible mistakes on the warrant.
Courtesy of Mark Ide.

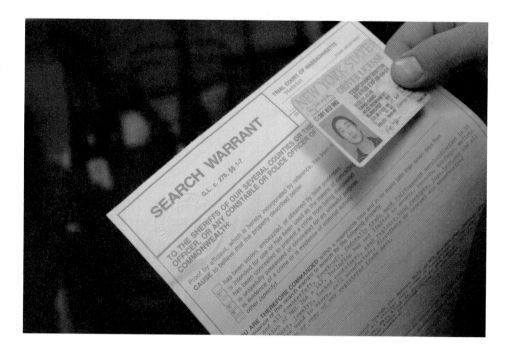

- *Only necessary force can be used in executing a search warrant.* The U.S. Code requires that officers announce their purpose and authority, and if refused admittance, break both outer and inner doors to gain entry. Denial need not be specific or even be inferred, such as the occupants refusing to answer the door.

- *Some states may authorize a "no-knock warrant."* If such a warrant is obtained, specific information must be contained in the affidavit justifying why the no-knock warrant is necessary.

Anticipatory Search Warrants

An anticipatory search warrant is a warrant based on an affidavit showing probable cause to believe that at some future time, particular evidence of a crime will be located at a particular place. Anticipatory warrants may not be executed until some specific event (other than the passage of time) has occurred. The specified events are called **triggering conditions**, and even though the warrant has been issued and is in the hands of the police, until the triggering condition has arisen, the search may not be carried out.

Anticipatory search warrants have been the subject of a great deal of litigation, much of that based on the argument that all anticipatory warrants are unconstitutional because they violate the Fourth Amendment requirement of probable cause. The contention of many defendants has been because, by definition, anticipatory search warrant affidavits show only that there will be probable cause to search the premises at some later time—not that there is at present probable cause to search—the Fourth Amendment requirement is not satisfied. Although this argument has been repeatedly rejected by various federal courts of appeals, the issue has recently come before the Supreme Court of the United States in the case of *United States* v. *Grubbs*, 377 F.3d 1072 (2004). Even though the case involved a warrant obtained by federal officers for a federal crime, the Supreme Court's opinion in that case is of value to all law enforcement officers and agencies in understanding anticipatory search warrants and their use.

FIGURE 5.7 Sample search warrant return.

SEARCH WARRANT RETURN

Received this writ _____ day of _____, 2007

Executed the same on the _____ day of _____, 2007 by going to the within designated place where I found and seized the following property, to-wit:

_____

_____

_____*(ITEMIZE PROPERTY HERE)*_____

_____

_____

and brought the same before the within named court.

_____
Sheriff - Peace Officer
Marshall - Policeman

Executed the same day on the _____ day of _____, 2007 by searching the within designated place, where I could find none of the above described property.

_____
Sheriff - Peace Officer
Marshall - Policeman

OFFICER'S FEES

Executing writ _____ $ _____

Mileage _____ Miles $ _____

Total: $ _____

_____
Sheriff - Peace Officer
Marshall - Policeman

United States v. Grubbs. Respondent Jeffrey Grubbs purchased a videotape containing child pornography from a website operated by an undercover postal inspector. Officers from the postal inspection service arranged a controlled delivery of a package containing a videotape to Grubbs' residence. A postal inspector submitted a search warrant application to a magistrate judge for the Eastern District of California, a copy of an affidavit describing the proposed operation in detail. The affidavit stated:

> Execution of the search warrant will not occur unless and until the parcel has been received by a person(s) and has been physically taken into the residence . . . at that time, and not before, the search warrant will be executed by me and other United States Postal Service inspectors, with appropriate assistance from other law enforcement officers in accordance with this warrant's command.

In addition to describing this triggering condition, the affidavit referred to two attachments, which describe Grubbs' residence and the items officers would seize. These attachments, but not the body of the affidavit, were incorporated into the requested warrant.

The magistrate judge issued the warrant as requested. Two days later, an undercover postal inspector delivered the package. Grubbs' wife signed for it and took the unopened package inside. The inspectors detained Grubbs as he left his home a few minutes later and then entered the house and commenced the search. Approximately 30 minutes into the search, Grubbs was provided with a copy of the warrant, which included both attachments but not the supporting affidavit that explained when the warrant would be executed. Grubbs consented to interrogation by the postal inspectors and admitted ordering the videotape. He was placed under arrest, and various items were seized, including the videotape. Grubbs subsequently pleaded guilty but reserved his right to appeal the denial of his earlier motion to suppress the evidence.

The Triggering Condition

To understand both the *Grubbs* case and the use of anticipatory search warrants in general, it is essential that the concept of the triggering condition be kept clearly in mind. The triggering condition is the anticipated future event that, when it occurs, gives rise to the necessary probable cause to search the premises. Even though the anticipatory search warrant has been issued, if the triggering condition has not yet occurred, the probable cause requirement of the Fourth Amendment has not yet been satisfied and the search is invalid.

The U.S. Supreme Court's decision in *Grubbs* upholds the constitutionality of anticipatory search warrants, provided that the following prerequisites are satisfied:

1. It must be true that if the triggering condition occurs, "there is a fair probability that contraband or evidence of a crime will be found in a particular place."
2. There is probable cause to believe that the triggering condition will occur.
3. The affidavit supporting the warrant provides that the magistrate was given sufficient information to evaluate both aspects of the probable cause determination.

It is apparent in the *Grubbs* decision, however, that it is not essential that the defendant be presented with a copy of the affidavit at the time that the search warrant is instituted nor that the defendant be told at the time of the search what the triggering condition was.

Warrantless Searches

mycrimekit

Review: Search and arrest warrants

Officers must remember that the rules applying to searches differ from those applying to arrests. An arrest and a search are two completely separate and distinct law enforcement procedures. For example, depending on certain statutory restraints, an officer might be empowered to make an arrest without an arrest warrant, provided that probable cause exists. In addition, arrests are permissible even when there is time for the officer to get a warrant. For searches, the rules are different. The Fourth Amendment says that all searches must be preceded by the officer's obtaining a search warrant. Regardless of how much probable cause an officer may have, if he or she searches without a search warrant, there is a legal presumption that the search is unconstitutional. Several exceptions have been developed in which a warrantless search is authorized under law:

- Consent searches
- Searches under exigent circumstances
- Searches incident to lawful arrest

- Stop-and-frisk searches
- Plain-view searches
- Automobile searches
- Open-field searches

Search by Consent

Police can search without a warrant when a suspect gives them permission to do so. Searches in this instance must, of course, be subsequent to an initial detention that was lawful. As a case in point, *Florida* v. *Royer* (1983) held that evidence obtained as a result of a **consent search** when the detention was made without probable cause is a violation of the defendant's Fourth Amendment rights and will be excluded.

CITY POLICE DEPARTMENT
CONSENT TO SEARCH

DATE _____

LOCATION _____

I, _____, having been informed of my constitutional right not to have a search made of the premises hereinafter described without a search warrant and of my right to refuse to consent to such a search, hereby authorize _____ _____, officers of the City Police Department, to conduct a complete search of my:

Premises ____

Curtilage ____

Vehicles ____

These officers are authorized by me to take from my premises any letters, papers, materials, or other property which they may desire, after receipting me for same. I further state that I am the proper person to give the consent and authorization referred to herein.

This written permission is being given by me to the above named officers(s) voluntarily and without threats or promises of any kind.

_____
Signature

WITNESSES:

_____

_____

_____

FIGURE 5.8 Sample consent to search form.

The consent search can be especially useful in cases in which officers have no legal basis for obtaining a search warrant. It is important to remember, however, that a consent search must be authorized voluntarily, with no coercion from officers. This was affirmed in *Bumper* v. *North Carolina* (1968) in a decision in which the U.S. Supreme Court held that a search is not justified on the basis of consent when consent was given only after the officer conducting the search asserted possession of a warrant. Although it is legal for officers to search on the word of the suspect, it is a better idea to have the person sign a consent-to-search waiver authorizing the search in writing. For the consent to be valid, officers must first establish that the person giving consent has legal authority to do so. Just because a suspect is present in a particular residence, he or she may not have legal authority to grant a search. Dominion and control can be verified through the seizing of utility bills, for example, that bear the name of the suspect and the associated address.

One interesting aspect of a consent search is that the suspect does not have to be given the *Miranda* warning or told that he or she has the right to withhold consent for the search to be valid (*Schneckloth* v. *Bustamonte*, 1973). In the event that the suspect changes his or her mind about the search, officers must cease searching or obtain a search warrant to continue.

Another problem with consent searches is that the person giving permission to search can limit the scope of the search. Permission to search can be withdrawn at any time, and any area or container within the search area can be specifically exempted. What if an area or container that might reasonably hold the object of the search isn't specifically exempted? In the case of *Florida* v. *Jimeno* (1991), the Court held that a person's general consent to search the interior of a car includes, unless otherwise specified, all containers in the car that might reasonably hold the object of the search. In this case a Dade County police officer began following a car after overhearing the driver, Enio Jimeno, make arrangements for a drug transaction over a pay phone.

When Jimeno failed to come to a complete stop before turning right at a stoplight, the officer pulled him over. The officer advised Jimeno that he was going to receive a traffic citation for failure to stop at the red light. Next, since he had reason to believe that Jimeno was involved with a drug transaction, the officer asked for permission to search the automobile. Jimeno agreed, claiming that he had nothing to hide. As a result of the search, the officer found 1 kilo of cocaine in a brown paper bag located under the passenger side floorboard. Jimeno was arrested and charged.

The issue here is that because Jimeno had not given specific permission to search the bag, the Florida courts ordered the cocaine suppressed as evidence. The courts claimed that although the officer was proper in asking for permission to search the vehicle, permission was not extended to the bag under the floorboard or any other containers in the car. The U.S. Supreme Court didn't agree. In his delivery of the majority opinion, Chief Justice William Rehnquist stated:

> The scope of a search is generally defined by its expressed object. [The officer] had informed Jimeno that he . . . would be looking for narcotics in the area. We think that it was . . . reasonable for the police to conclude that the general consent to search [the] car included consent to search containers within that car which might bear drugs.

Rehnquist further explained that a different degree of privacy should attach to a paper bag than to a locked suitcase and that it is probably unreasonable for an officer to think that a person who gives consent for a search of his vehicle has also given consent to pry open a locked bag inside the car. But it probably isn't unreasonable for the officer to open a paper bag under the same circumstances.

Rehnquist went on to say that "a suspect may of course delimit as he chooses the scope of the search to which he consents . . . but if his consent would reasonably be understood to extend to a particular container, the Fourth Amendment provides no grounds for requiring a more explicit authorization."

In a related case, *Florida* v. *Bostick* (1991), the U.S. Supreme Court permitted warrantless sweeps of inner-city buses. In *Bostick*, the Court ruled that law enforcement officers who approach a seated bus passenger and request consent to search the passenger's luggage do not necessarily "seize" the passenger under the Fourth Amendment. The test applied in such situations is whether or not a reasonable passenger would feel free to decline the request or otherwise terminate the encounter. In the *Bostick* case, the defendant was traveling from Miami, Florida to Atlanta, Georgia. When the bus stopped in Ft. Lauderdale, two police officers involved in drug interdiction efforts boarded the bus and, lacking reasonable suspicion, approached the defendant. After asking to inspect his ticket and identification, they then requested and were given consent to search the defendant's luggage for drugs. Cocaine was found as a result of the search.

The Florida Supreme Court ruled that the cocaine had been seized in violation of the Fourth Amendment. In doing so, the court noted that the defendant had been illegally seized without reasonable suspicion and that an impermissible seizure necessarily results any time that police board a bus, approach passengers without reasonable suspicion, and request consent to search luggage. The U.S. Supreme Court reversed the Florida court's decision and held that this type of drug interdiction effort may be permissible as long as officers do not convey the message that compliance with their request is required.

The Court noted that previous cases have permitted the police, without reasonable suspicion, to approach people in an airport for the purpose of asking questions, verifying identification, and requesting consent to search luggage.

Emergency Searches

In the case of an emergency or **exigent circumstances**, a search may also be conducted without a warrant provided that probable cause exists. As a general rule, the police are authorized to make an emergency warrantless search when the time it would take to get a warrant would jeopardize public safety or lead to the loss of important evidence. Here are some situations in which judges would most likely uphold a warrantless search:

- *A threat of the removal or destruction of evidence. Case example:* After a street drug arrest, an officer enters the house after the suspect shouts into the house, "Eddie, quick, flush our stash down the toilet." The officer arrests Eddie and seizes the stash.
- *A danger to life. Case example:* A police officer on routine patrol hears shouts and screams coming from a residence, rushes in, and arrests a suspect for spousal abuse.
- *The threat of a suspect escaping*

Any one of these circumstances may create an exception to the Fourth Amendment's warrant requirement. It is incumbent on investigating officers to demonstrate that a dire situation existed that justified their actions. Failure to do so will result in the evidence seized being deemed illegal. However, if a judge decides that an officer had time to obtain a search warrant without risking injury to people or the loss of evidence, the judge should refuse to allow into evidence whatever was seized in the course of the warrantless search. Judges always have the final word on whether police officers should have obtained warrants.

The need for emergency searches was first recognized by the U.S. Supreme Court in *Ker* v. *California* (1963) and *Cupp* v. *Murphy* (1973) when it decided that police may enter a dwelling unannounced in cases in which a delay in the search would result in the destruction of evidence. In a related decision, the court held that it was lawful for police to enter a residence without a warrant if they were in pursuit of a fleeing robber (*Warden* v. *Hayden*, 1967). In another case, *Mincey* v. *Arizona* (1978), the Supreme Court held that the "Fourth Amendment does not require police officers to delay in the course of an investigation if doing so would gravely endanger their lives or the lives of others." Finally, in the 1995 case of *Wilson* v. *Arkansas*, the Supreme Court ruled that police officers generally must knock and announce their identity before entering a dwelling or other premises with a search warrant. However, in certain emergencies, officers armed with a search warrant need not knock or identify themselves.

Searches Incident to Arrest

As we learned earlier, the *Chimel* decision authorized a search of an arrested suspect and the immediate area around him or her. This is justified by an officer's right to search a suspect for weapons before transporting him or her to jail. The area around the suspect is searched because it is considered lunging distance, where a suspect could conceivably acquire a weapon. When the suspect is arrested in a vehicle, the immediate area is defined as the entire passenger compartment of the vehicle, including closed but not locked containers (*New York* v. *Belton*, 1981). In circumstances in which a thorough search is desired pursuant to an arrest, a search warrant should be obtained.

Stop-and-Frisk Searches

In 1968, the Supreme Court of the United States declared in the case of *Terry* v. *Ohio* (1968)[1] that a police officer may stop a person for questioning if the officer reasonably suspects that the person has committed, is committing, or is about to commit a crime. It is not necessary that the officer have probable cause to arrest the individual at the time that the stop is made. All that is required is that the officer has a reasonable suspicion that the individual is involved in criminal activity. However, to be reasonable, this suspicion must be based on articulable facts that would lead a reasonable person to suspect that the individual is involved in criminal activity.

The Supreme Court further declared in *Terry* v. *Ohio* that an officer who has stopped a suspect may ". . . search for weapons for the protection of the police officer, where he has reason to-believe that he is dealing with an armed and dangerous individual."[2] This case is the landmark legal decision that grants officers the authority to conduct field interviews (also called "investigative detentions" or *Terry* stops) and pat-down searches (an investigative detention is commonly referred to as a "**stop and frisk**"). Numerous federal and state court decisions have interpreted and applied the principles of *Terry*. In addition, many states have enacted statutes dealing with field interviews and pat-down searches.[3]

Field Interviews versus "Consensual Encounters." The principles discussed here apply to field interviews only. They do not apply to so-called consensual or voluntary encounters. As noted earlier, an officer may conduct a field interview as defined in the policy (an investigative detention or *Terry* stop) only when he or she has a reasonable suspicion, based on objective facts, that the individual to be interviewed is engaged in criminal activity. Conversely, an officer who lacks "reasonable suspicion" as defined above may nevertheless approach a suspect and ask questions designed to produce evidence of criminal activity as long as the encounter is voluntary or "consensual."

The distinction is a critical one. Field interviews are "seizures" of the person within the meaning of the Fourth Amendment, and the discovery of any physical evidence during such an interview is valid only if Fourth Amendment considerations are met. On the other hand, consensual encounters are not seizures of the person. If the officer discovers evidence during the consensual encounter, it will normally be admissible in a trial even though there was no basis for "reasonable suspicion" at the time that the officer initiated the encounter. Thus, it is often desirable for the officer to approach a suspect in a manner that will make the initial contact a consensual encounter rather than a field interview.

Factors Defining a Field Interview.   The U.S. Supreme Court has held that a police–citizen encounter is consensual (i.e., does not amount to a seizure of the person) as long as the circumstances of the encounter are such that a reasonable person would feel that he or she was "free to leave," that is, to terminate the encounter and depart at any time.[4] The following factors, among others, may be considered by a court in determining whether the contact was a consensual encounter or a field interview (hereafter sometimes referred to as an "investigative stop"):

1. *Interference with the suspect's freedom of movement. Case example:* If officers position themselves or their vehicles in such a manner as to block the suspect's path, this indicates that the suspect is not free to leave and may render the encounter an investigative stop.

2. *Number of officers and their behavior. Case example:* Confrontation of the suspect by more than one officer may create an atmosphere of intimidation that will cause the courts to consider the contact an investigative stop. Excessive display of weapons, such as drawn or pointed firearms, will have the same effect. Even the prolonged or repeated display of badges or other police identification may be considered intimidating.[5] A threatening or bullying manner may lead to the same result.

3. *Physical contact with the suspect. Case example:* Any physical contact with the suspect for purposes of stopping or holding the individual or to search for weapons or evidence will almost certainly cause the contact to be considered a nonconsensual (i.e., an investigative) stop or even a full-fledged arrest.

4. *Retaining personal property of the suspect. Case example:* If the officer wishes the contact to be regarded as consensual, any personal property taken from the suspect, such as a driver's license or other identification, should be returned promptly to the suspect. Prolonged retention by the officer of such items may lead a court to conclude that the suspect was not free to leave.

An officer may ask the suspect to move to another area during the encounter without altering the consensual nature of the contact if it is made clear to the suspect that the request to move to another location is just that—a request only—and that the suspect is free to refuse the request.

One method of emphasizing the consensual nature of the encounter is for the officer to advise the suspect that the suspect has the right to refuse to answer questions, the right to refuse to consent to a search, and so forth. Such warnings may not be legally required under the existing circumstances, but if given, they will often persuade a court that any continuation of the encounter beyond that point was still voluntary on the part of the suspect. Even if the contact is not a consensual contact, it is still perfectly lawful if conducted in accordance with the principles applicable to investigative stops.

Initiation and Conduct of Field Interviews. The initiation of a field inter-view is justified only when an officer has reasonable suspicion that a suspect is engaged in criminal activity. This suspicion must be based on specific facts known to or observed by the officer that the officer can later articulate in detail to a court. Such facts may include the demeanor of a person (e.g., furtive behavior); the time of day or night; the area in which the encounter occurs; the inappropriateness of the suspect's presence in that area at that time; the fact that the suspect is carrying suspicious objects; objective evidence that the suspect may be armed (bulge in the clothing); and knowledge of the officer that a crime has recently been committed in that area, especially if the suspect matches the description of the perpetrator of the crime.[6]

In addition to the above, on January 12, 2000, the U.S. Supreme Court decided the case of *Illinois v Wardlow* ([98-1036] 183 Ill. 2nd 306, 701 N.E. 2d 484), which provides officers with an additional criterion for establishing rea-sonable suspicion to initiate a field interview. *Wardlow* deals with the common scenario in which a person notices police approaching and runs away to avoid them. In the past, it has generally been held by the courts that the act of fleeing from police does not, in and of itself, justify officers to pursue and stop the indi-vidual concerned. The *Wardlow* decision does not alter that basic fact, but it does permit officers to include fleeing as one more element that police may con-sider in determining whether reasonable suspicion exists sufficient to justify a *Terry* stop.

Officers must conduct the field interview in such a manner that the courts will not consider it an unlawful arrest. It must be remembered that in the view of the courts, an arrest may occur even though the actual words "you're under arrest" have not been uttered by the officer. Therefore, unless the stop produces probable cause to arrest the suspect, the officer should still conduct the field interview in a manner that will not convey the impression that the suspect is under arrest. For this reason, the officer should:

- Exercise reasonable courtesy and avoid intimidating or threatening behavior.
- Minimize physical contact, which may induce a court to treat the encounter as an arrest.
- Avoid detaining the suspect any longer than is absolutely necessary. One of the more common bases for judicial rulings that a stop has become an arrest is detention of the suspect for an excessive period of time.

In addition, any movement of the suspect from the point of initial contact, such as to an area where there is more light, should be limited to that which is reasonably necessary for officer safety and the determination of criminal involvement. However, it should be clearly understood here that notwithstand-ing cautions regarding the legal requirements for a field interview, officer safety should remain a paramount consideration and should be emphasized in all departmental policies.

Pat-Down Searches. As noted earlier, *Terry* v. *Ohio*, other court decisions, and various state statutes give officers the authority to conduct a pat-down search[7] or "frisk" of a suspect who has been the subject of a valid investigative stop if the officer reasonably believes that the suspect may possess a weapon.

The following points are vital when conducting a valid pat-down search:

- If the stop is invalid, the pat-down search is also invalid. Only a valid investigative stop based on reasonable suspicion of criminal activity justi-fies a pat-down search.

- The right to stop the suspect for questioning does not automatically give the officer the right to conduct the pat-down search. The erroneous belief that the right to stop automatically gives the officer the right to frisk is one of the more common errors made by police officers. In reality, even if the stop is valid, before a pat-down search may be conducted, there must be a separate basis for believing that the person who has been stopped may possess a weapon and may be a threat to the officer.

- Factors that may justify an officer reaching the conclusion that a suspect who has been validly stopped may possess a weapon include the type of crime suspected[8]; the circumstances of the stop (number of suspects, number of officers present, and time of day and location of the stop); the behavior of the suspect (belligerence); any visual indication that the suspect may be carrying a weapon (e.g., a bulge in the clothing); and any prior knowledge that the officer may have that this particular individual is or may be prone to violence.

- The pat-down search is limited to a "frisk" of the suspect's outer clothing only. It is not a full-scale search such as might be conducted after a valid arrest.[9] An officer may not reach into the suspect's clothing or pockets unless and until the presence of a weapon has been detected by the pat-down.[10]

The officer's belief that the suspect may be armed and dangerous must be both reasonable and actual. For the frisk to be valid, the officer's fear for his or her safety must be objectively reasonable and must actually exist. A federal circuit court has pointed out that an officer "cannot have a reasonable suspicion that a person is armed and dangerous when he in fact has no such suspicion."[11] Therefore, if the officer was not actually concerned for his or her own safety but frisked the suspect anyway, the frisk is illegal. When called on to justify the frisk, the officer must be prepared to make it clear that he or she was both reasonably and actually apprehensive for his or her safety.

Pat-down searches should, if possible, be conducted by officers of the same gender as the suspect. The fact that a male officer pats down a female suspect does not necessarily invalidate the pat-down, but it may lead to contentions of civil rights violations and hence to civil liability.

Frequently, a person who has been stopped for a field interview will have in his or her possession containers such as sacks, briefcases, or bags. Although "frisks" of such containers have sometimes been upheld by the courts, officers should not attempt to open these containers. Rather, the officer is instructed to place such items out of reach of the suspect during the field interview. This ensures the officer's safety while avoiding the risk of an unlawful search.[12]

State Court Decisions and Statutes. As noted earlier, the primary legal basis for field interviews and pat-down searches arises from the U.S. Supreme Court case of *Terry* v. *Ohio*. However, many states, including Illinois, New York, and Virginia, have statutes that govern these activities. These statutes may place restrictions on officers that are more stringent than those imposed by the U.S. Supreme Court. In addition, state constitutions may also place limits on an officer's authority to detain and frisk suspects that are more restrictive than those announced by the U.S. Supreme Court.

Plain-View Searches

Police officers have the opportunity to begin investigations or confiscate evidence without a warrant based on what they find in plain view and open to public inspection. This has become known as the **plain-view doctrine,** a doctrine first stated in the Supreme Court ruling in *Harris* v. *United States* (1968). A police officer found evidence of a robbery while inventorying an impounded vehicle. The court ruled that "objects falling in the plain view of an officer who has a right to be in the position to have that view are subject to seizure and may be used as evidence." This doctrine has been widely used by investigators in such cases as crimes in progress, accidents, and fires. An officer might enter an apartment, for example, while responding to a domestic disturbance and find drugs on a living room table. He or she would be within his or her rights to seize the drugs as evidence without having a search warrant. The criteria for a valid plain-view search were identified in *Coolidge* v. *New Hampshire* (1971). In that decision, the court identified three criteria that must be present:

1. The officer must be present lawfully at the location to be searched.
2. The item seized must have been found inadvertently.
3. The item is contraband or would be useful as evidence of a crime.

Before 1990, the courts required that all items found in plain view be found inadvertently, but in *Horton* v. *California* (1990), the Court ruled that "inadvertent discovery" of evidence is no longer a necessary element of the plain-view doctrine. Other cases supporting the plain-view doctrine include the 1958 *United States* v. *Henry* decision, in which the Court ruled that if an officer discovers evidence of another crime "unexpectedly," that evidence can be seized. In 1978, coinciding cases *Michigan* v. *Tyler* and *Mincey* v. *Arizona* concluded that while officers are present on a person's premises carrying out legitimate emergency responsibilities, any evidence in plain view is seizeable. In another case, the Court held that the officer needn't know that the evidence is even contraband, only that it is associated with a crime (*Texas* v. *Brown*, 1983). In this case, the officer's personal knowledge that heroin was transported in balloons was sufficient to seize a balloon without knowing exactly what it contained.

The plain-view doctrine has, however, been restricted by more recent court decisions, such as the case of *United States* v. *Irizarry* (1982), in which the court held that officers cannot move objects to gain a better view of evidence otherwise hidden from view. This view was affirmed in the case *Arizona* v. *Hicks* (1987), which stated that evidence seized must be in plain view without the need for officers to move or dislodge it. In *Hicks*, officers responded to a shooting in a second-floor apartment during which a bullet had been fired through the floor, injuring a man in the apartment below. The premises of James Hicks were in considerable disarray when investigating officers entered.

As the officers looked for the person who might have fired the weapon, they discovered a number of guns and a stocking mask that might have been used in some local robberies. The items were seized. But in one corner, officers noticed two expensive stereo sets. One of the officers approached the equipment, suspecting that it might be stolen, and read a few of the serial numbers from where it sat. But to read the remaining serial numbers, the equipment was moved away from the wall. After calling in the serial number, the officer learned that the equipment had, in fact, been stolen.

Hicks was then arrested and later convicted of armed robbery through use of the seized property. But on appeal, the U.S. Supreme Court decided that the search of Hicks's apartment became illegal when the officer moved the stereo set away from the wall to record the serial numbers. The Court explained that Hicks had a reasonable expectation of privacy, which means that the officers, although invited into the apartment, must act more like guests than inquisitors.

Automobile Searches

The precedent established for warrantless searches of automobiles is the automobile exception, or the *Carroll doctrine* (*Carroll v. United States*, 1925). This decision established that the right to search a vehicle does not depend on the right to arrest the driver but on the premise that the contents of the vehicle contain evidence of a crime. In this case, George Carroll, a bootlegger, was convicted for transporting intoxicating liquor in a vehicle, a violation of the National Prohibition Act. At the trial, Carroll's attorneys contended that the liquor need not be admitted into evidence because the search and seizure of the vehicle were unlawful and violated the Fourth Amendment. Because of the mobility of the automobile, the warrantless search under Carroll is justified. After the *Carroll* decision, there existed some uncertainty about the moving vehicle doctrine. Much of this doubt was laid to rest in 1970, however, when the U.S. Supreme Court reaffirmed the right of officers to search a vehicle that is moving or about to be moved out of their jurisdiction, provided that probable cause exists that the vehicle contains items that officers are entitled to seize.

Since the ruling of the *Carroll* doctrine, related cases have raised the question of whether officers searching under *Carroll* also have the right to search closed containers in a car. In a 1981 decision, the U.S. Supreme Court held that warrantless seizures of evidence in the passenger compartments of a car, after a lawful arrest, are valid (*New York v. Belton*, 1981). Before this decision, there was some confusion about the authority of police to search within the vehicle but outside the driver's "wingspan." The Court authorized a search of the entire passenger compartment of the vehicle, including the backseat. It also authorized the opening of containers in the vehicle that might contain the object sought. The following year, the Court held that after a lawful arrest, police may open the trunk of a car and containers found therein without a warrant, even in the absence of exigent circumstances (*United States v. Ross*, 1982). This case further defined the scope of police search-and-seizure authority in vehicle searches. The *Ross* case therefore has expanded the scope of warrantless searches only to what is "reasonable." It should be noted, however, that police may not open large containers taken from the car, such as footlockers, without a warrant, provided that there is time to obtain one.

In a high-impact case, *California v. Acevedo* (1991), much of the confusion about vehicle searches was eliminated. Federal agents in Hawaii intercepted a package of marijuana being sent via Federal Express to Santa Ana, California. At that time, officers staked out the Santa Ana Federal Express office. The man who claimed the package was then followed to his apartment, where he went inside and came back out a few minutes later with an empty carton, which he pitched into a dumpster. At that time, one officer left the area to obtain a search warrant while the other officers maintained surveillance on the residence.

Before the officer returned with the warrant, Acevedo drove up and entered the apartment. In about 10 minutes, he exited the apartment with an object in a paper bag that was about the same size as a brick of marijuana. Acevedo placed the bag in his vehicle trunk and began to drive away. In an effort to stop Acevedo before he would be lost, the officers stopped him and searched his trunk. The bag was discovered and was found to contain marijuana. Although the trial court found Acevedo guilty, on appeal, the California Court of Appeals ruled that the officer's probable cause was attached to the bag and not the vehicle; therefore, they should have obtained a warrant pursuant to the Chadwick

mycrimekit

Review: Warrantless searches

rule. The U.S. Supreme Court didn't agree. Its response included a statement by Justice Harry A. Blackmun, who wrote:

> The [Chadwick] rule not only has failed to protect privacy but it has also confused courts and police officers and impeded effective law enforcement. . . . We conclude that it is better to adopt one clear-cut rule to govern automobile searches and eliminate the warrant requirement for closed containers. We therefore interpret Carroll as providing one rule to govern all automobile searches—the police may search an automobile and containers within it where they have probable cause to believe contraband or evidence is contained.

Stated simply, the *Acevedo* case holds that if an officer has probable cause to believe that a container in an automobile holds contraband, the officer may open the container and seize the evidence, provided that the evidence is in fact contraband. Two subsequent cases further clarified the authority in which police officers may search vehicles.

The law on vehicle searches has changed dramatically over the past 15 years, enabling police officers more latitude in their search and seizure authority. For example, in *Pennsylvania* v. *Labron* (1993), the Supreme Court ruled that there is no need for a search warrant in vehicle searches if the vehicle is readily mobile, even if there is time to obtain a warrant. In a related case, the Court held that police officers with probable cause to search a car may inspect passengers' belongings found in the car that are capable of concealing the object of the search (*Wyoming* v. *Houghton*, 1999).[13]

Vehicle Inventory Search. In 1970, the U.S. Supreme Court reaffirmed the right of officers to search a vehicle that is moving or is about to be moved, provided that there is probable cause to believe that the vehicle contains items that are legally seizeable. In the *Chambers* v. *Maroney* (1970) case, the Court referred to the earlier case of *Carroll* v. *United States* and determined that a search warrant is unnecessary provided that probable cause exists that contraband is contained in the vehicle, that the vehicle is movable, and that a search warrant is not readily obtainable. This doctrine applies even if the vehicle has been driven to the police station by a police officer and there was time to secure a search warrant.

In the *Chambers* case, officers received a report that a service station had been robbed. After receiving a description of the station wagon the robbers were driving and a partial description of the suspects, officers stopped a vehicle matching the vehicle description and arrested the occupants. After the suspects were arrested, the officers took the vehicle down to headquarters to be searched. Although a search warrant could have been obtained, one was not. During the search, officers located two .38-caliber handguns concealed under the dashboard, some small change, and credit cards belonging to a service station attendant who had been robbed previously.

At the trial, the court rejected the search incident to lawful arrest because the search was made at the police station some time after the arrest. On appeal, however, the U.S. Supreme Court stated that there were alternative grounds for the search. When a vehicle is seized, its contents are routinely inventoried to prevent subsequent claims by the defendant that items were taken. The search and the inventory are, however, two separate processes under law but can be conducted simultaneously, as was the case in *Chambers*. Evidence located as a result of the inventory search is admissible in court. It has been recommended, however, that in the case of an automobile that is rendered immobile or one that has been transported to the police station, a search warrant should be obtained as a precautionary matter.

Open-Field Searches

In *Oliver* v. *United States* (1984), the U.S. Supreme Court reaffirmed its position that open fields are not protected by the Fourth Amendment. This differs from constitutional protection over buildings, houses, and the area surrounding them, known as *curtilage*. The curtilage is considered one's yard; thus, both the house and yard are protected and cannot be searched without a warrant or one of the exceptions mentioned. Open fields and pastures outside the curtilage are not protected by the Constitution; thus, searches made by the government of those areas are not considered "unreasonable."

In the *Oliver* case, police officers, acting on reports that marijuana was growing on Oliver's farm, proceeded to investigate, but without a warrant or probable cause. They drove past a locked gate with a sign that read "No Trespassing." However, a path was also observed leading around the side of the property. After following the path around the gate, officers found a field of marijuana located more than a mile from the house. Oliver was subsequently charged and convicted of manufacturing a controlled substance.

This case is significant because the Court essentially stated that a person's "reasonable expectation of privacy" under the Fourth Amendment does not apply when the property involved is an open field.

Defining Curtilage. In a 1987 decision, *United States* v. *Dunn*, the Supreme Court ruled that the warrantless search of a barn that is not part of the curtilage is valid. From this decision came four factors that laid out whether an area is considered a part of the curtilage:

1. The proximity of the area to the home
2. Whether the area is within an enclosure surrounding the home
3. The nature and uses of the area
4. The steps taken to conceal the area from public view

The *Dunn* decision, although still subject to imprecise application, is helpful because it narrows the definition of what buildings should be considered curtilage of the main residence.

Making an Arrest

The Fourth Amendment reads: "The right of the people to be secure in their persons, houses, papers, and effects, against unreasonable searches and seizures, shall not be violated, and no warrants shall issue, but upon probable cause, supported by Oath or affirmation, and particularly describing the place to be searched, and the persons or things to be seized." It has been said that an estimated 80 percent of a criminal investigator's duties are uneventful, routine, and unglamorous. But the successful completion of an investigation will end in the arrest of a suspect, who will then be prosecuted. This process is far from routine. It is the arrest that is one of the most critical aspects of an investigator's responsibilities. Arrests are always dangerous and often result in injury or even death of the arresting officer. Therefore, certain considerations must be kept in mind by professional investigators before exercising this important police function.

mycrimekit

Simulation: Search and seizure

Defining Arrest

One of the fundamental charges of criminal investigation is to identify a suspect in a crime and take him or her into custody. Indeed, when a suspect has been

FIGURE 5.9 Photo of investigator placing a suspect under arrest.

arrested pursuant to the filing of criminal charges or when an officer invokes the criminal process pursuant to the filing of charges, the officer must be familiar with certain critical legal guidelines.

What Is an Arrest?

The term **arrest** may take on many different interpretations. For example, it is the official interaction between a peace officer and a suspected lawbreaker when the suspect is captured and delivered before the court. It may also be construed as the simple restriction of one's freedom by an agent of the government. There may neither be an announcement "You're under arrest" by the arresting officer, nor may *Miranda* warnings be given. In some cases, the suspect may not even consider himself or herself to be under arrest. When a person is arrested, he or she forfeits many constitutional rights. Consequently, because of the severe legal implications, the arresting officer must ensure fair and lawful treatment of the arrestee and the legal process of criminal apprehension.

The Legal Arrest

The general test the courts consider to determine whether probable cause exists for an arrest is whether facts and circumstances within the officer's knowledge are sufficient to warrant a prudent person to believe a suspect has committed, is committing, or is about to commit a crime.[14] Laws of arrest vary from one jurisdiction to another, but peace officers are generally authorized to make an arrest on the authority of an arrest warrant for either a misdemeanor or a felony offense. In many cases, the only restriction placed on the officer in these circumstances is the time of day that the arrest is authorized. As a general rule, whereas misdemeanor arrest warrants are authorized only during the daytime hours, felony warrants are typically authorized for daytime or nighttime service. Under the strictest interpretation of the U.S. Constitution, a warrant should be required for all arrests. However, the courts have loosely interpreted this requirement in allowing officers to arrest without a warrant if they personally observe any violation of the law.

Realistically speaking, arrests result after a situation between the officer and suspect develops, whereupon the officer requests information from the suspect. Only when the suspect attempts to leave and tests the limits of the officer's response may the suspect realize that he or she is really under arrest. The "free to leave" test was created in 1994 in *Stansbury* v. *California* in an effort to create a test to determine the point at which an arrest had been made. The *Stansbury* case involved the interrogation of a suspected child molester and murderer, and the court attempted to clarify the issue of arrest. It held that "when determining when a person is in custody, the court must examine all of the circumstances surrounding the interrogation, but the ultimate inquiry is simply whether there [was] a formal arrest or restraint on freedom of movement of the degree associated with a formal arrest."

The most common type of arrest is that which follows the questioning of a suspect. After a decision to arrest is reached, the officer must come to the conclusion that a crime has been committed and that the suspect is probably the one who committed it. The presence of these elements constitutes the probable cause needed for a legal arrest. Under any circumstance, probable cause is the minimum requirement for arrest, and when a suspect is caught in the process of committing a crime, the officer has the immediate probable cause required for arrest. Most jurisdictions permit a felony arrest without a warrant when a crime is not in progress, provided that probable cause has been established. In the case of *Payton* v. *New York* (1980), the U.S. Supreme Court ruled that unless the suspect gives permission or an emergency exists, an arrest warrant is necessary if an arrest requires entry into a suspect's private residence.

In a related Supreme Court ruling, *County of Riverside* v. *McLaughlin* (1991), a person arrested without a warrant must generally be provided with a judicial determination of probable cause within 48 hours after arrest. Arrests are authorized under the following conditions:

- When the officer has probable cause to believe that the person to be arrested has committed a violation of the law "in his or her presence."
- When the officer has probable cause to believe that the person to be arrested has committed a felony but "not in his or her presence."
- When the officer has probable cause to believe that the person to be arrested has committed a felony whether or not a crime has been committed.

The in-presence requirement generally refers to the context of sight, but court rulings have supported prudent use of all five senses to support probable cause for a warrantless arrest. Other cases also have addressed the significance of the probable cause requirement. For example, *Draper* v. *United States* (1959) found that specific information as to the location of a suspect, when provided by a reliable informant, can also constitute probable cause for an arrest. In *Brinegar* v. *United States* (1949), the courts underscored the importance of the probable cause requirement as it relates to arrests by stating that a relaxation of the requirement would leave law-abiding citizens at the mercy of the personal whims of police officers.

Detention versus Arrest

What constitutes an arrest? How does an arrest differ from an investigative **detention**? There are many different types of situations in which it might appear that an officer has arrested someone but has not. Adams states that police intervention may be classified as a contact, a consensual encounter, an investigative detention, or an arrest:[15]

- *Contact.* In this situation, the subject is free to walk away if he or she so desires. It is the sole decision of the subject whether or not to cooperate with an officer.
- *Consensual encounter.* In this situation, the officer may not exert any authority over the subject. Officers can continue to seek the subject's cooperation but cannot demand it.
- *Investigative detention.* This is defined as something less than an arrest but more than a consensual encounter. Generally, this is when a person thinks that he or she cannot just walk away (*Terry* v. *Ohio*).
- *Arrest.* Act of placing a person in custody for a suspected violation of criminal law.

Probable Cause

- ☑ An officer has probable cause to make an arrest whenever the totality of facts and circumstances known to the officer creates a fair probability that a particular person is guilty of a crime.

- ☑ Probable cause is analogous to reasonable suspicion in all ways but one: Probable cause requires evidence that establishes a higher probability of guilt.

- ☑ The Fourth Amendment requires probable cause for four different purposes: (1) a warrantless arrest, (2) issuance of an arrest warrant, (3) issuance of a search warrant, and (4) warrantless search and seizure.

Investigatory Stops

Terry v. *Ohio* (1968) is the seminal case that recognized investigative stops (the investigative detention) as a separate category of seizures allowed on a lower degree of suspicion. Three constitutional requirements exist for a **Terry stop** to be lawful:

1. The officer must be able to point to objective facts and circumstances that would warrant a reasonable police officer to link the detainee's conduct with possible criminal activity.
2. The officer must proceed with the investigation as expeditiously as possible to avoid unnecessarily prolonging the period of involuntary detention.
3. The officer must stay within the narrow investigative boundaries allowed for reasonable suspicion in *Terry* stop situations.

To satisfy the reasonable suspicion standard, the officer must possess objective grounds for suspecting that the person detained has committed, is committing, or is about to commit a crime. To satisfy this standard, the officer must be able to point to specific facts that, taken together with irrational inferences that arise from them, provide a rational basis for suspecting the detainees of criminal activity.

Whether the facts known to the officer provided an objective basis for reasonable suspicion is determined from the vantage point of a trained police officer. Courts consider "rational inferences that arise from the facts," as well as the facts themselves, in deciding whether the officer's information was sufficient to satisfy the reasonable suspicion standard. Examples of how reasonable suspicion may affect criminal investigators are:

- *Criminal profiles.* Criminal profiles are groupings of behavioral characteristics commonly seen in a particular class of offenders. Although police are allowed to consider criminal profiles in evaluating the evidentiary significance of things they observe, the fact that a suspect exhibits characteristics included in the criminal profile is not a guarantee that a court will find that the officer possessed sufficient reasonable suspicion.

- *Tips from the public.* Police officers may not act on information received from members of the public without independent corroboration unless they have a rational basis for believing this information to be reliable.

- *Officer-to-officer information.* An officer who makes an investigatory stop (or an arrest) at the direction of another police department or officer need not be informed of the evidence that supports the action. However, if the officer making the stop lacks grounds to support the action, the stop will be constitutional only if the department or officer requesting the action had grounds to support it.

Investigatory stops are allowed on a lower degree of suspicion than arrests because they are designed to be less intrusive than arrests. When the police over-step the lawful boundaries of an investigatory stop, the stop automatically esca-lates into an arrest, resulting in a violation of the detainee's Fourth Amendment rights unless probable cause for an arrest has already been established.

Some investigatory techniques are too intrusive and too much like an arrest to be validated by reasonable suspicion alone. The police should never do the following unless they have probable cause for an arrest:

- Take a suspect against his or her will to the police station (*Hayes* v. *Florida*, 1985).
- Search a suspect for non-dangerous contraband without his or her consent.

Police should also avoid doing the following during a *Terry* stop:

- Give *Miranda* warnings before police have developed grounds for an arrest unless highly intrusive safety measures become necessary during the stop.
- Perform a weapons frisk without a reasonable suspicion that the detainees may be armed or dangerous.
- Transport detainees to a second location unless this action is necessary for officer safety or to further the investigation.
- Display weapons, use handcuffs, place detainees in a patrol car, or perform other acts traditionally associated with an arrest unless these precautions appear reasonably necessary for officer safety or to further the investigation.

When Is a Person Under Arrest?

In most cases, it is easy to determine when a person is under arrest: A suspect is taken into custody based on a warrant or probable cause. Handcuffs are applied, and the suspect is read his or her *Miranda* warning and transported off to jail. However, is a person under arrest simply when an officer displays his or her "authority" to arrest (e.g., turning on the red lights on a police car, ordering a person to stop)? The answer is that such actions may, indeed, not constitute a legal arrest.

The courts have held that a suspect is seized within the meaning of the Fourth Amendment whenever a law enforcement officer restricts their freedom to leave. This occurs when the suspect's liberty is restrained and brought under an officer's control, either through submission to a show of legal authority or physical restraint. For example:

- *Seizure by submission to a show of legal authority.* The test for whether there has been a show of authority is objective—whether a reasonable per-son in the suspect's place would feel that he or she was not free to ignore an officer's request and walk away.
- *Seizure by physical restraint.* If the suspect does not submit to an officer's show of legal authority, no seizure occurs until the suspect is actually brought under the officer's control. The free-to-leave "test" has been repeatedly adopted by the court as the test for a seizure.[16]

This issue was considered in the *California* v. *Hodari* (1991) case, where the court ruled that a Fourth Amendment seizure does not occur when law enforcement officers are chasing a fleeing suspect unless the officers apply physical force or the suspect submits to the officer's show of authority. A juvenile named Hodari was standing with three other youths on a street corner in downtown Oakland, California. When an unmarked police car was observed approaching, the youths ran in different directions. An officer exited the police car, pursued, and finally caught up with Hodari. Just before being tackled, Hodari tossed away a bag containing crack cocaine that was later used as evidence to convict Hodari of possession of cocaine.

On appeal, the California Court of Appeal held that Hodari had been constructively seized as soon as the chase began; therefore, an arrest had taken place. The officer's display of authority was sufficient to place him under arrest. Consequently, because there was no probable cause for the arrest before the cocaine was discovered, it was inadmissible as evidence. The conviction was overturned.

Upon review by the U.S. Supreme Court, the justices considered the issue of whether or not an arrest had been made. There was no doubt that the officer had displayed his authority, that he wanted Hodari to stop, and that the suspect recognized all of this. However, even though the suspect had not submitted to arrest, was an arrest made? In a majority decision, Justice Antonin Scalia said: "An arrest requires either physical force . . . or, where that is absent, submission to the assertion of authority." He later added: "Neither usage nor common-law tradition makes an attempted seizure a seizure." The conviction was reaffirmed.

When there is no physical contact between an officer and a suspect, the totality of the circumstances must be considered when deciding if an arrest has been made. It must be shown that the officer's words or actions would have led a reasonable person to believe that he or she was not free to leave before the officer attempts seizure of the person. Also, the person must somehow show his or her submission to the officer's authority before the seizure actually occurs. Other factors affecting the legality of an arrest include:

- The officer must have the appropriate legal authority to do so (e.g., jurisdiction).
- Arresting officers must be sure that persons arrested fall under the authority of the law (e.g., being physically placed into custody by the officer or submitting to the assertion of authority).

Related to U.S. Supreme Court decisions include the following:

- *County of Riverside* v. *McLaughlin* (1991). Detention of a suspect for 48 hours is presumptively reasonable. If the time to hearing is longer, the burden of proof shifts to the police to prove reasonableness. If the time to hearing is shorter, the burden of proof of unreasonable delay shifts to the suspect.

A *Terry* Stop Must Be:

1. Brief (90 minutes maximum)
2. Conducted efficiently so as to avoid unnecessarily prolonging the period of involuntary detention
3. Confined to investigating the suspicion that prompted the stop unless clear grounds for reasonable suspicion of unrelated criminal activity developed during the stop

- *Florida* v. *Bostick* (1991). The test to determine whether a police–citizen encounter on a bus is a seizure is whether, taking into account all the circumstances, a reasonable passenger would feel free to decline the officer's requests or otherwise terminate the encounter.

Use of Force

Police are granted specific legal authority to use force under certain conditions. But the authority of officers to use force is limited. Penalties for abuse of authority can be severe, so police officers must be clear as to what they can and cannot do. The management of force by police officers is a constant challenge facing law enforcement managers. Balancing issues of a violent society with the safety concerns of police personnel creates many obstacles and concerns in developing departmental policies and procedures. The prevailing police perspective is based on a serious concern for the welfare of officers who must cope with the constant threat of a violent society. In contrast, citizens are fearful that police officers may exceed their legal bounds and use force as a means of punishment rather than control.

Public awareness of police brutality was sparked by an unfortunate incident that occurred in Brooklyn, New York, during the summer of 1997. On Saturday, August 9, a fight between two women broke out in a bar, and the police were called. Haitian immigrant Abner Louima, a 30-year-old bank security guard, was taken into custody in connection with the incident. As Louima was being driven to the station house, he was beaten, and upon arrival he was stripped, searched, and sodomized with a wooden stick attached to a toilet plunger. Doctors examining Louima discovered he suffered a ruptured bladder, a punctured lower intestine, and several broken front teeth. Louima claimed that during the assault, the two arresting officers taunted him by saying, "That's yours, nigger," "We're going to teach you niggers to respect police officers," and "This is Giuliani time, not Dinkens time." (The latter comment was an apparent reference to the mayor's zero-tolerance policy, as well as his law-and-order approach to crime control.)

Police officers deal every day with persons who are violent, under the influence of drugs or alcohol, mentally deranged, or just desperate to avoid arrest. To cope, officers are granted specific legal authority to use force under constitutional law and the laws of most states. However, the authority of officers to use force is limited. Those limitations may be enforced through the use of criminal prosecution, civil lawsuits, and disciplinary actions. Our society recognizes three legitimate and responsive forms of force:[17]

1. The right of self-defense, including the valid taking of another person's life to protect oneself
2. The power to control those for whom some responsibility for care and custody has been granted an authority figure, such as a prison guard
3. The institution of a police group that has relatively unrestricted authority to use force as required

Police officers are taught that the penalties for abusing their authority to use force can be severe. To avoid harsh penalties, police officers must be aware of the rules that govern the use of force. Such rules are included in state law, federal law, and department policy. The federal standard for police use of force was established by the U.S. Supreme Court in *Graham* v. *Connor* (1989). In that

Fourth Amendment Requirements for a Constitutional Arrest

There are two types of arrests: formal (i.e., intentional) arrests and detentions that last too long or are too invasive to constitute a *Terry* stop.

☑ The Fourth Amendment requires probable cause for an arrest.

☑ An arrest warrant is mandatory under the Fourth Amendment only when the police make a nonconsensual entry into a private residence to arrest someone inside (*Payton v. New York*, 1980).

An arrest warrant has two advantages over an arrest without a warrant:

☑ It ensures that evidence seized during an arrest will be admissible.

☑ It immunizes the officer from a civil suit.

However, both of the advantages above will be lost if the officer:

☑ Deliberately or recklessly includes false information in his or her affidavit, or

☑ Fails to include enough factual information to enable a magistrate to make an independent determination as to whether probable cause exists for the arrest.

A defendant who is arrested without a warrant and not released on bail is entitled to a judicial determination of probable cause without undue delay after the arrest. Absent extraordinary circumstances, this detention must take place within 48 hours after a warrantless arrest.

case, the Court recognized that the police officer's duty to make arrests and to conduct searches and investigatory stops carries with it the authority to use force reasonably or to threaten the use of force. The *Graham* decision allows officers to use force for two reasons only: defense and control, not punishment. One must remember that the Fourth Amendment protects the "right of the people to be secure in their persons . . . against unreasonable searches and seizures and shall not be violated." Because a police officer's use of force constitutes a seizure, using excessive force is a violation of a citizen's rights under the Fourth Amendment.

Based on the totality of the circumstances, three key factors can be used to evaluate the extent of an officer's use of force:

1. The severity of the crime committed
2. Whether the suspect poses an immediate threat to the safety of the officer or others
3. Whether the suspect actively resisted arrest or attempted to evade arrest

When police are compelled to use force, a court will use the following standard to determine whether such force was reasonable. First, the officer's conduct will be compared with that of a "reasonable officer" confronted by similar circumstances. Second, when the judge and jury evaluate the officer's actions, they must do so from the "standing in your shoes" standard. This means they can only make use of information the officer had at the time that he or she exerted force; 20/20 hindsight cannot be considered in this analysis.

One of the confusing aspects about the use of force is that there are no clear-cut answers regarding how it is applied. Worse yet, there are many severe penalties

Use of Force in Making an Arrest or Other Seizure

Use of excessive force is regulated by three provisions of the Constitution: the Fourth, Eighth, and Fourteenth Amendments.

☑ The Fourth Amendment standard used to evaluate whether unconstitutional force has been used in making a seizure is whether a reasonable police officer on the scene would have considered this amount of force necessary. This is called the *objective reasonableness standard*.

☑ Physical force may be used for the following three purposes only:

1. To protect the officer or others from danger
2. To overcome resistance
3. To prevent escape

for police officers who take the wrong course of action on the street. We know that numerous dangerous situations confront police officers every day. From time to time, officers are required to use force—it's inevitable. After a police officer makes a decision to use force, his or her department and the courts will take considerable time scrutinizing the situation to determine if such actions were appropriate.

Remember, modern-day police officers must not only know how to use force techniques, such as the swinging of a baton, but must also know when to apply those techniques. The use of force by police officers stems from the premise that in a modern democratic society, citizens are discouraged by law from using force to solve personal disputes. Instead, they are expected to rely on the justice system to arbitrate and resolve conflicts. With few exceptions, such as cases involving self-defense, this restriction applies to most situations.

Understanding Reasonableness

Under the *Graham* decision, the Court identified three key factors based on the totality of the circumstances to use in evaluating an officer's use of **reasonable force**:

1. The severity of the crime committed
2. Whether the suspect posed an immediate threat to the safety of officers or others
3. Whether the suspect actively resisted arrest or attempted to evade arrest by flight

According to the *Graham* decision, active resistance to arrest includes any physical actions by the suspect that make the arrest physically more difficult to accomplish. Active resistance to arrest includes pushes and shoves as well as more obscure actions, such as holding on to the steering wheel while being removed from a car. An interesting finding of the *Graham* decision was an explanation of the standards under which officers' conduct should be judged by a jury and trial judge. First, the actions of the officer(s) will be compared to actions of a "reasonable officer" involved in a similar situation. Second, the Court said that when the judge and jury evaluate the officer from within the "shoes" of the officer under review, they must make their decision based on the information the officer had at the time that he or she took action. Thus, hindsight cannot be used to consider the behavior of the officers in question.

Levels of Force

In 1991, the Christopher Commission, which investigated the behavior of the Los Angeles Police Department in the Rodney King beating incident, found that there was a significant number of officers who regularly used force against the public and who often ignored department guidelines for the use of force. Under department guidelines, officers were required to exercise the minimum amount of force necessary to control a suspect. The Commission set forth guidelines that identify levels of force and the permissible use-of-force techniques within each level:

1. Social control (uniformed presence)
2. Verbal control
3. Weaponless control techniques (including pressure or pain holds), starting at "hands-on" with no pain, stunning (diffused impact with soft striking surfaces), and mechanical (skeletal)
4. Electronic control weapons
5. Chemical agents
6. Control instruments (equivalent to weaponless pressure or pain holds)
7. Impact weapons (equivalent to weaponless mechanical modes)
8. Firearms (and other means of force that could cause death or serious bodily damage when used)

Although it is important to consider this continuum in determining the various levels of force, it is also important to consider operational basics that apply to all police officers regarding the use of force. For example, experience tells us that although modern aerosol sprays can cause considerable discomfort, they seldom (if ever) result in bodily injury. In comparison, use of a baton may result in serious tissue damage, depending on the area targeted by the officer. So because using aerosol spray has a lower propensity for causing pain or injury, it has a low level of force.

Another example is the use of impact weapons, such as a baton or a flashlight. The flashlight has a greater propensity to create damage than the baton, and although the flashlight is commonly used as an impact weapon, it is not designed for this use. In comparing the two, it is easy to see that a flashlight would be on a higher level of force than a baton. Officers should constantly consider their options when approaching what they perceive to be a dangerous situation. In doing so, if the need to use force becomes a reality, proper application of force will be available quickly.

Deadly Force

In 1967, the President's Commission on Law Enforcement and the Administration of Justice noted that most police departments had no policy to guide them on the use of **deadly force**. At the time, most state laws were extremely broad in defining the circumstances under which officers could use deadly force. In its most commonly used parlance, the term *deadly force* refers to actions of police officers that result in the killing of a person. As mentioned above, police officers are legally authorized to use deadly force under certain circumstances.

As a rule, such actions result from situations in which persons are fleeing the police, assaulting someone, or attempting to use lethal force against another person (including a police officer). If deadly force is used improperly or illegally, the officers responsible may be criminally liable, and both the

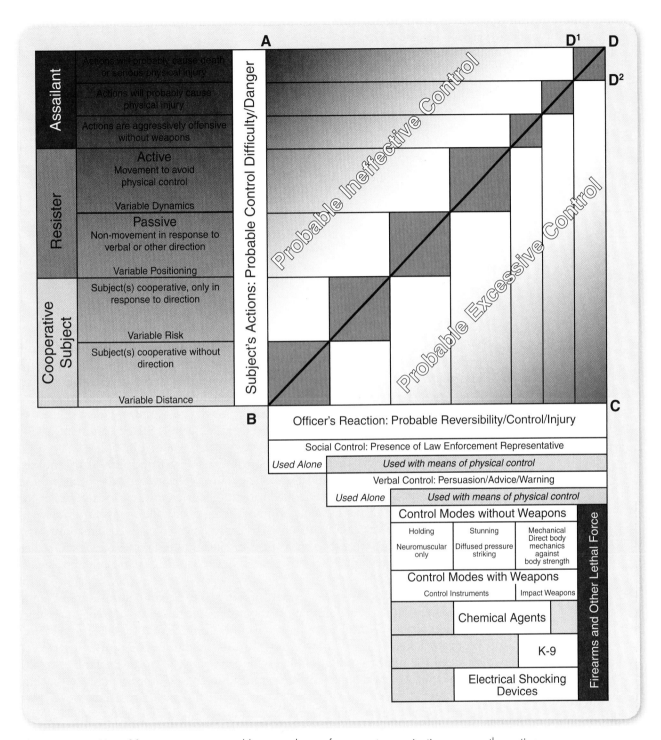

FIGURE 5.10 Use of force continuum used by many law enforcement organizations across the nation.

officers and the police department may be sued in a civil action. Most rules regarding the use of deadly force come from federal statutes and case law and, as a rule, are concerned with police use of deadly force to arrest fleeing felons engaged in nonviolent felonies. These cases are different from those pertaining to suspects committing violent felonies, such as murder, assault, rape, robbery, or other types of behavior that represent a substantial risk of bodily harm or death.

FIGURE 5.11 Decision model: The deadly force triangle. All three factors must be present to justify deadly force. *From Olson, D.T. (1998). Improving deadly force decision making. FBI Law Enforcement Bulletin February:1–8.*

The Fleeing-Felon Rule

Until the mid-1980s, the shooting of a suspect by police was tolerated by many police agencies. Although this is currently not the case, it was prevalent in the early development of policing, when most felonies were punishable by death and there was an assumption that all felons would avoid arrest at any cost. Therefore, the **fleeing-felon rule** was developed during a time when apprehension of felons was considered more dangerous than it is today. Police officers in those early days often worked alone and lacked sophisticated communications technology with which to track suspects who were wanted by police.

The concern was that felons would escape arrest and retreat to another community, where they could begin a new life of crime. As time went by and more efficient means were developed for apprehension, arrests became easier for law enforcement officials. For a period of time, police still relied on the ability to use deadly force even though some felons were not considered dangerous and posed no particular threat to the officer or the community. Before 1985, police officers were legally authorized by most states to use deadly force in apprehending fleeing felons.

Over the years, many states had modified the fleeing-felon rule, but some still allowed rather broad discretion about when to use deadly force. In a watershed decision by the U.S. Supreme Court in March 1985, it was determined that Tennessee's fleeing-felon law was unconstitutional. *Tennessee* v. *Garner* (1985) involved the police shooting and subsequent killing of an unarmed boy as the youth fled from an unoccupied house. In this case, the officer could see that the suspect was a youth and that he was unarmed. The officer argued, however, that if the youngster were able to leap a fence, he would be able to escape. The state statute in Tennessee at the time permitted officers to shoot fleeing felons to prevent escape. Pursuant to *Garner*, the Court ruled that for the use of deadly force by police to be lawful, it must be "reasonable." Reasonable deadly force is authorized under three circumstances:

1. To prevent an escape when the suspect has threatened an officer with a weapon

2. When there is a threat of death or serious physical injury to the officer or others

3. If there is probable cause to believe that the suspect has committed a crime involving the infliction or threatened infliction of serious physical injury and, when practical, some warning has been given by the officer

Summary Checklist

In this chapter, we consider the ways that information about crimes is documented by the criminal investigator. A properly documented case is one that is more likely to succeed in court. See how well you are able to answer the following questions in your checklist.

1. **What ways does the U.S. constitution guide investigators follow during the process of a search?**

   Of paramount importance in criminal investigations is the officer's ability to be aware of and work within constitutional (and departmental) guidelines.

   Under the Bill of Rights, citizens are basically guaranteed three classes of rights:

   - Privileges and immunities of citizens of the United States
   - Due process of law
   - Equal protection under the law

   Investigators must remember that they not only must have legal grounds to begin a search but that while conducting the search, they must not contaminate any evidence.

   - The probable cause requirement is at the heart of the police officer's authority to search, seize, and make arrests.
   - Probable cause is the minimum amount of information necessary to warrant a reasonable person to believe that a crime has been or is being committed by a person who is about to be arrested.

2. **Can you explain the significance of the exclusionary rule and how it relates to the responsibilities of a criminal Investigator?**

   The exclusionary rule states that courts will exclude any evidence that was illegally obtained even though it may be relevant and material.

   - The exclusionary rule originated with the 1914 case of *Weeks* v. *United States* and was expanded by the *Mapp* decision

   (*Mapp* v. *Ohio*, 1961), which applied it to both federal and state courts.

   - The U.S. Supreme Court has developed several exceptions to the exclusionary rule.

3. **Can you explain the utility of the search warrant in criminal investigations?**

   The search warrant is one of the most valuable tools in criminal investigation. It authorizes the search of homes, businesses, and vehicles of suspects; typically results in the arrest of multiple suspects; and expedites investigation and subsequent case closure.

   - Most searches occur without warrants being issued.
   - Evidence obtained through the use of a search warrant may be more readily accepted by courts than if seized without a warrant or incident to arrest.

   For the warrant to be legal, it must meet specific legal requirements:

   - It must be authorized by the proper official.
   - It must be issued only for specifically authorized objects.
   - It must be issued on probable cause.

   The search warrant process consists basically of three stages: the affidavit, the search warrant, and the search warrant return.

   - After it has been issued, the search warrant is basically an order by the court to execute it.

4. **Under what conditions can officers search without a warrant?**

   Depending on certain statutory restraints, an officer can make an arrest without an arrest warrant, provided that probable cause exists.

(continued)

Summary Checklist (Continued)

A number of exceptions to the search warrant requirement have been identified by the courts. These include:

- Consent searches
- Searches under exigent circumstances
- Searches incident to lawful arrest
- Stop-and-frisk searches
- Plain-view searches
- Automobile searches
- Open-field searches

5. What are the legal requirements for making an arrest?

The successful completion of an investigation will end in the arrest of a suspect. An officer has probable cause to make an arrest whenever the totality of facts and circumstances known to the officer creates a fair probability that a particular person is guilty of a crime. Arrests are authorized under the following conditions:

- When the officer has probable cause to believe that the person to be arrested has committed a violation of the law "in his or her presence"
- When the officer has probable cause to believe that the person to be arrested has committed a felony but "not in his or her presence"
- When the officer has probable cause to believe that the person to be arrested has committed a felony whether or not a crime has been committed

Investigatory stops are allowed on a lower degree of suspicion than arrests because they are designed to be less intrusive than arrests. In most cases, it is easy to determine when a person is under arrest: A suspect is taken into custody based on a warrant or probable cause. Handcuffs are applied, and the suspect is read his or her *Miranda* warning and transported off to jail.

6. Under what circumstances is an officer authorized to use force against a suspect?

Police are granted specific legal authority to use force under certain conditions. But the authority of officers to use force is limited.

- The federal standard for police use of force was established by the U.S. Supreme Court in *Graham* v. *Connor* (1989). In that case, the Court recognized that police officers' duty to make arrests and to conduct searches and investigatory stops carries with it the authority to use force reasonably or to threaten the use of force.
- The *Graham* decision allows officers to use force for two reasons only: defense and control, not punishment.

Physical force may be used for the following three purposes only:

- To protect the officer or others from danger
- To overcome resistance
- To prevent escape

Important Cases to Remember

California v. *Acevedo*
Carroll v. *United States*
Chambers v. *Maroney*
Chimel v. *California*
Coolidge v. *New Hampshire*
Florida v. *Bostick*

Florida v. Jimeno
Illinois v. Rodriguez
Mapp v. Ohio
Massachusetts v. Sheppard
Nix v. Williams
Oliver v. United States
Silverthorne Lumber Co. v. United States
Terry v. Ohio
United States v. Grubbs
United States v. Leon
United States v. Sokolow
U.S. v. Montoya de Hernandez
Weeks v. United States

Key Terms

affidavit

arrest

Bill of Rights

consent search

deadly force

detention

due process

exclusionary rule

exigent circumstances

fleeing-felon rule

plain-view doctrine

probable cause

reasonable force

scope of the search

search warrant

search warrant return

stop and frisk

Terry stop

triggering condition

Discussion Questions

1. Explain the roles played by the Fourth, Fifth, and Sixth Amendments in searches and seizures and how they relate to the investigative process.

2. Discuss the advantages of searching with a search warrant.

3. Identify conditions under which a search may be conducted without a search warrant.

4. List and discuss the four most popular techniques of searching a crime scene.

5. Explain the chain of custody and how evidence should be protected and stored.

6. Discuss the legal requirements of a legal arrest.

7. Discuss the ways that an investigative detention differs from arrest.

8. Explain the constitutional standards under which police use of force is identified.

mycrimekit™

Go to MyCrimeKit.com to explore the following study tools and resources specific to this chapter:

- *Practice Quiz:* Multiple-choice, true/false, short-answer, and essay questions.

- *Flashcards:* There are 19 key terms in this chapter. Flashcards test your knowledge of the chapter's key terms.

- *Web Links:* Check out the hotlink to *The New York Times* criminology articles.

- *Career Center:* Check out the hot links to interesting careers in criminal justice, criminology, and juvenile justice.

- *The Research Center:* Check out the Cybrary and research navigator for even more resources.

Notes

1. *Terry* v. *Ohio*, 392 U.S. 1 (1968).

2. Ibid.

3. State courts' decisions and statutes may place restrictions on officers not imposed by the Supreme Court of the United States.

4. See, for example *United States* v. *Mendenhall*, 446 U.S. 544 (1980); *Michigan* v. *Chesternut*, 486 U.S. 567 (1988).

5. Officers must, for reasons of both legality and personal safety, adequately identify themselves as police officers. Proper identification as a police officer does not render an encounter nonconsensual. It is only the excessive, unnecessary, or deliberately intimidating display of authority that affects the consensual nature of the encounter.

6. Knowledge by the officer that this particular individual has a criminal history or has been involved in criminal activity may also be considered. However, knowledge of a suspect's record shouldn't be the sole basis for the stop.

7. It should be noted that the term "pat-down" does not necessarily describe the proper technique for searching a suspect for weapons. It is a legal term, not a descriptive one. It refers to the fact that the search must be confined to contact with the suspect's outer clothing unless and until the presence of a weapon is detected.

8. Crimes involving violence or the use of weapons (e.g., murder or armed robbery) or crimes whose perpetrators often carry weapons (e.g., distribution of narcotics) may alone be sufficient to justify a pat-down search of any individual reasonably suspected of involvement in the crime. See, for example, *Landsdown* v. *Commonwealth*, 226 Va. 204, 308 S.E.2d 106 (1983).

9. A search is a full-scale attempt to locate evidence—that is, contraband or fruits, instrumentalities, or other evidence of a crime. It may include a complete examination of the suspect's clothing, including interior clothing, pockets, and the like. By contrast, a pat-down is a limited frisk of a suspect's outer clothing or a brief inspection of an object, vehicle, or area for the sole purpose of detecting weapons that may be used to harm the officer.

10. After the officer has detected the presence of a weapon or what the officer reasonably believes to be a weapon, the officer may reach into the clothing to remove the object. If the object proves to be a weapon, contraband, or other evidence that would justify an arrest, the officer may then place the individual under arrest and conduct a full-scale search of the person.

11. *U.S.* v. *Lott*, 870 F.2d 778 (1st Cir. 1989).

12. If the officer detects the presence of a weapon in the container, seizure of the weapon would be justified.

13. DEL CARMEN R. V. and J. T. WALKER (2000). *Briefs of leading cases.* Cincinnati, OH: Anderson.

14. *U.S.* v. *Puerta*, 982 F.2d 1297, 1300 (9th Cir. 1992).

15. ADAMS, T. (1990). *Police field operations*, 2nd ed. Upper Saddle River, NJ: Prentice Hall.

16. *Stansbury* v. *California*, 114 S. Ct. 1526, 1529 128 L.Ed2d 293 (1994); *Yarborough* v. *Alvarado*, U.S. Supreme Court No. 02-1684 (decided June 1, 2004).

17. PEAK, K. J. (1993). *Policing America: Methods, issues and challenges.* Upper Saddle River, NJ: Prentice Hall.

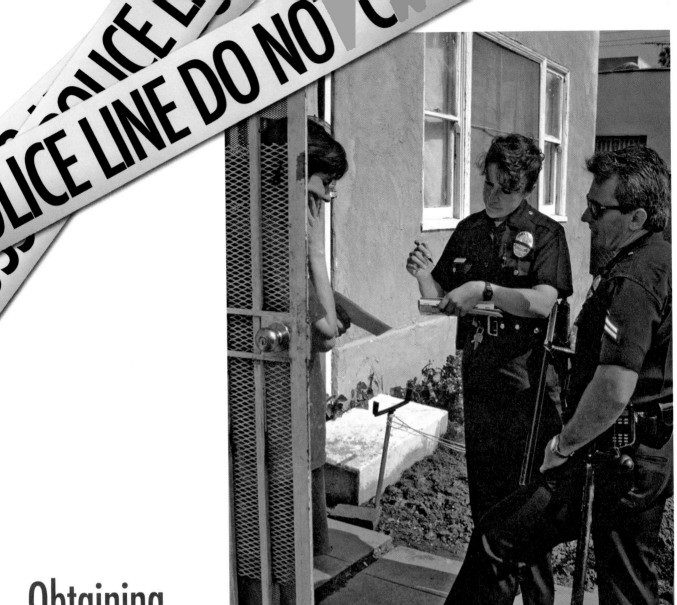

Obtaining Information

PART

3

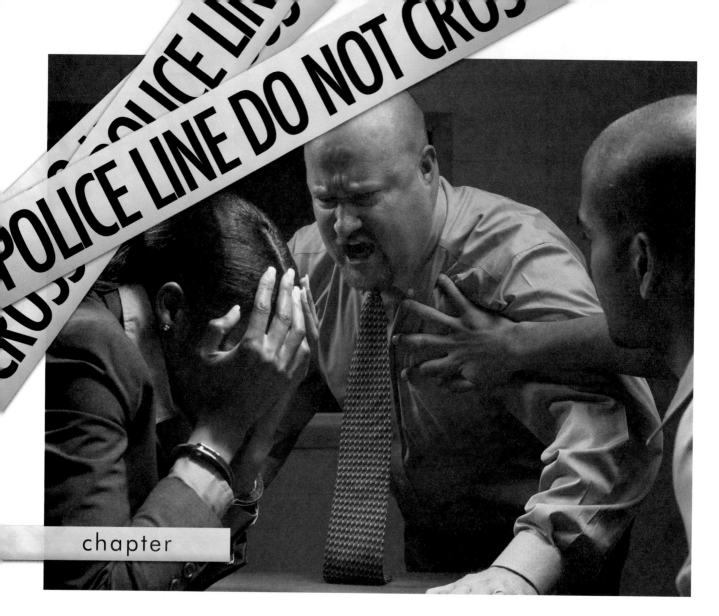

6

Interviews and Interrogations

This chapter will enable you to:

- Explain the distinctions between the interview and interrogation.
- Understand the significance of the *Miranda* decision.
- Appreciate the value of admissions and confessions.
- Explain the different techniques used in interviews and interrogations.
- Understand the process for taking a written statement.
- Realize the investigative utility of the polygraph exam.

Introduction

In their authoritative book, *Criminal Interrogation and Confessions*, Inbau and his associates illustrate the importance of gleaning information through interviews and interrogations. They state: ". . . the art and science of criminal investigation have not developed to a point where the search for and the examination of physical evidence will always . . . reveal a clue to the identity of the perpetrator . . . ."[1] In fact, experience has shown that in many cases, physical evidence is completely absent, and the only remaining approach is the interview of witnesses or the interrogation of the suspect him- or herself.

In cases in which physical evidence is identified and implicates a suspect, the investigator's job is still not finished. The matter of proof and prosecution remains. It is the duty of each investigator to attempt to secure a confession from suspects they have arrested. Again, legal considerations must always be kept in mind to ensure that all statements are admissible in court.

Interviews and interrogations are another fascinating aspect of criminal investigation. This is the phase of the investigation in which the investigator wears a different hat, so to speak. Putting the officer's psychological talents to work may come into play to enhance the chances of a suspect admitting his or her role in a crime.

Interview versus Interrogation

Investigators must make a clear distinction between the two processes of interviewing and interrogating suspects. An interview should precede every interrogation. Through an interview, investigators learn about the subjects and their needs, fears, concerns, and attitudes. They can then use this information to prepare themes or arguments to use during interrogations.[2]

To be a good interviewer or interrogator, the investigator must apply certain physical and psychological techniques to the person being interviewed to persuade him or her to divulge information. In the case of the interview, it is the investigator's job to create an atmosphere in which the subject can be relaxed enough to recall and explain details of a suspected crime. Conversely, when a criminal suspect is being interrogated, the investigator must gently and skillfully break down the suspect's defenses to gain an admission or confession and do so while staying within the constraints of constitutional law.[3] In some countries, physical and mental stress is used as ways to coerce information from both witnesses and suspects. It is generally accepted that a person will confess to anything if enough pressure or intimidation is applied. But is a "confession" really a truthful statement under these circumstances? Certainly not!

During the course of an investigation, an investigator will probably conduct many interviews and several interrogations. The distinction between an interview and an interrogation is often blurred, but it can be expressed in terms of the purpose of the contact. Inbau and his associates state that an **interview** is *nonaccusatory*.[4] It is a relatively formal conversation conducted for the purpose of obtaining information. Notes are taken, and major points are reviewed. Interviews, however, may involve virtually anyone, including informants, witnesses, victims, cooperating citizens, and even the suspect him- or herself. In brief, the interview process occurs either before the case focuses on a particular person or in a place where the suspect can clearly terminate the interview at any time.

By comparison, an **interrogation** is *accusatory*.[5] It is the systematic questioning of a person suspected of involvement in a crime for the purpose of obtaining a confession. Legal guidelines affecting the two activities differ considerably as the probability increases that the person being questioned may incriminate him- or herself.

The Interview Process

The interview is a form of communication used extensively by law enforcement. It is used in many ways to glean information from the subject being interviewed. For example, interviewing is used to screen job applicants, extract information from witnesses or victims of a crime, and obtain a confession from a criminal suspect. Interviews of cooperating citizens and witnesses are often conducted outside the office. More often than not, however, the investigator will have a more productive interview if it can be conducted at a location where the subject is mentally relaxed, such as his or her own home or place of business. Regardless of where the interviews are conducted, investigators should follow certain guidelines due to legal and technical considerations.

Investigators should take the time to prepare properly for the interview. Occasionally, this preparation must be done quickly and may consist of no more than a mental review of the details of the case, but some type of preparation should precede actual contact with the subject being interviewed. Generally, the most common interviews that investigators will conduct are with witnesses, cooperating citizens, victims, informants, and suspects. Let's look at the fundamentals of each of these.

Interviewing Witnesses, Citizens, and Victims

Investigators must remember that although the interview process is geared toward those believed simply to have information about a crime, witnesses often turn out to be suspects. Sources for interviews include the victim, witnesses, and the complainant. These subjects should be separated before questioning begins. The following considerations should be observed during the interview process.

- *Develop a plan of action.* To begin, the investigator should be familiar with pertinent data about the incident in question before initiating the interview. He or she should take care to develop questions designed to elicit the particular task at hand. For example, questions directed to a witness should be tailored to obtain specific facts for the police report. Questions that are prepared in advance will tend to add to the flow of conversation and give direction to the interview.

- *Conduct the interview in private.* It is sometimes easier to fulfill this requirement than others, depending on the circumstances. In all cases, it is important to provide interviewees with the greatest amount of privacy possible, both to encourage clarity of thought and to protect the confidentiality of the interview.

- *Place the interviewee at ease.* Most interviews involve a great amount of stress and emotional discord for the interviewee. This is usually created by a sense of uncertainty about the expectations of the investigator and the uniqueness of the situation. If a degree of fear develops in the person being interviewed, he or she may withhold information. Indeed, it is during the preliminary phase of the interview that the investigator's personality will be tested rigorously. The investigator should therefore take great care to make the person being interviewed as comfortable as possible and to build rapport. In addition, the investigator should attempt to uncover any reasons for the interviewee's reluctance to cooperate. It is also important to relax the person being interviewed because comments made by a calm person are easier to evaluate than those made by someone who is nervous. This can be accomplished by beginning the interview casually with friendly conversation. Certainly, a strained or awkward initial contact with the subject might convey the message that the investigator doesn't like something about the interviewee. A friendly approach will help defuse any negative feelings in the subject and reinforce positive ones.

- *Be a good listener.* After the communication barrier is lifted, the investigator must learn to let the interviewee speak freely. Indeed, this is a great shortcoming of many investigators because many feel the need to interrupt or share their personal opinions with interview subjects. It is the job of the interviewer to listen closely and evaluate not just *what* is being said but *how* it is being said. In short, it is the responsibility of the investigator to control the interview but not to dominate it.

- *Ask the right questions.* Not only is it important to know what questions to ask the subject but also how those questions should be asked. During the conversation, the investigator's emotions should be in check at all times, along with an attempt to make the questions easy to comprehend. In addition, the phrasing of questions is critical to the success of the interview. For example, close-ended questions, requiring a simple yes or no response, should be used sparingly. This type of question doesn't elicit personal information from the subject; it simply permits the person to confirm or deny information being offered. A preferable technique is to ask open-ended questions, which force the interviewee to relate in his or her own words what was observed. Hypothetical questions should also be avoided because they tend to make the interviewee guess at a certain response or to tell the interviewer what he or she wants to hear. Finally, the interviewer should avoid asking loaded, or leading, questions that contain the answer and require the person being interviewed to choose between the lesser of two evils.

- *Don't dispute the subject's answers.* The emotional reactions of the investigator must be kept under control at all times. After the subject gives his or her interpretation of what happened, the investigator can later go back and document any discrepancies.

- *Maintain control of the interview.* Frequently during an interview, the subject might try to steer the conversation away from the subject at hand. Again, proper preparation is the key to having a good plan and to staying on track.

- *Take brief notes.* After the interviewee begins to talk freely, the investigator should avoid interruptions. An attempt to take complete notes while a citizen is narrating a story will probably disrupt the flow of information. This generally occurs because the witness sees the investigator writing profusely and will slow down just to accommodate him or her. In doing so, the witness may become distracted and forget important details. Furthermore, some people are just naturally nervous speaking in the presence of someone recording everything they say. Brief notes are therefore the prescribed method of recording the conversation. These generally consist of names, addresses, and certain phrases that will outline the narrative for review. Most important, however, the investigator should listen carefully and not lose eye contact with the witness.

- *Adjourn the interview properly.* Just as the interview process begins with a proper introduction, it should also end appropriately. Generally, a concluding remark is appropriate, such as: "OK, you may leave—thank you for your time." It might also be advisable to summarize the interview briefly with the witness before dismissal. Such expressions of courtesy during and after the interview create a favorable impression and encourage further cooperation.

The Suspect Interrogation Process

During any case, it is important for information to be obtained by means of a direct interview with a suspect. As indicated earlier, it is not at all uncommon during the progress of a case for a person who was interviewed as a witness or victim to become a primary suspect at a later date. In that event, as the case progresses, the investigator can use information learned in the earlier interview.

Goals of the Interrogation

The interrogation is designed to match new information with a particular suspect to secure a confession. The goals of the interrogation process are as follows:[6]

- To learn the truth of the crime and how it happened
- To obtain an admission of guilt from the suspect
- To obtain all facts to determine the method of operation and the circumstances of the crime
- To gather information that enables investigators to arrive at logical conclusions
- To provide information for use by prosecutors in possible court action

Legal Requirements of the Interrogation

According to early English Common Law, the confession of a suspect was by far the most important type of evidence against an accused person. In many cases, failure to produce such evidence was equivalent to not having any evidence at all. Therefore, investigators vigorously pursued confessions at all costs, with little regard for the rights of those accused or the fairness of their methods. Techniques for obtaining the confession included submersion in water, stretching, branding, and other types of physical and psychological torture. Today, such tactics have been replaced with legal guarantees of fairness, such as the Bill of Rights, the Constitution, and statutes prohibiting the use of coercion or duress in the interrogation process. Still, the confession reigns as one of the most influential types of evidence in a court proceeding.

Safeguarding Against Police Misconduct

Several types of behavior have been identified as improper (even illegal) for police investigators and will result in any confession obtained from the suspect being deemed inadmissible by the courts. These behaviors include coercion or duress, physical constraint, unreasonable delay in arraignment, and refusing legal counsel during interrogation.

Coercion and Duress. Coercion and duress are similar in that they both create an environment of intimidation during the interrogation process. **Coercion** is defined as the use, or threat of use, of illegal physical methods to induce a suspect to make an admission or confession. **Duress** is the imposition of restrictions on physical behavior, such as prolonged interrogation and deprivation of water, food, or sleep. In *Brown* v. *Mississippi* (1936), the U.S. Supreme Court ruled that physical coercion used to obtain a confession was a violation of the Fourteenth Amendment. Following this ruling, the Court focused its attention on cases in which "psychological" rather than physical coercion was used to prompt a confession.

Methods of Coercive Interrogations

Confessions are extremely influential evidence that can often make or break a criminal case. After a confession is given, it is difficult to retract. Consequently, an admission of guilt can ultimately lead to substantial fines, imprisonment, and even execution depending on the nature of the case. It is difficult for most people to imagine why someone would risk such consequences and confess to committing a crime they know for certain they didn't commit. However, it happens more frequently than many realize. Methods used by inexperienced or unscrupulous police interrogators, such as deception, fear tactics, unreasonably long interviews, sleep or food deprivation, and either exaggerating or minimizing the crime. These methods are blamed for a large number of all documented false confessions.[7]

Fear tactics that include direct threats, intimidation, or actual physical abuse, have been known to coerce suspects into falsely admitting guilt to a crime. According to Richard Conti, such confessions are referred to as **coerced-compliant confessions**.[8]

An example of a coerced-compliant confession occurred in March 1983 after the murder of a woman from Pulaski County, Arkansas. Not long after the woman's murder, the police took into custody Barry Lee Fairchild, a young, mentally handicapped black man. Fairchild's lawyers said that while in custody, police interrogators forced their client to confess to the crime after they allegedly placed telephone books on his head and hit the books with blackjacks. It has been speculated that this method was likely used because it leaves no marks but causes considerable pain.[9] Fairchild was found guilty and executed for the murder in 1995, even though he continued to profess his innocence to the end.

Of the many coercive police tactics that have been identified over the years, physical abuse is one of the most brutal methods used to obtain a confession and is unconstitutional. But other less obvious techniques, such as the use of deception, trickery, and other psychological tactics, have also been discovered with greater frequency.[10] For example, in their authoritative book, *Criminal Interrogation and Confessions*, Inbau and associates state: "The use of such tactics is not only helpful but frequently indispensable in order to secure incriminating information from the guilty, or to obtain investigative leads from otherwise uncooperative witnesses or informants."[11]

Wakefield and Underwager state that another technique referred to as **maximization** is the exaggeration of evidence available, telling the person that the interrogator knows he or she is guilty or stressing the consequences of the crime.[12] The maximization method includes falsely telling suspects they have fingerprints linking them to the crime, that they failed a lie detector test, or that an acquaintance of the suspect witnessed him or her committing the crime. This technique can lead to false confessions. This occurs mostly in highly suggestible and confused suspects who actually begin to believe they are guilty of the crime they didn't commit. This is called **coerced internalization**.[13]

During the interrogation process, interviewers can also use minimization, whereby the seriousness of the crime is downplayed and the suspect believes he or she is less likely to get in trouble. This method can prompt a false confession, especially if it is coupled with other coercive techniques. For example, the interviewing detective might say, "You know, I think you're a really good person. I don't think you intended to do the harm that occurred in this case. Maybe it was an accident or maybe you were provoked or under the influence of some drug." The suspect may feel psychological pressure to satisfy the interrogator, especially if he or she admires or fears the interrogator, or the suspect may even believe what he or she is being told and thus falsely confess to the crime.

Another method used to get suspects to confess is to make them sit through long, drawn-out interrogations, which sometimes last more than hours. The suspect often goes without sleep, food, or both and gets so worn down emotionally and physically that he or she is more likely to give false statements in an attempt to end the torture. During such confessions, the police may feed suspects bits of information, which are incorporated into a confession. Similar to physical torture, extended interrogations that are accompanied by sleep and food deprivation are also unacceptable. A number of these techniques were documented as being used in the case of Stephanie Crowe.

Unreasonable Delay in Arraignments

Confessions obtained without coercion or duress may still be deemed unconstitutional and inadmissible if the suspect confessed before being allowed to see a magistrate within a reasonable period after arrest. The case of *McNabb* v. *United States* (1943) first illustrated this vital principle. In this case, McNabb, along with several members of his family, was involved in bootlegging. After the murder of several federal officers in Tennessee, McNabb was arrested for the crime. After his arrest, he was held in custody and was not taken before a magistrate for a considerable period. Subsequently, he confessed and was convicted. The court held that the government's failure to take McNabb before a committing officer was a violation of his constitutional rights; therefore, the confession was inadmissible. What made this case particularly significant is that for the first time, a confession, obtained voluntarily and freely, was still considered illegal because officers failed to comply with other constitutional procedures.

A subsequent ruling in *Mallory* v. *United States* (1957) reaffirmed that an officer making an arrest must take the accused, without necessary delay, before the nearest available magistrate and that an official complaint must be filed without delay. These decisions are based on the due process clause of the Fourteenth Amendment of the U.S. Constitution. The U.S. Supreme Court considers whether or not the case in its entirety represents a good picture of the civilized standards expected in this country.

The Suspect's Right to Legal Counsel

The legal guidelines to protect the rights of the accused were defined further by the U.S. Supreme Court in such cases as *Escobedo* v. *Illinois* (1964) and *Miranda* v. *Arizona* (1966). Surprisingly, before 1964, there were no legal rules requiring the presence of an attorney during the interrogation of a criminal suspect. In a ruling in May 1964, the U.S. Supreme Court reversed the conviction of a lower court because prosecutors had used incriminating statements made by the defendant to a friend that were overheard by a federal agent. The remarks were made after the defendant was indicted and while he was out on bail. The Court held that the statement was made by the defendant without the advice of his attorney, who he had already retained. So, according to the Court, the defendant was deprived of his Sixth Amendment right to an attorney.

In *Escobedo* v. *Illinois* (1964), Escobedo was arrested without a warrant and interrogated in connection with a murder. On the way to the police station, officers told Escobedo that he had been implicated as the murderer and that he should admit to the crime. He then requested to speak to an attorney. After arriving at the police station, his retained lawyer arrived and asked several times to speak with his client. His request was denied on several occasions. In addition, Escobedo requested to speak with his attorney on several occasions and was told that his attorney did not want to speak to him.

Subsequently, the defendant made an admission to the crime and was later found guilty.

The legal question here is: Does a suspect have a right to an attorney if he or she requests one during a police station interrogation? The answer is yes. Following this decision, states were directed to require police to advise every person arrested for a felony that they have a constitutional right to counsel and silence. Despite this, the guidelines for police in interrogation settings were still unclear.

The Miranda Warning. Two years after the *Escobedo* decision, the U.S. Supreme Court reversed an Arizona court's conviction in a kidnapping and rape case that further defined the *Escobedo* decision and the rights of the accused. In the *Miranda* v. *Arizona* (1966) case, a 23-year-old, Miranda, was arrested and transported from his home to the police station for questioning in connection with a kidnapping and rape. He was poor and uneducated. After two hours of questioning, officers obtained a written confession that was used against him in court. He was found guilty of the kidnapping and rape.

The legal question in this case is: Do the police have a responsibility to inform a subject of an interrogation of his or her constitutional rights involving self-incrimination and a right to counsel before questioning? Again, the answer is yes.

In addition to being informed of these rights, the suspect must also agree, freely and voluntarily, to waive them before police can begin questioning. Accordingly, the suspect may invoke his or her right to stop answering questions any time during the interrogation. Several court cases have arisen over the years that relate to *Miranda* and custodial interrogations. For example, *Rhode Island* v. *Innis* (1980) interpreted the meaning of interrogation by stating that in addition to direct questioning, interrogation also refers to any actions or remarks made by police that are designed to elicit an incriminating response.

In another case, *California* v. *Prysock* (1981), the U.S. Supreme Court found that **Miranda** **warnings** do not have to be given in any specific order or with precise wording. Furthermore, in *Edwards* v. *Arizona* (1981), the Court established a "bright line" rule for investigators. The Court found that "all" police questioning must be discontinued after a suspect who is in custody has requested an attorney, even if the *Miranda* warning was given a second time. However, in yet another related decision, *Oregon* v. *Bradshaw* (1983), the Court found that the *Edwards* decision doesn't apply if the suspect simply inquires, "What is going to happen to me now?" In this case, police were allowed to continue questioning the suspect. However, in *Minnick* v. *Mississippi* (1990), the Court ruled that after a custodial suspect requests counsel in response to *Miranda* warnings, law enforcement officers may not attempt to reinterrogate the suspect unless the suspect's counsel is present or the suspect initiates the contact with officers.

In related cases, it has been determined that probation officers need not read the *Miranda* warning to clients (*Minnesota* v. *Murphy*, 1984) and that the *Miranda* warning is not required during the issuance of traffic citations (*Berkemer* v. *McCarty*, 1984). The following year, in *Oregon* v. *Elstad* (1985), the Court decided that even though a confession was obtained before the *Miranda* warning was given, confessions obtained after it are admissible. In 1994, however, in the case of *Davis* v. *United States*, the Court put the burden on custodial suspects to make unequivocal invocations of the right to counsel. In the *Davis* case, a man being interrogated in the death of a sailor waived his *Miranda* rights but later said, "Maybe I should talk to a lawyer." Investigators

FIGURE 6.1 Sample waiver of rights form.

STATEMENT OF RIGHTS AND WAIVER	CITY POLICE DEPARTMENT	DATE
PLACE		
NAME	CASE NO. *(If applicable)*	

Before we ask you any questions, you must understand your rights. You have the right to remain silent. Anything you say can be used against you in court or other proceedings. You have the right to talk to a lawyer for advice before we ask you questions, and to have him with you during questioning. You have this right to the advice and presence of a lawyer even if you cannot afford to hire one. In such a case you have a right to have a court-appointed attorney present at the interrogation. If you wish to answer questions now without a lawyer present, you have the right to stop answering questions at any time. You also have the right to stop answering at any time until you talk to a lawyer.

You may waive the right to advice of counsel and your right to remain silent and answer questions or make a statement without consulting a lawyer if you so desire.

WAIVER

I ☐ have read ☐ had read to me   the statement of my rights shown above. I understand what my rights are and I elect to waive them. I am willing to answer questions and make a statement. I do not want a lawyer. I understand and know what I am doing. No promises or threats have been made to me and no pressure of any kind has been used against me. I was taken into custody at *(time)* _____ ☐ A.M. ☐ P.M., on *(date)* _____, and have signed this document at *(time)* _____ ☐ A.M. ☐ P.M., on *(date)* _____.

WITNESS	SIGNATURE OF PERSON WAIVING RIGHTS
WITNESS	

asked the defendant clarifying questions, and he responded, "No, I don't want a lawyer." Upon conviction he appealed, claiming that interrogation should have ceased when he mentioned a lawyer. The Court, in affirming the conviction, stated: "It will often be a good police practice for the interviewing officers to clarify whether or not [the defendant] actually wants an attorney."

Miranda Warning

A person being interrogated has the right to remain silent; any statement may be used in a court of law. The person also has the right to have an attorney present during questioning. If the suspect can't afford an attorney, one will be appointed for him or her before questioning.

The Public Safety Exception to Miranda. The public safety exception to *Miranda* was ruled on in *New York* v. *Quarles* (1984). This decision found that police officers who are reasonably concerned for public safety may question persons who are in custody and who have not been read the *Miranda* warning. The U.S. Supreme Court also found that subsequent statements are admissible in court. In this case, a woman complained to two officers that an armed man had just raped her. After giving the officers a description of the man, they proceeded to a nearby supermarket, where Benjamin Quarles was located. After a brief chase, the officers frisked Quarles and discovered an empty shoulder holster. After the suspect was in handcuffs, the officer asked Quarles where the gun was, and he nodded in the direction of some empty cartons and said, "It's over there." The gun was retrieved, and Quarles was arrested and read the *Miranda* warning.

> **MIRANDA WARNING**
> 1. You have the right to remain silent.
> 2. Anything you say can and will be used against you in a court of law.
> 3. You have the right to talk to a lawyer and have him present with you while you are being questioned.
> 4. If you cannot afford to hire a lawyer, one will be appointed to represent you before any questioning, if you wish.
> 5. You can decide at any time to exercise these rights and not answer any questions or make any statements.

FIGURE 6.2 Sample *Miranda* warning card carried routinely by officers and used after placing a subject in custody and before questioning.

When the case went to trial, the court ruled that under the requirements of *Miranda*, the statement "It's over there" and subsequent seizing of the weapon were inadmissible at the defendant's trial. On review, the U.S. Supreme Court acknowledged that Quarles should have been given the *Miranda* warnings. However, the Court recognized that the need to have the suspect talk was more important than the reading of the *Miranda* warning. The Court also ruled that if *Miranda* warnings had deterred the suspect from giving such information, the cost to society would have been much greater than the simple loss of evidence: As long as the gun remained in the pile of cartons, it posed a public safety hazard.

Defining Custody. *Miranda* applies only when testimonial evidence is being sought. In addition, it applies only to **custodial interrogations**, not to circumstances in which the suspect is free to leave. The custodial interrogation rule applies not only when the suspect has been arrested before questioning but also when his or her liberty has been restricted to a degree that is associated with arrest. Therefore, an interview itself can also be considered custodial even though no arrest has been made. It depends on the circumstances. For example, if the suspect is being questioned in a relaxed atmosphere at his or her own residence, the *Miranda* warning need not be given. Conversely, if the suspect is approached in his or her own home by officers possessing an arrest warrant, the *Miranda* warning must be given before questioning. In brief, the test is whether the interview is custodial, not whether the investigation has focused on a particular person being interviewed.

Preparation for the Interrogation

In preparation for an interrogation, the investigator should review all important details in the case and be prepared to seek answers to basic questions such as what, when, why, where, and how. In addition, the investigator should give some thought as to what information would be of the most value to the investigation. A series of questions can be drawn up and referred to unobtrusively during the interrogation.

The Interrogation Setting

In addition to the manner in which the interrogator treats the suspect, it is also important to consider the physical surroundings where the questioning occurs. Because of pressure from peers and family members who might be present at the scene, it is important to remove the suspect from familiar surroundings and take him or her to a location with a more sterile and less threatening atmosphere. A key psychological factor contributing to successful interrogations is privacy. This encourages the suspect to feel comfortable in unloading the burden of guilt. The structure of the interrogation setting should also be conducive to the obtaining of confessions. Its surroundings should reduce fear and therefore encourage the suspect to discuss his or her role in the crime. Consequently, the interrogation room should reflect a more businesslike atmosphere than a police-like environment.

The interrogation should be conducted in a room specifically designed for that purpose only. It should be isolated from the bustling activity of the rest of the office, the sound of police radios, overhead intercoms, and other interruptions. Ideally, a soundproof room best serves this purpose. The interrogation room should be well lit but not to the extent that its lights are glaring. In addition, it should be protected from interruptions and equipped with some means of communicating with the outside, such as a buzzer or office intercom. Furnishings should be minimal, consisting of chairs, preferably without a desk, and containing pencil and paper but otherwise nondescript, with no distracting decorations.

Ideally, no obstacles such as tables or desks should block the interviewer's full view of the subject's body. A large portion of nonverbal behavior emanates from the lower body, not just from the hands and face. Feet that fidget or point to the door communicate discomfort. If subjects sit behind a desk or table, the investigator should instruct them to relocate. Deceivers often use soda cans, computer screens, and other objects, both large and small, to form barriers between themselves—behaviors consistent with dishonesty.[14]

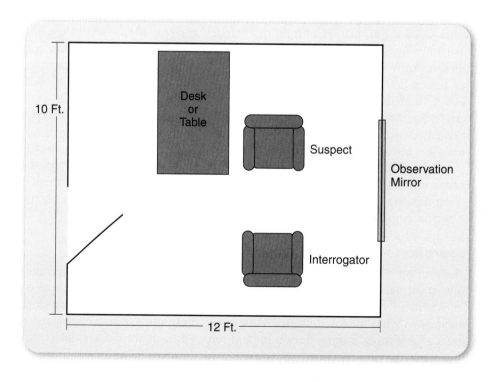

FIGURE 6.3 Physical layout of a police interrogation room.

The Interrogation Procedure

As a rule, two investigators handle the interrogation: One actually conducts the questioning, and the second acts as a witness to statements made by the suspect. Obviously, the two investigators should meet before the interrogation to discuss their "roles." Frequently, one investigator will assume one approach to the suspect, and the other will assume a different and sometimes contrasting style. The suspect may be more receptive to one approach than the other.

Interrogation Styles

Investigators have developed a variety of interrogation styles and techniques over the years. The decision to choose one style over the other may depend on many factors, including the personality of the suspect, the personality of the interrogator, and the nature of the case. Some of the most common styles of interrogation are described below.

- *Logical style.* In a case in which the evidence seems to be overwhelming, such as a drug trafficking case involving a drug purchase from an undercover agent, the investigator may try to appeal to the suspect's sense of logic. In doing so, the investigator, it is hoped, will persuade the suspect that cooperation is the only way the charges against him or her can be lessened. It is important to note here that promises of leniency to the suspect should not be made without direct authorization from the prosecuting attorney. The only promise that can be made is that his or her cooperation will be brought to the attention of the prosecutor for consideration of some kind of leniency.

- *Sympathetic style.* If the investigator thinks that the suspect is easily affected by an emotional appeal, the sympathetic approach might be a good technique. The interrogation is approached by speaking in low tones and will include expressions of concern and understanding for the suspect, his or her spouse, children, business, and so on. The investigator stimulates feelings of self-pity in the suspect when he or she blames others for his or her plight. Ideally, further relief of guilt is achieved by the suspect's agreeing to cooperate with the investigator.

- *Indifferent style.* In this technique, the investigator acts as though he or she does not really care if the suspect cooperates or not but thinks that he or she must go through the motions of making the opportunity available to the suspect. This style suggests that the investigator would rather see the suspect punished severely by the court rather than give him or her the opportunity to gain leniency through cooperation.

- *Face-saving style.* In this approach, the investigator attempts to give the suspect a "way out" that will justify his or her participation in the crime. By systematically rationalizing the suspect's actions up to the point of the violation, describing them as natural consequences of some other problem, the investigator tries to get the suspect to start talking about his or her actions. Periodically, the investigator interjects comments that tend to diminish the importance of the suspect's own involvement in the crime.

- *Egotistical style.* Here the investigator plays on the suspect's sense of pride and precision in the commission of the crime. It is pointed out how daring and difficult the crime was to implement and that it took a great degree of planning and intelligence to pull it off. This approach encourages the suspect to brag about his or her involvement in the crime and to provide additional details to impress the investigator.

FIGURE 6.4 Sample voluntary statement form.

**CITY POLICE DEPARTMENT
VOLUNTARY STATEMENT**

_____
Case #

_____
Date

I _____ am _____ years of age and
currently reside at _____ which is located in the city
of _____.

Statement:

_____

_____

_____

_____

_____

_____

_____

_____

_____

_____

_____

_____

_____

I have read this statement which consists of _____ page(s) and I affirm that it was given
voluntarily and that all the facts are truthful and accurate.

This statement was given at _____ (location) on the
_____ day of _____, 20__, at _____ (am) (pm).

_____
Signed

_____
Witness

_____
Witness

Verbal Symptoms of Deception

Because of certain psychological and cultural differences, a perceptive investigator can sometimes readily identify the manner in which people lie. For example, a trained listener can observe a pattern of evasiveness in the suspect and after a period is able to identify these statements as lies or efforts to deceive.

Liars and Lying. Lying requires the deceiver to keep the facts straight, make the story believable, and withstand scrutiny. When individuals tell the truth, they often make every effort to ensure that other people understand. In contrast, liars attempt to manage others' perceptions. Consequently, people unwittingly signal deception via nonverbal and verbal cues. Unfortunately, no particular nonverbal or verbal cue demonstrates deception.[15] The ability of an investigator to detect deceptive behavior depends largely on his or her ability to observe, catalogue, and differentiate human behavior. The more observations investigators make, the greater the probability of detecting deception. Here are some indicators of deceptive behavior:

> Research has shown that vocal changes occur 95 percent of the time when a person lies. A liar's speech rate and voice pitch will also increase 95 percent of the time.[16] In addition, liars will usually stall before giving an answer, to give them time to decide if they should lie or tell the truth, or to decide just how big a lie to tell. Liars will always attempt to con the investigator. They may choose to tell a big lie, a misleading statement, or the complete truth. In most cases, they will attempt to dodge the truth. For example, they may restate the question or ask to have it repeated. They might say "I can't remember" or that they don't understand the question. If the subject stammers, stutters, or has a mental block before answering the question, most of the time he or she is lying.[17]

Lying Techniques. Liars often lie by using *specifics*. For example, the suspect may say, "I don't even own a gun!" Although this could be a true statement at face value, he or she might have borrowed a gun to commit the crime but is relying on the fact that the statement is a true one, and the investigator will, it is hoped, infer that the suspect didn't commit the crime. Liars tend to admit only what the investigator can prove and deny what can't be proved. In addition, they sometimes make an issue out of trivial things. For example, if a suspect complains about the manner in which the government has treated him in the past, he is probably attempting to sway away from the real issue.

Physical Characteristics of Lying

Head Position

☑ *Tilted:* cooperative, interested, probably truthful

☑ *Jutting forward, no tilt, jaw up:* angry, aggressive, stubborn

☑ *Chin on chest, no tilt:* depressed, bored, probably lying

Eyebrows

☑ *Both raised with mouth partly open:* surprised, probably truthful

☑ *One raised:* confused, skeptical, probably truthful

☑ *Squeezed together and lowered:* angry, worried, confused

Eyes

☑ *Breaks eye contact (1 to 2 seconds is common):* suddenly tensed, probably lying; may not resume eye contact until a new subject is discussed

☑ *Looks at ceiling and blinks:* just decided to confess

☑ *Pupils fully dilated:* high degree of emotional arousal, probably lying

☑ *Closes eyes:* trying to mentally escape, probably lying

(continued)

Physical Characteristics of Lying Continued

☑ *Narrowed eyes:* looking for trouble, anticipating the worst

☑ *Rapid blinking:* nervous, probably lying

Hands

☑ *Covers both eyes:* probably lying

☑ *Hands over mouth:* probably lying

☑ *Hand on chin:* probably truthful

☑ *Touches or rubs nose while talking:* probably lying

☑ *Hands clasped together, holding back of head:* probably truthful

Legs

☑ *Men with crossed legs:* probably lying

Feet

☑ *Moves feet beneath chair:* probably lying

☑ *One foot tucked beneath the other:* probably truthful

Other lying techniques commonly used include the following:

- The suspect tries to confuse the interviewer by arguing about trivial points rather than addressing the real issues.
- A debating tactic is used in which the suspect tries to discount the investigator's argument in advance. For example, if the investigator makes a statement regarding a piece of evidence, the suspect replies, "You don't really expect anyone to believe that, do you?" The big lie or repeated assertion is based on the assumption that if you say something over and over, people will start to believe it. Repeated denial of the violation only reinforces the suspect's ability to lie.
- The "you don't understand" tactic is used by experienced liars to block an in-depth interrogation. This is attempted by saying, "You wouldn't understand," "You don't know how these things work," or "How would someone like you be expected to know?"
- The "loophole" liar is a dodger who is unsure just how much the investigator knows about the crime. Loophole liars typically respond by saying, "I can't remember" or "to the best of my recollection." This technique gives the person a way out in case he or she is later confronted with contradictory evidence.[18]

Why Suspects Cooperate and Confess

When we consider that self-destruction and self-condemnation are not normal human behavioral characteristics, it is perplexing why someone would openly confess to a crime. In addition, one could conclude that when a person is arrested and taken to a police station for questioning, he or she will not readily admit (and even choose to lie about) his or her part in a crime. Many criminals, particularly career criminals, have developed a keen sense of observation over the years. It is likely that this sense has aided them in the past in avoiding detection by police. Such criminals can easily see the direction in which an interrogation is going. Logically, then, one would think that the dialogue between the suspect and investigator would be brief. Strangely, because of complex psychological factors, this is not always the case.

Why do innocent people confess? A variety of factors may contribute to a false confession during a police interrogation. Many cases have included a combination of several of these causes. They include:

- Duress
- Coercion
- Intoxication
- Diminished capacity
- Mental impairment
- Ignorance of the law
- Fear of violence
- The actual infliction of harm
- The threat of a harsh sentence
- Misunderstanding the situation

Searching for Information

Depending on the crime in question and the particular suspect, it is logical to assume that many criminals follow the progress of the police through media accounts of the investigation. Still, they really don't have a good sense of exactly what the investigator knows and doesn't know about the suspect. It is the desire of the criminal to want to know exactly what the investigator knows about the crime. This "paranoia" frequently drives the suspect to accompany the investigator willingly to the police station for an interview. Once at the station, however, the suspect not only tries to learn what the investigator knows about the investigation but also attempts to lead him or her away from the focus of the investigation.

Closing the Communication Gap

Research indicates that most guilty persons who confess are, from the outset, looking for the proper opening during the interrogation to communicate their guilt to investigators.[19] Suspects also make confessions when they believe that cooperation is the best course of action. Before they talk, they need to be convinced that investigators are willing to listen to all the circumstances surrounding the crimes. Finally, suspects confess when interrogators are able to speculate correctly on why the crimes were committed. They want to know ahead of time that interrogators will believe what they have to say and will understand what motivated them to commit the crime.

Admission versus Confession

Although seemingly alike, there is a notable difference between the admission of a criminal act and the confession of one's complicity in a crime. An **admission** is a self-incriminating statement made by the suspect that falls short of an acknowledgment of guilt. It is, however, an acknowledgment of a certain fact or circumstance from which his or her guilt can be inferred. Conversely, a **confession** is direct acknowledgment by the suspect of his or her guilt in the commission of a specific crime or as being an integral part of a specific crime. For the confession to be lawful, the investigator must be mindful of the constitutional checks governing its admissibility.

False Confessions

For a number of reasons, innocent people sometimes confess to crimes they did not commit. These reasons include mental health issues and law enforcement tactics that place undue pressure on suspects to "cooperate."

Although it can be hard to understand why someone would falsely confess to a crime, psychological research has provided some answers. Moreover, in 2009, the Innocence Project reported that through DNA exonerations, the problem is more widespread than many people think. For example, in approximately 25% of the wrongful convictions overturned with DNA evidence, defendants made false confessions, admissions, or statements to law enforcement officials.[20]

The problem of false confessions can be illustrated by the case of Eddie Joe Lloyd. Lloyd was convicted of the 1984 murder of a 16-year-old girl in Detroit after he wrote to police with suggestions on how to solve various recent crimes. During several interviews, police fed details of the crime to Lloyd, who was mentally ill, and convinced him that by confessing he was helping them "smoke out" the real killer. Lloyd eventually signed a confession and gave a tape-recorded statement. The jury deliberated less than an hour before convicting him, and the judge said at sentencing that execution, which had been outlawed in Michigan, would have been the "only justifiable sentence" if it were available. In 2002, DNA testing proved that Lloyd was innocent, and he was exonerated. As mandated in a settlement with Lloyd's family, Detroit Police officials said in 2006 they would start videotaping all interrogations in crimes that could carry a sentence of life.[21]

A number of investigative practices can be identified that help safeguard against false confessions. One of these is recording the interrogation process (discussed earlier). For the recording of interrogations to be effective, the entire custodial interrogation must be recorded. Doing so will improve the credibility and reliability of authentic confessions, will better prepare the investigator's case for trial, and will help protect the rights of innocent suspects.

In some false confession cases, details of the crime are inadvertently communicated to a suspect by investigators during the questioning process. Later, when a suspect knows these details, the police take the knowledge as evidence of guilt. Often, threats or promises are made to the suspect off camera and then the camera is turned on for a false confession. Without an objective record of the custodial interrogation, it is difficult to gauge the reliability of the confession.

For law enforcement agencies, recording interrogations can prevent disputes about how a suspect was treated, create a clear record of a suspect's statements, and increase public confidence in the criminal justice system. Recording interrogations can also deter officers from using illegal tactics to secure a confession.

The Cognitive Interview Technique

mycrimekit

Review: Interrogations and confessions

Another widely accepted interviewing technique is the cognitive interview technique. As a rule, the cognitive interview technique is used for eliciting information from victims and witnesses, opposed to obtaining confessions from suspects. Two main forces were behind the development of the cognitive interview. The first was the need to improve the effectiveness of police interviews when questioning witnesses. The second was to apply the results of psychological research to this area, particularly the work of Elizabeth Loftus, whose research had already dispelled the myth that an eyewitness's memory operates like a video camera.[22] As a result, Ronald P. Fisher of Florida International University and Edward Geiselman of UCLA developed the technique of cognitive interviewing.

A number of differences can be identified between traditional interviewing techniques and the cognitive approach. For example, traditional interviewers attempt to bring out information by asking specific questions; they target a question for each content area that they need to address. For example, if an investigator needs to find out how tall the perpetrator was, then he or she asks the question, "How tall was the perpetrator?" And if the investigator wants to find out what was the angle of the plane that was approaching the airport, he or she would ask a direct question such as, "What was the angle of the plane as it approached the airport?"

The traditional interviewer asks many questions, each of which elicits a very brief response. The cognitive interview, on the other hand, is less directive and is in some ways a questionless interview. The goal is to ask as few questions as possible so that witnesses give you long narrative responses that each contains that much more information than a traditional interview. The objective is to try to elicit information, not extract information. The good interviewer tries to create a social environment so the witness generates information without having to wait for questions to be asked.

The two major subtypes of cognitive interviewing methods are think-aloud interviewing and verbal probing techniques.[23]

"Think-Aloud" Interviewing

The think-aloud interview derives from psychological procedures described by Ericsson and Simon (1980).[24] The term *think-aloud* is used to describe a very specific type of activity in which subjects are explicitly instructed to "think aloud" as they answer the survey questions. The interviewer reads each question to the subject and then records or otherwise notes the processes that the subject uses in arriving at an answer to the question. The interviewer interjects little else, except to say, "Tell me what you're thinking" when the subject pauses.[25]

The advantages of the "think-aloud" interview technique is that it elicits responses from the subject that are free from interviewer bias and that little formal training is required to prepare the interviewer for the use of the technique. The disadvantages are that it is easy for the subject to loose focus and stray from the task.[26]

Verbal Probing Techniques

As an alternative to the think-aloud, the use of verbal probing is the basic technique that has increasingly come into favor by cognitive researchers.[27] After the interviewer asks the survey question, and the subject answers, the interviewer then asks for other, specific information relevant to the question or to the specific answer given. In general, the interviewer "probes" further into the basis for the response. Examples of the probing technique include the following:

> "You stated that you saw the man entering her apartment. What means did he use to gain entry?
> "When you say you saw the men drive away, describe the manner that they were operating the car."

The advantages of the probing technique are that the investigator can control the interview with relative ease, and the subject of the interview can easily adjust to the method used by the investigator.[28]

Written Statements

Because the interrogation will generally produce much more information than is needed for the written statement, the investigator will have to decide what information he or she needs for preparation of the statement. A confession from the suspect should substantiate the elements of the charge or at least contain information related to the investigation. In addition, the statement of the confession should contain any details of extenuating circumstances or explanations offered by the suspect that might be grounds for additional inquiry. Several variables determine what methods are used to take the statement.

These include the intelligence level of the suspect, the amount and nature of information to be recorded, and the availability of stenographic services. In many cases, the suspect will be willing to give a verbal statement about his or her involvement in a crime but might be unwilling to have it written down at the time. If this occurs, the investigator should not interrupt the remarks being made by the suspect just to ask for a signed statement. Instead, after the suspect is finished giving his or her account of what happened, the investigator should ask if the suspect would be willing to sign (or write) a statement to that effect. The suspect should be assured that only the information given to the investigator will be included in the statement and that he or she will have the prerogative of not signing it if it is not accurate. The following techniques can be used if the suspect decides to sign the written statement:

- The suspect may respond orally to the investigator or a stenographer in response to questions. Responses are then written verbatim.
- The suspect may give a statement orally without direction from the investigator. This technique is the most desirable, provided that the end result is a clear and concise statement.
- The investigator could give the suspect a list of the important points to cover during the statement and suggest that he or she include these and other important points.
- The investigator may choose to write the statement according to the information given by the suspect in his or her oral statement.

If these techniques are adopted, the investigator must use the same phrases that were used by the suspect. The completed statement should then be shown to the suspect so that any changes can be made. Once corrections are in order, the statement is signed. The investigator should be careful to make the written statement reflect only one crime because in a criminal trial, the court will ordinarily not permit the introduction of evidence of additional crimes. Exceptions to this are when additional crimes tend to show intent, the identity of the defendant, or the scheme used in the commission of the crime in question. Therefore, the best policy is to obtain a separate written statement for each crime committed.

Structuring the Written Statement

The statement should begin with the place, date, and identification of the maker and the name of the person who is giving the statement. It is acceptable for the body of the statement to be in narrative or expository form. In addition, it should include all the elements of the crime as well as any facts that connect the suspect with the crime. If the investigator or stenographer prepares the statement, the suspect should be asked to read and sign each page at the bottom. To ensure that the suspect actually reads the statement, he or she should be asked to correct any typographical errors and to initial any corrections in ink. Finally, each page should be labeled "page _____ of _____ pages." The concluding paragraph should state that the suspect has read the statement consisting of so many pages and that the statement is "true and correct." After the suspect signs the statement in the space provided, two witnesses should sign it under the suspect's signature. Normally, the witnesses are the interrogators. Any more than two witnesses could leave the impression with the court that the suspect was intimidated by a large number of police at the time of the statement.

Recorded Statements

Frequently, the investigator will choose to record a statement made by a suspect. This can be especially advantageous when the suspect cannot read or write or when he or she is only fluent in a foreign language. One important point to remember is that when the investigator chooses to record the statement, the interrogation should still be conducted first. When it is time to record the statement, the investigator uses his or her notes from the first interrogation to develop the recorded statement. When the recording is complete, the recorded statement is then played back for the suspect to hear so he or she can verify that it is a true and accurate representation of what was said during the interrogation.

The Recording Procedure

The recording should begin with the investigator identifying him- or herself, the suspect, and any other investigators in the room (people entering and leaving the room during the interrogation should also be identified with corresponding times, but at the end of the recording). In addition, the opening remarks should include the location of the statement or interrogation, the time and date of the statement, and a statement by the investigator to the suspect as to why the statement is being recorded. After the important points of the statement are given, the investigator should ask the suspect if there are any additional comments that he or she would like to make.

Afterward, the investigator should state that the recorder is now going to be shut off and that the suspect can listen and verify its contents. After the suspect listens and verifies the recording, it is then turned back on, and he or she should verbally acknowledge that the contents accurately represent the statement and the recorder was not turned off or stopped at any time during the interrogation except for the time when the suspect reviewed the tape. Finally, the investigator states that the session is concluded and repeats the names of the persons in the room and the time and date of the statement. The recording should then be entered into evidence and processed appropriately.

Videotaped Confessions

On the basis of a national survey, it is estimated that one-third of all large police and sheriff's departments in the United States videotape at least some interrogations, a practice that is most common in cases of homicide, rape, and aggravated assault.[29] Proponents claim that videotaping has a number of benefits, such as deterring coercive behavior on the part of investigators and providing a more complete and accurate record of the confession for the judge and jury to evaluate the voluntariness and veracity of the defendant's statement.[30]

For evidentiary purposes, videotaped interrogations should provide a complete and objective record of police–suspect interaction. But the question is still raised—what is a complete and accurate record? For example, in an actual police confession in New York, police were convinced that they recorded a confession from a "neutral" camera angle. The camera was positioned behind the investigator and focused directly on the suspect. Although this may seem innocent enough, research suggests that it is not. On the basis of studies showing that people make causal attributions to factors that are visually salient, Lassiter and his colleagues taped mock interrogations from three different camera angles so that the suspect, the interrogator, or both were visible to mock jurors. The result was that those who saw only the suspect judged the situation as less coercive than those focused on the investigator. By directing visual attention on the suspect, the camera can lead jurors to underestimate the amount of pressure actually exerted by the "hidden" investigator.[31]

Recap Bias

An important related issue concerns whether jurors are shown a tape of the entire interrogation or merely a recap consisting of only the suspect's final confession. Recaps are common and take an average of 15 to 45 minutes.[32] On the question of whether they should be admitted into evidence, there are two possible bases for concern. First, the jury sees a final self-incriminating statement but not the circumstances that led up to it, perhaps increasing perceptions of voluntariness. Second, after recounting a story over and over again, a suspect is likely to show less emotion and appear unusually callous. In light of the fact that people are more forgiving of others who express remorse and apologize for their wrongdoings, recaps may bias the jury against the defendant.[33] At this point, empirical research is needed to examine these possible effects.

Framing the Tapes

A suspect often provides the police with a statement that is not a confession but is instead ambiguous (i.e., denying the charges but telling an implausible story). So what is the persuasive impact of an interrogation tape when the suspect maintains his or her innocence and goes to trial? One possibility is for the state to introduce the tape into evidence to highlight inconsistencies in the defendant's story. But another possibility is for the defense to show the tape and focus the jury's attention on the defendant's denials in the face of pressure.

To examine this question, in a 1990 study, Kassin, Reddy, and Tulloch had mock jurors watch a 45-minute "confession" of an actual murder suspect who asserted her innocence but told an implausible story. For some participants, the tape was introduced by the prosecution, who harped on the inconsistencies of the story; for others, it was shown by the defense lawyer, who noted that the defendant maintained her innocence despite pressure to confess (the tape was always followed by the lawyer's argument). Results showed that among participants, those who saw the tape being introduced by the prosecution rather than the defense were more likely to vote guilty.[34] With statements that are ambiguous enough to accommodate opposing interpretations, the adversarial advantage goes to the party that introduces the tape and frames it for the jury.

Use of the Polygraph

mycrimekit

Simulation: Interviewing the suspect

Of the mechanical devices that have been designed to aid investigators in obtaining information, the **polygraph**, or "lie detector," has proven to be of extreme value. Proper use of this tool can help an investigator determine a suspect's guilt or innocence. However, because of recent court rulings restricting the use of the polygraph in certain settings, the investigator should view this device as an aid only, not as a last resort or panacea.

The polygraph is designed simply to measure whether or not the person being tested is being deceptive. As the subject is asked different questions, the graphs observed by the operator will, it is hoped, indicate a truthful or a deceptive response. Indeed, the device does not actually do what its moniker indicates—it does not detect lies. What it does do is measure the physiological responses from the subject, including fear, anxiety, excitation, and other emotions. So the critical consideration in the use of a polygraph is not the machine itself but the operator's ability to interpret its results accurately.

Accuracy of the Polygraph

The criminal justice field is divided as to its acceptance of polygraph results. In fact, most courts do not accept the findings of a polygraph exam as absolute evidence except when stipulated to by all parties. Problems with the use of the polygraph have been in its application. Specifically, the machine should be used to identify statements as being false, not for the purpose of actually detecting lies.

The value of an examination can be looked at in two regards: reliability and validity. *Reliability* refers to the consistency of the examination's results. This can be shown through reproducing the examination repeatedly and obtaining the same results. Indeed, when properly administered, the polygraph can produce very reliable results. *Validity* refers to the accuracy of the examination. Validity can be affected by two considerations. First is the ability of the polygraph examiner to interpret the results of the examination accurately. Second, if the measurements that are recorded by the instrument fail to indicate lying directly, it lacks validity.

Administration of the Polygraph Exam

Before the exam occurs, the examiner will request certain information from the investigator. Such information includes the specific offense in question, a copy of the case file, a list of the different types of evidence, specific personal information about the subject, and any physical or psychological data about the subject, if known.

A polygraph examiner then attaches a probe to a person's chest and fingers to record his or her heart rate, respiration, and sweat gland activity during the course of questioning. Responses to questions are charted automatically, and from responses to both innocuous and relevant questions, the examiner can generally determine if the person is being deceptive.

Next, specific questions are structured, usually in a "yes" or "no" format. These questions are reviewed with the subject before he or she takes the test. This is to relax the person taking the test and, it is hoped, to elicit an admission of additional details of the alleged crime. When the test is completed, the subject is generally advised of the results in writing. If deception was detected, the subject might be interviewed about the weak points of the test. Frequently, this part of the process results in the subject's admitting to additional complicity in the crime.

Although the polygraph should not be considered a last-resort effort to obtain a suspect's confession, it can save money for the investigating agency. For example, it can weed out suspects in an investigation and let the focus of the investigation fall on specific persons.

Admissibility of Polygraph Results

Over the years, the courts have addressed various aspects of the issue of polygraph results and their admissibility in court. Clearly, the machine can only detect certain changes in the human body, and estimates are that such changes can be detected up to 95 percent of the time. Despite arguments in favor of the use of the polygraph, its results are not currently admissible as absolute evidence in court. One early court case upheld a ruling of a trial court that refused acceptance of the results of the polygraph (*Frye* v. *United States*, 1923). Later that same year, the court in *People* v. *Forts* considered the results of the polygraph inadmissible based on doubts about the instrument's reliability. The *State* v. *Bohner* (1933) case also failed to accept the results of the polygraph but acknowledged its usefulness. Exceptions occur, however,

A CLOSER LOOK

Is the Polygraph Junk Science?

Although the courts still call it "junk science," the lie detector or polygraph has never been so widely used by criminal justice agencies as a tool for determining the truth. In 1998, the U.S. Supreme Court ruled against the use of polygraph evidence in criminal court, but police agencies still rely on the polygraph exam to make critical personnel decisions from hiring to firing. Over the years, the percentage of police agencies using polygraphs to screen new employees increased from 16 percent in 1962, for example, to 62 percent in 1999, according to a study conducted by Michigan State's School of Criminal Justice. The same survey shows that police are confident of exam results—more than three-fourths believe that polygraphs are 86 to 100 percent reliable.

At the FBI, which employs over 11,000 agents, senior officials have requested permission to administer up to 225 polygraphs per year in investigations of suspected employee misconduct. That figure is in addition to the 3,000 tests given each year to new agents and witnesses and informants in major criminal investigations. The CIA, National Security Agency, Defense Department, Treasury Department, and many large police departments across the nation also depend on the polygraph. Failing a polygraph, as in the case of scientist Wen Ho Lee at Los Alamos National Laboratory in New Mexico, can end a career just as quickly as a guilty verdict. Lee was fired after he failed an FBI-administered polygraph in March 1999 and refused to cooperate with the government's investigation of Chinese espionage at the facility, which is the nation's premier weapons facility.

Fearing unwarranted invasions of individual privacy, Congress passed the *Employee Polygraph Protection Act* of 1988 to curb what had been a growing use of polygraph tests in private business. In 1998, the U.S. Supreme Court expressed concerns about the reliability of polygraphs when it upheld the military's ban on use of them in criminal trials. Yet government agencies still consider polygraphs a valuable personnel tool.

Thematic question

Given concerns about the accuracy of the polygraph and it admissibility in court, how can this investigative tool be used in the course of an investigation? Is it more prudent for a law enforcement organization to rely on cognitive interviewing techniques than the use of the polygraph to elicit admissions and confessions? Explain your response.

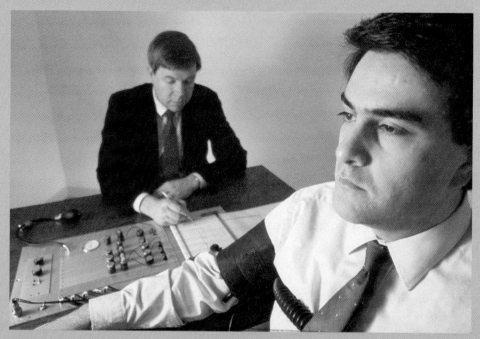

FIGURE 6.5 Photo of a man undergoing a polygraph test while answering questions from an examiner. Woodfin Camp & Associates, Inc.

Sources: Johnson, K. (1999). Government agencies see truth in polygraphs. *USA Today*, April 6:11A; McCarthy, S. (2000). The truth about the polygraph. Health & Body website. Available at: http://archive.salon.com/health/feature/2000/03/02/polygraph/index.html.

when all parties stipulate to the acceptance of the results before administration of the exam.

The Voice Stress Analyzer

An investigative tool gaining considerable popularity with law enforcement agencies is the voice stress analyzer (VSA). Unlike the computer polygraph, the VSA requires no wires be attached to the subject being tested. The VSA uses only a microphone plugged into the computer to analyze the subject's responses. As the subject speaks, the computer displays each voice pattern, numbers it, then saves each chart to file. Unlike the polygraph, drugs do not affect the results of the exam, and there are no known countermeasures that will cause the ubiquitous "inconclusive" results associated with the polygraph.

Rapidly supplanting the polygraph, the VSA has been used in many investigative situations such as homicide, sex crimes, robbery, white collar crimes, and internal affairs investigations, as well as pre-employment examinations for background investigators. The system has been used as an investigative tool for verifying statements of witnesses and denials of suspects and for determining the validity of allegations made against police officers.

Microtremors are tiny frequency modulations in the human voice. When a test subject is lying, the autonomic, or involuntary, nervous system causes an inaudible increase in the microtremor's frequency. The VSA detects, measures, and displays changes in the voice print frequency.

A laptop computer processes these voice frequencies and graphically displays a picture of the voice patterns. Furthermore, the VSA is not restricted to "yes" and "no" answers and is able to accurately analyze tape recordings of unstructured conversations.

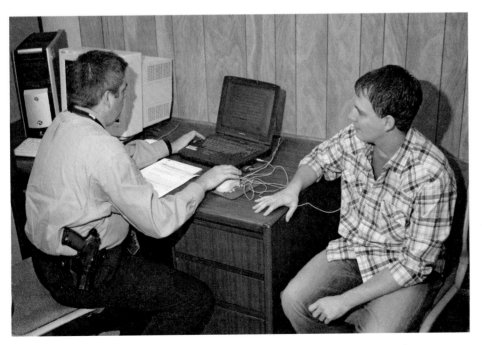

FIGURE 6.6 For many police organizations, the voice stress analyzer test, as shown here, has replaced the use of the polygraph because it is portable and more accurate and training is only a fraction of that required by polygraph training programs. Courtesy of Mike Himmel.

CASE IN POINT:

The Stephanie Crowe Murder Investigation

Interviews and interrogations can result in the incorrect implication of a suspect. This is illustrated in the case of 12 year-old Stephanie Crowe, who was found dead in her bedroom in Escondido, California, on January 20, 1998.

On that date at 6:30 A.M., the noise from Stephanie's alarm clock radio caused her grandmother, Judith Kennedy, to go the girl's room to see why Stephanie hadn't shut it off. Kennedy found her granddaughter wet with blood. Stabbed nine times through her bed covers, the petite brunette was dead. The six-year investigation, however, had more than its share of challenges and illustrates the consequences when officers are too quick to react to a confession that turns out to be false.

Police learned that six hours before Stephanie's body was discovered, witnesses saw Richard Raymond Tuite, a 28 year-old transient, standing in the Crowes' driveway looking up at their house. Another witness claimed she saw Tuite screaming and spinning around with his hands in the air in the proximity of the Crowes' house that night. Tuite's bizarre behavior that night, which also included his peering into windows of neighborhood houses, led to his being picked up by police the next morning as a possible suspect. The next day, Tuite was detained. The police questioned him about the murder. They took fingernail scrapings and clippings and photographs of him, confiscated his clothing and gave him a sweat suit, and released him. One detective later testified that Tuite was too "bumbling" to have killed the child so stealthily as to not wake her family. The police investigation quickly turned toward the family.

After Stephanie's body was discovered, the police separately interviewed each member of the entire Crowe family. They specifically focused their attention on Stephanie's 14-year-old brother Michael, who was questioned for 27 hours over a 3-day period. They also extensively interviewed two of his closest friends. By the time the interrogations ended, the police had obtained a confession from Michael and one of his friends and enough incriminating evidence from the third boy to file murder charges against them all.

Although the boys allegedly confessed, there was a great deal of doubt concerning the accuracy of their statements and the method used to get them. The police allegedly used lies, false promises, isolation from parents and attorneys, and even threats of

adult prison and predatory older inmates as persuasive techniques to get a confession.

The manner in which the boys claimed to have been interviewed prompted an investigation to determine whether they were coerced into confession. False confession expert Richard Leo analyzed the videotaped interrogations and came to a shocking conclusion. He determined that the interrogations were textbook examples of how not to question suspects, finding that it amounted to a form of psychological torture so coercive that the boys would have said almost anything to make it stop.

Investigators heard about sibling rivalry, about fantasy stories Michael Crowe had penned in which a brother and sister battle, and about a plot the trio of high school freshmen supposedly dreamed up to kill the seventh grader. In the interrogation, Michael Crowe wailed as he said he didn't remember killing his sister, but if the police had evidence pointing to him, then he must have done it. The boys quickly recanted. After much legal wrangling, most of their damning statements were excluded. One of the boys later testified he made up the story, stating, "[I would have] chewed off my own leg" to make the questioning stop. Before the murder trial even began, all charges against the boys were dropped because it became evident they had nothing to do with Stephanie's murder. The boys' exoneration rested on some key evidence—specks of Stephanie's blood that were found on two items of Tuite's clothing.

DNA testing of those items eventually linked Tuite to Stephanie's blood. After Tuite's arrest, many wondered why the DNA tests weren't conducted earlier and why Tuite wasn't held longer. Critics believed that the police were in such a hurry to solve the crime that they failed to conduct a proper investigation or even an ethical interrogation of suspects. In May 2004, Tuite was found guilty of voluntary manslaughter and sentenced to 13 years in a state prison. Resulting from the case were at least two books, a made-for-TV movie about the investigation, and some national media attention. In the meantime, the Crowe family sued the police department and prosecutors for violating Michael's civil rights during his interrogation.

Not only does this case illustrate the importance of conducting a proper and professional interrogation, but it also shows how when a suspect is incorrectly identified, the real perpetrator goes free. It is no small miracle that Tuite did not claim another

CASE IN POINT continued

victim after being released from his initial detention with police.

Thematic question: From a proactive investigative standpoint, in what ways can crimes such as this be prevented? Consider investigative efforts by both patrol officers and investigators.

Sources: Chacon, D. J. Verdict brings mixed reaction in Escondido. *Union-Tribunes SignonSanDiego.com*, May 26, 2004; Sauer, M. and J. Wilkens. Haunting questions: The Stephanie Crowe murder case. *Union-Tribunes SignonSanDiego.com*, May 11, 1999; Witt, A. and P. Schwartzman. Prince Georges prosecutor targets questioning; police must provide interrogation notes. *Washington Post*, June 7, 2001.

Summary Checklist

In this chapter, we consider the ways that information about crimes is documented by the criminal investigator. A properly documented case is one that is more likely to succeed in court. See how well you are able to answer the following questions in your checklist.

1. **Can you explain the difference between the investigative interview and an interrogation?**

   Investigators must make a clear distinction between the two processes of interviewing and interrogating suspects. An interview should precede every interrogation.

   - An interview is a relatively formal conversation conducted for the purpose of obtaining information.

   - An interrogation is the systematic questioning of a person suspected of involvement in a crime for the purpose of obtaining a confession.

2. **What is the process for conducting an investigative interview?**

   The investigator will have a more productive interview if it can be conducted at a location where the subject is mentally relaxed, such as his or her own home or place of business.

   - Sources for interviews include the victim, witnesses, and the complainant.

   - These subjects should be separated before questioning begins.

   - The investigator should be familiar with pertinent data about the incident in question before initiating the interview.

   - It is important to provide interviewees with the greatest amount of privacy possible

   - The investigator should take great care to make the person being interviewed as comfortable as possible and to build rapport.

   - It is the job of the interviewer to listen closely and evaluate not just *what* is being said but also *how* it is being said.

   The right questions should be asked:

   - Closed-ended questions, requiring a simple yes or no response, should be used sparingly.

   - A preferable technique is to ask open-ended questions that force the interviewee to relate in his or her own words what was observed.

   - Hypothetical questions should also be avoided.

3. **Can you explain the process of conducting a suspect interrogation?**

   The interrogation is designed to match new information with a particular suspect to secure a confession.

   - To learn the truth of the crime and how it happened

   - To obtain an admission of guilt from the suspect

   - To obtain all the facts to determine the method of operation and the circumstances of the crime

(continued)

Summary Checklist (Continued)

- To gather information that enables investigators to arrive at logical conclusions
- To provide information for use by prosecutors in possible court action

Coercion and duress are similar in that they both create an environment of intimidation during the interrogation process. These should both be avoided during the process.

Legal guidelines should also be observed such as the reading of the *Miranda* warning and the provision of an attorney after the suspect requests one.

4. Identify the procedures for conducting an interrogation.

In preparation of an interrogation, the investigator should review all important details in the case and be prepared to seek answers to basic questions such as what, when, why, where, and how.

A key psychological factor contributing to successful interrogations is privacy.

- The interrogation should be conducted in a room specifically designed for that purpose only. It should be isolated from the bustling activity of the rest of the office, the sound of police radios, overhead intercoms, and other interruptions.
- The decision to choose one interrogation style over the other can depend on many factors, including the personality of the suspect, the personality of the interrogator, and the nature of the case. Styles include logical, sympathetic, indifferent, facesaving, and egotistical.

The investigator should be aware of signs that suggest a suspect is lying.

- When individuals tell the truth, they often make every effort to ensure that other people understand. In contrast, liars attempt to manage others' perceptions.
- Liars often lie by using specifics.

Investigators should seek an admission or confession from the suspect.

- An admission is a self-incriminating statement made by the suspect that falls short of an acknowledgment of guilt.
- A confession is direct acknowledgment by the suspect of his or her guilt in the commission of a specific crime or as being an integral part of a specific crime.

5. Can you identify the known methods of improperly conducting an interrogation of a criminal suspect?

Methods used by inexperienced or unscrupulous police interrogators include deception, fear tactics, unreasonably long interviews, sleep or food deprivation, and either exaggerating or minimizing the crime. These are blamed for a large number of all documented false confessions. These methods include:

- Coerced-compliant confessions: Fear tactics that include direct threats, intimidation or actual physical abuse.
- Maximization: The exaggeration of evidence available, telling the person that the interrogator knows he is guilty or stressing the consequences of the crime.
- Coerced internalization: When highly suggestible and confused suspects actually begin to believe they are guilty of the crime they didn't commit.

6. How should a suspect statement be properly documented?

A confession from the suspect should substantiate the elements of the charge or at least contain information related to the investigation. In addition, the statement of the confession should contain any details of extenuating circumstances or explanations offered by the suspect that might be grounds for additional inquiry.

- The completed statement should then be shown to the suspect so that any changes can be made.
- After corrections are in order, the statement is signed.
- It is preferable to record the suspect's statement

7. **Compare and contrast the polygraph and the voice stress analyzer as investigative tools.**

   The polygraph, or "lie detector," has proved to be of extreme value.

- It is designed simply to measure whether or not the person being tested is being deceptive.
- Most courts do not accept the findings of a polygraph exam as absolute evidence except when stipulated to by all parties.

Unlike the computer polygraph, the VSA requires no wires be attached to the subject being tested.

- The VSA uses only a microphone plugged into the computer to analyze the subject's responses.

Key Terms

admission
coerced-compliant confessions
coerced internalization
coercion

confession
custodial interrogations
duress
interrogation

interview
maximization
Miranda warning
polygraph

Discussion Questions

1. Discuss the practical differences between the terms *interview* and *interrogation*.
2. Define *coercion* and *duress* and discuss how they taint the interrogation process.
3. Discuss how the *Escobedo* and *Miranda* cases affect the interrogation process.
4. Discuss the legal implications of the term *in custody*.
5. Describe the procedure for recording a suspect's statement.
6. Explain the uses of the polygraph in the interrogation setting.

mycrimeKit™

Go to MyCrimeKit.com to explore the following study tools and resources specific to this chapter:

- *Practice Quiz:* Multiple-choice, true/false, short-answer, and essay questions.
- *Flashcards:* There are 12 key terms in this chapter. Flashcards test your knowledge of the chapter's key terms.
- *Web Links:* Check out the hotlink to *The New York Times* criminology articles.
- *Career Center:* Check out the hot links to interesting careers in criminal justice, criminology, and juvenile justice.
- *The Research Center:* Check out the Cybrary and research navigator for even more resources.

Notes

1. INBAU, F., J. REID, J. BUCKLEY, and B. JAYNE (2001). *Criminal interrogation and confessions*, 4th ed. Gaithersburg, MD: Aspen Publishing.
2. VESSEL, D. (1998). Conducting successful interrogations. *FBI Law Enforcement Bulletin* October.
3. BOETIG, B. P. and A. BELLMEMER. (2008). Understanding Interrogation. *FBI Law Enforcement Bulletin* 77(10).
4. INBAU, F., J. REID, J. BUCKLEY, and B. JAYNE (2001). *Criminal interrogation and confessions*, 4th ed. Gaithersburg, MD: Aspen Publishing.
5. IBID.
6. TOUSIGNANT, D. D. (1991). Why suspects confess. *FBI Law Enforcement Bulletin* March:14–18.
7. LACAYO, R. (1991). Confessions that were taboo are now just a technicality. *Time*, April 8; LaPeter, L. Torture allegations dog ex-police officer. St. Petersburg *Times*, August 29, 2004; Liptak, A. Study suspects thousands of false convictions. *The New York Times*, April 19, 2004.
8. CONTI, R. P. (1999). The psychology of false confessions. *The Journal of Credibility Assessment and Witness Psychology* 2(1):13–26.
9. CHACON, D. J. Verdict brings mixed reaction in Escondido. *Union-Tribunes SignOnSanDiego.com*, May 26, 2004.
10. HUMES, E. Experts say false confessions come from leading questions, young suspects, high-pressure interrogations. Knight Ridder/Tribune News Service, October 28, 2004.
11. INBAU, F., J. REID, J. BUCKLEY, AND B. JAYNE (2001). *Criminal interrogation and confessions*, 4th ed. Gaithersburg, MD: Aspen Publishing.
12. WAKEFIELD, H. and R. UNDERWAGER (1998). Coerced or nonvoluntary confessions. *Behavioral Sciences and the Law* Autum:423–440.
13. IBID.
14. NAVARRO, J. and J. SCHAFER (2001). Detecting deception. *FBI Law Enforcement Bulletin* July.
15. IBID.
16. U.S. DEPARTMENT OF JUSTICE, DRUG ENFORCEMENT ADMINISTRATION (1988). *Drug enforcement handbook*. Washington, DC: U.S. Government Printing Office.
17. IBID.
18. EVANS, D. D. (1990.). 10 ways to sharpen your interviewing skills. *Law and Order* Aug:90–95.
19. COLEMAN, R. (1984). Interrogation: The process. *FBI Law Enforcement Bulletin* April:27.
20. INNOCENCE PROJECT web site (2009). Available at http://www.innocenceproject.org/understand/False-Confessions.php
21. IBID.
22. LOFTUS, E. F. and M. J. GUYER (2002). Who abused Jane Doe? The hazards of the single case history. *Skeptical Inquirer.* Available at http://www.csicop.org/si/2002-05/jane-doe.html.
23. FORSYTH, B. and J. T. LESSLER (1991). Cognitive laboratory methods: A taxonomy. In P. Biemer, R. Groves, L. Lyberg, N. Mathiowetz, and S. Sudman (Eds.), *Measurement errors in surveys.* New York: Wiley.
24. ERICSSON, K. A. & SIMON, H. A. (1980). Verbal Reports as Data. Psychological Review, 87, pp. 215-251.
25. WILLIS, G. B. (1999). *Cognitive interviewing: A "how to" guide.* Short course presented at the 1999 Meeting of the American Statistical Association: Research Triangle.
26. IBID.
27. IBID.
28. IBID.
29. GELLER, W. A. (1983). Videotaping interrogations and confessions. Washington, DC: Department of Justice, National Institute of Justice. *Research in Brief* March.
30. KASSIN, S. A. (1997). The psychology of confession evidence. *American Psychologist* 52(3):221–233.
31. LASSITER, G. D. and A. A. IRVINE (1986). Videotaped confessions: The impact of camera point-of-view on judgments of coercion. *Journal of Applied Social Psychology* 16:268–276; LASSITER, G. D., R. D. SLAW, M. A. BRIGGS, and C. R. SCANLAN (1992). The potential for bias in videotaped confessions. *Journal of Applied Social Psychology* 22:1838–1851.
32. GELLER, W. A. (1983). Videotaping interrogations and confessions. Washington, DC: Department of Justice, National Institute of Justice. *Research in Brief.*
33. ROBINSON, D. T., L. SMITH-LOVIN, and O. TSOUDIS (1994). Heinous crime or unfortunate accident? The effects of remorse on responses to mock criminal confessions. *Social Forces* 73:175–190.
34. KASSIN, S. M., M. E. REDDY, and W. F. TULLOCH (1990). Juror interpretations of ambiguous evidence: The need for recognition, presentation order and persuasion. *Law and Human Behavior* 14:43–55.

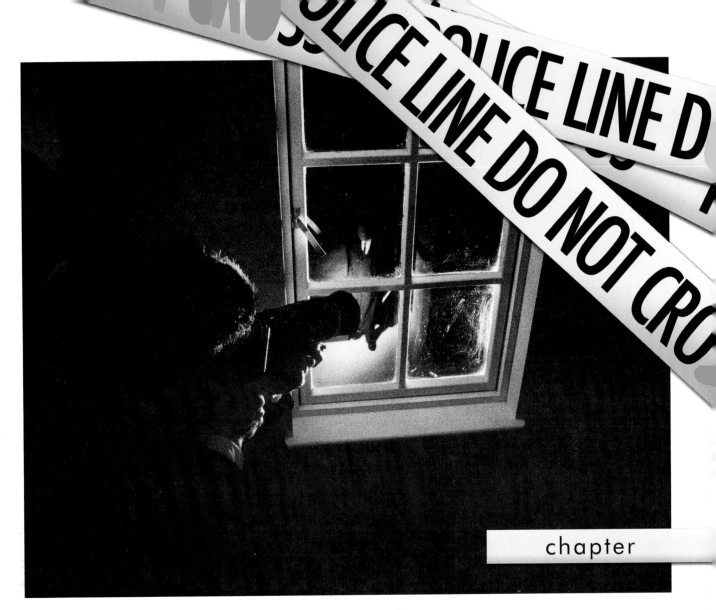

chapter

Criminal Intelligence and Surveillance Operations

7

This chapter will enable you to:

- Understand the roles and types of criminal intelligence.
- Identify the procedures of intelligence collection.
- Explain the types of flowcharting used in intelligence-gathering operations.
- Understand the usefulness of undercover investigations.
- Describe the steps and resources required to properly implement an undercover investigation.
- Explain the types of surveillance in criminal investigation as well as the benefits of a properly conducted intelligence operation.

Introduction

Information gathering, whether done consciously or unconsciously, is a regular part of a police officer's daily responsibilities.[1] The collection of criminal intelligence is another important function of the criminal investigative process and is one that has resulted in significant identification and arrest of major crime figures. Illustrating the importance of the intelligence function, leading expert in the field of terrorism and counterterrorist tactics Brian Jenkins made an argument regarding the need for developing criminal intelligence when he notes that:

> [P]hysical measures don't reduce terrorism—they only move the threat along. Society cannot invest enough resources to protect everything, everywhere, all the time. Someone wanting to set off a bomb in Manhattan to kill scores of people can do it. And reducing terrorism has nothing to do with access control or how thick you make the concrete wall. It requires going after the terrorists and taking their groups apart.[2]

Unfortunately, from a national level, the United States apparently lacks the intelligence capabilities necessary to adequately combat terrorism according to a major interagency study of federal capabilities and defenses. The 73-page report, commissioned by the U.S. Justice Department, pinpoints a lack of intelligence sharing on domestic terrorists as a significant problem and added that "the single most significant deficiency in the nation's ability to combat terrorism is a lack of information, particularly regarding domestic terrorism."[3]

Although the above deals specifically with domestic and international terrorism, the same observations hold true with regard to the prevention and interdiction of many other serious crimes. An effort to identify criminal groups and the persons who participate in and control them requires a systematic approach to information collection and analysis. Intelligence within the law enforcement context, whether of a tactical or strategic nature, refers to the collection, collation, evaluation, analysis, and dissemination for use of information relating to criminal or suspected criminal activities of a wide variety. Development of a systematic approach to this function within police agencies is essential to put what may otherwise be scattered—or even unrecorded—information and data to use in a constructive and concerted manner.

The History of Intelligence Collection

The collection of information for intelligence purposes has a long history. For hundreds of years, governments and their military forces have engaged in various activities to obtain intelligence about individuals and groups viewed as threatening. Although the origins of intelligence gathering by the police in the United States are difficult to determine, it appears that the intelligence function was first carried out by large-city police departments when immigrants first concentrated in urban centers of this country. Nationality groups thought to be threatening by virtue of their suspected involvement in vice, narcotics, racketeering, and organized criminal activities were singled out as the primary targets of police intelligence efforts.

The intelligence operations of federal, state, and local police agencies shifted focus over the decades based on perceived needs and threats. For example, during Prohibition, intelligence operations concentrated on crimes directly and indirectly related to alcohol smuggling and sales and its connections to organized crime. In the post–World War II era, intelligence was used to gather information on suspected Communist organizations, and during the Vietnam War period, it shifted more toward information gathering on political activists and dissidents, civil rights demonstrators, and antiwar protesters. Intelligence operations have long been used to aid in monitoring and building information on organized crime operations and are still widely used in this manner, although their focus has expanded to include the involvement of international conspiracies involved in drug trafficking. Most recently, intelligence operations have been directed at countering the threat of domestic and international terrorism. Considering the bombings of the World Trade Center (2001) and the federal building in Oklahoma City (1995) and the continued threat of terrorist activities, the need for law enforcement intelligence operations has become even more apparent.

Pitfalls of Intelligence Gathering

Although intelligence plays a key role in law enforcement operations, history tells us that it can also be the instrument of abuse if such operations are not properly organized, focused, and directed. Aggressive intelligence gathering operations that resemble fishing expeditions have been used improperly in the past to garner sensitive or confidential information on individuals for whom there is no reasonable suspicion of criminal activity. After it has been documented, such information can develop a life of its own if sufficient safeguards are not built into screening, reviewing, and managing intelligence files. If passed on to other law enforcement agencies as intelligence, it can form the basis for abuse of civil liberties and potential civil liability.

In the same manner, intelligence operations are misguided if they directly or indirectly gather information on persons based solely on their dissident political activities or views because they espouse positions or philosophies that are perceived to threaten conventional social or political doctrines, traditionally accepted social mores, or similar societal values or institutions. Use of law enforcement intelligence resources to intimidate, inhibit, or suppress such activities under the pretext of legitimate police concern for maintaining social order is at best misguided and, in the worst-case scenario, constitutes a threat to the principles of law enforcement in a democratic society.

The Usefulness of Intelligence

It is important to have an understanding and appreciation of potential abuses of criminal intelligence operations so intelligence gathering can be properly directed and information thus collected properly controlled and managed. That said, it is also important to reemphasize the indispensable role that criminal intelligence plays in support of law enforcement and the ultimate protection of society. Even though the Justice Department report is no doubt accurate in its assessment that this nation's intelligence resources are lacking in many regards, particularly with respect to the new threats of chemical, biological, and nuclear terrorists, it tends to overlook many of its successes.

This is probably nowhere better illustrated than in the efforts of local, state, and federal agencies in thwarting international and domestic terrorism in the United States. This concern came to the forefront after the September 11, 2001 attack on the World Trade Center and the Pentagon. It is worth noting that as devastating as these were, we often miss the fact that many attacks of a similar or even a potentially more devastating nature have been thwarted largely through the development and use of criminal intelligence.

Since the September 11, 2001 terrorist attacks, the United States has been fortunate to avoid subsequent terrorist attacks within its borders. But much of that is attributable to the efforts of enhanced intelligence resources. The vast majority of such incidents against the United States continues to be focused against U.S. targets abroad. The largest percentage of terrorist attacks in this country are bombings by special interest groups perpetrated against commercial establishments located in urban areas, such as the Animal Liberation Front, Up the IRS, and the Earth Night Action Group. Organizations such as these and right-wing groups such as the Aryan Nation, the Order, and Posse Comitatus are among the more threatening. At the same time, left-wing terrorist groups, such as the Marxist-oriented United Freedom Front, have been generally inactive since the 1980s due in part to the extensive number of arrests of group leaders during the past decade, largely serving as a credit to good intelligence operations.

Organized crime that has traditionally occupied a great deal of the focus of intelligence operations, while still a prominent threat, has experienced serious setbacks over recent years due largely to effective intelligence gathering operations and aggressive prosecution.

But domestic and international terrorism and organized crime are certainly not the only focus of criminal intelligence operations for state and local law enforcement agencies. State and local law enforcement share in the responsibility to counter these threats. Their input into regional and national intelligence databases is essential to this effort.

But state and local law enforcement agencies also are concerned with more provincial criminal matters. Defining these local criminal enforcement objectives and priorities forms the basis for needed information required to drive the intelligence function of individual agencies. Information gathering by individual officers is at the heart of any intelligence operation. Without the input of the officer on the beat, the generation of intelligence that can be returned to these officers for strategic and tactical purposes is not possible. Support of the agency's intelligence function is, therefore, the responsibility of every law enforcement officer who provides necessary information to fuel the process. And if raw information provides the indispensable material to fuel the intelligence function, a professionally organized system of information evaluation, collation, analysis, and dissemination is the refinement process that turns this raw information into useful products in support of law enforcement operations.

Intelligence, even the best of intelligence, does not produce decisions. Decisions on the use of law enforcement manpower and resources are made by command personnel who use intelligence constructively within the context of their professional experience. But without good intelligence to point the way and weigh the options, law enforcement executives are at a serious disadvantage.

Overt and Covert Intelligence Collection

Overt information collection includes personal interaction with people, many of whom are witnesses to crimes, victims of crimes, or the suspects themselves. To best facilitate the overt collection process, agency administrators should require officers from all divisions to document any information on suspected criminal activity and to pass on such information to intelligence officers. The patrol division can be especially instrumental in the overt intelligence collection process by noting any activity around residences or businesses operated by major criminals in the area. Findings should be reported on a special intelligence report form and forwarded to the proper investigators.

Covert information collection is the most common and includes a process known as **intelligence gathering.** This is a process of data collection on criminal acts that have not yet occurred but for which the investigator must prepare. Covert intelligence collection methods use physical surveillance, electronic surveillance, informants, and undercover officers. In this chapter, we discuss both the intelligence collection functions of criminal investigation and techniques for obtaining information through interviews and interrogation.

Criminal Intelligence and Criminal Investigation

The process of intelligence gathering originated as a function of the military but has now expanded to include "criminal" intelligence as it applies to domestic law enforcement. Despite its technological and scientific advancements, criminal intelligence gathering is one of the least understood aspects of criminal investigation. Additionally, it is probably one of the most valuable (yet underused) resources of the police function.

Defining Criminal Intelligence

To set the pace for this chapter, we should first attempt to define the term *criminal intelligence.* According to the federally funded RISS (Regional Information Sharing Systems) projects (discussed later in this chapter), criminal intelligence is defined as knowledge of past, present, or future criminal activity that results from the collection of information that, when evaluated, provides the user with a basis for rational decision making.[4] Many law enforcement agencies assign sworn personnel to the criminal intelligence division. However, many departments have difficulty adequately defining the mission of the intelligence unit or the tasks of officers working within it, so officers often conduct multiple duties within the unit. Some of these duties are not relevant to the intelligence collection objective. In a practical sense, because it serves the department by delivering information to line personnel, the role of intelligence personnel is more of a staff than a line function. Officers may therefore experience difficulty adjusting to their staff-related duties.

Technically, the role of intelligence personnel is to deliver information to line personnel. To absolve any confusion about the differences between the criminal intelligence function and the criminal investigation function, the four fundamental differences between the two are discussed next.

1. Criminal investigations are usually reactive in nature. Intelligence gathering, conversely, is a proactive function.

2. Criminal investigators generally work with deductive logic. This works by a logical progression through a sequence of events—the general to the specific. An example is collecting evidence from the crime scene, interviewing any witnesses, checking a suspect's criminal records, and so on.

   Intelligence unit personnel, conversely, exercise inductive logic. This affords them the luxury of beginning with the specific and expanding to the general.

3. Investigation case files are generally considered **open files**. They contain information developed for the purpose of eventually making an arrest and gaining a conviction in a court of law.

   In comparison, intelligence files are **closed files**. They contain information regarding ongoing criminal activity, but much of this information has not been verified as factual.

4. Intelligence files must therefore be maintained apart from criminal investigation files to prevent unauthorized inspection of data. The successful culmination of a criminal investigation is the arrest or conviction of a suspect in a crime. Successful intelligence operations are gauged by the cataloging of an intelligence product.

Types of Intelligence

The distinction between the different types of intelligence is often unclear because various methods are commonly used by different departments. To best understand the most common types of intelligence—strategic and tactical—the following definitions will be considered:

1. **Strategic intelligence** plays a role in the investigation of crimes by providing the investigator with a tool for long-range planning. Simply stated, it provides the investigator with information as to the capabilities and intentions of target subjects. Strategic intelligence has proved most useful in organizing long-range plans for interdiction in areas of criminal activity over extended periods.

2. **Tactical intelligence** targets criminal activity considered to be of immediate importance to the investigator. Specifically, tactical intelligence furnishes the police agency with specifics about individuals, organizations, and different types of criminal activity.

FIGURE 7.1 Intelligence report.

It is important to note that many police organizations have established criminal intelligence units that work with criminal investigators. These units are excellent resources of information for investigators who are following leads such as the identification of suspects, suspect associates, where suspects bank or hang out, what vehicles they drive, and other relevant information. On the national level, for example, the FBI is the lead agency for preventing and investigating intelligence activities on U.S. soil. In fact, it is the second highest priority for the FBI because foreign espionage poses a threat to the nation's national security.[5]

The FBI's counter-intelligence investigations have resulted in numerous arrests of suspects on American soil who have, in one way or another, compromised the safety and security of the nation. An example is the case of FBI Special Agent Robert Hanssen.

Hanssen was 56-year-old at the time of his arrest at a park in Vienna, Virginia, in February 2001. At the time, he was secretly placing a package containing classified information at a prearranged, or "dead drop," site for pick-up by his Russian handlers. On an estimated 20 occasions, Hanssen had received substantial sums of money from the Russians after clandestinely leaving packages for the KGB and its successor agency, the SVR, at dead drop sites in the Washington, DC, area. He also provided more than two dozen computer diskettes containing additional disclosures of information. Overall, Hanssen gave the KGB and SVR more than 6,000 pages of valuable documentary material. During the time of his illegal activities, Hanssen was assigned to New York and Washington, DC, where he held key counterintelligence positions. As a result of his assignments, Hanssen had direct and legitimate access to voluminous information about sensitive programs and operations. Hanssen used his training, expertise, and experience as a counter-intelligence agent to avoid detection to include keeping his identity and place of employment from his Russian handlers and avoiding all the customary "tradecraft" and travel usually associated with espionage. The turning point in this investigation came when the FBI was able to secure original Russian documentation of an American spy who appeared to the FBI to be Hanssen, which the investigation into his activities later confirmed.[6]

Procedures For Intelligence Gathering

The intelligence collection process should be thought of as a process of connecting a series of interrelated components of information. Failure on the part of the investigator to adequately connect any of these components could jeopardize the success of the investigation. Therefore, everyone associated with the collection process must have a keen understanding of the entire intelligence function and its various components. The intelligence function includes target selection, data collection, data collation and analysis, and dissemination.

Phase 1: Target Selection

Target selection is the first phase of the process. To obtain the greatest success, intelligence targets must be selected in a systematic manner. They may be based entirely on the utility, or size, of the target or available resources of the department. Factors for investigators to consider in selection of a suitable target include the following:

- Does this target conform to the unit's goals and objectives?
- Does the department (unit) have sufficient resources for the operation?
- What is the expected value of the target?

FIGURE 7.2 Intelligence target selection.

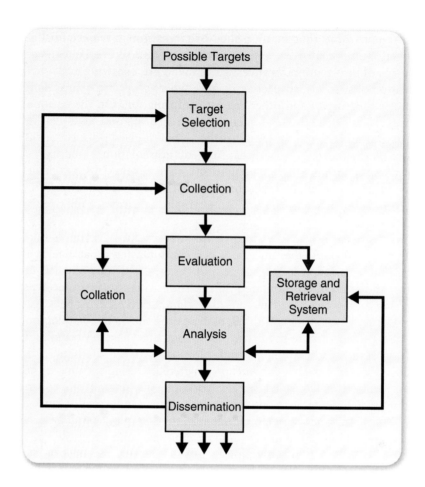

Factors to consider in selection of suitable intelligence targets include:

1. *Utility.* This is the worth of the successful result. If the desired information is collected, how valuable is the result? In determining target utility, consider the following:
   - Type of criminal activity
   - Amount and frequency of criminal activity
   - Impact of criminal activity

2. *Probability of success.* What are the chances of success with this target? In determining probability of success, consider:
   - Amount of effort to be expended
   - Experience and expertise of the intelligence unit personnel
   - Past success rate in similar operations
   - Availability of sources of information

3. *Required resources.* What resources are required to collect the desired information? When determining resources, consider the following:
   - Personnel hours—the primary required resource
   - Equipment
   - Confidential funds
   - Travel expenses
   - Amount of time required

4. *Objective.* The primary objective of selecting a target is to guarantee that intelligence efforts are focused toward targets that are an acceptable balance to merit or value, probability of a successful result, and resources used.

Phase 2: Data Collection

Collection of criminal information is the hallmark of the intelligence function and may be done overtly, covertly, or as a combination of both. Written policy should dictate exactly what types of information may or may not be gathered. Because the collection of both personal and sensitive information on individuals could be a high-liability issue for some communities, great care is warranted by the police agency. Generally, intelligence information regarding any suspected criminal activity can be gathered, such as the following:

- Drug trafficking
- Extortion
- Pornography
- Fraud
- Bribery
- Robbery
- Murder
- Gambling
- Prostitution
- Labor racketeering
- Fencing
- Burglary
- Forgery

In addition:

- Organizations that advocate the use of violence or other unlawful means to affect any unit of government
- Organizations that possess or attempt to control shipments of arms, explosives, or controlled chemicals or biological weapons for unlawful purposes
- Organizations that finance violent or unlawful activity
- Organizations whose actions constitute unlawful activity targeted toward other organizations or individuals
- Leaders of organizations such as those above

Information should not be gathered merely because of a person's membership in organizations unless such organizations meet the criteria set forth previously and are found to present a clear and present danger to society. Under no circumstances should information be gathered solely on the basis of race, creed, color, national origin, sexual preference, or political or religious beliefs. After the information is obtained, intelligence units are faced with the problem of maintaining a storage and retrieval system so that the information can become available when needed. Generally, this is done with a computer, but many departments prefer to rely on index cards as a simplified and more secure system. Information to be cataloged may originate from many different sources:

1. Information from investigators assigned to the intelligence unit
2. Information from nonintelligence departments of the agency, for example:
   - Offense reports
   - Arrest records
   - Field interrogation reports
   - Identification photographs
   - Fingerprint files
   - Warrant files
   - Traffic records
3. Information from other federal, state, and local jurisdictions

4. Information from sources other than law enforcement organizations, for example:

- Newspapers
- Trial records
- Telephone companies
- Public utilities

- Credit agencies
- Banks
- Professional associations
- Insurance companies

Phase 3: Data Collation and Analysis

The third phase in the procedure is the information collation process. *Webster's Dictionary* defines **collation** as "the process of comparing texts carefully" to clarify or give meaning to information. One example of collation is taking a deck of playing cards and arranging them into four piles, one pile for each suit, and in numerical order. Many different techniques are used by intelligence analysts to accomplish this function. These include linked data charts, different types of flowcharts, frequency distribution charts, and so on. Many of these are discussed later in the chapter. Following the collation of raw information is the analysis chase. This is the heart of any intelligence system, the procedure in which meaning is given to all of the otherwise fragmented parts of data collected. The analytical process involves data integration and clarification, inference development, inference testing, and finalizing inferences that are relevant and meaningful to the user (the intelligence product).

Phase 4: Dissemination

The **dissemination** stage of the intelligence process is the final stage, in which the process most commonly breaks down. As one intelligence analyst once remarked: "Possessing good intelligence information is like possessing gold nuggets because everybody wants as much as they can get but nobody wants to share what they have." Unless intelligence is shared through the law enforcement community in an interagency fashion, all of the effort and expense of collecting it could become meaningless. Most law enforcement agencies have strict guidelines, however, as to the release of information (e.g., who gets what information).

Analyzing the Information

The purpose of **analysis** is to make fragmented information flow in a logical sequence to make it purposeful to the user, such as taking a group of surveillance reports and arranging them in the order in which they occurred to determine primary suspects, locations most frequented, vehicles driven, and so on. Intelligence gathering can be problematic in and of itself. For example, when officers are working with large amounts of information regarding individuals and organizations, the sources of that information may be varied and unorganized and may include confidential informants, surveillance reports, police reports, investigative reports, and so on.

Link Analysis

To make sense out of the multitudes of information, a process known as *data description and integration* is used. Accordingly, one of the most common methods of data description and integration is link analysis. **Link analysis** charting is a technique designed to show relationships between individuals and organizations using a graphical visual design. It is used to show graphically transactions or relationships that are too large and confusing for one to assimilate through

CAREERS: DEA INTELLIGENCE RESEARCH SPECIALIST JOB DESCRIPTION

As a DEA Intelligence Research Specialists, you will have the opportunity to be a part of the nation's leading drug law enforcement agency. You will be recognized worldwide for your skills, commitment, and achievements in working closely with DEA Special Agents to conduct the most significant drug investigations and counter-drug operations within the U.S. and abroad. Need an exciting place to live? Our Intelligence Research Specialists positions are located in most major U.S. cities, other domestic areas, and foreign countries that need DEA's support in combating drug trafficking, violent crime, and terrorism. Come and use your intelligence skills at DEA to contribute to our nation's war on drugs and terrorism.

Qualifications:

DEA's Intelligence Division seeks candidates who have experience that demonstrates the ability to:

- Analyze information, identify significant factors, gather pertinent data, and develop solutions;
- Plan and organize work; and
- Communicate effectively orally and in writing.

Such experience may have been gained in administrative, professional, or technical positions.

Employment requirements:

Intelligence Research Specialists are subject to reassignment to any location in the United States depending on the needs of the DEA. All applicants must be available for relocation throughout their career with DEA and will be required to sign a statement to this effect when accepting an offer of employment.

Newly hired Intelligence Research Specialists must complete the Basic Intelligence Research Specialist Training Course. All applicants interested in applying for jobs at DEA must also be able to meet all DEA Employment Requirements and comply with DEA's Drug policy.

All applicants must meet the certain conditions of employment to be eligible for employment at DEA. These conditions include

- U.S. Citizenship
- Successfully pass a DEA administered drug test for illegal drugs
- Complete a DEA Drug Questionnaire to show compliance with the DEA Drug Policy (See DEA Drug policy for more information)
- Successfully pass a background investigation
- Register with the Selective Service System, if male and born after 12/31/1959

You will not be eligible for employment at DEA if you do not meet these requirements. All of theses requirements are thoroughly reviewed during the entire employment process. Please make sure you can meet all of these requirements before applying for a position with DEA.

Background Investigations

DEA, in its unique capacity as the world's eminent drug law enforcement agency, identifies, investigates, and targets for prosecution, organizations and individuals responsible for the production and distribution of illegal drugs. In many cases, our work is sensitive in nature. Therefore, all employees are required to go through an extensive background investigation. Once you have received and accepted a conditional offer of employment, DEA will initiate a background investigation. This investigation includes a credit and criminal records check; interviews of you, co-workers, employers, personal friends, educators, neighbors; and for some occupations a polygraph examination. Additionally, there are certain employment requirements employees must meet to be eligible for employment at DEA. Please use the following links to see if you meet the employment conditions.

DEA Drug Policy

Drug testing is required and continues throughout a career at DEA. Applicants who are found, through investigation or personal admission, to have experimented with or used narcotics or dangerous drugs, except those medically prescribed, will not be considered for employment with DEA. Exceptions to this policy may be made for applicants who admit to limited youthful and experimental use of marijuana. Such applicants may be considered for employment if there is no evidence of regular, confirmed usage and the full background investigation and results of the other steps in the process are otherwise favorable. Compliance with this policy is an essential requirement of all DEA positions.

Source: Drug Enforcement Administration, 2009 (Accessed in website: http://www.justice.gov/dea/resources/careers/opportunity/intel-research-spec.html

the reading of reports. Typically, decisions made using this method are accomplished through deductive reasoning.

There are several ways to illustrate this type of collation technique suitably. In all cases, the investigator must follow certain mechanical rules for the structure of the diagram. These include:

- Assembly of raw data (usually from a report)
- Selection of certain data points, such as names of individuals or organizations
- Construction of a collation matrix showing the data points
- Entry of the association points on the matrix
- Tabulation of the number of association points on the matrix
- Designation of the types of relationships by drawing different types of lines from one association point to another (usually accomplished by drawing dotted lines, solid lines, and so on)
- Relationship of individuals to organizations by constructing circles for individuals and boxes for businesses
- Examination of final diagram and recommendation(s) regarding a course of action

To illustrate the process of link analysis, consider the following scenario as if it were information from a surveillance report. The objective should be to determine the most appropriate target. Johnson and Taylor are long-time close associates and were cell mates in the Missouri State Prison in 1996. Every Tuesday during the month of October, Johnson met with Stephens at the Playboy Lounge for lunch. Public records reveal that Johnson is the sole owner of Equity Auto Sales. Taylor and Mullen are both employed at Tiger Beverage Company and have been observed on numerous occasions riding to work together.

On November 3, Johnson met Washington in the South Park Shopping Center parking lot at 3:00 P.M., and both sat in Washington's car for approximately 1.5 hours. After Johnson left, Washington drove to Anderson's residence.

The Role of the Intelligence Analyst

- ☑ To guide data collection
- ☑ To suggest operational recommendations
- ☑ To provide information to decision makers
- ☑ To assume a position of noninvolvement in policy formation

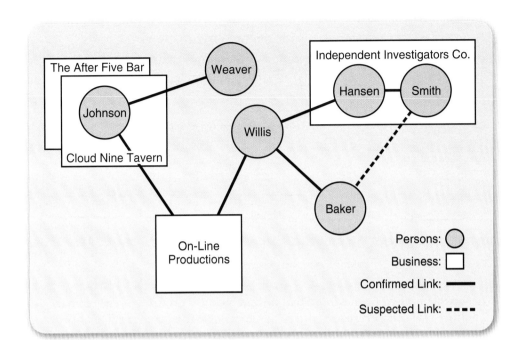

FIGURE 7.3 Hypothetical link analysis chart.

There, Anderson entered Washington's vehicle, and they drove away. The surveillance team lost them approximately two miles from Anderson's residence, due to heavy traffic. Two hours later, Washington and Anderson returned to Anderson's residence, and both went inside. On three separate occasions, Taylor has been seen with an unidentified man believed to be Stephens. "Pen register" records from Mullen's telephone reveal that several calls were made each day to Equity Auto Sales. The relationships in which each of the suspects is involved may reveal who is the most appropriate target. One can see how the method of link analysis can aid in an understanding of complex raw criminal information.

Flowcharting

Flowcharting is another common technique used in the data description and integration phase. Unlike the "frozen" nature of the link analysis diagram, the flowchart demonstrates a chain of events or activities over a period. Although use of flowcharts is not as common as link analysis, two types of flowcharts have emerged as the most useful in criminal intelligence collection: *event flow analysis* and *commodity flow analysis*. Both types of analysis give investigators a graphic display of a series of events that might be too complex if read in a report. There are no hard-and-fast rules regarding the construction of flowcharts; therefore, the analyst should try to maintain a degree of consistency throughout the chart regarding the symbols used.

Event Flow Analysis. Event flow analysis is usually conducted early in an investigation. Examples of flow analysis include charting a brief description of an event enclosed in a symbolic area such as a circle or rectangle. As different events are documented, they are connected by arrows to indicate the direction of the sequence. Consider the following scenario and observe how the information from a reliable informant can best be portrayed by using the event flowchart.

Kevin Johnson is a local businessman in town and owns three small businesses. On August 12, Johnson's Deli burned to the ground, and another of his stores, the Barbecue Shack, was vandalized. Later that night, Johnson's convenience store was bombed. Although Johnson couldn't say for sure who the

FIGURE 7.4 Hypothetical event flow analysis chart.

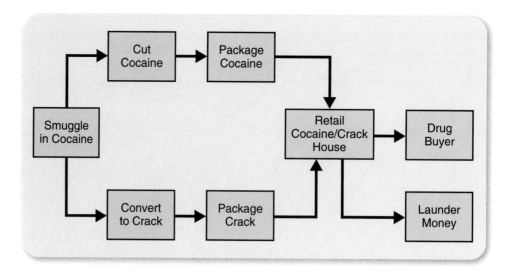

perpetrator might be, he noted that he had recently fired a 34-year-old part-time employee who had threatened Johnson as he left the property. This firing took place one week before the problems with the stores.

Commodity Flow Analysis. Commodity flow analysis may greatly simplify the investigative process by charting the logical flow of such commodities as drugs, money, and illegal arms shipments. For example, in a drug distribution network, if money can be traced from its origin to certain key individuals, an investigation will probably result in an arrest and conviction. This is particularly useful when the main drug kingpins don't typically possess the drugs themselves.

The structure of a commodity flowchart is generally the same as that of the event flowchart except that rather than descriptions of events being placed in circles or rectangles, persons or businesses are used. A scenario follows in which commodity flowcharting might best be used. Study this information from an investigation report and observe how the resulting flowchart illustrates and clarifies the facts and circumstances of the case.

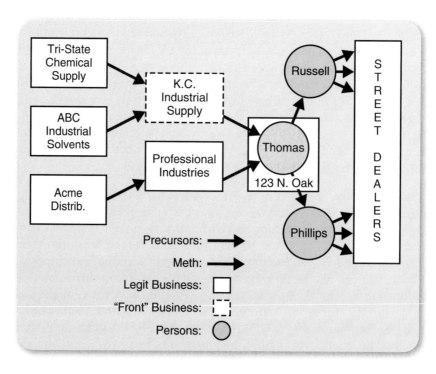

FIGURE 7.5 Hypothetical commodity flowchart.

Eddie Jaso purchased cocaine weekly from Sharon Martin. Jaso paid Martin about $20,000 per week on average. Undercover narcotics agents observed Jaso, along with Mario Barbisca and Timothy Freisen, selling cocaine to several known drug users at a local mall video arcade on several occasions over a period of one month. Records seized during a search of room 32 of the Bradford Hotel showed this location to be a trafficking site for drugs. The hotel's catering department served as a cover for the cocaine distribution network. Seized records also showed payments of about $40,000 per week each from Barbisca and Freisen to the catering department. Records revealed a monthly average of $300,000 in payments to Leonard Smith for various "supplies." Smith, a close associate of Freisen for the past two years, makes monthly deposits of about $500,000 to his accounts at Central Savings and Loan. He also makes large withdrawals on occasion. Both Smith and Freisen have records for drug trafficking.

The RISS Projects

The RISS program began with funding from the Law Enforcement Assistance Administration (LEAA) discretionary grant program. Since 1980, **RISS projects** have been placed under the Justice Department and have been funded on a yearly basis by the U.S. Congress. The primary basis for the establishment of the six RISS projects is to provide criminal justice agencies throughout established regions with a means by which criminal intelligence can be shared among member agencies. According to the Justice Department, intelligence-related services are provided to more than 150,000 sworn law enforcement officers in more than 1,700 criminal justice agencies throughout the United States. Specifically, the services offered member law enforcement agencies are:

- A centralized database
- Analysis of intelligence and investigative data
- Specialized equipment on loan
- Confidential funds
- Technical assistance
- Specialized training
- Access to telecommunications systems

All states throughout the country are placed in one of the six RISS regions:

1. *Western States Information Network:* Alaska, California, Hawaii, Oregon, Washington
2. *Rocky Mountain Information Network:* Arizona, Colorado, Idaho, Montana, Nevada, New Mexico, Utah, Wyoming
3. *Mid-State Organized Crime Information Center:* Illinois, Iowa, Kansas, Minnesota, Missouri, Nebraska, North Dakota, South Dakota, Wisconsin
4. *Regional Organized Crime Information Center:* Alabama, Arkansas, Florida, Georgia, Kentucky, Louisiana, Mississippi, North Carolina, Oklahoma, South Carolina, Tennessee, Texas, Virginia, West Virginia
5. *Middle Atlantic-Great Lakes Organized Crime Law Enforcement Network:* Delaware, District of Columbia, Indiana, Maryland, Michigan, New Jersey, New York, Ohio, Pennsylvania
6. *New England State Police Information Network:* Connecticut, Maine, Massachusetts, New Hampshire, Rhode Island, Vermont

The goal of the RISS projects is to aid state and local law enforcement agencies in the organizing and sharing of criminal intelligence. The very existence of the massive project illustrates the importance of criminal intelligence information in the field of criminal investigation.

Auditing and Purging Files

Intelligence files that are no longer accurate, or not relevant to the mission of the unit, do not pertain to investigative interests and activities, or contain insufficient supporting documentation are among those that should be purged. When files are deficient in one or more of these areas, consideration may be given to updating or improving them through validation and other means. However, when the basic information contained in these files is of such an age or of such poor quality as to make these efforts either too costly or unproductive, a decision should be made to purge the file. A record of any purged files should be maintained by the department.

Use of a qualified outside auditor is typically the best approach to purging intelligence files. This is because independent third parties remove much of the bias or the appearance of bias that may be evident when using in-house intelligence personnel. Although a yearly review of the files for purposes of purging useless materials is recommended, this does not preclude the destruction of files on an ad hoc basis when appropriate and with the approval of the intelligence or investigative unit.

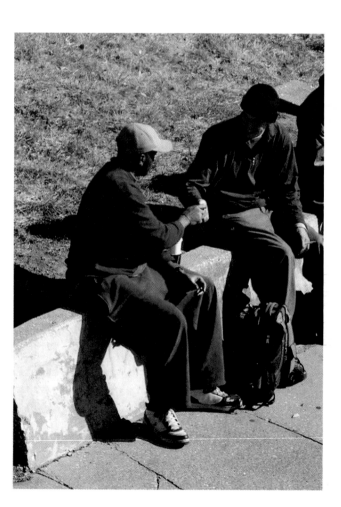

FIGURE 7.6 Photo of a crack cocaine transaction taken via stationary surveillance one-half block away.

Surveillance Operations

Similar to undercover operations, conducting surveillance requires using the team concept. The considerable resources required for surveillance draw personnel away from other investigative functions. The potential also exists for alerting the subject of the investigation to law enforcement's interest, which conceivably could compromise the covertness of not only the surveillance but the entire investigation as well. Proper preparation at the onset can make the difference between a productive surveillance and expending considerable resources without any results.[7] Perhaps the most challenging task in criminal investigation is to keep a suspect under surveillance without arousing his or her suspicions. Surveillance is a process that may take place under a variety of conditions for which the officer must be prepared. The teamwork concept is usually necessary because most surveillance operations involve more than one officer, one mode of travel, and one location.

A surveillance operation may be directed toward a person, a vehicle, or a location for the purpose of bringing an investigation into sharp focus. By identifying individuals in obtaining detailed information about their activities, the criminal investigator can accomplish the following:

- Obtain evidence of a crime
- Prevent the commission of an act or apprehend a suspect in the commission of an act
- Locate persons or watch their hangouts and associates
- Obtain probable cause for obtaining search warrants
- Obtain information for later use in an interrogation
- Develop leads and information received from other sources
- Obtain admissible legal evidence for use in court
- Protect undercover officers or corroborate their testimony

Preparing for the Surveillance

Before initiation of the surveillance, a study should be made of all files relating to the suspects, their activities in crimes, their working and neighborhood environments, and the vehicles involved in the case. In studying information relating to the suspects, the officer should focus on names and aliases used by suspects and detailed physical descriptions, including photographs when available. When possible, the suspect should be pointed out to the surveillance officers.

Identifying characteristics and mannerisms of the suspect should also be studied by the officers. The habits and normal routines of the suspects should be examined, as well as their probable suspicion of, and ability to elude, the surveillance operation. The identities and descriptions of known or suspected contacts or associates should be known, and the officer should be knowledgeable about the scope and extent of crimes and activities in which the suspects are involved.

The officers must also familiarize themselves with the type of neighborhood in which the operation will take place, concentrating on such aspects as the type of inhabitants, their dress, and their use of language. This information will assist the officers in blending in with the neighborhood.

The types of equipment used by surveillance officers are limited only by the improvisational ability of the officers themselves. For example, on a short-term surveillance of a building, the surveillance officers may use utility belts with tools and hard hats to adopt the appearance of public utility employees or may use some other type of "cover" equipment.

A physical reconnaissance should study the areas where the surveillance will take place and identify vantage points suitable for the officers. Similarly, traffic conditions should be observed, and the officers should become familiar with the names and locations of streets in the area, including locations of dead-end streets that may be used by the suspect to spot surveillance officers. The reconnaissance will also yield information on the neighborhood and its inhabitants that would not be in the police files.

The officer must mentally and physically prepare him- or herself for surveillance operations. The officer needs to realize that he or she must be patient and possess endurance. Perseverance is needed while waiting for the suspect to appear or to doggedly follow a suspect through the same routine day after day.

The officer must be alert and resourceful because regardless of careful planning, there are always many unanticipated occurrences in surveillance work. The officer must develop keen powers of observation and memory because often he or she is unable to write down all events, descriptions of contacts, or times as they occur. Furthermore, the officer must prepare a logical explanation for being in a particular place at a particular time in the eventuality that he or she is approached by the subject and accused of following him or her.

The officer must address and adopt the demeanor of local inhabitants to blend into the setting. The type of clothing to be worn will determine whether concealment of weapons or use of personal radios jeopardizes the operation. Ideally, the officer should have an ordinary appearance to avoid attracting the suspect's attention. Doing so will better ensure that the officer is able to blend in to the target's environment. The officer must have the ability to act naturally under all circumstances as if he or she belongs at that scene.

Officers should also have such items as caps, jackets, and glasses available to quickly change appearance if needed. Flexibility and versatility are the keys to any surveillance. A change of clothing may suffice for one individual, but another may use clothing to suggest a trade or service. The clothing and behavior should be coordinated to communicate some cover or excuse for being in a neighborhood.

Foot Surveillance

Generally, the foot surveillance technique is used only during relatively short distances or to maintain contact with a suspect after he or she has left a vehicle. There are four principal methods for conducting a moving surveillance on foot: one-officer surveillance; two-officer surveillance; ABC method; and the progressive, or leapfrog, method.

One-Officer Surveillance. The single-officer technique is extremely difficult to conduct because the suspect must be kept in view at all times and close contact is required to enable the officer to immediately observe the suspect if he or she enters a building, turns a corner, or makes other sudden moves.

Two-Officer Surveillance. This method affords greater security against detection and reduces the risk of losing the suspect. On streets that are crowded with pedestrian or vehicular traffic, both officers should normally remain on the same side of the street as the suspect. The first officer trails the suspect fairly closely. The second officer remains some distance behind the first. On a less crowded street, one officer should walk on the opposite side of the street nearly abreast of the suspect. To avoid detection, the two officers should make periodic changes in their positions relative to the suspect.

ABC Method. By using a three-officer surveillance team in this technique, the risk of losing the suspect is further reduced. Under most conditions, this method provides greater security against detection. The ABC method also permits a greater

Surveillance Kit Checklist

- ☑ Department two-way radio
- ☑ Handheld portable radio with spare battery
- ☑ Cellular phone
- ☑ Digital camera with telephoto lens (if available) with extra storage media and spare battery
- ☑ Digital video camera
- ☑ Stabilizing device such as a tripod
- ☑ Binoculars or thermal-imaging device
- ☑ Detailed road maps, compass, or GPS navigation device
- ☑ Flashlight with extra batteries
- ☑ Change of clothing, including hat and toiletries
- ☑ Food and water
- ☑ Cash, including coins for toll lanes
- ☑ Extra set of car keys
- ☑ Towels and glass cleaner
- ☑ Equipment bag to contain above items

variation in the position of the officers and allows an officer who suspects he has been spotted by the suspect to drop out of close contact. Under normal traffic conditions, officer "A" keeps a reasonable distance behind the suspect. Officer "B" follows "A" and concentrates on keeping "A" in view. Officer "B" also checks if an associate of the subject is being used to detect the surveillance (countersurveillance). Officer "C" walks on the opposite side of the street slightly behind the suspect. On streets with little or no traffic, officers "B" and "C" may be on the opposite side of the street, or officer "C" may be in front of the suspect. On crowded streets, however, all three officers should generally be on the same side of the street. The lead officer should follow closely to observe the suspect at intersections or if he or she enters a building. As with the two-officer method, the officers should frequently alter their positions relative to the suspect to avoid detection.

When the suspect approaches an intersection and there is a probability that he or she might turn, officer "C" across the street should reach the intersection first. By pausing at the corner, officer "C" can watch the suspect and signal his or her actions to officers "A" and "B." If "C" signals that the suspect has turned the corner and stopped, both "A" and "B" may have to cross the intersection and proceed to a point out of the suspect's view and rely on "C" to signal them when the suspect continues on his way. Whether or not the suspect stops, turning the corner provides an opportunity to rotate the positions of the officers.

To communicate with each other, surveillance officers must have agreed on some basic hand signals. These hand signals must be simple and given in such a manner as not to attract attention. When possible, small, easily concealed personal radios can be used by the team.

Progressive, or Leapfrog, Method. In the progressive, or leapfrog, method of surveillance, the suspect is observed intermittently as he or she moves along a certain habitual route. The surveillance officer stations him- or herself at a fixed point until the suspect disappears from view. If a suspect follows the same route each day, the destination may be determined without constant surveillance. The officer should station himself each day where the suspect disappeared from view the previous day. More than one officer can be used to extend the period of observation. This method may be of value in locating hideouts or meeting places when the risk of trailing a suspect is too great.

Use of this method is not common because of the time involved and the probability of obtaining poor results. There is no assurance that the suspect will either go to the same destination or take the same route every day. However, a modified version may be useful when a suspect's rounds are routine or his or her contacts are known but his or her source or base of operation is unknown. The suspect can be followed until the risk of detection is too great. The surveillance can then be canceled for that day and reinstituted the next day at the location where the previous day's surveillance was called off.

Difficulties in Surveillance Operations

Problems that may be encountered when conducting foot surveillance are infinite, but there are certain common difficulties that preplanning may help to resolve. For example, if the suspect enters a building, at least one officer should follow the suspect inside unless the building is a private home or small shop or if entry would expose the officer. In the case of a large public building with many exits, all officers should follow the suspect into the building. It is prudent for one officer to remain in the lobby or at the door to spot the suspect if he or she leaves the building.

If a suspect enters a restaurant, at least one officer should enter behind the suspect to note any contacts made inside. If possible, the officer should pay his or her check before the suspect to be prepared to leave with the suspect. In some cases, it is desirable for the officer to leave shortly before the suspect and wait for him or her outside. Doing so could give the suspect the impression that he or she is not being observed by the surveillance officer.

If the suspect registers in a hotel, the room number and length of anticipated stay may be obtained from a manager or desk clerk. However, these employees should not be asked for information until it is determined that they can be trusted. If the hotel management is cooperative, it may be possible to obtain a room near the suspect, which can be used as a surveillance base. All in-room outgoing telephone numbers dialed by the suspect are normally recorded by the hotel switchboard operator. These records should be examined for leads. Trash from the suspect's room should not be overlooked, although trespassing to retrieve this or any other possible evidence without a search warrant is not permitted.

A clever suspect, discovering that he or she is under surveillance, may not reveal this knowledge but may attempt to lose the followers by means of false contacts or decoys. For example, when attempting a surveillance on a suspected illicit drug exchange, the suspect may leave a package full of worthless papers or materials with the contact, thereby causing unwary officers to redirect or discontinue their surveillance, leaving the suspect free to make his or her real contacts unobserved. Similarly, the suspect may attempt to lead the officer into a trap. A thorough knowledge of the locality, tempered with good judgment and alertness to realize when trailing becomes too easy, is a good defense against such traps. If a suspect resorts to trickery, it is good policy to change surveillance officers. Some common methods that a suspect may use to detect foot surveillance are:

- Stopping to tie a shoelace while looking for followers
- Stopping abruptly and looking at people to the rear or reversing course and retracing his or her steps

- Stopping abruptly after turning a corner or alternately walking slowly and rapidly
- Arranging with a friend in a shop or other place to watch for surveillants behind him or her
- Riding short distances on buses and taxis or circling the block in a taxi
- Entering a building and leaving immediately via another exit
- Watching in lobby and restaurant mirrors to see who is coming and going
- Starting to leave a location quickly and then suddenly turning around to see if anyone else also suddenly rises
- Opening and closing the hotel door to indicate that he or she has left the room and then waiting inside the room with the door slightly ajar to see if anyone leaves an adjacent room

Vehicle Surveillance

As is the case with foot surveillance, there are four types of vehicular surveillance, or **mobile surveillance**: the one-, two-, and three-car surveillance and the leapfrog method. If only one car is available for surveillance, its position should be behind the suspect car, the distance varying with the amount of traffic in the area. In city traffic, no more than two vehicles should be permitted between the suspect's car and the surveillance vehicle. In rural areas, it is advisable to give the suspect a good lead. If intersections and road forks are far between, the lead can be extended to a point where the suspect car may be even temporarily lost from view over hills or around curves. When possible, there should be another car between the surveillance vehicle and the suspect car. At night, the surveillance vehicle should not have its headlights on high beam unless absolutely necessary to maintain contact. Similarly, all other unnecessary lights on the car should be off.

Whenever possible, the surveillant's car should be occupied by two officers—one driver and one observer to take notes. The second officer can also take over surveillance on foot if necessary. Seating arrangements and appearance of these two officers should be changed periodically to avoid recognition by suspects. The officers should prepare for emergencies by carrying food, raincoats, tire chains, and any other items appropriate for the circumstances of the surveillance. Many agencies install switches (kill switches) on surveillance cars to enable the officers to darken lights, shut off running lights, or shut off individual lights needed to change the vehicle's appearance.

When conducting a two-car surveillance in city areas during daylight hours, both cars should be behind the suspect's car. Occasionally, one car may operate on a parallel route, timing itself to arrive at intersections just before the suspect to observe his route at the intersection. This method is also highly suitable for use at night in suburban areas.

In a three-car surveillance, parallel routes can be more readily used, and the positions of the cars can be changed frequently enough to prevent discovery of the surveillance. One car may be used to lead the suspect vehicle while observing it through the rearview mirror.

The leapfrog surveillance with cars is very similar to leapfrog surveillance on foot. In this type of surveillance, for example, the suspect's vehicle may be observed intermittently as it proceeds along its suspected route. From a fixed position, the officers watch the suspect vehicle disappear from view. After a number of such surveillances, the suspect's final destination is finally determined. This particular approach of the leapfrog surveillance is often impractical due to the greater distances that can be covered by car. For this reason, it would be more beneficial if the surveillance officers followed the suspect's car until the risk of detection is too great, whereupon the surveillance is called off for that day. The

FIGURE 7.7 Detective conducting a "moving" or vehicle surveillance. A properly conducted moving surveillance requires the investigator in the lead vehicle (known as the "eyeball") maintaining constant communication with other surveillance units to alert them as to the actions of the target vehicle. *Courtesy of Mike Himmel.*

next time the suspect makes his or her scheduled trip, the officers can initiate their surveillance at the geographical point the previous surveillance was ended.

As with foot surveillance, the suspect who believes he or she may be being followed can resort to various techniques to detect the surveillance automobile. Some of the most common techniques include:

- Alternating fast and slow driving or parking frequently
- Stopping suddenly around curves or corners or speeding up a hill and then coasting slowly downhill
- Driving into dead-end streets or pulling into driveways

Once a suspect has confirmed his or her suspicion, he or she can use a variety of techniques to elude automobile surveillance. Some examples are:

- Committing flagrant traffic violations such as making U-turns, driving against traffic on one-way streets, and running through red lights
- Using double entrances to driveways—in one entrance and out the other
- Cutting through parking lots
- Driving through congested areas
- Deserting the vehicle beyond the blind curve or corner

Stakeouts, or "Stationary Surveillance"

When a **stakeout** is used, officers watch from a **stationary surveillance** vantage point such as a room, house, or camouflaged outdoor fixture located near the premises being observed. A stakeout is the tactical deployment of police officers in anticipation of the commission of a crime at a specific location. The anticipated perpetrators may be known individuals or may be suspects known only by their mode of operation (MO). The purpose of the stakeout is to arrest the suspect(s) during the attempted or actual commission of a crime.

Stakeouts almost always involve enforcement actions against armed criminal suspects. Therefore, the safety of officers and bystanders should always be of primary concern. The objectives of criminal arrest should never supersede the need to protect officers and civilians against unreasonable risks.

Briefings

The briefings preceding deployment of a stakeout should be of two types:

1. The first type is the dissemination of information by detective personnel. The detectives in charge of the case should provide the assigned officers with all information concerning the suspect(s) and his or her MO. This

should include, when available, photos or composites, suspect armament, and the suspect's potential for violence based on previous crimes. Is the suspect armed? Has the suspect used his weapon? Has the suspect taken hostages? Does the suspect appear to be in control or is the suspect he under the influence of alcohol or drugs? Does the suspect run after committing the crime or calmly exit the location? Is there a getaway car with a driver? What is the possibility of outside accomplices? Does there appear to be inside help? Are the suspects "counter jumpers," or do they position or station themselves in a particular area or manner? As these and related issues are discussed, one can begin to formulate the tactical actions that officers must take.

2. The second type of briefing is provided by those officers who surveyed, or "advanced," the assigned location. An *advance* consists of assessing a potential stakeout location and developing an initial tactical plan. The advance should be the responsibility of the stakeout supervisor or senior officer(s) with stakeout experience. Organization, manpower deployment, and related concerns should be the responsibility of supervisors with tactical knowledge.

Investigative Procedures

Generally, a stakeout consists of an inside team and an outside team of two officers each. The **outside team** is normally designated as the arrest team. Enforcement action should not be taken by the inside team unless a life-threatening situation develops. After the subjects have exited the stakeout location, the inside team is also responsible for securing the location to ensure that the suspects do not reenter and possibly create a barricade or hostage situation.

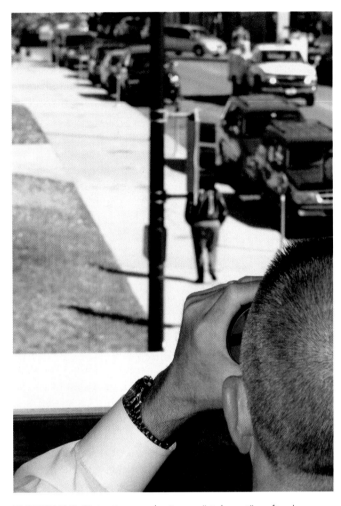

FIGURE 7.8 Detective conducting a "stakeout" or fixed surveillance. Such operations are tedious and time consuming but often net valuable information regarding the actions and routines of suspects. Courtesy of Mike Himmel.

Although the outside team is normally the arrest team, assignment of this responsibility is ultimately based on factors associated with the specific stakeout location. For example, normally crowded public stores are not generally the best location for an arrest confrontation. But less trafficked locations, such as exclusive jewelry stores that use controlled public access, would be preferable over a busy public street. These and related factors concerning the stakeout location should be addressed during the stakeout advance, and a decision should be made on team responsibilities by the detail supervisor.

The **inside team** is responsible for briefing officers concerning their actions if a crime occurs. They should ensure that employees do not initiate any independent action and should remove any privately owned weapons. All employees must understand that they should not inform anyone that police are present, nor should they seek assistance from the stakeout team for crimes such as shoplifting. If necessary, uniformed officers may respond as usual to handle these offenses. Such incidents should be handled as quickly as possible, and uniformed officers should exit the area after the call for service has been handled. The investigators must conduct themselves in a normal and inconspicuous manner at all times. They should also be cautioned to lie prone on the floor if gunfire develops.

If the inside team is not going to observe from a concealed position, employees must be inconspicuous in their particular setting. If employees wear distinctive attire, then so must the inside team. There is always a possibility that the suspects may inspect a location before committing the crime, so stakeout officers must appear to be part of the local operation. All police equipment must be concealed, and radios must be turned off. Any private security should be dismissed and should leave the area. If the absence of private security would be obvious, security personnel may be permitted to stay, but they should not be armed and should be thoroughly briefed as to their role.

The investigators should be informed that no police action will be taken inside, with the exception of actions necessary to save lives, so as to relieve any unnecessary anxiety on the part of employees. Employees must also ensure that there is nothing on the premises, such as a scanner, that would reveal the stakeout operation. If any employee displays obvious signs of stress, serious consideration should be given to removing that employee with the cooperation of the location's management personnel.

If there is any suspicion that an officer may be involved with the suspects, an inside team should not be deployed, and no one outside of the police agency should be notified of the stakeout operation. In such instances, assigned officers should conduct the stakeout from a covert observation post outside the location.

Concealment of the outside team is a concern that officers sometimes overlook. Just as suspects survey prospective target locations from inside, they also frequently survey the surrounding area. Stakeouts that do not adhere to good concealment practices risk detection. There is simply no way, for example, that two officers can sit in a vehicle or use the same disguise for an extended period of time without being conspicuous.

A sedan is frequently used but may not be the best available option for the outside team. If a sedan is preferred, however, one officer should sit in the front seat and one in the right rear seat. The officer in the rear seat should position himself so he or she has a clear view of activities to the rear of the vehicle. This positioning is necessary because there have been cases in which officers have been fatally wounded while seated together in the front of their vehicle and unable to see suspects approaching from the rear.

Underground parking, carports, and residential driveways also provide concealment and allow officers some freedom of movement. Vans and other businesses or residences are also frequently used. Whatever the location, the observation post should be selected with the understanding that it could be in place for an extended period of time.

The response of the outside team to the stakeout location should be tested, taking into account changing traffic patterns at different times of the day. Experience has shown that 30 seconds should be considered the maximum allowable response time for the outside team to get to the stakeout. To reduce response time, outside teams should not situate themselves on the opposite side of major thoroughfares and should either minimize the number of intersections that must be crossed or eliminate them altogether.

Entry and exit of the inside team to the stakeout location are extremely important. All equipment, particularly weapons, must be concealed, and officers should not arrive at the location at the same time. After they are inside, the first officer should contact the designated manager or person in charge. Officers should seek a private area to brief the manager on stakeout procedures and then reevaluate the situation for safety. If circumstances that could affect safety have sufficiently changed since the advance was conducted, the officers should contact a supervisor immediately and, if necessary, redeploy until the problem(s) can be resolved.

The physical environment of a stakeout is one of the most problematic issues should the use of firearms be needed. Regardless of whether an officer is stationed inside or outside the location, all officers must visually inspect the entire location with background in mind. For example, plateglass windows from floor to ceiling or plasterboard walls are unacceptable background materials if the use of firearms becomes necessary by the inside team.

Officers should be positioned to minimize interior backgrounds. A standard procedure in this regard is to station one officer undercover, at a point in the facility well above eye level. This positioning provides several advantages. If the use of firearms is required, this officer will be firing downward, thus minimizing or eliminating background problems. It also provides for greater visibility and strategic advantage. With one officer in this position providing cover, the second inside officer can be used to collect the suspect's weapons and frisk and handcuff the subject if an arrest must be made inside the stakeout location.

The inside team should alert the arrest team as soon as anything unusual is suspected. Radio contact with the arrest team should be maintained as long as possible to describe the suspects and the types of weapons being carried, anticipated exit route, and other pertinent information that would assist the arrest team and promote their safety.

Weapon readiness is also an important consideration. When shotguns are used, a round should be chambered with the safety on. Shotguns should never be leaned against a wall, table, or other object but should be laid flat when not being held. Semi-automatic handguns should also be in a ready condition with the safety on. There is no time to chamber a round when needed instantly in a tactical situation. In addition, when disengaging the safety in such instances, it should be done as quietly as possible. Placing a finger on each side of the safety release when disengaging is a good way to ensure silence.

Exiting a location is as critical as entering. Officers should exercise the same caution in leaving the location as they did when entering. As a stakeout continues, fatigue may become a factor. Officers and supervisors should be alert to signs of fatigue, and personnel should be rotated as necessary. This is particularly the case with inside team officers, whose level of preparedness and stress is greatest. Rotation can help to alleviate this constant tension as well as allow other officers to become knowledgeable about other duties of the stakeout operation.

Post-Stakeout Procedures

The potential for the use of deadly force is a part of nearly all stakeouts. However, this potentiality does not constitute grounds for an exception to existing policies and procedures that govern the use of deadly force in individual agencies. The safety of officers and citizens alike and overall reverence for human life remain important issues. As in other circumstances, officers should use deadly force only as a last resort after all other reasonable alternatives are exhausted.

If a suspect is shot, he or she should be disarmed and handcuffed immediately. Officers should not diagnose the condition of the suspect to determine whether handcuffs are required. Instances exist in which presumably dead or incapacitated suspects have inflicted serious injuries on unsuspecting officers. The suspect's weapon should also be secured. If the officer is not familiar with the weapon, he or she should handle it only to the degree necessary until it can be rendered safe.

After the arrest, the surrounding area should be checked for accomplices and getaway cars and the immediate area secured as a crime scene as soon as possible. In addition to ambulances, a call should be made for assistance from uniformed support personnel. These calls should be made by telephone because police radio communications are frequently monitored by the news media and the public.

All plainclothes officers should display proper ID and be easily identified as police officers because responding officers may not be aware that the location was a stakeout. Raid jackets are relatively inexpensive, easily obtainable, and easily recognized.

After the location is secured, standard procedures for handling a crime scene should be used. The area should be roped off or isolated, evidence should be preserved, and witnesses should be located and identified. Information to be released should be channeled only to assigned press relations officers. Officers involved in the incident should not be subjected to press interviews and should not make public statements.

Electronic Surveillance and Wiretaps

With the growing use of high technology to investigate crime and uncover violations of criminal law, courts throughout the nation are evaluating the applicability of constitutional guarantees with regard to high-tech surveillance. Recent technology makes possible increasingly complex forms of communication. One of the first Supreme Court decisions involving electronic communications was the 1928 case of *Olmstead* v. *United States*. In the *Olmstead* case, bootleggers used their home telephones to discuss and transact business.[8] Agents tapped the lines and based their investigation and ensuing arrests on conversations they overheard. The defendants were convicted and eventually appealed to the high court, arguing that the agents had, in effect, seized information illegally without a search warrant in violation of the defendant's Fourth Amendment right to be secure in their homes. The Court ruled, however, that telephone lines are not an extension of the defendant's home and therefore are not protected by the constitutional guarantee of security. However, subsequent federal statutes have substantially modified the significance of the *Olmstead* decision.

Recording devices carried on the body of an undercover agent or informant were ruled to produce admissible evidence in *On Lee* v. *U.S.* (1952) and *Lopez* v. *U.S.* (1963).[9] The 1967 case of *Berger* v. *New York* permitted wiretaps and "bugs" in instances in which state law provided for the use of such devices and officers had obtained a warrant based on probable cause.[10]

The Court appeared to undertake a significant change of direction in the area of electronic eavesdropping when it decided the case of *Katz* v. *U.S.* (1967). Federal agents had monitored a number of Katz's telephone calls from a public phone using a device separate from the phone lines and attached to the glass of a phone booth. The Court, in this case, stated that a warrant is required to unveil what a person makes an effort to keep private, even in a public place. In the words of the Court, "the government's activities in electronically listening to and recording the petitioner's words violated the privacy upon which he justifiably relied while using a telephone booth and thus constituted a search and seizure within the meaning of the Fourth Amendment."

In *Lee* v. *Florida* (1968), the Court applied the Federal Communications Act to telephone conversations that might be the object of police investigation and held that evidence obtained without a warrant could not be used in state proceedings if it resulted from a wiretap.[11] The only person who has the authority to permit eavesdropping, according to that act, is the sender of the message.

The Federal Communications Act, originally passed in 1934, does not specifically mention the potential interest of law enforcement agencies in monitoring communications. Title III of the Omnibus Crime Control and Safe Streets Act of 1968, however, mostly prohibits wiretaps but does allow officers to listen to electronic communications when (1) an officer is one of the parties involved in the communication, (2) one of the parties is not the officer but willingly decides to share the communication with the officer, or (3) officers obtain a warrant based on probable cause. In the 1971 case of *U.S. v. White*, the Court held that law enforcement officers may intercept electronic information when one of the parties involved in the communication gives his or her consent, even without a warrant.[12]

In 1984, the Supreme Court decided the case of *U.S. v. Karo*, in which Drug Enforcement Administration (DEA) agents had arrested James Karo for cocaine importation.[13] Officers placed a radio transmitter inside a 50-gallon drum of ether purchased by Karo for use in processing the cocaine. The device was placed inside the drum with the consent of the seller of the ether but without a search warrant. The shipment of ether was followed to the Karo house, and Karo was arrested and convicted of cocaine trafficking charges. Karo appealed to the U.S. Supreme Court, claiming that the radio beeper had violated his reasonable expectation of privacy inside his premises and that, without a warrant, the evidence it produced was tainted. The Court agreed and overturned his conviction.

Minimization Requirements for Electronic Surveillance

The Supreme Court established a minimization requirement pertinent to electronic surveillance in the 1978 case of *U.S. v. Scott*.[14] **Minimization** refers to the requirement that officers take every reasonable effort to monitor only those conversations, through the use of phone taps, body bugs, and the like, that are specifically related to the criminal activity under investigation. As soon as it becomes obvious that a conversation is innocent, the monitoring personnel are required to cease listening. Problems arise if the conversation occurs in a foreign language, if it is "coded," or if it is ambiguous. For example, in one wiretap operation, heroin traffickers referred to a pound quantity of product as an "elbow" or "LB." Investigators were aware of this street term and were able to continue monitoring the conversation. It has been suggested that investigators involved in electronic surveillance maintain logbooks of their activities that specifically show monitoring of conversations as well as efforts made to minimize noncriminal conversations.

The Electronic Communications Privacy Act of 1986

In 1986, Congress passed the Electronic Communications Privacy Act (ECPA), which brought major changes in the requirements law enforcement officers must meet to intercept wire communications (involving the human voice). The ECPA deals specifically with three areas of communication: (1) wiretaps and bugs, which enable officers to listen to criminal conversations; (2) pen registers, which record numbers dialed from a telephone; and (3) tracing devices, which determine the number from which a call emanates. The act also addresses the procedures to be followed by officers in obtaining records relating to communication services, and it establishes requirements for gaining access to stored electronic communications and records of those communications. The ECPA basically requires that investigating officers obtain wiretap-type court orders to eavesdrop on ongoing communications. The use of pen registers and recording devices, however, is specifically excluded by law from court order requirements.[15]

A related measure, the Communications Assistance for Law Enforcement Act (CALEA) of 1994, appropriated $500 million to modify the U.S. phone system to allow for continued wiretapping by law enforcement agencies. The law also specifies a standard-setting process for the redesign of existing equipment that would permit effective wiretapping in the face of coming technological advances. The law essentially requires telecommunication carriers, as defined by the act, to ensure law enforcement's ability, pursuant to a lawful court order, to intercept communications notwithstanding advanced telecommunications technologies. In 2003, federal and state judges approved 1,442 wiretap requests, and approximately 4.3 million conversations were intercepted by law enforcement agencies throughout the country. Approximately one-third of all intercepted conversations were classified as "incriminating."[16]

The Telecommunications Act of 1996

Title V of the Telecommunications Act of 1996 made it a federal offense for anyone engaged in interstate or international communications to knowingly use a telecommunications device "to create, solicit, or initiate the transmission of any comment, request, suggestion, proposal, image, or other communication which is at the scene lewd, mischievous, filthy, or indecent, with intent to annoy, abuse, threaten, or harass another person." The law also provides special penalties for anyone who "makes a telephone call . . . without disclosing his identity and with intent to annoy, abuse, threaten, or harass any person at the called number who receives the communication" or who "makes or causes the telephone of another repeatedly or continuously to ring, with the intent to harass any person at the called number; or makes repeated phone calls" for the purpose of harassing a person at the called number.[17]

A section of the law, known as the Communications Decency Act (CDA), criminalizes the transmission to minors of "patently offensive" obscene materials over the Internet and other computer communications devices. Portions of the CDA, however, were invalidated by the U.S. Supreme Court in the case of *Reno* v. *ACLU* (1997).[18]

Thermal Imaging

In 1996, the California appellate court decision in *People* v. *Deutsch* identified the kinds of issues that are likely to be encountered as the United States and law enforcement expand its use of high technology.[19] In this case, judges faced the question of whether a warrantless scan of a private dwelling using a thermal imaging device constitutes an unreasonable search within the meaning of the Fourth Amendment. These devices, also known as **forward-looking infrared** (FLIR) systems, measure radiant heat energy and display their readings as thermographs. Images that a thermal imager produces can be used (as in the case of Dorian Deutsch) to reveal unusually warm areas or rooms that might be associated with the cultivation of drug-bearing plants, such as marijuana. Two hundred cannabis plants, which were being grown hydroponically under high-wattage lights in walled-off portions of Deutsch's home, were seized after an exterior thermal scan of the home by a police officer who drove by the residence at 1:30 A.M.

Satellite-Assisted Surveillance

Shortly after Laci Peterson disappeared in Modesto, California on Christmas Eve 2002, her husband Scott assured police that he had nothing to do with it. The police, however, were suspicious. Without Peterson's knowledge, they received court permission to attach **Global Positioning System (GPS)** tracking devices to the undersides of three vehicles he was known to drive. The devices, which use cell phone networks and signals from orbiting satellites to pinpoint land locations, indicated that twice in January 2003, Peterson drove to a San Francisco Bay marina near where the bodies of his wife and unborn son washed ashore three months later.

Scott Peterson was subsequently arrested and charged with the murder of his wife and unborn child. Prosecutors in the case used data gathered by the GPS devices as part of a body of evidence suggesting that Peterson was guilty.

The use of GPS in the Peterson case reflects how police across the nation are turning to such devices for surveillance, eavesdropping, and other tasks that traditionally have been performed by uniformed officers and detectives. Recent improvements in cell phone technology and in the quality of satellite signals allow investigators to track and record a vehicle's movements in real time and display the information on a map displayed on a laptop computer.

A CLOSER LOOK

The Mechanics of Thermal Imaging

In its simplest terms, thermal imagers operate like the human eye, but are much more powerful. Energy from the environment passes through a lens and is registered on a detector. In the case of the thermal imager, that energy is in the form of heat. By measuring very small relative temperature differences, invisible heat patterns are converted by the thermal imager into clear, visible images that can be viewed by the operator through a viewfinder or monitor. Thermal imagers are usually very sensitive and can detect temperature variations smaller then 0.1°C.

Thermal imagers "see" nothing more than the heat emitted by all objects in the camera's field of view. They do not see visible light, nor do they see rays or beams of energy. Thermal imagers are completely passive and non-intrusive. Because these devices see heat and not light, they can be used for both daytime and nighttime operations.

Thermal imagers can be compared with image intensifiers, which are another type of night vision technology and one that has been used by law enforcement and the military for years. In contrast to image intensifiers, thermal imagers are unaffected by the amount of light in a scene and will "bloom" or shut down indirect light. Unlike image intensifiers, thermal imagers can see through dust, smoke, light fog, clouds, haze, and light rain because infrared wavelengths are longer than visible wavelengths of light.

Because the officer had not anticipated entering the house, he proceeded without a search warrant.

A California court ruled that the scan was an illegal search because "society accepts reasonable expectation of privacy" surrounding "non-disclosed activities within the home."

In a similar case, *Kryllo* v. *U.S.* (2001), the U.S. Supreme Court reached much the same conclusion. Based on the results of a warrantless search conducted by the officers using a forward imaging device, investigators applied for a search warrant of Kryllo's home.[20] The subsequent search uncovered more than 100 marijuana plants that were being grown under bright lights. The Court held "where, as here, the government uses a device that is not in general public use, to explore details of a private home that would previously have been unknowable without physical intrusion, the surveillance is a Fourth Amendment search, and is presumptively unreasonable without a warrant."

Thematic Question

The Kryllo case and the use of thermal imaging had raised many important questions regarding the right of the people to be safe from criminality and their concurrent right to be free from intrusive police surveillance. If you had to make concessions in either regard, which would you choose: your right to privacy against government intrusion or the ability of the police to conduct surveillance into suspected criminal's homes to identify criminal activity? Explain your response.

A typical GPS tracking device is about the size of a paperback book and can be affixed to a car's undercarriage with a magnet. The cost for such a device is minimal, at about $1,000. As of the writing of this text, questions over whether police need a court's permission (a court order) to use GPS devices in investigations have become the subject of concern in state and federal courts across the nation.

Wiretaps and property searches ordinarily must be authorized by a state or federal judge, who determines whether such tactics are needed to investigate a crime. The surveillance on public roads ordinarily does not require such court orders. Because GPS devices are a substitute for ordinary visual surveillance, many police departments believe they can be used without a court order. Civil rights advocates are concerned that the technology has advanced to where police can track thousands of people anywhere, anytime, and police don't have to give a reason.

As of the preparation of this text, there are no records of how often GPS is being used nationally in criminal investigations. However, an examination of recent criminal investigations has revealed that its use is somewhat common. For example:

1. In May 2004, a Honolulu police unit that locates stolen automobiles parked a car with a GPS tracker in a high-crime area. The "bait" car was stolen and located quickly. Police arrested the driver.

2. In 2002, criminal investigators in Nassau County, New York, used two GPS devices to track a car driven by burglary suspect Richard Lacey. Prosecutors used GPS records to show that the car was in the vicinity of several homes at the time they were burglarized.

3. In 2000, the FBI in Las Vegas used two GPS devices that had been built into a car to eavesdrop on the targets of an investigation into organized crime. The device, offered as a safety accessory by some car makers, allows lost or endangered drivers to be located quickly if they are calling for help.

4. In 1999, in Spokane, Washington, GPS devices on the Ford pickup and the Honda Accord driven by murder suspect William Bradley Jackson led police to the grave of his missing nine-year-old daughter, Valiree. The GPS data indicated that Jackson made two trips to the site in the three weeks after he reported the girl missing. He was convicted of murder and sentenced to 56 years in prison.

The first GPS devices were developed by the military in the 1980s and read signals transmitted by a network of 24 satellites. The device calculates its location based on its distance from each satellite. A built-in modem and antenna transmit information similar to a cell phone call. Experts suggest that the system can be accurate, down to a nanosecond and within 20 feet. Criminal investigators claim GPS devices have distinct advantages over human trackers in that they can operate around the clock without a break, and they're less likely to lose track of the targets or to be noticed.

Courts are just beginning to address issues raised by GPS use in criminal investigations. In the *Jackson* case in Washington state, police argued that the devices do not require a court order because they provide the same information as a visual search. The state's court of appeals agreed, finding that the GPS devices used to track Jackson were "merely sense augmenting" and revealed information open to "public view" as Jackson traveled county roads. However, the state supreme court disagreed stating that under Washington's state constitution, GPS

FIGURE 7.9 How GPS tracking works in criminal investigation. Copyright 2004, USA Today. Reprinted with permission.

surveillance requires a court order because it amounts to a search. In September 2003, Justice Barbara Madsen wrote in an opinion joined by all nine of the court's justices: "the intrusion into private affairs made possible with the GPS devices is quite extensive . . . vehicles are used to take people to a vast number of places; they can reveal preferences, associations, personal habits and foibles." She continued to say that "GPS can provide a detailed picture of one's life."

However, the murder conviction in the Jackson case was upheld because Spokane County investigators took the precaution of getting a court order, even as they argued that it wasn't needed. It is possible that federal courts could reach a different conclusion because the U.S. Supreme Court, for more than 20 years, has authorized law enforcement to plant electronic transmitters on vehicles without a warrant and to track them, as long as the vehicles do not enter private property.

In addition to tracking criminal suspects, some law enforcement agencies also use GPS devices to check on the activities of their own employees. For example, between 1999 and 2003, law enforcement agencies in Des Moines, Iowa; Omaha, Nebraska; Orlando, Florida; and other cities have used GPS devices on police cars to track the cars' whereabouts during duty hours. In one case, in Clinton Township, New Jersey, in 2001, five officers were let go after their handwritten activity logs conflicted with information collected by GPS devices. In this case, one night shift officer reported that he had spent about two hours checking the security of a residence and several local businesses. The global positioning data indicated that his cruiser had been parked at a McDonald's restaurant the entire time.

Summary Checklist

In this chapter, we consider the ways information about crimes is documented by criminal investigators. A properly documented case is one that is more likely to succeed in court. See how well you are able to answer the following questions in your checklist.

1. **Can you explain the function of intelligence gathering and its uses?**

The collection of criminal intelligence is another important function of the criminal investigative process, and one that has resulted in significant identification and arrest of major crime figures.

Development of a systematic approach to this function within police agencies is essential to put what may otherwise be scattered—or even unrecorded—information and data to use in a constructive and concerted manner.

- After it has been documented, such information can develop a life of its own if sufficient safeguards are not built into screening, reviewing, and managing intelligence files. If passed on to other law enforcement agencies as intelligence, it can form the basis for abuse of civil liberties and potential civil liability.

2. **Can you distinguish between overt and covert intelligence collection?**

- Overt information collection includes personal interaction with people, many of whom are witnesses to crimes, victims of crimes, or the suspects themselves.
- Covert information collection is the most common and includes a process known as intelligence gathering.

3. **Are you able to distinguish between criminal intelligence and criminal investigation functions?**

Criminal intelligence is defined as knowledge of past, present, or future criminal activity that results from the collection of information that,

when evaluated, provides the user with a basis for rational decision making.

Criminal investigations are usually reactive in nature. Intelligence gathering, conversely, is a proactive function.

- Investigation case files are generally considered open files. They contain information developed for the purpose of eventually making an arrest and gaining a conviction in a court of law.
- In comparison, intelligence files are closed files.

4. **Can you identify the procedures for intelligence gathering?**

The intelligence collection process should be thought of as a process of connecting a series of interrelated components of information.

- Target selection is the first phase of the process.
- Data collection is the second phase to the process.
- The third phase in the procedure is the information collation process.
- The dissemination stage of the intelligence process is the final stage.

Intelligence can be analyzed through techniques such as link analysis and flowcharting. Resources of proper collection of information can be found in such projects as the RISS projects, which provide financial and logistical support.

5. **What ways can surveillance be useful in criminal investigations?**

- Conducting surveillance requires using the team concept.
- Perhaps the most challenging task in criminal investigation is to keep a suspect under

surveillance without arousing his or her suspicions.

- Before initiation of the surveillance, a study should be made of all files relating to the suspects, their activities in crimes, their working and neighborhood environments, and the vehicles involved in the case.

- In studying information relating to the suspects, the officer should focus on names and aliases used by suspects and detailed physical descriptions, including photographs when available.

6. Can you identify the various techniques for conducting surveillance of suspects?

Generally, the foot surveillance technique is used only during relatively short distances or to maintain contact with a suspect after he or she has left a vehicle.

- The four principle methods for conducting a moving surveillance on foot are one-officer surveillance; two-officer surveillance; the ABC method; and the progressive, or leapfrog, method.

As is the case with foot surveillance, there are four types of vehicular surveillance (or mobile surveillance): the one-, two-, and three-car surveillance and the leapfrog method.

When a stakeout is used, officers watch from a stationary surveillance vantage point such as a room, house, or camouflaged outdoor fixture located near the premises being observed.

- A stakeout is the tactical deployment of police officers in anticipation of the commission of a crime at a specific location.

- Generally, a stakeout consists of an inside team and an outside team of two officers each.

7. In what ways should investigators be knowledgeable of electronic surveillance techniques?

With the growing use of high technology to investigate crime and uncover violations of criminal law, courts throughout the nation are evaluating the applicability of constitutional guarantees with regard to high-tech surveillance.

- Recent technology makes possible increasingly complex forms of communication.

- The Supreme Court established a minimization requirement pertinent to electronic surveillance in 1978.

- In 1986, Congress passed the Electronic Communications Privacy Act (ECPA), which brought major changes in the requirements law enforcement officers must meet to intercept wire communications.

Investigators must be aware of other applicable laws that regulate their actions in the use of electronic surveillance techniques.

Key Terms

analysis

closed files

collation

covert information collection

dissemination

flowcharting

forward-looking infrared

Global Positioning System (GPS)

inside team

intelligence gathering

link analysis

mobile surveillance

open files

outside team

overt information collection

RISS projects

stakeout

stationary surveillance

strategic intelligence

tactical intelligence

Discussion Questions

1. Define the goal of the intelligence function as it pertains to the collection of criminal information.

2. List and discuss the four fundamental differences between criminal investigation and criminal intelligence gathering.

3. List and discuss the four phases of the intelligence process.

4. Discuss the basic differences between event and commodity flowcharting.

5. Explain the ways a cover story can be established and the various concerns in doing so.

6. Explain the relationship and role of the undercover officer and the support officer.

7. Explain the role and function of surveillance operations.

8. Compare and contrast the different types of surveillance methods.

mycrimekit™

Go to MyCrimeKit.com to explore the following study tools and resources specific to this chapter:

- *Practice Quiz:* Multiple-choice, true/false, short-answer, and essay questions.

- *Flashcards:* There are 20 key terms in this chapter. Flashcards test your knowledge of the chapter's key terms.

- *Web Links:* Check out the hotlink to *The New York Times* criminology articles.

- *Career Center:* Check out the hot links to interesting careers in criminal justice, criminology, and juvenile justice.

- *The Research Center:* Check out the Cybrary and research navigator for even more resources.

Notes

1. Botsch, R. B. (2008). Developing street sources: Tips for patrol officers. *FBI Law Enforcement Bulletin* 77(9).
2. Interview with Brian Michael Jenkins. (1994). *Omni*, 17(2):77.
3. Suro, R. (1998). U.S. lacking in terrorism defenses: Study cites a need to share intelligence. *The Washington Post*, April 24:A-18.
4. U.S. Department of Justice (1988). *Intelligence collection and analytical methods training manual.* Washington, DC: Drug Enforcement Administration.
5. FBI Website. Counterintelligence. Available at http://www.fbi.gov/hq/ci/cointell.htm.
6. FBI Website. Famous cases: Robert Philip Hanssen Espionage case. Available at http://www.fbi.gov/libref/historic/famcases/hanssen/hanssen.htm.
7. Nason, J. (2004). Conducting surveillance operations: how to get the most out of them. *FBI Law Enforcement Bulletin* May.
8. *Olmstead* v. *U.S.*, 277 U.S. 438 (1928).
9. *On Lee* v. *U.S.*, 343 U.S. 747 (1952); *Lopez* v. *U.S.*, 373 U.S. 427 (1963).
10. *Berger* v. *New York*, 388 U.S. 41 (1967).
11. *Lee* v. *Florida*, 392 U.S. 378 (1968).
12. *U.S.* v. *White*, 401 U.S. 745 (1971).
13. *U.S.* v. *Karo*, 468 U.S. 705 (1984).
14. *U.S.* v. *Scott*, 436 U.S. 128 (1978).
15. For more information on the ECPA, see Fiatal, R. A. (1988) The Electronic Communications Privacy Act: Addressing today's technology. *FBI Law Enforcement Bulletin* April:24–30.
16. The Administative Office for The United States Courts (2003). Wiretap Report. Available at uscourts.com.
17. Telecommunications Act of 1996, Public Law 104, 110 Statute 56.
18. *Reno* v. *ACLU*, 117 S. Ct. 2329 (1997).
19. *People* v. *Deutsch*, 96 C.D.O.S. 2827 (1996).
20. *Kyllo* v. *U.S.*, 533 U.S. 27 (2001).

Management of Informants and Undercover Operations

This chapter will enable you to:

- Describe the types of people used as informants.
- Identify various areas of concern in the use of informants.
- Understand the various motivations of informants.
- Document and process an informant properly.
- Maintain control of an informant during an investigation.
- Protect an informant's identity.
- Understand the problems most commonly associated with the use of informants.
- Understand the usefulness of undercover investigations.

- Describe the steps to properly implement an undercover investigation.
- Understand the resources required for a successful undercover investigation.
- Explain the benefits of surveillance in criminal investigation.
- Identify the different types of surveillance operations.

Introduction

Over a 10-month period beginning in 2003, motorists in Ohio were terrorized by a sniper firing random shots at vehicles along Interstate 270 that killed at least two persons. The two dozen shootings had struck a variety of targets such as cars, trucks, buses, schools, and homes in the Columbus area. Initially, investigators had little to go on in their investigation and publicly expressed their frustration in not having developed a suspect in the shootings. But finally in early 2004, ballistic tests on a 9mm handgun connected Charles McCoy, Jr., to the Ohio Interstate shootings as well as at least eight other shootings.

In March 2004, McCoy checked into the Budget Suites Hotel in Las Vegas, Nevada, at 3:00 A.M. under his own name. That evening, Conrad Malsom, a 60-year-old unemployed car salesman who lived in Las Vegas, spotted McCoy reading a *USA Today* article about himself in the sports betting parlor of the Stardust Casino. The two even shared a pizza as Malsom got a closer look. As they talked, Malsom learned where McCoy was staying and even took a sheet of paper containing some notes that McCoy was writing down. Malsom called the Las Vegas police, who arrested McCoy outside his hotel at 2:45 A.M. the following day.

The concept of informants in society is nothing new. In fact, both police and civilians attempt from time to time to encourage public participation in solving crimes. One well-known program is Crimestoppers, which encourages citizens to engage in "anonymous" informing to assist police in developing suspects in crimes or to catch criminals in the act of committing them. Although some people complain that Crimestoppers makes "snitches" out of law-abiding citizens, others argue that it is simply a system of public responsibility similar to the old days of the "hue and cry," when all citizens assumed responsibility for public order.

FIGURE 8.1 Suspected sniper Charles McCoy, Jr., was turned in by informer Conrad Malsom in Las Vegas, Nevada, in March 2004. AP Wide World Photos.

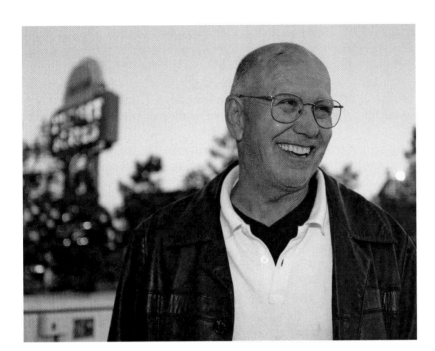

FIGURE 8.2 Tipster Conrad Malsom notified police of the whereabouts of Charles McCoy, the Ohio Interstate sniper. Joe Cavaretta, AP Wide World Photos.

In addition to allowing tipsters to call the police anonymously, many informants receive cash rewards for their cooperation. The amount of the reward depends on the "quality of information" provided by the citizen—that is, information that results in an arrest. All communication between the police and the citizen is accomplished by the assignment of a number to the caller. That number is used in lieu of a name for the remainder of the citizen–police relationship, negating the need for the police ever to know the true name of the tipster.

Along lines similar to Crimestoppers are efforts by victims of crimes to convince the community to become more involved with identifying known criminals and reporting violators to police. One example of this is the well-known television show *America's Most Wanted*. The show has helped track down more than 800 fugitives.[1] Other shows, including *Unsolved Mysteries* and *U.S. Customs*, have had similar success.

Another public forum for locating criminals has been around longer than the television shows discussed above is the FBI's Top Ten Most Wanted list. The FBI has maintained its Most Wanted list since 1950, and although it was once a mainstay in crime fighting, it has all but lost its appeal in today's high-tech age of television, computers, and the Internet. Still, it is designed to encourage citizen participation in sharing information with the police about crime and criminals who are wanted. The Most Wanted list was invented by a wire service reporter and later adopted by the publicity-driven director of the FBI, J. Edgar Hoover. As of 1997, 422 of the 449 fugitives who appeared on the list have been captured, a 94 percent success rate.[2]

In its earliest stages, when few Americans owned television sets, the Most Wanted list contained bank robbers, burglars, and car thieves, criminals who dominated the crime scene. Today's Most Wanted list includes cop killers, drug dealers, and international terrorists who aren't even in the country.[3] Skeptics argue that the list has outlived its usefulness because of the age of modern technology (the Internet, electronic billboards, and television). In 1992, the U.S. Post Office discontinued putting Top 10 posters on its walls. Perhaps it could be argued that the FBI's "list" has become ineffective, especially with the advent of so many different high-tech media showcasing the nation's fugitives. Of late, some victims have taken the initiative to seek help from the public by using their own money and resources.

During August 1997, the parents of murder victim JonBenet Ramsey ran their fourth advertisement in a local newspaper appealing for help from the public. The ad included samples of handwriting from the ransom note and commented that "the killer appears to be obsessed with technocrime movies and phrases from them."[4] In addition, the ad included quotes from the movies *Dirty Harry* and *Speed* that the family claimed were similar to the ones used in the ransom note.

In any case, whether it is a paid police informant or an anonymous tip, police rely heavily on information from the public to solve crimes. Experience has shown that a primary component of crime control is proactive law enforcement. Proactive investigations include vice cases such as drug trafficking, prostitution, and gambling, in which investigators actually seek out potential crimes and intervene "before" the crimes occur. Accordingly, the use of *informants* as a source of criminal information in such crimes has proved to be invaluable. Consequently, law enforcement officers are insistent in protecting the identities of their sources so that the well-being of the informants will not be jeopardized and so they will continue to be of use to the officer in future criminal investigations. (Note: Informants are also commonly called *informers*, *confidential informers*, or *cooperating individuals* (CIs), but in this book, they are referred to as *informants*.)

One of the most exceptional examples of informant use was the 1963 testimony of Joseph Valachi, a former Mafia soldier. Valachi's highly publicized role as an informant with the FBI resulted in the convictions of several management figures in the American Mafia. This case raised questions and public concern about the appropriateness of law enforcement officers using "criminals to catch criminals." Another high-visibility case involved Tommaso Buscetta, a crime family boss in Palermo, Sicily, who testified against numerous other Mafia bosses during the mid-1980s. His testimony was instrumental in the arrest and subsequent prosecutions of an estimated 450 fellow Mafiosos. Nevertheless, many misconceptions still exist about the value and utility of the criminal informant. For example, some think that police officers who are using an informant will be tolerant of that person's criminal lifestyle and might be less willing to report criminal wrongdoing on the part of the informant. Although through the years some improprieties have been documented regarding the use of informants, the value of such persons has proved immense in the prosecution of many high-level crime figures and in aiding law enforcement in understanding the inner workings of sophisticated criminal organizations.

In addition, some people believe that in dealing closely with informants, police officers may themselves become tainted and their positions compromised. In this chapter, we consider the role of informants in criminal investigations and how best to manage the information provided by them.

Who Are Informants?

Although the word **informant** has many negative synonyms, such as "snitch" and "stoolie," the term could best be defined as "anyone who provides information of an investigative nature to law enforcement."[5] Exclusions to this definition, of course, are victims of crime who have reported specific criminal activity to law enforcement. This makes their role more that of a complainant.

Indeed, the informant is most typically used in cases in which there is no complainant. These typically include vice and victimless crimes such as drug violations, gambling, and prostitution. Because informants can be virtually anyone in a community, a good investigator should consider anybody with whom he or she comes in contact as a potential source of criminal information. That is, the premise of locating a knowledgeable informant is to realize that someone somewhere is aware of various crimes committed. It is therefore the investigator's responsibility to locate and develop relationships with such people.

Generally, people who become informants can be classified into four general groups:

1. *Average citizens.* Although not necessarily a criminal source, people falling into this group may still be an excellent source of information. Most good investigators have several informants of this type who are contacted periodically for leads. Examples of these informants are waitresses, bartenders, dancers, and private investigators.

2. *Fellow law enforcement officers.* On an average day, investigators exchange valuable information with other investigators many times. Although much of this information is between "friends" who are investigators, a considerable amount is also exchanged by officers working in other units within the department. In addition, investigators who befriend officers with other local, state, or federal agencies can also benefit from useful information about criminals and criminal activity.

3. *Mentally ill persons.* It is unfortunate, but a percentage of informants fall into the category of mentally ill or deranged. An experienced investigator can detect when such persons are simply fabricating information or passing on news stories or gossip. One should also consider, however, that although an informant is mentally ill, his or her information might still have some validity.

4. *Criminals or their associates.* Without question, criminal informants have proven to be most valued in many police investigations. These are people who are currently, or have been, associated with a particular criminal element and are therefore in an excellent position to supply firsthand information about criminal activity. Informants are a dynamic group of people who come from diverse backgrounds and frequently view their role in different ways. For example, informant one may give information with no reservations about his or her identity becoming known. Conversely, others may have valuable information to render but may do so only with the understanding that their identities remain concealed. Those falling into the latter category typically want their identities to be kept secret for their own protection and because if their true identities become known, their function as informants would be ended.

Using Informants

Although a frequent source of valuable information, the use of an informant in a criminal investigation can be problematic. Therefore, the use of an informant should not be considered if similar results could be achieved through other means. Problems that stem from the use of informants are due to three variables. First, informants are often difficult to control. Many of them have been criminals for long periods and are very independent by nature. This independence sometimes results in the informant's attempting to manipulate the investigator and manage the investigation.

Second, an informant can become a source of public embarrassment for the law enforcement agency. For example, an informant might be arrested for a high-visibility crime during the time that he or she is working with the police.

FIGURE 8.3 Police informant working as a mechanic relays information to undercover police officer in front of truck, San Rafael, CA.

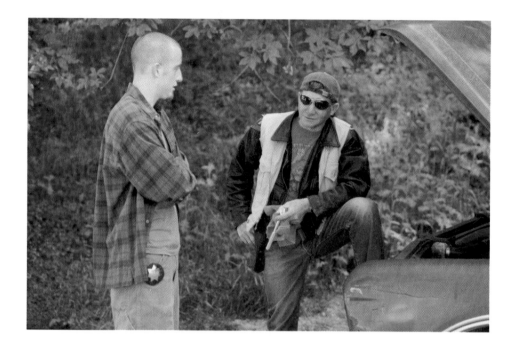

The local media could then make headlines that could jeopardize the investigation in which the informant was involved. Such situations are sometimes unavoidable but can usually be minimized with proper management techniques.

A third area of concern is the informant's questionable **credibility** in court. Depending on the role of the informant in the investigation, he or she might have to testify in court proceedings. A good defense council can expose the criminal background of such people and show that their testimony is not to be believed. If this is accomplished, juries will have difficulty finding the defendant guilty "beyond a reasonable doubt." After the decision has been made to use the services of an informant, he or she can be used in a number of ways:

- Make observations in areas where strangers would be suspect
- Furnish information from a source not readily available to the investigator
- Conduct "controlled" undercover transactions or introduce undercover agents to criminal suspects
- Collect intelligence information (e.g., determine street prices of drugs and identify suspects, their associates, and their residences)

The criminal investigator has the responsibility to evaluate every informant used. This saves time and effort if it is determined that the informant's information is unreliable or that the informant harbors a hidden agenda. Thus, the motive is extremely important to identify with each informant candidate because it may directly affect the credibility of the case.

Informant Motivations

Successful recruitment and management of informants pivots on the investigator's ability to recognize the **motivation** of the informant. Because the negative stigma of being an informant is so great in the United States, it is sometimes difficult to develop such people successfully. Police occasionally consider average citizens as informants provided that they are willing to offer relevant information in an investigation. The motivation of such people is a sense of civic duty.

As one might guess, mentally ill informants (depending on their illness) are motivated by very different reasons. These reasons are usually very complicated and difficult to determine, and frequently, information furnished by these

**CITY POLICE DEPARTMENT
COOPERATING INDIVIDUAL AGREEMENT**

I, _____, the undersigned, state that it is my intent to associate myself, of my own free will and without any coercion or duress, with the City Police Department as a cooperating individual.

As a cooperating individual, I understand and agree that I have no police powers under the laws of the state of (____) and have no authority to carry a weapon while performing my activity as a cooperating individual. Further, I understand and agree that my only association with the city of (____) is as a cooperating individual on a case-by-case or time-to-time basis as an independent contractor, and not as an employee of the police department. Any payment I receive from the City Police Department will not be subject to federal or state income tax withholding or social security. I understand that it is my responsibility to report any income and also that I am not entitled to either workmen's compensation or unemployment insurance payments for anything I do as a cooperating individual.

In consideration for being allowed to associate with the City Police Department as a cooperating individual, and in consideration for any payment I may receive, I agree to be bound by the following terms and conditions and procedures while so associated.

1. I agree that under no circumstances will I purchase or possess any controlled substances or suspected controlled substances without the direction and control of a police officer and then will make a purchase only with monies supplied by him.

2. I agree not to use or sell, dispense, or transfer any controlled substance except that I may use any controlled substance prescribed to me by a licensed physician.

3. I agree to maintain a strict accounting of all funds provided to me by the City Police Department and I understand that misuse of city funds could be grounds for criminal prosecution against me.

4. I agree not to divulge to any person, except the officer with whom I am associated, my status as a cooperating individual for the City Police Department unless required to do so in court, and shall not represent myself to others as an employee or representative of the City Police Department nor use the department or any of its officers as personal references or as credit or employment references.

5. I understand that any violation of the above listed provisions may be grounds for my immediate removal as a cooperating individual and that any violation of law may result in my arrest and prosecution.

I understand that association with the City Police Department as a cooperating individual may involve strenuous physical activity and may become hazardous to my physical well-being and safety. Nevertheless, it is my desire to associate myself with the department, on an independent contractor basis, as a cooperating individual. I am associating myself with the department in this status freely and without any coercion or duress. In consideration for being accepted as a cooperating individual, I release and discharge the City of (____), the City Police Department and its elected officials, officers, employees, and agents from all claims, demands, actions, judgments, and executions which I may have or acquire and subsequently claim to have against the City for personal injuries and property damage I may sustain which arises out of or in connection with my association with the city. I make this release for myself, my heirs, executors, and administrators. Also, I agree not to maintain any action against the City of (____), the City Police Department, or its elected officials, officers, employees, or agents for personal injuries and property damage I sustain which arise out of or in connection with my association with the City Police Department.

_____
Cooperating Individual

_____
Date

WITNESSES:

_____
Officer

_____
Officer

FIGURE 8.4 Sample informant agreement.

persons is worthless to the investigator. When a mentally ill informant gives valuable information, however, the person may be motivated by the same reasons as those that motivate criminal informants. Indeed, the criminal informant is the most valuable of all informant categories. As indicated, these people pose many legal, moral, and ethical considerations not generally associated with the other three categories. Motivations for a criminal informant fall into a number of categories:

- *The fearful informant.* Many persons agree to cooperate with law enforcement when fear is the chief motivator. Fear comes in many forms, such as fear of detection by law enforcement or retribution from criminal associates. Typically, this incentive arises when a person is arrested for an offense and fears being convicted and imprisoned. Given the opportunity, the arrestee may choose to provide information to investigators in exchange for leniency. Investigators must be careful not to make any promises to persons arrested without the consent of the prosecutor, who is generally vested with such authority. The investigator may, however, advise the informant that such a recommendation may be made pending any cooperation.

- *The financially motivated informant.* "Mercenary" informants give information in exchange for a fee. Often, the financially motivated informant will prove to be a valuable contributor to the investigation. Such persons may, however, attempt to manipulate the investigation to prolong payments to them. This is typically done by extending the investigation through providing misleading information or by "setting up" suspects in criminal violations that they are not predisposed to commit (i.e., entrapment).

- *The revengeful informant.* Revenge is not uncommon to the criminal underworld, and wrongs committed by one criminal against another are commonly settled outside the law. Frequently, however, informants motivated by revenge can produce favorable investigative results. Although those motivated by revenge are seldom concerned about revealing their identity in court, investigators must be careful to recognize an exaggerated or embellished story. In addition, such persons frequently have drifting allegiances and may reconcile with their former adversaries midway through the investigation, thus ruining credibility and jeopardizing the well-being of investigators.

- *The egotistical informant.* Many people take great delight in passing on information to others. Informants falling into this category may also be of great value to an investigator. This motivation is sometimes dubbed the *police complex* because of a person's desire to associate with law enforcement. It is typically characterized by a small-time criminal alleging to have inside information on high-level crime figures.

- *The perversely motivated informant.* People who display a perverse motivation are those who inform with a hidden benefit or advantage to themselves. Sometimes informants with this motivation are trying to eliminate their competition, learning investigative techniques, determining if any of their criminal associates are under investigation by police, or learning the identity of undercover officers. In all cases, the investigator must be aware of such motivations to avoid "setups" and compromising situations.

- *The reformed informant.* Informants characterized by this motivation act out of a sense of guilt from wrongdoing. Such informants are rare but when encountered may provide reliable information to the investigator.

Documenting Your "Source"

Proper management of informants is essential in avoiding unethical, immoral, or unprofessional allegations later in an investigation. The investigator must remember that informants belong to the agency and are not the "personal" resource of the investigator. This understanding will ensure that a system of checks and balances through records and verification of information can be officially maintained.

All candidates for informants should be well documented. They should, therefore, be fingerprinted, photographed, and carefully interviewed by investigators before being used as an informant. Interviews should reflect the informant's true name and any aliases, address, employment history, and so on. In addition, criminal records, if any, should be verified through the National Crime Information Center as well as through local and state law enforcement agencies. All such procedures should be contained in an official informant file established specifically for that person. The file should then be indexed by number, not by name, and that number should be used in all subsequent reports referring to the informant.

During the informant interview, the interviewer must be careful to solicit certain information. Some typical questions asked potential informants include:

- What is his or her motivation?
- Has the informer been reliable in the past?
- What is the intelligence of the informant?
- How does he or she know about the violation?
- Does he or she have a personal interest, and if so, what?
- Does he or she have direct knowledge?
- Does he or she have access to additional knowledge?
- Does he or she harbor any vengeance toward the suspect?
- Is he or she withholding some kind of information?
- Has he or she lied about information in the past?
- Is he or she willing to testify in court?

After the informant responds to the preceding questions, the investigator should have adequate information to proceed with a final evaluation of the person's potential worth. If the informant poses more of a liability than a benefit, he or she should be eliminated from further consideration.

Maintaining Control

Customarily, the investigator who develops an informer is the one who is assigned to him or her. A cardinal rule in working with informants is for the investigator to command control of the investigation, not the informant. This is sometimes difficult to accomplish because many informants possess strong, manipulative personalities. Although informants should be asked frequently for their opinions, each suggestion should be considered carefully. Additionally, investigators must be careful not to promise anything they cannot deliver (e.g., money, a reduced charge, relocation of their family, police protection).

Control of informants is best achieved through frequent personal contacts with them. These interactions are the best method for debriefing informers and maintaining rapport with them. The officer assigned should make most, if not all, contacts with informants. Doing so reduces additional demands of the informant and ensure the person's allegiance to the control officer. Another critical area of instruction for the informant is **entrapment**. Criminal suspects must be given an "opportunity" for the commission of a crime and not the "motivation" for doing so. If the entrapment issue is not remembered during the course of an investigation, the case may result in the dismissal of charges against the suspect and a soiled reputation for the department.

Protecting the Informant's Identify

Experience has shown that defendants may attempt to injure, intimidate, or even murder people working with the police. Accordingly, investigators bear an ethical and professional responsibility to safeguard the identities of informants and their families to the best of their ability. During initial interviews, investigators should advise potential informants that it is impossible to guarantee the confidentiality of their identities absolutely but that all efforts will be made to do so. In fact, the U.S. Supreme Court has ruled that the identities of informants may be kept secret if sources have been explicitly assured of confidentiality by investigating officers or if a reasonably implied assurance of confidentiality has been made. Measures that can be taken by the investigator to protect an informant's identity include:

- Limiting direct contact with the informant to one investigator or the "control" agent (unless the informant is of the opposite sex, in which case, two investigators should be present); meetings should be brief and held where neither party will be recognized
- Minimizing telephone conversations between control agents and informants in the event that someone is listening in on the line
- Selecting different locations to meet
- Warning informants about discussing their associations with the police to anyone, including their friends and spouses

The U.S. Supreme Court addressed the issue of protection of the informant's identity in court. In *U.S. Department of Justice v. Landano* (1993), the Court required that an informant's identity be revealed through a request made under the federal Freedom of Information Act. In that case, the FBI had not specifically assured the informant of confidentiality, and the Court ruled that "the government is not entitled to a presumption that all sources supplying information to the FBI in the course of a criminal investigation are confidential sources."

Legal Considerations

Information gathering is a complex process that raises many ethical and legal questions regarding the techniques used by investigators. For example, when police pay informants for information, critics argue that the informant might be tempted to entrap persons into committing crimes so that the informant can realize some income. Another common use of informants is *flipping*. This is a procedure in which an arrested person is given the choice of providing information to police in exchange for dropping their charges. Flipping is a widely used procedure requiring approval of the local prosecutor, but it still raises questions about the ethical appropriateness of the procedure.

Simply put, the informer's primary role is to provide probable cause to police for arrests and search warrants. The case of *Aguilar v. Texas* (1964) established a two-pronged test to the effect that an informant's information could provide probable cause if both of the following criteria are met:

- The source of the information is made clear
- The police officer has a reasonable belief that the information is reliable

The two-pronged *Aguilar* test was intended to prevent the issuance of warrants on the basis of false or fabricated information. But two subsequent cases have provided exceptions to the two-pronged test. *Harris v. United States* (1968) acknowledged the assumption that when an informant provided information that was damaging to him or her, that information was probably true. In the *Harris* case, an informant told police that he had purchased nontax-paid whiskey from another person.

Because the information actually implicated the informant in a crime, it was taken at face value as being true even though it failed the second prong of the two-pronged test. In 1969, the case of *Spinelli* v. *United States* created an exception to the requirements of the first prong. In that case, the U.S. Supreme Court ruled that some information can be so highly specific that it must be accurate even if its source is not revealed. Then, in 1983, in *Illinois* v. *Gates*, the Court adopted a totality of circumstances approach, which held that sufficient probable cause for issuing a warrant exists where an informant can reasonably be believed on the basis of everything that is known by the police.

Under the *Gates* decision, however, the Court held that although it is still important to consider the two-pronged test, each part of the test should be viewed separately and independently. The totality of the circumstances approach, therefore, permits any deficiencies of one part of the test to be overcome by the other with available evidence. In their decision, the Court stated:

> For all these reasons we conclude that it is wiser to abandon the two-pronged test established by our decisions under *Aguilar* and *Spinelli*. In its place we reaffirm totality of the circumstances analysis that traditionally has informed probable cause determinations. The task of using the magistrate is simply to make a practical, common-sense decision whether, given all the circumstances set forth in the affidavit before him, including the "veracity and basis of knowledge" of persons supplying hearsay information, there is a fair probability that contraband or evidence of a crime will be found in a particular place. And the duty of a reviewing court is simply to ensure that the magistrate had a "substantial basis for conclud[ing]" that probable cause existed.

In 1990, the case of *Alabama* v. *White* was reviewed by the Supreme Court, which held that an anonymous tip, even in the absence of other corroborating information about a suspect, could form the basis for an investigatory stop when the informant accurately predicts the "future" behavior of the suspect. The Court reasoned that the ability to predict a suspect's behavior demonstrates a significant degree of familiarity with the suspect's affairs.

Federal Protection of the Informant

If the case in which the informant testifies involves organized crime, the informant is eligible to enter the federal **Witness Security (WITSEC) program**. The WITSEC program, developed in 1971 and operated under the U.S. Marshal's Service, is designed to relocate government informants, providing them with new names, social security numbers, and other identification. Although a controversial program, it enjoys a 92 percent success rate in convictions of organized crime members by persons entering the program.

Other Problems with Informants

As indicated earlier, working with informants can be problematic. In addition to concerns of entrapment and ethical, moral, and criminal activity on the part of the informant, there are several other areas of concern:

- *Investigators becoming too friendly with informants.* Because investigators and their informers work together closely, it is possible that an officer can become caught up in an informant's personal problems. Certainly, the investigator should lend a sympathetic ear when possible, but investigators should be cautioned that becoming too close to an informant could jeopardize the investigator's level of control over the person.

- *Informants of the opposite sex.* Over the years, many investigators have fallen victim to allegations of sexual misconduct with informants of the opposite sex. Although some have proved truthful, many have had no basis but resulted in disciplinary action against the officer and a termination of the investigation. To avoid such allegations, a second officer should always accompany the investigator. The location of meeting spots with informants should also be considered very carefully, particularly if a second officer is not present.

- *Crimes committed by the informant.* During initial meetings between the investigator and potential informants, officers should stress that any criminal activity on the part of the informant will not be tolerated. History has shown that after being arrested for a crime, informants will sometimes mention the name of their control officer in hopes of being released or of receiving special treatment.

- *Officers who "own" their informants.* Over the years, some corrupt officers have claimed that meetings between themselves and criminals were in fact meetings with informants. Informants should be considered the "property" of the entire department and should be sufficiently documented. This avoids any allegations of misconduct on the part of investigators if seen with known criminals.

At times, information provided by informants is of such value that informants are paid for the information they supply. The investigator should be careful not to pay for information that has not been verified or that is not considered useful in the investigation. Accordingly, informant payments should be sufficiently modest as to avoid defense accusations of entrapment. When this occurs, the defense will maintain that the investigator's payment to the informant was so high that the informant was enticed into "setting up" the suspect solely for the monetary reward.

Undercover Operations

Undercover operations are an important part of the criminal investigation function but one that is highly specialized and not practiced by all law enforcement agencies. Investigators require specialized training to successfully perform this function. Stories abound regarding both investigative successes and failures in this area. From a practical standpoint, undercover work and surveillance are viable options for police investigators because they provide considerable information that is not otherwise available through traditional investigative methods.

For example, in February 2009, the U.S. Drug Enforcement Administration (DEA) arrested 52 persons in California, Minnesota, and Maryland as part of *Operation Xcellerator*. This investigation targeted the Sinaloa Cartel, a major Mexican drug trafficking organization.

In recent years, the Sinaloa Cartel has been responsible for bringing multi-ton quantities of narcotics, including cocaine and marijuana, from Mexico into the United States through distribution cells in the United States and Canada. They are also believed to be responsible for laundering millions of dollars in drug money. Suspects in this investigation were charged with engaging in a continuing criminal enterprise by violating various felony provisions of the Controlled Substances Act, conspiracy to import controlled substances, money laundering, and possession of unregistered firearms.[6]

The subjects of undercover operations and surveillance are discussed in this chapter because of their close relationship with each other and because of their importance to the investigative function. Typically, undercover work has been associated with drug enforcement, but it is a tool that can be useful in the investigation of a number of criminal activities.

Overview

Undercover operations have been used by police agencies for decades. However, they present many problems and concerns for the department because of the delicate nature of undercover work and the officer's role in determining whether someone is committing criminal violations.[7] Undercover work forces the officer to assume a different identity and, sometimes, a lifestyle that thrusts him or her into the criminal subculture, where he or she can be tempted to do things that would otherwise be immoral or even illegal (e.g., using illegal drugs). This has the potential to exact a heavy price on individual officers because, depending on the nature of the assignment, they may be separated from family, friends, and other department members for extended periods of time.

Undercover work is street-level work at its best (or worst, however you wish to view it). Officers are required to participate in undesirable activities, and those who remain in undercover positions for too long a period may begin to adopt the very behaviors of the criminals they are investigating, including undesirable mannerisms and foul language at the least. Even worse, the department can become involved in illegal activities during the course of an investigation. For example, New York City undercover officers ran a pornographic bookstore as part of an undercover sting operation. Officers, as part of their undercover investigation, purchased 1,200 pornographic films and resold them for considerable profit. After eight months, the officers finally arrested several film distributors.

Langworthy observes that some undercover operations result in additional criminal activities.[8] As a result of his analysis of a Birmingham undercover anti-fencing operation, he concluded that the operation caused a substantial amount of crime by creating a market for stolen goods. If the police operation had not existed, no market would have existed, and criminals would have stolen less.

Any undercover operation is subject to claims of entrapment. Officers are permitted to do things that provide the opportunity for a suspect to commit a crime, but they may not induce someone to commit a crime. Because undercover operations generally may be initiated without prior judicial authorization, the results are subject to strict scrutiny by the courts. Allowing police to make the decision to initiate an undercover operation based on mere suspicion has been the subject of much criticism.[9] Recognizing the magnitude of the problem, the FBI now requires that large-scale undercover operations first be reviewed by their Criminal Undercover Operations Review Committee.

Informants are particularly useful and often necessary in the investigation of vice crimes. They can be problematic, however, because police sometimes overlook illegal acts committed by informers to pursue their investigations. For example, narcotics users or lower-level dealers may be allowed to continue violating the law to make cases against their suppliers. Consequently, to move up the distribution network, undercover officers may find it necessary to cooperate with dealers who are selling a significant amount of drugs.

A 1989 informant management case in Cleveland resulted in disastrous consequences for the department.[10] Officers of the narcotics unit enlisted the help of Arthur Feckner, one of the city's major wholesalers, to arrest his supplier. The investigation, which resulted in the seizure of more than 100 pounds of cocaine, caused enormous problems for the department. Allegations surfaced that the police allowed Feckner to continue to sell drugs in a housing project to finance their drug investigation. Detectives maintained that they believed the money came from the sale of his assets and collection of debts from past drug sales. However, Feckner says he sold $20 million worth of drugs with the knowledge of the police.

Undercover operations require a number of decisions. Administrative discretion is exercised in determining what activities will be pursued, and operational discretion is exercised in determining who will be targeted for investigation. Because police do not have the resources to investigate every crime, they engage in selective enforcement, enforcing only particular types of violations or targeting specific types of offenders. The decision-making process for vice crimes is subject to the factors previously discussed. The most important criterion for officers is the seriousness of the offense.[11] Most forms of vice, when considered alone, could be viewed as relatively minor crimes. However, in the current political climate, which emphasizes "zero tolerance," possession of even small amounts of drugs is viewed as serious. Officers are therefore much less likely to use size discretion in their decision to arrest in drug cases.

Understanding Undercover Work

The use of undercover agents is not recommended for every police organization because of resources required for a successful undercover operation. These resources include manpower, training, funding, specialized equipment, and other unique resources.

Police administrators must be careful in the selection of the proper candidate(s) for undercover work. Not every police officer can function properly and professionally in an undercover capacity. Typically, an undercover officer works with minimal direct supervision.[12] As such, officers can be exposed to a number of enticements, which could result in the compromising of the officer's integrity or the investigation. Because of this, the undercover officer must have considerable personal integrity.

One of the greatest challenges to undercover officers is the development of skills that maximize their efforts to match wits with some of the most intelligent and artful criminals on the street. Undercover assignments are either performed in the short term or long term (or "deep cover"). Short-term undercover operations are normally considerably safer for the officer than those that are **deep cover**. Short-term operations permit the help of surveillance officers and protection that undercover agents working in a deep-cover capacity do not have. However, the benefits of working a deep-cover undercover operation allow an undercover agent time to gain total trust of the criminal suspect to the point of openly discussing criminal operations. This is a great advantage to an undercover agent because as a rule, criminals are very suspicious about meeting new "clients" who could be (and sometimes are) police informers or undercover officers.

While no two cases are exactly the same, Motto and June point out that there are certain elements common to each undercover operation: the introduction, the acceptance, the buy, the arrest, covering the informant, and the "after action."[13]

The informant typically makes the "introduction" of the undercover operative to the suspect. This is the initiation of the case. From this point on, the "acceptance" phase takes over when the undercover agent is either accepted or not. In the event the suspect does not accept the officer, it might be necessary for the informant to meet the suspect at a later time without the undercover officer to determine why the suspect was suspicious. In the event the officer is not accepted, the informant can bring in a second officer with a different cover story. This time, both the officer and informant will try to overcome the difficulties experienced during the first contact.

After the introduction, there is a short period of "bobbing, weaving, and circling": The suspect gets to know or feel if he or she can trust the undercover officer. If a feeling of trust is established, the conversation will quickly turn to the criminal activities in which the suspect is involved.

In the case of an undercover drug operation, for example, this conversation generally results in the undercover agent asking for or obtaining samples, and the suspect will quote the purchase price. After the samples have been delivered and the undercover agent has had an opportunity to examine them, the purchase price is discussed.

This purchase, or the "buy," may or may not go through. In other words, a decision must be made whether or not to arrest a suspect when he or she delivers the contraband (also known as a **buy-bust**) or to take that action after subsequent deliveries (known as a **buy-walk**). If it is determined that the investigation should continue, no arrests should be made and nothing should be done to arouse the suspect's suspicion or to identify accidentally the true role of the undercover operative. This is known as *covering the informant.*

In drug investigations, the first buy is usually a small one whereby the agency doesn't mind losing its **seed money** so that the undercover officer can make a bigger purchase at a later time. Subsequent purchases of contraband are known as the "after action." As a rule, the second purchase or, if necessary, several subsequent purchases. are large enough to warrant not only the appearance of a suspect but also some of the people connected with him or her. These individuals could be present in several capacities, including countersurveillance, protection, main participants, or equal partners, and perhaps even higher-ups. Sometimes it is necessary because of the development of circumstances surrounding the case to arrest a suspect when an initial delivery is made.

Preparing for Undercover Assignments

Undercover work can be defined as assuming a fictitious identity and associating with known or suspected criminals for the purpose of collecting information or evidence on criminal activity. All undercover work has the potential for considerable danger. It requires that officers establish a cover story (which may or may not be blown at any time during the investigation) and that they associate closely with individuals who may be armed, unpredictable, under the influence of drugs, or mentally unstable.

Personnel Considerations. The selection, management, and retention of effective undercover employees (UCEs) pose significant challenges to local, state, federal, and international law enforcement agencies. UCEs face unique experiences and stressors that set them apart from their overt counterparts and place them at increased risk for psychological injury, disciplinary action, and other adverse personal and professional consequences.[14]

Given the inherent dangers of undercover work, the selection and training of personnel must be meticulous. Consideration must be given to the particular goals and resources of the unit, the officers' personalities, their professional backgrounds, and their physical and mental conditions. In addition, an officer's proficiency with firearms, good reporting skills, and the ability to keep a cool head and use common sense under stressful conditions must be carefully weighed by police supervisors. Because of concern for officer safety and the increasing potential for agency liability, the days of undercover officers working the streets in deep cover and under minimal supervision are becoming less common.

Those being considered for undercover assignments should be disabused of any myths created by television and popular media stereotypes. Undercover work is not a glamorous job providing the agent with expensive meals, luxurious sports cars, and unheard-of electronic gadgetry. Conversely, it is also not a duty that requires an officer to isolate him- or herself from family and friends and become a drug-using martyr.

Most undercover work consists of a brief meeting between the agent and a suspect, an exchange of dialogue, and a transaction—usually a purchase of contraband such as a quantity of illegal drugs, stolen property, or illegal weapons. Deep-cover assignments, that is, assignments that require agents to operate with minimal protection over extended periods of time, are not as widely used and require specialized training.

Although required to work one on one with a suspected drug dealer, undercover officers must also realize that both their safety and the overall success of the investigation require equal participation by all unit members. Each officer's role (undercover contact, surveillance officer, radar officer, and officers assisting in arrest) is of equal importance. Even though every officer within the unit must maintain his or her caseload, each should regard the overall mission of the unit as an effort of a team rather than of one individual.

Functions of Undercover Officers. There are two general functions for officers within the undercover unit. The **undercover (UC) officer** contacts individuals or infiltrates establishments or organizations suspected of being involved in criminal activity. Usually, such contacts are possible because the officer's appearance, mannerisms, dress, and overall demeanor are similar to those of the suspect. Considerable time and money are spent in carefully cultivating the officer's ability to function effectively in this capacity, so the true identity of the undercover officer should be protected at all times.

The **support officer** (sometimes called an intelligence, cover, or tactical officer) is a plainclothes officer who works with the undercover unit but not in an undercover capacity. Support officers assist undercover officers by observing the illicit transactions (e.g., an illegal drug transaction) in which they, or their informers, are involved. Support officers also participate in drug raids at the culmination of an investigation, interview arrestees, and perform other functions within the unit that would otherwise jeopardize or expose the identity of the undercover agent.

Because criminal enterprises differ in their resources, methods, procedures, and philosophies, the operational distinctions between undercover and support officers may not be feasible in some agencies. In such circumstances, officers may be required at different times to perform both functions.

Equipment. To approach any covert investigation effectively, one of the first orders of business is to determine what equipment is necessary. The choice of equipment will, of course, vary according to the agency's financial resources, the size of the unit, the mission, and the type of assignment at hand. However, when considering an equipment purchase, careful thought should be given to its purpose and user, its usefulness, and its durability.

Undercover investigators require equipment that is different from that given to support officers. In addition, equipment assigned to a criminal investigator might be regularly carried with him or her in an assigned vehicle. Therefore, it may experience much wear and tear from moving around in the trunk of a car or the back of the van, or it may suffer from drastic changes in weather conditions due to changing humidity, temperature, or dust particles, for example.

Vehicles. As a rule, each vehicle owned by the agency should be assigned a separate number, and a maintenance and repair file should be kept on each vehicle. The kinds of vehicles the agency should own and the equipment the vehicles should contain depend on how they will be used. Following are some examples.

Support Officer Vehicles. Vehicles for a support officer should generally be nondescript such as two-door sedans or commonly observed SUVs in plain colors such as white, tan, gray, or dark blue. Exotic or expensive sports cars might be advantageous in short-term undercover assignments, but they will also be easily remembered or identified (**burned**) as police vehicles by nervous or attentive suspects during any moving surveillance.

Vehicles should also be assigned to match the driver. For example, a more expensive car should be assigned to an appropriately dressed agent; a sports car should be assigned to an investigator who fits the role of someone who would typically drive one. If local laws permit, seized vehicles, if in good condition, are good assets and can provide a constant source of plausible vehicles for the undercover unit. Undercover personnel should not use vehicles assigned to support officers. Support officers' vehicles need to be outfitted differently from those assigned to undercover officers. These vehicles should have more standard "police-type" electronics that benefit them but would identify, or "burn," an undercover investigator. Support officer vehicles are sometimes equipped with "kill switches." These are standard toggle switches, usually concealed in the glove box and wired so that a single headlight, the tail lights, or brake lights can be turned off. This is beneficial in nighttime surveillance to change the appearance of the vehicle when a suspect is looking for surveillance through his or her rearview mirror (see the section on surveillance methods in Chapter 7).

Undercover Officer Vehicles. Vehicles used by undercover investigators should not be equipped like support officer vehicles. Undercover vehicles must be kept "clean." Criminal suspects will often be inside the undercover vehicle, and it is common for them to examine the vehicle for a possible police radio or hidden wires to microphones or even to check the vehicle registration. Consequently, anything the suspect discovers in the vehicle should be placed there purposely to support the officer's cover story.

The Undercover Working Environment

Although undercover operations have unique benefits, they also have a serious downside. On one hand, undercover is an investigative method by which officers can see firsthand the inner workings of criminal organizations. Officers can converse and strategize with their criminal targets and learn the ways criminal minds work. Conversely, this close interaction may place officers in jeopardy because they might inadvertently reveal something inconsistent with their cover story. Furthermore, exposure to criminal elements in a close, undercover capacity for extended periods of time might result in the undercover officer's acting and speaking in a manner other than he or she is accustomed, even when off duty, reflecting poorly on the officer's credibility.

To minimize problems associated with undercover operations, a certain degree of preparation is imperative. This includes establishing a sound cover story and understanding specialized infiltration techniques.

The Cover Story

A prerequisite for assuming an undercover role is to establish a **cover story**. Simply defined, the cover story is a fictitious story that the agent will convey to suspects concerning his or her background, including his or her name, address, hometown (or area), and employment, if applicable. Other details may be included, but it is a good idea to keep the cover story simple in case an agent must deal with inquisitive criminal suspects.

The cover story should fit with the area and people involved with the investigation. When an officer chooses to associate him- or herself with a particular town or area, it should be one with which the officer is already familiar, in case he or she later meets someone from that area. Officers should remember that mixing a partial truth with the cover story makes an officer more believable to the suspect.

When claiming a place of employment, the officer should choose one that cannot be easily checked out by suspects. This is more of a problem in rural areas because people are more likely to know each other. It may be desirable to choose an out-of-town place of employment that requires a lot of travel or to present a fictitious job in which the officer is self-employed, thus making it harder for criminal suspects to verify. Whatever story is chosen, the officer should be provided with business cards, customized stationery, credit cards, checking and savings account books, and other supporting credentials to corroborate the cover story. Moreover, the officer should be familiar with the profession chosen for the cover story for the same reasons he or she should be familiar with the purported hometown.

The officer's appearance and mannerisms should also fit the cover story. If the officer claims to be an oil field worker, for example, it might be out of character for the officer to be seen by the suspect in an expensive business suit. On the other hand, if the officer's cover story is that of financier for a big money deal, then expensive clothing might be more appropriate. It might also be necessary for an undercover officer to wear expensive jewelry to help convince sellers of his or her cover story. Depending on the nature of the investigation, expensive jewelry can sometimes be borrowed from local stores for short periods; however, the safety and security of the jewelry are the responsibility of the undercover officer.

Protecting the Undercover Officer's Cover

After the cover story has been established, the undercover officer is committed to it. Certainly the basics—name, hometown, and location—cannot easily be changed without jeopardizing the officer's safety and the integrity of the investigation. Even if changes are not necessary, however, the undercover officer must be able to detect and withstand attempts by suspects and their associates to test and invalidate the officer's cover story.

Typically, suspects will barrage the officer with questions in an attempt to catch any inconsistency in the cover story. If they are successful, or believe they are, suspects usually attempt to frighten or intimidate the officer into admitting he or she is a law enforcement agent or into abandoning the investigation out of fear for their personal safety.

Panic is the undercover officer's worst enemy. Officers must realize two important things: paranoia is common among drug dealers and no matter what suspects say they know about the agent, many times they're just attempting to lock the officer into an admission for which they have no proof. If the officer keeps the cover story general, most questioning and suspicion should be easily overcome. Moreover, if the officer has been properly trained and responds to the suspects according to his or her training, a bond of trust may develop between the officer and suspects, which can pave the way to a successful investigation.

Different criminals use different methods to expose undercover police agents. Even though good field training should prepare undercover personnel for most of these obstacles, not every confrontation can be anticipated. Undercover personnel should remember that most questions about their cover story are bluffs, and they should remain calm and confident, discounting the challenges presented without appearing scared, intimidated, or paranoid.

An investigator should also be aware that criminals can be quite tricky and cunning when trying to expose possible police infiltration. For example, they may:

- Attempt to intoxicate the officer in the hope that he or she will say something inconsistent with the cover story while under the influence of alcohol.

- Use prostitutes, girlfriends or boyfriends, or associates to attempt to seduce the officer; in doing so, the upper torso will be felt for body mikes, the waist area for weapons, and pockets for police credentials or anything else indicating an association with police work.
- Ask the officer questions about his or her cover story when the suspects already know the answer; the suspects hope to observe nervousness on the part of the officer.
- Ask the officer to furnish drugs to a friend or an associate knowing that it is against regulations for a law enforcement officer to do so.
- Ask the officer to consume drugs furnished by the suspect.
- Attempt to learn information about the officer's family (spouse, children, other relatives, or friends) so that an officer's story can be more easily verified.
- Ask the officer to perform various illegal acts.
- Attempt to rummage through the officer's car or personal belongings to locate police-related material or information showing that the officer was lying about his or her cover story.
- Ask the undercover officer excessive questions to see how many he or she is willing to answer before becoming suspicious or angry.

Infiltration

After a cover story is established, a methodical process of infiltration must take place to uncover criminal wrongdoing and its associated evidence. During infiltration, a relationship is established between the officer and a suspect. Frequently, an officer finds it difficult to meet or establish any rapport with the suspect without the help of an informant. In some cases, however, informants may cause more trouble for the officer and the investigation than they are worth; therefore, their use should be carefully considered. Infiltration requires inventiveness and originality on the officer's part because he or she might have to create his or her own opportunity to speak with the suspect.

After contact has been made between the officer and the suspect, the suspect's confidence must be gained as soon as possible. An officer can best accomplish this by learning the interests of the suspects (e.g., jobs, the opposite sex, local bars, motorcycles, cars, drugs), which the officer can then discuss. Context must be regularly attempted throughout the investigation to maintain rapport with the suspect.

When working without an informant, it might be necessary to canvass a target area. The undercover officer can expedite the investigation by revealing intelligence on target suspects and locations, concentrating on areas with high levels of crime that might provide investigative leads. Typical starting places might be bars, nightclubs, or taverns, which can be excellent sources of intelligence for undercover officers. Much can be learned just by being present at these locations; generally people do not have a reasonable expectation of privacy when "openly" conversing in public in such places as a bar. The undercover agent can simply overhear otherwise private or guarded information about their suspects' names, types of criminal activities, places of employment, and vehicles they drive. After the officer learns such information and it appears that the information might be useful in showing criminal activity, it should be properly documented in intelligence reports. The lack of such properly generated intelligence reports accounts for the loss of much valuable criminal information to the unit.

A CLOSER LOOK

Becoming a DEA Special Agent

A DEA Special Agents are a select group of men and women from diverse backgrounds whose experience and commitment make them the premier federal drug law enforcement agents in the world. Applicants must be at least 21 years of age and no older than 36 at the time of their appointment.

Education. The most competitive candidates possess a bachelor's or master's degree, along with a grade point average (GPA) of 2.95 or higher. Special consideration is given to candidates with degrees in criminal justice/police science or related disciplines; finance, accounting, or economics; foreign languages (with fluency verified) in Spanish, Russian, Hebrew, Arabic, dialects of Nigerian languages, Chinese, Japanese; computer science/information systems; and telecommunications, electrical engineering and mechanical engineering.

Depending on scheduling and candidate availability, the DEA's hiring process may take 12 months or longer. Hiring involves a multi-step process that includes the following phases:

- Qualifications review
- Written and oral assessment and panel interview
- Urinalysis drug test
- Medical examination
- Physical task test
- Polygraph examination
- Psychological assessment
- Background investigation
- Final hiring decision

Training. All applicants must successfully complete all phases of the hiring process and remain most competitive to receive a final offer of employment. For more information, contact your nearest DEA field division recruitment office. Scheduling times and locations are handled by the local recruitment coordinators. Special Agent candidates are required to successfully complete a 16-week Basic Agent Training (BAT) program at the DEA Training Academy in Quantico, Virginia.

Through this program, instruction and hands-on training are provided in undercover, surveillance, and arrest techniques; defensive tactics and firearms training; and the basics of report writing, law, and drug identification and recognition. In addition, applicants participate in a rigorous physical fitness program.

Duty Station. Between the 8th and 12th weeks of the training, applicants are provided with final duty station assignments. Mobility is a condition of employment. Assignments are made based upon DEA's current operational needs.

Mobility. Mobility is a condition of employment. Special Agents are subject to transfer throughout their career based on the needs of the agency.

Salary. DEA Special Agents are generally hired at the GS-7 or GS-9 level, depending on education and experience. The salary includes federal Law Enforcement Officer base pay plus a locality payment, depending on the duty station. Upon successful graduation from the DEA Training Academy, 25% availability pay will be added to the base and locality pay. After graduation, the starting salaries are approximately $49,746 for a GS-7 and $55,483 for a GS-9. After four years of service, Special Agents are eligible to progress to the GS-13 level and can earn approximately $92,592 or more per year.

Drug Use Policy. The DEA is charged with enforcement of the Federal Controlled Substances Act; therefore, all applicants must fully disclose any drug use history during the application process. Applicants whose drug use history is outside of acceptable parameters will not be considered for employment. All DEA employees are subject to random urinalysis drug testing throughout their careers.

The Physical Task (PT) Test. The PT test determines if potential candidates can withstand the rigors of Special Agent training. Candidates must be in excellent physical condition to pass this test.

If a candidate fails the first PT test, administered in the field, a second test must be successfully taken within 30 days. A second failure will cause the candidate's application process to be discontinued. Candidates are encouraged to train to ensure that they are prepared to successfully complete this test.

A CLOSER LOOK CONTINUED

Background investigation. A background investigation (BI) is one of the final steps in the application process that seeks to discern a comprehensive snapshot of applicants. The investigation provides information on applicants' personal history, education and work experience, personal and professional references, as well as other necessary checks. The time it takes to complete the BI is dependent on the type and scope of investigation being conducted.

Thematic question

Considering drug enforcement agents often work in a proactive undercover capacity, to what extent do you think that doing so unfairly targets persons for investigation who have not yet committed a crime? Explain your response.

Source: U.S. Drug Enforcement Administration: DEA Special Agents. Available at http://www.dea.gov/job/agent/faqs.html#question002.

It should be noted that although bars, nightclubs, and taverns can be lucrative sources of information, officer safety is greatly reduced in these settings. If two undercover officers are available, it is a good idea to assign both of them to a particular tavern, working independently of each other. This accomplishes two goals: It gives both officers additional backup, and it provides each officer the chance to identify different suspects in criminal groups operating within the tavern.

If a tavern is to be infiltrated, the undercover officer has several potentially good targets to consider. The first people contacted may not be offenders but might know those who are. Without being too aggressive, the undercover officer might consider befriending one of the following people in the bar:

- *Bartender.* Bartenders may or may not be involved in criminal activity, but they will most likely know of any criminal activity occurring and who is responsible.
- *Waitresses.* Waitresses are also frequently aware of an array of criminal activity taking place within the bar.
- *Bar customers* (regulars). Regular customers in a tavern might also be good players to befriend; they, too, often know who might be involved in criminal activity.

Sometimes an informant will arrange a transaction for the purchase of contraband and a first-time meeting between a contraband dealer and the undercover officer. In this case, the seller will have some degree of suspicion about the officer, and some initial questioning should be anticipated. At this point in the investigation, the officer should remember a few guidelines:

1. The officer should not let the suspect question him or her any more than if the roles were reversed. Some questioning is understandable and justifiable, but it can become excessive. If this occurs, the officer should deal with it the best way possible, perhaps by acting angry, advising the seller that he's too inquisitive and that the deal is either on or it is not. This should help convince the seller that the officer is aware of what the suspect is attempting to do and that he or she is being manipulated. Undercover officers will find that subsequent transactions are usually much easier because the dealer feels confident because he or she has not been arrested as a result of dealing with the officer.

2. While working in a bar, an officer might purchase drinks or pay for pool or video games to start a conversation with a suspect. However, officers

must be careful to abide by established police policy regarding the consumption of alcoholic beverages while on duty. Most law enforcement agencies permit officers to consume liquor while working undercover, but because an officer's judgment may be impaired and because he or she might become less likely to remember necessary facts, this must be done with considerable discretion. Furthermore, in case it becomes an issue in court later, the officer should drink as little as possible in order to avoid attacks on the officer's credibility by defense attorneys after the case goes to trial.

3. If the undercover assignment takes the officer to the suspect's house, in addition to taking additional safety precautions, the officer must recognize that this is a good opportunity to learn new information about the suspect. The officer should mentally map out all entrances, exits, and windows that the suspect may use for escape during a possible future raid. The officer should mentally note the number on the telephone, which might furnish a lead to the name of a new associate later. Discreetly observing mail lying out in the open may also reveal the names of associates or roommates. Finally, noting the presence of controlled substances and their hiding places, in addition to any weapons, may be useful later when obtaining a search warrant or conducting a raid.

4. Officers should remember that the practice of lying and deceiving is common for drug dealers. If the officer gets caught in a lie, he or she should never become prematurely paranoid and fear that his or her cover has been blown. The officer should react with disinterest or perhaps even laugh it off for the suspect's benefit. It is best to try to justify the line by claiming that he or she doesn't "want too many people knowing too much about my personal business." The suspect will most likely identify with and respect such an explanation.

Risks in Undercover Assignments

For investigators assignee to undercover roles, two principal problems can be identified that may pose problems for both the investigator and his or her agency. The first is the problem of maintaining the "criminal" identity, and the second area is the process of reintegration back into normal investigative duties. The maintenance of identity problems are those that are associated with adopting of and living of a double life in a new environment.

Stress in Relationships. Undercover work is one of the most stressful jobs that a police officer can undertake.[15] The largest cause of stress for investigators working undercover is the requirement that they distance themselves from friends, family, and their normal environment. This simple isolation can result in the onset of depression and anxiety. There are no data on the divorce rates of undercover agents, but considerable tension in relationships has been known to develop. This can result from a need for secrecy and an inability to share work problems, the unpredictable work schedule, personality and lifestyle changes, and the length of separation. These factors can all result in problems for relationships.[16]

Stress from Uncertainty. Stress can also result from an apparent lack of direction of the investigation or not knowing when it will end. The amount of elaborate planning, risk, and expenditure can also place pressure on an agent to succeed, which can cause considerable stress.[17] The stress that an undercover agent faces is considerably different from that faced by investigators who are not assigned to undercover assignments and whose main source of stress results from pressures by the administration and the general bureaucracy of police work.[18]

Because the undercover agent is removed from the bureaucracy, it may result in another problem. Because they do not have the usual controls of a uniform, badge, constant supervision, a fixed place of work, or (often) a set assignment, combined with their continual contact with the criminal underworld (members of the opposite sex, pressure and manipulation from criminal suspects, alcohol, availability of illicit drugs, and opportunities to earn or seize large amounts of illicit money), increase the likelihood for corruption.[19]

Development of Alcohol or Drug Abuse. This stress may be instrumental in the development of drug or alcohol abuse in some agents. These agents are more prone to the development of an addiction because they experience greater stress than other police, they are isolated, and drugs are often very accessible.[20] Police, in general, have very high alcoholism rates compared with people in most occupational groups, and stress is cited as a likely factor.[21] The environment that agents work in, including taverns, bars and private residences of criminal suspects, often involves considerable exposure to the consumption of alcohol, which in conjunction with the stress and isolation may result in alcoholism.[22]

Feelings of Personal Guilt. There can also be some guilt associated with working undercover because of the need to essentially betray the trust of those (criminal suspects) who have come to trust you. According to Marx, this can cause anxiety or even, in very rare cases, sympathy with those being targeted.[23] This is especially true with the infiltration of political groups because often the agent shares similar characteristics, such as class, age, ethnicity, or religion, with those they are infiltrating. This could even result in the conversion of some agents.[24]

Problems of Reintegration. The lifestyle led by undercover agents is very different than that for other areas in law enforcement, and it can be quite difficult to reintegrate back into normal duties. Agents work their own hours, they are removed from direct supervisory monitoring, and they can ignore the dress and etiquette rules.[25] So the resettling back into the normal police role requires the shredding of old habits, language, and dress. After working such free lifestyles, agents may have discipline problems or exhibit neurotic responses. They may feel uncomfortable and take a cynical, suspicious, or even paranoid worldview and feel continually on guard.[26]

CASE IN POINT:

The Anti-Snitch Movement

It was strange enough for prosecutors and police to see the T-shirt with a traffic-sign message: "STOP SNITCHING," but one of those T-shirts was about to show up in court with a matching baseball cap. Worse yet, the wearer was a prosecution witness for Pittsburgh's Prosecutor Lisa Pellegrini.

In March of 2006, Rayco "War" Saunders— ex-con, pro boxer, and walking billboard for an anti-snitch movement— sparked a coast-to-coast debate involving everyone from academics to police to rappers. Pellegrini, while thinking "witness intimidation," told Saunders to lose the hat and reverse the shirt.

Saunders, claiming "First Amendment" rights, refused. He left the courthouse, shirt in place. Case dismissed.

The attitude of "don't be a snitch" is common throughout many communities and, in some cases, even condoned. While the Mafia's traditional blood oath of silence, "Omerta," has been broken by turncoat after turncoat, in some inner-city neighborhoods, the call to stop snitching is galvanizing. Some say it's an attempt by drug dealers and gangsters to intimidate witnesses, but others say it's a legitimate protest against law enforcement's overreliance on criminal informers.

CASE IN POINT continued

Take the case of Busta Rhymes, the hip-hop star who refused to cooperate with police investigating the slaying of his bodyguard, Israel Ramirez, on February 5, 2006, outside a Brooklyn studio where Rhymes was recording a video with other rap performers. Police claimed that although Rhymes and as many as 50 others may have witnessed the shooting, no one came forward—reminiscent of the echo of silence that followed the unsolved murders of rappers Tupac Shakur, The Notorious B.I.G., and Run-DMC's Jam Master Jay.

Although some argue that it's logical for a witness to a crime to want to talk to the police, others say that because of growing animosities between the police and the public, *not* being an informer is the honorable thing to do.

Informers have always been a key investigative tool but at the same time have been viewed as a necessary evil. In some cases, if a drug dealer needs to make a deal, he or she will tell on friends or family alike if necessary. It may not be right, but it's the only answer for some people. In some cases, criminal informers who are allowed to remain free commit more crimes, return to crime after serving a short prison sentence, frame other people for crimes they didn't commit, or tell prosecutors anything they want to hear.

According to a study by the Northwestern University Law School's Center on Wrongful Convictions, 51 of the 111 wrongful death penalty convictions since the 1970s were based in whole or in part on the testimony of witnesses who had incentives to lie. Based on federal statistics, one of every four black men from 20 to 29 years of age is incarcerated, on probation, or on parole and under pressure to snitch. Estimates are that one in 12 of all black men in the highest crime neighborhoods throughout the nation is a criminal informant.

Hence the backlash—"stop snitching." The slogan appeared in Baltimore in 2004 as the title of an underground DVD featuring threatening gun-wielding drug dealers and a brief appearance by NBA star and Baltimore native Carmelo Anthony. Whatever its intent, the stop snitching movement concerns officials who are already enraged about witness reluctance and witness intimidation. State and local governments spend a fraction of what the federal government devotes to witness protection and informant management, although in March 2006, Pennsylvania restored $1,000,000 for that purpose. This move came as more than half a dozen witnesses recanted earlier testimony in the trial of men accused in the Philadelphia street shooting death of a third-grade boy.

The movement has created problems for law enforcement across the country because without informers, many cases cannot be properly investigated. "Stop Snitching" T-shirts have been banned from a number of courthouses across the nation. In Boston, Mayor Thomas Menino sent police officers into the stores to remove "Stop Snitching" T-shirts from the shelves. In Maryland, the crime of witness intimidation was elevated from misdemeanor to felony, and in Baltimore, police made a DVD of their own called "Keep Talking."

Sources: HAMPSON, R. (2006). Anti-snitch campaign riles police, prosecutors. *USA Today*, March 29:1A–2A; Scolville, D. (2007). How to develop informants. Police. *The Law Enforcement Magazine*. Available at http://www.policemag.com/Articles/2007/08/How-to-Develop-Informants.aspx.

Summary Checklist

In this chapter, we consider the ways information about crimes is documented by criminal investigators. A properly documented case is one that is more likely to succeed in court. See how well you are able to answer the following questions in your checklist.

1. **Do you know the type of citizen who typically becomes an informant for the police?**

   The term "informant" could best be defined as "anyone who provides information of an investigative nature to law enforcement."

- The informant is most typically used in cases in which there is no complainant. These typically include vice and victimless crimes such as drug violations, gambling, and prostitution.

- Generally, people who become informants can be classified into four general groups: the average citizen, fellow law enforcement officers, mentally ill persons, and criminal or their associates.

2. Can you describe the methods and procedures for using an informant?

The use of an informant in a criminal investigation can be problematic. Therefore, his or her use should not be considered if similar results could be achieved through other means.

Problems that stem from the use of informants are due to three variables:

- They are often difficult to control
- They have been criminals for long periods of time
- They vary independent by nature

Other problems include:

- An informant can become a source of public embarrassment for the law enforcement agency
- The credibility of the informant in court is questionable

The investigator must have the ability to recognize the motivation of the informant. Motivations include:

- Financial motivations
- Revenge
- Egotistical persons
- Perversely motivated persons
- Self-reformed persons

3. Can you explain the ways that an informant should be documented and controlled?

All candidates for informants should be well documented. They should, therefore, be fingerprinted, photographed, and carefully interviewed by investigators before being used as informants.

All such procedures should be contained in an official informant file established specifically for that person.

- Typically, the investigator who develops an informer is the one who is assigned to him or her

Many informants possess strong, manipulative personalities.

- Although informants should be asked frequently for their opinions, each suggestion should be considered carefully

Control of informants is best achieved through frequent personal contacts with them.

- These interactions are the best method for debriefing informers and maintaining rapport with them
- The officer assigned should make most, if not all, contacts with the informant
- Investigators must always consider that the informant may be attempting to "entrap" the subject and avoid such situations

Another common use of informants is flipping. This is a procedure in which an arrested person is given the choice of providing information to police in exchange for dropping their charges.

- Flipping is a widely used procedure requiring approval of the local prosecutor, but it still raises questions about the ethical appropriateness of the procedure

4. Do you know the usefulness of undercover operations in criminal investigation?

Undercover operations are an important part of the criminal investigation function but one that is highly specialized and not practiced by all law enforcement agencies.

- Investigators require specialized training to successfully perform this function

Undercover work forces the officer to assume a different identity and, sometimes, a lifestyle that thrusts him or her into the criminal subculture, where he or she can be tempted to do things that would otherwise be immoral or even illegal (e.g., using illegal drugs).

Undercover work allows the investigator to observe without being known as a law

(continued)

Summary Checklist (Continued)

enforcement officer. Because of this, he or she is able to identify evidence of crime in a number of categories.

Police administrators must be careful in the selection of the proper candidate(s) for undercover work.

- Not every police officer can function properly and professionally in an undercover capacity.
- Typically, undercover officers work with minimal direct supervision.

Undercover assignments are either performed in the short term or long term.

5. **Can you identify the steps that investigators must prepare for undercover assignments?**

All undercover work has the potential for considerable danger. It requires that officers establish a cover story (which may or may not be blown at any time during the investigation) and that they associate closely with individuals who may be armed, unpredictable, under the influence of drugs, or mentally unstable.

Officers being considered for undercover assignments should be disabused of any myths created by television and popular media stereotypes. Undercover work is not a glamorous job providing the agent with expensive meals, luxurious sports cars, and unheard-of electronic gadgetry.

- Most undercover work consists of a brief meeting between the agent and a suspect, an exchange of dialogue, and a transaction—usually a purchase of contraband such as a quantity of illegal drugs, stolen property, or illegal weapons.

There are two general functions for officers within the undercover unit.

- The undercover officer who contacts individuals or infiltrates establishments or organizations suspected of being involved in criminal activity.
- The support officer (sometimes called an intelligence, cover, or tactical officer) is a plainclothes officer who works with the undercover unit but not in an undercover capacity.

Undercover officers must be assigned a nondescript vehicle in which to operate. A prerequisite for assuming an undercover role is to establish a cover story.

- The cover story is a fictitious story that the agent conveys to suspects concerning his or her background
- The officer's appearance and mannerisms should also fit the cover story.

After a cover story has been established, a methodical process of infiltration must take place to uncover criminal wrongdoing and its associated evidence.

Key Terms

burned

buy-bust

buy-walk

cover story

credibility

deep cover

entrapment

informant

motivation

seed money

support officer

undercover (UC) officer

Witness Security (WITSEC) program

Discussion Questions

1. List and describe the four groups of people that most commonly become informants for law enforcement.

2. List and discuss the advantages and benefits of using informants in criminal investigations.

3. What are the various motivations for becoming involved with law enforcement as an informant?

4. List and discuss other problems that arise in the management of informants.

5. Compare and contrast the ways an undercover operation can benefit and hinder a criminal investigation.

6. List the considerations in preparing for an undercover operation.

7. From a management standpoint, what concerns are there regarding investigators working in an undercover capacity?

mycrimekit™

Go to MyCrimeKit.com to explore the following study tools and resources specific to this chapter: Flashcards: There are 13 key terms in this chapter.

- *Flashcards:* test your knowledge of the chapter's key terms.
- *Web Links:* Check out the hotlink to The New York Times criminology articles.

- *Career Center:* Check out the hot links to interesting careers in criminal justice, criminology, and juvenile justice.
- *The Research Center:* Check out the Cybrary and research navigator for even more resources.

Notes

1. ANON. (1996). Police upset by cancellation of *America's Most Wanted*. *USA Today*, May 16.
2. PUENTE, M. (1997). A no longer most wanted list. *USA Today*, July 29:3A.
3. IBID.
4. GRAY, P. (1997). A heart in her hand. *Time*, Aug. 23:43.
5. U.S. DEPARTMENT OF JUSTICE, DRUG ENFORCEMENT ADMINISTRATION (1988). *Drug enforcement handbook*. Washington, DC: U.S. Government Printing Office.
6. DRUG ENFORCEMENT AGENCY. (2009). Hundreds of alleged Sinaloa cartel members and associates arrested in nationwide takedown of Mexican drug traffickers. Available at http://www.usdoj.gov/dea/pubs/states/newsrel/2009/la022509.html.
7. ADAMS, T. (2001). *Police field operations*, 5th ed. Upper Saddle River, NJ: Prentice Hall.
8. LANGWORTHY, R. (1989). Do stings control crime? An evaluation of a police fencing operation. *Justice Quarterly*, 6:28–45.
9. SCHOEMAN, F. (1986). Undercover operations: Some moral questions. *Criminal Justice Ethics*, 5(2):16–22.
10. TURQUE, B. and J. STOFFEL (1989). Fury over an unholy alliance: How Cleveland cops teamed up with a drug dealer. *Newsweek*, May 8:26.
11. BLACK, D. (1971). The social organization of arrest. *Stanford Law Review*, 23:1087–1111; LAFAVE, W. (1965). *The decision to take a suspect into custody*. Boston, MA: Little, Brown and Company; SMITH, D. A. and C. VISHER (1981). Street-level justice: Situational determinants of police arrest decisions. *Social Problems* 29:167–178.
12. LYMAN, M. D. (2007). *Practical drug enforcement*, 3rd ed. Boca Raton, FL: CRC Press.
13. MOTTO, C. J. and D. L. JUNE (2000). *Undercover*, 2nd ed. Boca Raton, FL: CRC Press.
14. KRAUSE, M. (2008). Safeguarding undercover employees: A strategy for success. *FBI Law Enforcement Bulletin* 77(8).
15. GIRODO, M. (1991). Symptomatic reactions to undercover work. *The Journal of Nervous and Mental Disease* 179(10):626–630.
16. MARX, G. (1988). *Undercover: Police surveillance in America*. Berkeley: University of California Press.
17. IBID.
18. BROWN, J. (1990). Sources of occupational stress in the police. *Work & Stress* 4(4):305–318. Available at http://www.informaworld.com/smpp/content~content=a782548838~db=all.
19. MARX, G. (1988). *Undercover: Police surveillance in America*. Berkeley: University of California Press.
20. IBID.
21. IBID.
22. GIRODO, M. (1991). Drug corruptions in undercover agents: Measuring the risks. *Behavioural Science and the Law* 9:361–370.
23. MARX, G. (1988). *Undercover: Police surveillance in America*. Berkeley: University of California Press.
24. IBID.
25. GIRODO, M. (1991). Personality, job stress, and mental health in undercover agents. *Journal of Social Behaviour and Personality* 6(7):375–390.
26. MARX, G. (1988). *Undercover: Police surveillance in America*. Berkeley: University of California Press.

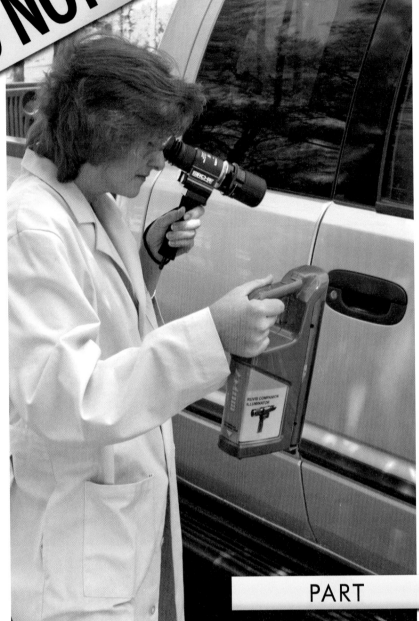

Crimes Against Persons

PART

4

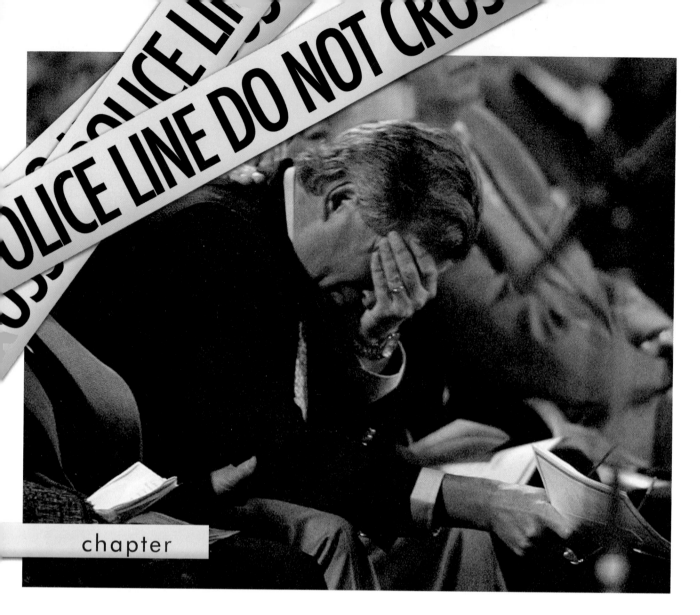

9 Death Investigations

This chapter will enable you to:

- Identify the various modes of death.
- Understand the duties of the responding officer.
- Learn the fundamentals of protecting the crime scene.
- Learn techniques used in identifying victims.
- Understand the methods used in estimating time of death.
- Understand the significance of defense wounds.
- Interpret entrance and exit wounds.
- Identify the characteristics of an autoerotic death.

chapter

Introduction

The brutal murder of six-year-old JonBenet Ramsey on Christmas night in 1996 shocked America. Just as the Lindbergh baby kidnapping and murder seven decades earlier had seared the nation's consciousness, this murder—of a beautiful and talented child in a wealthy Boulder, Colorado home—renewed every parent's worst nightmare: No child was truly safe, not even tucked in at home on Christmas night.

JonBenet's murder—particularly as the days went by and no arrests were forthcoming—quickly became a national obsession, featured day after day on network news, television tabloid programs, talk radio, newspapers, and magazines. Her image displayed across television screens countless times, often showing her in a fancy red cowgirl outfit, singing "I want to be a cowboy sweetheart," or dancing across the stage in a glittering Las Vegas showgirl outfit, complete with heavy makeup. Her unusual first name became so well known that like Cher and Madonna, she no longer had need of a last name.

The public's shock at the murder soon spread to dismay at the Boulder Police Department's investigation—a dismay fed by a steady flow of leaks from the Boulder County District Attorney's office about the inept police investigation being conducted. Specifically, it became known that the police had badly botched the initial investigation by failing to seal off the crime scene. It also appeared as though the police were treating the primary suspects—JonBenet's parents—with kid gloves by not only acquiescing to their refusal to be interviewed at police headquarters but also to being interviewed separately. Fueled with such information, the media, especially tabloid television and talk radio shows, were quick to blame JonBenet's parents, John and Patsy Ramsey. Some in the media began to point the finger directly at her father. Others implied it was her mother who had garroted the girl. Some speculated the crime had to have been committed by both parents. The tabloids even raised the possibility that her brother, Burke, who was just shy of 10 years old at the time, murdered JonBenet.

As of the preparation of this book, this case continues unsolved. A grand jury met for over a year, only to disband in October of 1999 without handing down an indictment or even issuing a report, an option that was open to it. Boulder Police Chief Mark Beckner admitted that the case files have been put in storage, although he said some more "forensic testing" was going on. The then newly elected Boulder district attorney, Mary Keenan, promised to look into the case. Nothing seemed to come of it. In April of 2003, she issued a statement saying she concurred with a federal court in Georgia's contemporaneous finding that JonBenet was most likely murdered by an intruder. Two months later, Keenan shifted responsibility for the case away from the Boulder Police Department to the district attorney's office, and she hired Tom Bennett as lead investigator of the case, directing him to focus his probe on the premise that an intruder killed JonBenet.

During the intervening three years, the case all but dropped from public view. The death of Patsy Ramsey on June 24, 2006—of ovarian cancer at age 49—briefly brought the case back into the spotlight. And then on August 16, 2006, the long-dormant case appeared back in the headlines across the world when a 41-year-old child-sex offender by the name of John Mark Karr was arrested in Bangkok, Thailand, at the request of the Boulder District Attorney's Office. Karr was extradited back to Boulder at which time DNA results from the JonBenet crime scene failed to link Karr to the crime. As the Boulder District Attorney faced considerable criticism for Karr's premature extradition, his candidacy as JonBenet's killer was dismissed.

In all societies, the instances of homicide and wrongful death have endured as top concerns for law enforcement officials. Considered as one of the gravest social problems, law enforcement plays an important role in investigating the facts and circumstances surrounding each such case. An estimated 15,500 people are murdered every year, and most of these (an estimated 85 percent) involve people who knew each other (e.g., friends, neighbors, family members).

Murder and non-negligent manslaughter, as defined in the Uniform Crime Reporting (UCR) Program, is the willful (non-negligent) killing of one human being by another. The classification of this offense, as for all other offenses that make up the Crime Index, is based solely on police investigation as opposed to the determination of a court, medical examiner, coroner, jury, or other judicial body. The program does not include deaths caused by negligence, suicide, or accident; justifiable **homicide**; and attempts to murder or assaults to murder, which are scored as aggravated assaults.

The extent of homicide (identified as "murder" by FBI statistics) in the United States is reflected in the Uniform Crime Report published by the FBI. For example, statistics show that nationwide in 2007, an estimated 16,929 persons were murdered, a 0.6 percent decline from the 2006 estimate. The 2007 figure was, however, 2.4 percent higher than the 2003 level. Statistics also show that murder accounted for 1.2 percent of the overall estimated number of violent crimes. In 2007, there were an estimated 5.6 murders per 100,000 inhabitants.[1]

Types of Wrongful Death

Murders may occur in sprees, which involve killings at two or more locations with almost no time break between murders. John Allen Muhammad, 41, part of the "sniper team" that terrorized the Washington, D.C. area in 2002, was arrested along with 17-year-old Jamaican immigrant Lee Boyd Malvo in the random shootings of 13 people in Maryland, Virginia, and Washington over a three-week period. Ten of the victims died. In 2003, Muhammad and Malvo were convicted of capital murder; Muhammad was sentenced to die. Malvo was given a second sentence of life without the possibility of parole in 2004, after he struck a deal with prosecutors in an effort to avoid the death penalty.

MURDER TREND: COMPARATIVE RATES

Year	Number of Offenses	Rate per 100,000 Inhabitants
2006	15,972	149.4
2007	15,707	147.6
Percent change	−0.6	−1.3

Source: From Federal Bureau of Investigation. (2008). *Crime in America, 2007. Uniform crime reports.* Washington, DC: U.S. Government Printing Office.

In contrast to spree killing, mass murder entails "the killing of four or more victims at one location, within one event." Recent mass murderers have included Timothy McVeigh (the antigovernment Oklahoma City bomber) and Mohammed Atta and the terrorists he led in the September 11, 2001 attacks against American targets.

Yet another kind of murder, serial murder, happens over time and officially "involves the killing of several victims in three or more separate events." In cases of serial murder, days, months, or even years may lapse between killings.

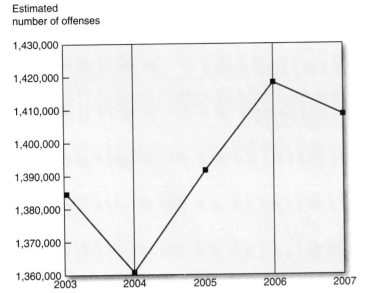

Estimated number of offenses

FIGURE 9.1 Violent crime offense, five-year trend, 2003 to 2007. *FBI, Crime in the United States, 2008.*

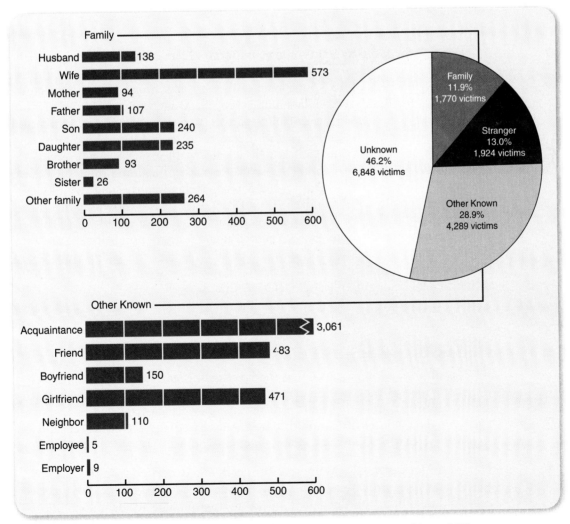

FIGURE 9.2 Murder by relationship: percent distribution. *FBI, Crime in the United States, 2008.*

FIGURE 9.3 The actual scene of a violent crime resulting from a homicide. Imagine you are the crime scene investigator. What evidence do you see here that must be carefully preserved and documented? *Courtesy of Mike Himmel and the Missouri State Highway Patrol.*

Some of the more infamous confessed serial killers of recent years are Wichita BTK murderer Dennis Rader; Jeffrey Dahmer, who received 936 years in prison for the murders of 15 young men (and who was himself later murdered in prison); Ted Bundy, who killed numerous college-age women; Henry Lee Lucas, now in a Texas prison, who confessed to 600 murders but later recanted (yet was convicted of 11 murders and linked to at least 140 others); Otis Toole, Lucas's partner in crime; cult leader Charles Manson, who is still serving time for ordering followers to kill seven Californians, including the famed actress Sharon Tate; Andrei Chikatilo, the Russian "Hannibal Lecter," who killed 52 people, mostly schoolchildren; David Berkowitz, also known as the "Son of Sam," who killed six people on lovers' lanes around New York City; Theodore Kaczynski, the Unabomber, who perpetrated a series of bomb attacks on "establishment" figures; Seattle's Green River killer, Gary Leon Ridgway, a 54-year-old painter who confessed in 2003 to killing 48 women in the 1980s; and the infamous "railroad killer," Angel Maturino Resendiz.

Modes of Death

mycrimekit

Interactive: Murder and manslaughter

It is of primary importance that the investigator learn the manner in which the victim died as soon as possible after discovery of the body. Although much of this information is learned from the autopsy, much can also be discovered through careful examination of both the deceased and the crime scene. Modes of death can be divided into four general categories:

1. *Accidental death.* Many types of death are associated with this category, including drowning, falling, automobile wrecks, and accidental drug overdose. Often, murders are disguised to appear to be accidental in nature.

2. *Natural death.* Deaths from natural causes include heart attack, stroke, disease, and old age. In many circumstances, the deceased will have been

under a doctor's care, but often people are found, and their mode of death is questionable. For example, a person might have been forced to consume certain drugs that can cause death, but the symptoms indicate death from "natural" causes (e.g., heart attack).

3. *Suicide.* Methods of committing suicide are numerous and include stabbing, shooting, drug overdose, and carbon monoxide poisoning. As with other modes of death, investigators should be sure that the cause of death was actually suicide and not murder designed to look like suicide.

4. *Murder.* Murder is one person intentionally causing another person to die. Many different situations can result in a person's death. These include:

- Wounds from handguns and shotguns
- Cutting and stabbing wounds
- Blunt-force injuries
- Extraordinary modes of death such as poisoning and death by asphyxia (strangulation)

Legal Characteristics of Homicide

Criminal investigators encounter wrongful death in many ways. Some victims are killed by accident, others in the heat of passion, and still others for profit. Therefore, it is incumbent on the professional investigator to be clear as to what laws best describe the alleged crime. Under law, categories of homicide are generally divided into two distinct classifications: murder and manslaughter. Murder is considered the most serious of all statutory crimes and is defined as the purposeful, premeditated, and unlawful taking of the life of a human being by another person. Persons found guilty of murder receive the harshest of sentences, which may include life imprisonment or the death penalty. Many states classify murder in different degrees, typically first and second. For example, first-degree murder is considered the most serious and includes, as one of the elements, premeditation and preplanning. Second-degree murder is a lesser offense but requires that the person "attempted" to kill his or her intended victim (e.g., a domestic argument that erupts into a physical altercation resulting in the death of one of the parties).

FIGURE 9.4 License plate—blood on the back matched the victim. The victim was beat up on the trunk of the vehicle and subsequently raped and killed. The investigator noticed a small crescent-shaped cut under the victim's eye and theorized that the corner of a license plate could have imparted the cut. When a suspect was developed, investigators took the license plate off his vehicle and found this stain. The DNA matched the victim. Courtesy of Missouri State Highway Patrol Crime Laboratory.

Manslaughter is the deliberate killing of another person and is typically classified into two subcategories: voluntary and involuntary. *Voluntary manslaughter* generally refers to the killing of another person out of an act of passion but lacks premeditation. For example, a man arrives at his home to find his wife with another man. The husband then loses his temper and immediately shoots the man. The key element here is that the scene must erupt into passion and must be followed immediately by the act of murder without premeditation or "cool reflection" about the incident.

Involuntary manslaughter usually refers to the accidental or nonintentional death of another human being, with severe negligence. Examples of involuntary manslaughter include a motorist who is exceeding the speed limit by 30 miles per hour and hits a child playing in the street. If the driver were traveling at the speed limit, he or she would have been able to stop in time to miss the child. Other examples of involuntary manslaughter include the reckless handling of a firearm, resulting in someone's death, and leaving dangerous poisons or drugs in reach of children.

Elements of Homicide

Legal elements of the crime of homicide vary from one state to another but do exhibit some commonalties.

MURDER

- *First degree.* A person commits the crime if he or she knowingly causes the death of another person after deliberation on the matter.
- *Second degree.* A person commits the crime if he or she knowingly causes the death of another person while committing a criminal act and not acting under the influence of sudden passion.

MANSLAUGHTER

- *Involuntary.* A person commits the crime if he or she recklessly causes another person's death.
- *Voluntary.* A person commits the crime if he or she causes the death of another person by being certain of taking the victim's life and acting in the heat of passion.

The Preliminary Investigation

Homicide investigations are usually reactive in nature and are typically initiated by a telephone call to a local law enforcement agency notifying them of some aspect of the offense. Such calls may be a simple request for assistance by an injured person, a call stating "shots were fired," or a report of some form of violence that was observed (e.g., a man or woman being beaten). Rarely, however, does this initial call contain enough information to determine exactly what is occurring or what has occurred. Investigators on the scene typically learn such details.

The first officer to respond to a suspected homicide call is generally a patrol officer arriving a short time after the call is received. The actions taken at the time of arrival may have a critical bearing on the subsequent course of the investigation. Some of the most critical of these are featured in this section. Responding officers might encounter:

- A man who directs the officer to the crime scene
- A crime scene that might be in an isolated place that is untouched and easily safeguarded

- A crime scene that might be filled with people milling around, acting confused, shouting, or crying
- A killer who might either still be on the scene or may have just exited
- A victim who may be dead or may still be alive but in need of medical attention
- A crime scene in a public place that may be difficult to secure

In all situations, the first officer on the scene has several principal concerns:

- Determine if the victim is dead or alive
- Contact medical help for the victim if needed
- Apprehend the perpetrator if still present on the scene
- Make the appropriate notifications if the perpetrator has left the scene
- Safeguard the crime scene
- Detain any witnesses

After these fundamental steps are dealt with, the officer must become what could be termed **scene-conscious**. That is, he or she must become aware of the crime scene situation and be prepared to take certain immediate actions, the focus being identifying any aspects of the scene that might be subject to chemical change, change by dissipation, or change because something was moved.

Protecting the Crime Scene

After the preliminary duties have been performed, the responding officer must protect the crime scene from unauthorized persons who may move, destroy, or otherwise contaminate evidence. It is important for civilians and unauthorized police personnel alike to be denied entrance to the scene. Experience has shown that probably no aspect of the homicide investigation is more open to error than the preservation and protection of the crime scene.[2] Death scenes can be expected to produce an abundance of evidence. All such evidence will enable the investigators to determine the manner of death, weapons used, time of death, and other pertinent information.

Taking Notes at the Scene

Complete notes are critical during the early stages of the homicide crime scene investigation. Because details are of such vital importance, both the investigating and responding officers should take notes. In fact, these notes could later become decisive evidence in the prosecution of the suspect(s). Crime scene notes in a homicide investigation should include the following:

- Names of officers on the scene
- Names and addresses of witnesses at the scene
- Name and address of the person notifying the police
- Manner of entry/exit of the perpetrator to the crime
- Description of weather conditions

As indicated earlier, investigators should also be prepared to draft a sketch of the scene. The sketch should show all critical aspects of the homicide crime scene, such as the location and position of the body; location of any weapons; and positions of furniture, clothing, and other types of evidence. The sketch will prove to be of value later in the investigation when reports are being finalized and in preparing for court.

Identifying the Victim

Homicide crime scenes can vary greatly from one case to the next. For example, in one case, the body might be charred as a result of a fire designed to cover up evidence. In another, the body might have been chopped up and parts distributed over a broad geographical area. In other cases, bodies have been recovered in lakes and rivers and offer little or no immediate clues as to their identity. In all circumstances, the body must be identified.

The Deceased Victim

If the victim is obviously deceased, the officer should not attempt to authorize the removal of the body until after the crime scene has been processed. This will allow valuable time for the identification process. Efforts in identifying the victim may begin with a cursory inspection of the victim's personal effects and clothing. Papers in the possession of the victim may make the identification process easy, particularly if certain items are present (e.g., a driver's license, personal letters).

Witnesses can also provide useful identification information of the victim if known to them. Other people might be able to offer positive identification, such as parents, friends, neighbors, or spouses. A good practice for investigators is to have more than one person identify the remains to avoid a case of mistaken identity. In addition, it is also a sound policy to corroborate positive identifications by additional evidence.

Other identifiers that investigators should look for include:

- *Wounds and blood.* Investigators can also tell if the body has been moved by inspecting wounds and blood around the body. If wounds indicate severe bleeding and little blood is on the scene, the body may have been moved. Blood type and DNA evidence are also options that might be considered by investigators.
- *Fingernail scrapings.* Technicians at the morgue will also look for fingernail scrapings. This evidence might turn up hair, skin, blood, or fibers that might be useful in developing a suspect.
- *Fingerprints of the deceased.* The deceased's fingerprints can be taken by using an ink roller on each finger. Next, while strips of fingerprint paper are placed in a curved holder such as a spoon, each finger is placed against the strip and an impression is taken. Rigid joints can be loosened by working the finger back and forth several times.

The Victim Who Is Still Alive

In cases in which the victim is still alive or conscious, he or she might be willing to give information such as the name of his or her assailant, a description of the assailant's clothing, and the type of automobile the assailant was driving. After this information is learned, it should be passed on to the communication center for broadcast to other officers and departments.

Dying Declaration

If the victim is badly wounded and believes that he or she is dying, the officer should treat his or her statement as a **dying declaration**. Under the Federal Rules of Evidence, a dying declaration is admissible if the proponent of the statement can establish:

- Unavailability of the declarant
- The declarant's statement is being offered in a criminal prosecution for murder or in a civil action

- The declarant's statement was made while under the belief that his or her death was imminent
- The declarant's statement must relate to the cause or circumstances of what the declarant believed to be his or her impending death[3]

Consider this example: Suppose Rachel stabs Steve and then runs away, and a police officer happens upon Steve as he lies in the street, bleeding to death. If Steve manages to sputter out with his last words, "I'm dying—Rachel stabbed me" (or even just "Rachel did it"), the officer can testify to that in court.

The declarant (here, Steve) does not actually have to die for the statement to be admissible, but he or she needs to have had a genuine belief that he or she was going to die, and the declarant must be unavailable to testify in court. In the above scenario, if Steve were to recover instead of dying and were able to testify in court, the officer would no longer be able to testify to the statement. It would then constitute hearsay and not fall into the exception. Furthermore, the statement must relate to the circumstances or the cause of the declarant's own death. If Steve's last words are, "Rachel killed Kayla," that statement will not fall within the exception and will be inadmissible (unless Rachel killed Steve and Kayla in the same act).

Furthermore, as with all testimony, the dying declaration will be inadmissible unless it is based on the declarant's actual knowledge. Suppose, for example, Steve bought a cup of coffee at the coffee shop and was stricken with food poisoning. If his dying last words were, "The supplier who sold them the coffee mix must have used a contaminated packing machine," that statement would be inadmissible despite the hearsay exception because Steve had no way of knowing anything about the conditions in which the coffee was packed.

In U.S. federal courts, the dying declaration exception is limited to civil cases and criminal homicide prosecutions, although many states copy the Federal Rules of Evidence in their statutes and some permit the admission of dying declarations in all situations.

Estimating the Time of Death

If the wrongful death appears to have been a homicide, all areas around the body become important in determining the time of death. The time of death in a homicide case, particularly when there are no witnesses, is one of the most critical variables in its investigation. It may convict a murderer, break an alibi, or even eliminate a suspect. Time may come into play if the deceased had an appointment with someone around the time of his or her death. In addition, in cases of exclusive opportunity, in which only certain persons are present with the victim, husbands or wives, boyfriends or girlfriends, and so on, may become likely suspects.

Changes in the Body: Decomposition

Simply stated, death occurs when vital functions of the body are halted. These include functions of breathing and circulation. In addition, investigators should observe other changes.

After death occurs, human decomposition takes place in five stages. The process of tissue breakdown may take from several days up to years. At all stages of decomposition, insect activity occurs on the body, as detailed below.

Stage 1: The Fresh Stage. The fresh stage of decomposition occurs during the first few days after the death. There are no physical signs of decomposition during this time. However, homeostasis of the body has ceased, allowing cellular and soft tissue changes to occur because of the process of autolysis, the destruction of cells and organs due to an aseptic chemical process. At this point, the body enters *algor mortis*, the cooling of the body's temperature to that of its surroundings.

When the body's cells reach the final stage of autolysis, an anaerobic environment is created, that is, an environment in which oxygen is not present. This allows the body's normal bacteria to break down the remaining carbohydrates, proteins, and lipids. The products from the breakdown create acids, gases, and other products that cause production of volatile organic compounds (VOCs) and putrefactive effects. VOCs are produced during the early stages of human decomposition.[4]

Substances produced during the fresh stage of decomposition attract a variety of insects. *Diptera* insects begin to lay their eggs on the body during this stage, especially member of the Calliphoridae family of insects.[5] If the body is on the ground or buried in soil, there is also considerable insect activity by the insects that live in the soil around the body. The reasoning for this is simple: A dead human body serves as an excellent source of decaying matter to feed on and as such, a hospitable environment.

Stage 2: The Putrefaction Stage. Odor, color changes, and bloating of the body during decomposition are the results of putrefaction. The lower part of the abdomen turns green due to bacteria activity in the cecum. Bacteria break down hemoglobin into sulfhemoglobin, which causes the green color change. A formation of gases enters the abdomen, which forces liquids and feces out of the body. The gases also enter the neck and face, causing swelling of the mouth, lips, and tongue. Due to this swelling and misconfiguration of the face, identification of the body can be difficult.

Bacteria also enter the venous system, causing blood to *hemolyze*. This leads to the formation of red streaks along the veins. This color soon changes to green through a process known as *marbelization*. It can be seen on the shoulders, chest and shoulder area, and thighs. The skin can develop blisters containing fluid. The skin also becomes fragile, leading to skin slippage, making it difficult to move a body. While in this condition, body hair comes off easily. The color change of the discoloration from green to brown marks the transition of the early stage of putrefaction to the advanced decompositional stages.

During the putrefaction stage of decomposition, the majority of insect activity again comes from members of the Calliphoridae family (included are Formicidae, Muscidae, Sphaeroceridae, Silphidae, Lepidoptera, Hymenoptera, Sarcophagidae, Histeridae, Staphylinidae, Phalangida, Piophilidae, Araneae, Sepsidae, and Phoridae). As with the fresh stage of decomposition, if the body is on the ground or buried in soil, there is also considerable insect activity by soil-inhabiting arthropods.[6]

Stage 3: The Black Putrefaction Stage. After the body goes through the bloating stage, it begins the black putrefaction stage. At this point, the body cavity ruptures, the abdominal gases escape, and the body darkens from its greenish color. These activities allow for a greater invasion of scavengers, and insect activity increases greatly. This stage ends as the bones become apparent, which can take anywhere from 10 to 20 days after death depending on region and temperature. This period is also dependent on the degree to which the body is exposed.

During the black putrefaction stage of decomposition, insects that can be found living in the body are *Calliphoridae* larvae, *Staphylinidae*, *Histeridae*, *Gamasid* mites, *Ptomaphila*, *Trichopterygidae*, *Piophilid* larvae, parasitic wasps, *Staphylinid* larvae, *Trichopterygid* larvae, *Histerid* larvae, *Ptomaphila* larvae, *Dermestes*, *Tyroglyphid* mites, *Tineid* larvae, and the *Dermestes* larvae.[7]

Some insects can also be found living in the soil around the body such as *Isopoda*, *Collembola*, *Dermaptera*, *Formicidae*, *Pseudoscorpiones*, *Araneae*, *Plectochetos*, *Acari*, *Pauropoda*, *Symphyla*, *Geophilidae*, and *Protura*. The types of insects differ based on where the body is, although *Diptera* larvae can be found feeding on the body in almost all cases.[8]

It is important to note that the identification of insects has proven to be one way that the time of death can be determined. Examining the larvae of insects found on the body accomplishes this. Investigators should consider contacting an entomologist (insect expert) for advice at this stage of the investigation. This technique studies the various stages of growth of each larva before it develops into an adult insect. Houseflies, for example, deposit eggs on the remains of the corpse, usually in the area of the eyes, mouth, nostrils, and wounds. The eggs then become maggots and feed on the body. Typically, the time span for the hatching of the maggot is 24 hours.

The developmental stage depends on the type of insect in question. An entomologist can identify the specific insect and determine an estimated time span for its development as well as the season in which the death occurred. The recommended procedure is for all insects to be placed into alcohol for preservation.

Stage 4: The Butyric Fermentation Stage. After the early putrefaction and black putrefaction phases have taken place, the body begins mummification, in which the body begins to dry out. The human carcass is first mummified and then goes through adipocere formation. Adipocere (grave wax) formation is the loss of body odor and the formation of a cheesy appearance on the cadaver. Mummification is considered a post-active stage because there is less definite distinction between changes, and they are indicated by reduced skin, cartilage, and bone. Mummification is also indicated when all of the internal organs are lost due to insect activity.[9]

Stage 5: The Dry Decay Stage. When the last of the soft tissue has been removed from the body, the final stage of decomposition, skeletonization, occurs. This stage encompasses the deterioration of skeletal remains and is the longest of the decomposition processes. Skeletonization differs markedly from the previous stages, not only in length but also in the deterioration process itself.

The strength and durability of bone stems from the unique protein–mineral bond present in skeletal formation. Consequently, changes to skeletal remains, known as *bone diagenesis*, occur at a substantially slower rate than stages of soft tissue breakdown. As the protein–mineral bond weakens after death, however, the organic protein begins to leach away, leaving behind only the mineral composition. Unlike soft tissue decomposition, which is influenced mainly by temperature and oxygen levels, the process of bone breakdown is more highly dependent on soil type and pH, along with the presence of groundwater. However, temperature can be a contributing factor: Higher temperature leads the protein in bones to break down more rapidly. If buried, remains decay faster in acidic-based soils than in alkaline soils. Bones left in areas of high moisture content also decay at a faster rate. The water leaches out skeletal minerals, which corrode the bone, leading to bone disintegration.[10]

The Forensics of Decomposition

Various sciences study the decomposition of bodies. These sciences fall under the general topic of forensics because the usual motive for study of the decomposition of human bodies is to determine the time and cause of death for legal purposes:

- *Forensic pathology* studies the clues to the cause of death found in the corpse as a medical phenomenon.

- *Forensic entomology* studies the insects and other vermin found in corpses; the sequence in which they appear, the kinds of insects, and where they are found in their life cycle are clues that can shed light on the time of death, the length of a corpse's exposure, and whether the corpse was moved.[11]
- *Forensic anthropology* is the branch of physical anthropology that studies skeletons and human remains, usually to seek clues as to the identity, race, and sex of their former owner.[12]

The University of Tennessee Anthropological Research Facility (better known as the "Body Farm") in Knoxville, Tennessee has a number of bodies laid out in various situations in a fenced-in plot near the medical center. Scientists at the Body Farm study how the human body decays in various circumstances to gain a better understanding of decomposition.[13]

Factors Affecting Decomposition

The rate and manner of decomposition in an animal body are strongly affected by a number of factors. In roughly descending degrees of importance, they are:

- Temperature
- The availability of oxygen
- Prior embalming
- Cause of death
- Burial and depth of burial
- Access by scavengers
- Trauma, including wounds and crushing blows
- Humidity or wetness
- Rainfall
- Body size and weight
- Clothing
- The surface on which the body rests
- Foods and objects inside the specimen's digestive tract (bacon opposed to lettuce)

The speed at which decomposition occurs varies greatly. Factors such as temperature, humidity, and the season of death all determine how fast a fresh body will skeletonize or mummify. A basic guide for the effect of environment on decomposition is given as Casper's law (or ratio): If all other factors are equal, then when there is free access of air, a body decomposes twice as fast than if immersed in water and eight times faster than if buried in earth.

The most important variable is a body's accessibility to insects, particularly flies. On the surface in tropical areas, invertebrates alone can easily reduce a fully fleshed corpse to clean bones in less than two weeks. The skeleton itself is not permanent; acids in soils can reduce it to unrecognizable components. This is one reason given for the lack of human remains found in the wreckage of the *Titanic*, even in parts of the ship considered inaccessible to scavengers. Freshly skeletonized bone is often called "green" bone and has a characteristic greasy feel. Under certain conditions (normally cool, damp soil), bodies may undergo saponification and develop a waxy substance called adipocere caused by the action of soil chemicals on the body's proteins and fats. The formation of adipocere slows decomposition by inhibiting the bacteria that cause putrefaction.

In extremely dry or cold conditions, the normal process of decomposition is halted—by either lack of moisture or temperature controls on bacterial and enzymatic action—causing the body to be preserved as a mummy. Whereas frozen mummies commonly restart the decomposition process when thawed, heat-desiccated mummies remain so unless exposed to moisture.

Other Visual Evidence of Decomposition

Body Color. After the victim dies, circulation of blood through the arteries and veins ceases. As the body settles, color in the lips and nails disappears as the blood settles into the lower capillaries of the body. The blood then changes from red to a dark purplish color as it loses its oxygen. This is the beginning of lividity, which we discuss later.

Changes in Eyes. The eyes are the most sensitive part of the human body and, in death, do not react to light, touching, or pressure. In addition, the eyelids may remain open; the pupils may become irregular in size and shape and typically become milky and cloudy in color within 8 to 10 hours of death.

Temperature of the Body. In life, a person's body maintains a body temperature of 98.6° F. Even after death, there may not be a loss of body heat because the body will tend to adapt to the temperature of its environment. The rate of cooling can, however, be a primary determinant as to the time of death. For example, a corpse will feel cool to the touch from 8 to 12 hours after death and will remain the same temperature as its surroundings for about 24 hours after death. Several factors can contribute to the rate in which a body loses heat. The greater the difference between the body and the environment, the faster the body will cool down.

Water and air temperature are the most important contributing factors. The temperature of the body before death can influence its temperature after death occurs. Predeath conditions such as stroke, sun stroke, and strangulation generally result in a higher body temperature at the time of death. One reliable method for determining body temperature is to insert a thermometer into the rectum of the deceased (do not insert a thermometer into the wound). The medical examiner will usually place a thermometer in the victim's liver. Body temperature can also be raised by the victim's excessive body fat or heavy clothing.

FIGURE 9.5 Postmortem lividity located on the back of a murder victim shows where blood has pooled after death.
Courtesy of Mike Himmel and the Missouri State Highway Patrol.

The International Association of Chiefs of Police (IACP) offers a working formula to determine the estimated time of death when it is thought to be less than 24 hours:

$$\frac{98.6 \text{ (normal temp.)} - 2 \text{ (rectal temp.)}}{1.5 \text{ (avarage rate of heat loss)}} = \text{no. of hours since death}$$

Rigor Mortis. Rigor mortis, the process of stiffening, or contraction of body muscles after vital functions cease, is generally considered a poor indicator of time of death. As a rule, rigor mortis sets in two to four hours after death, but many variables may contribute to "rigor." Contrary to popular belief, rigor mortis starts at the same time throughout the entire body. However, it is first observed in the jaws and neck.[14] It then tends to progress in the head-to-foot direction. At the time of completion, typically 8 to 12 hours after death, the torso, jaws, neck, and upper and lower extremities are "stiff as a board." Once in this state, the body resists any change in position.

Postmortem Lividity. As indicated earlier, when a body's vital functions cease, blood settles to the bottom side of the body because of gravity. A purplish **lividity** stain forms on the skin of the body closest to the surface on which it is lying. So if a body is lying on its stomach and the lividity stain is on its back, the body has probably been turned over. Postmortem lividity may appear anywhere between one-half hour to four hours after death. It is sometimes valuable in determining whether or not a body has been moved, depending on the state of the lividity. If it is determined that the body has been moved, the officer must ask why—perhaps another police officer turned over the body. Generally speaking, however, after lividity has set in for 12 hours, the body will not diminish in color and will remain unchanged.

Animals. A body discovered outdoors (and in some cases indoors) will sometimes be mutilated by wild animals. Bodies that have been mutilated will give the appearance of having been grossly injured, but that will not necessarily be evidence of a postmortem attack. Investigators must be careful not to draw false conclusions.

Bodies Found in Water. As described in the preceding section, marine life can also damage and distort dead bodies found in water (floaters). Generally, a forensic pathologist will have to be consulted to distinguish postmortem injuries from those that occurred in life. Experience has shown that bodies found in air will have decomposed twice as fast as those found submerged in water.

Gunshot Wounds as Evidence

mycrimekit

Review: Wrongful death

Several factors can affect the type of wound inflicted by a firearm. Such wounds may resemble a stab wound at first, but certain physical characteristics may vary, depending on the type of caliber weapon used, the distance between the shooter and victim, and whether the lethal bullet had ricocheted off another object. To understand the firearm wound best, let's discuss the effect that a firearm has on the human body. Vernon Geberth states that when a firearm is discharged, several things can occur:[15]

- Fire or flames are emitted from the barrel
- Smoke follows the flame
- The bullet emerges from the barrel

FIGURE 9.6 Blood drops and spatter are common on violent crime scenes and when properly documented can tell the investigator the distance from its origin or point of impact and direction of travel (trajectory). *Courtesy of Mike Himmel and the Missouri State Highway Patrol.*

FIGURE 9.7 Blood and biological evidence must be properly stored for preservation. This refrigerator is used for storage of blood evidence. *Courtesy of Mike Himmel and the Missouri State Highway Patrol.*

- Additional smoke and grains of both burned and unburned gunpowder follow the bullet out of the barrel
- The material spreads outward from the barrel as it is emitted
- If the firearm is close to the targeted surface, much of this material will be deposited on it

In addition, if the surface is farther away, less of the material will be deposited. Depending on the material or clothing present on the body, it is sometimes possible to predict the distance between the firearm and the victim.

In the case of a contact wound, where the muzzle of the weapon was held against the body when discharged, certain residue will be present. Soot is always present in such wounds, with powder particles identified in at least half of cases.[16] These particles are often difficult to readily identify, however, and may require expert analysis.

Assessing the Severity of Gunshot Wounds

When assessing the likely severity of gunshot wounds, there are numerous variables which include the following, considered either singly or in concert.[17]

- *The particular type of weapon used.* Rifles are generally more destructive than handguns. For example, a close-range abdominal wound inflicted by a 7.62 NATO rifle will be much more severe than one inflicted by a .38 revolver from the same distance.
- *The caliber of the weapon.* A wound from a small-diameter bullet will generally be less severe than a wound inflicted by a larger diameter bullet when the velocities are the same. The cartridge designation is generally an approximation of bullet diameter and is of value to the gun knowledgeable in estimating other characteristics (e.g., velocity, weight, design).
- *The design of the bullet used and its velocity.* Expanding bullets are more damaging than non-expanding ones. Of the non-expanding bullets, flat or very blunt-nosed bullets are more damaging than more pointed bullets because the more pointed bullet may push some tissue aside. Heavier bullets penetrate more deeply than lighter bullets at the same velocity.
- *The range at which the victim was shot.* Wounds inflicted from a distance of 16 feet will invariably be more severe than those fired from a range of 1600 feet if all other factors are equal. The velocity of a bullet (and therefore its destructive potential) gradually reduces as it travels from the muzzle of a firearm.
- *The path of the wound.* Initial entry is generally a poor guide because it is only a single point.
- *The number of wounds inflicted.* Frequently, gunshot wound victims have been hit multiple times. For example, being hit once is less severe than suffering four separate wounds. In much the same way, an individual pellet from buckshot is comparatively small, but because victims are usually hit by large numbers of pellets simultaneously, the degree of injury is severe, particularly when the wound is inflicted at close range.

Even nonfatal gunshot wounds frequently have severe and long-lasting effects, even after the victim has made a successful recovery.[18] Typically, the consequences involve some form of major disfigurement or permanent disability. As a rule, all gunshot wounds are considered medical emergencies that require immediate hospital treatment.

Gunshot wounds consist of two basic types: entrance and exit wounds. Determining whether the wound in question is an entrance or an exit wound can have an overwhelming effect on the outcome of the case. Although the medical examiner makes this determination, in many cases he or she might not come to the crime scene, and the initial determination will be made by the investigator.

Entrance Wounds

Generally, the wound where the projectile entered the body is smaller than the exit wound, but there have been well-documented exceptions to this. The hole will usually be a neat, clean hole with an abrasion mark around it accompanied by a blackish-gray ring around the edges. Minimal bleeding will typically be observed.

Exit Wounds

An exit wound is usually a larger wound than the entrance wound, with a ragged or torn appearance. The exit wound usually has a larger amount of blood around it than the entrance wound.

Smudging

Smudging is usually a ring that results from gunpowder being deposited around the wound. It has a dirty appearance and can usually be wiped off. The significance of smudging is that it indicates that the victim was close to his or her assailant, although the firearm was not actually touching the skin.

Tattooing

Tiny pinpoint hemorrhages may result from the discharge of unburned powder being deposited into the skin. Called *tattooing*, these marks cannot be wiped away. One issue of critical importance in investigating gunshot wounds is the determination of whether or not the victim was murdered or died from suicide. The presence (or absence) of powder burns not only helps in making this determination but also helps the investigator decide the distance between the victim and the firearm.

FIGURE 9.8 When a handgun is fired, gunpowder and primer residues emit from the barrel. If fired from close range, these residues (called stippling) can possibly be found on the skin of both the shooter and the victim. *Courtesy of Forensic Technology WAI, Inc.*

FIGURE 9.9 Dual gunshot wounds to the head with stippling. *Courtesy of Mike Himmel and the Missouri State Highway Patrol.*

Understanding Gunshot Residue

For decades, gunshot residue (GSR) has been considered evidence that a specific person fired a handgun. But in recent years, GSR has been somewhat discredited and its usefulness limited, if not disregarded. To best understand the role of GSR in death and shooting investigations, it is instructive to understand the operation of a handgun.

If one inspects the back of a bullet larger than a .22, a small circle in the center (known as "centerfire") can be seen. This is a short, sealed cylinder containing primer. When the trigger is pulled, the hammer of the gun strikes this cylinder, and the shock of that blow causes the primer to explode. This explosion blows out into the large chamber of the casing, where the gunpowder is, causing the gunpowder to catch fire. The burning of the gunpowder is what expels the bullet away from the casing, down the barrel of the gun, and out the open end.[19]

Tiny particles of this primer material (GSR) are also expelled from the front of the gun. They can also "leak" from the breechblock area when the gun is fired, either from the open back of the chamber in revolvers or when chamber opens and the cartridge is ejected in automatics. As a result, GSR can settle on the hand of the shooter.

Primer is generally made up of barium nitrate and antimony sulfide; however, most .22 ammunition does not have antimony, and rare brands have neither antimony or barium.[20] It also contains lead styphnate, but because lead is commonly found in the environment, the presence of it on a person's hands is not considered significant. Therefore, most GSR detection techniques concentrate on barium and antimony.[21]

Most gunpowder used today is "double base," which means it is a combination of nitroglycerin and cellulose nitrate (commonly and incorrectly known as nitrocellulose).[22] GSR tests used to range from the now-discredited "paraffin test," which essentially tested for the nitrates from the gunpowder to "atomic absorption."

Atomic absorption involves swabbing the suspect's hands with cotton swabs and then soaking them in an acid solution. The solution is exposed to high temperatures, and a light reads the absorption rate of the atomized solution. This is a time-consuming and time-limited process because the swabs have to first be "digested," then spun, then diluted with deionized water (in different concentrations for barium and antimony) in tiny sample cups that are placed in an automated machine, a spectrometer.[23]

Atomic absorption only shows that the element is present but not in what form. Moreover, barium and antimony can also be found in other sources such as firecrackers, paint, and some industrial settings. Accordingly, locating these elements on a suspect's hands does not prove that he or she fired a gun or even that he or she handled a gun. Rather, it is only an "indication" that he or she was in the general area of a fired gun.[24]

GSR is composed of extremely tiny particles that can be easily removed from the skin. For example, all the shooter has to do is wash his or her hands thoroughly; also, normal human movement and activity can remove the particles as well. To a great extent, this is the reason why deceased victims' hands are bagged in paper (not plastic as is often depicted in television shows)—to preserve the GSR particles. Most labs will not test samples collected from living persons more than 6 hours after the shooting. This doesn't apply to deceased persons because they're not moving around or using their hands after death.[25]

From this comes the determination that although the presence of GSR doesn't prove someone did fire a gun, the absence of GSR doesn't prove they didn't. As such, attorneys and forensic scientists disagree on the usefulness of GSR evidence. For example, prosecutors often say that GSR on the defendant's hands proves that he or she is the killer. On the other hand, defense attorneys argue that the absence of GSR on the defendant's hands proves that he or she is not the killer. Consequently, in recent years, the legal community has become increasingly disenchanted with circumstantial evidence and more interested in evidence that provides a higher degree of scientific certainty, such as DNA. For this reason, a number of crime laboratories across the nation have discontinued GSR analysis.[26]

In summary, the practical use of GSR is limited because it fails to prove, with certainty, that a suspect fired a weapon. It's use, however, can be corroborative if considered with other evidentiary factors.

Defense Wounds

Defense wounds are characteristic of a struggle between a victim and an assailant. Such wounds may appear on the body of the victim and may take many forms. For example, in a fatal stabbing, slashing wounds on the hands of the victim may indicate that the victim grabbed the knife during a struggle, only to have it pulled back by the killer. These wounds are usually deep and concentrated on the palms and the undersurface of the fingers. Other indicators of a struggle are bruises on the forearms of the victim of a beating, indicating that the victim was attempting to defend him- or herself from attack by the assailant. In addition, a victim of a shotgun killing might have shot from the shotgun blast embedded in his or her hands or forearms.

Shotgun Wounds

Second only to the handgun, the most common weapon with which officers are confronted is the shotgun. A shotgun shell may project anywhere from 200 small pellets (birdshot) to nine larger (buckshot) to one large lead projectile called a *slug*. The shotgun remains one of the most effective killing weapons because of its capability for massive tissue destruction. It remains a choice of many criminals because all that is required, in many cases, is simply pointing the weapon in the general direction of the victim, and, after discharge, some contact is typically made. In addition, the appearance of the shotgun commands respect from all who face it, making it an effective tool of intimidation. From an

FIGURE 9.10 X-ray of a shooting victim showing locations of bullets in skull. Courtesy of Mike Himmel and the Missouri State Highway Patrol.

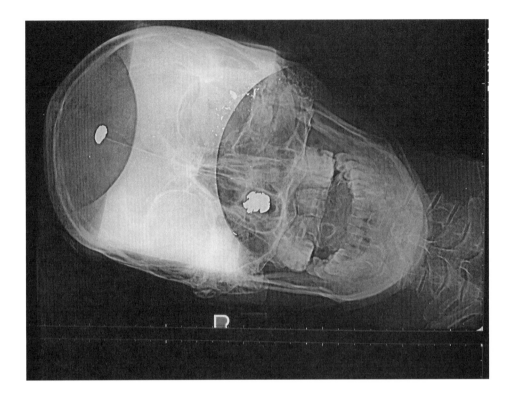

evidentiary standpoint, the shotgun wadding usually remains in the skin of the victim if discharged within 10 feet. Shotgun wadding can tell the investigator three things:

1. The type of shot used.
2. The gauge of gun used.
3. Possible evidence to help identify the gun used.

FIGURE 9.11 One of two bullets recovered from the skull of a shooting victim. Courtesy of Mike Himmel and the Missouri State Highway Patrol.

Best Practices: Keys to a Successful Homicide Unit

- ☑ No more than five cases per year as a primary for each detective
- ☑ Minimum of two two-person units responding initially to the crime scene
- ☑ Case review by all involved personnel within the first 24 to 72 hours
- ☑ Computerized case management system with relational capacity
- ☑ Standardized and computerized car-stop and neighborhood-canvass forms
- ☑ Compstat-style format
- ☑ Effective working relationships with medical examiners and prosecutors
- ☑ No rotation policy for homicide detectives
- ☑ Accessibility to work overtime when needed
- ☑ Cold case squads
- ☑ Investigative tools, such as polygraph, bloodstain pattern analysis, criminal investigative analysis, and statement analysis
- ☑ Homicide unit and other personnel work as a team

Source: Keel, T. (2008). Evaluating best practices for homicide units. *FBI Law Enforcement Bulletin* 77(2).

Pitfalls in Homicide Investigations

A recurring theme throughout this book is that the loss of crucial evidence in any criminal case can result in either the guilty party going unpunished or innocent parties being wrongfully incarcerated. This premise certainly applies to wrongful death investigations. In addition, carelessness in the processing of the crime scene can result in undue anguish to families. A study conducted by pathologist Alan Moritz concluded that there are several pitfalls that have been most commonly identified by veteran death investigators in the United States:[27]

System Errors

- Assumption that the case is not provable
- Inadequate staffing of the investigative unit
- Lack of awareness about the objective of the investigation
- Insufficient training
- Alteration of the scene before the investigator's arrival
- Inadequate photographic documentation at the scene
- Inadequate sketches
- Inadequate attention to detail
- Poor documentation
- Failure to follow up leads on a timely basis
- Overlooking evidence

Body Mistakes

- Failure to record body information thoroughly at the scene
- Assumption of identification based on circumstantial evidence
- Mishandling and mislabeling of bodies
- Failure to recognize, record, and safeguard personal property

FIGURE 9.12 A shotgun used in a homicide is being tagged as evidence. All firearms associated with crimes must be carefully documented.
Courtesy of Mike Himmel.

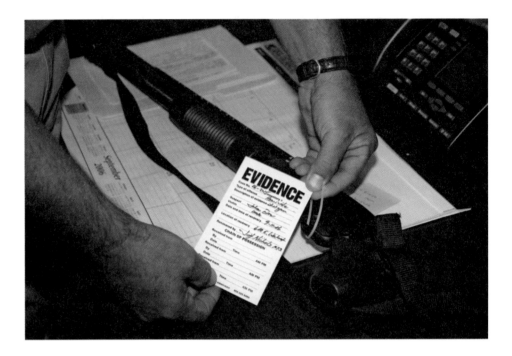

- Failure to notify next of kin in a timely, humane manner
- Trace evidence
- Follow-up errors
- Failure to report critical facts that determine what examinations need to be performed
- Failure to complete a timely and accurate death investigation report
- Failure to develop the victim's family and social history
- Failure to prepare for courtroom testimony

Personal Pitfalls

- Fallacy that length of service ensures competence
- Jumping to conclusions
- Failure to verify information received from other sources
- Talking too much and too soon to the wrong people
- Cutting corners

Recognizing these (and other) pitfalls will, it is hoped, alert investigators to the possibility that the investigation may be in jeopardy. As soon as problems are identified, the investigator can plan to avoid these pitfalls and discover solutions to problems rather than create more complications.

Serial, Mass, Sensational and Spree Murders

As mentioned in the beginning of this chapter, serial, mass, and sensational homicide add to the complexity of murder investigations. Such crimes generally have a psychodynamic component that can be very difficult to detect and understand. Because of this component, it is usually a logical decision to incorporate the expertise of psychology professionals in the investigation. For simplicity, let's now define the terms *serial*, *mass*, and *sensational murder*.[28]

FIGURE 9.13 Robert Kenneth Stewart attends a hearing in Moore County Superior Court in Carthage, N.C., Thursday, May 28, 2009. Stewart was charged with killing eight people at Pinelake Health and Rehabilitation Center nursing home in Carthage in March 2009. AP Photo/Gerry Broome.

Serial murder is the murder of separate victims with time breaks as short as two days to as much as weeks or even months between victims. Examples of serial murderers are the Hillside Strangler in California and Ted Bundy, who traveled across the United States leaving a trail of victims. In 1991, serial killer-cannibal Jeffrey Dahmer was arrested in connection with 17 murders in Milwaukee. A search of his apartment revealed 15 dismembered bodies, including a head found in the refrigerator, a heart discovered in the freezer, and a vat of acid for disposing of leftover body parts.

Mass murder consists of four or more murders in a single incident within a short span of time. A recent example of a mass murder is the March 29, 2009, Carthage nursing home incident. In this case, a gunman opened fire at the Pinelake Health and Rehab Nursing Home in Carthage, North Carolina killing eight people, including one employee of the facility, a nurse, before being shot and apprehended by a responding police officer.[29] The shooter was Robert Stewart, who was charged with eight counts of first-degree murder on the day of the shooting. Stewart's estranged wife was a nurse at the nursing home.

Sensational murder is murder that arouses intense public interest. For example, on August 1, 1966, in Austin, Texas, Charles Witman killed his wife and mother. He then went to the University of Texas tower and, with a rifle, shot and killed 14 people. *Lust murders* (also a subclass of serial murder) also commonly attract public interest because of the instances of torture and violence that are typically associated with this type of crime. These types of crimes often involve some type of psychotic motivation, as in the Tylenol poisonings in Chicago, the Atlanta child killings, the California Night Stalker case, and the Son of Sam case in New York.

Spree murder is killing in a rampage fashion. It is defines as someone who embarks on a murderous assault on his or her victims (two or more) in a short time in multiple locations. The U.S. Bureau of Justice Statistics defines a spree killing as "killings at two or more locations with almost no time break between murders."[30] According to the FBI, the general definition of spree murder is two or more murders committed by an offender or offenders, without a cooling-off period; the lack of a cooling-off period marks the difference between a spree murder and a serial murder. The category has, however, been found to be of no real value to law enforcement because of definitional problems relating to the concept of a "cooling-off period."[31]

An example of a spree murder is the Virginia Tech massacre that was a school shooting consisting of two separate attacks approximately two hours apart on April 16, 2007. These took place on the campus of Virginia Polytechnic Institute and State University (Virginia Tech) in Blacksburg, Virginia. The perpetrator, Seung-Hui Cho, killed 32 people and wounded many others before committing suicide.[32]

National Center for the Analysis of Violent Crime

Renowned FBI Agent Robert K. Ressler conceived the National Center for the Analysis of Violent Crime (NCAVC) in 1981 during a conversation with then–Quantico Director Jim McKenzie. Jim McKenzie supported the idea.

The mission of the NCAVC is to coordinate investigative and operational support functions, criminological research, and training in order to provide assistance to federal, state, local, and foreign law enforcement agencies investigating unusual or repetitive violent crimes (serial crimes). The NCAVC also provides investigative support through expertise and consultation in nonviolent matters such as national security, corruption, and white-collar crime investigations. Former President Ronald Reagan gave it the primary mission of "identifying and tracking repeat killers."

The NCAVC uses the latest advances in computer and investigative strategies to combat serial and violent crime. Violent Criminal Apprehension Program (ViCAP), PROFILER (a robot, rule-based expert system programmed to profile serial criminals), and Criminal Investigative Analysis Program (CIAP) are other programs designed to investigate serial crime.

VICAP specifically works by identifying and linking the signature aspects in violent serial crimes. The signature of a crime is the intrinsic part of the crime that the criminal must include in order for him or her to be satisfied and thus is present in every crime committed by the same person (although the signature does evolve over time).[33]

Today, every division in the FBI is mandated to have an NCAVC coordinator also known as a "profiling coordinator." The NCAVC or profiling coordinator acts as a liaison to the local law enforcement agencies. Typical cases for which NCAVC services are requested include child abduction or mysterious disappearance of children, serial murders, single homicides, serial rapes, extortions, threats, kidnappings, product tampering, arsons and bombings, weapons of mass destruction, public corruption, and domestic and international terrorism. Research and training programs support the operational services of the NCAVC. Requests for NCAVC services are typically facilitated through NCAVC coordinators assigned to each FBI field office.

The NCAVC is further organized into three components: Behavioral Analysis Unit (BAU), East and West Regions; Child Abduction Serial Murder Investigative Resources Center (CASMIRC); and ViCAP.[34]

Homicide Information Sharing System

Another example of a successful information sharing system is the Washington State Homicide Information Sharing System (HITS). The HITS system developed out of a research project funded by the National Institute of Justice

(NIJ). Initially, it was designed to record information on homicides in Washington State between 1981 and 1986. As part of the project, HITS operators contacted each of the state's 273 police and sheriff's departments, as well as each of the 39 county medical examiner or coroner's offices, county prosecuting attorney's offices, the Department of Vital Statistics, and the Uniform Crime Report (UCR) Unit of the Washington Association of Sheriffs and Police Chiefs, to determine the number of murders in the State during this period.[35]

Working with law enforcement agencies in the state, researchers eventually entered more than 1,300 murder files into the HITS system. All known cases were identified by name, case number, and the jurisdiction responsible for the investigation.

The HITS, housed in the Criminal Justice Division of the Attorney General's Office, was originally funded as part of the Community Protection Act of 1990. The Community Protection Act funding for the HITS unit came on the heels of several high-profile cases, including serial killers:

- Ted Bundy
- Gary Ridgway, aka the "Green River killer"
- Wesley Allen Dodd
- Child molester and mutilator Earl Shriner

The Dodd case, in particular, demonstrated the need for statewide information sharing on violent offenders. Before killing three young boys in Clark County, Dodd had been implicated in child luring and molestation in the Tri-Cities and King County areas.

By the time Dodd moved to Clark County, however, he was just another transient offender able to evade law enforcement's statewide view of his propensity for harming young children. He did so by simply moving to another county and another jurisdiction each time he came under the scrutiny of local law enforcement.

At the time, an offender's crossing into another jurisdiction crippled the sharing of information by law enforcement. It is interesting to note that after his conviction, Dodd outlined some of the "holes" in the state's criminal justice system in a handwritten letter to Washington Attorney General Ken Eikenberry. Dodd described himself as a sexual predator, who was basically "ignored" by law enforcement authorities as he moved from community to community.

At the time of its origination, the HITS Unit gathered data related solely to homicide. Over time, the need to capture sex-related and other crime data became apparent. The HITS Unit recognized that gathering more than just homicide data was critical to realizing the full potential of the system. As a result, the HITS Unit currently collects, codes, maintains, and most importantly, shares, data about nearly 65,000 cases.

The HITS database now collects other crimes and incidents that do not rise to the level of rape or homicide. As with rape and homicide, this number continues to grow every day. The data captured in this file typically involve other crimes that have occurred and are historically predatory in nature, such as:

- Non-rape sexual assaults (e.g., molestation, fondling, incest)
- Sex offender registration and changes of address forms
- Child luring
- Stalking

- Child pornography (Internet and non-Internet related)
- Identity theft
- Suspicious circumstances (e.g., children approached on the way to school, bloody clothing found, abandoned vehicles, missing persons)[36]

The HITS system has proven to be a beneficial system in sharing information between law enforcement agencies in the Northwest. As with VICAP, such information sharing systems allow investigators to quickly learn what is occurring in other jurisdictions so a rapid investigative response can be made.

Autoerotic Death

An **autoerotic death** represents one of the most bizarre and complex crime scenes of all. In this type of wrongful death investigation, a body (typically, male) will be discovered in a partially suspended position, nude, or clad only in feminine attire. The actual cause of death in this type of case will probably be asphyxia, but until properly investigated, the mode of death could be diagnosed as suicide or homicide when actually it is an "accidental" death.

Vernon Geberth states that most of the literature of autoeroticism focuses on young boys and older men who gain sexual gratification through a predetermined ritualistic exercise.[37] Over the years, bodies have been discovered in many different conditions, including being completely nude, partially nude, or dressed in women's attire. Use of a ligature is also common and is designed to restrict the flow of oxygen (hypoxia) to the victim during sexual orgasm. Basically, the sensation of choking is believed to heighten the sexual stimulation of the participant. Rob Hazelwood and his associates have identified three ways that autoeroticism may result in death:[38]

1. Failure with the physiological mechanism
2. Failure in the self-rescue device
3. Failure on the part of the victim's judgment and ability to control a self-endangering fantasy scenario

When a possible autoerotic death is under investigation, the investigator should ask him or herself the following:

- Is the victim nude or sexually exposed?
- If male, is he dressed in women's attire?
- Is there evidence of masturbation?
- Is a ligature present?

In the article "Death During Dangerous Autoerotic Practice," Hazelwood suggests several criteria that can be used by the criminal investigator to determine an autoerotic death:[39]

- Evidence of a physiological mechanism for obtaining or enhancing sexual arousal that depends on either a self-rescue mechanism or victim's judgment to discontinue its effect
- Evidence of solo sexual activity
- Evidence of sexual fantasy aids (e.g., pornography, vibrators, mirrors)
- Evidence of prior erotic practice (e.g., photographs)
- No apparent suicidal intent

As indicated, most autoerotic cases involve men, but it is important to realize that women are sometimes involved. For example, what might appear to be a sexual slaying with bondage and suffocation of the victim may actually be an accidental death of a woman who was practicing autoeroticism. One such case involved a 35-year-old woman who was discovered dead by her nine-year-old daughter. The woman was nude and lying on a small-shelved area in the rear of her bedroom closet. She was on her stomach, and an electric vibrator with a hard rubber massaging head was between her thighs and in contact with her vulva. The vibrator was still operating when she was discovered. Attached to the nipple of her right breast was a clothespin, which was compressing the nipple. Around the victim's neck was a nylon stocking that was positioned in loop fashion and fastened to a shelf bracket above the victim's head.

The lower portion of her body was supported by the shelf, and her upper body rested on her arms, which were extended downward in a "push-up" fashion. The victim placed clothespins on her nipples to cause discomfort and used the ligature around her neck to reduce the oxygen flow. She obviously intended to support her upper-body weight with her arms, but she lost consciousness, and the weight of her body, hanging from the nylon stocking, caused her to strangle. Investigators should consider any hanging or suffocation crime scene as a possible autoerotic death, especially if the clues described are present. In addition, the investigator may face problems convincing family members that the victim died accidentally (as a result of autoeroticism) rather than as a result of suicide or murder. Therefore, a sympathetic approach when dealing with family members is highly recommended.

Suicide

Suicide can be defined as the deliberate taking of one's own life. It has been said that as soon as an apparent suicide has been discovered, the responding officer should question his or her first impression at the scene. Statistics showing the instance of suicide is alarming. For example, in 2009, the American Foundation for Suicide Prevention showed that 33,000 people in the United States die by suicide every year. Statistics also show:

- A person dies by suicide about every 16 minutes in the United States.
- 90% of all people who die by suicide have a diagnosable psychiatric disorder at the time of their death. (More than 60 percent of all people who die by suicide suffer from major depression. If one includes alcoholics who are depressed, this figure rises to more than 75 percent.)
- 83% of gun-related deaths are the result of a suicide, often by someone other than the gun owner.
- Firearms are used in more suicides than homicides.[40]

Homicide and suicide appear to have many similarities, and the two are often difficult to distinguish. For example, if the case is actually a suicide but appears to be a murder, the responding officer may waste valuable time processing the scene as though it were a homicide. Conversely, if the scene is processed as a suicide when it is actually a homicide, valuable evidence will be damaged or lost.

Certain questions should present themselves to the officer at a wrongful death crime scene. For example, did there appear to be a struggle? Are defense wounds present on the victim? This situation will call on the investigator's powers of observation and common sense.

Reasons for Concern about Suicides

- ☑ The cause of death is an index to society's health.
- ☑ Suicides are the largest group of potentially preventable deaths.
- ☑ Insurance companies are usually liable for double indemnity in accidental deaths.

Evidence of Suicide

Of primary importance to the investigator is to secure the crime scene to protect evidence of the crime. At least until a complete search of the area has been conducted, individuals should not be allowed to move about the crime scene. This includes police officers and family members of the deceased. From an evidentiary standpoint, most wrongful death crime scenes will produce an abundance of physical evidence. The scene should therefore not be disturbed until the search is complete. All objects left at the scene should be left in their original condition. Such objects include shell casings, weapons, notes, and other items.

The Suicide Note

A suicide note or death note is a message left by someone who later attempts or commits suicide. It is estimated that 12 to 20 percent of suicides are accompanied by a note.[41] Although the suicide note has traditionally been the manner in which the victim expresses his or her feelings about his or her death, this should not always be taken as absolute proof of a suicide. The suicide note should be viewed with some suspicion, and elements of it must be scrutinized. For example, if handwritten, an attempt should be made to compare the handwriting on the note with the deceased to see if it is authentic. Investigators should also try to locate the supply of paper from which the note was taken. After it has been located, impressions might be identified on the pad to verify that the note was prepared at a certain location. The content of the note might also indicate a motive for the suicide. It may be a confession to a crime, an appeal for understanding, or even a method of placing guilt on those left behind. Because paper is such an excellent preserver of fingerprints, the note should be handled very carefully and protected as valuable evidence. After it has been collected, it should be delivered to the crime laboratory for handwriting analysis.

Reconstructing the Death

The investigator should attempt to reconstruct the circumstances surrounding the death of a suicide victim. In doing so, the question should be asked: Could the victim logically have killed him- or herself this way? The reconstruction process uses objects found at the crime scene and attempts to make inferences that can, it is hoped, be translated into theories about the commission of the crime. In this process, assumptions should not be made unless supported by some type of evidence. One misconception, for example, is that a gunshot entry wound is always smaller than its exit wound. Another misconception is that suicides by hanging are always accomplished by the total suspension of the victim's body. Again, this assumption is incorrect.

Materials Used

Years of experience have shown that certain self-inflicted wounds happen in a somewhat predictable fashion. Therefore, certain conclusions can be drawn by studying the locations and characteristics of specific injuries. Such conclusions may support certain probabilities about the commission of the act. Persons choosing suicide generally select a method that is as painless as possible. Exceptions to this are cases in which a mentally ill person purposely inflicts immense pain on him- or herself during the suicide. When completing the act, victims will often "personalize" their actions. For example, they might push aside clothing that tends to get in the way of a knife or gun barrel, enabling the weapon to come in direct contact with the skin. In addition, female victims will typically commit the crime while being careful not to disfigure their face. Persons choosing to hang themselves will be careful to place the rope or ligature directly against their skin and not around their shirt collar.

Motives for Suicide

One's behavior can be a good indicator as to why or whether he or she chooses suicide. Indeed, if there is no apparent reason for the victim to consider suicide, homicide should be considered to be the manner of death. Impulses displayed by people who commit suicide are complex and difficult to understand. Therefore, investigators will find difficulty in totally understanding this radical course of action and should be satisfied with explanations that might, at least on the surface, appear sketchy. For example, reasons for suicide have included old age, bad health, a failing love affair, marital problems, financial problems, and fear of arrest or imprisonment. When such indicators exist, the investigator should interview friends, family, neighbors, co-workers, and anyone else who might be able to furnish answers to investigators. Other information can be verified through traditional means. For instance, if the apparent reason for suicide is financial problems, such information can be verified through a check of the victim's financial affairs.

During interviews, the investigator should look for comments made by the victim to his or her associates about suicide. For example, the victim might once have remarked to a close friend, "If that ever happened, I'd kill myself." Or the victim may have stated, "she/he would be better off without me." In all cases, however, such remarks should be verified if at all possible because a false suicide threat might be used to cover up a murder.

CASE IN POINT:

Evidence in the JonBenet Ramsey Murder Case

The murder of six-year-old JonBenet Ramsey over a decade ago remains one of the most disturbing unsolved crimes in recent history. Figure 9.14 is a rough sketch of the Ramsey house and the locations where each piece of evidence was located. Consider the amount of evidence, how it relates to the crime and other pieces of evidence, and the complicated process of investigating wrongful death cases.

1. *The corpse.* Six-year-old JonBenet's 45-pound corpse was found in the basement's wine cellar. According to police reports, John Ramsey said he found the body covered with a white blanket, a Colorado Avalanche sweatshirt, and a pink

Barbie nightgown. This last item was JonBenet's favorite possession.

The dead child's long blonde hair was done up in two loose ponytails. Duct tape covered and sealed her mouth. John Ramsey is said to have ripped this tape off after he removed the coverings from the body. According to information leaked from grand jury hearings, police determined that a fiber found on the sticky part of the tape matched that of a garment Patricia Ramsey was wearing on the night of the killing. However, others point out that the fiber could have become adhered after John Ramsey threw the ripped-off tape on the floor.

CASE IN POINT continued

The dead girl was dressed in a crewneck top decorated with a sequined star on the chest and long white underpants, which were extensively stained with urine. The autopsy reported that the child's bladder was empty when she died.

Beneath, she wore white panties imprinted with a rosebud pattern. The panties were also stained with urine as well as a small amount of blood. Additional amounts of blood were found around her genitals; her vagina showed signs of penetration and abrasion, but no semen was found in, on, or around the body.

She wore a gold cross and chain around her neck; a gold bracelet on her wrist was inscribed with "JonBenet 12-25-96." On her left palm was a heart drawn in red ink. Two pieces of white synthetic cord were involved in the killing. One was wrapped around the girl's neck and had strands of her hair entangled in its knot. The other was tied around her wrist. The neck cord was also entangled with a broken length of paintbrush handle that is believed to have been used to make a strangulation garrote. Police have matched the wooden handle to a paintbrush found in Patricia Ramsey's oil painting gear.

According to the Boulder coroner, John E. Meyer, the primary cause of death was strangulation. Based on autopsy information, other medical authorities have suggested that she was hit on the head first and strangled later. Although the girl had been struck with a blunt object hard enough to open an 8-inch-long skull fracture, the blow did not break the skin, a fact that suggested to police that the object was padded in some manner.

2. *The kitchen flashlight.* During their searches of the Ramsey home, police seized a number of objects that could have been used to inflict the skull-cracking blow. These included a hammer, golf clubs, several baseball bats, and a large rubber-coated flashlight that was found on the kitchen counter on the morning the child's body was discovered. The flashlight has received special attention by police, including analysis at the Colorado Bureau of Investigation laboratory. The results of those forensic tests are not known.

3. *The basement.* The corpse was found in what the family called the wine cellar. The cement-floored space had its own door and contained a collection of bottled wine as well as other household items commonly stored in basements, such as old cans of house paint. Then–Boulder police chief Rick French searched the basement on the morning JonBenet was reported missing but said he did not look in the small wine cellar room.

Fleet White, a retired oil company executive and neighbor of the Ramsey family, who helped in the morning search for JonBenet, is reported to have told police that prior to the arrival of French that he had inspected the wine cellar room and saw nothing there. Later that day, John Ramsey said he looked in the wine cellar for the first time and saw the body of his daughter lying on the floor.

Police found the overall basement area to be acoustically well insulated from much of the rest of the house. Tests found that screams in the basement were actually easier to hear outside the building than from the family bedrooms on the second floor. Residents in the vicinity said they heard a child's screams between midnight and 2:00 A.M. on the night that JonBenet died.

4. *Forensic contamination.* Authorities say that John Ramsey and a police officer disturbed, destroyed, or contaminated important forensic clues when each moved the body shortly after Ramsey said he first discovered it. Ramsey lifted the corpse from the floor of the wine cellar, carried it upstairs, and put it down on the floor of the foyer near the top of the stairs. A short time later, detective Linda Arndt lifted the corpse from that spot and moved it into the living room near the Christmas tree before she called her office to report a homicide. In addition, throughout the day, police allowed the Ramseys to host a crowd of friends and neighbors in the house. Dozens of people roamed the rooms, cleaning kitchen counters and appliance surfaces as they prepared to lay out spreads of bagels, coffee, and other snacks for themselves.

5. *The train room.* Another room in the basement was called the train room because it contained a large table for model train setups. The table was covered in artificial grass, traces of which are believed to have been found in JonBenet's hair.

6. *The Swiss army knife.* A Swiss army knife owned by nine-year-old Burke Ramsey was also recovered from an undisclosed spot in the basement. The knife was reported to be one of the young boy's prized possessions.

CASE IN POINT continued

FIGURE 9.14 Murder of JonBenet Ramsey: Location of evidence in the Ramsey house.

7. *The ransom note.* One of the most vital and controversial clues of the case is the handwritten ransom note that Patricia Ramsey says she found on the staircase near the kitchen. The note, which demanded an amount of money that was exactly equal to John Ramsey's Christmas bonus, also contained references to other aspects of the Ramseys' personal lives that would not be known to outsiders. According to police, a rough draft or "practice" version of the note was written on a pad seized from an undisclosed location inside the house. News leaks from both sides of the investigation have indicated that various handwriting experts have reached dramatically different conclusions about whether the writing was similar to Patricia Ramsey's.

8. *The 9-1-1 call.* At 5:51 A.M. on December 26, Patricia Ramsey dialed 9-1-1 and reported her daughter missing, but she failed to put the handset back in its cradle when she hung up. The 9-1-1 connection remained live, continuing to record sounds from within the Ramsey house. The police later turned that 9-1-1 recording over to the Aerospace Corp. in southern California for enhancement. That enhanced tape constitutes one of the most controversial and mysterious aspects of the case. In the recording, Burke Ramsey can reportedly be heard asking his parents, "What did you find?" His father, John Ramsey, can reportedly be heard harshly silencing the boy. Patricia Ramsey reportedly can be heard screaming, "Help me, Jesus, help me, Jesus." Among the reasons the tape is important is because it appears to directly contradict John and Patricia Ramsey's statements to police that Burke was asleep during the early morning commotion.

CASE IN POINT continued

9. *The victim's bedroom.* JonBenet and her brother, Burke, had separate bedrooms on the second floor near the top of the staircase leading up from the kitchen area.

10. *The pineapple chunks.* The coroner reported finding pineapple in the victim's small intestine, indicating that she had eaten the fruit just hours before she died. It has been reported that pineapple was one of her favorite snacks. But the Ramseys said that JonBenet was asleep when they arrived home from a Christmas party the night before and that they put her right to bed around 10:00 P.M. after changing her clothes as she continued to sleep.

11. *Unlocked windows and doors.* Police found that six ground-floor windows and the kitchen-area door to the exterior of the Ramsey house were not locked the night of the killing.

12. *Kitchen door pry mark.* An attorney for the Ramseys has pointed to a pry mark on the doorjamb of the kitchen door that leads to the exterior of the building as part of the "substantial evidence" that points toward an intruder as the killer. However, police characterized the mark as a "possible" pry mark, and a locksmith who inspected the house in the wake of the slaying said there was no evidence of a forced entry.

13. *The broken basement window.* The glass of a ground-level basement window at the back of the basement was broken. Police said John Ramsey broke the window months before and didn't repair it. There was dirt at the base of the window that could have resulted from someone squeezing in through the small opening.

14. *The blue suitcase.* Police found a blue suitcase propped below the broken basement window that some suggest could have been used by someone climbing out through the opening.

15. *DNA specimens.* The issue of DNA has been the subject of inaccurate media reports that were later corrected. For instance, shortly after the killing, *Newsweek* magazine reported that semen was found on the dead girl's thigh. That report was later retracted. However, authorities collected blood and hair samples from every member of the Ramsey family as well as a number of people with whom JonBenet was in contact in the days before her death. It is known that DNA experts from the FBI, the Colorado Bureau of Investigation, and several other DNA testing laboratories across the country have been consulted or retained by both sides of the investigation. The exact details of the DNA findings are not known.

16. *A stun gun.* More conjecture than fact is the continuing suggestion (which has not been confirmed) that an electric stun gun may have been involved. The autopsy report made no mention of stun gun marks on the body. However, *New York* magazine reported that among the many videotapes found in the Ramsey house was an instruction program about how to use a stun gun. A rear neighbor to the Ramsey house, Margaret Dillon, was questioned by detectives about stun guns. Another neighbor, Scott Gibbons, reported seeing "strange lights" in the Ramsey home that some have suggested could have been the flash of a stun gun.

CASE IN POINT:

The Investigation of the "BTK" Killer

Dennis Lynn Rader (born March 9, 1945) is a serial killer who murdered at least ten people in Sedgwick County (in and around Wichita), Kansas, between 1974 and 1991. He was known as the BTK killer (or the BTK strangler), which stands for bind, torture, and kill, an apt description of his modus operandi (MO).

The BTK's Modus Operandi, "MO"

Using personal jargon for his killing equipment, Rader casually described his victims as his "projects"

and at one point likened the murders of his victims to killing animals by saying he "put them down."

Rader created what he called a "hit kit," a briefcase or bowling bag containing the items he would use during murders: guns, tape, rope, and handcuffs. He also packed what he called "hit clothes" that he would wear for the crimes and then dispose of.

Rader developed a pattern for his murders. He would wander the city until he found a potential victim. At that point, he would stalk the person until he

CASE IN POINT continued

knew the pattern of the person's life and when would be the best time to strike. He would also get acquainted with his potential victims if they were his coworkers, making them easier to track down and identify. Rader often would stalk multiple victims at a time, so he could continue the hunt if one victim didn't work out. At the time of the murder, Rader would break into the house, cut the phone lines, and hide until his victim came home.

Rader would often calm his victims by pretending to be a rapist who needed to work out some sexual fantasies on them. This caused many of his victims to be more cooperative and even help him, thinking that once the rape was over, he would leave them alone. Instead, Rader would kill them.

The name BTK, chosen by Rader for himself, also dictated his methods. Rader bound, tortured, and killed his victims. Rader would strangle his victims until they lost consciousness, then let them revive, then strangle them again. He would repeat the pattern over and over again, forcing them to experience near-death, becoming sexually aroused at the sight of their struggles. Finally, Rader would strangle them to death.

Rader's victims included:

- 1974: Four members of one family (Joseph Otero; his wife, Julie Otero; and two of their five children, Joseph Otero II and Josephine Otero) and another separate victim, Kathryn Bright
- 1977: Shirley Vian
- 1977: Nancy Fox
- 1985: Marine Hedge
- 1986: Vicki Wegerle
- 1991: Delores Davis

Police officials say there is no reason to believe Rader was responsible for any other murders. He collected items from the scenes of the murders he committed and reportedly had no items that were related to any other killings.

Evidence in the BTK Investigation: Letters

Rader was particularly known for sending taunting letters to police and newspapers. There were several communications from BTK during 1974 to 1979. The first was a letter that had been stashed in an engineering book in the Wichita Public Library in October 1974 that described in detail the killing of the Otero family in January of that year.

In early 1978, he sent another letter to television station KAKE in Wichita claiming responsibility for the murders of the Oteros, Shirley Vian, Nancy Fox, and another unidentified victim assumed to be Kathryn Bright. He suggested a number of possible names for himself, including the one that stuck: BTK. He demanded media attention in this second letter, and it was finally announced that Wichita did indeed have a serial killer at large.

In his 1978 letter, Rader wrote the following (written verbatim):

I find the newspaper not writing about the poem on Vain unamusing. A little paragraph would have enough. I know it not the media fault. The Police Chief he keep things quiet, and doesn't let the public know there a psycho running around lose strangling mostly women, there 7 in the ground; who will be next?

How many do I have to Kill before I get a name in the paper or some national attention. Do the cop think that all those deaths are not related? Golly -gee, yes the M.O. is different in each, but look a pattern is developing. The victims are tie up-most have been women-phone cut-bring some bondage mater sadist tendencies-no struggle, outside the death spot-no wintness except the Vain's Kids. They were very lucky; a phone call save them. I was going to tape the boys and put plastic bags over there head like I did Joseph, and Shirley. And then hang the girl. God-oh God what a beautiful sexual relief that would been. Josephine, when I hung her really turn me on; her pleading for mercy then the rope took whole, she helpless; staring at me with wide terror fill eyes the rope getting tighter-tighter. You don't understand these things because your not under the influence of factor x. The same thing that made Son of Sam, Jack the Ripper, Havery Glatman, Boston Strangler, Dr. H.H. Holmes Panty Hose Strangler OF Florida, Hillside Strangler, Ted of the West Coast and many more infamous character kill. Which seems senseless, but we cannot help it. There is no help, no cure, except death or being caught and put away. It a terrible nightmare but, you see I don't lose any sleep over it. After a thing like Fox I come home and go about life like anyone else. And I will be like that until the urge hit me again. It not continuous and I don't have a lot of time. It take time to set a kill, one mistake and it all over. Since I about blew it on the phone-handwriting is out-letter guide is to long and typewriter can be traced too. My short poem of death and maybe a drawing; later on

CASE IN POINT continued

real picture and maybe a tape of the sound will come your way. How will you know me. Before a murder or murders you will receive a copy of the initials B.T.K. , you keep that copy the original will show up some day on guess who?

May you not be the unluck one!

P.S.

How about some name for me, its time: 7 down and many more to go. I like the following How about you?

'THE B.T.K. STRANGLER', 'WICHITA STRANGLER', 'POETIC STRANGLER', 'THE BOND AGE STRANGLER' OR PSYCHO' THE WICHITA HANGMAN THE WICHITA EXECUTIONER, 'THE GAROTE PHATHOM', 'THE ASPHIXIATER'.
B.T.K

A poem was enclosed titled, "Oh Death to Nancy." In 1979, he sent two identical packages, one to an intended victim who was not at home when he broke into her house and the other to KAKE. These featured another poem, "Oh Anna Why Didn't You Appear," a drawing of what he had intended to do to his victim, as well as some small items he had pilfered from Anna's home. Apparently, Rader had waited for several hours inside the home of Anna Williams on the 600 block of South Pinecrest. Not realizing that she had gone to her sister's house for the evening, he eventually got tired of the long wait and left.

All of Rader's communications were poorly written, with many misspellings and incorrect grammar usage. It was theorized at times that the writing style was a ruse to conceal his intelligence, but it turns out Rader really does write that way in his everyday life even though he earned a college degree in 1979.

In 1988, after the murders of three members of the Fager family in Wichita, a letter was received from someone claiming to be the BTK killer in which he denied being the perpetrator of this crime. He did credit the killer with having done admirable work. It was not proven until 2005 that this letter was in fact written by the genuine BTK killer, Rader, although he is not considered by police to have committed this crime.

In March 2004, he began a series of 11 communications from BTK that led directly to his arrest in February 2005. The *Wichita Eagle* newspaper received a letter from someone using the return address Bill Thomas Killman. The writer claimed that he murdered Vicki Wegerle on September 16, 1986, and enclosed photographs of the crime scene and a photocopy of her driver's license, which had been stolen at the time of the crime.

In May 2004, a word puzzle was received by KAKE. In June, a package was found taped to a stop sign in Wichita containing graphic descriptions of the Otero murders. In July, a package was dropped into the return slot at the downtown public library containing more bizarre material, including the claim that he, BTK, was responsible for the death of 19-year-old Jake Allen in Argonia, Kansas, earlier that same month. This claim was found to be false, and the death remains ruled as a suicide.

In October 2004, a manila envelope was dropped into a UPS box in Wichita containing a series of cards with images of terror and bondage of children pasted on them. Also included was a poem threatening the life of lead investigator Lt. Ken Landwehr and a false autobiography giving many details about his life. These details were later released to the public as though possibly factual, but the police were mostly trying to encourage the killer to continue to communicate until making a major mistake.

In December 2004, Wichita police received another package from the BTK killer. This time the package was found in Wichita's Murdock Park. It contained the driver's license of Nancy Fox, which was noted as stolen at the scene of the crime, as well as a doll that was symbolically bound at the hands and feet with a plastic bag tied over its head.

In January 2005, Rader attempted to leave a cereal box in the bed of a pickup truck at a Home Depot in Wichita, but the box was at first discarded by the owner. It was later retrieved from the trash after Rader himself asked what had become of it in a later message.

A surveillance tape of the parking lot from that date revealed a distant figure driving a black Jeep Cherokee leaving the box in the pickup. In February, there were postcards to KAKE and another cereal box left at a rural location that contained another bound doll symbolizing the murder of 11-year-old Josephine Otero. Rader asked the police that if he put his writings onto a floppy disk if the disk could be traced or not. He received his answer in a newspaper ad posted in the *Wichita Eagle* saying it would be OK.

On February 16, 2005, he sent a floppy disk to Fox TV station KSAS in Wichita. Forensic analysis quickly determined that the disk had been used by the Christ Lutheran Church in Wichita, plus the name Dennis. An Internet search determined that Rader was president of this church. He was arrested on February 25.

After his arrest, Rader stated he chose to resurface in 2004 for various reasons, including the release of the book *Nightmare in Wichita—the Hunt*

CASE IN POINT continued

for the BTK Strangler by Robert Beattie. He wanted the opportunity to tell his story his own way. He also said he was bored because his children had grown up and he had more time on his hands.

Rader's Arrest

The BTK killer's last known communication with the media and police was a padded envelope that arrived at FOX affiliate KSAS-TV in Wichita on February 16, 2005.

- A purple 1.44-MB Memorex floppy disk was enclosed in the package.
- Also enclosed were a letter and a photocopy of the cover of a 1989 novel about a serial killer (*Rules of Prey*).
- A gold-colored necklace with a large medallion was also in the envelope.
- Police found meta-data embedded in a Microsoft Word document on the disk that pointed to Christ Lutheran Church, and the document was marked as last modified by "Dennis."
- A search of the church Web site turned up Dennis Rader as president of the congregation council. Police immediately began surveillance of Rader.

Sometime during this period, police obtained a warrant for the medical records of Rader's daughter, Kerri. A tissue sample seized at this time was tested for DNA and provided a familial match with semen at an earlier BTK crime scene. This, along with other evidence gathered before and during the surveillance, gave police probable cause for an arrest.

Rader was stopped while driving near his home and taken into custody shortly after noon on February 25, 2005. Immediately after, law enforcement officials—including a Wichita Police bomb unit truck, two SWAT trucks, and FBI and ATF agents—converged on Rader's residence near the intersection of I-135 and 61st Street North.

Once in custody, Rader talked to investigators for hours, confessing right away. Twelve DVDs were filled with Rader's confession.

Observations

The BTK investigation illustrates the complexity of criminal investigation, evidence, and prosecution. Such cases also show how difficult it is for those who sit as jurors to decipher the truth in a criminal trial.

CASE IN POINT:

The Investigation of the Green River Killer

For 20 years, the bodies of a number of murdered young prostitutes and runaway girls periodically washed up in the Green River, approximately 45 miles from Seattle. By 2004, the total number of victims came to 48, and in addition to the Green River, their remains had shown up in ravines, airports, and freeways, with two of them discovered in Oregon. The victims were strangled. In time, the killer became known as the Green River Killer.

Over the years, the investigation into the murders produced a considerable amount of evidence but nothing sufficiently conclusive to justify the arrest of a suspect. Finally, in early 2004, 54-year-old Gary Leon Ridgway, a slight man with thick glasses, married three times and the father of one child, was charged with all 48 murders. Ridgway was a longtime painter at Kenworth Truck Co.

Ridgway had been a suspect since 1984, when one of the victim's boyfriends reported that he last saw her getting into a pickup identified as Ridgway's. But Ridgway said he did not know the victim, Marie Malvar. A police investigator in Des Moines cleared him as a suspect. Later that year, Ridgway contacted the King County Green River Task Force ostensibly to offer information about the case—and passed a polygraph test.

Investigators continued to suspect him, however, and in 1987 searched his house and took a saliva sample. It was 13 years before technology caught up to their suspicions and they could link that saliva sample to DNA taken from the bodies of three of the earliest victims. Ridgway was arrested on November 30, 2001, and later pleaded guilty to seven killings. But facing DNA evidence and the prospect of the death penalty, he began cooperating and trading information for his life.

He confessed to 42 of the 48 listed killings, as well as six not listed. Furthermore, he led investigators

CASE IN POINT continued

FIGURE 9.15 Gary Ridgway, seated to the left side of his attorney, Mark Prothero, was dubbed the "Green River Killer" almost 20 years ago after the bodies of some of his 48 victims showed up in Washington State's Green River, about 45 miles from Seattle. *Elaine Thompson/AP Wide World Photos.*

to four sets of previously undiscovered human remains. It turned out that the killings had continued long after investigators thought they had stopped. The last victim on the list disappeared in 1984, but one of the cases Ridgway plead to involved a woman killed in 1990 and another in 1998. Ridgway's pleas to the 48 murders gave him the dubious distinction of having more convictions than any other serial killer in the nation's history.

For example, John Wayne Gacy, who preyed on men and boys in Chicago in the 1970s, was convicted of 33 murders; Ted Bundy, whose killing spree began in Washington State, confessed to killing more than 30 women and girls but was convicted of killing only three before he was executed in Florida.

Ridgway's Motives and Method of Operation

Ridgway stated that his motive for the killings was "to kill as many women as I thought were prostitutes as I possibly could." Ridgway continued:

> I picked prostitutes as victims because I hate prostitutes and did not want to pay them for sex. I also picked prostitutes because they were easy to pick up without being noticed. I also knew they would not be reported missing right away, and might never be reported missing. I picked prostitutes because I thought I could kill as many of them as I could without getting caught.
>
> In most cases, when I murdered these women, I did not know their names. Most of them I liked. . . . I killed them the first time I met them and do not have a good memory of their faces. I killed so many women that I have a hard time keeping them straight. . . . I killed most of them in my house on Military Road, and I killed a lot of them in my truck, not far from where I picked them up. . . . I killed some of them outside. . . . I remember leaving each woman's body in the place where she was found.
>
> Another part of my plan was where I put the bodies of these women. Most of the time I took the women's jewelry and their clothes to get rid of any evidence and make them harder to identify. I placed most of the bodies in groups, which I call clusters. I did this because I wanted to keep track of all the women I killed. I liked to drive by the clusters around the country and think about the women I placed there.

Here are Ridgway's accounts of only a few of his murders:

- Wendy Lee Coffield: "I picked her up, planning to kill her. After killing her, I placed her body in the Green River."
- Debra Bonner: "I picked her up planning to kill her. After strangling her to death, I placed her body in the Green River."
- "I strangled Debra Estes to death. I picked her up, planning to kill her. After killing her, I buried her body near the Fox Run Apartments in Federal Way."
- "I strangled Carol Christensen to death. I picked her up, planning to kill her. After killing her, I placed her body in a wooded area in Maple Valley."

Chapter 9 Death Investigations

CASE IN POINT continued

- "I strangled Denise D. Bush to death. I picked her up planning to kill her. After killing her, I left her body just off a dirt road in the neighborhood of Riverton. I later transported some of her remains to a place just off the Bull Mountain Road, near Tigard, Oregon. I left the remains there with the remains of Shirley Sherrill. I did this to throw off police investigators so I could continue killing prostitutes."

CASE IN POINT:

Checklist: Suicide Shootings and Stabbings

Shootings

- Firearm suicides are common.
- Handguns are used more commonly than rifles.
- An aid such as a string or stick is commonly used.
- A weapon tightly clenched by the victim indicates suicide.
- Gunpowder residue should be located on the "gun hand" of the victim using a firearm. Location of the wound can be used in determining if shooting was self-inflicted. A forensic examination to determine the distance between the gun muzzle and the wound can often distinguish between homicide and suicide.

Stabbings

- Self-inflicted stab wounds are commonly in the chest area.
- When there are a large number of stab wounds in the victim, investigators should be suspicious.
- Generally, the body will be located at the point of the act, indicating no struggle with an assailant.
- The depth of a wound does not necessarily indicate the length of the weapon.
- The instrument, when located, must be well preserved in its original condition.
- Generally, there will be no "defense wounds" located on the victim of a suicide, but hesitation wounds might be mistaken for defense wounds.

Summary Checklist

In this chapter, we consider the ways information about crimes is documented by criminal investigators. In all societies, the instances of homicide and wrongful death have endured as top concerns for law enforcement officials. Considered as one of the gravest social problems, law enforcement plays an important role in investigating the facts and circumstances surrounding each such case. A properly documented case is one that is more likely to succeed in court.

See how well you are able to answer the following questions in your checklist.

1. Do you understand the various types and modes of wrongful death cases?

It is of primary importance that the investigator learn the manner in which the victim died as soon as possible after discovery of the body. Modes of death include:

- Accidental death
- Natural death
- Suicide
- Murder

2. Can you identify the legal characteristics of homicide?

It is incumbent on the professional investigator to be clear as to what laws best describe the alleged crime.

(continued)

Summary Checklist (Continued)

Under law, categories of homicide are generally divided into two distinct classifications: murder and manslaughter.

- Murder is considered the most serious of all statutory crimes and is defined as the purposeful, premeditated, and unlawful taking of the life of a human being by another person.

- Manslaughter is the deliberate killing of another person and is typically classified into two subcategories: voluntary and involuntary.

3. Can you explain the steps of the preliminary investigation of a wrongful death case?

The first officer to respond to a suspected homicide call is generally a patrol officer arriving a short time after the call is received. The actions taken at the time of

arrival may have a critical bearing on the subsequent course of the investigation.

The officer must become aware of the crime scene situation and be prepared to take certain immediate actions, the focus being identifying any aspects of the scene that might be subject to chemical change, change by dissipation, or change because something was moved.

The responding officer must protect the crime scene from unauthorized persons who may move, destroy, or otherwise contaminate evidence.

Complete notes are critical during the early stages of the homicide crime scene investigation.

Witnesses can also provide useful identification information of the victim if known to them.

4. Do you know the means in which a person's death can be estimated?

If the wrongful death appears to have been a homicide, all areas around the body become important in determining the time of death.

The time of death in a homicide case, particularly when there are no witnesses, is one of the most critical variables in its investigation. Notable changes in the body include:

- Body color
- Changes in the eyes
- Temperature of the body
- Rigor mortis
- Postmortem lividity

5. Do you know the characteristics of a gunshot wound?

Physical characteristics may vary, depending on:

- The type of caliber weapon used
- The distance between the shooter and victim
- Whether the lethal bullet had ricocheted off another object.

In the case of a contact wound, where the muzzle of the weapon was held against the body when discharged, certain residue will be present.

Generally, the wound where the projectile entered the body is smaller than the exit wound, but there have been well-documented exceptions to this.

An exit wound will usually be a larger wound than the entrance wound

Tiny pinpoint hemorrhages may result from the discharge of unburned powder being deposited into the skin. Called tattooing, these marks cannot be wiped away.

3. **Can you distinguish between serial, mass, and sensational murders?**

Serial, mass, and sensational homicide add to the complexity of murder investigations. Such crimes generally have a psychodynamic component that can be very difficult to detect and understand. Examples include:

- Serial murder is the murder of separate victims with time breaks as short as two days to as much as weeks or even months between victims.

- Mass murder consists of four or more murders in a single incident within a short span of time.

- Sensational murder is murder that arouses intense public interest.

Autoerotic death and suicide present special challenges for criminal investigators and must be properly identified for subsequent investigation.

Key Terms

autoerotic death

dying declaration

homicide

lividity

manslaughter

mass murder

murder

rigor mortis

scene-conscious

sensational murder

serial murder

spree murder

suicide

Discussion Questions

1. List and discuss the duties of the responding officer in a homicide case.
2. What notes should be taken at a wrongful death crime scene?
3. Discuss the importance of determining the time of death at a homicide crime scene.
4. What is meant by the terms *rigor mortis* and *postmortem lividity*? How is an understanding of these terms important to the investigation of a wrongful death?
5. To what extent do wounds play a role in understanding the facts and circumstances surrounding a wrongful death?
6. Explain the problems encountered by investigators in a wrongful death that is believed to be autoerotic.
7. Discuss what evidence should be located in the investigation of a suspected suicide.
8. What are the distinctions among serial, mass, and sensational murders?

mycrimekit

Go to MyCrimeKit.com to explore the following study tools and resources specific to this chapter:

- *Practice Quiz:* Multiple-choice, true/false, short-answer, and essay questions.
- *Flashcards:* There are 13 key terms in this chapter. Flashcards test your knowledge of the chapter's key terms.

- *Web Links:* Check out the hotlink to *The New York Times* criminology articles.
- *Career Center:* Check out the hot links to interesting careers in criminal justice, criminology, and juvenile justice.
- *The Research Center:* Check out the Cybrary and research navigator for even more resources.

Notes

1. Federal Bureau of Investigation. (2008). *Crime in America, 2007. Uniform crime reports.* Washington, DC: U.S. Government Printing Office.
2. GEBERTH, V. (1990). *Practical homicide investigation,* 2nd ed. New York: Elsevier.
3. See Rule 403. Available at; http://federalevidence.com/rules-of-evidence.
4. STATHEROPOULOS, M., & A. AGAPIOU, ET. AL. (2007). Environmental aspects of VOCs evolved in the early stages of human decomposition. *Sci Total Environ* 385(1-3):221–227.
5. EBERHARDT T.L., AND D. A. ELLIOT (2008). A preliminary investigation of insect colonisation and succession on remains in New Zealand. *Forensic Science International* 176(2-3):217–223
6. IBID.
7. SMITH, K. G. V. (1987). *A manual of forensic entomology.* Cornell University: Press: Ithaca, NY; p. 464.
8. IBID.
9. IBID.
10. BUCKBERRY, J. (2000). Missing, presumed buried? Bone diagenesis and the under-representation of Anglo-Saxon children. Available at http://www.assemblage.group.shef.ac.uk/5/buckberr.html.
11. SMITH, K. G. V. (1987). *A manual of forensic entomology.* Cornell University Press:464; Kulshrestha, P., and D. K. Satpathy. (2001). Use of beetles in forensic entomology. *Forensic Science International* 120(1-2):15–17
12. SCHMITT, A., E. CUNHA, AND J. PINHEIRO. (2006). *Forensic anthropology and medicine: Complementary sciences from recovery to cause of death.* Humana Press: NY: p. 464; Haglund, W. D., and M. H. Sorg. (1996). *Forensic taphonomy: The postmortem fate of human remains.* Boca Raton, FL: CRC Press:636.
13. IBID.
14. GEBERTH, V. (1990). *Practical homicide investigation,* 2nd ed. New York: Elsevier.
15. IBID.
16. DI MAIO, V. J. M. (1985). *Gunshot wounds: Practical aspects of firearms, ballistics, and forensic techniques.* New York: Elsevier.
17. MAHONEY, P. F., J. RYAN, A. J. BROOKS, AND C. W. SCHWAB. (2004) *Ballistic trauma—A practical guide,* 2nd ed. Springer
18. KRUG E. E. (Ed.). (2002). *World Report on Violence and Health.* Geneva: World Health Organization.
19. Note that some small caliber bullets, such as .22s, may have the primer crimped into the rim of the bullet instead of in a center cylinder, and the hammer can strike the bullet anywhere on the rim to fire the slug. This is known as "rimfire."
20. CENTERS FOR DISEASE CONTROL AND PREVENTION, Agency for Toxic Substances and Disease Registry. (2007). *Toxicological profile for barium and barium compounds.*
21. Magnetic susceptibility of the elements and inorganic compounds, in *Handbook of chemistry and physics,* 81th edition. Boca Raton, FL: CRC Press; United States Geological Survey. (2009). *Antimony statistics and information* Available at http://minerals.usgs.gov/minerals/pubs/commodity/antimony/.
22. BROWN, G. I. (1998). *The big bang: A history of explosives.* Sutton Publishing: UK.
23. FIREARMS ID.COM. Gunshot residue test results. Available at http://www.firearmsid.com/A_distanceResults.htm.
24. IBID.
25. BYKOWICZ, J. (2005). Convictions tied to controversial gun-residue test: Prosecutor's office counts several cases over 5 years; Defenders seek further review. *Baltimore Sun,* March 27.
26. GUZMAN, D. (2007). Judge rules out gunshot residue evidence in murder trial. *Houston News,* October 29. Available at http://www.click2houston.com/news/14452905/detail.html.
27. MORTIZ, A. R. (1981). Classical mistakes in forensic pathology. *American Journal of Forensic Medicine and Pathology* 2(4):299–308.
28. GEBERTH, V. (1986). Mass, serial and sensational homicides. *Law and Order* October:20–22.
29. BBC NEWS. (2009). Man kills eight at US care home. Available at http://news.bbc.co.uk/2/hi/americas/7971065.stm.
30. CHARALAMBOUS, N. AND M. DILLMAN. (2006). No evidence of spree killer yet, police say. *Anderson Independent-Mail News,* December 17.
31. FEDERAL BUREAU OF INVESTIGATION. *Serial murder — Multi-disciplinary perspectives for investigators.*
32. COMMONWEALTH OF VIRGINIA. *Report of the Virginia Tech Review Panel..* Available at http://www.governor.virginia.gov/TempContent/techPanelReport.cfm. Cho shot and wounded another 17 people and caused injury to six others as they tried to flee.
33. FEDERAL BUREAU OF INVESTIGATION.. *National Center for the Analysis of Violent Crime.* Available at http://www.fbi.gov/hq/isd/cirg/ncavc.htm.
34. IBID.
35. WASHINGTON STATE OFFICE OF THE ATTORNEY GENERAL. *Homicide Investigation Tracking System.* Available at http://www.atg.wa.gov/page.aspx?ID=2352
36. IBID.
37. IBID.
38. HAZELWOOD, R. R., A. W. BURGESS, AND N. GROTH (1985). Death during dangerous autoerotic practice. In *Social Science and Medicine* 15(suppl E):129–133.
39. IBID.
40. AMERICAN FOUNDATION FOR SUICIDE PREVENTION. (2009). National statistics. Available at http://www.afsp.org/index.cfm?fuseaction=home.viewpage&page_id=050FEA9F-B064-4092-B1135C3A70DE1FDA.
41. SHIOIRI T., A. NISHIMURA, K. AKAZAWA, et al. (2005). Incidence of note-leaving remains constant despite increasing suicide rates. *Psychiatry and Clinical Neurosciences.* 59(2):226–228.

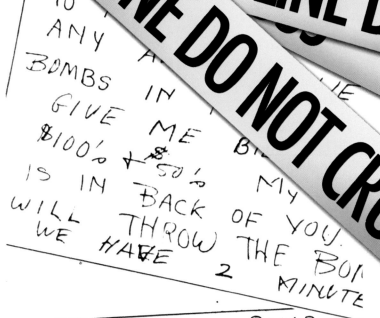

Robbery

10

This chapter will enable you to:

- Understand the motivations behind the crime of robbery.
- Identify the legal elements of the crime of robbery.
- List the steps to follow in the preliminary investigation of robbery offenses.
- Identify various types of physical evidence found in robberies.
- Appreciate the role of the witness in a robbery investigation.
- Explain the function of the neighborhood canvass during a preliminary investigation.

Introduction

On Friday, February 28, 1997, two Los Angeles patrol officers were driving by a bank at 9:30 A.M. when one of the officers glanced into a bank window and saw a customer being shoved by someone holding what appeared to be a shotgun. The officers summoned help and one of the biggest shoot-outs in the city's history ensued. The bank was in fact being robbed and the two gunmen, clad in bulletproof body armor, exited the bank and began unloading hundreds of rounds from fully automatic AK-47 rifles.

The shoot-out was broadcast live via a news helicopter, and all of America watched in horror as the two robbers, showing little emotion, calmly walked down the street as they emptied and reloaded their weapons over and over again. In a matter of minutes, buildings, police cars, and parked vehicles were permeated with bullet holes. The shoot-out, which drew almost 300 LA police officers, lasted about 30 minutes and ultimately ended with the death of both robbers. Sixteen bystanders and police officers were wounded in the shoot-out, but miraculously, no one other than the robbers was killed.

Robbery ranks among the most serious and feared criminal offenses because it involves both threatened or actual violence and a loss of property to the victim. It is also a particularly significant crime because of the psychological trauma suffered by its victims.

Robbery Offenses

Robbery, often confused with the crime of burglary, is a personal crime and involves face-to-face contact between the victim and offender. Weapons may be used or strong-arm robbery may occur through intimidation, especially where gangs threaten victims by their sheer numbers. Purse snatching and pickpocketing are not classified as robbery under the Uniform Crime Reporting Program but are included under the category of larceny theft.

Understanding Robbery

The primary motivation for robbery is to obtain money, although some juvenile robbers are also motivated by peer influence and the quest for "thrills." Drug and alcohol use is also common among street criminals and may influence their decisions to choose a particular criminal technique. Indeed, statistics reveal that robbers who use drugs are twice as active as those who do not.[1] Clearly, the distinct advantage of robbery over some other type of crime is that it is quick, easy, and requires little planning or preparation.

Most of what we have learned about robbery is descriptive information about trends and patterns. Statistics show that many robberies do not result in physical harm to the victim or extensive loss, but one in three does involve actual injury. These injuries range from bruises and black eyes to life-threatening gunshot or knife wounds. The statistics, as cited above, are staggering regarding the instance of robbery in the United States.

Defining Robbery

Robbery is defined as the theft or attempted theft, in a direct confrontation with the victim, by force or the threat of force or violence. The range of events commonly associated with robbery is reflected in the vernacular expressions for the crime, including such terms as *holdups*, *muggings*, and *stickups*. A child "rolled" for his lunch money and a bank teller confronted by a gun-toting gang are also both robbery victims.

Victims of burglary often claim that they were "robbed." Such incidents are not actually robbery unless the burglar encounters someone in the structure and uses force or threatens them as a means of completing the theft. For example, pocket picking and purse snatching are not really robberies unless the victim resists and is overpowered.

The Uniform Crime Reporting Program defines *robbery* as the taking or attempting to take anything of value from the care, custody, or control of a person or persons by force or threat of force or violence or by putting the victim in fear.[2]

Trends

In 2008, the FBI reported that during 2007, the estimated number of robberies (445,125) decreased 0.5 percent from the 2006 estimate. However, the five-year robbery trend (2003 data compared with 2007 data) showed an increase of 7.5 percent. The 2007 estimated robbery rate (147.6 per 100,000 inhabitants) showed a decrease of 1.2 percent compared with the 2006 rate.[3]

The proceeds the criminals net as a result of their crimes are surprisingly low. For example, in 2007, the average dollar loss per robbery offense was $1,321. The highest average dollar loss was for banks, which lost $4,201 per offense. Furthermore, firearms were used in 42.8 percent of robberies based on supplemental data received from law enforcement agencies.[4]

Consequences of Robbery

In the sense that most robbers are motivated by economic gain, robbery could be considered a property crime. However, judged by the value of property taken in robberies, it is not a particularly serious crime. The loss sustained in most robberies is less than $100. It is, of course, the violent nature of the crime that makes it a crime against persons and a serious violation of criminal law. Among the other consequences of the crime, robbery creates a sense of widespread anxiety and defensive behavior. For example, an elderly couple was robbed at gunpoint one summer evening in the parking lot of their favorite restaurant. Although less than $75 was taken and no one was physically hurt, they chose not to return to the restaurant for fear of falling victim to robbers a second time. Other types of defensive behavior include carrying a weapon and moving to the suburbs to avoid the likelihood of becoming a victim of a robbery.

ROBBERY TRENDS

Year	Number of Offenses	Rate per 100,000 Persons
2006	447,403	149.4
2007	445,125	147.6
Percent change	−0.5	−1.2

Source: From Federal Bureau of Investigation. (2008). *Crime in America, 2007. Uniform crime reports.* Washington, DC: U.S. Government Printing Office.

Elements of Robbery

State laws are very specific regarding the definition of robbery. As indicated, many people confuse the term *robbery* with *burglary*, but clearly some elements of the crimes differ considerably. For example, an apartment dweller might claim that his apartment was "robbed" when in actuality it was burglarized. Accordingly, a person might claim she the victim of robbery when, in fact, she was the victim of a larceny. The distinction between these offenses is evident in the elements of the crime.

FIGURE 10.1 Robbery location: percent distribution, 2007. *From Federal Bureau of Investigation. (2008). Crime in America, 2007. Uniform crime reports. Washington, DC: U.S. Government Printing Office.*

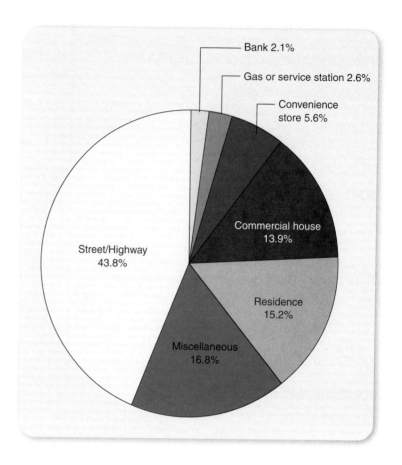

The elements of robbery vary depending on certain attributes of the crime. These attributes may include inflicting serious physical injury on the victim or being accompanied by an accomplice during commission of the crime. Because of these differences, many states have chosen to divide robbery into first, second, and third degrees, depending on the seriousness of the act.

Types of Robbery

Attempts have been made to classify and explain the character and dynamics of robbery. In a study conducted in London, McClintock and Gibson found that robbery follows one of five patterns:[5]

1. *Robbery of persons employed in positions placing them in charge of money or goods.* Examples are robberies of banks, stores, offices, jewelry stores, or other sites where money changes hands. The instance of these types of robberies has decreased in recent years.

2. *Robbery in open areas.* This includes muggings, street robberies, and purse snatchings. Crimes of this nature constituted an estimated 30 percent of violent crimes in 2007.

3. *Robbery on private premises.* This represents crimes in which robbers break into homes and rob residents.

4. *Robbery after preliminary association of short duration.* These types of robberies typically occur as a consequence of a chance meeting in a nightspot or party or after a sexual encounter.

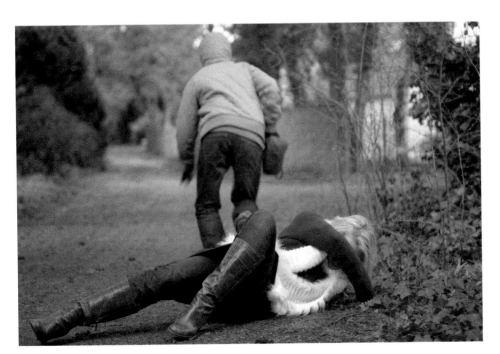

FIGURE 10.2 Photo of a "snatch-and-grab" robbery (mugging). Such crimes often take place in isolated areas where there are few, if any, witnesses. *Courtesy of Alamy Images.*

5. *Robbery after previous association of some duration between victim and offender.* These are considerably less common than stranger-to-stranger robberies, which account for an estimated 75 percent of robberies.[6]

In accordance with the preceding typologies, the following examples of common robberies should be considered. Notice the addition of crimes such as school and vehicle robberies.

Commercial Robberies: Stores and Banks

The **commercial robbery** typically occurs at the end of a workweek and during the evening and very early morning hours. Typical targets of the commercial robber are stores and businesses located close to major thoroughfares, such as main streets, highways, and interstates. Such locations offer the offender a quick and easy means of escape. In addition, stores employing only one or two employees make prime targets for a bandit.

Because many robberies are committed by persons with criminal records, their methods of operation (MOs) can sometimes be established easily. After it has been identified, the MO can be compared with other robberies with similar MOs to identify a suspect. Convenience stores represent a growing target for robbers. Convenience stores are the target for an estimated 6 percent of all commercial robberies. The growing numbers of such businesses have contributed to their victimization by robbers. Many stores have a policy of keeping only a minimal amount of cash on the premises to deter would-be robbers. Others use video cameras to record business transactions and customers in the store.

Legal Elements of Robbery

☑ Forcibly steal property

☑ Using force or threatening the immediate use of physical force against another person

Bank robbery represents a much greater property loss than other types of robbery but accounts for only an estimated 2 percent of all robberies.[7] Bank robberies are both state and federal crimes; therefore, they fall under the jurisdiction of local, state, and federal law enforcement. The FBI is summoned in these cases because any banking institution federally insured by the Federal Deposit Insurance Corporation (FDIC) falls under federal jurisdiction. These include federal banks, federal credit unions, and federal savings and loan companies. Typically, the investigation of such offenses will involves the collective talents and resources of investigators in each jurisdiction.

The most common method of bank robbery is a threat with a visible firearm, most typically a handgun. Most of the remaining robberies are perpetrated with the use of a demand note passed to the teller. In this case, the note can be a valuable piece of evidence if the robber fails to ask for its return. In addition, in the majority of bank robberies, the perpetrator acts alone in the facility, but accomplices may be waiting in an escape vehicle outside. At times, lookouts are also used to spot police cruisers.

One of the best tracing clues in a robbery is the vehicle used in the escape. Such clues vary from one offense to another. For example, the professional robber's getaway vehicle may be rented or stolen and may have stolen license plates. This enables the suspects to ditch the vehicle or the plates after they have left the area of the robbery. Conversely, an amateur robber often uses his or her own vehicle. The complexion of bank robbery has changed in recent years due to an increase in the number of branch banks, which tend to be located in such a way as to be highly vulnerable to robbers.

A CLOSER LOOK

Brazen Bank Robbers

In 1995, a pair of holdup men who were thought to have robbed at least 18 Midwestern banks were also playing a kind of cat-and-mouse game with the FBI. They wore FBI logos during their holdups, used agents' names when they rented their getaway cars, and wrote letters to the newspapers making fun of the FBI. The "Midwestern Bank Bandits," as they called themselves, concentrated on banks in Kansas, Iowa, Wisconsin, Nebraska, Ohio, and Kentucky. The pair adopted a clear method of operation:

- They spent no more than five minutes in a bank.
- They prohibited tellers from touching cash so the tellers couldn't rig a moneybag with a dye bomb. Instead, they leaned over the counter and grabbed the cash themselves.
- They purchased old used cars before each robbery and signed FBI office chiefs' names on the titles.

- They sometimes wore clothing bearing the logos of the FBI and the ATF.
- They sometimes slowed their pursuers by leaving behind such items as a package they said contained explosives or a grenade pin or taut string tied to the glove compartment door of their getaway car, giving the appearance of a booby trap.

Thematic Question

Research bank robberies in your area and see (1) the locations most commonly robbed, (2) the physical makeup of the suspected robbers, and (3) what techniques were used to commit the crime. To what extent have these factors assisted the police or hindered the successful apprehension of the robbers?

Street Robberies

The most common type of robbery is the one committed on public streets and alleyways. Most street robberies (also called *muggings*) are committed with a weapon, typically a handgun and usually take place at night, and both the robber and victim are usually on foot. Suspects in street robberies are apt to be teenagers, usually young men. The unarmed **street robbery** is also common in many cities. In this case, the victim is approached by two or more attackers who, through their numbers, intimidate the victim, reducing their willingness to resist. Those who are most likely to become victims of street muggers are elderly individuals and people who are drunk in public. Both categories of victims pose no immediate threat to robbers, are slow to react, and will probably not offer resistance. The unarmed robber relies on opportunity rather than a strategic plan in selecting a victim. The most likely victim is one who walks alone on a secluded street after dark.

Residential Robberies

The **residential robbery** is one of the most terrifying types of robberies because an armed intruder breaks into a home and holds residents at gun or knifepoint. Often, these crimes begin as burglaries but "convert" to robberies after the intruder discovers that there is someone home and chooses to use violence as a means of completing the theft. One common type of residential robbery is when someone who has a right to be in the house, such as an invited guest, commits the crime. Indeed, according to the National Institute of Justice (NIJ), 54 percent of all residential robberies are committed by acquaintances.[8]

School Robberies

The NIJ concludes that an estimated 3.2 percent of noncommercial robberies occur in schools every year. This averages out to be an estimated one million school-related robberies annually. Accordingly, the victimization rate for youths ages 12 to 19 is about 1 percent per year. A **school robbery** fails to meet the stereotypic type of robbery in that it is not stickups or mugging but, for the most part, is an instance of petty extortion or a "shakedown" of students or teachers. Ironically, few of these robberies have resulted in property loss. The average dollar loss is typically less than $1.[9]

Characteristics of Robbery

- ☑ About one in 12 victims experiences serious injuries such as rape, knife or gunshot wounds, broken bones, or being knocked unconscious.
- ☑ Most robberies are committed by two or more people.
- ☑ About half of all completed robberies involve losses of $82 or less; 10 percent involve losses of $800 or more. Most theft losses are never recovered.
- ☑ Offenders display weapons in almost half of all robberies.
- ☑ Robbers use guns in about 40 percent of robberies.
- ☑ Offenders using weapons are more likely to threaten than actually attack their victims.
- ☑ In almost nine of 10 robbery victimizations, the robbers are male.
- ☑ More than half of all robbery victims are attacked. Female robbery victims are more likely to be attacked than are male victims.
- ☑ Victims age 65 and older are more likely to be attacked than younger victims.

Vehicle Robberies

On October 5, 1997, an armored car with $17 million in cash was stolen from its Loomis Wells Fargo and Company warehouse. After a five-month police search, a 28-year-old former Loomis employee, David Scott Ghantt, was arrested in Cozumel, Mexico, together with six others. At the time of Ghantt's arrest, about $14 million was still missing. The police were tipped off because someone noticed that one of the suspects had moved from a trailer park to a $650,000 home, purchased a BMW automobile, and paid for breast implants for his wife—all with cash.

One year earlier, the largest armored car heist in U.S. history occurred in Jacksonville, Florida, where an employee pulled a gun on two coworkers and stole $18.8 million in cash. The robber, Philip Noel Johnson, was arrested five months later as he was attempting to cross the Mexican border. In that theft, all but about $186,000 was recovered from a mountain home in North Carolina.

The victim of the vehicle robbery is often the driver of the vehicle, as illustrated in the example above. Such vehicles often include delivery vehicles, taxicabs, buses, and so on, while the people involved make easy targets for the robber because they frequently work alone and in sparsely populated areas of town. A delivery vehicle, for example, is most vulnerable when it is arriving for a delivery or after a delivery has been made. Sometimes the robbers opt for the cash given the driver after delivery has been made.

Taxi drivers are vulnerable because they are required to work alone and cruise all areas of town. The most common MO for a taxi robbery is for the driver to be asked to drive to an address in a secluded part of town, where the robber makes his or her move. A preventive measure taken by some taxi companies is the placement of a protective shield between the driver and passenger seats. Robberies of buses generally occur during layoff points where there are few passengers. A new trend in vehicle robberies emerged in Miami, Florida, in 1991—the **smash-and-grab robbery**. The robbers stake out streets and exit ramps from airports, and when automobile drivers come to a stop at a street light, the robbers approach the car, break the window, and hold up the driver at gunpoint.

FIGURE 10.3 Images made by a surveillance camera and released by the Dewitt County (IL) Sheriff's Department show William Ginglen robbing the Bank of Kenney in Kenney, Illinois, on July 12, 2004. Ginglen pleaded guilty in July to seven counts of armed bank robbery on December 29, 2005. *Courtesy Redux Pictures.*

Types of Robbers

Conklin developed a well-known typology of robbers.[10] Rather than focusing on the nature of robbery incidents, Conklin organized robbers into the following types:

- *Professional robber.* The professional robber is characterized as having a long-term commitment to crime as a source of livelihood, planning and organizing crimes before committing them, and pursuing money to support a particular lifestyle. Professionals may be robbers exclusively or may be involved in other types of crime as well. The professional robber recognizes robbery as a type of crime that is quick, direct, and profitable. The "pro" might typically effect three or four "big scores" a year to support him- or herself, all well planned, and sometimes while working in groups with specifically assigned tasks for all group members.

- *Opportunistic robber.* The opportunist will steal to obtain small amounts of money when he or she identifies what seems to be a vulnerable target. Examples of opportunist targets are cab drivers, drunks, and elderly people. The opportunist is typically a younger perpetrator who does not plan the crime well (e.g., use of weapons, getaway car). Typically, he or she operates in the environment of a juvenile gang.

- *Drug addict robber.* The drug addict robber robs to support his or her drug habit. Unlike the professional, he or she has a low commitment to robbery because of its danger but a high commitment to theft because it supplies much-needed funds. Although the addict is less likely to use a weapon, he or she is more cautious than the opportunist. When desperate for funds, however, he or she will be less careful in selecting victims and carrying out the crime.

- *Alcoholic robber.* Excessive consumption of alcohol may cause some persons to enter into robbery as a criminal alternative. Alcoholic robbers plan their crimes randomly and give little consideration to victim selection, escape, or circumstances under which the crime will be committed.

The First Officer on the Scene

After receiving a radio call, the first officer's initial responsibility is to arrive at the scene as quickly and safely as possible. Of the two, safety should be emphasized more so than swiftness. The decision to use equipment such as emergency lights and siren is left to the officer's judgment and may depend on several considerations. Factors influencing the decision to use emergency equipment include:

- Distance to be traveled to the crime scene
- Amount of traffic
- Time of day of the call
- Inability to clear traffic
- Need to halt assault of a victim

Next, the officer should summon assistance and be prepared to wait for backup before attempting to enter the robbery location. When approaching the scene, he or she should be on the lookout for fleeing subjects and persons sitting in parked cars. These might be accomplices or lookouts working with the robber. Police vehicles should be parked a reasonable distance from the robbery location. After removing the keys from the patrol car, the officer should take a shotgun and approach the location cautiously on foot.

The first officer on the scene should cover the most likely exit from the robbery location. After assessing the situation, it is his or her job to direct other responding officers to cover other escape routes. If possible, a determination should be made as to whether or not the robbery is still in progress before officers enter the building.

If the robbery is still in progress, entry into the structure should not be authorized. It is likely that robbers might exit the structure on their own, especially if they are unaware that the police are at the location. If the suspect sees the police, the officer should make every attempt to convince him or her to surrender. If it cannot be determined whether or not a crime is still in progress, officers covering the front should enter together. Under no circumstances should the first-arriving officer enter the location without assistance. Once on the scene, the officer should apprehend the suspect if possible. First aid should then be rendered if victims have been injured. Finally, witnesses should be located and questioned.

The Preliminary Investigation

When responding to calls in which the robbers have already left the scene, officers must prioritize the care of any injured parties. In addition, they must keep in mind that the robbery scene is a crime scene, where valuable evidence may be present. Therefore, possible locations of fingerprints and other evidence should be protected. Next, witnesses should be located and statements taken regarding descriptions of the suspects and their vehicles so that a "flash" description can be broadcast.

When obtaining description information from witnesses, officers should first separate them to minimize discussion about the robbery and provide officers with separate suspect description sheets. It is important during this stage of the investigation to get descriptions while the witnesses' recollection of the crime is still fresh. Officers should remember that although speed is crucial at this stage of the preliminary investigation, so is accuracy. A second broadcast is required after further questioning of the witnesses is conducted. The purpose is to correct any errors broadcast in the original transmission and to provide district officers with additional details. The correct form of broadcast is typified by the following example:

Robbery. Seventh Heaven Convenience Store, 308 Granada, at 2330 hours by two suspects.

Suspect 1. Male, white, 18 to 25 years of age, 6 feet 2 inches, 210 pounds, long brown hair, full beard, sunglasses, wearing black "Poison" T-shirt and faded blue jeans and white tennis shoes. Suspect in possession of proceeds from robbery: brown paper bag containing approximately $350 cash.

Suspect 2. Female, white, 20 to 22 years of age, 5 feet 4 inches, 120 pounds, wearing red tank top and blue jean shorts, dirty white tennis shoes. Suspect has long brown hair pulled back and is armed with a small semiautomatic handgun, possibly .32 caliber.

Escape. Both suspects were last seen driving east on Broadway in an older model light tan Ford Mustang, Texas license, with the first two digits believed to be "RW." The paint on the car is faded, and its top is rusted.

The supplemental broadcast should contain as much important information as possible, and when significant information is unavailable, its omission should be so stated. For example, in the preceding scenario, it is not mentioned whether either suspect had a coat. Stating that details are not available at the time of the broadcast will let officers know that there is a possibility that the suspects might, in fact, be wearing coats. The intent here is to eliminate unnecessary inquiries from the field regarding such items.

The Neighborhood Canvass

Typically, a robbery investigation takes weeks or even months to complete. A logical starting place, however, is a canvass of the area surrounding the location of the robbery. Specifically, investigators should consider the suspect's most

A CLOSER LOOK

The "Typical" Robbery

The most common type of robbery is of the individual. And the most common place for it is on your way to and from your car. Nearly half of all robberies occur on the streets and in parking lots. Another 14 percent happen in locations like subway and train stations, indoor ATMs, and other locations. It is always important to recognize when you are entering a "fringe area," where the likelihood of being robbed increases.

There is more than a 60 percent chance that you will face a weapon when robbed. That is, however, a statistical norm across all types of robberies. The odds of facing a weapon go up significantly if you are being robbed by only one person. Strong-arm tactics tend to be the domain of the pack; the individual mugger tends to prefer weapons—and guns are the most common.

Weapons

Although all robberies are felonies, the use of a weapon tends to bring about stiffer penalties. Although all robberies are considered violent crimes, it is common for states to upgrade the class of felony if a weapon is used in the commission of a robbery. That means the person who is robbing you is risking a much greater prison sentence if he or she is caught and convicted. And this doesn't bother the robber.

The weapon of choice is a gun. It is fast and easy to get, and because most robberies happen at point-blank range, requires very little training to hit the target. All the robber has to do is point in the general direction and pull the trigger until either he or she runs out of bullets or you are on the ground screaming in pain. Guns are used in

up to 40 percent of all robberies, and knives and other weapons are used in another 20 percent. Again, these numbers are a national average that incorporates every kind of robbery.

Needless to say, guns, knives, and other weapons make up 100 percent of all *armed* robberies. And weapons are the norm for robberies of establishments.

Strong Arm

Many people do not realize that 40 percent of all robberies are committed by strong-arm tactics. That doesn't sound too bad until you realize that this means you are being mugged by a wolf pack. A varying number of individuals surround you and then either threaten or proceed to pilfer your possessions. That means 10 or so people proceed to pummel you, and often after you are on the ground, they continue to kick and stomp you.

Furthermore, most states recognize both an extreme disparity of force and the shod human foot on a downed individual as legal justification for the victim to use lethal force to protect him- or herself from immediate death or serious bodily injury—both of which can, and often do, occur during a strong-arm robbery. It doesn't matter if they don't have weapons, ten people stomping a person can kill or hospitalize him or her for months just as well as one person with a weapon.

Packs of young criminals roaming or loitering in an area are a serious danger sign, one that should be avoided at all costs. People should not walk into their midst. Doing so would be literally walking into the lions' jaws.

A CLOSER LOOK CONTINUED

What makes these kinds of robberies even more difficult is how often they will be explained away as "we were just messin' witcha." And because no weapons have been displayed, it is difficult for prosecutors to prove intent in such cases. Until the robbery has actually occurred, there is no clear-cut crime even if the group is displaying or menacing with a weapon.

Home Invasion Robbery

Home invasion robberies have become common in the past decade. In areas where automatic garage doors are standard, a tactic often used is to follow the victim home and then either pull into the garage or jump out of the car and rush the person before the garage door closes.

In other areas, entry through the front door is common. Whether this is achieved by simply ringing the doorbell and crashing the door when the person answers it, through deceit (e.g. "My car broke down; can I use your phone?"), or just kicking in the door depends on the robbers.

Although an individual can do a home invasion, these types of robberies tend to be the domain of packs and gangs. And they tend to be armed as well. This is because they expect there to be multiple people at home.

Fortunately, many of the best protections against a home invasion robbery will also keep your home safe from burglars.

FIGURE 10.4 Robbery is considered a violent crime because it places the victim in fear of death or serious bodily injury, as depicted here. Michael Newman, PhotoEdit, Inc.

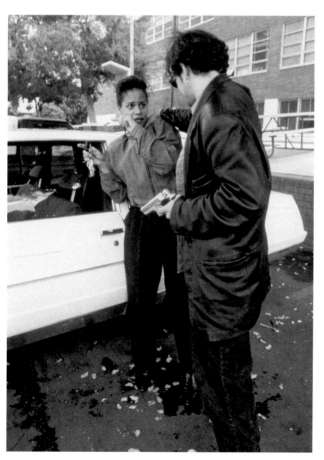

likely escape route and question residents and business owners in the area. In addition, while the canvass is in progress, officers should look for evidence discarded by the suspect during his or her escape. Because many citizens are apprehensive about the presence of officers at their residence, investigators should immediately state their intended purpose is to place the citizen at ease. It is also important for the officer to stress the significance of all information, regardless of how meaningless it appears to the citizen. Specific questions include whether the citizen observed anyone meeting the description of the suspect or the getaway vehicle. Additionally, it should be determined if anyone heard anything of interest to the officer, such as a car door slamming, gunshots, or tires screeching.

The **neighborhood canvass** is also critical in the event that the robber is hiding somewhere close to the robbery location. Therefore, investigators should look in parked cars, dumpsters, and alleyways for the hidden suspect. In addition, local motels or hotels in surrounding towns and car rental companies should also be checked. When speaking to residents in the area of the robbery, it is advantageous to have a sketch of what the suspect looks like. The sketch could also be circulated throughout the community along with the establishment of a "tip line" for anonymous information.

Typical MO Information for Robbery

- ☑ Type of location robbed
- ☑ Time and day of week
- ☑ Type of weapon used
- ☑ Use or threatened use of force
- ☑ Verbal statements made
- ☑ Vehicle used
- ☑ Object(s) stolen
- ☑ Number of suspects
- ☑ Use of disguises
- ☑ Other peculiarities

The Robber's Method of Operation

Studies have shown that many people who commit a robbery are often repeat offenders, or recidivists. Therefore, it is important to document the techniques and **method of operation (MO)** used by the suspect. An MO focuses on the behavior of the criminal during the commission of a crime. For example, the location of the robbery, such as a bank or convenience store, may identify certain groups of suspects. Other factors include the type of weapon used; the dress of the robber(s); and the amount of money, merchandise, drugs, and so on, taken.

In addition to the age, gender, height, and race of a suspect, it is important to document specific behavior during a crime. Such behavior might indicate nervousness (or calmness) or could indicate that a person was under the influence of drugs at the time.

The treatment of the victim(s) could also have a bearing on the investigation. For example, was violence used? If so, what were the injuries? Was the victim kicked, beaten, shot, or struck with the weapon? Other actions might also be significant, such as:

- Did the suspect cut the telephone wires?
- Were the victims locked up?
- Were the victims tied up or gagged?

Investigators should remember that because of a lack of abundant physical evidence, robbery scenes may suggest other types of evidence. MOs in connection with any available physical evidence may help identify the perpetrator and ultimately prove a case.

Physical Evidence

The crime scene should be processed as soon as possible after physical evidence has been identified. Evidence in robberies may take several forms, including fingerprints, **binding material,** and fired cartridges. The value of fingerprints at a robbery crime scene is immense, so it is essential to conduct a thorough search of all surfaces in or near the scene that the robbers might have touched.

Physical Evidence in Robberies

- ☑ Blood (if applicable)
- ☑ Fingerprints
- ☑ Notes from the robber
- ☑ Binding material
- ☑ Fired cartridge

These surfaces include countertops, doors and door handles, cash registers and computers, and any furniture encountered by the suspects. In particular, if the robbers handled any paper products (e.g., notes to bank tellers), such surfaces are particularly good for preserving latent prints and should be protected and processed.

Binding material, if located, may include strips of tape, such as duct or masking tape, cloth strips, wire, rope, or any material used to incapacitate the victim. In the event that rope is used as a restraining device, care should be taken not to destroy any knots. These can be used to link the suspect with any specialized technique of tying knots. Such items can be used as comparison items in the event that similar material is later found in the possession of suspects.

Shell casings or cartridges may also provide important evidence of a robbery. Such items may bear latent prints of perpetrators or identify the type of weapon used for the crime. In fact, rifling (impressions) on the sides of casings may be used in linking a specific gun with a crime.

In the case of bank robberies, some banks may use bait money to aid in capturing the robbery suspect. When used, bait money is placed in a specially designated bin in a teller's cash drawer. This cash has had its serial numbers prerecorded in the event that it is later found in a suspect's possession. In other cases, when bait money is removed from a drawer, a silent alarm will be set off, notifying local police that a robbery is in progress.

The Role of Witnesses

mycrimekit

Video: Robbery

Because of the violent nature of the crime of robbery and the imminent threat of injury, witnesses are not likely to remember many specific details of a robbery. It is important, however, that officers attempt to gather as much information as possible from any witnesses. It is vital that witnesses be separated so that their individual perceptions of what happened won't influence other witnesses. Experience has shown that an exchange of dialogue between witnesses might unconsciously alter the way in which some witnesses "recall" an event. After the witnesses have been separated, interviews should be conducted regarding both the event and details about the robber(s).

People at the scene of a robbery will be afraid, confused, and even angry. Because of the emotionally charged environment, officers should expect to receive somewhat different interpretations of what occurred from the witnesses because no two people will perceive a situation in exactly the same way. In fact, if the stories are too similar, the investigator should question the truthfulness of the witnesses' stories. The details regarding perpetrators should be as specific as possible. Information should be sought regarding specifics, such as scars, tattoos, jewelry worn, and other particulars about the suspects. Leading questions asked by the investigator might help draw out these details. Leading questions include:

- What did you notice most about the robber's appearance?
- What were the most noticeable features about the robber's face?
- Was there anything unique or unusual about the robber's manner of speech?

Such questions encourage witnesses to stop and think about specific details regarding a crime.

Summary Checklist

In this chapter, we consider the ways information about crimes is documented by the criminal investigator. A properly documented case is one that is more likely to succeed in court. See how well you are able to answer the following questions in your checklist.

1. **Do you understand the various types of robbery offenses?**

   Robbery, often confused with the crime of burglary, is a personal crime and involves face-to-face contact between the victim and the offender.

   The primary motivation for robbery is to obtain money, although some juvenile robbers are also motivated by peer influence and the quest for "thrills."

   Robbery is defined as the theft or attempted theft, in a direct confrontation with the victim, by force or the threat of force or violence.

2. **Can you discuss the different types of robbery?**

   Robberies occur in different ways and under various circumstances. These include:

   - The commercial robbery typically occurs at the end of a workweek and during the evening and very early morning hours.

   - Bank robbery represents a much greater property loss than other types of robbery but accounts for only an estimated 2 percent of all robberies

   - Street robberies are the most common type of robbery committed on public streets and in alleyways.

   - The residential robbery is one of the most terrifying because an armed intruder breaks into a home and holds the residents at gun- or knifepoint.

   - School robberies represent an estimated 3.2 percent of noncommercial robberies that occur every year.

   - Vehicle robberies include delivery vehicles, taxicabs, buses.

3. **Do you know the duties of the first officer on the scene of a robbery?**

   After receiving a radio call, the first officer's initial responsibility is to arrive at the scene as quickly and safely as possible. Of the two, safety should be emphasized more so than swiftness.

   The officer should summon assistance and be prepared to wait for backup before attempting to enter the robbery location.

   The first officer on the scene should cover the most likely exit from the robbery location.

   If the robbery is still in progress, entry into the structure should not be authorized.

   (continued)

Summary Checklist (Continued)

When responding to calls in which the robbers have already left the scene, officers must prioritize the care of any injured parties.

Witnesses should be located and statements taken.

- It is important to get suspect descriptions from witnesses while their recollection of the crime is still fresh.

A neighborhood canvas should be performed beginning at the most logical place and working outward.

- Specific questions include whether the citizen observed anyone meeting the description of the suspect or the getaway vehicle.

4. Do you know the various methods of operation of robbers?

 The most common type of robbery is of the individual. And the most common place for it is on your way to and from your car.

Studies have shown that many people who commit a robbery are often repeat offenders, or recidivists.

- It is therefore important to document the techniques and method of operation (MO) used by the suspect.
- An MO focuses on the behavior of the criminal during the commission of a crime.
- In addition to the age, gender, height, and race of a suspect, it is important to document specific behavior during a crime.

The crime scene should be processed as soon as possible after physical evidence has been identified.

The value of fingerprints at a robbery crime scene is immense, so it is essential to conduct a thorough search of all surfaces in or near the scene that the robbers might have touched.

It is vital that witnesses be separated so that their individual perceptions of what happened won't influence other witnesses.

Key Terms

bank robbery

binding material

commercial robbery

method of operation (MO)

neighborhood canvass

residential robbery

school robbery

smash-and-grab robbery

street robbery

Discussion Questions

1. What are the most common motivations for the commission of the crime of robbery?

2. Discuss the distinction between someone who has been robbed and someone who has been burglarized.

3. List and discuss the elements of the crime of robbery.

4. Discuss the importance of the flash description during the preliminary investigation phase of a robbery.

5. Explain the different types of physical evidence that should be sought in a robbery investigation.

6. Describe the responsibilities of the first officer responding to the scene of a robbery.

7. What is a neighborhood canvass, and how does it relate to a robbery investigation?

8. How is an understanding of the robber's MO valuable in investigating a robbery?

mycrimekit™

Go to MyCrimeKit.com to explore the following study tools and resources specific to this chapter:

- **Practice Quiz:** Multiple-choice, true/false, short-answer, and essay questions.

- **Flashcards:** There are nine key terms in this chapter. Flashcards test your knowledge of the chapter's key terms.

- **Web Links:** Check out the hotlink to *The New York Times* criminology articles.

- **Career Center:** Check out the hot links to interesting careers in criminal justice, criminology, and juvenile justice.

- **The Research Center:** Check out the Cybrary and research navigator for even more resources.

Notes

1. NATIONAL INSTITUTE OF JUSTICE. (1987). *Investigators who perform well*. Washington, DC: U.S. Department of Justice.
2. FEDERAL BUREAU OF INVESTIGATION. (2006). *Crime in America, 2005. Uniform Crime Reports*. Washington, DC: U.S. Government Printing Office.
3. FEDERAL BUREAU OF INVESTIGATION. (2008). *Crime in America, 2007. Uniform Crime Reports*. Washington, DC: U.S. Government Printing Office.
4. IBID.
5. McCLINTOCKI, F. H. and E. GIBSSON. (1961). *Robbery in London*. London: Macmillan:15.
6. IBID.
7. IBID.
8. NATIONAL INSTITUTE OF JUSTICE. (1990). *Computer crime: The new crime scene*. Washington, DC: U.S. Department of Justice.
9. NATIONAL INSTITUTE OF JUSTICE. (1983). *Robbery in the United States: An analysis of recent trends and patterns*. Washington, DC: U.S. Government Printing Office.
10. CONKLIN, J. (1972). *Robbery and the criminal justice system*. New York: J.B. Lippincott:1–80.

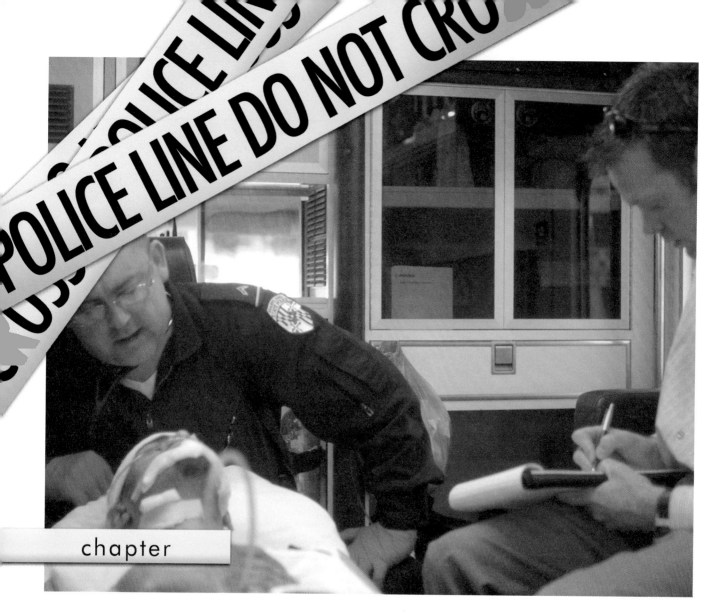

11

Assault and Related Offenses

This chapter will enable you to:

- Describe the legal definition of assault.
- Identify various types of assault.
- Understand the problem of domestic violence and recent assault legislation.
- Explain the methods of investigating stalking cases.
- Identify symptoms of possible child abuse.
- List and discuss the steps in investigating child abuse.
- Understand techniques of rape victim interviews.
- Identify evidence in rape cases.

Introduction

In December 2004, police charged five Indiana Pacers basketball players and seven Detroit Pistons fans after a mass brawl erupted during a game. The fight, which was aired on national television, was sparked by a dispute over a foul. Pacers teammates Jermaine O'Neal, Ron Artest, David Harrison, Anthony Johnston, and Stephen Jackson were all charged with misdemeanor assault and battery. Detroit fan John Green was charged with two counts of simple assault for throwing cups and ice at Artest. Another fan, Bryant Jackson, was charged with felony assault for throwing a chair into the crowd. In September 2005, Artest, O'Neal, and Jackson were each sentenced to one year of probation and ordered to complete 60 hours of community service.

The pattern of assault is similar to that of homicide. One might say that the difference between the two is that the victim survived. Assaults can occur many ways: For example, a rock is thrown by one teen at another, a wife breaks a bottle over her husband's head during a domestic squabble, a drug dealer beats up a customer who steals his drugs. These are all forms of assault. Many "traditional" crimes are also accompanied by assaults against victims. For example, robbery, drug dealing, sexual assault (rape), and loan sharking all frequently contain some aspect of the crime of assault.

Studies of assault cases have revealed that most victims of assault (two-thirds to three-fourths of cases) are acquainted with their attacker. In addition, it is common for such victims to choose not to file charges against their attackers. If charges are filed, many victims later choose not to follow through with prosecution, particularly if the parties are related or are close friends. Such realities can make investigation of these types of crime difficult and frustrating.

Trends

In 2008, the FBI reported the instances of aggravated assault nationwide during 2007 at an estimated 855,856 aggravated assaults. The two- and 10-year trends indicate that the estimated number of aggravated assaults in 2007 declined less than 1 percent (-0.6) compared with the offense estimates from 2006 and

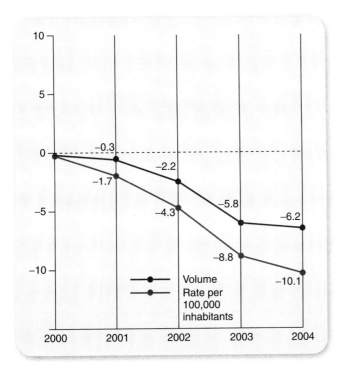

FIGURE 11.1 Aggravated assault percentage change chart.

declined 12.4 percent from the 1998 estimate. The FBI shows that the rate of aggravated assaults in the Nation was estimated at 283.8 offenses per 100,000 inhabitants in 2007. In 2007, 21.4 percent of the aggravated assaults for which law enforcement agencies provided expanded data involved a firearm.

AGGRAVATED ASSAULT TREND

Year	Number of Offenses
2006	860,853
2007	855,856
Percent change	–0.6

Source: FBI, Crime in the United States, 2008.

Legal Classifications of Assault

Although states often define *assault* differently, some general definitions will be considered. The terms *assault* and *battery* were formerly used to distinguish between threats and actual contact between suspect and victim. Today, many revised state statutes categorize threats and actual physical contact as **simple assault** and **aggravated assault**. These are defined as follows.

Simple Assault

- *Threats by one person to cause bodily harm or death to another.* Investigators must identify evidence to show specific intent to commit bodily injury; an injury received as a result of an accident is not an assault. A suspect's words and actions or any injuries to the victim may demonstrate intent. The injury must be to another party; injury to property or self-inflicted injury, regardless of its seriousness, is not assault.

- *Purposely inflicting bodily harm on another.* Bodily harm or injury and simple assault need not cause severe physical pain or disability. The degree of force necessary in simple assault may range from a push or a slap to slightly less than that required for the great bodily harm that is characteristic of aggravated assault.

AGGRAVATED ASSAULT, TYPES OF WEAPONS USED AND PERCENT DISTRIBUTION WITHIN REGION, 2007

Region	Total all Weapons*	Firearms	Knives or Cutting Instruments	Other Weapons (e.g., Clubs, Blunt Objects)	Personal weapons (e.g., Hands, Fists, Feet)
Total	100.0	21.4	18.8	34.2	25.7
Northeast	100.0	15.2	20.9	33.9	30.1
Midwest	100.0	22.2	17.4	31.2	29.2
South	100.0	23.4	19.5	34.5	22.6
West	100.0	19.9	17.3	35.4	27.4

*Because of rounding, the percentages may not add to 100.0.

Aggravated Assault

Aggravated assault includes the elements of simple assault plus an element relating to the severity of the attack. Aggravated assault is usually committed with a weapon or by some means likely to produce great bodily harm or death.

- *High probability of death.* The assault is considered aggravated if it is committed by any means so severe that any reasonable person would think it would result in a high probability of death. For example, a strike to the head sufficient to cause unconsciousness or coma, a gunshot or knife wound that causes heavy bleeding, or burns inflicted over a large area of a person's body would be considered aggravated assault.

- *Serious, permanent disfigurement.* Permanent disfigurement includes such things as loss of an ear or part of the nose or permanent scarring of the face or other parts of the body that are normally visible. It cannot be a temporary injury that will eventually heal and not be evident.

- *Loss or impairment of body members or organs.* Regardless of the part of the body affected, a charge of aggravated assault is supported by the loss or permanent impairment of body members or organs or by maiming.

Only one of these additional elements is needed to show aggravated assault, although two or all three are sometimes present. Some states do not require that there be permanent or protracted injury or loss if the weapon used in the assault is a dangerous weapon that causes fear of immediate harm or death. As with simple assault, the act must be intentional, not accidental.

FIGURE 11.2 Bruising on the thigh from assault by blunt instrument. *Courtesy of Mike Himmel.*

Legal Elements of Simple Assault

☑ Threats by one person to cause bodily harm or death to another

☑ Purposely inflicting bodily harm on another

Legal Elements of Aggravated Assault

☑ High probability of death

☑ Serious, permanent disfigurement

☑ Permanent or protracted loss or impairment of the function of any body member or organ or other severe bodily harm

Self-Defense

Under criminal law, persons may defend themselves and their property, and it is not necessary for the victim to wait until he or she has been physically assaulted before acting in **self-defense.** To do so, however, the elements of a threat should at least be present. It is on this point that the law makes a distinction in the interpretation of the word *threat.* For example, derogatory gestures or name calling between two persons does not give one the right to use violence or force against the other (*Naler* v. *State*, 1933). There are many cases, however, in which legal force is permitted under the law. For example, the law recognizes that persons are under no legal obligation to retreat from an attack. However, if escape from the attacker is possible without killing him or her, the victim must do so.

Conversely, if in trying to escape, the victim risks further peril, lethal force to defend one's self is allowed. Accordingly, if a situation erupts to the point where force is used by the victim to defend him- or herself, the degree of force should be no more than a reasonable person, under the same circumstances, would be justified in using. Therefore, the type of force used must be only enough to rebuff the attack, and no more. Any display of excessive force used to "punish" the attacker can be interpreted by the courts as an assault in and of itself.

The Preliminary Investigation

In the event that an assault has been committed and the suspect is not on the scene, the call turns into an investigation. Experience has shown that most victims of assault know their attackers. After arriving on the scene, first aid should be administered to the victim, or if necessary, the victim should be transported to the hospital. If this is necessary, an officer should accompany the victim in the event that he or she tries to discard any evidence. If the victim is taken to the hospital, the accompanying officer should question the attending physician to determine if an assault has actually been committed. A brief examination by the physician should disclose whether or not the victim is being truthful about the origin of his or her injuries.

Officers arriving on the scene of an assault should do the following:

- Control and disarm those involved in the altercation.
- Provide medical aid to injured people.
- Separate suspects.
- Protect the crime scene.
- Give the *Miranda* warning if applicable.
- Obtain preliminary statements.
- Photograph any evidence observed.
- Collect and preserve evidence.
- Reconstruct the crime.

Documenting the Elements of Assault

An assault that does not involve a dangerous weapon and results in no serious injury is a relatively minor crime. In comparison, aggravated assault is an extremely serious crime. Investigators can establish intent by determining the events that led up to the assault. The suspect's exact words and actions should be documented, and statements should be taken from the victim and any witnesses.

Responding officers should also establish the severity of the assault by taking photographs and describing all injuries in their notes. The size, location, number, color, depth, and amount of bleeding of any injuries must also be carefully described. Some bruises do not become visible for several hours or even days, so assault victims should also be advised that additional photographs will need to be taken later. An oral or written statement should be obtained from qualified medical personnel regarding the severity and permanence of the injuries and any impairment of bodily functioning. Next, the means of the attack and the exact weapon used must be determined (e.g., gun, knife, fists).

Protecting the Crime Scene

The crime scene must be protected to preserve evidence, and photographs should be taken. This is done to document that an altercation actually occurred. It is also advisable for the investigator to photograph the victim's injuries as soon as possible. If this is not done, medical personnel might bandage the wounds without adequately documenting or describing them beforehand, making a description difficult to obtain.

Initial Questioning

Stating the obvious, the simple task of inquiring about "what happened" is one of the criminal investigator's most important duties. Although many people are reluctant to talk with police officials, others cooperate out of a sense of civic duty, and such statements can make the difference between the success and failure of an investigation.

Questioning the Victim. The victim and any witnesses should be questioned next. When interviewing the victim, the investigator should ask the victim the facts surrounding the incident to determine that an assault actually did occur. Next, investigators should have the victim describe how the weapon was used (if there was one) and if there was any motive for the attack.

Questioning the Witnesses. It is also important to locate and question any impartial witnesses who can verify or corroborate the victim's story. Such people might be difficult to locate, however, because they may be friends of the attacker or might be afraid of retribution by the suspect. If possible, statements should be taken from anyone who witnessed the assault. Additionally, it might be advisable to canvass the neighborhood to locate residents who might have heard or observed something relevant to the case. The questioning of witnesses might also reveal threats made by either the attacker or the victim that might have fueled the altercation.

Searching the Crime Scene

As with all crime scenes, a thorough search for evidence should be conducted as soon as possible. In many cases, a brief search can even be made while the victim is still on the scene. When searching, the investigator should look for weapons (this may include broken bottles, ashtrays, or other objects), footprints or fingerprints, and trace evidence (e.g., pieces of torn clothing, lost buttons, hair). In the event that the victim cannot accompany the investigator during the search, it would be a good idea to return to the scene at a later time with the victim and have him or her recount the occurrence. The victim might be able to point out evidence that might have been missed during the initial search.

mycrimekit

Video: Aggravated assault

Domestic Violence

In the 1970s, if a woman telephoned police to complain about being assaulted by her husband, she had little hope of getting him arrested. By the 1980s, a revolution was well under way in the manner that police responded to domestic

FIGURE 11.3 Black eye of domestic violence victim. *Courtesy of Mike Himmel.*

violence. As of 1984, few arrests were made in domestic violence cases that had no visible injury. In fact, at the time, 22 states barred police from making warrantless arrests in cases they had not personally witnessed. By 1988, many police departments had started treating domestic violence as a crime against the state, as though it had been committed by a stranger.

A growing fear of liability put pressure on police to adopt new policies. For example, in 1984, a jury in Torrington, Connecticut, awarded a $2.3 million judgment against the police department for failing to protect a woman and her son from repeated violence by her husband. One year earlier, he had stabbed her 13 times and broken her neck while the police were at her house responding to her 9-1-1 call.

By 1980, all but six states had adopted some form of domestic violence legislation. The new laws provided for funding for shelters, established more effective procedures, and created "protection orders" to prohibit men from abusing their wives. By 1987, more than half the nation's major police departments had adopted "pro-arrest" policies, which require officers to make an arrest unless they could document a good reason not to do so.

A 1984 study in Minneapolis found that an arrest plus a night in jail cut in half the risk of repeat violence against the victim in the following six months compared with the other two standard approaches: advising the couple to calm down and ordering the suspect to leave his home for six hours. Critics have argued that the mandatory arrest policy may do more to incite violence against women than to cure it.

The Investigative Response to Domestic Violence

Responding to domestic violence calls is one of the most unpleasant duties for police officers. In some cases, officers not trained properly for this type of duty may have preconceptions or biases that it is simply a "family matter" and not a real policing issue. However, domestic assault calls are often dangerous for the police. This is because the highly emotional atmosphere accompanying domestic abuse situations, the raw violence often displayed, the family lives destroyed, and the victim's frequent hesitancy to prosecute or seek shelter all place a heavy burden on the officers sent to such disturbances. Still, an appropriate and effective police response to all domestic calls is warranted.

Response to such calls may be initiated by the dispatcher, who can save hours of legwork by exploring with the victim her frame of mind and that of the potential attacker. From that point on, responding officers' actions are critical. What responding officers do upon arrival often determines what happens in court, whether an effective arrest will be conducted, and whether or not proper evidence will be collected. Domestic violence calls are complicated in that they may unfold simple battery, assault, kidnapping, trespassing, murder, stalking, terroristic threats, spousal rape, or many other types of criminal violations. Police investigators should never assume that the parties involved in a domestic dispute are merely involved in a minor squabble.

Typically, patrol officers respond to domestic violence calls. When that occurs, officers should not park their patrol car within view of the location to which they are responding. Doing so may allow the suspect to see the officers coming and to become even more enraged at the thought of going to jail. This could result in the infliction of additional injuries on the victim or provide the suspect with time to gather weapons with which officers could be assaulted.

After officers have entered the location of the domestic violence call and have secured the area, the investigation begins. The first rule is to interview the suspect and victim separately. Upon first contact with the suspect, the *Miranda* warning should not be read to the suspect. At this point, until a determination has been made as to the nature of the dispute and the relationship between the suspect and victim, the suspect is not under arrest for domestic violence. The parties are simply under detention for investigation because police officers have reasonable suspicion to detain them. This is a critical point in the investigation. Because of their agitated emotional state, many domestic violence suspects make spontaneous admissible statements that can be used against them later in court. The officers should reduce the level of tension at the scene by separating and talking to the participants. The officers must also consider the safety of the participants and any children present.

Any evidence that would lead an officer to make an arrest in any other situation also applies to spousal abuse situations. Most states allow arrests based on probable cause. In line with the probable cause standard, police officers should arrest all abusers who are not acting in self-defense and issue an arrest warrant even if the offender is absent. Finally, officers should be careful not to detain a potential abuser any longer than other offenders.

Twenty states now mandate police to make an arrest in domestic violence incidents if there is a protective or restraining order against the attacker. A number of states make it mandatory for an officer to make an arrest if there is probable cause, even without an assigned complaint by the victim. In Nevada, for example, if the police have sufficient reason to believe that a person, within the preceding four hours, committed an act of domestic violence or spousal battery, they are required to arrest the person if there are no mitigating circumstances.

Officers should not base their decisions regarding arrest on their perception of the willingness of the victim or witness to testify. The victim need not sign a complaint. If the assault was a mutual assault, that is, both people involved committed assault, officers must try to determine the **primary physical aggressor** and arrest that person. Some factors to consider in making this determination include:

- Prior domestic violence involving either person
- The relative seriousness of the injuries inflicted upon each person involved
- The potential for future injury
- Whether one of the alleged assaults was committed in self-defense
- Any other factor that helps the officer decide which person was the primary physical aggressor

As with any criminal investigation, evidence must be collected. In domestic violence cases, evidence includes photographs of injuries, victims' statements, prior police reports, doctor or hospital reports, weapons used, damaged clothing or other property, and statements from neighbors and other witnesses. It should be made clear to the victim that an "order of protection" may be obtained from the court to help prevent further assaults.

Legal Approaches to Domestic Violence

In many cities, a high percentage of female victims request that battery charges be dropped or refuse to testify against the abuser after he has been arrested. In response to this, prosecutors in many cities with vigorous prosecution philosophies are increasingly adopting a controversial policy of "no drop." For example, in San Diego, if the victim won't testify, prosecutors use tapes from the woman's 9-1-1 calls and testimony from neighbors and police to build a case.

Protection Orders. For many women who have become leery of the criminal justice system but are threatened by their violent partners, **protection orders** have become an option. Now used in all 50 states and the District of Columbia, protection orders are often backed up by the threat of jail. In some cases, judges can establish temporary custody for children, forbid telephone threats or harassment, and make the husband pay financial support or leave his home.

A temporary protection order can be issued the same day the woman requests it and can be put in effect for a year or longer. In comparison, a woman can wait for months for a criminal prosecution to come to trial or years for a property settlement from a divorce decree. On the other hand, in some states, protection orders amount to nothing more than a cruel hoax on victims. Husbands or boyfriends have killed women while under protection orders.

Elder Abuse

As baby boomers approach retirement, we see the aging population growing larger each year. With this increase in the elder population, a growing concern is that of elder abuse. Some experts characterize it as a "hidden problem" similar to that of spousal abuse 25 years ago.[1]

In a general sense, elder abuse can be defined as "a single, or repeated act, or lack of appropriate action, occurring within any relationship where there is an expectation of trust which causes harm or distress to an older person."[2]

Although there are common themes of elder abuse across nations, there are also unique manifestations based on history, culture, economic strength, and societal perceptions of older people within nations themselves. The fundamental common denominator is the use of power and control by one individual to affect the well-being and status of another, older individual.

There are several types of abuse of older people that are universally recognized as being elder abuse, including:

- *Physical.* Hitting, punching, slapping, burning, pushing, kicking, restraining, false imprisonment or confinement, or giving too much medication or the wrong medication

- *Psychological or Emotional.* Shouting, swearing, frightening, blaming, ridiculing, constantly criticizing, ignoring, or humiliating a person; a common theme is a perpetrator who identifies something that matters to an older person and then uses it to coerce an older person into a particular action

- *Financial.* I Illegal or unauthorized use of a person's property, money, pension book or other valuables (including changing the person's will to name the abuser as heir), often fraudulently obtaining power of attorney, followed by deprivation of money or other property, or by eviction from the person's own home

- *Sexual.* Forcing a person to take part in any sexual activity without his or her consent, including forcing them to participate in conversations of a sexual nature against their will
- *Neglect.* Depriving a person of food, heat, clothing, comfort, or essential medication

In addition, some jurisdictions also recognize the following as elder abuse:

- *Rights abuse.* Denying the civil and constitutional rights of a person who is old but not declared by court to be mentally incapacitated; this is an aspect of elder abuse that is increasingly being recognized and adopted by nations
- *Self-neglect.* Elderly persons neglecting themselves by not caring about their own health or safety.[3]

Institutional abuse and racial abuse are not usually included in such categories because they tend to denote the motivation or circumstances, rather than the manifestation of abuse. That is not to suggest that institutional practices, often marginalized as examples of "poor practice," do not form a major aspect of elder abuse or that racially motivated abuse is not a significant area of concern.

The core feature of this definition is that it focuses on harms where there is "expectation of trust" of the older person toward their abuser. Thus, it includes harm by people the older person knows or with whom they have a relationship, such as a spouse, partner, family member, friend, neighbor, or people that the older person relies on for services (e.g., volunteer worker, social worker, bank worker, or solicitor). Many forms of elder abuse are recognized as types of domestic violence or family violence.

Perpetrators of elder abuse can include anyone in a position of trust, control, or authority. Some perpetrators may "groom" an older person (befriend or build a relationship with the person) to establish a relationship of trust. The majority of abusers are relatives, typically the spouse or partner or sons and daughters, although the type of abuse differs according to the relationship. In some situations, such abuse is "domestic violence grown old," a situation in which the abusive behavior of a spouse or partner toward another continues into old age.[4]

In some cases, the older abuser becomes the older victim, and the younger victim becomes the younger abuser. In other situations, it is older people attempting to care and support other older people and failing, in the absence of external support. With sons and daughters, it tends to be financial abuse, justified by a belief that it is nothing more than the "advance inheritance" of property, valuables, and money.

Within paid care environments, abuse may occur for a variety of reasons. Some abuse is institutional in that it is a consequence of practices or processes that are part of running of a care institution or service. Some abuse is the willful act of cruelty inflicted by a single individual upon an older person. And some abuse is a consequence of lack of knowledge, lack of training, lack of support, or insufficient resourcing. Sometimes this type of abuse is referred to as "poor practice," although it is important to recognize that this term reflects the motive of the perpetrator (the causation) rather than the impact on the older person. With the aging of today's population, there is the potential that elder abuse will increase unless it is more comprehensively recognized and addressed.

Cases involving violence against society's elders include sexual assault and homicide. In one case, a son withheld insulin from his diabetic mother "because it cost too much." In fact, cases have shown that most elder abuse is caused by

A CLOSER LOOK

Profiling the Batterer[36]

The profiles of abusive men have been fairly consistent. They tend to be manipulative, persuasive actors. They believe women should be subordinate, although they are often quite dependent on their spouses or girlfriends. They are cons: smart, charming, and cunning. Once they spot vulnerable women, they put on their best behavior and treat women with great respect, but the real anger they feel for women is just below the surface. Many batterers don't beat women out of a fit of rage but rather after some premeditation. In some cases, men have ripped out the telephone wires just before beating their spouses, which prevents the victims from calling 9-1-1 for help. Economic considerations are also a reason why battered women stay with their abusive partners. The cruel choice for battered women is often whether to be beaten or to be poor.

Psychologists have likened battering relationships to the Stockholm syndrome, in which hostages, over time, identify with their captors. Entangled in an intimate relationship that often begins as romance, many women come to agree with their partner's view of them as worthless. Often, a batterer goes into a "honeymoon" period just after a beating, persuading his partner that he will reform.

family members and caregivers rather than strangers. Getz illustrates several of the one million typical cases of elder abuse that occur each year:[5]

- A deputy found an elderly man abandoned by his children with no heat or hot water in his home. The bed was saturated with urine, and the man was covered with his own excrement. His body was covered with lesions and sores that were infested with maggots. One of his feet had to be amputated.

- A home health aide, previously convicted of dealing in stolen property and grand theft, was assigned by a hospital in Sun City, Florida, to care for an 86-year-old man after open heart surgery. The worker and her husband systematically drained his assets to buy cars and gamble, took out a $22,000 mortgage on his home, and attempted to divert his direct-deposit checks to their own use before they were finally caught.

- Officials closed the Riverside Nursing Home in Tampa, Florida, and removed 19 residents on stretchers after administrators ignored repeated citations and scores of deficiencies. One resident restricted to a soft-food diet died from choking on a hot dog. Another was treated for dehydration and malnutrition after not being fed for five days.

It is becoming clear that police need special legal tools with which to deal with elder abuse, especially because so many of the violations against the elderly are not criminal in nature. Methods for investigating elder abuse should follow the standard for other criminal investigations, beginning with the preliminary investigation, identification of evidence, documentation of evidence, and location of witnesses to support the evidence.

Stalking

To some, the crime of stalking is a recent social phenomenon, but in actuality, newspapers have featured many stories about stalking over the course of the past two decades. For example, in 1982, movie actress Theresa Saldana was stabbed by a Scottish drifter who believed that he was sending her to heaven. In 1988, TV actress Rebecca Schaefer was shot dead by a stalker as she opened the door of her Hollywood home. She had been followed for months. Such incidents and the subsequent stalkings of Madonna, David Letterman, and other celebrities have led all 50 states and the District of Columbia to pass anti-stalking laws since the beginning of the 1990s.

Despite the growing interest in stalking, research on the subject has been limited to studies of small, underrepresentative, or clinical samples of known stalkers; law journal reviews addressing the constitutionality and effectiveness of specific anti-stalking statutes; and case studies of individual stalkers. Empirical data have been lacking on important questions, which include:

- How much stalking is there in the United States?
- Who stalks whom?
- How often do stalkers overtly threaten their victims?
- How often is stalking reported to the police?
- What are the psychological and social consequences of stalking?

In a 1998 research brief prepared by the National Institute of Justice (NIJ) for the Centers for Disease Control and Prevention, some of these answers were provided. The data are from the National Violence Against Women (NVAW) survey and a nationally representative telephone survey of 8,000 U.S. women and 8,000 U.S. men.[6]

Legal definitions of stalking vary widely from state to state, but the term generally refers to harassing or threatening behavior that a person engages in repeatedly, such as following a person, appearing at a person's home or place of business, making harassing telephone calls, leaving written messages or objects, or vandalizing a person's property. Some states include in their definition such activities as lying in wait, surveillance, nonconsensual communication, telephone harassment, and vandalism. These actions may or may not be accompanied by a credible threat of serious harm, and they may or may not be precursors to an assault or murder.

Most stalking laws require that to qualify as a stalker, the perpetrator must have made a credible threat of violence against the victim, others include in their requirements threats against the victim's immediate family, and still others require only that the alleged stalker's course of conduct constitutes an implied threat.

Using a definition of stalking that requires victims to feel a high level of fear, the NVAW survey found that 8 percent of women and 2 percent of men in the United States have been stalked at some time in their lives. Based on U.S. Census estimates of the number of women and men in the United States, one of every 12 U.S. women (8.2 million) has been stalked at some time in her life and one of every 45 U.S. men (2 million) has been stalked at some time in his life.[7]

Who Stalks Whom?

Although stalking is a gender-neutral crime, women are the primary victims of stalking and men the primary perpetrators. Seventy-eight percent of stalking victims identified by the NVAW survey were women, and 22 percent were men. Thus, four out of five stalking victims are women. Overall, 87 percent of the stalkers as defined by victims were male.[8]

Although the stereotypical stalking incident has been portrayed in books and movies, such as the movie *Fatal Attraction*, as a male victim pursued by a jealous, obsessive woman, many stalking cases involve men stalking men. In 1997, a male stalking case achieved high notoriety, as film producer and director Steven Spielberg was stalked by 31-year-old bodybuilder and would-be screenwriter, Jonathan Norman. Norman was convicted in a Los Angeles court in March 1997.

Spielberg, whose studio had turned down an unsolicited script from Norman, could have been targeted both as a celebrity and as an authority figure.

Experts say that the motive can also be romantic jealousy—gay men are the most likely victims of male-on-male stalking. But male stalking is often linked to the high-profile positions that the targets hold in society. For example, students stalk professors, attractive celebrities are pursued by lonely men looking for famous buddies, and business and political leaders can become objects of hate when consumer complaints turn ugly. Researchers say that men stalk other men for primarily the same reasons that they stalk women: a complex mix of mental and personality disorders that can include schizophrenia, drug dependency, narcissism, and antisocial behavior. Some of the problems with male stalking are that men are more reluctant than women to report being stalked and can have trouble getting police to take them seriously. Furthermore, public services for stalking victims, such as spouse-abuse shelters, are still oriented to the most frequent targets—women.

Although only a small percentage of stalking victims are actually physically attacked, psychological and social consequences are also common. About one-third of women and one-fifth of men who have been stalked sought psychological counseling as a result of their victimization. More than one-fourth of stalking victims said their victimization caused them to lose time from work. This included attending court hearings, meeting with psychologists or other mental health professionals, meeting with attorneys, and avoidance of contact with the assailants. For those victims who are stalked, the behavior lasts only a relatively short period of time—about two-thirds of all stalking cases last a year or less.

The crime of stalking generally refers to some form of repeated harassing or threatening behavior. A stalker is someone who intentionally and repeatedly follows and tries to contact, harass, or intimidate another person. The Violence Against Women Grants Office adds: "Legal definitions of stalking vary widely from state to state. Though most states define stalking as the willful, malicious, and repeated following and harassing of another person, some states include in their definitions such activities as lying in wait, surveillance, nonconsensual communication, telephone harassment, and vandalism."[9] Other experts have asserted that although statutes vary from one state to another, most define stalking as a course of conduct that would place a reasonable person in fear for his or her safety and that the stalker attempted and did, in fact, place the victim in fear.

Forms of Stalking

Three broad categories of stalking have been identified, based on the relationship between the stalker and the victim:

1. In **intimate or former intimate stalking**, the stalker and victim may be married or divorced, current or former dating partners, serious or casual sexual partners, or former sexual partners. An estimated 70 to 80 percent of stalking cases fall into this category.

2. In **acquaintance stalking**, the stalker and victim know each other casually. They may be neighbors or coworkers. They may have even dated once or twice but were not sexual partners.

3. In **stranger stalking**, the stalker and victim do not know each other at all. This behavior is characterized by the stalker developing a love obsession or fixation of another person with whom he or she has no personal relationship. Cases involving public figures and celebrities fall into this category.

Brody notes that the growth in popularity of e-mail, along with use of the Internet, has spawned **cyberstalking**.[10] This informal term refers to preying on a victim through his or her computer. Some people say that cyberstalking is the crime of the twenty-first century. Using the Internet to harass, intimidate, and terrorize takes an old problem and adds a diabolically futuristic twist. The types of victims vary: from politicians who get death threats via e-mail to women whose nude photographs, real or doctored, are posted on the Web. Although the average stalking case is serious enough, add the Internet component, and it becomes even more frightening because the stalker could be anyone, anywhere in the world.

Online, stalkers often hide behind false addresses and names and even impersonate their victims. Such a case happened in Los Angeles when a relationship soured and a 51-year-old security guard took to the Internet for revenge. Using his ex-girlfriend's real name, address, and telephone number, the guard went into electronic chat rooms and solicited rough sex during the summer of 1998. He engaged in sexually explicit conversations posing as his ex-girlfriend and introducing the idea of rape. In one instance, he said: "I want you to break down my door and rape me." Six men did, in fact, show up, and it was simply good fortune that the woman was unharmed. During the summer of 1999, the security guard was sentenced to six years in prison.[11]

The state of California has reacted aggressively to cyberstalking by updating statutes that once applied only to physical or telephonic harassment. Today, it is also illegal to harass or terrorize anyone using devices such as pagers, fax machines, or computers.

The range of sentencing for cyberstalking follows the range for physical stalking, which can be anywhere from no jail time at all to a maximum of four years. Prosecutors are often able to enhance the sentences by adding other charges. However, the U.S. Department of Justice estimates that only about one-third of states have followed California's lead. The department recommends that all states review their statutes to make them technologically neutral. The fact that cybercrime crosses jurisdictional lines is a problem for prosecutors. For example, suppose that a threatening message is sent from a computer in Michigan to a computer in California. Who investigates? Who gets the search warrant? And if evidence is turned up in Michigan, can it be used in California?

The first multi-jurisdictional computer forensic laboratory in the country was established in 1999 in San Diego, California. It aims to identify cyberstalkers, who often operate with little fear of getting caught. Participants include the FBI and the San Diego police, sheriff, and district attorney's office. In 1998, the unit prosecuted Dwayne Comfort, a student at the University of San Diego, who terrorized five female classmates by sending them sexually explicit e-mail that made it clear that he was watching their every move.[12]

The Justice Department released a report in September 1999 that said that based on the number of people who have access to the Internet, there might already have been tens of thousands of victims of cyberstalking.[13] The phenomenon is so new, the report says, that no hard statistics have been compiled. However, experts do know from their experience with ordinary stalking that women are far more likely to be stalked than men.

Some experts predict that the problem is likely to grow because using the Internet to stalk is relatively easy. Technically sophisticated stalkers can generate multiple messages throughout the day without even being present to push the send button. The anonymity they enjoy encourages some who would never have physically stalked a victim to do so with abandon on the Internet. The bad news for victims is that many law enforcement agencies don't have the sophisticated equipment or training that is often needed to track electronic stalkers.

The U.S. Justice Department has noted that all 50 states and the District of Columbia have general stalking laws, some of which can be applied to Internet stalking offenses, and that a number of states have added laws specifically targeting cyberstalking.[14]

Occurrence of Stalking

Research suggests that women are the primary victims of stalking and men the primary perpetrators. Furthermore, stalking is more prevalent than previously thought: 8 percent of women and 2 percent of men surveyed said that they had been stalked at some time in their lives. In addition, 1 million women and 371,000 men are stalked annually in the United States. According to the Department of Justice: "60 percent of women are stalked by spouses, former spouses, live-in partners, or dates, while 70 percent of men are stalked by acquaintances or strangers."[15]

The Investigative Response to Stalking

Typically, the police response to stalkers has been to issue restraining orders. Unfortunately, such orders are often ineffective: 69 percent of women and 81 percent of men have reported that stalkers violate such orders. Because of the proven ineffectiveness of restraining orders, the perceived inability of the criminal justice system to handle stalkers effectively, and victims' fear of antagonizing stalkers, many stalking incidents go unreported. An estimated 50 percent of all stalking victims report their stalking cases to the police, and about 12 percent of all stalking cases result in criminal prosecution. Of those offenders convicted for stalking, most were sentenced "for violations of protection orders that had been issued by the court in domestic violence cases."[16]

In dealing with stalkers, an investigator should encourage a victim to make a police report of the incidents and document the harassment. These records can serve as the basis for legal action against the stalker. In many cases, the crime of stalking requires that the victim actually suffers substantial emotional distress because of the stalker's conduct. Consequently, investigators may demonstrate such victim distress through documentation of the victim's response to the harassment. Such documentation may include answers to the following questions. Has the victim:

- Moved to a new location?
- Obtained a new phone number?
- Put a tap on the phone?
- Told friends, coworkers, or family members of the harassment?
- Given photos of the defendant to security?
- Asked to be escorted to the parking lot and work site?
- Changed work schedule or route to work?
- Stopped visiting places previously frequented?
- Taken a self-defense course?
- Purchased pepper spray?
- Bought a gun?
- Installed an alarm system?

Responses to these questions can indicate the victim's state of mind to help prove that element of the crime. In 1996, a federal law prohibiting interstate stalking was also enacted. Such legislation makes stalking a specific crime and empowers law enforcement to combat the stalking problem. Anti-stalking laws describe specific threatening conduct and hold the suspect responsible for proving that his or her actions were not intended to frighten or intimidate the victim.

What is an Order of Protection?

Basic Elements of a Valid Order of Protection

Any court order of protection should be presumed valid if all of the following are found:

- The order gives the names of the parties.
- The order contains the date the order was issued, which is prior to the date when enforcement is sought.
- If the order has an expiration date, the date of expiration in the order has not occurred.
- The order contains the name of the issuing court.
- The order is signed by or on behalf of a judicial officer.
- The order specifies terms and conditions against the abuser.

Verifying the Terms and Conditions of an Order of Protection

Verification is not required under Federal law and may be necessary only if the order does not appear valid on its face. In some cases, the enforcing jurisdiction's law may require verification if the protected party cannot furnish a copy of the order.

Verification can be accomplished by any of the following methods:

- Confirm the elements of an order in the NCIC Protection Order File.
- Review the elements of an order in state or local registries of protection orders in the issuing jurisdiction.
- Confirm the elements of an order if previously filed with designated authorities in the enforcing jurisdiction.
- Draw upon personal knowledge of the officer or information obtained through an interview.

FIGURE 11.4 What is an order of protection?

Sexual Assault

On August 5, 1996, recently released serial rapist Reginald Muldrew struck again, this time breaking into the apartment of a Gary, Indiana, woman; putting a pillow over her face; and then raping and threatening to kill her. But this time things went a little awry. As he was leaving his victim's residence, the 48-year-old rapist was chased by and critically beaten by a group of teenagers. The police soon arrived and arrested him. Suspected of more than 200 sexual assaults in the Los Angeles area, Muldrew earned himself the nickname of the "pillowcase rapist."

Sadly, cases such as this aren't all that atypical. One doesn't have to look far to read in the newspapers of yet another incident involving criminal sexual misconduct. Because of intense media (and public) interest, such cases tend to raise the consciousness of society regarding the plight of both victims and their perpetrators. Generally speaking, most sex crimes, rape in particular, are thought to be grossly underreported by victims. In fact, an estimated 50 percent of all sexual assaults are believed to go unreported to authorities. Perhaps this could be attributed to the intense personal nature of such offenses and because victims are too embarrassed or humiliated to report the incident. Indeed, studies have revealed that many victims would rather just forget such crimes than go through the agony of reliving them through police interviews and courtroom testimony. In addition, many perpetrators have turned out to be the friends, relatives, and acquaintances of the victims, creating an even greater disincentive for bringing about formal charges.

Although many different types of sex-related crimes exist, this chapter focuses on the crime of rape. Let's take a broader look at some of the most common types of rape that one might consider as an investigative priority. These include forcible rape and acquaintance rape.

The Role of the Sex Crime Investigator

Historically, the police investigator of sexual crimes has faced a somewhat different professional hurdle than that of most investigators. Many officers, including others in his or her own department, may view this job as a sort of "garbage collector" of the street. In fact, those who commit such crimes are also viewed by many as garbage that must be removed immediately.

Conversational topics involving sex are probably the most socially guarded in our society. Accordingly, many sexual disorders are among the most misunderstood in our culture, and those vested with investigating sex offenders are sometimes viewed as being tainted somehow by the very caliber of criminal whom they investigate.

The professional investigator of sexual crimes seeks out opportunities to become more proficient in investigations through reading, attendance at seminars, or job-related courses.[17] This includes staying abreast of recent research on offender typologies and underlying motivations for the various types of offenses encountered and the emotional impact (short and long term) of sexual crimes on victims. Without doubt, he or she must remain current in the field.

Forcible Rape

In a very broad sense, the term **rape** has been applied to a wide variety of sexual attacks and, in popular terminology, may include same-sex rape and the rape of a male by a female. Use of the term *forcible rape* for statistical reporting purposes by law enforcement agencies, however, has a specific and somewhat different meaning. The Uniform Crime Reports (UCR) defines a forcible rape as "the carnal knowledge of a female forcibly and against her will." By definition, rapes reported under the UCR program are always of females. In contrast to what may be an emerging social convention, in which male rape is a recognized form of sexual assault, the latest edition of the *Uniform Crime Reporting Handbook*, which serves as a statistical reporting guide for law enforcement agencies, says: "Sex attacks on males are excluded [from the crime of forcible rape] and should be classified as assaults or 'other sex offenses,' depending on the nature of the crime and the extent of the injury." Although not part of the UCR terminology, some jurisdictions refer to same-sex rape as sexual battery. Sexual battery, which is not included in the UCR tally of reported rapes, is intentional and wrongful physical contact with a person without his or her **consent** that entails a sexual component or purpose. Statutory rape, in which no force is involved

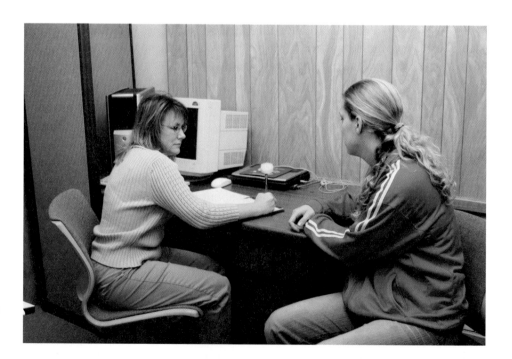

FIGURE 11.5 Female detective interviewing a sexual assault victim. Courtesy of Mike Himmel.

with a girl below the age of consent, is not included in rape statistics, but attempts to commit rape by force or the threat of force are included.

Forcible rape is the least reported of all violent offenses. The FBI estimates that only one of every four forcible rapes is reported to the police. An even lower figure was reported by a 1992 government-sponsored study, which found that only 16 percent of rapes were reported. The victim's fear of embarrassment has been cited as the reason most often given for non-reports. Previously, reports of rape were usually taken by seemingly hardened desk sergeants or male detectives who may not have been sensitive to the needs of female victims. In addition, the physical examination that victims had to endure was often a traumatizing experience in itself. Finally, many states routinely permitted the women's sexual history to be revealed in detail in the courtroom if a trial ensued. All of these practices contributed to considerable hesitancy on the part of rape victims to report victimizations.

The past few decades have seen many changes designed to facilitate accurate reporting of rape and other sex offenses. Trained female detectives often act as victim interviewers, physicians have been better educated in handling the psychological needs of victims, and sexual histories are no longer regarded as relevant in most trials.

Rape is frequently committed by a man known to the victim, as in the case of date rape. Victims may be held captive and subjected to repeated assaults. In the crime of heterosexual rape, any female—regardless of age, appearance, or occupation—is a potential victim. Through personal violation, humiliation, and physical battering, rapists seek a sense of personal fulfillment and dominance. In contrast, victims of rape often experience a diminished sense of personal worth; increased feelings of despair, helplessness, and vulnerability; a misplaced sense of guilt; and a lack of control over their personal lives.

Contemporary research holds that forcible rape is often a planned violent crime, which serves the offender's need for power rather than sexual gratification. Statistically speaking, however, most rapes are committed by acquaintances of the victims and often betray a trust or friendship. Date rape, which falls into this category, appears to be far more common than believed previously. Recently, the growing number of rapes perpetrated with the use of the "date rape drug" Rohypnol has alarmed law enforcement personnel. Rohypnol is an illegal pharmaceutical substance that is virtually tasteless. Available on the black market, it dissolves easily in drinks and can lead anyone who unknowingly consumes it to be unconscious for hours, making the person vulnerable to sexual assault.

Trends

In 2008, the FBI reported in the *UCR* that the estimated number of forcible rapes (90,427) in 2007 decreased 2.5 percent from the previous year. The 2007 estimated number of forcible rapes decreased 3.7 percent from the 2003 estimate and declined 2.9 percent from the 1998 estimate. The rate of forcible rapes in 2007 was estimated at 59.1 offenses per 100,000 female inhabitants, a 3.0 percent decrease compared with the 2006 estimated rate of 60.9. Based on data reported to the UCR program in 2007, rapes by force accounted for 92.2 percent of reported rape offenses, and assaults to rape attempts accounted for 7.8 percent of reported rapes.

Legal Aspects of Rape

According to common law, there are three elements to the crime of rape when the female is over the age of consent:

1. Carnal knowledge (penetration).
2. Forcible submission.
3. Lack of consent.

Penetration, as an essential element of rape, means generally that the sexual organ of the male entered the sexual organ of the female. Court opinions have held that penetration, however slight, is sufficient to sustain a charge of rape. There need not be an entering of the vagina or rupturing of the hymen; entering of the vulva or labia is usually all that is required. It is important during the victim interview that investigators clearly establish that penetration occurred with the penis. Penetration of a finger is not rape, although it is, of course, another form of assault.

FORCIBLE RAPE TREND

Year	Number of Offenses	Rate per 100,000 Inhabitants
2006	92,757	31.0
2007	90,427	30.0
Percent change	−2.5	−3.2

In many states, the victim must have resisted the assault and her **resistance** must have been overcome by force. The amount of resistance that the victim is expected to have displayed depends on the specific circumstances of the case. The power and strength of the aggressor and the physical and mental ability of the victim to resist vary in each case. The amount of resistance expected in one

(A)

(B)

FIGURE 11.6 Part of the victim's broken button was located at the scene of the sexual assault, and part was discovered on the clothing of the suspect. Ballistics comparison made a positive match (photos A and B).
Courtesy Missouri State Highway Patrol Crime Laboratory.

case will not necessarily be expected in another situation. It can be expected that one woman would be paralyzed by fear and rendered mute and helpless by circumstances that would inspire another to fierce resistance or that a woman may be rendered incapacitated by drugs such as Rohypnol or GHB (see Chapter 16).[18] For the most part, there must be resistance on the part of the woman before there can be a foundation for a rape charge.

The kind of fear, however, that would render resistance by a woman unnecessary to support a case of rape includes a fear of death or serious bodily harm, a fear so extreme as to preclude resistance, or a fear that would render her incapable of continuing to resist. On the other hand, consent prior to penetration may remove the criminal character of rape from the subsequent intercourse. Of course, it is problematic in some cases whether the consent was voluntary or coerced or whether resistance was possible or even prudent on the part of the victim. As one state ruled, "There is no definite standard fixed for the amount of resistance required in rape cases. Resistance is not necessary where it would endanger the complainant's safety or when she is overcome by superior strength or paralyzed with fear."[19] This ruling may reflect the position of some state courts, although other states require more demonstrable evidence of resistance to rape. In any event, most recognize that there is a wide difference between consent and submission by force or threat of force: Consent may involve submission, but submission does not necessarily imply consent.

Corroboration

In the absence of a statute requiring corroboration, common law has traditionally held that the unsupported testimony of the victim, if not contradictory, is sufficient to sustain a conviction of rape. Some states, to provide safeguards against unfounded accusations of rape, have laws that require corroborative evidence. Corroboration is supportive evidence that tends to prove that a crime was committed. It lends credence to the allegation that the crime occurred and need not be proved beyond doubt.

Investigators should pay close attention to corroborative evidence even if it is not required by statute. Corroboration of a rape offense can take physical forms such as semen stains on clothing, bruises, cuts, and medical evidence of sexual intercourse. Corroborating evidence can also be circumstantial, such as statements and observations of witnesses. Although in some jurisdictions, rape can be proved by the sole testimony of the victim, it is not common. Medical and scientific evidence are of prime importance and often directly influence the successful prosecution of a case.

Date Rape

Typically, people believe that most rapists and victims were strangers to one another. But a disturbing trend in rapes indicates that many victims and offenders were acquainted before the crime was committed. For example, **date rape** is becoming more frequent on college campuses. It has been estimated that 20 percent of all college women have been victims of rape or attempted rape. One self-report survey conducted on a Midwestern campus found that 100 percent of all rapists knew their victims beforehand.[20]

Another troubling phenomenon is campus gang rape, in which a group of men attacks a defenseless or intoxicated woman. Well-publicized rapes have taken place at the University of New Hampshire, Florida State University, Duke University, and Pennsylvania State University.

As the interview progresses, the investigator should encourage the victim to recollect any additional identifying characteristics of the assailant. Such inquiries should be phrased so as not to appear to be probing. If the victim's memory is not jogged through these inquiries, the investigator should proceed with the interview.

FIGURE 11.7 Sexual assault evidence collection kit. *Courtesy of Mike Himmel and the Missouri State Highway Patrol.*

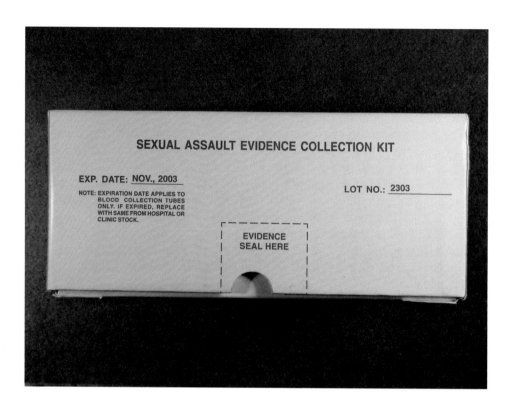

Victim Interview Checklist

☑ Interviewers should be sensitive to the needs and concerns of the victim.

☑ All victims react differently to incidents of sexual assault.

☑ Police officers react differently to sexual assault victims.

☑ The interviewer must display a genuine interest in the welfare of the victim.

☑ Victim interviews demand patience and perseverance.

☑ Interviewers should ask brief open-ended questions.

☑ It should be established whether the victim knows the suspect.

☑ Descriptions of the suspect and his vehicle must be acquired if available.

☑ Leading questions should not be asked.

☑ Official police jargon should not be used.

☑ Victims should be walked through the crime scene to indicate what the suspect may have touched.

☑ The victim needs to feel that she has regained control of her life.

☑ Investigators must anticipate what information the victim might want to know.

☑ Investigative procedures should be explained carefully if the investigator is asked to do so.

☑ The interview should never be rushed.

Evidence in Rape Cases

As with all investigations, the identification, collection, and preservation of evidence are the primary responsibility of the investigator. Rape cases are somewhat unique in that evidence may present itself in three general areas:

1. On the crime scene
2. On the victim
3. On the suspect (or at locations occupied by the suspect)

Additionally, evidence in rape cases may take many forms. Therefore, after the responding officer has given the rape victim aid, a determination of the circumstances surrounding the attack must be made. When immediate medical attention is required, the officer on the scene may make initial inquiries about the assault while waiting for the ambulance to arrive. The victim should be asked to:

- Describe what happened.
- Describe the assailant.
- Describe the attacker's vehicle.
- Describe the location where the crime occurred.

If the incident was fairly recent, a flash description of the suspect or his vehicle should be given to the dispatcher for possible broadcast. After the crime scene investigation is under way, the investigator should determine if there is any physical evidence to be collected. Typically, the rape victim will scratch the skin or tear the hair of her attacker, and evidence may be present under her fingernails. For example, a single strand of hair may reveal the gender, race, and age of the attacker. Such evidence is seizable by investigators and extremely valuable in court.[21]

The clothing of the victim can also provide valuable information (e.g., stains, blood, soil, grass stains, trace evidence). As early as possible, clothing should be

FIGURE 11.8 Sexual assault evidence kit contents—vaginal, oral, and rectal swabs. Courtesy of Mike Himmel and the Missouri State Highway Patrol.

FIGURE 11.9 Sexual assault evidence kit contents—envelopes for hair combings. Courtesy of Mike Himmel and the Missouri State Highway Patrol.

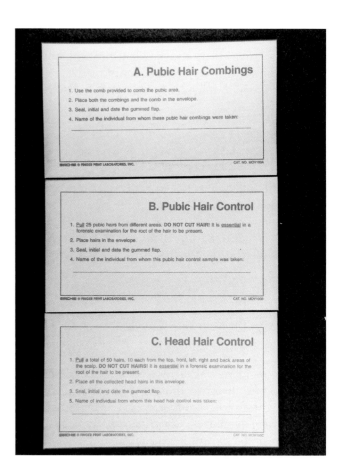

Rape Evidence Checklist

☑ Photograph all physical injuries of the victim.

☑ Note the clothing of the victim (e.g., torn, dirty, missing buttons).

☑ Examine the hair (both victim and suspect) for foreign fiber, debris, and blood.

☑ Obtain fingernail scrapings for clothing fibers, skin, blood, hair, and so on.

☑ Obtain blood samples from the victim.

☑ Obtain pubic hairs from both the victim and the suspect (this includes standards for comparison).

☑ Obtain vaginal swabs from the victim (the attending physician should acquire at least two).

☑ Obtain anal and oral swabs from the victim.

☑ Allow wet articles to air dry using fresh air, not heated air.

☑ Ensure that the victim has a cervical exam by a physician of her choosing.

☑ Obtain a written report from the examining physician.

collected from the victim and preserved for laboratory analysis. Other types of evidence that should be considered are bedsheets, mattress, towels and washrags, discarded facial tissues, robes, and sofa or chair cushions. The investigator is limited only by his or her imagination when considering the types and locations of such articles.

If a suspect is in custody, the necessary legal instrument (i.e., court order) should be secured to obtain hair and blood standards to compare with those found on the victim.

The Rape Evidence Kit. Preassembled kits for rape evidence collection can be found in many different configurations and can be quite useful to the investigator. Typically included are directions for proper use to avoid confusion and error. Hazelwood and Burgess note that commonly included are forms covering (1) medical examination and interview of the victim, (2) consent or release concerning authority to disseminate victim-related information, (3) consent or release regarding evidence obtained from the victim, and (4) chain of custody documentation.[22]

These documents are best constructed as a cooperative effort between local law enforcement and medical professionals who treat sexual assault victims. Many evidence recovery procedures can be incorporated into a rape evidence collection kit. The following is a general list of some essential elements of the kit:

- Head hair brushing comb
- Pubic hair brushing comb
- Packages for head and pubic hairs collected (both known and suspected samples)
- Vaginal swabbings
- Oral swabbings
- Anal swabbings
- Fingernail scrapings
- Miscellaneous debris collection

The acquisition of known biological samples is basically the same for both the victim and the suspect. Accordingly, trace evidence can be collected in a similar fashion. In fact, the components of the victim-oriented assault kit serve as a good guide for kits used on a suspect.

Investigative Procedures: The Crime Scene Investigation. An officer's first duty at the scene of a rape is to aid the victim and obtain medical attention immediately if required. If the attack was brutal and the victim is suffering from wounds, briefly question the victim about the attack if she is able to speak. Questions relating to what happened, where the attack took place, and a description of or information about the assailant are pertinent basic facts. This initial attempt to secure information should be made whenever possible while awaiting the arrival of an ambulance or during transport to medical facilities. In turn, the dispatcher should be contacted immediately with this information.

Usually upon arriving at a rape scene, officers will find the victim of a sexual assault under severe emotional stress ranging from hysteria to deep depression. She may be sobbing uncontrollably, excited to the point of incoherence, or in a state of shock. In cases in which the victim was drugged, she may be confused and unsure of what happened to her. When encountering any of these situations, officers must comfort the victim and reassure her that she will be all right and that she has nothing more to fear. A victim in this mental state may best be comforted by another woman such as a female officer, a family member, a friend, or a victim advocate. Such individuals should be summoned as quickly as possible if not objectionable to the victim.

The crime scene should be secured and a search for physical evidence begun as soon as possible. Quite often, the victim will pull hair or tear the assailant's clothes or scratch his face and accumulate skin tissue or bloodstains under her fingernails. The victim's clothing can also provide valuable information. This should be collected and forwarded to the crime laboratory with other trace evidence for analysis.

Clothing: When a rape occurs in the home, the victim should be requested by the responding officer not to change her clothing, shower, or touch anything in the area until officers arrive at the scene to give her instructions. Responding officers should assume custody of all the clothing worn at the time of the attack so they may be examined for blood or seminal stains, hair fibers, and other physical trace evidence that may lead to the identification, apprehension, and conviction of a suspect. If the location of the crime makes the immediate recovery of the clothing impractical, the victim should be informed that an officer will collect her garments at the hospital for transfer to the crime laboratory. In these situations, arrangements should be made with a friend or a relative to bring a change of clothing for the victim to the hospital. The number of persons handling the victim's clothing must be restricted. Concerted efforts to protect the integrity of the specimens and to guard the chain of possession also require that evidence be properly marked, packaged, and labeled to facilitate future identification.

The clothing of a rape victim, especially the undergarments, as well as the clothes of a suspect, should be analyzed by crime laboratory technicians for semen stains, bloodstains, hair, and other physical traces, such as soil and grass stains. Scientific analysis of the evidence may link a suspect to the crime, or it may indicate that a suspect is not the person who should be sought.

Recovered clothing should be carefully handled to protect the evidentiary value of the stains it may contain. Seminal traces and bloodstains are highly brittle when dry and may be brushed off the clothing. Clothing should be covered with paper before folding and each item individually placed in an evidence bag.

Semen: Seminal traces may be located by ultraviolet radiation because of their fluorescent qualities. Semen is highly proteinaceous serum normally containing a great number of spermatozoa. These traces are usually found on underclothing of the victim, the suspect, or both and may also be located on bedding, mattresses, towels, automobile cushions, and similar types of materials found at or near the crime scene or in the possession of a suspect. Ultraviolet light or an acid phosphatase color test is helpful in identifying semen on these and other surfaces. Vaginal secretions and some other material will react to the latter test but not at the same speed as semen. A positive test requires that the material be subjected to microscopic examination for confirmation.

Bloodstains may also be found in similar locations. Both semen and blood samples can be subjected to DNA analysis.

Hair: It is fairly common to find a reciprocal transfer of evidence in crimes involving bodily contact. As such, it is not unusual to find hair of the offender transferred to the body or clothing of the victim and, in turn, to discover some of the victim's hair on the suspect.

Recovered hair is usually subjected to microanalysis at the crime laboratory. The results of this examination can generally narrow the search for a suspect. A single strand of hair may identify the race, sex, approximate age, and the true color of the hair of its host. The analysis can also determine the portion of the body that the hair is from such as the scalp, chest, arm, leg, or pubic region.

Although the crime laboratory examination leads to general identification characteristics of a suspect, a positive finding may suggest the implication of an individual whereas a negative finding may disprove an erroneous theory. By the same token, hair found on a suspect's clothes can be examined and identified as being similar to that of the victim.

Investigative Procedures: The Forensic Examination. The forensic examination is arguably the most critical component in the aftermath of a sexual assault. The exam has two main goals: to treat the assault survivor for medical injuries and to collect evidence that may lead to the arrest, prosecution, and conviction of the offender. Exams are usually conducted by a sexual assault forensic examiner, or SAFE—a medical professional who has received specialized education and has fulfilled clinical requirements to perform medical forensic examinations. SAFEs can be nurses (often called sexual assault nurse examiners, or SANEs), doctors, or even physician assistants. Rape victims should receive medical attention and undergo an examination as soon as possible after the incident.

All sexual assault survivors have the right to a properly conducted exam in which they are treated with dignity, compassion, and respect. In September 2004, former U.S. Attorney General John Ashcroft released the Attorney General's National Protocol for Sexual Assault Medical Forensic Examinations (SAFE Protocol), which offers guidance for communities that want to develop a response that is sensitive to sexual assault victims and promotes offender accountability. Produced by the Office on Violence Against Women and based upon "best practices" from around the country, the SAFE Protocol also examines the roles of other members of the sexual assault response team (SART), which include law enforcement officers, prosecutors, victim advocates, and forensic scientists.

A recent study funded by NIJ examined the efficacy of SANE or SART interventions as tools in the criminal justice system. The study findings indicate that in communities with these programs, sexual assault cases are reported more quickly. In cases involving SANE or SART interventions, the average time between the assault and the report is 5.6 days compared with 33 days in cases without these interventions.[23] According to the researchers, cases with SANE or SART interventions have more evidence available and are more likely to have victim participation. Furthermore, they found that this intervention is a significant factor in the identification and arrest of suspects, is a strong predictor that charges will be filed, and increases the likelihood of conviction.[24]

The victim has the right to be examined by a physician of her choice. However, for practical reasons, this should be generally discouraged. A private practitioner or a hospital staff physician is often reluctant to be specific in officially reporting findings or to take time from a busy work schedule to testify in court. Gentle persuasion and tact will usually influence an unwilling victim or her parents to allow a physician or sexual assault nurse examiner from a public institution to conduct the examination. A written statement or report should be obtained from the attending physician or nurse after the victim has been examined. This record is extremely important at the trial to sustain the victim's allegation that she was raped.

The medical examination usually consists of a visual examination of the vaginal area to determine if there is evidence of tissue damage (lacerations, abrasions, contusions) or other indication of physical trauma that is logically connected with the assault. Smears should be obtained from the vaginal passage to determine the presence or the absence of sperm. However, the presence of sperm merely corroborates that the victim had sexual intercourse, not necessarily that she had been raped. In cases in which a drug-facilitated rape is probable, urine and blood samples should be taken.

If the crime of rape occurs, the victim should be checked out by a medical doctor with training in conducting SAFE exams or a specially trained nurse. If possible, a female law enforcement agent should be present to maintain the chain of custody.

NATIONALLY RECOGNIZED SEXUAL ASSAULT FORENSIC EXAMINATION CHECKLIST

Check all items as provided during the sexual assault forensic exam.

- ☑ Utilized appropriate evidence collection kit (city, county or state forensic lab)
- ☑ Completed screening exam for Emergency Medical Condition
- ☑ Activated bedside advocacy
- ☑ Activated interpreter
- ☑ Interventions for disabilities
- ☑ Obtained history of assault (including narrative)
- ☑ Obtained history of drug facilitated sexual assault (if indicated)
- ☑ Obtained consent for evaluation and treatment
- ☑ Obtained consent for evidentiary SAFE exam
- ☑ Obtained consent for photography
- ☑ Obtained consent for drug screening (if drug facilitated assault indicated)
- ☑ Obtained consent for release of information to all appropriate agencies
- ☑ Obtained consent for law enforcement activation (per patient request)
- ☑ Collected urine for drug facilitated sexual assault
- ☑ Collected underwear worn during or immediately after the assault
- ☑ Collected clothing, as forensically indicated, in brown paper bags, sealed and labeled
- ☑ Obtained swabs & smears from all areas that victim states were bitten or licked
- ☑ Obtained swabs & smears from appropriate areas as identified using an alternative light source
- ☑ Collected blood standard (if forensically indicated)
- ☑ Utilized crime scene investigators for bite mark impressions (if forensically indicated)

- ☑ Collected oral swab for DNA Standard (if forensically indicated)
- ☑ Collected oral swabs & smear (if orally assaulted)
- ☑ Collected anal swabs & smear (if forensically indicated)
- ☑ Collected vaginal swabs & smear (if forensically indicated)
- ☑ Collected cervical swabs & smear (if forensically indicated)
- ☑ Collected penile swabs & smear (if forensically indicated)
- ☑ Collected head hair standard (if forensically indicated)
- ☑ Collected pubic hair standard (if forensically indicated)
- ☑ Completed toluidine dye exam (if forensically indicated)
- ☑ Completed X-rays (if indicated)
- ☑ Completed CTs (if indicated)
- ☑ Collected unknown sample(s) (if forensically indicated)
- ☑ Collected fingernail scrapings (if forensically indicated)
- ☑ Photography: (with colposcope or digital)
- ☑ Genital photography by forensic examiner
- ☑ Non-genital photography by forensic examiner
- ☑ Less than 10 photos
- ☑ More than 10 photos
- ☑ Forensic evidence storage/log (as indicated)
- ☑ Completion of DHSS Adult Female, Adult Male, or Child Sexual Assault Exam Form
- ☑ Confidential forensic patient file separate from general hospital medical records
- ☑ Forensic exam conducted by forensically trained physician or healthcare provider such as Sexual Assault Nurse Examiner (SANE)

Source: U.S. Department of Justice, National Protocol for Sexual Assault Medical Forensic Examinations (9/04)

If the victim dies before the physical examination, she should not be examined by the attending physician. Instead, the body should be examined by the posting physician or the medical examiner. This procedure is followed to reduce the number of persons examining the body. Also, an examination before the posting process may destroy or remove important evidence.

The medical examination of a deceased victim should include other body cavities such as the anus, mouth, and ears. Scrapings should also be taken from under the fingernails. A thorough examination is necessary to determine the kind of sexual assault suffered by the victim and to obtain specimens of blood that could possibly be the assailant's. In some instances, assailants insert foreign objects into body cavities before or after the death of the victim. In instances of death, officers should provide the medical examiner with all information surrounding the assault and death of the victim.

Investigative Procedures: The Interview. Although the victim interview is one of the key components of a rape investigation, it can also be one of the more difficult functions for a criminal investigator. The difficult and, in many ways, specialized nature of these interviews has been a major reason for the introduction and use of rape crisis specialists to assist in these cases. Most agencies do not have such specialized personnel resources, but many agencies have found it helpful to utilize female officers individually or in conjunction with a male officer for such interviews. Female officers, even without specialized training, are generally effective in mitigating some of the anxiety and apprehension that rape victims have concerning the interview process and related investigatory activities. Significant additional benefits can be realized for both the victim and the criminal investigation if the same female officer can be assigned to assist the victim throughout the investigation and prosecution of the case.

Most rape investigations should incorporate a preliminary and subsequent in-depth interview with the victim. The initial interview conducted at the crime scene should be limited to gathering basic facts about the crime sufficient to identify the victim and to describe and locate the offender on a timely basis. The ability of the responding officer or investigator to gather this information will depend greatly on the emotional and physical condition of the victim and the professional and interpersonal skills of the interviewer. However, it is ill advised to attempt to fully explore the events and circumstances surrounding the crime at the scene of the incident. The emotional condition of rape victims generally precludes their ability to clearly focus and to articulate accurate and complete details of the incident. Even in cases in which a victim appears to be under control, officers should be aware that the victim's emotional state may cause her to cloud certain facts, and in cases in which the victim was drugged, she may have blacked out during the assault. Officers should be sure to clarify such information at a later time during an in-depth interview session.

By gathering complete information during the in-depth interview, officers avoid the need to repeatedly question the victim at later dates. Repeated interviews require the victim to relive the experience again and again. A structured interview that will cover all pertinent areas is one of the better means of avoiding such repetitive questioning.

The investigative goal of the police officer in interviewing a rape victim is to determine if and how the crime occurred. It is from the statements made by the victim to the officer that the essential elements of the offense and the direction of the investigation are established. The prosecutor and eventually the court must be given a well-balanced account of the offense describing the actions of the offender, any accomplices, and the victim. It is the investigator's responsibility to provide the court with the explanation and clarification it seeks. Part of the story may be obtained from the analysis of physical evidence, but the eyewitness account of the victim or other persons fills in the missing portions of the picture presented to the court.

Because the interview process may be considered as a routine operation, the police officer may, if not careful, project a feeling of lack of concern for the victim as a person. The danger is that the victim may be left with the impression that she is being treated as an object of physical evidence rather than as a human being. This eventuality must be avoided for its own sake as well as for the good of the investigation. It is by the personal and sensitive communication of the interview that the victim's cooperation is gained and her emotional well-being maintained. If the officer treats the victim impersonally, her confidence will be shattered, the interview will be unsuccessful, and the victim may suffer further emotional stress. The following points should be kept in mind when conducting the in-depth interview.

Officer Attitude: When interviewing a rape victim, the officer must realize that, from the victim's viewpoint, what has occurred is a violent and perverted invasion of her "self." Furthermore, the officer must be constantly aware of personal sexual attitudes and prejudices as well as the subtle and not-so-subtle ways in which they emerge. Special care should be exercised so that the rape victim is not placed in the position of perceiving herself as being guilty because of the personal nature of the crime and the social stigma attached to it. Maintaining professionalism throughout the interview will help the officer obtain an accurate report of the crime without causing the victim to experience unnecessary anxiety.

The interviewer's approach should be informal and natural in order to put the victim at ease. Words should be used that are appropriate to the victim's age, intelligence, and social class. Slang or colloquialisms may be appropriate in alluding to matters indirectly related to the offense, but medical terms should be used to refer to the various sexual organs and parts of the body (e.g., penis, vagina, vulva). In some instances, an officer may have to define terms to the victim before the interview. This adds a degree of dignity to the confidential relationship one should establish, indicates respect for the private parts of the body, and helps allay doubt or misgiving about the officer's sincerity and interest.

Physical Setting: It is unreasonable to expect a rape victim to respond to detailed questioning while she is uncomfortable or in physical pain. The victim may have been beaten as well as raped. If the rape has occurred outdoors, the victim and her clothing will probably be soiled. Sometimes the victim has been urinated on or has been forced to commit oral sodomy. Under conditions such as these, the preliminary interview should be brief, and the in-depth follow-up interview should be conducted after the victim has been medically examined and treated and her personal needs, such as washing and changing clothes, have been met.

Officers often interview a rape victim at the hospital or other medical facility where the victim is being treated. Most hospitals meet the basic requirements of appropriate physical setting for an interview. The physical surroundings of most hospitals provide desired privacy and a professional care environment that can restore confidence in the victim.

Outside the hospital, the interview should take place in a comfortable setting where there is privacy and freedom from distraction. A crowded office or similar location where the interview is subject to interruption is inappropriate. The reluctance of a rape victim to discuss intimate details of the crime will generally increase if there are other people present. This may include persons who would be close to the victim under otherwise normal conditions, such as a husband or boyfriend.

Opening Remarks: The opening remarks represent a critical point at which an officer must gain the victim's confidence and let her know that a major part of the officer's function is to help and to protect her. The officer should make clear his or her sympathy for and interest in the victim. By doing this, the officer contributes to the immediate and long-term emotional health of the victim and lays the foundation of mutual cooperation and respect on which an effective interview is built.

Ventilation Period: After the opening remarks, the officer should allow the victim to direct the conversation into any area of concern to her. This "ventilation" period gives the victim an opportunity to relieve emotional tension. During this time, the officer should listen carefully to the victim and provide answers to questions as appropriate and reassurance when necessary.

Investigative Questioning: After a ventilation period, the victim should be allowed to describe what occurred in her own words and without interruption.

As the victim provides details about the rape, she will also relate a great deal about herself. Her mood and general reaction, her choice of words, and her comments on unrelated matters can be useful in evaluating the facts of the case. It is important in such an interview that the police officer be humane, sympathetic, and patient. He or she should also be alert to inconsistencies in the victim's statements. If the victim's story differs from the originally reported facts, the officer should point out the discrepancies and ask her to explain them in greater detail. The officer should phrase questions in simple language, making sure that she understands the question. It is best if the questions are presented in a manner that encourages conversation rather than implies interrogation. Often a rape victim will omit embarrassing details from her description of the crime. Officers should expect a certain amount of reluctance on the part of the victim to describe unpleasant facts. The officer should explain that certain information must be discussed to satisfy the legal aspects of rape and pursue the investigation. He or she may add that the same questions will be asked in court if the case results in a trial. In a majority of cases, the attack is premeditated, and in about 80 percent of the cases,[25] the rapist has known or has seen the victim before the assault. Because of this, certain types of questions should be asked. The victim should be asked if, and how long, she has been acquainted with the offender. The circumstances of their meeting and the extent of any previous relationship, including any prior sexual relations, should be explored. Although previous sexual acts with the accused will not absolve the offender at this point in the investigation, knowledge of them helps to establish the nature of the relationship with the offender, as well as prepare for possible prosecutorial problems. If it is determined that the victim had known the rapist before the incident, he should be identified and interviewed. If the offender is unknown, the officer must get a detailed description of him, including his clothing, speech mannerisms, and related identifying characteristics. The officer should determine whether the offender revealed any personal facts such as area of residence or places he frequented. Questions should be asked related to the presence of any accomplices, use of weapons, and make and model of any vehicle involved, among other pertinent factors.

With the increasing prevalence of date rape drugs such as Rohypnol and GHB, there are new problems that arise during investigations. The victim may have little or no memory of the assault and may not be sure whether or not an assault took place. The questioning should focus on the events leading up to the incident, the beverages ingested, and who provided them. The officer should question the victim as to any unusual side effects she experienced, as well as typical effects on the victim from alcohol and drugs.[26]

Concluding the Interview: As a result of having been raped, many victims suffer long-term emotional problems. Because of this, it is appropriate for the officer conducting the interview to determine whether the victim has sought assistance for any such problems. It is generally advisable to inform the victim that emotional reactions to rape are common and that counseling is advisable. Victims who are not familiar with available community resources to assist in these matters should be provided with information on referral agencies.

Actual versus False Complaints

There have been many misconceptions regarding rape, one of which is the prevalence of false reports. Approximately 1 to 6 percent of rape reports are fictitious, no greater than the incidence of false reports for other crimes.[27] A victim's reactions and appearance may lead an officer to question the validity of the complaint, but a victim's reactions can be quite varied. Even a jovial attitude displayed by a rape victim is not abnormal. Another reason officers question the validity of rape reports is the prior sexual involvement a victim may have had with an offender. But this is not conclusive. Even prostitutes are subjected to sexual assault, which includes the humiliation and trauma of the crime.

Profiling the Rapist

As with the investigation of many other types of crimes, one of the best methods for solving rape and sexual assault cases is to understand the offender's motivations. The use of the rapist **profile** can aid the criminal investigator in understanding the behavioral patterns of the suspect. Profiling will not solve rape cases but will assist in the investigation by focusing on confirming certain events at a crime scene or by eliminating suspects.

Profiles have been of value to law enforcement agencies when investigators review their investigative files and attempt to apply the information to the case. Similarly, profiles can be used to "match" profile characteristics to newly developed suspects who come into only minimal contact with the investigators.

Research by such experts in the field as A. Nicholas Groth, Ann Burgess, and Robert Hazelwood has led to an improved understanding of rapists and their victims. Groth, a leading expert on sex crimes, describes the role of both the "power" and the "anger" rapist. Groth has developed the main premise behind the rapist profile in his typologies.[28] The **power rapist** has been subdivided into two personality types: the power-reassurance rapist and power-assertive rapist. The **anger rapist** has also been subdivided into two categories: the anger-retaliatory rapist and the anger-excitation rapist.

The Power-Reassurance (Manhood) Rapist.

The power-reassurance rapist has the primary motivation of power over his victim. Accounting for an estimated 81 percent of rapes that are reported, the term *power* does not imply that he desires to harm his victim physically in any way; he does not. Indeed, his psychological disorder focuses on how he perceives his manhood or lack of it. The pre-offense behavior of the power-reassurance rapist includes fantasies about having a sexual affair with a member of the opposite sex. Because of his obsession with proving his manhood, his fantasies revolve around "successful" sexual relations with his partner. It is thought that these fantasies center around a relationship that most of the "normal" population enjoys regularly.

Criminal investigations of this type of rapist show that he will usually deploy a particular "plan of attack." If the rapist persists in his attacks, his plan will become more and more refined but also more easily predicted by investigators. In particular, this class of rapist will usually select victims through prior observation or stalking. This may be accomplished through prowling, voyeurism, and so on, typically conducted in residential areas. Statistically, attacks occur in the victim's residence after dark and close to the rapist's own neighborhood. Additionally, he will use weapons of opportunity and verbal threats in his attack.

Profile of the Power-Reassurance Rapist[29]

☑ Rapes between midnight and 5 A.M. every 7 to 20 days

☑ Selects victims by watching and window peeping

☑ Seeks women about his own age who are living alone and attacks in their home

☑ Uses a weapon of opportunity

- ☑ Covers the victim's face or wears a ski mask to prevent identification
- ☑ Asks the victim to remove her clothing
- ☑ Performs vaginal sex; may experience premature ejaculation or impotence
- ☑ Asks the victim to say that she likes his sexual performance
- ☑ Is socially inadequate, a loner, lives alone or with parents, has a menial job, frequents porno theaters and shops, has been arrested for window peeping or burglary
- ☑ Has no vehicle; first rapes within walking distance of his home

Victim Characteristics of the Power Rapist[30]

- ☑ The victim is usually of the same race as the attacker.
- ☑ The victim will probably be alone at the time of initial contact.
- ☑ The victim will have been evaluated by the attacker as one who probably won't resist attack.
- ☑ The attacker considers her to be meek, nonaggressive, or easily dominated.
- ☑ Physical size is commonly used in the rapist's consideration of victims.
- ☑ The victim is typically attacked through a "surprise" method.
- ☑ The rapist hopes that she will yield to his "initial" advance.
- ☑ If the rapist does not get the desired initial response from the victim, he will probably flee the scene.

Profile of the Power-Assertive Rapist[31]

- ☑ Rapes between 7 P.M. and 1 A.M., every 20 to 25 days
- ☑ Selects a victim of opportunity; may meet her in a bar or date two or three times
- ☑ Selects a woman about his own age, uses an overpowering or con approach, dominates victim, rapes indoors or outdoors
- ☑ Uses a weapon of choice
- ☑ Uses no mask, may attempt to hide his face, won't let victim look at him
- ☑ Is a macho type, body conscious, athletic; frequents singles bars; has a hard-hat job or is a truck driver
- ☑ Is married or divorced, has been arrested for domestic disturbance or crimes against property
- ☑ Has a flashy vehicle: sports car or four-wheel-drive pickup

Ironically, studies have shown that after the attack, the offender is likely to apologize to the victim—hence the nickname "gentleman rapist." He may actually view his actions as nonthreatening to the victim and serving only to satisfy his personal needs. Investigations have also revealed that the attacker will sometimes take a personal article from the victim as a souvenir.

The Power-Assertive Rapist. The second profile occurs in an estimated 12 percent of rape attacks and involves the assertive personality of the rapist. It is the desire of this person to demonstrate his manhood to the victim through sexual assault. Research has shown that this type of rapist seldom plans his attacks and is an opportunist by nature. His victims are, however, typically of the same race and age group as the assailant. Many such offenders have chosen the bar scene as their hunting ground and may typically choose a bar close to the place where they live or work.

The power-assertive rapist will probably use the con approach with his victim, and after he gets her in a location where he can make his attack, he will use a moderate degree of force. After the assault, he will probably threaten his victim with retaliation if she reports him. As with the previous type of offender, he will also desire an object from the victim as a souvenir, such as an article of clothing. The power-assertive rapist is also thought to be a repeat offender whose future targets are difficult to predict.

The Anger-Retaliatory Rapist. The anger-retaliatory rapist profile is that of a person who vents his anger and frustration toward the opposite sex by punishing them. The punishment is based on either real or imagined wrongs that they have perpetrated against him (or the male population in general). Sexual assault is the means by which he chooses to humiliate them.

This category of rapist, which accounts for an estimated 5 percent of all rapes, typically includes pre-offense behavior that involves a significant stressor that typically relates to women. Studies show that this can usually be traced back to the offender's family or work relationships. For example, a rapist's stressor may be a woman who continually demeaned him in his early home life, resulting in stress buildup inside. After storming out of his residence, he comes across an unsuspecting woman who he designates as the target of his rage and frustration. Such an assault is usually spontaneous and results from improper management of that stressor.

Profile of Anger-Retaliatory Rapist[32]

- ☑ Rapes any hour of day or night, at irregular 6- to 12-month intervals, after fight with wife or "put-down" by a woman
- ☑ Selects a victim of opportunity, in his own neighborhood or near work
- ☑ Selects a woman his same age or older, uses a "blitz" attack
- ☑ Uses a weapon of opportunity: fists, feet, club; beats victim before, during, and after sexual assault
- ☑ Performs anal and then oral sex and vaginal sex; has possible retarded ejaculation
- ☑ Uses much profanity and degrading language
- ☑ May have arrests for domestic disturbance, speeding, or fighting on the night of the rape

☑ Is a loner, drinker, troublemaker, has an explosive temper, sports fan, laborer, construction worker

☑ Is a married man, abuses wife and children; has been arrested for fighting, family disputes, drinking

☑ May have any type of vehicle

Victim selection is usually somewhere near the attacker's residence, and she may possess physical characteristics similar to those of the female stressor in his life (e.g., the same age, the same hairstyle). His characterization of the attack on the victim may sound something like: "She was just in the wrong place at the wrong time." This rapist will typically use a blitz-type attack, with the use of force before, during, and after the attack. Although the actual assault is fairly brief, it is typically violent, and the rapist uses any resistance on the part of the victim to fuel his own anger.

The Anger-Excitation Rapist. Of all of the rapist profiles discussed, the anger-excitation rapist is the most dangerous. The anger-excitation rapist has a strong propensity toward sadism and is prone to severely injure or even murder his victim. In addition, he enjoys the victim's response to the infliction of pain, usually resulting from torture. The planning stage of the attack is done meticulously by this type of rapist, who harbors images and fantasies about sadistic sexual acts with his victims. Typically, every stage of the attack is carefully thought through.

Victims may have certain traits exhibited by women in the rapist's life with whom he has experienced conflict. Research has shown that this type of rapist will usually use a weapon to gain control of the victim while exposing himself to minimum risk of harm or detection. After the victim is in his control, he will use excessive and brutal force to maintain both psychological and physiological control of her.

Profile of the Anger-Excitation Rapist[33]

☑ Assaults are extremely well planned.

☑ His violent fantasies are acted out during the assault.

☑ Gloves and mask are included in the rape kit.

☑ The victim's resistance fuels the attacker's rage.

☑ Victim selection is day or night at irregular intervals.

☑ Brutal force is used to control his victim.

☑ While inflicting pain on the victim, the attacker is usually calm.

☑ The victim's clothes are usually cut off her.

☑ Video recordings are usually made of the assault.

☑ The sadistic rapist has no remorse.

☑ He may attempt to hide his face by wearing a hood or mask.

The Rapist's Approach

For a more complete profile of the perpetrator, it is important that the investigator document the method of approach used by the attacker. Three such forms of behavior exhibited by rapists are offered by Hazelwood and Burgess:[34]

1. *Con approach.* The victim is approached openly with a subterfuge or "cover." Typically, the attacker is friendly and offers some type of assistance or requests directions.
2. *Blitz approach.* Immediate physical assault is used to subdue the victim. This approach leaves no opportunity to cope verbally or physically and frequently involves the use of a gag or blindfold.
3. *Surprise approach.* The attacker waits for the victim in a secluded area where he won't be discovered and then approaches on his own volition (e.g., hiding in the backseat of an automobile or stepping out from behind a wall).

Methods of Control

Through the careful interview of the victim, investigators should attempt to determine the method of control used by the attacker. This is a significant component to the profiling process in which similar characteristics might be identified in the examination of other rape offenses. According to Hazelwood and Burgess, the use of force may include four levels of severity:[35]

1. *Minimal force.* Little or no force is used, but minimal slapping may be used to intimidate.
2. *Moderate force.* The repeated hitting or slapping of the victim in a painful manner is accompanied by the use of profanity.
3. *Excessive force.* The victim is beaten on all or most parts of her body.
4. *Brutal force.* Sadistic torture and intentional infliction of physical and emotional pain are used.

Studies have revealed that rapists reveal a great deal about themselves during the course of the attack through verbal remarks and comments. This makes it extremely important for the investigator to elicit specific information from the victim as to what the attacker said during the assault, specifically comments regarding demands made of the victim as well as compliments made to the victim during the attack.

Another important step in the investigation is to determine whether or not the attacker stole any items from the victim that might serve as a token or "prize" by which to remember the victim. Such items can be valuable evidence if recovered by police and used as evidence in court.

Summary Checklist

In this chapter, we consider the crime of assault and related offenses such as domestic violence and rape. Investigators must keep basic evidentiary considerations in mind when conducting investigation of assault. These include properly following preliminary investigation protocols, interviewing the victims and witnesses, and identifying evidence.

The pattern of assault is similar to that of homicide. One might say that the difference between the two is that the victim survived. Assaults can occur many ways.

Studies of assault cases have revealed that most victims of assault (two-thirds to three-fourths of cases) are acquainted with their attacker.

1. Do you know the legal aspects of assault?

Many revised state statutes categorize threats and actual physical contact as simple assault and aggravated assault.

- Simple assault is generally threats by one person to cause bodily harm or death to another.

- Aggravated assault includes the elements of simple assault plus an element relating to the severity of the attack.

2. Can you describe the preliminary investigation stages of assault investigations?

Most victims of assault know their attackers.

After arriving on the scene, either first aid should be administered to the victim, or if necessary, he or she should be transported to the hospital.

- Control and disarm those involved in the altercation.

- Provide medical aid to injured people.

- Separate suspects.

- Protect the crime scene.

- Give the *Miranda* warning if applicable.

- Obtain preliminary statements.

- Photograph any evidence observed.

- Collect and preserve evidence.

- Reconstruct the crime.

Responding officers should also establish the severity of the assault by taking photographs and describing all injuries in their notes.

3. Do you know the investigative aspects of domestic diolence and stalking?

Responding to domestic violence calls is one of the most unpleasant duties for police officers.

What responding officers do upon arrival will often determine what happens in court, whether an effective arrest will be conducted, and whether or not proper evidence will be collected.

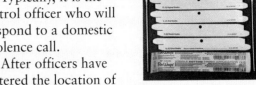

Typically, it is the patrol officer who will respond to a domestic violence call.

After officers have entered the location of the domestic violence call and have secured the area, the investigation begins.

- The first rule is to interview the suspect and victim separately.

Any evidence that would lead an officer to make an arrest in any other situation also applies to spousal abuse situations.

Officers should be careful not to detain a potential abuser any longer than other offenders.

If the assault was a mutual assault, that is, both people involved committed assault, officers must try to determine the primary physical aggressor and arrest that person.

For many women who are threatened by their violent partners, protection orders have become an option.

The crime of stalking is another crime commonly encountered. The term generally refers to some form of repeated harassing or threatening behavior. This includes:

- Following a person

- Appearing at a person's home or place of business

- Making harassing telephone calls

- Leaving written messages or objects

- Vandalizing a person's property

Women are the primary victims of stalking and men the primary perpetrators.

Although only a small percentage of stalking victims are actually physically attacked, psychological and social consequences are also common.

4. Can you identify the investigative and legal aspects of rape and evidence in rape cases?

Most sex crimes, rape in particular, are thought to be grossly underreported by victims.

(continued)

Summary Checklist (Continued)

Many perpetrators have turned out to be the friends, relatives, and acquaintances of the victims

The term *rape* has been broadly applied to a wide variety of sexual attacks and, in popular terminology, may include same-sex rape and the rape of a male by a female.

The Uniform Crime Reports (UCR) define a forcible rape as "the carnal knowledge of a female forcibly and against her will."

- By definition, rapes reported under the UCR Program are always of females.

Some jurisdictions refer to same-sex rape as sexual battery.

Statutory rape occurs when no force is involved with a female younger than the age of consent.

Forcible rape is the least reported of all violent offenses.

Forcible rape is often a planned violent crime, which serves the offender's need for power rather than sexual gratification.

A disturbing trend in rapes indicates that many victims and offenders were acquainted before the crime was committed.

Rape cases are somewhat unique in that evidence may present itself in three general areas:

- On the crime scene
- On the victim
- On the suspect (or at locations occupied by the suspect)

The crime scene should be secured and a search for physical evidence begun as soon as possible.

Areas often containing biological evidence include clothing, semen, hair, and blood

Rape victims should receive medical attention and undergo an examination as soon as possible after the incident.

5. **Do you know the different rapist profiles?**

The use of rapist profiles can aid criminal investigators in understanding the behavioral patterns of suspects.

Profiles can be used to "match" profile characteristics to newly developed suspects who come into only minimal contact with the investigators.

The power rapist has been subdivided into two personality types:

- The power-reassurance rapist and power-assertive rapist

The anger rapist has also been subdivided into two categories:

- The anger-retaliatory rapist and the anger-excitation rapist

Investigation of the crime of rape must also include documentation of the offender's approach and methods of control. This information will help the investigator identify the rapist's method of operation.

Key Terms

acquaintance stalking

aggravated assault

anger rapist

consent

cyberstalking

date rape

intimate or former intimate stalking

power rapist

primary physical aggressor

profile

protection orders

rape

resistance

self-defense

simple assault

stranger stalking

Discussion Questions

1. List and describe various types of assault.
2. Describe the stages of investigation for the crime of assault.
3. Discuss recent models of legislation in which police deal with domestic abuse.
4. Explain the problem of stalking and the investigative response to it.
5. Discuss the problem of date rape and why it is such a difficult crime to investigate.
6. What are the legal elements of rape?
7. Discuss the major points to remember when interviewing a rape victim.
8. What types of evidence should be sought in a rape case?
9. What are some of the evidentiary concerns that investigators must face when investigating a rape case?

mycrimekit

Go to mycrimekit.com to explore the following study tools and resources specific to this chapter:

- *Practice Quiz:* Multiple-choice, true/false, short-answer, and essay questions.
- *Flashcards:* There are 16 key terms in this chapter. Flashcards test your knowledge of the chapter's key terms.
- *Web Links:* Check out the hotlink to *The New York Times* criminology articles.

- *Career Center:* Check out the hot links to interesting careers in criminal justice, criminology, and juvenile justice.
- *The Research Center:* Check out the Cybrary and research navigator for even more resources.

Notes

1. GETZ, R. J. (1995). Protecting our seniors. *Police* September:40–43.
2. THE NATIONAL COMMITTEE FOR THE PREVENTION OF ELDER ABUSE. Psychological abuse. Available at http://www.preventelderabuse.org/elderabuse/psychological.html.
3. DE BENEDICTIS, T., & J. SEGAL (2007). *Elder abuse types, signs, symptoms, causes, and help.* Available at http://www.helpguide.org/mental/elder_abuse_physical_emotional_sexual_neglect.htm
4. IBID.
5. IBID.
6. NATIONAL INSTITUTE OF JUSTICE, CENTERS FOR DISEASE CONTROL AND PREVENTION (1998). *Stalking in America: Findings from the National Violence Against Women survey.* Washington, DC: U.S. Department of Justice, Office of Justice Programs.
7. IBID.
8. IBID.
9. VIOLENCE AGAINST WOMEN GRANTS OFFICE (1998). *Stalking and domestic violence: The third annual report to Congress under the Violence Against Women Act.* Washington, DC: U.S. Department of Justice (NCJ-172204).
10. BRODY, J. (1998). Deep disorders drive stalkers, experts say. *Star Tribune,* August 30:E5.
11. ALVORD, V. (1999). Cyberstalkers must beware of the law. *USA Today,* November 8:22A; National Institute of Justice (1997). The crime of stalking: How big is the problem? *Research Preview* 10–11; National Institute of Justice, Centers for Disease Control and Prevention (1998). *Stalking in*

America: Findings from the National Violence Against Women survey . Washington, DC: U.S. Department of Justice, Office of Justice Programs; Willing, R. (1998). Men stalking men: Stalkers often gravitate toward positions of power. *USA Today,* June 17:1A.
12. NATIONAL INSTITUTE OF JUSTICE, CENTERS FOR DISEASE CONTROL AND PREVENTION (1998). *Stalking in America: Findings from the National Violence Against Women survey* . Washington, DC: U.S. Department of Justice, Office of Justice Programs.
13. ALVORD, V. (1999). Cyberstalkers must beware of the law. *USA Today,* November 8:22A.
14. IBID.
15. TJADEN, P., and N. THOENNES (1998). Prevalence, incidence, and consequences of violence Against women: Findings from the National Violence against Women Survey. National Institute of Justice. *Research in Brief.* Washington, DC: U.S. Department of Justice.
16. IBID.
17. LANNING, K. W. and R. R. HAZELWOOD (1988,.). The maligned investigator of criminal sexuality. *FBI Law Enforcement Bulletin* September:1–10.
18. See for example, The American Prosecutors Research Institute. (1999). *The prosecution of rohypnol and GHB related sexual assaults.*
19. *PEOPLE V. MCCANN,* 76 Ill. App. 3rd 184, 186, 394 N.E.2d 1055, 1056 (2d Dist. 1979).
20. MEYER, T. (1984). Date rape: A serious campus problem that few talk about. *Chronicle of Higher Education* December 5.

21. GRIFFITHS, G. L. (1985). The overlooked evidence in rape investigations. *FBI Law Enforcement Bulletin* April:8–15.

22. HAZELWOOD, R. and A. BURGESS (1987). *Practical aspects of rape investigation.* Boca Raton, FL: CRC Press.

23. ROSE, K. (2007). Sexual assault virtual training takes responders from exam room to courtroom. *National Institute of Justice Journal* No. 258, October.

24. IBID.

25. HEISE, L. L. (1993). Reproductive freedom and violence against women: Where are the intersections? *Journal of Law, Medicine & Ethics* 21(2): 206–216.

26. See, for example, *Drug facilitated sexual assault: Rohypnol and GHB. Training key #509* Alexandria, VA: International Association of Chiefs of Police, 1999.

27. LEDRAY, L. E. (1994). *Recovering from rape.* New York: Henry Holt and Company:227.

28. GROTH, A. N., et al. (1977). Rape: Power, anger and sexuality. *American Journal of Psychiatry*, 134:1239–1243.

29. IBID.

30. IBID.

31. IBID.

32. IBID.

33. IBID.

34. HAZELWOOD R. and A. BURGESS (1987). *Practical aspects of rape investigation.* Boca Raton, FL: CRC Press.

35. IBID.

36. HEISE, L., and J. ROBERTS (1990). Reflections on a movement: The U.S. battle against women abuse. In M. SCHULER (Ed.). *Freedom from violence: Women's strategies round the world.* Line Village, NV: Copperhouse Publishing:5–12.

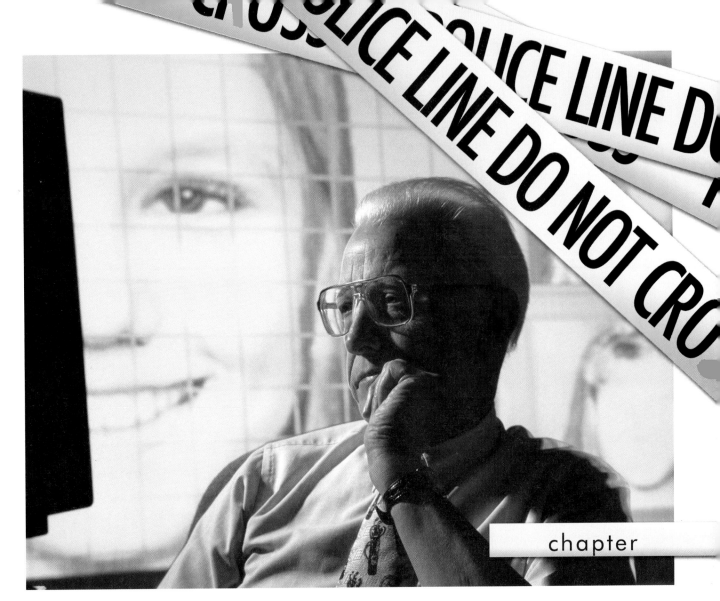

Missing and Abducted Persons

12

This chapter will enable you to:

- Understand the complexity of the nation's missing persons problem.
- Discuss the first responder's role in missing persons cases.
- Identify the steps in investigating missing and abducted persons.
- List and discuss the different categories of missing and abducted persons.
- Explain police supervisor responsibilities in missing persons cases.
- Identify guidelines for interviewing suspects in missing persons and abduction cases.
- Understand the investigator's role in missing and abducted persons cases.

chapter

Introduction

On June 10, 1991, 11-year-old Jaycee Lee Dugard was abducted from a school bus stop within sight of her stepfather, Carl Probyn, who was standing in their home in South Lake Tahoe, California. Probyn saw two people in a gray sedan (possibly a Mercury Monarch or Mercury Zephyr) make a U-turn at the school bus stop where Dugard was waiting, and forced her into the car despite her struggles. He then gave chase on a bicycle but he was unable to overtake their vehicle. For almost 20 years, Probyn remained a suspect in Jaycee's disappearance. Eighteen years later, on August 26, 2009, Jaycee appeared in the office of her alleged kidnapper's parole officer in California, and her identity was confirmed the following day.[1]

Arrested for Jaycee's kidnapping were 58-year-old Phillip Craig Garrido along with his wife 55-year-old Nancy Garrido, of Antioch, California. The investigation into the kidnapping revealed that Jaycee was kept in a concealed area behind Garrido's house in Antioch, California for 18 years. Jaycee gave birth to two daughters, now aged 15 and 11, during this time. Jaycee's abductor, Garrido, fathered the children. While Jaycee and her daughters never went to school or saw a doctor, they remained physically healthy.

The details of Jaycee's abduction are disturbing. After the abduction, the Garridos took Dugard to their home in a low-rent, unincorporated area within northeast Antioch. They later built a privacy fence around the property, which already had several large trees in the yard. Phillip Garrido was found to have violated his parole and was returned to federal prison from April to August of 1993.[2]

While she was captive, Dugard had access to the business phone and had an email account. One customer of the printing business indicated that she never hinted to him about her childhood abduction or true identity. Her two daughters told others she was their older sister.

In 2006, one of Garrido's neighbors called 9-1-1 to inform them that there were tents in the backyard with children living there and that Garrido was a "psychotic" with sexual addictions. A deputy sheriff spoke with Garrido at the front of the house for about 30 minutes and left after telling him there would be a code violation if people were living outside the property. After Dugard was found in August 2009 the local police issued an apology.

On August 24, 2009, Garrido went to a University of California, Berkeley police office seeking permission to hold a special Christian event on campus referred to as a part of his "God's Desire" program. He spoke with UC Berkeley special events manager Lisa Campbell. Campbell found his behavior odd and asked him to make an appointment for the next day. She notified campus police officer Ally Jacobs, who ran a background check on Garrido and learned he was on parole for rape.

Garrido arrived the next day with two girls, aged 11 and 15, whom he introduced as his daughters. At the meeting Jacobs noticed that the girls' behavior displayed some of the same detachment and religious fervor as their father, along with their drab dresses. When asked about a bump near her eye, the younger girl suggested that it was congenital and untreatable, which, because of the way she said it, seemed to Jacobs to be rehearsed. Jacobs later stated about the meeting that the girls "had this weird look in their eyes like brainwashed zombies." After the meeting, Jacobs attempted to contact Garrido's parole officer to express her concern about the welfare of the two girls.[3]

The next day, the parole office talked to Jacobs and was shocked to learn that Garrido had children. He called Garrido and asked him to come in for a parole meeting. Later that day Garrido arrived at the meeting with his wife, the two girls, and Jaycee Dugard, whom they all referred by the name "Allissa".

FIGURE 12.1 (A) Photo of Phillip Craig Garrido (B) Photo of Jaycee Lee Dugard

After being separated from Garrido for a further interview, the three were discovered to be Dugard and two children she had borne. Garrido and his wife were then arrested by local police. An FBI agent put Dugard on the telephone with her mother Terry Probyn, who at first thought the call was a prank. Dugard retained custody of her children and was soon reunited with her mother.

The Jaycee Dugard case is an example of the tragedy of missing persons, cases and how difficult such cases are to investigate. In the Jaycee Dugard case, she was missing for 18 years and gave birth to two daughters fathered by her abductor. Jaycee's case demonstrates the need for a swift investigative response to child abductions to identify and capture those involved in abductions and return victims safely to their homes.

A Look at the "Big Picture"

Although this chapter addresses missing and abducted persons in general, it focuses primarily on the thousands of children who are discovered missing each year. The magnitude of the missing and abducted problem is complex, multifaceted, and disturbing. For example, there are different types of missing children cases, including family abductions; endangered runaways; nonfamily abductions; and lost, injured, or otherwise missing children. National estimates for the number of missing children are from incidence studies conducted by the U.S. Department of Justice's Office of Juvenile Justice and Delinquency Prevention.

In 2009, the National Center for Missing and Exploited Children reported the following instances of missing and abducted children:

- 797,500 children (younger than age 18 years) were reported missing in a one-year period of time studied resulting in an average of 2,185 children being reported missing each day.
- 203,900 children were the victims of family abductions.
- 58,200 children were the victims of non-family abductions.

- 115 children were the victims of "stereotypical" kidnapping. (These crimes involve someone the child does not know or someone of slight acquaintance who holds the child overnight, transports the child 50 miles or more, kills the child, demands ransom, or intends to keep the child permanently.)[4]

Statistics show that there are an estimated 100 cases per year in the U.S. in which a child is abducted and murdered. The victims of these cases are "average" children leading normal lives and living with normal families, typical low-risk victims. The vast majority of them are girls (76 percent), with the average age being slightly older than 11 years of age. In 80 percent of cases, the initial contact between the victim and killer is within 1/4 mile of the victim's residence.[5]

Profiling the Abductor

A kidnapping is the type of abduction that is most harmful to the child, both psychologically and physically. Many child abductions also involve some type of sexual abuse. An earlier study funded by the Justice Department's Office of Juvenile Justice and Delinquency Prevention (OJJDP) provided additional insight on the child abduction problem. This 1997 survey examined 600 abduction cases across the nation. The findings were very similar to those of the **National Incidence Studies of Missing, Abducted, Runaway and Throwaway Children (NISMART)** project.[6]

More than half (57 percent) of child abduction murders are committed by a killer who is a stranger to the victim. Family involvement in this type of case is infrequent (9 percent). However, the relationship between the victim and the killer varies with the gender and age of the victim. Whereas the youngest girls, one to five years old, tend to be killed by friends or acquaintances (64 percent), the oldest young women, 16 to 17 years old, tend to be killed by strangers (also 64 percent). The relationship between the killer and victim is different for the male victims. The youngest male victims (one to five years old) are most likely to be killed by strangers (also 64 percent), as are teenage boys (13 to 15 years old, and 16 to 17 years old, 58 percent).[7]

The average age of killers of abducted children is around 27 years old. They are predominantly unmarried (85 percent) and half of them (51 percent) either live alone (17 percent) or with their parents (34 percent). Half of them are unemployed, and those that are employed work in unskilled or semi-skilled labor occupations. Therefore, the killers can generally be characterized as "social marginals."

Almost two-thirds of the killers (61 percent) had prior arrests for violent crimes, with slightly more than half of the killers' prior crimes (53 percent) committed against children. The most frequent prior crimes against children were rape (31 percent of killers) and other sexual assault (45 percent of killers). Sixty-seven percent of the child abduction murderers' prior crimes were similar in method of operation (MO) to the murder that was committed by the same killer.

Commonly, the killers are at the initial victim–killer contact site for a legitimate reason (66 percent). They either lived in the area (29 percent) or were engaging in some normal activity. Most of the victims of child abduction murder are victims of opportunity (57 percent). Only in 14 percent of cases did the killer choose his victim because of some physical characteristic of the victim. The primary motivation for the child abduction murder is sexual assault. After the victim has been killed, 52 percent of the bodies are concealed to prevent discovery. In only 9 percent of cases is the body openly placed to ensure its discovery.

A unique pattern of distance relationships exists in child abduction murders. The initial contact site is within 1/4 mile of the victim's last known location in 80 percent of cases. Conversely, the distance between the initial contact site and the murder site increases to distances greater than 1/4 mile (54 percent). The distance from the murder site to the body recovery site again decreases to less than 200 feet in 72 percent of cases.

It was discovered that once the murder investigation has begun, the name of the killer is known to the police within the first week in 74 percent of cases.[8]

The Elizabeth Smart kidnapping emphasizes several characteristics that child abductors seem to have in common. First, they most often have a prior visual sighting of the victim, and the initial contact is frequently made at or near the home. Secondly, the motivation for the crime is often sexual in nature. The victim is usually a girl younger than age 14 years, and the suspect is an unemployed white male with a criminal record. Although the alleged kidnapper, Brian Mitchell, was 20 years older than the NISMART average, he fit the profile reasonably well. Elizabeth Smart could be considered a very lucky victim. That's because girls her age who are abducted under similar circumstances stand a very good chance of being killed.

The duration of a kidnapping episode was usually less than 24 hours (90 percent). Only fewer than 10 percent last longer than one day. Nonfamily abductions show the same patterns, although 30 percent of them last less than even three hours. The most dramatic difference between nonfamily abductions and kidnappings is in the treatment of the victim. In 99 percent of nonfamily abductions, the child is returned alive. In kidnappings, a safe return occurs only 57 percent of the time. Ominously, the child suffers a sexual or physical assault in an astounding 86 percent of the stereotypical kidnappings. These findings powerfully emphasize the extreme danger of these events and the urgency of police interaction as soon as possible.

Stereotypical kidnapping, in which a child is abducted and either assaulted or held for ransom, is a crime that first appeared in the United States in the late nineteenth century. During the 1920s, it became entrenched in the public consciousness when a series of child abduction cases terrified parents across the country.

Types of Missing Children Cases

In general, missing children cases fall into three basic categories, nonfamily abduction, family abduction, and runaway (or lost).

The **nonfamily abduction** case, in which a child is removed without authorization from his or her family by force or trickery, is the most complex and dangerous type of missing child case. In this situation, time is of the essence because the child is considered to be in great danger. Many experts believe that the first few hours after an abduction are the most dangerous for children.

Also included in this category are abductions of newborns and infants from health care facilities, malls, grocery stores, and public transportation facilities, as well as other public places where the mother's or child care provider's attention may be diverted. Although the snatching of newborns is not a crime of epidemic proportions, naturally, it causes tremendous trauma for the parents or guardians. The offender almost always is a woman and generally does not harm the baby because she usually abducts the child in order to have a baby of her own.

The second type of case is the **family abduction,** which generally occurs in conjunction with divorce and separation. In this type of case, the noncustodial parent removes the child from the care of the custodial parent and may flee to another state or even another country with the child. The child may be at risk with the noncustodial parent. There have been recent cases across the nation in which the child of a family abduction was murdered by the noncustodial parent, who then committed suicide. Family abductions are often very complex cases involving court orders, child protection services, and hidden agendas, as well as raw emotions and sometimes extreme possessiveness toward the children on the part of one or both parents.

The third type of missing child case involves the **runaway or lost child,** who could be in great danger depending on such factors as age, maturity, and intelligence. The voluntary runaway child is the most common missing child case encountered by law enforcement officers.

Abductions via the Internet

Some child abductions have been connected to the Internet as a result of the easy access both the child and predator have to this worldwide communications network. Susceptible preteens and teens are sometimes lured into false friendships in Internet "chat rooms" and then kidnapped from a prearranged meeting place. In other cases, the abductor may send the child money and a bus ticket to meet in another state. Children and teens who get involved in chat room conversations on the Internet have no way to know exactly who they're talking to. One of the many attractions of chat rooms is the anonymity they provide. People can be anyone they choose to be online, where real identities are hidden and fictitious names and personalities emerge.

In one case, a preteen boy was lured to San Francisco by an adult male pedophile with a large collection of child pornography. The youth told his friends at school and showed them the bus ticket and money he was sent. His friends revealed this information to the police only after the boy was reported missing. A nationwide search was initiated, and they were questioned.

How do investigators determine if a missing child case involves an Internet lure? A computer in a child's room or home with an Internet connection can steer the investigation in this direction, especially if the parents or guardians reveal that the child spent a lot of time "online" and talked about new friends made via "chat rooms." Another clue is the sudden disappearance of the child for no apparent reason (e.g., there was no recent fight between the child and parents, yet the child was gone one day when the parents returned from work). In a case like this, the investigator should check to see whether the child took any favorite possessions, a suitcase, duffle bag or backpack, clothes, or money. Missing possessions indicate a runaway, but runaways are not always what they appear to be.

Other clues to the child's disappearance can be found on the computer itself. The computer may yield electronic mail (e-mail) saved on the hard drive, a disk, or a printout. The child may have left notes in schoolbooks that would provide clues, such as the online friend's address, phone number, or e-mail address. Before searching computers for data and evidence, the investigator should consult with the department attorney as well as agency computer specialists because complex investigations involving computer systems and online access services present unique technical, operational, and legal problems.

Because of the threat Internet predators pose, there have been efforts to use the Internet as a resource to prevent child abduction or to help the families of those who have been abducted. Many organizations have set up websites where users can go to gain knowledge or contribute help to stopping child abduction. Among these are the organizations Enough is Enough and National Center for Missing and Exploited Children, which have partnered with the online community MySpace to help keep the Internet a safe place for children. MySpace also features pages and groups dedicated to helping find missing children.[9]

Legislative History of Child Abduction

In today's increasingly technological world, many people's views concerning police and criminal investigation have become distorted by what they see on television. Those unfamiliar with investigations of missing persons often have

FIGURE 12.2 Photo of Sara Lunde, age 13 years, who was abducted and found dead on April 16, 2005. Convicted sex offender 36-year-old David Onstott was indicted by a Florida grand jury one month after Sara's disappearance.

watched television shows wherein FBI agents respond and take over all manner of missing person cases, which they then successfully resolve within the 1-hour time frame. Many of the general public believe, based on such shows, that the FBI automatically responds to any case involving a missing person. In reality, the local "cop on the beat" usually arrives as the first law enforcement officer on the scene and begins the investigation.[10] At one time, no federal agency had responsibility or jurisdiction to investigate these cases. Kidnapped, lost, or

FIGURE 12.3 Jessica Lunsford's family and Jessica at a press release after her abduction in 2005. Jessica's abduction and murder resulted in the passing of Jessica's law.

missing people were considered a problem best dealt with by local law enforcement. This changed dramatically, however, with the 1932 kidnapping of Charles Lindbergh's infant son.

As the first person to fly solo across the Atlantic Ocean, Charles Lindbergh became one of America's most notable heroes. This was an incredibly courageous undertaking. In 1927, planes were not reliable; navigation over water was dangerous because there were no landmarks; and choosing additional fuel over the weight of a radio, Lindbergh had no way to communicate if problems arose. After his successful flight, the young hero faced all of the positive and negative aspects of becoming immensely famous. Without a doubt, the most heartbreaking result of this notoriety occurred in 1932, when kidnappers abducted the Lindbergh's baby son from a bedroom in their Hopewell, New Jersey, home and left a ransom note. Several days later, the child was found dead. Local authorities in Hopewell and the New Jersey State Police shared jurisdiction for the investigation, which made national headlines. Although both kidnappers were caught, convicted, and executed, the public was appalled that the vast resources of the federal government could not be immediately focused on a case of this magnitude. Congress responded later that year with the passage of the Federal Kidnapping Act,[11] which allowed the use of federal agencies in kidnapping cases.

Few changes occurred in the investigation of missing children from 1932 until 1968. As society changed and divorce became more prevalent, child custody issues took on increasing importance.[12] During a divorce proceeding, one parent normally was awarded custody of the child or children.

To change this, all the other parent had to do was go to another state, find a judge to issue a conflicting order that granted that parent custody, and simply not return to the state where the first order was issued. Although the second ruling could be challenged, it was a long, expensive process that often proved unsuccessful. In 1968, the U.S. Congress addressed this with the passage of the UniformChild Custody Jurisdiction Act (UCCJA),[13] which made the practice of moving to another state for the purpose of changing custody illegal. Unfortunately, conflicting court orders still were issued, causing confusion for law enforcement officers when parents reported their children as missing. Which court order to enforce had to be decided on a case-by-case basis.

The problem of missing children continued to grow. During the 1980s, the federal government enacted several measures that provided law enforcement with tools necessary to investigate these cases. In 1980, Congress passed the Parental Kidnapping Prevention Act to strengthen the UCCJA and allowed states to use the Federal Parent Locator Service to obtain address information on noncustodial parents who abducted their children. This act also authorized the use of the Fugitive FelonAct[14] against these same individuals. In 1982, Congress changed National Crime Information Center (NCIC) rules to allow the entry of missing children into the system. Before this, police had to obtain a warrant for the noncustodial parent's arrest. At the time, most jurisdictions considered these cases strictly as civil matters and would not issue warrants, which meant that the vast majority of children taken by a noncustodial parent were not eligible for entry into NCIC. The Missing Children Act of 1982[15] allowed the entry of these missing children even though the noncustodial parent would not be charged with a crime. Two years later, Congress revisited this issue yet again and passed the Missing Children's Assistance Act (MCAA),[16] creating a national clearinghouse for missing children and authorizing research to determine the extent of the problem within this country.

Globalization also has played a role in this field. Congress recognized this and, in 1988, ratified the Hague Convention treaty on missing children with the passage of the InternationalChild Abduction Remedies Act,[17] whereby the U.S.

Department of State would become involved in noncustodial parental abductions in which the abducting parent takes the victim outside the boundaries of the United States.

As the research ordered by the MCAA of 1984 started to come in, society began to recognize the extent of the problem with missing and exploited children. In 1990, Congress again stepped up and passed the National Child Search Assistance Act (NCSAA),[18] mandating law enforcement agencies to enter each reported missing child (younger than 18 years of age) into NCIC, including all reported runaways. NCSAA also increased the involvement of the **National Center for Missing and Exploited Children (NCMEC)** with law enforcement throughout the country. In 1993, those in law enforcement involved in combating international kidnapping received additional support from Congress with the passage of the International Parental Kidnapping Crime Act,[19] making it a felony for a person to remove a child from the United States in an attempt to interfere with lawful court orders granted in custody matters.

Finally, in 1994, Congress passed the Jacob Wetterling Crimes Against Children and Sexually Violent Offender Registration Act,[20] designed to determine the number of sex offenders and provide law enforcement with a readily accessible database with possible suspect information should a child go missing. Later modification under Megan's law permits law enforcement to provide information on registered sex offenders to the general public, resulting in numerous publicly accessible websites. Congress made this act stronger in 2006 with federal penalties for failure to register. In 2007, a national database will begin operating.

This brief look and the changing legislation in this area shows that the focus and extent of this problem has changed dramatically, especially since 1980. However, the law enforcement community still does not know its true extent because the NCMEC receives fewer than 200 stranger-abduction reports annually.[21] What the profession has learned from the growing statistics compiled by the NCMEC, coupled with supporting legislation passed over the years, is that an ongoing problem exists with noncustodial parental abductions. These crimes—most states consider them felonies—normally are committed against children because the abductors refuse to accept the lawful issuance of a court order.[22]

A CLOSER LOOK

Megan's Law and Jessica's Law

Megan's Law

Megan's law is an informal name for laws in the United States requiring law enforcement authorities to make information available to the public regarding registered sex offenders. Individual states decide what information will be made available and how it should be disseminated. Commonly included information includes the offender's name, picture, address, incarceration date, and nature of crime. The information is often displayed on free public websites but can also be published in newspapers, distributed in pamphlets, or distributed through various other means.

At the federal level, Megan's law is known as the Sexual Offender (Jacob Wetterling) Act of 1994 and requires persons convicted of sex crimes against children to notify local law enforcement of any change of address or employment after release from custody (prison or psychiatric facility). The notification requirement may be imposed for a fixed period of time—usually at least 10 years—or permanently. Some states may legislate registration for all sex crimes, even if no minors were involved. It is a felony in most jurisdictions to fail to register or fail to update information.

A CLOSER LOOK CONTINUED

Megan's law provides two major information services to the public: sex offender registration and community notification. The details of what is provided as part of sex offender registration and how community notification is handled vary from state to state, and in some states, the required registration information and community notification protocols have changed many times since Megan's law was passed. The Adam Walsh Child Protection and Safety Act supplements Megan's law with new registration requirements and a "three-tier" system for classifying sex offenders according to their risk to the community.

Jessica's Law

Jessica's law is the informal name given to a 2005 Florida law, as well as laws in several other states, designed to punish sex offenders and reduce their ability to reoffend. A version of Jessica's law has been introduced on the federal level, known as the Jessica Lunsford Act.

Jessica's law is the name commonly used by the media to designate all legislation and potential legislation in other states modeled after the Florida law. Forty-two states have introduced such legislation since Florida's law was passed.

The law is named after Jessica Lunsford, a young Florida girl who was raped and murdered in February 2005 by John Couey, a previously convicted sex offender. Public outrage over this incident spurred Florida officials to introduce this legislation. Among the key provisions of the (Florida) law are a mandatory minimum sentence of 25 years in prison and lifetime electronic monitoring of adults convicted of lewd or lascivious acts against a victim less than 12 years old. In Florida, sexual battery or rape of a child younger than 12 years old is punishable only by life imprisonment with no chance of parole.

Sources: Levenson, J. S. and L. P. Cotter. (2005). The effect of Megan's law on sex offender reintegration. *Journal of Contemporary Criminal Justice* 21(1):49–66. doi:10.1177/1043986204271676; Levenson, J. S., D. A D'Amora, and A. L. Hern. (2007). Megan's law and its impact on community re-entry for sex offenders. *Behavioral Sciences & the Law* 25(4):587–602. doi:10.1002/bsl.770; Welchans, S. (2005). Megan's law: Evaluations of sexual offender registries. *Criminal Justice Policy Review* 16(2):123–140. doi:10.1177/0887403404265630; Wilson, D. (2009). Appleton attorney fights "Jessica's law" on mandatory sex offender sentencing. *Post-Crescent*, March 21, Florida Statute 800.04; Florida Statute 947.1405; Florida Statute

Amber Alerts

In 2003, Congress took a monumental step in fighting child abductions with the passage of the Prosecutorial Remedies and Other Tools to End the Exploitation of Children Today Act, or, more commonly, the PROTECT Act.[23] Considered by many to be the most comprehensive legislation designed to ensure the safety of children ever passed, the PROTECT Act also created the AMBER (America's Missing: Broadcast Emergency Response) Alert system. The Amber Alert is a partnership involving law enforcement, other government agencies, and the news media to produce public service announcements about certain abducted children whose cases meet identified criteria.[24]

Critics and those unfamiliar with the system ask why some children appear more important than others; all children are equally important. In a perfect world, every case would be handled the same, but not all cases lend themselves to the same investigative tools. Sheer volume dictates that the news media cannot become involved in the investigation of all missing children.[25] Moreover, to maintain the intense impact of the alerts, authorities must use them judiciously. Recognizing these realities, those who designed AMBER Alert targeted the stranger abductor. Further evaluation, however, revealed that children often were in more danger from noncustodial parental abductors and other family members than from unknown "bogeymen." Therefore, the system was modified to include the issuance of alerts involving family members.[26]

Dallas, Texas, was the first community to create and use a system involving the media in an attempt to locate missing children. In 1996, a man grabbed 9-year-old Amber Hagerman from her bicycle, threw the screaming child into the pickup truck he was driving, and left the area. Amber was found murdered four days later, and her homicide remains unsolved. A concerned citizen contacted a local radio station and suggested that it broadcast missing children alerts similar to those concerning inclement weather. Within 5 years, this commonsense approach to a difficult problem achieved national acceptance.

With the goal of effectively recovering endangered children, how do authorities decide if a missing child fits the criteria specified for broadcast? The U.S. Department of Justice, the organizing agency nationwide, recommends that law enforcement agencies:

- Reasonably believe that an abduction has occurred.
- Believe that the child is in imminent danger of serious bodily injury or death.
- Have enough descriptive information about the victim and the abduction to issue an AMBER Alert to assist in the recovery of the child.
- Know that the abducted child is 17 years of age or younger.
- Have entered the child's name and other critical data elements, including flagging it as a child abduction, into NCIC.

Although not specified within this list, other issues are implied. For example, the request for the alert must come from a law enforcement agency. A police report must be on file (a requirement for entry into NCIC). A recent picture of the child and an adequate description of the clothing worn when he or she was abducted are helpful but not required. Additionally, the abduction must have occurred recently, preferably within five hours but possibly as long as 24 hours. Of importance, agencies should remember that no required waiting period exists for entering a missing person into NCIC. As soon as they receive the report, they can enter the information.

Finally, AMBER Alert is only one tool in a criminal investigator's toolbox. After all, child abductors, including noncustodial parents, are dangerous criminals, and officers can use the same tools to apprehend them as they do any other type of potentially violent offender.

Some critiques of the Amber Alert program have argued that it is not appropriate in every missing child case. Instead, sometimes what is needed is a broader, coordinated effort to locate a missing child. Accordingly, the Child Abduction Response Teams (CART) teams were developed. CART teams complement the AMBER program by providing a way for a community response to all missing children's cases, even those that don't meet the criteria for an AMBER Alert. CART teams are organized regionally and are designed to meet the demographic and geographic needs of the community. CART can also be used to recover runaway children if they are younger than age 18 years and in danger.

Training typically includes an actual child abduction case study, components on response planning, and first responder protocol, to name a few of the subjects that are addressed in each regional training session. CART includes law enforcement investigators, forensic experts, AMBER Alert coordinators, search and rescue professionals, policymakers, crime intelligence analysts, victim service providers, and other interagency resources.[27]

Code Adam

Code Adam is an internationally-recognized "missing child" safety program in the United States (and Canada), originally created by Wal-Mart retail stores in 1994. It is named in memory of Adam Walsh, the 6-year-old son of John Walsh (the host of Fox Network's *America's Most Wanted*). Adam was abducted from a Sears department store in Florida in 1981 and was later found murdered. Today, many department stores, retail shops, shopping malls, supermarkets, amusement parks, and museums participate in the Code Adam program. Legislation enacted by Congress in 2003 now mandates that all federal office buildings use the program.[28]

Wal-Mart, along with the NCMEC and the departments of several state attorneys general, has offered to assist in training workshops for other companies to implement the program. Social scientists point out that the fear of child abduction is out of all proportion to its incidence. In particular, they point to the long-term persistence of retail kidnapping narratives in urban legends to highlight how parents have been sensitized to this issue for generations before the Adam Walsh case.[29]

Companies that do implement the program generally place a Code Adam decal at the front of the business. Employees at these businesses are trained to do the following six steps, according to the National Center for Missing & Exploited Children:

1. If a visitor reports a child is missing, a detailed description of the child and what he or she is wearing is obtained. Additionally, all exterior access to the building is locked and monitored; anyone approaching a door is turned away.

2. The employee goes to the nearest in-house telephone and pages Code Adam, describing the child's physical features and clothing. As designated employees monitor front entrances, other employees begin looking for the child.

3. If the child is not found within 10 minutes, law enforcement is called.

4. If the child is found and appears to have been lost and unharmed, the child is reunited with the searching family member.

5. If the child is found accompanied by someone other than a parent or legal guardian, reasonable efforts to delay their departure will be used without putting the child, staff, or visitors at risk. Law enforcement will be notified and given details about the person accompanying the child.

6. The Code Adam page will be canceled after the child is found or law enforcement arrives.

The Investigative Response

From an investigative standpoint, child kidnapping is one of the most emotionally charged and difficult criminal cases for law enforcement officers. Time is the merciless enemy. In 1997, the U.S. Office of Juvenile Justice Delinquency and Prevention (OJJDP) reported that most children (74 percent) who are murdered during stranger kidnappings are killed within the first few hours of the event. Therefore, it is imperative that investigators use every tool available to them, including the awesome power of the media.

By its very nature, abduction must take priority over many types of cases. Research has indicated that strangers who commit the offense with the intention of fulfilling a sexual desire often murder their victims within three hours.[30] In contrast, noncustodial parents may take the child to use as a weapon against their former significant other. So, in either situation, time may be very short. The person responsible for the investigation must be called immediately to the scene. No agency would assign a homicide investigator a case the next morning and then reconstruct the incident from police reports.

Abductions can be even more complex than some murders. As with all violent suspects, law enforcement officers use proven methods to locate them. All of these and more also come into play during the investigation of an abduction.

As with any other investigations, however, the best efforts by police may not lead to a quick resolution of a case. If the incident is a stranger abduction, law enforcement administrators must be prepared for the anger of the family to be redirected toward their agency. These family members are hurt and, especially if the victim is not recovered, need closure. When this is lacking, they react like any other human being and find somewhere to refocus their anger. Departmental procedures prepared in advance can help investigators cope with such difficulties and reassure the family that authorities are doing all they can.[31]

Noncustodial parental abductions can prove equally dangerous to a child. Often, the suspect takes the child and starts another life outside the investigating agency's jurisdiction. Again, investigators need to recognize and use the methods they would in any other criminal investigation. In most states, a noncustodial parental abduction is a felony. Even before charges are filed, however, the law enforcement agency can enter the child, the suspect, and the suspect's vehicle into NCIC. If the department cross-references all of the information, it will alert officers in other jurisdictions, who may stop the suspect on a traffic violation and possibly recover the child. The custodial parent then can make arrangements to retrieve the child. After the felony warrant is on file and if investigators believe the suspect has fled their jurisdiction, the FBI can help obtain a warrant for unlawful flight to avoid prosecution. This enables a wide variety of federal resources to come into play, including the Federal Parent Locator Service, which coordinates with such agencies as the Internal Revenue Service, the U.S. Social Security Administration, and the U.S. Department of Agriculture to monitor the issuance of checks and notifies law enforcement if the suspect registers for or receives any type of public assistance.

Early in the investigation, agencies may want to request an off-line search from NCIC. Usually, abductions are planned, and within minutes of the act, the suspect may have left the jurisdiction with the child. Often, the abductor may drive too fast, leading to a stop on a traffic violation. The custodial parent may not even know that an abduction has occurred before the suspect has fled the state. An off-line search can show the location of the stop, thereby giving investigators an indication of the abductor's possible destination.

In 2005, this tactic worked for an investigator in Indianapolis, Indiana. A mother was allowed to make an unsupervised visitation with her child, a ward of the state because of the woman's history of drug abuse and neglect. When the mother did not return as scheduled, a child protective services worker made a police report. Officers had no idea which direction the woman would go. An off-line search revealed that an officer in Missouri had stopped her for a traffic violation only a few hours after she had picked up the child for the visit before the Indianapolis police received the report of the missing child. Through a variety of tools, including federal assistance agencies, the Indianapolis investigator tracked the woman to Long Beach, California, where detectives located the suspect and her children living in a van under a bridge. Extradited to Indianapolis, she was prosecuted and convicted on the felony charge. The judge in the case felt that she would continue to be a danger to her children and sentenced her to a prison term.[32]

The Initial Call for Assistance

The initial response to a missing child call is perhaps the most crucial component of the investigation. The manner in which patrol officers respond to the initial call often determines whether the child is found quickly and returned home safely, remains missing for months or years, or is never found.

In most law enforcement agencies, the patrol officer is the first responder to missing child calls. Therefore, all patrol officers need to be trained to respond to such calls efficiently, compassionately, and professionally—paying particular attention to safeguarding evidence, quickly obtaining as much information as possible about the child and the circumstances, interviewing witnesses, and at the same time calming and reassuring the parents or guardians of the missing child. But before the patrol officer even arrives on the scene, information about the missing child should be relayed from the dispatcher to the responding officers. Dispatch operators, working with a standard list of predetermined questions, should gather pertinent information from the caller and relay it to the responding officers. After the dispatch operator has calmed the caller, basic facts and information can be gathered to help the responding officers, including a brief description of the missing child and information about a possible abductor(s).

Dispatch personnel should, to the degree possible, also provide responding officers with an overview of any agency records concerning the child and family, such as (1) history of violence or child abuse calls, (2) criminal activities of family members or other persons living at the address (e.g., arrests, narcotics), (3) runaway reports on the child or siblings, and (4) juvenile delinquency reports on the child or siblings. In addition, dispatch personnel should check to determine if there have been recent problems regarding children in the neighborhood. Such information could disclose many things such as complaints about prowlers, indecent exposure incidents, attempted abductions, convicted child molesters living in the neighborhood, and the like.

Department policy should provide for an immediate city- or countywide radio alert to all other patrol units and all neighboring law enforcement agencies. Even though such an alert may not contain precise factual information about the missing child or circumstances in this early stage, these immediate radio broadcasts often result in prompt, safe recoveries, particularly when a small child has simply wandered away from home and become lost.

A judgment must be made as to when a person is to be declared as "missing" and the corresponding issue of when a missing persons report should be filed. The responsibility for these determinations lies primarily with knowledgeable reporting parties: persons who are in a position to know the behavioral patterns and character of the individual involved—such as parents, guardians, or close personal friends—and who are also often the best judges of what is highly unusual, irregular, or suspicious behavior with regard to the individual's whereabouts. As such, there should be no mandatory waiting period for filing a missing persons report, and such reports should be allowed to be filed either personally or by telephone. The response by law enforcement includes steps to be taken by the responding officer, the supervisor at the scene, and the case investigator.

Responding Officer Responsibilities

The patrol officer initially establishes the seriousness of the complaint about a missing child, safeguards the scene, gathers crucial facts, and conducts preliminary interviews of witnesses. For this reason, patrol officers must learn to become as thorough as they can in responding to missing child reports. Assumptions about such cases must be avoided or officers may overlook crucial information and evidence.

To initiate a successful missing persons investigation, the first responder must focus on quickly gathering factual information and safeguarding potential evidence. This is particularly the case with regard to missing children, whether they may be abducted, runaway, or lost. This may also be true of some elderly persons or others who, because of physical or mental disability or reduced functioning, are not fully capable of taking care of themselves. The elderly, especially those suffering from Alzheimer's disease or similar problems, present specific concerns as the subjects of missing persons reports. Open terrain searches for missing persons in general also require adherence to professionally recognized search management principles. Some of the most widely accepted principles of searching for missing persons are discussed later in this chapter.

The patrol officer who responds to the call is best suited to obtain the details of the initial account, particularly because the officer patrols the area or neighborhood and is likely to notice any unusual activities or suspicious persons. The officer should respond to the call promptly, since the time factor is often crucial, especially in cases involving abductions by strangers.

In 1994, the NCMEC developed a checklist for first responders in missing children cases, listing tasks an officer should complete to ensure a successful investigation.[33] These steps are general, but they do provide a framework for the officer's actions.

The Sixteen Steps of Investigation

Sixteen tasks commonly associated with the responsibilities of the first responder are identified in this chapter. However, it is recognized that in the real world, many tasks of first responders, supervisors, and investigators are not distinctly or conveniently divided between these respective agency personnel. The following 16 steps are those that should nominally be taken by officers. It should be understood that not every step may pertain to all situations nor do the steps need to be addressed in the exact order in which they are presented in this book.

Step 1: Interview parents or the person who made the initial report to the emergency operations center (EOC). This interview should be conducted in an area where interruptions are minimal and preferably in private. The purpose of the interview is to obtain a complete description of the missing child, circumstances of how the child came to be missing, and information necessary to make an initial definition and assessment of the type of case.

Case example: The complainant may be the operator of a preschool who reports that the child was approached by a man whom the child called "Daddy."

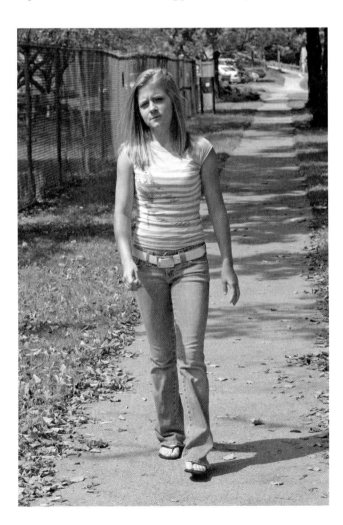

FIGURE 12.4 Stephanie Quackenbush stands on the sidewalk in Albany, New York, where in 2005 she escaped from a man who tried to abduct her. She later testified at the attacker's trial. *Courtesy of Tim Roske.*

The man then put the child in a car and left without speaking to any of the adults at the school. One of the teachers, however, obtained the license tag number of the car. Further questioning of the complainant reveals that the child's parents are divorced and engaged in a bitter custody dispute, although the court has awarded custody to the mother. The officer can make a preliminary assessment that this is a family abduction that may not warrant calling in additional personnel. *Consider another case example:* The mother of a five-year-old girl calls from the mall reporting her daughter missing; the line of questioning and initial actions of the responding officer should be very different from the above because all initial signs point to a possible abduction by a stranger.

Step 2: Verify that the child is in fact missing. Here the officer needs to make certain that the child cannot be located on the premises or nearby. In the preschool case above, three teachers and 40 children (ranging in age from two through five) saw the missing boy (age three) run and greet his father and then leave in the car. At the mall, a search of the grounds by security officers failed to turn up the missing five-year-old girl. However, when the patrol officer asked the mother if she had checked her vehicle in the parking lot, the mother said no. The officer went with the mother to the parking lot and found the girl asleep on the back floor of the family van, which had been left unlocked. The little girl said she was tired and went to take a nap without telling her mother because "Mommy was talking to the lady about the furniture, and Mommy told me not to interrupt when grown-ups are talking to each other. So I just came to the van to take a nap." Case closed.

Before beginning an area search, ask those at the scene if a search has already been conducted, and if so, what areas were covered. Officers should never assume that searches conducted, often by distraught parents or others, have been performed in a thorough manner. However, under exigent circumstances, prior search efforts may help officers focus on other alternatives even if their intention is to research those same areas as time permits. The officers should make a quick check of the house and grounds for small children, looking in such places as closets, refrigerators, large boxes and vehicles in garages, storage sheds, under shrubbery, in doghouses, under beds, and behind furniture. The child may have been playing hide-and-seek with an imaginary playmate and fallen asleep. In the case of teenagers overdue home by several hours, the officer should ask the parents if they've checked their answering machine for messages. Perhaps the teenager left a note in the kitchen explaining the absence, and the parents did not find the note. A variety of possible explanations are possible in apparent missing persons cases depending on the circumstances involved, and concerned parents sometimes overlook the obvious.

Step 3: Verify the child's custody status. With divorce so prevalent in the United States and custody battles a common denominator in the lives of many children, the patrol officer should ask the parent if there has been a divorce or separation and, if so, which parent has primary legal custody. If there has been a marital breakup, the officer should raise the issue of a possible abduction of the child by the **noncustodial parent.** Another area of inquiry involves possible emotional problems affecting the child; if the child is taking the parental breakup badly and falsely assuming blame, the child may have run away. All of these issues must be explored, no matter how insensitive the questions may seem under the circumstances.

Step 4: Identify the circumstances of the disappearance. Did the child disappear from home or from the residence of a relative or friend? Is the child missing after a visit with a noncustodial parent? Is the child missing from a public place, such as a shopping mall, park, amusement center, or school playground?

Was the child seen talking to a stranger? Did the child disappear while the parent or guardian's attention was focused elsewhere, such as paying for a purchase or loading groceries into a vehicle? The NCMEC lists several unusual circumstances that alert the first responding patrol officer to "pull out all the stops" by requesting additional personnel, supervisory and investigative assistance, and any special support units that may be needed, such as K-9 and helicopters. The need for other resources, such as assistance from other law enforcement agencies, fire department search and rescue teams, neighborhood watch teams, and others, can be determined by a field supervisor. Unusual circumstances that may require such additional resources include the following:

- The missing child is 13 years old or younger.
- The missing child is believed to be out of the zone of safety for his or her age and developmental stage.
- The missing child is mentally incapacitated, has attempted or threatened suicide, or has a history of self-destructive behavior.
- The missing child is drug dependent, including prescribed medication or illegal substances, and the dependency is potentially life threatening.
- The missing child has been absent from home for more than 24 hours before being reported to the police.
- Based on available information, it is believed that the missing child is in the company of adults who could endanger his or her welfare.
- Based on available information, it is determined that the missing child is in a life-threatening situation.
- The absence is inconsistent with the child's established patterns of behavior, and the deviation cannot be readily explained.
- Other circumstances are involved in the disappearance that would cause a reasonable person to conclude that the child should be considered "at risk."

When one or more of these circumstances is present, the patrol officer should take immediate action and call for mobilization of additional resources. It is always better to overreact when a child's life may be in danger. Resources can be demobilized quickly if it is determined later that they are not needed.

Step 5: Determine when, where, and by whom the missing child was last seen. For example, if the child disappeared while the parent or guardian was paying for groceries, did any of the cashiers, store employees, or other shoppers see the child leave the store with anyone? If the child disappeared while walking to school, did any residents or delivery persons on the child's route witness the child getting into a vehicle? Interview everyone who may have been in a position to see the child.

Step 6: Interview the individuals who last had contact with the child. It is especially important to interview the child's friends if the child is a preteen or teenager. Friends of older children often know more about the child's attitudes, emotions, and plans than the parents or guardians. Perhaps friends will reveal that the child is having trouble with his father and is staying with another friend. A teacher may reveal that the child's noncustodial parent came to the school to get permission to remove the child from school because the child was being taken to a dental appointment. In the case of a child missing from a public place, it is important to interview those persons operating stores, concessions, or amusements that may have attracted the child's attention, leading the child to wander away from parents or guardians. For example, if a small boy wandered into a video arcade, was given quarters by an adult man to play games, and then left the arcade with the man, the operator of the arcade should be able to provide a description of the circumstances and the suspect, along with time frames.

Step 7: Identify the child's zone of safety for his or her age and developmental stage. Try to determine how far the child could travel from the spot where last seen before he or she would most likely be at risk of being injured or exploited. This perimeter should define the first immediate search zone under many circumstances.

Step 8: Make an initial determination of the type of incident. Based on the available information, determine whether the incident appears to be a nonfamily abduction; family abduction; endangered runaway; or lost, injured, or otherwise missing person. This initial classification will help the officer begin investigative actions. To make the initial classification, the officer should analyze the information already gathered. However, officers must be extremely cautious in **labeling,** or classifying, a missing child case, because the classification process will affect the way initial evidence or information is gathered. As the NCMEC advises, even if the initial information suggests a classification into a category considered to be "less urgent," officers should run "parallel investigations" that take all possibilities into account until the case category is clearly determined.

Step 9: Obtain a detailed description of the missing child, suspected abductor(s), vehicles, and the like. If several people are at the scene, each person should be interviewed separately by the officer to obtain descriptions of a possible suspect and vehicle. Witnesses should not be interviewed in the presence of other witnesses because there is a tendency on the part of some to "go along"—either consciously or unconsciously—with a description given by another witness. As most officers know, the perception and recall of witnesses can be faulty, and when they use each other to fill in missing details in their memory, important details may be lost.

Step 10: Relay detailed descriptive information to the EOC for relay to other law enforcement agencies and information referral sources. Supervisors, in consultation with the public information officer or agency chief executive, may decide at this time to provide descriptive information to the news media to generate assistance from the public in locating the missing child or encouraging any witnesses to come forward.

Step 11: Ensure that any remaining persons at the scene are identified and interviewed and information is properly recorded. To aid in this process, take pictures or videotape everyone present, if possible. Note the name, address, and home or business telephone numbers of each person. Determine each person's relationship to the missing child, if any. Note information that each person may have about the child's disappearance. Determine when or where each person last saw the child. Ask each one: "What do you think happened to the child?" Obtain the names, addresses, and telephone numbers of the child's friends and other relatives and friends of the family. Friends, relatives, and neighbors may reveal that there are problems in the home, the child is frequently abused (either verbally or physically), the father or "live-in" boyfriend has a "hot temper," or the mother drinks during the day and screams at the kids. This type of sensitive information may be elicited by the officer; the person being interviewed can be assured of privacy and told that the information provided will not be given to family members. Such information can provide important clues to investigators as to the type of case: a homicide by parents or guardians with lies told to police to cover up the crime, a stranger abduction, or a "runaway" or abused child.

Step 12: Continue to update the emergency dispatcher and other appropriate department personnel. Periodically update the public information officer or department spokesperson. If there is no media relations officer or supervisor on the scene handling these duties, the senior officer at the scene may be asked to provide periodic updates to media personnel. Under such circumstances, the officer must follow the agency's media relations policies and procedures, being careful not to release information that could jeopardize an investigation, falsely accuse individuals, or inadvertently implicate anyone in a crime.

Step 13: Obtain and record permission to search houses or buildings. This includes any locations where the incident took place or where entry is required to conduct the investigation. To search a house or apartment, obtain the permission of the owner or renter. In the case of a building, such as a shopping mall or store, obtain the manager's permission or the permission of any private security firm working on the premises. Be sure to search any surrounding areas, including vehicles, parking lots, storage sheds, garbage containers, truck trailers at loading docks, warehouse areas behind stores, construction sites, shrubbery, culverts, and other places of concealment.

Even if the child was reported missing from a public place, such as a shopping mall, it is highly advisable to seek permission for a thorough search of the child's home. In some recent cases, the child was murdered in the home, leaving bloodstain evidence, and after disposing the body, the parents or guardians drove to a public place (e.g., mall, gas station), called the police and reported that the child had been abducted from that location. By not searching the home, vital evidence of a crime can be lost.

Step 14: Secure and safeguard the crime scene. This includes securing the area where the incident took place or the location at which the child was last seen as a crime scene in order to safeguard vital evidence. The patrol officer must take control of the immediate area where the incident occurred and establish an appropriate perimeter to avoid destruction of vital evidence.

It is not uncommon for even well-intentioned citizens at a public site to overrun a crime scene, inadvertently destroying or otherwise carrying off such evidence as fibers, hair, cigarette butts, dropped credit card slips and driver's licenses, a weapon, or other possessions with fingerprints. Pedestrian and vehicular traffic at such locations can also destroy any scent trails that may be used by canine teams to track the missing child. Under exigent circumstances and until backup arrives, the patrol officer may obtain assistance from store managers, private security officers, school principals, and other trusted authority figures to block off crime scenes. As soon as possible, backup should be requested to help safeguard a potential crime scene.

At the child's home or crime scene, items of evidential value and other personal effects that may assist in locating the child should be protected and, if appropriate, collected. These include, but are not limited to, the child's personal articles such as a hairbrush; diary; photographs; and items with the child's fingerprints, footprints, or teeth impressions. The contents and appearance of the child's room and residence should be noted. If possible, photographs or videotapes of these areas should be taken.

The child's current bedsheets can be collected, if appropriate, for use by search dog teams and, under some circumstances, may be necessary for later crime laboratory analysis. Recent photos and family videos may also be useful for release to the media if this option becomes necessary. In many cases, widespread use of a child's photo in the media has precipitated telephone tips that have successfully concluded investigations.

The officer should also obtain a set of the child's fingerprints if the parents have had a set prepared as a crime prevention measure. If a fingerprint card is not available, items should be secured from the child's room that are likely to contain prints, such as a smooth plastic or metal toy, drinking glass, TV remote control, comic books, or game boxes.

Officers should adhere to established department policies and procedures for crime scene processing. However, in addition, when investigating cases of missing children, officers are advised to treat the crime scene processing assignment with a "worst-case scenario" in mind.

Step 15: Obtain photos, videotapes, and any other identifying information on suspects. In particular, any photos of the suspect should be relayed to the shift commander as soon as possible. In some cases, the first responder may be able to secure photos or videos. For example, store security cameras may provide valuable videotape. In other cases, such as an abduction by a noncustodial parent, the custodial parent or child's school may be able to provide a current photograph, address, place of employment, and other identifying information. When a license tag number can help identify a suspect, the state department of motor vehicles can generally quickly provide a photo. If the suspect has an arrest record, photos may be available in local, state, or federal law enforcement records systems.

Step 16: Prepare reports and make all required notifications. Ensure that information about the missing child is entered into the FBI's NCIC Missing Persons File and that any information on a suspected abductor is entered into the NCIC Wanted Persons File.

FIGURE 12.5 26 year-old Vinson Filya, who abducted 14-year-old Elizabeth Shoaf as she stepped off a school bus in 2006. Shoaf was kept in an underground bunker, where she text messaged her mother from Filyaw's cell phone while he slept. Copyright 2006, USA Today. Reprinted with permission.

The NCMEC recommends that a law enforcement agency take several other steps to publicize the incident, to receive tips from the public and obtain help with a widespread search. These measures, which are usually carried out by administrative personnel rather than the first responder or patrol officer, include:

1. Ensure that the details of the case have been reported to the NCMEC.

2. Prepare and update bulletins for local law enforcement agencies, state missing children's clearinghouses, FBI, and other appropriate agencies.

3. Prepare a flyer or bulletin with the child's and suspected abductor's photographs and descriptive information. Distribute it in appropriate geographical regions.

4. Secure the child's latest medical and dental records. These may be necessary to positively identify the child.

5. Establish a telephone hotline to receive tips and leads from the public.

6. Establish a leads management system to prioritize leads and ensure that each one undergoes a review and follow-up.

The Investigator's Role

Many of the duties of the investigator in a missing or abducted child case are the same as those used in conducting almost any type of investigation. Indeed, some have been referenced in foregoing chapters related to the first responding officer and supervisory responsibilities. However, investigative officers can take eight basic steps to help ensure a successful outcome in a missing or abducted child case. These procedures are geared more toward nonfamily abduction cases and situations in which a child disappears and could be in danger. Family abduction and runaway (or lost) child investigative procedures are covered in depth in the NCMEC's manual.

Step 1: Obtain a detailed briefing from the first responding officer and other on-scene personnel. The investigator should debrief the first responding officer before conducting any interviews with family members of the missing child or witnesses who may have been identified in the early stages of the case. A thorough debriefing of the first responder will help the investigator analyze the information in order to formulate an approach to upcoming interviews of family members and witnesses.

Step 2: Verify the accuracy of all descriptive information. The verification process should include all other details developed during the preliminary investigation. At this, point the investigator should begin interviewing the missing child's family members and possible witnesses to determine the facts and sort out any conflicting information obtained by the first responder and other officers on the scene.

Step 3: Obtain a brief recent history of family dynamics. This process will help the investigator hypothesize about various possibilities involving the disappearance of the child. Was the family the truly loving, close-knit family the mother tearfully described to the first responder? Or were there previous police calls to the residence for domestic disturbances? Has the child's school reported the family to social service agencies for possible abuse of the child? Is there a large life insurance policy on a four-year-old child? If so, why? Is the missing little girl an "ugly duckling" with a learning disability while the mother is the glamorous "prom queen" type with a live-in boyfriend who spends all his money on drugs

FIGURE 12.6 A hole in the ground where Filyaw kept hostage Elizabeth Shoaf less than one mile from her home. Courtesy of Jim Davenport, AP Wide World Photos.

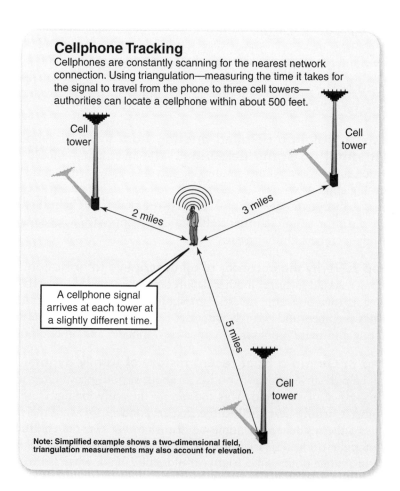

FIGURE 12.7 Cell phone tracking technology that resulted in the locating of Elizabeth Shoaf. USA Today.

and alcohol? Answers to such questions, often obtained from neighbors, friends of the child, and other family members, can offer invaluable insights to what may have happened to the child and where the child may now be located.

Step 4: Explore the basis for conflicting information. Information offered by witnesses and other individuals may not coincide. As such, the investigator needs to conduct in-depth fact-finding interviews with all witnesses, friends, and relatives of the child and the child's parents or guardians necessary to resolve those conflicts. It is at this point that the investigator may consider asking the parents or guardians to submit to a polygraph examination.

After the investigator has interviewed all relevant persons, it is necessary to again meet with the first responder, fellow investigators, and the supervising officer to "compare notes" and work through any conflicting information gathered in the course of the investigation. This collaborative process should provide the investigative staff with a solid foundation upon which to structure the future direction of the case.

Step 5: Review and evaluate all available information and evidence. At this point, an information management system becomes a critical tool in the investigative process. The investigator should designate another investigator, a crime analyst, or a patrol officer to serve as the case information manager, centralizing all data as they are gathered, making comparisons, and keeping track of leads and tips. Appointing one person to be in charge of all information pertaining to the case helps ensure that valuable data will not become misdirected and possibly lost.

Depending on the resources available to the agency, data may be computerized or incorporated into a simple card system, in which facts are indexed for cross-reference and easily available for prompt review. The method of filing does not matter as long as the system works for the investigator in charge of solving the case.

After the incoming data and evidence have been organized, reviewed, and evaluated, the investigator can develop and execute an investigative follow-up plan and secure necessary additional resources, personnel, and specialized services.

Step 6: Develop an investigative plan for follow-up. By evaluating evidence and the information gathered from interviews of police officers, witnesses, the child's parents or guardians, and others, the investigator can prepare a follow-up plan, which may include the following tasks:

1. Conduct more in-depth interviews with specific people who have been questioned previously.
2. Set up lead-tracking policies and procedures.
3. Gather more complete background information on the missing child, parents or guardians, and possible suspects.
4. Reevaluate the scene and conduct a more detailed search.
5. Canvass the neighborhood to locate potential witnesses and information.
6. Search the child's home even if the child is missing from another location.
7. Obtain search warrants when consent for a search is denied.
8. Administer polygraph examinations to the parents or guardians if officers and investigators suspect they are not telling the truth or something seems awry.
9. Contact social service agencies and the child's school to determine whether the child's family was the subject of abuse investigations or had other problems that may be significant to the progress of the investigation.

Step 7: Determine what additional resources and specialized services are required. At this point, the investigator's assessment of the type of incident (e.g., abducted child, possible abduction, family abduction, lost child, or runaway) should help determine what additional assistance may be needed both from within the department and from outside agencies. For example, the investigator may have been told by a relative of the child that the child's parents appeared in family court to answer child neglect charges. The investigator can save time by asking the police juvenile officer to follow up this lead with the family court and social service agency assigned to the family's case. The juvenile officer could also contact teachers where the missing child attends school and might even interview parents of the child's playmates.

If an abduction is suspected and it can be assumed that the child may be transported to another jurisdiction, the investigator may want to contact the FBI for help, along with the NCMEC, state police, state missing children clearinghouses, and other law enforcement agencies in the region. An excellent checklist for investigating Internet-related missing children's cases is provided in the NCMEC manual.

Step 8: Execute an investigative follow-up plan. The procedures initiated by the investigator depend on the type of case—runaway, family kidnapping, suspected abduction by a stranger, or lost child. Although the procedures are similar to those involved in investigating other major cases, investigators should be aware that the missing or abducted child case may bring the added factor of emotional stress and that the degree of stress will vary depending on the circumstances of the case.

The 2003 Child Protection Act (Amber Alerts)

In September 2006, Vinson Filyaw, a 26-year-old unemployed construction worker, approached 14-year-old Elizabeth Shoaf as she stepped off her school bus in Lugoff, South Carolina. Posing as a police officer, Filyaw used handcuffs to restrain Elizabeth and dragged her back to a bunker located near his rural trailer home. Filyaw told Elizabeth that the entrance to the bunker was booby-trapped and warned her that if she tried to escape or if anyone tried to rescue her, a bomb would detonate. While Filyaw had Elizabeth in his custody, he sexually assaulted her.

For 10 days, family members, police, and volunteers conducted a sweeping search for Elizabeth but found few clues. Elizabeth engineered her own remarkable rescue by snatching Filyaw's cell phone as he slept and sending a text message to her mother describing the location where she was being held. Investigators using cell phone tracking technology traced the call to Filyaw's cell phone. Investigators deducted Elizabeth's kidnapper was, in all likelihood, a known sex offender who was suspected of a sexual assault against a 12-year-old relative.

Using the signal from a nearby cell tower to triangulate her location, authorities began scouring the area and were able to rescue her. Police also seized a cache of pornography, canned goods, cheap generic cigarettes, homemade hand-grenades, and incendiary devices fashioned out of black powder from fireworks. They did not, however, find Filyaw.

After a failed attempt to hijack a car to make his escape, Filyaw was found walking along the side of Interstate 20. He was charged with kidnapping, first-degree sexual assault, impersonating a police officer, and possession of incendiary devices.

This case illustrates the seriousness and reality of child abductions and points to the need for community and police cooperation in the investigative phase. It also shows the importance of Amber Alerts and how they provide much-needed and timely information regarding child abductions.

In April 2003, President George W. Bush signed into law the so-called Child Protection Bill, which encourages states to establish **Amber Alert** systems to quickly post information about child abductions. The measure was hailed as an important milestone in the protection of America's children because when a child is reported missing, the case becomes a matter of the most intense and focused effort by law enforcement.

The law also enhanced penalties for youth abductions and child sex crimes, boosted funding for missing and exploited children programs, and increased penalties on those convicted of child pornography, including images created digitally.

The Amber Alert system makes use of radio, television, roadside electronic billboards, and emergency broadcast systems to disseminate information about kidnapping suspects and victims soon after the abduction of a child younger than age 18 years is reported. In such cases, authorities say, the child could be killed or seriously injured a short time after being kidnapped.

The alerts, named after a 9-year-old Texas girl, Amber Hagerman, who was kidnapped and killed in 1996, are in effect in 41 states at the time of this writing. Amber's mother, Donna Norris, attended the bill-signing ceremony along with the survivors of two high-profile kidnapping cases, Jacqueline Marris and Tamara Brooks, two California teenagers rescued in the first use of the system in that state, and Utah teen Elizabeth Smart, whose father, Ed Smart, called for a national Amber Alert system after her recovery in March 2003.

One of the primary purposes of the new law is to encourage states to develop Amber Alert systems of their own. Attorney General John Ashcroft stated the bills aim to create a "seamless" system across the country. After the signing of the bill, an Amber Alert coordinator was appointed at the Justice Department to assist states and was designated $10 million for the establishment of the initiative.

Interviewing Suspects in Abductions

After a suspect has been identified, the investigator must carefully plan an interview to gain as much information as possible without violating the suspect's constitutional rights. A checklist of sample questions to ask a suspect may include:

- What do you think should happen to someone who would do this?
- Have you ever done this before?
- Have you ever thought of doing this before?
- Did you do it?
- Do you know who could have done this?
- Explain to me why . . .
- Do you keep a diary, calendar, notebook, or computer? Can I look at it?
- Have you ever been arrested for this type of crime before?
- Have you ever been questioned about this type of crime before?
- Do you own, possess, or have access to (items described by witnesses)?
- Do you know this child? His or her family? The family's business?
- Is there any reason why someone would accuse you of this?
- If it becomes necessary, would you . . . (submit to a polygraph, give fingerprints, stand in a lineup)?
- Would you let me search your . . . (car, house, storage locker, other places)?

- How do you react to stress?
- What is your general mode of transportation?
- Do you drive around a lot? Go places unannounced?
- What are your sleeping habits?
- Do you ever lie? If so, how frequently, under what circumstances, and why?

During the interview, treat the subject with consideration but be firm. As soon as the interview begins, size up the subject—is he or she intelligent, emotional, or very self-assured? Be prepared for the interview by gathering as many facts as possible about the incident before confronting the subject.

As the interview progresses, the effective investigator may obtain more answers by being a good listener—letting the subject talk, not trying to manipulate what the subject is saying. Concentrate on how the subject answers questions as much as what he or she says. Also watch the subject's body language and facial expressions. Encourage the subject to tell it in his or her own words, emphasizing that the subject should tell you all the facts. At the same time, do not be visibly shocked by anything the subject says—if an investigator shows shock by facial expressions or a look of disgust, the subject could begin to gain the upper hand in the interview. If necessary, the investigator should be empathetic. Be patient and do not expect to obtain answers to all questions quickly. Ask questions that require more than a yes or no answer. Some examples are:

- Tell me what happened then . . .
- I'd like to hear more about . . .
- And what happened then . . . ?

Don't rush the subject; set aside sufficient time for a thorough interview. Be direct and professional—do not make the subject guess what information is needed. Allow the subject to "save face" if embarrassing questions are asked. If the subject feels humiliated, the interview may come to an abrupt halt. Avoid using technical terms or police slang.

As the interview is drawing to a close, try to get the subject to help time-orient the facts, putting them in chronological order. Be aware of what the subject did not say during the interview.

One of the most important procedures to follow throughout the interview is to observe the subject's due process rights (Fourth and Fifth Amendments). Throughout the missing or abducted child investigation, be certain to take all precautions to observe the legal rights of any potential suspects so that a successfully investigated case will not be lost in court.

CASE IN POINT:

The Abduction of Elizabeth Smart

In 2002, 14-year-old Elizabeth Smart was abducted at gunpoint from her home in Salt Lake City. After a considerable amount of publicity and a search conducted by literally thousands of police and volunteers, investigators were unable to develop solid leads in the case. It wasn't until Elizabeth's own younger sister recalled a workman who visited the Smart home in 2001 that a suspect was developed.

On March 12, 2003, almost nine months after she was abducted, Brian David Mitchell, 49, was arrested and charged with kidnapping. Elizabeth was found in his custody and safely returned to her parents. During her captivity, she was allegedly sexually assaulted several times. Later, it was discovered that her mother, Lois Smart, had picked up Mitchell off the street in downtown Salt Lake City in 2001 and

CASE IN POINT continued

brought him home to do some minor chores. Mitchell had spent several hours raking leaves and repairing the roof. During that time, he also observed Elizabeth, who was home at the time.

Sources: CNN News. (2002). *Interview with Jake and Kathleen Garn,* June 18. Available at http://transcripts.cnn.com/TRANSCRIPTS/0206/

18/ltm.01.html; Cosgrove-Mather, B. (2004). Elizabeth Smart, one year later. CBS News, May 24. Available at http://www.cbsnews.com/stories/2004/03/03/national/main603816.shtml; Smart, T. (2005). *In plain sight: The startling truth behind the Elizabeth Smart investigation.* Chicago: Chicago Review Press.

CASE IN POINT:

Investigating the Disappearance of Stacy Peterson

On October 18, 2003, Bolingbrook, Illinois Police Officer Drew Peterson married Stacy Ann Peterson (Cales). Stacy, Peterson's fourth wife, went missing on October 28, 2007, and was officially reported missing in the early hours of October 29, 2007, after her sister, Cassandra Cales, failed to hear from her when expected. Drew Peterson claimed that Stacy called him at 9 P.M. on Sunday to tell him

that she had left him for another man and that she had left her car at Bolingbrook's Clow International Airport.

Peterson had a 29-year career as a police officer. He began working with the Bolingbrook Police Department in 1977. A year later, he was assigned to Metropolitan Area Narcotics Squad, and in 1979, he was awarded "Police Officer of the Year" from the

FIGURE 12.8 Photo of Stacy Peterson.

CASE IN POINT continued

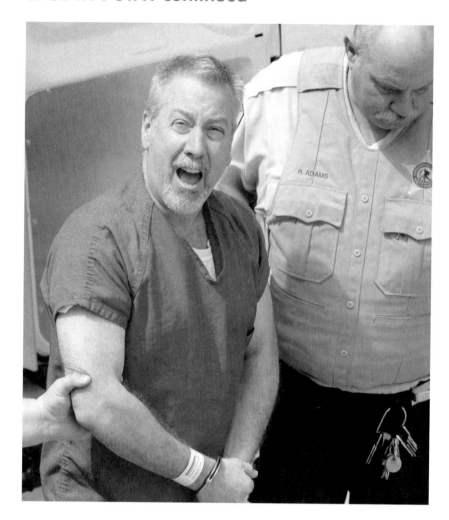

FIGURE 12.9 Photo of Drew Peterson.

department. In 1985, he was fired from the Bolingbrook Police Department after the village board of police and fire commissioners found him guilty of disobedience, conducting a self-assigned investigation, failure to report a bribe immediately, and official misconduct. He had been indicted two months earlier on charges of official misconduct and failure to report a bribe.

Indictments alleged that Peterson solicited drugs in exchange for information about his agency. The charges were later dropped. Special prosecutor Raymond Bolden said at the time that the charges were not provable. Peterson won reinstatement with the department in March 1986. Judge Edwin Grabiec ruled that police and fire commissioners lacked sufficient evidence to find Peterson guilty of the charges. Peterson was also accused of using excessive force for allegedly breaking the thumb of an arrestee in May 2007. The charges were later dismissed on the grounds that Peterson was not present during the arrest nor on duty that day.

After Stacy's (his fourth wife) disappearance on October 28, 2007, Peterson retired as a Bolingbrook police sergeant on December 2007. On November 15, 2007, the Bolingbrook Police Pension Board voted to allow Peterson to collect his pension of $6,067.71 per month, stating current law gave them no option because Peterson had not been convicted of a crime.

Peterson's wives: Peterson's first wife was Carol (Hamilton) Brown. The two were married from 1974 to 1980 and divorced after she learned about his infidelity. Peterson's second wife was Victoria Connolly, who he married in 1982. Connolly has alleged a history of abuse during her 10-year marriage to Peterson, as has her daughter, who lived in the household during this time, from the age of 8 to 17 years. In 2007, Connolly stated that Peterson "was a legend in his own mind." The couple divorced after Peterson started dating Kathleen Savio, who later became his third wife. Peterson's divorce from Carol Brown was finalized on February 18, 1992. He married Savio two months later.

Peterson and Savio were married until their divorce on October 10, 2003. Reportedly, between 2002 and 2004, police were called out to the Peterson house 18 times on domestic disturbance calls. On March 1, 2004, Kathleen Savio's body was found in a waterless bathtub. Her death was initially ruled an accidental drowning by a coroner's jury that included a police officer who personally knew Peterson and assured the other jurors that Peterson was "a good man who would never hurt his wife."

However, after Stacy Peterson's disappearance, Savio's body was exhumed and underwent forensic examination on November 16, 2007. Dr. Michael Baden, a former New York City chief medical examiner who conducted the examination at the request of Savio's relatives and Fox News, concluded that she died of drowning following a struggle when her body was placed in the bathtub. Illinois State Attorney James Glasgow told the press that after examining evidence in the case, he believed that the death was a "homicide staged to look like an accident." On February 21, 2008, Glasgow announced that a pathologist determined that Savio's death was a homicide, adding that the death had been investigated as such reopening the case after the exhumation.

The investigation: The Illinois State Police, along with agents from the FBI, investigated a number of leads in Stacy's disappearance and the death of Kathleen Savio. Four search warrants were executed on Drew Peterson's property after Stacy's disappearance, including seizure of his vehicle and Stacys vehicle and of Drew's 11 firearms.

A long-time friend of Peterson, Rick Mims, admitted that he and Peterson bought three blue containers from a cable company where they both worked part time in 2003. Mims also provided photos of the containers to police and has sold his story to the tabloids for an undisclosed sum of money. Peterson's stepbrother, Thomas Morphey, who has a history of drug and alcohol addiction, attempted suicide two days after allegedly helping Drew carry a large blue plastic container from Peterson's Bolingbrook home to his sport utility vehicle, fearing he may have helped dispose of the body of Stacy Peterson.

Neighbors reported seeing Peterson and another man hauling a 55-gallon barrel, large enough to hold a person, out of the house shortly after Stacy's disappearance. There were also reports of truckers referring to the containers, but their stories were treated as not credible after it was found they were not in the Bolingbrook area at the times they claimed.

One theory was that Stacy Peterson was romantically involved with Scott Anthony Rossetto or his brother Keith Rosetto, both of Shorewood, Illinois. Both Rosetto brothers denied this allegation. Investigators have speculated that Peterson's body may have been dumped near Rossetto's home in an effort to frame him as the killer.

On May 7, 2009, Peterson was indicted by the Will County Grand Jury and arrested for the murder of his third wife, Kathleen Savio. Bail was set at $20 million. While being arrested, Peterson joked, "I guess I should have returned those library books." As of the writing of this text, Drew Peterson has not been convicted of either the death of Stacy Peterson or Kathleen Savio.

Thematic question: Among other important questions, do you believe, based on evidence set forth in this section, that Drew Peterson was responsible for the deaths of Stacey Peterson, Kathleen Savio, or both? To what extent does the evidence support your conclusion, and what additional evidence should be identified to support or refute the criminal charges?

Sources: Walberg, M. & J. Napolitano. *Expert: 3rd wife was slain.* Chicago Tribune. 17 November 2007; Hosey, J. and J. Lundquist. *The man Stacy turned to.* The Bolingbrook Sun. 18 November 2007; Slife, E., *EXCLUSIVE: Peterson's second wife tells her story.* Chicago Tribune. 16 November 2007. Peterson case: Did cops protect one of their own? November 30; Fox Chicago. (2007). Drew Peterson is Now Accused of Police Brutality. myfoxchicago.com, December 17; Fox News. (2007). Missing mom Stacy Peterson's family wants husband, Drew, to take lie detector test, November 30; NBC5.com Chicago. (2007). Peterson's family demands Drew take lie detector test, November 27; Fox News. (2009). Drew Peterson charged with murdering third wife, held on $20M bond, May 7. Available at http://www.foxnews.com/story/0,2933,519392,00.html; Savio V. (2007). Peterson complaint. Available at http://www.scribd.com/doc/14542696/Savio-v-Peterson-Complaint; Slife, E. (2007). Peterson's second wife tells her story. Chicago Tribune, November 16; Tarm, M. (2007). Relatives try to confront Ill. officer. Available at ABC News.com, November 17.

Summary Checklist

The magnitude of the missing and abducted problem is complex, multifaceted, and disturbing. For example, there are different types of missing children, including family abductions; endangered runaways; nonfamily abductions; and lost, injured, or otherwise missing children. See how well you are able to answer the following questions in your checklist.

(continued)

Summary Checklist (Continued)

1. Do you understand the extent that missing and abducted persons are a Problem?

- Over the past 26 years, reports of missing persons have increased sixfold, from roughly 150,000 in 1980 to about 900,000 in 2006.

- In 2005, an alarming 2,300 Americans were reported missing every day.

- The U.S. Justice Department identified 840,279 missing persons cases in 2001.

- The National Center for Missing Adults in Phoenix, Arizona, consistently tracks about 48,000 "active cases."

- Slightly more than half—about 25,500—of the missing are men. About four out of 10 missing adults are white, three of 10 black, and two of 10 are Latino.

- About half of the roughly 800,000 missing juvenile cases in 2005 involved runaways, and another 200,000 were classified as family abductions related to domestic or custody disputes.

- According to the NISMART survey, more than 203,900 children are abducted by a family member in America each year.

- NISMART concluded that 69 percent of abduction victims were female and 80 percent were younger than 14 years old.

2. Can you identify the different types of abductions?

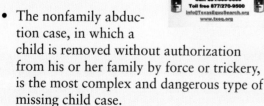

Missing children cases fall into three basic categories, nonfamily abduction, family abduction, and runaway (or lost).

- The nonfamily abduction case, in which a child is removed without authorization from his or her family by force or trickery, is the most complex and dangerous type of missing child case.

- The family abduction generally occurs in conjunction with divorce and separation.

- The runaway or lost child is the third category.

Some child abductions have been connected to the Internet as a result of the easy access both child and predator have to this worldwide communications network.

3. Do you know the Legislative history of dealing with missing and abducted children?

At one time, no federal agency had responsibility or jurisdiction to investigate these cases. Kidnapped, lost, and missing people were considered a problem best dealt with by local law enforcement.

- In 1968, the U.S. Congress addressed this with the passage of the Uniform Child Custody Jurisdiction Act (UCCJA), which made the practice of moving to another state for the purpose of changing custody illegal.

- In 1980, Congress passed the Parental Kidnapping Prevention Act to strengthen the UCCJA and allowed states to use the Federal Parent Locator Service to obtain address information on noncustodial parents who abducted their children.

- In 1982, Congress changed National Crime Information Center (NCIC) rules to allow the entry of missing children into the system.

- The Missing Children Act of 1982 allowed the entry of these missing children even though the noncustodial parent would not be charged with a crime.

- In 1988, the International Child Abduction Remedies Act was passed, whereby the U.S. Department of State would become involved in noncustodial parental abductions in which the abducting parent takes the victim outside the boundaries of the United States.

- In 1990, Congress again stepped up and passed the National Child Search Assistance Act (NCSAA), mandating law enforcement agencies to enter each reported missing child (younger than

18 years of age) into NCIC, including all reported runaways.

- in 1994, Congress passed the Jacob Wetterling Crimes Against Children and Sexually Violent Offender Registration Act, designed to determine the number of sex offenders and provide law enforcement with a readily accessible database with possible suspect information if a child goes missing.

The passing of these laws demonstrates that the focus and extent of this problem has changed dramatically, especially since 1980.

In 2003, Congress took a monumental step in fighting child abductions with the passage of the Prosecutorial Remedies and Other Tools to End the Exploitation of Children Today Act, or, more commonly, the PROTECT Act.

- The PROTECT Act also created the AMBER (America's Missing: Broadcast Emergency Response) Alert system.

4. Can you identify the steps in the investigative process for child kidnapping?

By its very nature, abduction must take priority over many types of cases.

- Research has indicated that strangers who commit the offense with the intention of fulfilling a sexual desire often murder their victims within three hours.

Abductions can be even more complex than some murders.

Early in the investigation, agencies may want to request an off-line search from NCIC.

The initial response to a missing child call is perhaps the most crucial component of the investigation.

- The manner in which patrol officers respond to the initial call often determines whether the child is found quickly and returned home safely, remains missing for months or years, or is never found.

Before the patrol officer even arrives on the scene, information about the missing child should be relayed from the dispatcher to the responding officers. This should include:

- History of violence or child abuse calls
- Criminal activities of family members or other persons living at the address (e.g., arrests, narcotics)
- Runaway reports on the child or siblings
- Juvenile delinquency reports on the child or siblings

5. Do you know the investigator's role in investigating child abductions?

Many of the duties of the investigator in a missing or abducted child case are the same as those used in conducting almost any type of investigation.

There are eight basic steps that investigative officers can take to help ensure a successful outcome in a missing or abducted child case.

These procedures are geared more toward nonfamily abduction cases and situations in which a child disappears and could be in danger.

- Obtain a detailed briefing from the first responding officer and other on-scene personnel.
- Verify the accuracy of all descriptive information.
- Obtain a brief recent history of family dynamics.
- Explore the basis for conflicting information.
- Review and evaluate all available information and evidence.
- Develop an investigative plan for follow-up.
- Determine what additional resources and specialized services are required.
- Execute an investigative follow-up plan.

Key Terms

Amber Alert
Code Adam
family abduction
labeling

National Center for Missing and
Exploited Children (NCMEC)
National Incidence Studies of
Missing, Abducted, Runaway and

Throwaway Children (NISMART)
noncustodial parent
nonfamily abduction
runaway or lost child

Discussion Questions

1. List and discuss the three types of missing persons cases discussed in this chapter.

2. Explain the significance of the NISMART data on abducted children.

3. Explain how it can be determined if a missing child case is a result of an Internet lure.

4. List and discuss the duties of a responding officer to a missing person call.

5. List and discuss the steps that a criminal investigator should follow in the investigation of a missing person.

6. Discuss the origin, function, and utility of Amber Alerts.

7. Identify the types of questions that should be asked of a suspect in a child abduction case.

mycrimekit™

Go to MyCrimeKit.com to explore the following study tools and resources specific to this chapter:

- *Practice Quiz:* Multiple-choice, true/false, short-answer, and essay questions.

- *Flashcards:* There are nine key terms in this chapter. Flashcards test your knowledge of the chapter's key terms.

- *Web Links:* Check out the hotlink to The New York Times criminology articles.

- *Career Center:* Check out the hot links to interesting careers in criminal justice, criminology, and juvenile justice.

- *The Research Center:* Check out the Cybrary and research navigator for even more resources.

Notes

1. See: http://www.nydailynews.com/news/national/2009/09/01/2009-09-01_phillip_garrido_charged_with_kidnapping_jaycee_lee_dugard_told_court_he_stalked_.html

2. See: http://www.telegraph.co.uk/news/worldnews/northamerica/usa/6101545/Jaycee-Lee-Dugard-walks-into-police-station-18-years-after-disappearance.html

3. Moore, Matthew (2009). "Jaycee Lee Dugard walks into police station 18 years after disappearance". The Register, August 27. http://www.telegraph.co.uk/news/worldnews/northamerica/usa/6101545/Jaycee-Lee-Dugard-walks-into-police-station-18-years-after-disappearance.html

4. J. Wolak, K. Mitchell, and D. Finkelhor (2006). *On-line victimizations of youth.* Washington, D.C.: Office of Juvenile Justice Programs. National Center for Missing and Exploited Children.

5. Flores, J. R. (2002). *National Incidence Studies of Missing, Abducted, Runaway and Throwaway Children (NISMART).* Washington, DC: U.S. Department of Justice, October.

6. Flores, J. R. (1999). *Non-family abducted children: National estimates and characteristics.* Washington, DC: Administrator of Office of Juvenile Justice and Delinquency Prevention.

7. Flores, J. R. (2002). *National Incidence Studies of Missing, Abducted, Runaway and Throwaway Children (NISMART).* Washington, DC: U.S. Department of Justice, October. This study commissioned by the US Department of Justice, Office of Juvenile Justice and Delinquency Prevention found that there were only approximately 115 stereotypical stranger abductions in 1999.

8. Ibid.

9. Ibid.

10. Allender, D. (2007). Child abductions: Nightmares in progress. *FBI Law Enforcement Bulletin* 76(7).

11. 18 U.S.C. § 1201(a)(1)

12. Ibid.

13. 19 U.S.C, Chapter 16.

14. 18 U.S.C. § 1073.

15. 28 U.S.C. § 534.
16. 42 U.S.C. § 5771.
17. 42 U.S.C. §§ 11601-11610.
18. 42 U.S.C. § 5779.
19. 18 U.S.C. § 1204.
20. 42 U.S.C. § 14071.
21. The FBI's Uniform Crime Reporting Program has no category for abductions per se. It has a listing in Part II offenses for those against family and children, but because Part I offenses take precedence, a child abducted and raped will be counted as a forcible rape in most agencies.
22. ALLENDER, D. (2007). Child abductions: Nightmares in progress. *FBI Law Enforcement Bulletin* 76(7).
23. 18 U.S.C. § 2252.
24. For additional information, access U.S. Department of Justice Office of Justice Programs. Amber Alert. Available at http://www.amberalert.gov.
25. National Center for Missing & Exploited Children. Available at http://www.missingkids.com.
26. ALLENDER, D. (2007). Child abductions: Nightmares in progress. *FBI Law Enforcement Bulletin* 76(7).
27. IBID.
28. CROFT, R. (2006). Folklore, families and fear: Understanding consumption decisions through the oral tradition. *Journal of Marketing Management* 22(9/10):1053-1076.
29. IBID.
30. IBID.
31. The NCMEC can be contacted as a source for both model policies and excellent training, which it provides at no cost to a wide variety of agencies working with children.
32. ALLENDER, D. (2007). Child abductions: Nightmares in progress. *FBI Law Enforcement Bulletin* 76(7).
33. National Center for Missing and Exploited Children (1994). *Missing and abducted children*. Available at www. missingkids.com.

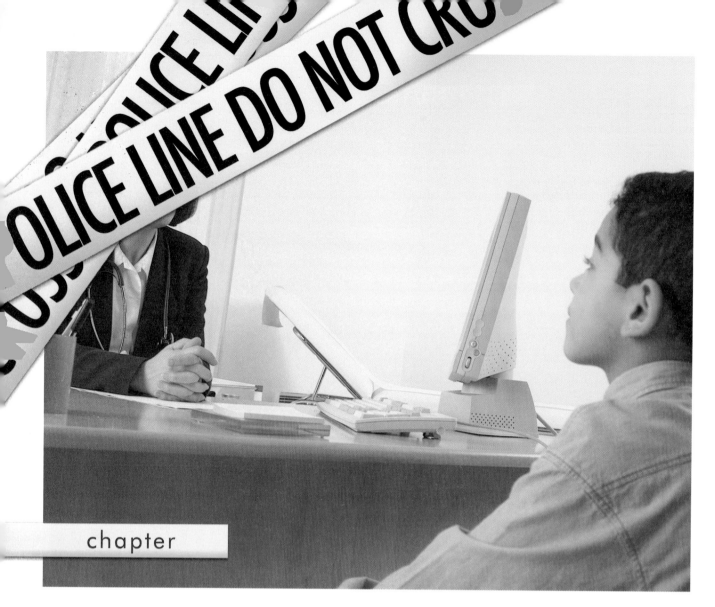

13

Crimes Against Children: Child Abuse and Child Fatalities

This chapter will enable you to:

- Describe the roles and distinctions between the pedophile and the child molester.
- Understand the problem of child abuse and the investigator's response to the problem.
- Identify various techniques of child molestation investigations.
- Discuss the role of the medical profession in cases involving sexual misconduct with children.
- Identify interview techniques for child victims of sexual misconduct.
- Understand problems associated with placing children on the witness stand in criminal trials.

Introduction

In March 2004, emergency crews in Crystal Lake, Illinois, responded to a call for assistance at the home of 44-year-old Kathy Leonard. When they arrived they found Leonard's son, 15-year-old Seamus M. Leonard, who had cerebral palsy, lying dead amid piles of trash. Emergency personnel commented to local media that the condition of this victim was worse than any victim they had ever seen. McHenry County State's Attorney Gary Pack told *The Crystal Lake Northwest Herald*, "It would bring anyone to tears."

A subsequent autopsy revealed the boy died of pneumonia; malnutrition was listed as a contributing cause. Six other children, ages three to 17 years, who also lived in the home, were placed in protective custody under the State Department of Children and Family Services.

After the discovery, the home was deemed uninhabitable by the city's building department and county health department. Case workers from the Illinois Division of Children and Family Services had actually visited the home in January 2003, one year earlier, after a domestic violence complaint. They claimed that there were no indicators of child neglect during their visit. Leonard was arrested and charged with involuntary manslaughter in the death of her son.

The Abuse of Children

The Leonard case illustrates the complexity of **child abuse** cases. The numbers of child abuse cases, of course, reflect only those cases that come to the attention of the police. Statistics show that many more cases exist. In fact, every year in the United States, tens of thousands of children die from a variety of causes, including illness, diseases, accidents, suicides, and homicides. Each death is a heartbreaking event for the child's family and a tragic loss for society.

When a child's death is sudden and unexpected, the tragedy is compounded if law enforcement is unable to conduct a proper investigation. If the investigation is flawed, two outcomes—neither acceptable—are very real possibilities. First is that an innocent person will be suspected or accused of either a crime that did not occur or a crime for which the person has no responsibility. Secondly a real crime will remain undetected or unsolved and the person responsible for the fatal maltreatment of the child will never be identified or brought to justice.

Although the vast majority of child deaths are related to natural causes or accidents, all sudden and unexpected child deaths must be properly investigated. Every day, at least four children in the United States die from maltreatment. Only by thoroughly investigating all sudden and unexpected child deaths can society be certain that maltreatment is not involved. Professionally conducted investigations of child fatalities ensure that innocent people are not falsely accused of wrongdoing and guilty people are not allowed to escape arrest and prosecution and possibly harm another child.

The Scope of the Problem

The problem of child abuse is a considerable public concern and statistics are alarming. For example, in 2006, the National Center for Victims of Violent Crime reported the following:[1]

- An estimated 896,000 children were victims of maltreatment (neglect or abuse)
- Fifty-two percent of child maltreatment victims were girls and 48 percent were boys

- Fifty-four percent of all child victims were white, 26 percent were African American, and 11 percent were Hispanic. American Indians or Alaska Natives accounted for 2 percent of victims and Asian-Pacific Islanders accounted for 1 percent of victims
- Approximately 40 percent of child victims were maltreated solely by their mothers, another 19 percent were maltreated solely by their fathers, and 18 percent were abused by both parents. Child victims abused by a non-parental perpetrator accounted for 13 percent of the total
- The youngest children (from birth through age three years) were the most likely to experience recurring maltreatment
- Children abused by someone other than a parent were 16 percent less likely to experience recurrence than children who were abused by their mother
- Victimization rates are inversely proportional to the age of the child—the older the child, the less likely he or she is to be maltreated
- In 2002, an estimated 1,400 children died due to child abuse or neglect. Five percent of child molesters released from prison commit a new sex offense within three years of their release
- Twenty-nine children were murdered by their babysitters in 2003
- Victims of child abuse comprised 21 percent of the recipients of crime victim compensation in 2003

Nearly 3 million cases of child abuse and neglect were reported in 1993, according to the National Committee on the Prevention of Child Abuse (NCPCA), a 23 percent increase in only five years. Of these cases, about 1,300 resulted in death. However, these reported cases represent only a portion of all actual instances of child abuse. In addition, the escalation of drug abuse in the United States has added another tragic dimension to the child abuse problem.

Child abuse, in all its varied forms, is a symptom of a pathologic social environment in general and a signal of a family in distress in particular. The greater availability of highly addictive and generally more affordable drugs, such as crack cocaine, has added more impact on families with children who are already at risk as well as created additional cases of drug dependency and family crises. The debilitating and all-consuming nature of these drugs directly fuels the environment that fosters child abuse and neglect.

One of the traditional problems in dealing effectively with child abuse has been the inability of the two lead investigative authorities—social welfare and law enforcement agencies—to work together in a strategic manner. These agencies often work along parallel lines with one another, each addressing its respective component of the same individual or family problem. Obvious reasons for this are based on differences in philosophy and training of personnel as well as the administrative and statutory demands under which they must work. Although the duties and responsibilities of these two components cannot and should not join, there are points at which they do intersect.

After a situation of abuse or neglect has been reported to law enforcement authorities, it has often already reached a point where permanent or irreparable damage has been enacted upon the child. Law enforcement and social welfare agencies share a responsibility in seeing that children do not become the targets of adult violence and parental neglect. Routine sharing of information by these agencies in a strategic manner, when permissible and appropriate, can often prevent child abuse or neglect from taking place. The point at which social welfare problems start to become law enforcement matters often represents a critical juncture for the welfare of the children involved. The key is often to determine the appropriate point for law enforcement intervention. This is generally best performed by pooling the interests and capabilities of welfare officers, law enforcement prosecutors, and relevant others in a team approach to meet the needs of specific cases.

Child Fatalities: The Nature of the Problem

Awareness of some basic dynamics in issues is critical to effective investigations of child fatalities. Research and experience have shown that children are most at risk of dying of maltreatment during the first four years of life. In fact, 40 percent of children who are victims of fatal maltreatment are infants (younger than one year old), and 75 percent are younger than five years old.[2] The Centers for Disease Control and Prevention have reported that the chances of being murdered are greater on the day of birth than at any other point in a person's life. Caring for children during their preschool years can be very stressful for parents and other caretakers. Faced with a young child's persistent problems with sleeping, feeding, and toilet training, a caretaker may lose control and assault the child in anger or may cause injury while punishing the child. Some inexperienced caretakers have unrealistic expectations about what is appropriate child behavior and what children are even capable of doing in the early stages of their development. In these cases, caretakers can become angry because they view a child's crying or bedwetting as an act of defiance rather than being normal behavior for a young child. The deadly combination of an angry adult and a physically vulnerable child can result in fatal or life-threatening injuries to the child.

For the most part, child fatalities can be categorized as either acute or chronic maltreatment. These are discussed next.

Acute Maltreatment. **Acute maltreatment** means that the child's death is directly related to injuries suffered as a result of a specific incident or abuse or act of negligence. In such cases, the child has not been previously abused or neglected.[3]

In cases involving acute physical abuse, the caretaker may have fatally assaulted the child in either an inappropriate response to the child's behavior or a conscious act to hurt the child. Offenders of cases of **shaken baby syndrome (SBS)**, in which a child's brain is injured from violent shaking, often cite the child's crying as the "triggering event."[4]

In cases of acute neglect, a caretaker's one-time failure to properly supervise the child may result in a fatal injury. A common example is a fatal drowning that occurs when an infant is briefly unsupervised in a bathtub. Children have also sustained fatal gunshot wounds when caretakers fail to properly secure loaded firearms. Some states have statues that specifically assign criminal responsibility to an individual who makes a firearm accessible to a child, either intentionally or through failure to properly secure the weapon. The penalty for this crime may be increased if the child's possession of a firearm results in either injury or death to the child or another person.[5]

Chronic Maltreatment. In **chronic maltreatment** cases, the child's death is directly related to injuries caused by neglect occurring over an extended period of time. Battered child syndrome is an example of chronic physical abuse (discussed later in this chapter). Although the direct cause of death in a battering case is usually a specific injury (often brain trauma), numerous indications of former maltreatment—old and new injuries and possible signs of neglect—are also typically present. Depriving a child of food for a significant period of time is a common form of chronic physical neglect. In cases of chronic abuse or neglect, a history of the child's previous maltreatment often will appear in either Child Protective Services (CPS) or medical records. In fact, in 2000, 38 percent of all children who died of abuse or neglect had prior current contact with a CPS agency.[6]

How Child Fatalities Differ from Other Types of Homicide

All persons involved in the investigation of a child fatality must understand that these cases differ from typical homicides in many regards, including the causes of death, the offender's motivations and legal culpability for the crime, the methods used to inflict the fatal injuries, the types of injuries that the victim sustained, the forensic and physical evidence involved, and the investigative techniques used. In the following discussion, some of the unique issues criminal investigators may encounter are discussed.

Delayed Death. Many maltreatment deaths involve a delay between the time the child sustains the fatal injury and the subsequent death of the child. Although this may also be true with any serious injury, it often happens in cases of abuse of head trauma and in cases involving internal injuries to the chest and abdomen. Note that abusive head trauma (AHT) is the most common type of fatal injury and maltreatment death and includes brain trauma resulting from SBS and other types of direct blunt trauma to the brain. Experiences show that the investigator will be called to the hospital about a severely injured child being treated or surviving on life support and will learn that the prognosis for survival is slim. Depending on the injuries sustained, the child may survive anywhere from hours to days.

This delayed death scenario can also occur when a child is severely scalded from an immersion burn, suffers an infection or other medical complications arising from the injuries, and then dies weeks or months after the incident occurred. That child may also suffer brain trauma and lapse into a coma for months, only to die eventually from pneumonia or some other medical complication. Even though the abuse was not the immediate cause of death in these situations, the manner of death would still be most likely ruled a homicide because the original abuse was the basis for the medical complication that resulted in the child's death.

Witnesses and Accomplices. Another common factor in maltreatment cases is the absence of a witness to the actual incident of abuse or neglect that caused the child's life threatening or fatal injury. Similar to other homicides in which a person may be killed in a public place, maltreatment murders almost always occur in a private location, such as the family's home.

Accomplices are also rare in maltreatment cases. It is unusual for two or more persons to participate in the child's fatal maltreatment. Far more common is the situation in which one person is aware that another (e.g., a spouse, girlfriend, or boyfriend) is abusing or neglecting a child but fails to report the maltreatment or take steps to protect the child. In some cases, the person who is aware of the abuse may actually interfere with the investigation by lying or purposely misleading investigators or even tampering with physical evidence. In such cases, these persons will be held legally responsible for their role in the child's death.

Although an investigation may not present an opportunity to turn accomplices against each other (as is often the case in adult homicide cases), it may be possible to convince the person not actually involved in the abuse or neglect to testify about how the suspect treated the child. More and more states are limiting spousal immunity in child abuse cases and other circumstances. To obtain cooperation, it is often possible to charge a reluctant witness with failure to report suspected child abuse or failure to protect the child. In some cases, these persons may actually have been involved in fatal maltreatment and can be charged as accomplices in the child's death.

Weapons. Maltreatment murders of children rarely involve traditional weapons such as firearms, knives or blunt objects. Typical weapons include hands, feet, household items, and scalding water. Often, death results and injuries are caused by shaking, slamming, blunt-force trauma, scalding, starvation, neglectful supervision, and various other forms of physical abuse and neglect. Investigation is unlikely to turn up a weapon that will directly link the offender to the crime in the way that ballistic evidence links a suspect's gun to a victim's death. The exception may be a human bite mark or an instrument such as an electrical extension cord that leaves a distinct pattern injury.

Trace Evidence. In most cases of fatal child maltreatment, trace evidence such as fingerprints and DNA will be of far less value than it might be in other crimes. For example, if a child who lives with both parents is beaten to death at the home, the mere presence of the parents' fingerprints at the scene links neither of them to the crime. Exceptions are cases in which the offender sexually assaulted or bit the child and DNA evidence is involved.

Circumstantial Evidence. Because most fatal child maltreatment cases lack witnesses or any direct evidence tying a specific individual to the crime, these cases may often rely on circumstantial evidence. Specifically, the investigator must prove that only the suspect could have committed the crime. Two critically important steps are to establish that the suspect was the only person with the child at the time of the fatal injury and to prove that the injury was not accidental.[7]

Internal Injuries. In many child fatalities, the victim's injuries may not be visible at first. The symptoms or signs of some injuries may begin to appear hours or even days after the child sustained the injuries. Most fatal injuries of children involve trauma to the brain and the internal organs of the abdomen and chest. These injuries can only be detected with medical procedures such as radiographs (x-rays), computed tomography (CT) and magnetic resonance imaging (MRI) scans, and the forensic autopsy. Unless the child's injuries are visible externally, the death may appear natural at first. The investigator must not jump to conclusions based solely on an external examination of the child's body. This is especially true for an infant whose death may appear to be from natural causes such as SIDS.

Motives. Child maltreatment murderers are, by definition, committed by persons responsible for the care and supervision of the victim. For example, in 2001, an estimated 83 percent of these fatalities involved a parent, and 17 percent involving nonparent caretakers.[8] The motives in these cases differ from those typically found in homicide cases. Caretakers generally do not kill their children for revenge or greed during the commission of a violent crime such as a robbery or sexual assault. This is not to suggest that on occasion children will not be murdered by sadistic or violent caretakers. In many child fatalities, the victim is subjected to violent assault because of crying, bedwetting, or feeding problems or because the caretaker has feelings of resentment, frustration, or hatred for the child.

The Role of Child Protective Services and the Police

As with other types of criminal investigations such as arson, an unusual aspect of child fatality cases is the involvement of an agency other than law enforcement in the investigation. Typically, CPS has legal authority to be involved in the investigation of a child's death if a parent or other member of the household is suspected. It should be noted, however, that the CPS role is very different from the law enforcement role.[9]

The role of CPS is to determine whether maltreatment was involved in the child's death, identify the responsible party, and then take appropriate action to protect any surviving siblings. CPS does not determine whether anyone committed a crime nor are CPS personnel trained as criminal investigators or trained to collect evidence or interrogates suspect offenders. It is therefore important that law enforcement and CPS communicate and coordinate their efforts during the course of the investigation. One coordinated investigation is always preferable to two separate investigations. In fact, at least 30 states have either mandated or authorized implementation of multidisciplinary teams to investigate child maltreatment.[10]

The role of the criminal investigator is to determine whether a crime has been committed and who is responsible. Accomplishing this involves analyzing old and new injuries revealed by an autopsy and by a review of the child's medical history, thoroughly investigating the death scene, collecting and examining evidence, interviewing witnesses, and interrogating suspects.

Although it is important that law enforcement and CPS coordinate their efforts, it is imperative that the police assume the leadership role in the investigation. This is necessary because of the legal and practical issues involved in obtaining evidence and confessions. Only a police investigator has the training, expertise, and legal mandate to execute search warrants, collect and evaluate evidence, interrogate suspects, and file criminal charges.

If the CPS investigator prematurely confronts a parent of a suspected fatal child abuse, the police investigator will find it more difficult, if not impossible, to successfully interrogate that same individual at a later time. It must be remembered that both police and CPS investigators are acting under statutory requirements. Only if these two social actors coordinate their efforts and use their respective resources will the investigation succeed.[11]

Responsibilities of the First Responder

Police officers dispatched to the location of a seriously injured or deceased child—the "first responders" on the scene—have a number of important responsibilities to carry out before investigators arrive. This assumes that paramedics have already reached the scene and are in the process of attending to the child.

The officer's first priority is to identify and secure the potential crime scene or location where the child was injured or discovered. It is important to remember that the scene may involve more than one room in a house and may also involve the outdoors. Officers should then assess the situation and request additional support as necessary, including additional officers to help secure the scene, crisis counselors, paramedics, personnel from the corners or medical examiner's office, and the detectives or investigators who will conduct the investigation. The first responder should clear all individuals from the scene and make sure that nobody enters the area where they could trample or otherwise contaminate or remove evidence.[12] This can be very difficult to achieve because family members may be very emotional and may not want to leave the deceased child. Patience and diplomacy will encourage cooperation in most cases.

While securing the scene, first responders should be observant. They should look at what is happening and listen to what people are saying. Until the officers have time to write down their observations, they must make mental notes of anything that may be relevant. Without attempting to conduct thorough interviews of the parents or caretakers, the first responder should identify who discovered the child and then find out whether anyone attempted first aid or moved, dressed, or bathed the child. This information should be given to the investigators as soon as they arrive.

As soon as the scene is secure, one officer should be charged with maintaining the log of all personnel who enter the scene. The first responders should also ensure that nobody opens or closes the windows; uses the commode; or disposes of anything, including trash, the child's clothing, medicine, or anything else until the scene has been processed and photographed. Furthermore, until the investigator arrives, the first responder should obtain the names of those present and their relationships to the child. The officers should allow no one to leave the location until this information is obtained.

Collecting Evidence

If the investigator suspects that a child's life-threatening injuries or death may be the result of maltreatment, immediate action is needed to preserve the crime scene and to collect any evidence. Evidence collection includes photographing the victim and searching the location where the investigator believes the injuries occurred. Before searching any possible crime scene, the investigator must determine whether a search warrant or consent to search is necessary. If there are any doubts, the investigator should consult the legal adviser. In most cases of child deaths, there is no exception to the Fourth Amendment requirement for a search warrant for valid consent to search.

The search of the scene should include the following:

- Ensure that scale diagrams are made of the layout and that photographs, a video, or both are taken. Photographs should show the general location and progress to specific items of interest.

- Consider as evidence prescription or over-the-counter medicine the child was taking and other medicine or substances the child may have ingested. If it is not practical to remove such medicine from the scene because someone else in the household needs it, document the information on the label.

- It appears that the child may have died of malnourishment, the investigator may want to take an inventory of the amount of baby food or formula that is present. Whatever is found should be documented and photographed.

- If evidence is located that the caretaker has been abusing alcohol or other substances, this evidence should also be carefully documented.

- Trash cans inside and outside the residence should also be searched for possible evidence such as bloodstained clothing; items used to clean up blood, vomit, urine or feces; and implements used to injure the child, such as wooden spoons, belts, and electrical extension cords.[13]

Interviewing Witnesses

Conducting timely, thorough interviews of witnesses contributes greatly to the success of a child fatality investigation. The list of potential witnesses varies from case to case but typically includes the deceased child's siblings and parents, the child's caretakers immediately before the death or during the time the child appeared to be in medical distress, neighbors, law enforcement first responders, paramedics, medical providers, and anyone else who may have relevant information about the child or the events leading to the injury or death.

As stated in Chapter 6, an interview differs significantly from an interrogation. It is important to understand the difference between these two police functions. An interview is a nonconfrontational conversation between two people in which information is exchanged. In comparison, an interrogation is an attempt to obtain a confession from a suspect who is believed to have committed a crime. In an interview, the person being questioned may have knowledge the investigator needs. Because the person is not under arrest and formal charges have not been filed, it is usually not necessary to give "Miranda warnings" at this point. The Miranda requirement in this regard, however, may be governed by state law in the respective jurisdiction of the crime. The following considerations should be kept in mind during the course of interviewing witnesses.[14]

- The interview should be conducted as early in the investigation as practical.
- Witnesses should be interviewed separately.

- It should be determined what a witness actually observed and knows first-hand and what someone else may have told them. For example, if a witness states that a child fell from the couch, it is important for the investigator to determine whether the person actually saw the child fall or is just repeating something someone else told him or her. If the investigator later determines that the child did not fall from the couch, the person who told the witness that this occurred may actually have caused the child's injury, as demonstrated by giving false information to conceal his or her actions.

- After witnesses provide a verbal account, a formal statement should be taken. This applies to caretakers, neighbors, first responders, paramedics, medical professionals, and anyone else who has information about the event. It is preferable to record the statement electronically (audio or videotape) or ask the witness to write or type it in affidavit format and then have the witness sign it. The value of the formal statement is that it documents the witness' version of the events and locks the witness into that story. The investigator then can verify or disprove that account during the course of the investigation. A person originally identified as a witness may later be identified as a suspect. Having properly documented the formal statement prevents that person from changing his or her story as additional facts emerge.

- Other children residing in the home of the deceased child can also be important witnesses. They may have observed or heard something directly related to the death and may have knowledge of the child's prior maltreatment. They might even know who is responsible. It is important that someone who has specific training on how to interview children conduct all interviews with child witnesses. If the criminal investigator does not have this training, someone should be located who does to conduct the interview. These interviews are often conducted at child advocacy centers (CACs), CPS, or victim or witness programs available in the community.

- Witnesses should be provided the opportunity to give a narrative account of what they actually know about the event under investigation. For example, in a case in which child was brought to the hospital after having a seizure, the parent should be asked to tell everything that happened to the child in the previous 72 hours. It is important that the investigator does not interrupt with questions or requests to repeat part of the account.[15] It is far better to hear the entire story and then ask about things that were not mentioned or that need clarification.

- In some cases, it may be appropriate to request that a witness or a possible suspect take a polygraph or voice stress analyzer test. Although the results of these tests are not admissible in court, they can be useful in subsequent interviews and interrogations.[16]

Evidence from the Autopsy

The autopsy will determine the official cause of death (e.g., blunt force trauma, drowning) and manner of death (e.g., natural, accidental, homicide, suicide, undetermined). The criminal investigator should observe the autopsy if at all possible. The information learned from the autopsy will better prepare the investigator for subsequent interviews and interrogations.

The pathologist can provide information about the child's injuries, including those related to the death and those previously inflicted, and about the child's general state of health before death. It is important to ask for details to explain whether a single event or multiple factors caused or contributed to the death.[17]

In turn, the investigator can tell the pathologist what he or she has learned from interviews and record checks. In many cases, the pathologist's knowledge can offer an opinion regarding the possibility that the child's injuries occurred in the manner described by witnesses. The pathologist may also be able to estimate the time of death based on the child's stomach contents and investigative notes about the child's last meal.[18]

Documentation of the Case

The official case file must document the entire investigation from the time law enforcement received the initial call to the time criminal charges are filed. It must include all copies of official police reports, investigators' notes, medical records, the autopsy report and pictures, crime scene pictures, the 911 recordings, witness statements, search warrants, newspaper articles, background investigation on the suspect, and any other relevant information or records obtained during the investigation.

Because most of the information in the official file will be subject to the discovery process by defense attorneys investigators need to be thoroughly familiar with the files contents. A defense attorney may attempt to impeach the investigator's testimony on the witness stand by obtaining statements from the investigator that contradict the evidence in the case file.[19]

When entering notes in the case file, investigators should refrain from including personal opinions and ideas outside the scope of their professional knowledge. These include things such as time of death, body temperature, and cause of death. Finally, a check should be made of the CPS investigator's case file for additional items that should be contained in the police case file.[20]

Interrogating Suspects

Proper interrogation of a suspect may be instrumental in identifying the person responsible for the child's injuries. Absent any direct evidence showing who is responsible (which is almost never the case), the suspect's voluntary confession of guilt is probably the most powerful evidence that can be presented at trial. However, a suspect's written or electronically recorded voluntary statement is of little value unless it is admitted into evidence. The defense attorney will almost always challenge a suspect's confession by claiming coercion or some other violation of the client's rights under the Fourth, Fifth, Sixth or Fourteenth Amendments. Accordingly, the investigator must be thoroughly familiar with the case law in his or her state as it relates to obtaining confessions and the admissibility of confessions as evidence.

Investigators must carefully document that the suspect's constitutional rights are protected and that all applicable departmental procedures and state laws have been followed. At a bare minimum, the case file should contain the following documentation:

- Whether the suspect was under arrest at the time of the interrogation or was just brought in for questioning
- When the interrogations started and how long they lasted
- How long and at what time the suspect was allowed to use the restroom or to have something to eat or drink
- The names of any individuals who participated in the interrogation or observed it
- Whether the suspect had any physical impairments or medical problems that could interfere with the ability to speak, hear, or understand what was being said
- The suspect's level of formal education and whether the suspect can read and write[21]

Suspects should be interrogated as early in the investigation as possible. Investigators can usually begin as soon as the cause and manner of death are known (even if the official autopsy report has not been written) and the evidence indicates who the suspect is. In some cases, it may be best to interrogate the suspect before the autopsy is conducted. The following guidelines will assist in conducting a proper interrogation:

- Dress in business or casual clothes, not a uniform.
- If the suspect does not speak English and an interpreter is needed, make sure the interpreter is an expert in the suspect's language.
- Have another investigator observe the interrogation. If the investigator's agency does not videotape interrogations, then the observer can at least rebut any allegations that the suspect was mistreated or coerced into a confession.

If the confession cannot be obtained, everything the suspect says should be documented. This is helpful because a suspect who is not confessing to causing the child's fatal injuries may offer an explanation of the injuries and surrounding events that is implausible or can be refuted by evidence.

Even if the suspect confesses, the confession may be suppressed at trial for a variety of procedural and legal reasons. This is one reason why the investigator must not stop working on the case even when a confession has been obtained. Rather, the investigator should continue to investigate any new leads and interview anyone he or she thinks might have relevant information.

Child Physical Abuse

In addition to child fatalities, child physical abuse remains a serious problem. As with the investigation of child fatalities, the investigative response to child physical abuse must be timely and thorough. *Child abuse* is a generic term that incorporates a variety of purposeful acts resulting in injuries to a child. Probably the most dramatic of these and the most often reported to the police is physical child abuse that results in death or serious injury. However, child abuse is far more pervasive and often more subtle. For example, as stated earlier, physical battering may be the result of a parent's momentary fit of anger, or it may be part of an ongoing abusive situation. In the case of sexual abuse situations within families, offenses are more frequently calculated and may form a long-term pattern of sexual abuse. Physical neglect of a child's needs for nourishment or medical care, reckless disregard for his or her safety, and failure to provide food or medical care are all elements of the child abuse and neglect problem.

The physical effects of child abuse are only part of a child's injuries. The psychological and emotional impact of abuse frequently have long-term consequences for the child. Many children blame themselves for the abuse, adopting the feeling that they are bad and deserve the abusive treatment. Others may adopt the long-lasting perception that violence is a natural, even acceptable, component of family life and interpersonal relationships. As a consequence, many abused children carry to the next generation the same type of treatment that they endured. Other children translate physical abuse into later criminal violence. The fact that so many violent offenders have histories of child abuse and neglect is testimony to the fact that child abuse is often an intergenerational phenomenon. As such, it is important not only for the current victim but also for future generations to identify child abuse whenever possible and to bring appropriate enforcement and treatment to bear on the problem.

Investigative Resources

The point at which an investigation of child abuse begins depends largely on the reporting party or agency and the degree to which a case of abuse, neglect, or abandonment can be legally established. For example, abused children who require immediate medical attention suggest a point of investigative departure through interviews with medical staff. In most cases, investigation of child abuse requires contact with one or more sources of information depending on the nature of the complaint and the perceived scope of the abuse. Basic types of questions can be identified for conducting interviews with individuals who report child abuse. Such inquiries are generally warranted before direct contact is made with the family and the child.

Other basic types of information available through the police department should also be collected early in the investigation. This includes such information as the existence of criminal records or charges against any members of the family or court protection orders that may have been filed against any family members. Other general sources of investigative information can be gathered from a variety of resources in the community. These are reviewed in the following sections.

Emergency Room Personnel and Medical Examiners

In the worst-case scenario—the death of a child—a medical examiner may be the primary source of contact for investigative purposes. Police departments in general and investigative personnel in particular must develop a good working relationship with the medical examiner's office. In these and related circumstances, a collaborative relationship generally proves to be far more productive than either the police or medical personnel working independently. The investigative officer should be present at the autopsy or at the initial examination of the body and should brief the examining physician on the circumstances of the alleged accident if information is available. This also holds true for emergency room physicians who treat a child after a presumed serious but nonfatal accident. In both cases, physical examinations may reveal certain types of injuries that confirm or suggest abuse. These include the following:

1. *External signs.* Some injuries have identifiable patterns that can be linked to specific objects used in an attack. For example, one may be able to identify bite or scratch marks; coat hanger or hot iron impressions; fingertip marks caused by tight gripping; straight, curved, curvilinear, or jagged lesions that may indicate whipping by specifically shaped objects; and scald or peculiar burn marks.

    The location of some injuries is also indicative of abuse. These include injuries to the genitals, buttocks, and rectal areas, as well as trauma to the torso, upper arms, and thighs. These and related injuries are particularly incriminating if they are not accompanied by other relatively common injuries suffered by children, such as skinned knees and bruises to the elbows, shins, and forehead, or by other injuries that would have probably been received as part of the accident. For example, most often children who are involved in accidents also display these signs of typical childhood play. On the other hand, children who are abused may show few or none of these signs and, except for the abusive injuries, may even appear well groomed and dressed.

    There may also be signs of old injuries to various parts of the body that are in different stages of healing. Some children seem to be accident prone and may accumulate a variety of injuries over time. However, injuries that are not common to childhood and that appear to have been received over a period of time can be signs of a steadily escalating cycle of abuse.

In all cases of suspected abuse, injuries should be photographed in color to assist in establishing the extent of damage and the age of injuries at later trial presentation.

2. *Internal signs.* As noted, some injuries are not characteristic of childhood activities and common accidents. For example, it is very unlikely that pre-toddlers would be able to break a major bone, such as a thigh or upper arm bone, or other smaller bones given the children's lack of mobility and the inherent difficulty in breaking the bones of young children. Some fractures will be apparent externally. Others, particularly older fractures, require radiologic examination to be identified. The nature of some fractures provides almost indisputable evidence of abuse. These include spiral fractures, indicating vigorous handling, shaking, or twisting, and fractures to the rear and upper part—occipital and varietal bones, respectively—of the skull, suggesting that the child was swung by the feet into a solid object or suffered a blow to the head. Subdural hematomas, without evidence of contusions on the scalp, or skull fractures may suggest violent shaking of an infant, causing whiplash of the child's head and subsequent internal injuries.

Like the emergency room physician, the medical examiner may be confronted by a child whose history, pattern, or extent of injuries does not correlate with the alleged cause of death. Also typical of the abused child is an inordinate parental delay in seeking medical attention, evidence of administration of home remedies for a serious injury, a history of prior visits to different emergency rooms, frequent changes of physicians, any prior diagnosis of "failure to thrive," even multiple emergency room visits with a well child. If any of these situations are encountered, one should consider child abuse as likely.

Based on the judgment of a physician, the diagnosis of one or more of these suspicious injuries may be sufficient evidence to conclude that the child suffered from abuse. These injuries are particularly incriminating when they do not correlate with parental explanations of how they were incurred. This underscores the importance of a close and ongoing communication between police investigating officers and physicians. Examining physicians must be kept informed about the course of the investigation and the types of questions that should be answered as the result of their examination. A child who suffers from physical abuse is termed a **battered child**. Battered children suffer from a wide array of abuses, including minor assaults to severe beatings, which in some cases cost them their lives. Because of the privacy and nature of the crime, such victims often have nowhere to turn. Child abuse is aggravated by high levels of unemployment, poor parenting skills, stress, marital conflict, and a general lack of information about child development.

As with any assault case, evidence is a primary objective. Bruises, bloody clothes, dramatic changes in a child's behavior, and statements from possible witnesses are all important. Special care must be afforded the interview of a child victim because children are imaginative and highly susceptible to suggestion. Because of this, the use of specially trained child interviewers is recommended to secure a competent statement from the child victim.

Battered Child Syndrome

Battered child syndrome is a tragic and disturbing phenomenon. Unfortunately, it is a crime that is often successfully hidden by its perpetrators. Law enforcement has an important role to play in uncovering cases of battered child syndrome and

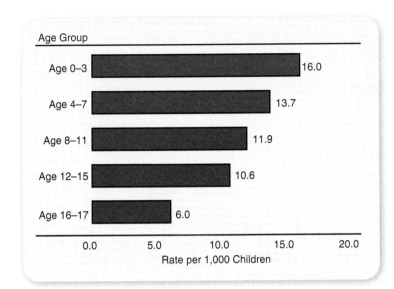

FIGURE 13.1 Child Victimization Rates by Age Group, 2002. According to this chart, the largest victimized age group is the youngest, with a rate of 16.0 per 1,000 children of the same age group. *U.S. Department of Health & Human Services, Administration for Children and Families.* (2003).

gathering evidence for successful prosecution. Investigators must have a working knowledge of battered child syndrome and what it means to an investigation. *Battered child syndrome* is defined as the collection of injuries sustained by a child as a result of repeated mistreatment or beating. If the child's injuries indicate intentional trauma or appear to be more severe than could reasonably be expected from an accident, battered child syndrome should be suspected. In such cases, an investigator must do more than collect information about the currently reported injury. A full investigation requires interviewing possible witnesses about other injuries that the child may have suffered, obtaining the caretaker's explanation for those injuries, and assessing the conclusions of medical personnel who may have seen the victim before.

The issue of whether information on the victim's prior injuries or medical condition will be admissible at trial should be left up to the prosecutor. However, an investigator's failure to collect such information leaves the prosecutor without one of the most important pieces of corroborative evidence for proving an intentional act of child abuse. Evidence of past inflicted injuries may also be the only information available to help the prosecutor distinguish between two

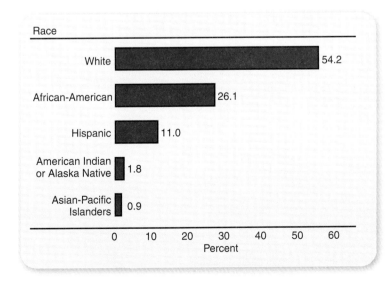

FIGURE 13.2 Percentage of child victims by race, 2002. This chart shows that 54.2 percent of all victims were white, 26.1 percent were African American, and 11 percent were Hispanic. *U.S. Department of Health & Human Services, Administration for Children and Families.* (2003).

or more possible perpetrators in the current case and may help refute claims by the child's parents or caretakers that injuries suggestive of physical abuse were caused by an accident.

Recognizing Abuse

There are several signs of abuse that officers can identify while assessing the situation. For example, if the child has an injury that is inconsistent with the explanation given by the parents, abuse might have occurred. If the officer is told that a child's hand was severely scalded in water by "accident," the officer should question why the child didn't take the obvious action of withdrawing his hand. It would be logical to suspect that someone forcibly held the child's hand in the water.

Other injuries can also be good indicators of child abuse (e.g., cigarette burns, bruises, cuts that appear to be nonaccidental in origin). In addition, abused children sometimes have bite marks appearing on the abdomen, scrotum, and buttocks.[22] Most typically, however, abuse takes the form of severe and numerous beatings going far beyond normal disciplinary measures. Such evidence includes injuries in different stages of healing or complications stemming from old injuries that are not explained sufficiently by the parents.

Taking the Initial Report

State laws generally require certain persons to report instances of child abuse, neglect, and sexual abuse. These persons include school officials, medical personnel, attorneys, social workers, and others. Such reports can be made verbally or in writing to the state department of family or child services, the welfare department, the juvenile court, or a local law enforcement agency. Typically, special forms are used for child abuse and molestation cases, and laws require immediate action. Initial child abuse reports are confidential in nature and contain the child's name, address, and age as well as information on the child's parents or legal guardians.

In addition, the name and address of the person suspected of abusing the child are documented as well as the nature of the alleged offense. In the case of an emergency circumstance or one that appears to be life threatening for the

FIGURE 13.3 Photo of physical abuse of a child. Here the feet of this child were forcibly held against a heater by a parent. Courtesy of Science Photo Library.

Justifications for Officers Making an Arrest

☑ Injury to the child is severe.

☑ Evidence of a serious crime exists.

☑ It seems likely that the suspect will flee the scene.

☑ There is a disturbance of the peace.

☑ The suspect seems to pose a danger to others.

child, the police can remove the child from the home provided that the welfare or juvenile justice official taking the report deems it necessary. All allegations will be investigated by local law enforcement.

The Initial Police Response to Child Abuse

The time factor is crucial in the law enforcement response to suspected child abuse. Complaints are sometimes logged during or shortly after a battering incident; therefore, the safety of the child is the utmost priority for the responding officer. Consequently, the responding officer's first task is to get medical attention for the child. In the absence of any immediate danger to the child, most state laws require that officers at least attempt to resolve any problems before physically removing the child from the home. In the event that the child is facing imminent danger, of course, removal from the home is appropriate.

The second responsibility of the responding officer is to determine if a crime has, in fact, been committed. If such determination is made, the officer should conduct a criminal investigation accordingly, such as identifying evidence. Subsequent to the investigation, it may be necessary to take a suspect into physical custody.

Steps in Investigating Battered Child Syndrome

Investigators confronted with the case of possible child abuse or child homicide must overcome the unfortunately frequent societal attitude that babies are less important than adult victims of homicide and that natural parents would never intentionally harm their own children. When battered child syndrome is suspected, the investigator should always:

- Collect information about the "acute" injury that led the person or agency to make the report
- Conduct interviews with medical personnel who are attending the child
- Review medical records from a doctor, clinic, or hospital
- Interview all persons who had access to or custody of the child during a time in which the injury or injuries allegedly occurred. Caretakers should always be interviewed separately; joint interviews can only hurt the investigation
- Consider any statements the caretakers made to anyone concerning what happened to the child to require medical attention
- Conduct a thorough investigation of the scene where the child was allegedly hurt

Interviews with Medical Personnel

It is important for the investigator to contact all medical personnel who had contact with the family, such as doctors, nurses, admitting personnel, emergency medical technicians (EMTs), ambulance drivers, and emergency room personnel.

- Talk with those who provided treatment for the child about the diagnosis and what treatments were used. The attending physician will often be able to express at least an opinion that the caretaker's explanation did not "fit" the severity of the injury. However, failure to obtain an opinion from the attending physician should not end the investigation.
- Speak with any specialists who assisted the attending physician.
- Have someone knowledgeable about medical terms translate them into layperson terms so that the exact nature of the injuries is clear.
- Obtain available medical records concerning the injured child's treatment, including records of any prior treatment. (Note: If only one caretaker is suspected of abuse, the nonabusive caretaker may need to sign a release of the records. If both are suspected, most states have provisions that override normal confidentiality rules in the search for evidence of child abuse. Procedures for obtaining these records must be confirmed in each state.)
- Interview the child's pediatrician about the child's general health since birth and look for a pattern of suspected abusive injuries.

It is absolutely vital that photographs of the child be taken as soon as possible after a child has been brought to the treatment facility. Most clinics and hospitals have established procedures for photographing injuries in obvious cases of abuse, but when the injuries are more subtle, they may overlook the need for photographs. The investigator should make sure that medical personnel take and preserve photographs or that the investigating team takes them.

Other Important Sources of Information

Interview siblings, other relatives, neighbors, family friends, teachers, church associates, and others who may know about a child's health and history. People who surround the child and are part of his or her life are sometimes overlooked as sources of background information for a child abuse or homicide prosecution.

Review emergency medical (EMT) records or 911 dispatch tapes. These records are frequently overlooked but can be valuable sources of information. Families with one or more emergencies may in fact be abusing their children and not just being hit by a long streak of "bad luck."

After the family history has been obtained, request any police reports that may be held by law enforcement agencies in the jurisdiction where the family lives. Also check the child welfare agencies' files on the family. Collect additional family history concerning connections between domestic violence and child abuse; substance abuse and child abuse; and other connections, even apparently unrelated arrests or charges. These records may be helpful in piecing together the complicated picture of what happened to the child this time and who was responsible.

Consultation with Experts

Identifying experts is important to the child abuse investigator. If the investigator does not have a basic knowledge of the causes of young children's injuries, experts should be consulted. Attending training conferences can provide the investigator with a great deal of basic knowledge and help establish a network of experts.

Interviews with Caretakers

A major trait of abuse by caretakers is either complete lack of an explanation for critical injuries or explanations that do not account for the severity of the injuries. The investigation must not be dictated solely by caretakers' early explanations because after they learn that their excuses don't match the medical evidence, they will come up with new ones.

In child homicide cases, for example, investigators will learn quickly about "killer couches," "killer stairs," and "killer cribs." Abusers freely use these terms in their explanations of the child's death. However, studies show that children do not die from falls from simple household heights; they usually do not even suffer severe head injuries from such falls.

In nearly every case of actual abuse, caretakers will not be consistent in their explanations of the injuries over time. Sometimes the changes are apparent from statements that abusers have made to others. Additional interviews may be needed to document the changes in explanations and to follow up on additional information that the investigation uncovers.

The Crime Scene Investigation

Caretakers' changes in explanations often mean that investigators must visit the home or the scene of the injury more than once. The ideal time to obtain such evidence is immediately after the child's injury is reported before the caretakers have an opportunity to tamper with the scene. If the caretakers do not consent to a search of the scene, a search warrant may be necessary. The strongest evidence of the need for a search warrant is the medical evidence supporting what probably happened to the child and the caretakers' inconsistent or absent accounts of the events.

Whatever explanation caretakers offer for a child's injury or injuries, it is vital that the investigator secure physical evidence. He or she must be thorough in obtaining photographic evidence of the location where the injury took place because physical evidence and records must be preserved, for example:

- The crib from which the child allegedly fell
- The child's "environment," including bedding on the bed or in the crib and on other beds in the home
- Any toys or objects on which the child allegedly landed
- In cases in which the child was apparently burned, a record of any sinks, bathtubs, and pots or pans containing water. In addition to testing the temperature of the standing water, the temperature of water from the water heater and from each tap should be tested. The temperature setting of the water heater should also be checked. This may help disprove an allegation that the child accidentally turned on the hot water. Other sources of heat in the home should be documented, regardless of the caretakers' initial explanation of what burned the child.
- A complete photographic or videotape record of the home or other location in which the injuries allegedly occurred, focusing on areas that the caretakers have already identified as the site of the particular trauma (e.g., stairs, bed or crib, or bathtub).

The investigator should be trained by his or her local crime laboratory personnel on the types of evidence that can and should be processed in preserving these cases:

- If the child suffered apparent cigarette burns, collecting cigarette butts found in the home may facilitate analysis of the burn patterns.
- If the case involves a combination of sexual and physical abuse, collecting the child's clothing and bedding may allow identification of what happened and who was involved.

- If the child shows evidence of bite marks, saliva swabbing should be done to allow positive identification of the biter.
- If the child has suffered a depressed skull fracture, any objects the approximate size of the fracture should be seized for appropriate analysis.

Shaken Baby Syndrome

SBS is a form of child abuse that occurs when an abuser violently shakes an infant or small child, creating a whiplash-type motion that causes acceleration–deceleration injuries. The injury is estimated to affect between 1,200 and 1,600 children every year in the United States.[23] In shaken baby cases, it is common for there to be no external evidence of trauma.[24] Injuries from impacts with hard objects may accompany SBS; this combination of shaking with striking against a hard object is sometimes termed the *shaken impact syndrome* or *shaken/slam syndrome*.

Victims of SBS are age 3 years and younger. Typically, most child victims are younger than 18 months. The motion required to injure a child often results in bleeding inside the head and may cause irreversible brain damage, blindness, cerebral palsy, hearing loss, spinal cord injuries, seizures, learning disabilities, and even death. It can be traced historically from the mid-1500s and was officially named and defined in 1974. The classic medical symptoms associated with infant shaking include:

- Retinal hemorrhaging (bleeding in the back of the eyeball), often bilaterally (in both eyes)
- Subdural or subarachnoid hematomas (intracranial bleeding, most often in the upper hemispheres of the brain, caused by the shearing of the blood vessels between the brain and the dura mater of the arachnoid membrane)
- Absence of other external signs of abuse (e.g., bruises), although not always. Symptoms include breathing difficulties, seizures, dilated pupils, lethargy, and unconsciousness

According to all credible studies in the past several years, retinal hemorrhaging in infants is, for all practical purposes, conclusive evidence of SBS in the absence of a good explanation. Good explanations for retinal hemorrhaging include:

- A severe auto accident in which the baby's head either struck something with severe force or was thrown about wildly without restraint during the crash
- A fall from several stories onto a hard surface, in which case there are usually other signs of trauma, such as skull fractures, swelling, and intracranial collection of blood

Simple household falls, cardiopulmonary resuscitation (CPR), and tossing a baby in the air in play are not good explanations for retinal hemorrhaging. There simply is not enough force involved in minor falls in play activities to cause retinal hemorrhage or the type of severe life-threatening injuries seen in infants who have been shaken.

In most cases of SBS, there is no skull fracture and no external sign of trauma. The typical explanation given by caretakers is that the baby was "fine" and then suddenly went into respiratory arrest or began having seizures. Both of these conditions are common symptoms of SBS.

The shaking necessary to cause death or severe intracranial injuries is never an unintentional or nonabusive action. Rather, such injuries are caused by a violent, sustained action in which the infant's head, which lacks muscular control, is violently swept forward and backward, hitting the chest and shoulders. The action occurs right in front of the shaker's eyes. Experts say that an observer watching the shaking would describe it as "as hard as the shaker was humanly capable of shaking the baby" or "hard enough that it appeared the baby's head would come off." In almost every case, the baby begins to show symptoms such as seizures or unconsciousness within minutes of the injury. The baby may have difficulty breathing, or his or her breathing may stop completely.

SBS occurs primarily in children 18 months of age or younger. It is most often associated with infants younger than one year old because their necks lack muscle control and their heads are heavier than the rest of their bodies. An infant cannot resist the shaking, but a toddler can, to some extent. Although the collection of injuries associated with SBS is sometimes seen in toddlers, it is rare and is always a sign of extremely violent and severe action against the child.

Munchausen Syndrome by Proxy

Munchausen syndrome is a psychological disorder in which a patient fabricates symptoms of disease or injury in order to undergo medical tests, hospitalization, or even medical or surgical treatment. To command medical attention, patients with Munchausen syndrome may intentionally injure themselves or induce illness in themselves. In cases of **Munchausen syndrome by proxy**, parents or caretakers with Munchausen syndrome attempt to bring medical attention to themselves by inducing illness in their children. The parent then may try to resuscitate or have paramedics or hospital personnel save the child. The following scenarios are common occurrences in these cases:

- A child's caretaker repeatedly brings the child in for medical care or calls paramedics for alleged problems that cannot be documented medically.
- The child experiences "seizures" or "respiratory arrest" only when the caretaker is there, never in the presence of neutral third parties or in the hospital.
- When the child is hospitalized, the caretaker turns off the life support equipment, causing the child to stop breathing, and then turns everything back on and summons help.
- The caretaker induces illness by introducing a mild irritant or poison into the child's body.

Indications of Munchausen Syndrome

Caution is required in the diagnosis of fabricated or induced illness (FII). Many of the items below are also indications of a child with organic but undiagnosed illness. An ethical diagnosis of Munchausen syndrome must include an evaluation of the child, the parents, and the family dynamics. Diagnoses based only on a review of the child's medical chart can be rejected in court. An adult care provider who is abusing the child often seems comfortable and not upset over the child's hospitalization. Medical professionals need to monitor that adult's visits to the child while in the hospital in case that adult does things to make the child sicker. In addition, in most states, medical professionals have a duty to report such abuse to legal authorities.[25]

- A child who has one or more medical problems that do not respond to treatment or that follow an unusual course that is persistent, puzzling, and unexplained

- Physical or laboratory findings that are highly unusual, discrepant with history, or physically or clinically impossible
- A parent who appears to be medically knowledgeable or fascinated with medical details and hospital gossip, appears to enjoy the hospital environment, and expresses interest in the details of other patients' problems
- A highly attentive parent who is reluctant to leave the child's side and who him- or herself seems to require constant attention
- A parent who appears to be unusually calm in the face of serious difficulties in the child's medical course while being highly supportive and encouraging of the physician, or a parent who is angry; devalues staff; and demands further intervention, more procedures, second opinions, and transfers to other, more sophisticated, facilities
- The suspected parent may work in the health care field him- or herself or profess interest in a health-related job
- The signs and symptoms of a child's illness do not occur in the parent's absence (hospitalization and careful monitoring may be necessary to establish this causal relationship)
- A family history of similar or unexplained illness or death in a sibling
- A parent with symptoms similar to the child's medical problems or an illness history that itself is puzzling and unusual
- A suspected emotionally distant relationship between parents; the spouse often fails to visit the patient and has little contact with physicians even when the child is hospitalized with serious illness
- A parent who reports dramatic, negative events, such as house fires, burglaries, or car accidents, that affect him or her and their family while the child is undergoing treatment
- A parent who seems to have an insatiable need for adulation or who makes self-serving efforts for public acknowledgment of his or her abilities[26]

These indicators may or may not provide the need for further investigation but should be taken seriously until such time the allegations have been proven invalid.

Investigative Guidelines

- ☑ Consult with all possible experts, including psychologists.
- ☑ Exhaust every possible explanation in the cause of the child's illness or death.
- ☑ Find out who had exclusive control over the child when the symptoms of the illness began or at the time of the child's death.
- ☑ Find out if there is a history of abusive conduct toward the child.
- ☑ Find out if the nature of the child's illness or injury allows medical professionals to express an opinion that the child's illness or death was neither accidental nor the result of a natural cause or disease.
- ☑ In cases of hospitalization, use covert video surveillance to monitor the suspect. Some cases have been solved in this fashion.
- ☑ Determine whether the caretaker had any medical training or a history of seeking medical treatment needlessly. Munchausen syndrome by proxy is often a multigenerational condition.

Sudden Infant Death Syndrome

Sudden infant death syndrome (SIDS) is the diagnosis given for the sudden death of an infant 1 month to 1 year of age that remains unexplained after a complete investigation, which includes an autopsy, an examination of the death scene, and a review of the victim's medical and family history. SIDS is a recognized medical disorder. Infants who succumb to the syndrome appear healthy before the incident, even to a physician. At this time, there is no strong evidence to suggest that SIDS can be stopped because the first and only symptom is death. SIDS appears to occur after an infant has been put down for sleep. Victims may have been down for sleep for as little as 10 minutes. Studies show that there are no apparent signs of a struggle or suffering. Although SIDS is associated with an infant's sleep time and often occurs in the crib, the event may occur anywhere the infant is sleeping. SIDS events have occurred in infant seats, car seats, strollers, and in the parents' bed.

SIDS is not a positive finding; rather, it is a diagnosis made when there is no other medical explanation for the abrupt death of an apparently healthy infant. When a baby dies from shaking, intracranial injuries, peritonitis (inflammation of the peritoneum, the membrane that lines the abdominal cavity), apparent suffocation, or any other identifiable cause, SIDS is not even considered a possibility. SIDS rarely occurs in infants older than age seven months and almost never is an appropriate diagnosis for a child older than 12 months.

Research shows that SIDS can occur at anytime between one month of age and one year of age; however, 91 percent of SIDS deaths occur before the age of six months, with the highest concentration occurring between two months and four months of age. The syndrome affects all races and socioeconomic groups. Environmental, behavioral, and physical influences may put some infants at greater risk for SIDS, and conversely, many SIDS victims meet no specific risk factors. Some general risk factors have, however, been identified. These include:

- Mother younger than 20 years of age
- Late or no prenatal care
- Premature infants
- Low birth weight infants
- Drug and alcohol use during pregnancy
- Smoking (mothers who smoke during and after pregnancy triple the risk of SIDS in their infants)[27]

SIDS cases must be approached with great sensitivity. However, before SIDS can be determined to be the cause of death, investigators must ensure that every other possible medical explanation has been explored and that there is no evidence of any other natural or accidental cause for the child's death.

An investigator's suspicions should be aroused when multiple alleged SIDS deaths have occurred under the custody of the same caretaker. Statistically, the occurrence of two or three alleged SIDS deaths in the care of the same person strongly suggests that some degree of child abuse was involved. Whenever there is evidence that the child who has died was abused or that other children in the family have been abused, SIDS is not an appropriate finding.

Even when there is no affirmative medical finding of the cause of death, prosecution may still be possible. In some cases, experts can explain what occurs when a child is suffocated and can render a medical opinion that suffocation is one of the ways that someone could cause the child's death without leaving obvious medical signs.

Sexual Abuse of Children

The abuse of children can take many forms. In addition to possible physical danger posed by an abusive caregiver or parent, a child can also be traumatized by being sexually abused. Consider the 1995 case when an 11-year-old testified that she was molested during sexual orgies supposedly staged by a Pentecostal preacher in Wenatchee, Washington. The child also testified that her foster father, who happened to be Detective Bob Perez, lead police investigator in the case, also physically abused her. Prosecutors charged 28 persons in the case, charging that they forced 50 children to have sex with each other and with adults in two sex rings. Nineteen people either pleaded guilty or were convicted in the case; only one person was acquitted. In yet another case, the Boy Scouts have dismissed more than 1,800 scoutmasters suspected of molesting children between 1971 and 1991; some of those dismissed may have moved to other troops to continue their abuse.[28]

In recent years, the problem of child sexual abuse has generated increased attention and is becoming more openly discussed than ever before. Child abuse can take a number of insidious forms. An example is the case of Catholic Priest John J. Geoghan, who was a key figure in the Roman Catholic sex abuse cases that rocked the Boston Archdiocese in the late 1990s and early 2000s. Geoghan's case eventually led to the resignation of Boston's archbishop, Cardinal Bernard Francis Law, on December 13, 2002.

Over a 30-year career in six parishes, Geoghan was accused of sexual abuse involving more than 130 children. Charges were brought in Cambridge, Massachusetts, concerning accusations of a molestation that took place in 1991. Geoghan was defrocked in 1998. In January 2002, he was found guilty of indecent assault and battery for grabbing the buttocks of a 10-year-old boy in a swimming pool at the Waltham Boys and Girls Club. In 1991, Geoghan was sentenced to nine to 10 years in prison.

Numerous civil lawsuits resulted from Geoghan's actions because lawyers argued that the archdiocese had transferred Geoghan from parish to parish despite warnings of his behavior. On August 23, 2003, while in protective custody at the Souza-Baranowski Correctional Center in Shirley, Massachusetts,

FIGURE 13.4 Photo of former Catholic Priest John Geoghan with his attorney at trial. Courtesy of AP Wide World Photos.

Geoghan was trapped in his cell, strangled, and stomped to death by another inmate, Joseph Druce.

Statistics also point out that child sexual abuse is a growing problem. Although it is difficult to estimate the incidence of child sexual abuse, stories of abuse such as those discussed above illustrate the seriousness of the problem. In one study by Diana Russell, women in the San Francisco area were surveyed, and Russell found that 38 percent had experienced intrafamilial or extrafamilial sexual abuse by the time they reached age 18 years.[29] A more recent survey of Minnesota students in grades six, nine, and 12 revealed that about 2 percent of the boys and 7 percent of the girls had experienced incest, while 4 percent of males and 13 percent of females had experienced extrafamilial sexual abuse. Although the percentage of abused girls is smaller than that found by Russell, research by Glenn Wolfner and Richard Gelles indicates that up to one in five girls suffers sexual abuse.[30]

Although these results are alarming, it is probable that they still underestimate the true incidence of child sexual abuse. It is difficult to get people to respond to questions about child sexual abuse, and many victims either are too young to understand their abuse or have repressed their memory of such incidents. Of course, children may be inhibited because parents are reluctant to admit that abuse occurred. In one study, 57 percent of children referred to a clinic because they had sexually transmitted diseases claimed not to have been molested despite irrefutable evidence.[31]

As with the previous categories of sexual criminal activity, much misunderstanding exists regarding the sexual abuse of children. This category of offense includes:

- *Exploitation.* The use of children for illegal activities such as prostitution and pornography
- *Incest.* Sexual relations between children and their parents
- *Child sexual abuse.* The sexual molestation of children, as well as seduction and statutory rape

The Child Protection Act of 1984 describes child pornography as a highly organized business that focused on runaways and homeless youth and one that operates on a national basis. It provided for increased penalties for adults involved in it and pointed out that such acts are injurious to the physical and emotional well-being of the child. In addition to this act, most states have passed legislation addressing child abuse and the sexual exploitation of children.

The basis of sexual misconduct with children is **pedophilia,** which is sexual attraction to children. A surprising number of people share this preference, and some are more willing than others to make physical overtures toward satisfying their desires. Surprisingly, there have been groups formed to promote sex with children. Such groups produce manuals and literature to support their perspective and have actually approached legislatures to restructure or eliminate laws governing "age of consent."

One such group, Paedophilia (British spelling), asserts that its members possess a natural sexual attraction toward children and that the attraction is as natural as the attraction of a man to a woman. Indeed, this group even suggests that for some, the sexual attraction to children is as natural as certain people's orientation toward homosexuality or heterosexuality and may therefore be impossible to change. Groups sharing similar goals and desires are:

- The René Guyon Society
- The North American Man/Boy Love Association
- The Pedophile Information Exchange

- The Child Sensuality Circle
- The Pedo-Alert Network
- Lewis Carroll Collectors Guide

All of these groups advocate adult–child sex and the changing of laws that make it a crime.[32] In any case, it is clear that a subculture exists regarding this problem and that a great deal of misunderstanding also exists about how best to deal with the situation. In addition to these organizations, yet another category of child sexual offender exists: the stereotypic child molester or child rapist. Unlike people associated with the above-mentioned organizations, this class of offender usually conducts deeds individually with the victim.

In any case, the investigation of sexual offenses involving children must be handled carefully through the use of technical investigative techniques and training. Additionally, investigators must have an in-depth understanding of the underground subculture of groups or individuals who exploit children sexually through incest, child pornography, prostitution, and molestation.

The Preliminary Investigation

In the early phase of the investigation, the investigator must collect as much information about the charge as possible. This is typically done by interviews with people who are most closely associated with the child. Assuming that such persons are not suspects in the case, they could provide the investigator with information regarding any abnormalities in a child's physical appearance as well as unusual behaviors and actions by the child. In the event that the person being questioned becomes a suspect, investigators should be careful to avoid accusations or passing judgment. In addition, if the subject develops into a suspect during the interview, the officer must remember to afford the subject all of his or her due process rights under the Fourth, Fifth, and Fourteenth Amendments.

The Forensic Interview

For the most part, the child abuse investigation begins with information provided by the child victim. Obtaining this information is a vitally delicate task that normally requires a forensic interview of the child to determine whether he or she has been abused. In the case of a criminal investigation, the forensic interview can be conducted by a law enforcement officer or a member of child welfare or CPS, provided they are properly trained to do so. As such, child abuse investigations typically represent a collaborative effort between law enforcement and social service professionals.

In addition to yielding the information needed to make a determination about whether abuse or neglect has occurred, forensic interviewing provides evidence that will stand up in court if the investigation leads to criminal prosecution. Properly conducted forensic interviews are legally sound in part because they ensure the interviewer's objectivity; use non-leading, non-suggestive techniques; and emphasize careful documentation of the interview. Generally, the forensic interview is used only during the assessment portion of a child abuse investigation and involves only the children who are the subject of the investigation.[33]

Although of vital importance in investigations in which it is likely substantiation will lead to criminal prosecution, such as cases of physical, sexual, or emotional abuse, forensic interviews occur in virtually all child abuse investigations. When responding to reports of neglect, at the point when investigators begin exploring the allegations with a child, they should approach this as a forensic interview opposed to a casual conversation.

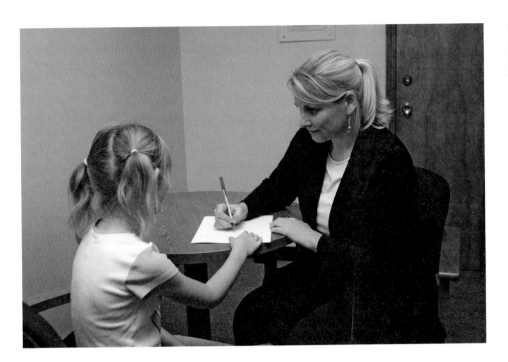

FIGURE 13.5 Interviews with possible child abuse victims must be conducted with specially trained personnel.

Why Are Forensic Interviews Needed?

The reason forensic interviews are needed is because most perpetrators deny the abuse and most acts of maltreatment are not witnessed, the victim's statement is critical evidence in child abuse cases. Yet developmental issues, such as children's varying abilities to recall events and use language, as well as the trauma they may have experienced, complicate efforts to obtain information about the abuse. The forensic interview is designed to overcome these obstacles.[34]

The goal of the forensic interview is to obtain a statement from a child in an objective, developmentally sensitive, and legally defensible manner.[35] To ensure facts are gathered in a way that will stand up in court, forensic interviews are carefully controlled. For example:

- The interviewer's statements and body language must be neutral.
- Alternative explanations for a child's statements are thoroughly explored.
- The results of the interview are documented in such a way that they can bear judicial scrutiny.

In many jurisdictions, the backgrounds and professions of the persons who conduct forensic interviews vary from community to community and from investigation to investigation. Sometimes these interviews are conducted only by child welfare workers or law enforcement investigators in the field; sometimes another secondary forensic interview is conducted by a therapist or other specially trained professional in a controlled, child-friendly environment.

The Initial Interview

In most jurisdictions, state child welfare investigators conduct the initial forensic interview because state laws often require that after a report is received that a child has been physically, emotionally, or sexually abused, there must be an immediate face-to-face contact with the child. During this meeting, which must typically occur within 24 hours after the report is made, child welfare workers assess risk and determine whether steps need to be taken to ensure the child's immediate safety. When police investigators discover a possible child abuse case, he or she can contact state child welfare workers and then observe the interview.[36]

The location of the interview is an important consideration toward establishing the proper atmosphere for the child interview. Not only should the interview room specifically designed—comfortable, quiet, and free from distractions—but there should also be only one interviewer responsible for interviewing the child.

In joint investigations, such as those involving police investigators and child service workers, both may be present, but only one should be in the primary role. Moreover, to protect against outside influence, no person having a direct relationship with the child can be present, even for support. A trained victim advocate may accompany the child during the interview. The interview room needs to be equipped with non-intrusive video and audio equipment, and all interviews must be recorded. Such recordings document the interviewer's technique and capture the child's demeanor and statements.

The initial forensic interview can be influenced by a number of factors. These include the specific circumstances being investigated (e.g., the child may need to be referred for a medical examination, which is often accompanied by a secondary forensic interview); the investigating officer's proximity to and ability to access forensic interviewing resources, such as a local CAC; the protocols and procedures adopted by each agency; and the interviewer's skill and comfort level.

One of the objectives of forensic interviewing is to reduce the number of times children are interviewed. The concern is contamination of the child's memory of the incident(s) being investigated. Research and clinical experience indicate that the more times a child—especially a young child—is interviewed about alleged abuse, the less reliable and legally defensible that child's testimony may become.[37]

Lauren Flick, a psychologist who has conducted more than 3,000 child interviews, describes contamination this way:

> If I am the first person to talk to a child about an event, that event is like a design on the bottom of a swimming pool filled with clear water—it is easy to read. But each conversation this child has with someone about the alleged abuse clouds the water. If he has talked with his principal, parents, a police officer, etc., it can be very hard or impossible to discern the design at the bottom of the pool.[38]

The Secondary Forensic Interview

More in-depth forensic interviews sometimes occur after the initial stages of an investigation. These are usually conducted by specially trained psychologists or professionals with graduate-level education in the areas relevant to this type of interviewing. Furthermore, these interviews usually take place at centers that facilitate the interview process—therapists and doctors sometimes have such facilities, as do most providers of child medical evaluations.

CACs are also excellent resources for forensic interviewing. CACs offer comfortable rooms with children's furniture, toys, interviewing props, and other aids for observing and documenting interviews. Law enforcement and child welfare agencies are encouraged to work with CACs to avoid delays that can be detrimental to the overall success of the investigation.

Multidisciplinary Investigations

In most jurisdictions, forensic interviews can, and often are, multidisciplinary. This means that more than one agency participates in or observes the interview. The two agencies most commonly involved in multidisciplinary investigations are child welfare workers and law enforcement. Other participants can include representatives of mental health, the district attorney's office, and others. Advocates of the multidisciplinary approach argue that they:

- Reduce the number of child interviews, thereby reducing stress on the child. Repeatedly asking a child to relive abuse amounts to revictimization.
- Improve evidence quality so that perpetrators can be held accountable for harming children and the public can be protected.[39]

Close collaboration and joint investigation of serious child physical and sexual abuse by child welfare workers and law enforcement is common.

Techniques of Forensic Interviewing

Because forensic interviews can play a pivotal role in investigations of sexual and emotional abuse of children, criminal investigators need to know how they are conducted. There are many ways to conduct the forensic interview, and there is no single model or method endorsed unanimously by experts in the field. Some of the many forensic interviewing models in use today include the child cognitive interview, step-wise interview, and narrative elaboration. Similar to many of the others in existence, these three interview types have been shown to be more effective in helping children recall information than standard interviewing techniques.

Despite the different styles of interviews, there are some basic elements common to most forensic interviews. These include phases such as introduction, rapport building, developmental assessment (including learning the child's names for different body parts), guidelines for the interview, competency assessment (during which, among other things, it is determined if the child knows the difference between lying and telling the truth), narrative description of the event or events under investigation, follow-up questions, clarification, and closure.[40]

Forensic interviews may also incorporate the use of aids and props, such as anatomically detailed dolls, anatomical diagrams, dollhouses, puppets, and so on. Despite the differences that exist in the approaches interviewers take, it is possible to get a general sense of what a forensic interview is like. To do this, the step-wise interview will be examined.

The Step-Wise Interview

Developed by researcher John Yuille and his colleagues, the step-wise interview uses techniques to:

- Minimize any trauma the child may experience during the interview
- Maximize the amount and quality of the information obtained from the child while at the same time minimizing any contamination of that information
- Maintain the integrity of the investigative process for the agencies involved[41]

The steps in this method begin with the most open, least leading, least suggestive form of questioning and, if necessary, proceed to more specific and more leading questioning.[42] Basic questions fall into four categories and each carries different risks of influencing answers.

- *Open-ended questions.* These are invitations to provide information about an event or activity or prompts to elaborate on previously given information.
- *Specific questions.* These focus the inquiry or ask directly about a particular topic. These questions are often used to clarify information given by the interviewee.

- *Leading questions.* These are to be used with extreme caution. Such questions contain information that has not previously been mentioned by the interviewee.
- *Suggestive questions.* These are seldom used in forensic interviews. They are questions that imply or include an expected answer.[43]

Open-ended questioning is recommended for the forensic interview because any influence of the interviewer is reduced and the probability of the resulting information being accurate is increased. Specific questions and sometimes leading questions are necessary to clarify information given by the interviewee, but the interviewer should quickly return to open-ended questioning. Leading questions may be necessary at times, but remember that these are "high-risk questions" in the forensic setting. In all cases, suggestive questions must be avoided in the forensic interview.

The step-wise method begins with a rapport-building phase during which the interviewer puts the child at ease by asking questions about the child's interests. During this phase, the rules for the interview are discussed (e.g., "If you are unsure about an answer, please say so") and the child's level of development (e.g., linguistic, cognitive), body language, and affect are assessed. The child is commonly asked to recount two specific past experiences, such as a school outing. The interviewer uses these narratives as a basis for assessing the level of detail the child ordinarily conveys and as a way to teach the child to tell a story in a way that fits with the "rules" of the interview.

The interviewer then introduces the topic of concern with a general question such as, "Do you know why we are talking today?" The objective at this phase is to encourage the child to give an unprompted, free narrative account of the event under investigation. Younger children are less responsive to this kind of prompt. After the child has exhausted his or her free narrative, the interviewer moves to questioning.

This begins with open-ended questions and then, if necessary, the interviewer proceeds to use specific but non-leading questions, closed questions, and leading questions. As the interviewer descends in this hierarchy of questions, he or she can have less confidence in the accuracy of the child's responses, which make them less useful either for drawing a conclusion about abuse or as forensic evidence. The interviewer ends the step-wise interview by thanking the child for participating, asking if the child has any questions, and explaining what will happen next.[44]

Physical Evidence in Child Sexual Molestation Cases

- ☑ Camera or video equipment used for taking photographic images of the victim engaged in sexual acts with the offender
- ☑ Notebooks, diaries, papers, or anything else linking the offender to the victim
- ☑ Negatives or undeveloped film that depict the victim (or other juveniles)
- ☑ Magazines, books, or movies depicting juveniles in sexual situations
- ☑ Newspapers, magazine clippings, or other publications listing phone numbers with other sexual interests that might tend to identify juveniles involved with the suspect
- ☑ Evidence of occupancy, such as bills, letters, rent receipts, or other mail or correspondence showing that the suspect resides at a particular location or is in control of a particular location
- ☑ Any items of physical evidence belonging to the victim or used by the subject in sexual acts

Children as Witnesses

One of the most compelling reasons children are such formidable victims is the fact that they may be considered incompetent witnesses in the courtroom. Indeed, many such cases rely heavily on testimony from child victims. If the incident really happened, the child can be irreparably scarred, but if it didn't, the accusation can ruin the life of the accused. Until about a decade ago, there was little discussion of the possibility of false allegations in child sexual abuse cases. In recent years, however, skepticism has grown, partly because of sophisticated studies showing that witnesses, especially younger ones, can be influenced by the biases of interviewers.

In 1989, the McMartin Preschool case involved nine children who accused staff members at a suburban Los Angeles day care center of wholesale sexual molestation. After what some newspapers called the longest criminal trial ever, charges against the school's founder, Virginia McMartin, and four teachers were dropped. The determination as to whether or not a child should be considered as a competent witness rests with the discretion of the courts. Experienced investigators suggest that children usually tell the truth to the best of their ability and that when they lie, it is to get out of trouble, not "into" trouble.

Factors considered by the trial judge were the child's age, intelligence, and sense of moral and legal responsibility. A child will be deemed competent to testify if he or she possesses the capacity to observe the events, recollect and communicate them, and understand questions and answer intelligently with an understanding of the duty to speak the truth.[45] In short, the child must understand that some form of punishment will result if the truth is not told. In the absence of clear physical evidence such as rectal or vaginal abrasions, it is difficult to distinguish false allegations from truthful ones. Typically, interviewers will have the child demonstrate the abuse incident with an anatomically correct doll. Some courts, however, have ruled out these dolls because they view them as suggestive.

David Raskin, a forensic psychologist at the University of Utah, devised a form of interview designed to show the quality of a child's story. Derived from experimental work done in Germany in the 1950s, the interview allows the child to begin the interview with a free narrative, holding off prompting as long as possible. A series of questions then follows and is succeeded by a validity assessment that looks for shifts of focus, reappearing elements, and digressions. Raskin asserts that when people anchor events in their memory, they are not told in a straightforward manner. Specifically, most people correct themselves,

Characteristics of Child Victims[46]

- ☑ In the 8- to 16-year-old age group
- ☑ Unsupervised
- ☑ From unstable home environments
- ☑ From low- or average-income families
- ☑ Subject to abrupt changes in moods
- ☑ Not necessarily delinquent
- ☑ In possession of more money than normal, new toys, new clothes, and so on (gifts from the molester)
- ☑ Withdrawn from family and friends

add elements momentarily forgotten, and redescribe the event. The technique is based on the premise that when someone is inventing a story, it is difficult for them to proceed in this fashion.

The Child Molester

Child molesters represent the most common type of pedophile. The term *pedophile* is commonly used by medical treatment and law enforcement and psychology professionals alike and generally refers to one who engages in some form of child sexual exploitation. The specific images of the **child molester** conjured up by society vary greatly. Such images range from child molesters who coax or pressure their victims into sexual activity to the more violent child rapist who overpowers and threatens his or her victims and all variations in between. In reality, the child molester is not a crazed psychopath but more accurately is a product of his or her own emotional immaturity.

Herman Goldstein defines this offender as "a significantly older person who engages in any type of sexual activity with individuals legally defined as children."[47] The term *pedophile* is also associated with *child molester*, although the two terms may not portray the same type of person, that is, a pedophile, one whose sexual orientation is toward children, may harbor thoughts of sexual relations with children but may never act out such fantasies. Conversely, however, it might be a safe assumption to consider most child molesters as pedophiles, as their sexual desires are, indeed, manifested by sexual assault.

In most cases of abuse, only one child and one adult are involved, but cases involving several adults and several children have been reported as well. For example, a 54-year-old man who had previously won a community award for his work with youth was arrested for child molestation involving boys as young as 10 years old. The man would encourage and photograph sexual acts between the boys, such as mutual masturbation and oral and anal sex. He would then have sex with one of them.[48]

A study of 229 convicted child molesters revealed the following information. Nearly 25 percent of their victims were younger than six years of age. An additional 25 percent were ages six to 10 years old, and about 50 percent were 11 to 13 years old. Fondling of the child was the most common sexual behavior, followed by vaginal and oral–genital contact. Bribery was most often used to gain the participation of the victims.[49] Studies have shown that pedophiles have the highest recidivism rate of all sex offenders, approximately 25 percent.[50] Incidents of child molestation are believed to be one of the most underreported types of crime. This can be attributed to several phenomena, including embarrassment on the part of the child, fears of bearing the blame for the incident, a fear of being labeled after the incident is exposed, apprehension about the court process, concern that no one will believe the child victim, and fear of reprisal by the offender.

For investigative purposes, the child molester can be viewed as falling into two distinct typological categories: situational and preferential. The **situational molester** doesn't necessarily suffer from any specified psychological disorder but may commit such crimes because of one of several external factors. These include intoxication, drug abuse, mood or mental conditions, or other social conditions. In contrast, the **preferential molester** has sexual desires focusing on children and typically has a more identifiable psychological disorder.

Accordingly, studies of child molesters have revealed two psychological types: fixated and regressed.[51] The **fixated child molester** is one whose primary sexual orientation is toward children and whose sociosexual maturation develops as a result of unresolved conflicts in his or her development. With this offender, children have always been the focus of sexual interests, and sexual contacts with age mates have been situational but never preferred. The child molester will probably not be a stranger to the victim, that is, statistics have shown that such offenders are not only commonly known but are also frequently related to their victims. Examples are:

- A natural parent or other family member, including a stepfather, stepmother, or uncle
- A trusted adult, neighbor, boyfriend, or familiar person
- A remote acquaintance (e.g., coworker of one of the child's parents)

The **regressed child molester,** however, represents a clear (but possibly temporary) departure from a primary orientation toward age mates, as the child becomes a substitute for an adult partner. Unlike the fixated offender, regressed child molesters did not previously exhibit preferences for younger persons in their formative years. Rather, when adult relationships develop conflicts and become emotionally unfulfilling, sexual attraction to children emerges.

Investigating the Molester

It is important for any investigator to understand, as fully as possible, the methods used by child sex offenders. When an investigator understands the molester's desires and intentions, he or she can more adequately seek out the proper evidence for prosecution. For example, investigations have shown that child molesters frequently collect pornography and child erotica. Such items aid the prosecution in establishing intent or motive of some offenders. Pornography fuels the desires that child molesters harbor for sexual contact with children.[52] Studies have also shown that child sexual assault is frequently a premeditated act, that is, offenders might only casually consider a particular course of action (fantasizing) without a specific plan or act, or they might take a more overt action in stalking and abducting their victim.

Premeditation and Intent

The circumstances of any given incident can show premeditation on the part of the molester. For example, in one such case, a man boarded a transit bus loaded with children. The offender was then seated next to a young girl approximately 10 years old, and during the bus ride, the man's arm came to rest on the child's inner thigh or upper leg. Subsequent investigation revealed that the same man was frequently among a group of children at the time a local school let out and had no business being there. Here he also used his "hand trick" as was used on the bus.[53]

As this case illustrates, premeditation may be demonstrated through comparing different situations with which the same suspect was involved and establishing a mode of operation. As indicated, investigators should remember that molesters frequent places where there are children in their target group. This will help establish the molester's intent and might also help establish probable cause to stop, detain, identify, and possibly arrest offenders.

In conclusion, both the medical and legal professions have made great strides in identifying non-accidental trauma inflicted on children and the suspected sexual abuse of them. This progress accounts for what appears to be an increase in the number of identified child abuse homicides. Sadly, however, there will always be some children who die of abuse that is never discovered. Children deserve investigators' best efforts to turn over every stone in cases involving any suspicion of abuse of children.

FIGURE 13.6 Dean Arthur Schwartzmiller smiles with his attorney Melinda Hall in a San Jose, California courtroom on January 29, 2007, as he was sentenced to 150 years to life for sexually abusing two 12-year-old boys. Courtesy Paul Chet.

FIGURE 13.7 Two girls, aged 7 and 9 years, ride their bikes in front of the home of convicted child molester Dean Schwartzmiller, in San Jose, California. Paul Sakuma, AP Wide World Photos.

The Pedophile/Child Molester

- ☑ Has access through family, enticement, or
- ☑ Lures the child, or tricks the child into sex acts; sometimes pressures the child into sexual activity
- ☑ Gives gifts or rewards to the child
- ☑ Cautions his or her victims against disclosure
- ☑ Frequently explains that the activity must be kept a "secret" between the offender and the child
- ☑ Gives the child attention, acceptance, recognition in exchange for sex
- ☑ Often targets children with disabilities who are loners
- ☑ May target the child of a single parent who may have no male figure in the immediate family
- ☑ May be a child rapist (forcible)
- ☑ Overpowers and controls the child much as do adult rapists
- ☑ Uses physical force or threats
- ☑ Is part of a small minority of sex offenders of children

Summary Checklist

In this chapter, we examine child abuse and its many forms. Depending on the nature of the offense, investigators must consider specific indicators that a crime occurred and evidence to support a possible criminal charge.

The number of child abuse cases, of course, reflect only cases that come to the attention of the police. It is likely that many more cases exist. Forms of assault against children may include physical harm, sexual abuse, emotional abuse, and neglect and often include forms of pushing, shoving, slapping, and whipping.

See how well you are able to answer the following questions in your checklist.

1. **Are you able to explain the nature and extent of the child abuse problem?**

    - In 2006, the National Center for Victims of Violent Crime reported that an estimated 896,000 children were victims of maltreatment (neglect or abuse).

- *Child abuse* is a generic term that incorporates a variety of purposeful acts resulting in child injuries.

- The physical effects of child abuse are only part of a child's injuries. The psychological and emotional impact of abuse frequently have long-term consequences for the child.

- According to the National Committee on the Prevention of Child Abuse (NCPCA), nearly 3 million cases of child abuse and neglect are reported each year.

2. **Can you identify the investigative aspect of battered child syndrome?**

    The point at which an investigation of child abuse begins depends largely on the reporting party or agency and the degree to which a case of abuse, neglect, or abandonment can be legally established.

    Some injuries have identifiable patterns that can be linked to specific objects used in an attack.

(continued)

Summary Checklist (Continued)

Investigators must have a working knowledge of battered child syndrome and what it means to an investigation.

- Battered child syndrome is defined as the collection of injuries sustained by a child as a result of repeated mistreatment or beating.

- If the child's injuries indicate intentional trauma or appear to be more severe than could reasonably be expected from an accident, battered child syndrome should be suspected.

There are several signs of abuse that officers can identify while assessing the situation. For example, if the child has an injury that is inconsistent with the explanation given by the parents, abuse might have occurred.

State laws generally require certain persons to report instances of child abuse, neglect, or sexual abuse.

- These persons include school officials, medical personnel, attorneys, social workers, and others.

The time factor is crucial in the law enforcement response to suspected child abuse.

The responding officer's first task is to get medical attention for the child.

It is important for the investigator to contact all medical personnel who had contact with the family, such as doctors, nurses, admitting personnel, emergency medical technicians (EMTs), ambulance drivers, and emergency room personnel.

If the investigator does not have a basic knowledge of the causes of young children's injuries, experts should be consulted.

3. Do you know the investigative guidelines for child homicide?

The more carefully planned out a killing is, the less likely a medical explanation for the death will be found.

Most injuries resulting from abuse are much more subtle than poisoning, beating, bludgeoning, shooting, or strangulation.

Investigators must be aware that children do not die from simple falls.

When presented with a child who has died under suspicious circumstances in which there is no obvious sign of abuse, the investigator should ask an experienced pediatrician to help locate a specialist whose medical expertise can help make sense of a confusing picture.

4. Are you Able to Identify the Signs of Shaken Baby Syndrome?

SBS occurs primarily in children 18 months of age and younger.

It is most often associated with infants younger than one year old because their necks lack muscle control and their heads are heavier than the rest of their bodies.

In most cases of SBS, there is no skull fracture and no external sign of trauma.

According to all credible studies in the past several years, retinal hemorrhaging in infants is, for all practical purposes, conclusive evidence of SBS in the absence of a good explanation.

5. Do you know the problem of munchausen syndrome by proxy and how to detect it?

Munchausen syndrome is a psychological disorder in which a patient fabricates symptoms of disease or injury in order to undergo medical tests, hospitalization, or even medical or surgical treatment.

Parents or caretakers who have Munchausen syndrome attempt to bring medical attention to themselves by inducing illness in their children.

Investigators should:

- Consult with all possible experts, including psychologists.

- Exhaust every possible explanation in the cause of the child's illness or death.

- Find out who had exclusive control over the child when the symptoms of the illness began or at the time of the child's death.

6. Can you identify the investigative steps in child sexual abuse?

Child abuse can take a number of insidious forms.

Statistics of child sexual abuse underestimate the true incidence of child sexual abuse.

Child sexual abuse includes the following forms:

- *Exploitation.* The use of children for illegal activities such as prostitution and pornography.
- *Incest.* Sexual relations between children and their parents or other relatives.
- *Child sexual abuse.* The sexual molestation of children, as well as seduction and statutory rape.

The basis of sexual misconduct with children is pedophilia or sexual attraction to children.

In the early phase of the investigation, the investigator must collect as much information about the charge as possible.

- This is typically done by interviews with people who are most closely associated with the child.
- The child victim must also be forensically interviewed.

Child victim interviews must be conducted by investigators who are specially trained in child forensic interview techniques.

- These persons may be police investigators or members of the social services or the psychological community.

Many such cases rely heavily on testimony from child victims.

7. Do you understand the traits of the child molester?

Child molesters are the most common type of pedophiles.

- The term pedophile is commonly used by medical treatment and law enforcement and psychology professionals alike and generally refers to one who engages in some form of child sexual exploitation.

The term *pedophile* is also associated with child molesters.

For investigative purposes, child molesters can be viewed as falling into two distinct typological categories: situational and preferential.

- The situational molester may commit such crimes because of one of several external factors such as intoxication, drug abuse, mood or mental conditions, or other social conditions.
- The preferential molester has sexual desires focusing on children.

Studies of child molesters have revealed two psychological types: fixated and regressed.

- The fixated child molester is one whose primary sexual orientation is toward children.
- The regressed child molester, however, represents a departure from a primary orientation toward age mates because the child becomes a substitute for an adult partner.

Key Terms

acute maltreatment	chronic maltreatment	regressed child molester
battered child	fixated child molester	shaken baby syndrome (SBS)
battered child syndrome	Munchausen syndrome by proxy	situational molester
child abuse	pedophilia	sudden infant death syndrome (SIDS)
child molester	preferential molester	

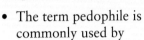

Discussion Questions

1. Discuss the distinctions between child physical and sexual abuse.

2. Describe some of the physical indications of child abuse.

3. Describe the "typical" child molester and how the actual offender differs from the stereotypical offender.

4. Explain the importance of the forensic interview.

5. Discuss the steps that investigators should follow when investigating suspected child abuse.

6. List and explain the various "syndromes" of child abuse.

mycrimekit™

Go to MyCrimeKit.com to explore the following study tools and resources specific to this chapter:

- *Practice Quiz:* Multiple-choice, true/false, short-answer, and essay questions.

- *Flashcards:* There are 14 key terms in this chapter. Flashcards test your knowledge of the chapter's key terms.

- *Web Links:* Check out the hotlink to *The New York Times* criminology articles.

- *Career Center:* Check out the hot links to interesting careers in criminal justice, criminology, and juvenile justice.

- *The Research Center:* Check out the Cybrary and research navigator for even more resources.

Notes

1. CHILDREN'S BUREAU. (2004). *Child maltreatment.* Washington, DC: U.S. Department of Health and Human Services. Available at http://www.acf.dhhs.gov/programs/cb/publications/cm02.

2. WALSH, B. (2005). *Investigating child fatalities.* Washington, DC: United States Department of Justice, Office of Justice Programs, Office of Juvenile Justice and Delinquency Prevention, August.

3. BONNER, B. L., S. M. CROW, AND M. B. LOUGE. (2002). Fatal child neglect. In Dubowitz H (Ed.). *Neglected children.* Thousand Oaks, CA: Sage Publications:156–173.

4. IBID.

5. BRIERE, J., L. BERLINER, J. A. BULKLEY, ET AL. (Eds). (1998). *The APSAC handbook on child maltreatment,* 2d ed. Thousand Oaks, CA: Sage Publications.

6. WALSH, B. (2005). *Investigating child fatalities.* Washington, DC: United States Department of Justice, Office of Justice Programs, Office of Juvenile Justice and Delinquency Prevention, August.

7. IBID.

8. KOCHANEK, K.D. AND B.L. SMITH. (2002).Deaths: Preliminary data for 2002. *National Vital Statistics Reports* 52(13):27; National Clearinghouse on Child Abuse and Neglect Information (NCCANI). (2003). *Child abuse and neglect fatalities: Statistics and interventions. Fact sheet.* Washington, DC: U.S. Department of Health and Human Services, Administration for Children and Families, NCCANI, August.

9. PENCE, D. AND C. WILSON. (1994). *Team investigation of child sexual abuse.* Thousand Oaks, CA: Sage Publications.

10. WALSH, B. (2005). *Investigating child fatalities.* Washington, DC: United States Department of Justice, Office of Justice Programs, Office of Juvenile Justice and Delinquency Prevention, August.

11. PENCE, D. AND C. WILSON. (1994). *Team investigation of child sexual abuse.* Thousand Oaks, CA: Sage Publications.

12. WALSH, B. (2005). *Investigating child fatalities.* Washington, DC: United States Department of Justice, Office of Justice Programs, Office of Juvenile Justice and Delinquency Prevention, August.

13. IBID.

14. ZULAWSKI, D.E. AND D. E. WICKLANDER. (1993). *Practical aspects of interview and interrogation.* Boca Raton, FL: CRC Press.

15. IBID.

16. WALSH, B. (2005). *Investigating child fatalities.* Washington, DC: United States Department of Justice, Office of Justice Programs, Office of Juvenile Justice and Delinquency Prevention, August.

17. REECE, R. M. (Ed.). (1994). *Child abuse: Medical diagnosis and management.* Malvern, PA: Lea and Febiger.

18. IBID.

19. COOK, N. AND M. Hermann (1996). *Criminal defense checklists.* Deerfield, IL: CBC.

20. IBID.

21. WALSH, B. (2005). *Investigating child fatalities.* Washington, DC: United States Department of Justice, Office of Justice Programs, Office of Juvenile Justice and Delinquency Prevention, August.

22. GEBERTH, V. (1990). *Practical homicide investigation,* 2nd ed. New York: Elsevier.

23. National Center for Injury Prevention and Control. (2006). *Child maltreatment: Fact sheet.* Centers for Disease Control and Prevention (CDC). Available at http://www.cdc.gov/ncipc/factsheets/cmfacts.htm.

24. American Academy of Pediatrics: Committee on Child Abuse and Neglect. (2001). Shaken baby syndrome: Rotational cranial injuries. Technical report. *Pediatrics* 108(1):206–10. Available at http://pediatrics.aappublications.org/cgi/content/full/108/1/206.

25. ELDER W., I. C. COLETSOS, AND H. J. BURSZTAJN. (2010). In F. J Domino (Ed). *Factitious disorder/Munchhausen syndrome.*

The 5-minute clinical consult, 18th edition. Philadelphia: Wolters Kluwer/Lippincott.

26. VENNEMANN B., M. G. PERDEKAMP, W. WEINMANN, ET AL. (2006). A case of Munchausen syndrome by proxy with subsequent suicide of the mother. *Forensic Science International*. 158(2-3):195–199.

27. PROTECTIVE AND FAMILY SERVICES, State of Texas. Available at http://www.dfps.state.tx.us/child_care/information_for_child_care_professionals/sbs_sids.asp.

28. GEISSINGER, S. (1993). Boy Scouts dismissed 1,800 suspected molesters from 1971–1991. *Boston Globe*, October 15:3.

29. RUSSELL, D. (1983). The incidence and prevalence of intrafamilial and extrafamilial sexual abuse of female children. *Child Abuse and Neglect* 7:133–146.

30. WOLFNER, G. and R. GELLES (1993). A profile of violence toward children: A national study. *Child Abuse and Neglect* 17:144–146.

31. LAWSON, L. and M. CHIFFEN (1992). False negatives in sexual abuse disclosure interviews. *Journal of Interpersonal Violence* 7:532–542.

32. GOLDSTEIN, H. (1977). *Policing a free society*. Cambridge, MA: Ballinger, p. 1.

33. SORENSON, E., B. L. BOTTOMS, AND A. PERONA. (1997). *Handbook on intake and forensic interviewing in the children's advocacy center setting*. Washington, DC: Office of Juvenile Justice and Delinquency Prevention.

34. SAYWITZ, K. J. AND G. S. GOODMAN. (1996). Interviewing children in and out of court. In J. BRIERE, L. BERLINER, J. A. BULKLEY, ET AL. (Eds.). (1998). *The APSAC handbook on child maltreatment*, 2d ed. Thousand Oaks, CA: Sage Publications:297–317.

35. IBID.

36. SORENSON, E., B. L. BOTTOMS, AND A. PERONA. (1997). *Handbook on intake and forensic interviewing in the children's advocacy center setting*. Washington, DC: Office of Juvenile Justice and Delinquency Prevention.

37. SAYWITZ, K. J. AND G. S. GOODMAN. (1996). Interviewing children in and out of court. In J. Briere, L. Berliner, J. A. Bulkley, et al. (Eds.). (1998). *The APSAC Handbook on child maltreatment*, 2d ed. Thousand Oaks, CA: Sage Publications:297–317.

38. FLICK, J. AND J. CAYE. (2001). *Introduction to child sexual abuse (curriculum)*. Chapel Hill, NC: UNC-CH School of Social Work.

39. AMERICAN PROFESSIONAL SOCIETY ON THE ABUSE OF CHILDREN. (1997). *Investigative interviewing in cases of alleged child abuse*. Chicago: Cordisco Steele, L. and C.N. Carnes. (2002). *Child centered forensic interviewing*. International Society for Prevention of Child Abuse and Neglect. Available at http://www.ispcan.org/TCBYAUTHOR.htm.

40. Cordisco Steele, L. and C.N. Carnes. (2002). *Child centered forensic interviewing*. International Society for Prevention of Child Abuse and Neglect. Available at http://www.ispcan.org/TCBYAUTHOR.htm.

41. YUILLE, J.C., R. HUNTER, R. JOFFE, AND J. ZAPARNIUK. (1993). *Interviewing children in sexual abuse cases*. In G. Goodman and B. Bottoms (Eds.), *Understanding and improving children's testimony: Clinical, developmental and legal implications*. New York: Guilford Press.

42. GRAY, J. (ED.). (1994). Improving investigations: Strategies for professionals. *Virginia Child Protection Newsletter* 44 (Winter):8–12.

43. FALLER, K. C. (1993). *Child sexual abuse: Intervention and treatment issues*. Washington, DC: US DHHS Administration for Children and Families. Available at http://nccanch.acf.hhs.gov/pubs/usermanuals/sexabuse/index.cfm; Finkelhor, D. (1994, summer/fall). Current information on the scope and nature of child sexual abuse. *The Future of Children* 4(2). Available at http://www.futureofchildren.org/information2826/information_show.htm?doc_id=74226.

44. YUILLE, J.C., HUNTER, R., JOFFE, R., & ZAPARNIUK, J. (1993). Interviewing children in sexual abuse cases. In G. Goodman & B. Bottoms (Eds.). *Understanding and Improving children's testimony: Clinical, developmental and legal implications*. New York: Guilford Press; Flick, J. and J. Caye. (2001). *Introduction to child sexual abuse (curriculum)*. Chapel Hill, NC: UNC-CH School of Social Work; Sattler, J. M. (1998). *Clinical and forensic interviewing of children and families*. San Diego: Jerome M. Sattler Publishing, Inc.

45. KLOTTER, J. (1990). *Criminal law*, 3rd ed. Cincinnati, OH: Anderson.

47. GOLDSTEIN (1977). *Policing a free society*. Cambridge, MA: Ballinger.

48. BURGESS, A. W., C. R. HARTMAN, AND M. P. MCCAUSLAND. (1984). Response pattern in children and adolescents exploited through sex rings and pornography. *American Journal of Psychiatry* 141:656–662.

49. ERICKSON, W. D., N. H. WALBEK, AND R. K. SEELY (1988). Behavior patterns of child molesters. *Archives of Sexual Behavior* 17:77–86.

50. IBID.

51. GROTH, A. N. AND J. BIRNBAUM (1981). *Men who rape: The psychology of the offender*. New York: Plenum Press.

52. GOLDSTEIN (1977). *Policing a free society*. Cambridge, MA: Ballinger

53. IBID.

Crimes Against Property

PART

5

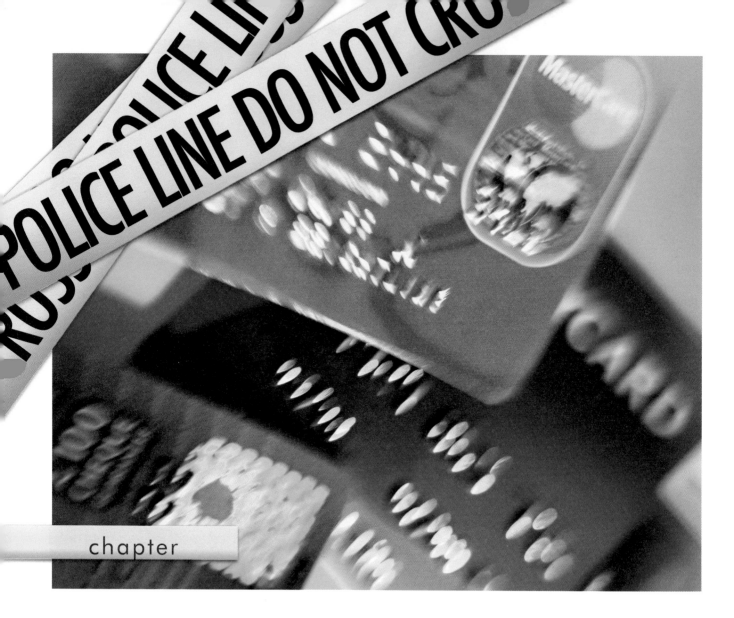

14

Theft-Related Offenses

This chapter will enable you to:

- Discuss the steps in the preliminary investigation of burglaries.
- Consider the various types of evidence required in a burglary case.
- Describe how to trace stolen property.
- Understand the problems of forgery and fraud.
- Define the various types of embezzlement.
- Understand the problem of shoplifting.
- Understand the extent of the motor vehicle theft problem.

Introduction

The crime of **burglary** is generally considered a covert crime in which the criminal works during the nighttime, outside the presence of witnesses. The burglar has often been portrayed in the media as a cunning masked person who is quick to elude police. In actuality, burglars are represented by virtually every creed, gender, and color and may indeed be skillful in their techniques, but they may also be bungling amateurs. In fact, it is estimated that opportunists commit most burglaries. Burglary for the most part is a **property crime**. The crime differs from robbery because burglars are more concerned with financial gain and less prepared for a violent altercation with the victim. Their goal is to steal as much valuable property as possible and sell what they steal (usually to a fence, who has connections to dispose of the property before police can discover it).

Burglary

The Uniform Crime Reports (UCR) program uses three classifications of burglary: forcible entry, unlawful entry or no force used, and attempted forcible entry. In most jurisdictions, force need not be used for a crime to be classified as burglary. Unlocked doors and open windows are invitations to burglars, and the crime of burglary consists not so much of a forcible entry as it does the intent of the offender to trespass and steal.

Many people fear nighttime burglary of their residence. They imagine themselves asleep in bed when a stranger breaks into their home, resulting in a violent confrontation. Although such scenarios do occur, daytime burglaries are more common. Many families now have two or more breadwinners, and because children are in school during the day, some homes—and even entire neighborhoods—remain unoccupied during daylight hours. This shift in patterns of social activity has led to growing burglary threats against residences during the daytime.

Trends

According to the FBI, in 2007, there were an estimated 2,179,140 burglaries, a decrease of 0.2 percent compared with 2006 data. Burglary accounted for 22.1 percent of the estimated number of property crimes committed in 2007. Of those, 61.1 percent involved forcible entry, 32.4 percent were unlawful entries (without force), and the remainder (6.5 percent) were forcible entry attempts. Burglary is a relatively common crime that costs victims billions of dollars every year. For example, in 2007, burglary offenses cost victims an estimated $4.3 billion in lost property; overall, the average dollar loss per burglary offense was

BURGLARY TRENDS

Year	Number of Offenses	Rate per 100,000 Inhabitants
2006	2,183,746	729.4
2007	2,179,140	722.5
Percent change	−0.2	−0.9

Source: Federal Bureau of Investigation. (2008). *Crime in the United States—2007.*

FIGURE 14.1 Burglary: Percent change. *From Federal Bureau of Investigation. (2008). Crime in the United States—2007.*

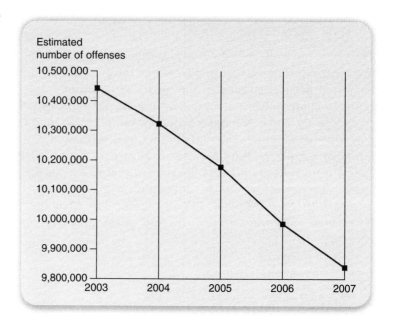

$1,991. Burglary of residential properties accounted for 67.9 percent of all burglary offenses, with 57.4 percent taking place during the day and 42.6 percent at night.[1]

Burglary versus Robbery

A distinction should be made between the terms *burglary* and *robbery* because they are commonly confused. Burglary is considered a property crime in which the thief seeks to avoid direct contact with people during commission of the crime. In addition, locations of burglaries are usually unoccupied homes or businesses where no witnesses are present. The crime of robbery is quite different. Here, the robber chooses to confront his or her victim at a location where witnesses are present. Robbery is therefore classified as a crime against persons. In this chapter, we examine burglary.

Why Criminals Burglarize

Burglary is an appealing alternative to the criminal because it offers a quick opportunity to acquire money or other valuables on short notice. Drug addicts have typically been associated with burglaries because they need a constant source of cash with which to purchase drugs. Some burglars are violent in nature, but experience has shown that they usually try to avoid confrontations during the commission of their act. In fact, many actually flee the area when confronted.

Elements of Burglary

Although the elements of the crime are defined by each state's criminal code, many differences exist regarding these laws. Some commonalities, however, are also present and are generally reflected in the elements of the crime.

Burglary is a crime against the dwelling that is violated. Accordingly, no violence need be directed toward any occupants. As a rule, after the burglar is inside the structure, no additional felony need be committed for the legal elements of the crime to be met. Exceptions are when the person believes that the structure he or she is entering is open to the general public. Decisions as to the validity of this claim are typically left up to the jury.

How a Thief Works

Although many jurisdictions report an increase in daytime burglaries, some occur at night, typically between 7 and 12 P.M. It is during those hours that a burglar becomes most inconspicuous on the street. In selecting a target, the burglar will look for certain things to indicate that a structure is vacant. These include:

- Newspapers collecting in the front of the residence, indicating that no one has been home for a while
- Empty garage left open
- House with too many lights on or just one light left on

When a daytime burglary occurs, it is usually during the time that most people are working. To approach the residence, a more innovative burglar may pose as a salesperson, insurance agent, public utility worker, or other "legitimate" person. This permits him or her to verify that no one is home. After it is determined that the residence is vacant, either a quick, forceful entry can be made into the house, or the burglar can look for a tree or large bush that might cloak a window, which he or she can then use to enter the house unnoticed by neighbors.

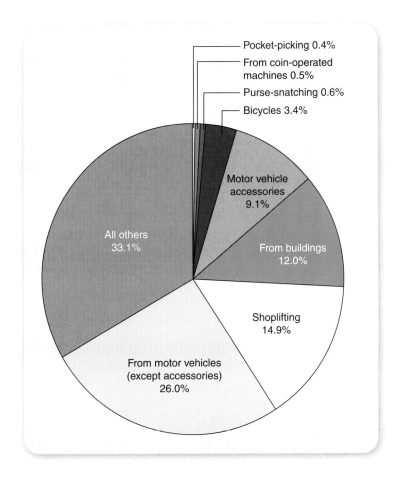

FIGURE 14.2 Larceny–theft: percent distribution, 2007. *From Federal Bureau of Investigation. (2008). Crime in the United States— 2007.*

Types of Burglaries

Burglaries can be divided into two general categories: residential and commercial. Residential burglars may focus on apartments or houses and usually work the higher-income areas of town. In both cases, the experienced burglar will be familiar with preventive measures used by residents. Such measures are sometimes easily defeated through knowledge of how they work. For example, an apartment dweller was careful in placing a steel rod in the track of the sliding glass door leading to the patio area before he left town. The burglar, however, simply removed the six screws securing the "nonmovable" piece of glass next to the sliding door, slid the pane of glass to the side, and entered the apartment. After the burglar is inside the structure, money is most typically sought, but other valuables might be taken as well.

Warehouses, stores, taverns, and restaurants are all common targets of commercial burglaries. Occasionally, employees of companies will be implicated in such thefts because they have direct knowledge of the types of merchandise in stock and locations of cash.

ATM Burglaries

In February 1998, six people in Orlando, Florida were charged in connection with three ATM (automated teller machine) thefts after a predawn gun battle with police. The suspects were thought to be connected with a Yugoslav–Albanian–Croatian crime ring that targets ATM machines nationwide. In another February 1998 case, three people in Los Angeles were charged with burglarizing seven bank ATMs. In one case, one suspect disabled the alarms in the machines and then destroyed the surveillance tapes while the other two served as lookouts.

Burglaries of ATMs are one new form of burglary that is on the increase. The ability of banks to provide increased security measures, along with the proliferation of small, freestanding ATMs, has become a concern for criminal investigators. In 1997, there were more than 200 ATM burglaries (and attempted burglaries) compared with 70 in 1992. This compares with a reduction of bank robberies, down 13 percent during 1997.[2] Of course, the use of ATMs is also up considerably in recent years. In 1997, there were 11 billion ATM transactions compared with 4 billion in 1985. The amount stolen from ATMs ranges from $15,000 to $250,000, so the "take" for a successful burglar can be fairly substantial.

Types of Burglars

Criminals who commit property crimes can be categorized into one of two groups: amateurs or professionals. Although both pose a problem to society, each group has special characteristics.

Elements of Burglary

Burglary is committed when a person:

- ☑ Knowingly breaks or
- ☑ Remains in
- ☑ A building or structure belonging to another
- ☑ For the purpose of committing a crime therein

Inside lights remaining off at night indicating no one is home

Newspapers collecting on driveway or yard indicating that owners are away

Shrubs are not trimmed

Area around the home is not properly lighted

House keys located around the home

Windows or doors left unlocked

No vehicles located in the driveway or in front of the home indicating that owners are away

FIGURE 14.3 Drawing showing how a house can be an attractive target to a burglar. Research shows that the average burglar spends no more than five minutes trying to break into a home.

The Amateur Burglar. The amateur burglar might travel a broad geographical area in search of the best opportunities for stealing. Many such persons resort to more personal contact with victims, such as purse snatching, muggings, or even robbery. The amateur thief is sometimes armed and can pose a serious threat to communities in which he or she operates.

FIGURE 14.4 Pry marks such as these are often evidence of a forcible entry. Courtesy of Mike Himmel and the Missouri State Highway Patrol.

FIGURE 14.5 A. Heel of suspect's shoe that was seized as evidence. **B.** Comparison imprint of the suspect's shoe heel found at the scene of a burglary; the matching shoe was seized in the investigation. Courtesy of Mike Himmel and the Missouri State Highway Patrol.

Juveniles pose another type of amateur thief. Most juveniles are opportunists who search for homes and businesses with unlocked doors or open windows. It is also characteristic of juveniles to resort to needless destruction of property during the commission of their crimes. In one case, three juveniles entered a residence to steal some liquor, but while they were there, they carved their initials in a grand piano, broke record albums in half, and spray-painted obscenities on the walls. Juvenile burglars sometimes go to the kitchen and consume food from the cabinets or refrigerator during the commission of the crime. In these cases, fingerprints may be lifted from the walls, cabinets, and so on for later use in identifying a possible suspect.

The Professional Burglar. The professional thief represents a unique criminal type. Such a person takes a great deal of time in planning a crime to avoid detection and net the greatest cache of property possible. The "pro" commonly relies on the expert use of tools for entry into otherwise secure structures. He or she might also consider making a bogus burglary call to another part of town to occupy the local police, thus giving him or her more freedom in his work. Pros typically drive trucks or vans, which conceal and transport their tools. Fake company names may even be painted on the sides of vehicles to deter suspicion by neighbors.

The Preliminary Investigation

The patrol division is usually the first to respond a burglary call. The first thing officers should do is determine whether a crime is currently in progress. If so, an ample number of officers should be dispatched to prevent the escape of the suspect(s). Officers approaching the burglary location should do so quietly without warning emergency lights or siren. En route, officers should also be on the lookout for persons fleeing the scene. It is also important for each officer to know exactly which fellow officers are responding to the call. As a rule, the first officer to receive the call will assume responsibility for placement of assisting officers.

FIGURE 14.6 **Left.** Tire track evidence documented and preserved at a burglary scene. **Right.** Tire matching tire impressions from the scene. Investigators must remember to photograph all tread on the suspect tire to capture the section of tread that touched the ground. *Courtesy of Mike Himmel and the Missouri State Highway Patrol.*

After arriving, great care should be taken not to slam car doors, to turn down police radios, and to avoid the jangling of keys while approaching the residence. In addition, officers should approach the residence on both the front and back sides in the event that the suspect attempts to flee.

Indications of Burglary

At the scene, certain reliable indicators that a burglary has been (or is being) committed can be observed (e.g., open doors or windows). Sometimes a burglar who makes his or her entrance through a window will remove the glass. This makes it difficult for the officer to detect a break-in with only a superficial glance. So when checking glass, the officer should look for a reflection with the use of a flashlight. Sometimes burglaries can be detected by spotting debris on the floor from shelves or counters. Also, debris can be found around desks and cabinets. Other indicators include vehicles parked near the suspect location for no apparent reason or trucks parked close enough to a building to permit access to a roof or to conceal a window or door. In the case of a building burglary, a burglar alarm is another indicator of possible entry. Although wind, stormy conditions, or malfunctions can set off some alarms, the responding officer should not assume anything. Every alarm situation should be responded to as though it were a burglary in progress.

Yet another sign of a burglary in progress is a person serving as a lookout. Lookouts may be on, in, or near buildings or sitting in cars. Burglars have been known to use such tactics as parking a car a few feet down the street, raising the car's hood, using citizens-band walkie-talkies, or just blowing the horn as a signal that police are approaching.

Approach with Caution!

Officers should enter the structure with weapons drawn, using their flashlights for illumination rather than room lights. This is done as a precaution to avoid the forming of silhouettes. In addition, officers should hold flashlights to their sides while flashing them sporadically to avoid making targets of themselves. After the location has been secured, or "flushed" for suspects, certain aspects of the scene should be documented.

- Document the time of the call.
- Record details about the type of structure.

- Record and document the method of entry and exit used by the suspect.
- Determine the whereabouts of the owner.
- Log all items of property taken and their original locations.
- Discuss with neighbors whether they noticed anything suspicious.

If no suspects are located in the structure, investigators should follow the preliminary investigation steps outlined in Chapter 3. If suspects are thought to be inside the burglary location, entry should not be considered until sufficient backup has arrived and each officer knows the exact location of other officers at the time of entry.

Physical Evidence

Experience has shown that most burglars are convicted on circumstantial evidence. Therefore, any physical evidence located at the burglary crime scene is critical to the case. In addition to forensic evidence such as broken glass, tool marks, and fingerprints at the burglary crime scene, other evidence should also be sought by the investigator. In the case of safe burglaries, safe insulation can be used to link the suspect to the crime scene.

Investigative Techniques in Burglary Cases

- ☑ Determine the point of entry.
- ☑ Check to see if a window or door was forced open.
- ☑ What type of tool was used?
- ☑ Are there tool marks?
- ☑ Is there evidence of lock picks?
- ☑ Look for footprints, tire tracks, and so on.
- ☑ Look for other trace evidence such as cigarette butts, fibers, hair, pieces of broken tools, and so on.
- ☑ Sketch the scene.
- ☑ Interview victims and witnesses.
- ☑ Make a list of property taken (include serial numbers).
- ☑ Make a list of all persons on the crime scene.

FIGURE 14.7 Bolt cutters are considered a pinching type of tool and have interactive blades that oppose each other. Courtesy of the Missouri State Highway Patrol.

FIGURE 14.8 A copper wire that was cut by a pair of bolt cutters (*right*). Notice how the cut is peaked (*arrows*) and not flat. A microphotograph of the copper wires (*left*). The bolt cutters in Figure 14.7 were identified as cutting this copper wire. Courtesy of the Missouri State Highway Patrol.

FIGURE 14.9 Burglary tools. Courtesy of Mike Himmel.

Possession of Burglary Tools

Possession of **burglary tools** is considered a separate felony offense by most jurisdictions. If circumstances surrounding the confiscation of the tools indicate that they were intended for use in a burglary, possession of them is usually sufficient for a conviction, even though a burglary has not yet been committed.

Many legitimate uses, of course, can be found for the tools and materials. The investigating officer should therefore determine if possession of the tools is legitimate and if there is any criminal "intent" present that would support criminal charges. Burglary tools can consist of numerous items.

Tracing Stolen Property

After a successful burglary has occurred, the thief will probably seek to get rid of the stolen property as soon as possible. To this end, a **fence** is used. The fence is a person who buys and sells stolen property with criminal intent.

The Fence

Fencing operations can range from professional to highly unorganized. For example, a nonprofessional fence might simply take a trunk full of stolen property in his or her vehicle to a location such as a factory parking lot, where workers on break can come for "good deals." A professional fence may operate from an otherwise legitimate business such as a pawnshop or used furniture store. People operating in this fashion don't necessarily consider themselves criminals but yet seldom question the lawful ownership of property they receive. From this fixed location, the fence purchases property on a random basis from thieves in the area. This arrangement tends to foster a degree of dependency between the thief and the fence, each needing the services of the other.

Proving the Receipt of Stolen Property

Establishing proof of a fencing operation is a grueling and time-consuming task. However, a fence is most vulnerable during the possession and storage of stolen property. Although many arrests result from lengthy investigations, many are made when suspected stolen property is identified. This is sometimes necessary when there is a risk of losing the property and confiscation is required. As a first rule of thumb, the property in question must be identified as stolen, a task that is more difficult than it may first seem. For instance, many suspected thieves are in possession of property that bears no identification numbers. Without some type of identification number, positive identification is extremely difficult.

In addition, many companies fail to maintain adequate inventory control. Poorly kept records also make it difficult to trace property even when identification numbers are present. Another category of untraceable goods is **fungible goods**, items such as tools, liquor, and clothing that are indistinguishable from others like them. In the absence of some type of identifying numbers, such items are virtually untraceable. To convict a thief for a property offense in this category, investigators must prove that the suspect received stolen property. Laws addressing stolen property also include possession, concealment, and sale of stolen property. Because evidence in this category is sometimes difficult to obtain, investigators might have to rely on circumstantial evidence for prosecution.

One method of showing possession of stolen property is to locate the property on the premises of the suspect. This finding, however, may not be sufficient to prove "criminal intent." It is helpful to show that the stolen goods are in close proximity with personal goods owned by the suspect. This will avoid the defense that the stolen goods were in the possession of someone else living at the same residence.

Circumstantial Evidence

Other than the evidence discussed previously, investigators might need to rely on circumstantial evidence to prove receipt of stolen property. Such evidence is described as follows:

- Did the suspect pay for the merchandise with a check or cash?
- Was the property purchased for considerably lower than the normal retail price?
- Does the suspect have a receipt for the property?
- Were the stolen items isolated from other items in storage?
- Is there property from several different thefts present at the location?

After property has been retrieved, a determination should be made as to how it got there. The owner of the property should examine it and make a positive identification. In many cases, a secondhand store or pawnshop owner can make a positive identification of a fence.

Larceny–Theft

In 2002, 25-year-old Ted Roberts and 22-year-old Tiffany Fowler were arrested in Orlando, Florida and charged with stealing moon rocks from the Johnson Space Center in Houston, Texas. Roberts had been working as a student intern at the center, and Fowler was a Space Center employee. Officials realized that the lunar samples, along with a number of meteorites, were missing when they discovered that a 600-pound safe had disappeared from the Houston facility. They had been alerted to the loss by messages placed on a Web site run by a mineralogy club in Antwerp, Belgium, offering "priceless Moon rocks collected by Apollo astronauts" for sale for up to $5,000 per gram. Roberts and Fowler were arrested by federal agents pretending to be potential buyers for the moon rocks.

Probably the most commonly committed crime of personal gain is larceny–theft. It is defined as the unlawful taking, carrying, leading, or riding away of property from the possession of another. Larceny–theft is one of the eight Index crimes according to the UCR. Generally, the two terms are considered synonymous. In some states, criminal law recognizes simple larceny (e.g., shoplifting) and grand larceny (e.g., auto theft). In most cases, what distinguishes one form of larceny from another is the dollar amount of the items stolen. Often, when anything stolen is valued under $200, the charge is simple larceny, while stolen property valued in excess of that figure is grand larceny. As a rule, thefts of any amount are considered larceny. The following offenses are examples of larceny:

- Pocket picking
- Breaking into coin machines
- Purse snatching
- Shoplifting
- Stealing bicycles
- Stealing motor vehicles
- Stealing valuables left in unattended buildings
- Stealing motor vehicle accessories

Larceny–Theft Offenses

There are many types of larceny–theft offenses, and their rate of occurrence is considerable. A lack of witnesses or other "concrete" evidence makes larceny a difficult crime to solve. Although there are many different types of larceny–theft offenses, in this book we attempt to discuss only a few of the most problematic. Before the investigator can determine whether a crime has been committed, he or she must understand the legal elements.

mycrimekit

Video: Burglary

Elements of Larceny–Theft

A person commits the crime of larceny–theft if he or she:

- ☑ Takes and carries away
- ☑ The personal property
- ☑ Of another
- ☑ Without consent and with the intent to steal.

LARCENY—THEFT TREND

Year	Number of Offenses	Rate per 100,000 Inhabitants
2006	6,607,013	2,206.8
2007	6,568,572	2,177.8
Percent change	−0.6	−1.3

Source: Federal Bureau of Investigation. (2008). *Crime in the United States—2007.*

In larceny–theft investigations, the state must show that there was a "taking," at least for a brief time, and that the defendant had control over the property "of another." The taking must be deliberate and with the intent to steal.

The UCR defines larceny–theft as the unlawful taking, carrying, leading, or riding away of property from the possession or constructive possession of another. It includes crimes such as shoplifting, pocket picking, purse snatching, thefts from motor vehicles, thefts of motor vehicle parts and accessories, and bicycle thefts, in which no use of force, violence, or fraud occurs. In the UCR program, this crime category does not include embezzlement, confidence games, forgery, or worthless checks. Motor vehicle theft is also excluded from this category inasmuch as it is a separate Crime Index offense.

Trends

In 2008, the FBI reported that there were an estimated 6.6 million (6,568,572) larceny-thefts nationwide during 2007. Larceny-theft is a pervasive crime that accounted for an estimated 66.7 percent of all property crimes and costs to victims at an estimated $5.8 billion dollars in lost property in 2007. The average value of property taken during larceny-thefts was $886 per offense.[3]

Forgery and Fraud

Theft crimes in the form of forgery or fraud accounted for 54 percent of the 28,012 white-collar felony dispositions in 1993. In addition, fraud constituted 38 percent, and embezzlement made up 8 percent of white-collar dispositions. Fraud cases may be enigmatic in nature. For example, in 1992, physician Cecil Jacobson (the sperm doctor) was convicted of secretly fathering the children of as many as 75 of his patients through artificial insemination. In this case, the federal jury ruled that he wrongfully used his sperm instead of that of anonymous donors to impregnate patients after promising to use donors who resembled their husbands and that he used hormone injections to trick women into thinking they were pregnant and then told them they'd miscarried, ensuring that they would return.

Check Fraud

Despite all the talk of electronic banking, one low-tech device is increasingly popular: the checkbook. Just as check writing has boomed, so has check fraud. According to the American Bankers Association, check fraud is a growing concern, costing banks $12.2 billion in 2006.[4] In addition to its impact on banks is its effect on consumers. For example, check fraud leads to higher fees for bounced checks, and when a person is a victim of check fraud, dealing with it can impose a severe hardship in reconciling and closing an account and dealing

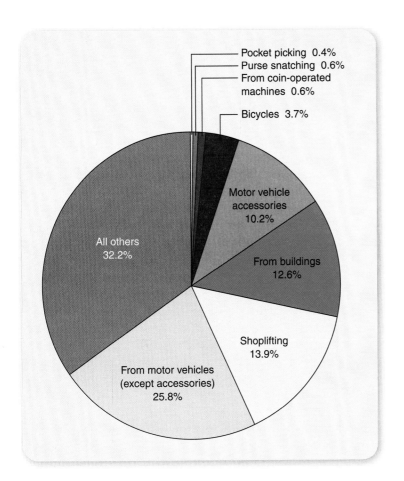

FIGURE 14.10 Larceny–theft: percent distribution, 2007. Because of rounding, the percentages may not add up to 100. *From Federal Bureau of Investigation. (2007). Crime in the United States—2006.*

with creditors seeking payment for merchandise purchased with bogus checks. Why is there an increase in check fraud? The American Bankers Association responds with several reasons:

- The proliferation of personal computers and high-quality copiers, which make it easier and less expensive to forge copies of checks
- Checking account customers who don't safeguard their account numbers
- Competition for business, which discourages some banks from stepping up procedures to detect and combat fraud because it might inconvenience customers

Criminals realize that check forgery is not only lucrative, but because it is a nonviolent crime, their chances of being prosecuted are unlikely. Bands of criminals often travel from region to region targeting different banks and payroll accounts. After infiltrating an employer and forging documents, they can walk off with as much as $300,000 per day.

Forgery of a victim's personal check involves acquiring both the check and a form of identification of the victim. He or she must then be able to forge the victim's name on the instrument successfully to the point that it closely resembles the original. In addition to the signature, amounts of checks can sometimes be altered to represent larger amounts. This can be accomplished in several ways. For example, the amount $10 can be altered to read $100 simply by adding a zero onto the designated amount and then altering the written portion of the

A CLOSER LOOK

$40 Million Check Fraud Ring

In April 1996, law enforcement agencies began targeting a group of people who allegedly operated a fraudulent check-cashing scheme in the United States and abroad. On June 12, 2000, nine persons, primarily Nigerian nationals, were arrested in the Los Angeles area for their involvement in a check scheme that involved more than $40 million. All of those arrested pleaded guilty. Federal agents identified five of the nine people as the ringleaders of the scheme.

Theft of Credit Cards and Checks

Those involved in this scheme illegally obtained millions of dollars by stealing not only credit cards but also blank and completed checks. The stolen completed checks ranged from roughly $10,000 to more than $2 million. Checks addressed to businesses and high-tech customers were stolen by mail carriers with the U.S. Postal Service. Checks were also stolen from company mailrooms before they were sent and after they were received. Usually, the targeted businesses, including Toyota and Disney, were large corporations known to write many checks. Dozens of companies did not discover the

missing money until reviewing their checking records, months after the thefts.

Most of the stolen checks were then given to forgers who prepared them for deposit by changing the payee names and dollar amounts of the check. Some checks were deposited after only the endorsements were forged. The altered checks were deposited into accounts in banks and brokerages in the United States, Indonesia, Senegal, Germany, England, and Hong Kong; these accounts were established using false personal or business names. In some instances, account names were established that were similar to the names of the targeted businesses.

With the stolen money in their false accounts, those involved in the scheme wrote checks, purchased cashier's checks, withdrew cash, and transmitted money by wire transfer.

Here's how the scheme worked: A check worth more than $160,000 was stolen from a large entertainment company, altered, and deposited into a bank account controlled by one of the defendants. The money in the account was then divided into 33 cashier's checks and distributed to members of the gang.

instrument. Forgery of government checks is another growing problem in many parts of the country. Many such checks, such as welfare and unemployment payments, are mailed in groups at regular intervals and are sometimes stolen directly from mailboxes.

Banking institutions often consider the government check as legitimate because of its "official" appearance. Therefore, its legitimacy often goes unquestioned. Once passed, the forged government check may go undetected for months before the crime is discovered. Another method of forgery includes the use of fictitious checks drawn on a nonexistent firm or person. These schemes, called **check kiting**, are commonly encountered by law enforcement authorities. Kiting consists of drawing cash on accounts made up of uncollected funds. By using two different banking institutions, the kiter may use funds from one bank to cover checks drawn on another. Each time the bank pays out funds against the account balance, the kiter has been successful in cheating the bank out of its own funds.

Banks are responding with new methods designed to stop bank fraud. For example, in 1995, the Texas Banking Association began experimenting with a new program in which a thumbprint is required from nonaccount holders who wish to cash checks. The thumbprints are kept on file only until the check clears. Pilot programs in Nevada and Arizona have resulted in a 40 to 80 percent reduction in check fraud losses.[5] Other services, such as the Duplex/BEI Check Fraud Prevention Program, aid banks in identifying patterns of criminal behavior to single out suspicious checks before they lose money. For example, a criminal opens an account with a small amount of money and waits a few months to deposit a fraudulent check for $80,000. He or she then withdraws the money after two business days, knowing that the bank is required to make the money available promptly. By the time the bank finds out that a check is counterfeit, a criminal is already gone with the money.

Investigating Check Forgery

One problem presenting itself in forgery cases is when the victim desires only restitution from the suspect and is unwilling to follow through with prosecution. The posture of the victim must therefore be determined early by the investigating law enforcement agency; otherwise, the police simply become a collection agency for the victim, and much valuable time is lost. To deal with this problem, many law enforcement agencies ask the forgery victims to sign a written agreement in which they agree to prosecute. Failure to sign the agreement would result in future claims of forgery being declined for investigation by the police. Witnesses in a check fraud case may include employees who both accepted and deposited a forged instrument.

A logical first step of the forgery investigation is to interview the person who was the recipient of the bad check: the acceptor. This is probably the most important source of investigative leads. After all, the acceptor is a witness to the crime, and he or she alone can describe the actual circumstances surrounding the crime. The investigator should consider asking the acceptor the following questions:

- What remarks did the suspect make during passing of the check?
- Was the check written or signed in the presence of the acceptor?
- What credentials, if any, were offered as identification?
- What was the suspect's description? (This should include physical, dress, mannerisms, and so on.)
- Was the customer a repeat customer or known to the acceptor?
- What type of transportation was used to and from the institution?

Responses to these inquiries, along with the investigator's personal evaluation of the competency of the acceptor, may help identify the suspect. The depositor is the next player who should be interviewed. This is the actual person whose account was used to draw funds from. The depositor should be asked to examine the forged check for anything that might be observed from it. If the signature on the check is not that of the depositor, a statement to that effect should be made to the investigator. Next, the investigator should inquire as to whether another party was allowed to use the depositor's account.

An affidavit should then be acquired from the depositor along with standards of the depositor's handwriting as it appears on his or her checks. The depositor should be asked how the suspect may have acquired the stolen checks. In the event that the depositor claims that checks were stolen during a burglary, the offense report should be pulled and reviewed. It is in the investigator's interest at this point to identify a possible discrepancy between the statement of the depositor and information from an offense report. Finally, the instrument itself must be secured as evidence and a receipt for it should be issued to the victim.

Embezzlement

Embezzlement is a low-profile crime that typically consists of employees of organizations stealing large amounts of money over a long period of time. Embezzlement is also extremely difficult to detect. Those who are successful in the embezzling of funds can cause extensive fiscal damage to victim organizations, frequently resulting in their financial ruin.

The crime of embezzlement is increasing at 15 percent per year and has an estimated annual cost of $4 billion.[6] The number of people arrested for embezzlement, however, has increased 40 percent since 1985, indicating that more employees are willing to steal from their employers, more employers are willing to report instances of embezzlement, or law enforcement officials are more willing to prosecute people involved with the crime of embezzlement.

Embezzlement is usually defined under individual state statutes dealing with grand theft. Generally speaking, however, it can be described as a fraudulent appropriation of property by a person to whom that property has been entrusted. Although the elements of the crime may vary, some common elements can be generalized:

- A trusting relationship exists between the suspect and the victim.
- The perpetrator had lawful possession of the pilfered belongings at some time during the relationship.
- The property was stolen or converted to a form of possession that was contrary to the trust relationship.
- There was criminal intent to deprive the lawful owner of the property, either temporarily or permanently.

The element of trust is critical in establishing the crime of embezzlement. For example, a bank teller has the lawful right to handle a bank's cash. Secretly taking quantities of that cash for his or her own personal use, however, is a form of possession that is contrary to the trust relationship with the bank.

Investigating Embezzlement

A primary element of the crime of embezzlement is the element of trust. So, to investigate this type of crime, the investigator must show that the suspect first accepted the property in the scope of employment and then misappropriated it

---

Crime Prevention Key: Avoiding Becoming a Victim of Check Fraud

☑ Don't give your checking account number or the numbers at the bottom of your checks to people you don't know, including people who say they are from your bank. They have no business requesting such information.

☑ Reveal checking account information only to businesses you know are reputable.

☑ Guard your checkbook. Report lost or stolen checks immediately.

☑ Properly store or dispose of canceled checks.

☑ Report any inquiries or suspicious behavior to your banker, who will take steps to protect your account and to notify authorities.

☑ Do not leave your ATM receipt at the ATM because these receipts contain account your information. Dispose of it safely and securely.

for his or her own use. Intent is relatively easy to demonstrate in these cases, however, because it usually requires some form of concealment or secrecy, such as altering business records. The investigation of embezzlement allegations is a tenacious and time-consuming task because paper trails are sometimes difficult to follow. Yet the investigator must be able to explain fully to a prosecutor, judge, and jury how the crime was committed and offer convincing evidence to support the findings of the case. This task can be especially perplexing when dealing with a company whose record-keeping practices are already haphazard.

Because many embezzlement cases require a degree of accounting expertise, investigators lacking such expertise may become frustrated, and the successful outcome of the case may then be jeopardized. The most common way of overcoming this obstacle is for the investigator to solicit the victim's help in providing technical support during the investigation. Company executives and consultants outside the company are generally willing and able to explain specific accounting processes. Embezzlers usually prefer to steal cash because it is both difficult to trace and easy to conceal. Investigators may, however, find this to be an advantage. For example, if an employee is found to be spending significantly large amounts of cash, he or she might also be hard-pressed to explain the origin of the money.

To seek a complaint, the investigator must put together a complete investigative file on the suspect and all circumstances surrounding the violation. The file should contain the following:

- A complete investigative report that identifies specific funds that were taken without authorization
- Methods used for the pilfering
- Photocopies of all checks and related documents pertaining to the theft(s)
- A statement of determination outlining the economic and psychological impact of the crime on its victim

Categories of Embezzlement

Many different types of embezzlement exist. These vary depending on the degree of trust that exists between the suspect and victim, but they typically fall into one of several categories discussed below.

Theft of Currency. The most common form of embezzlement is the theft of cash from a trusted party. Although a serious crime, such thefts are usually for modest amounts of money that may not be considered all that financially damaging to the victim company. Theft schemes most commonly used include:

- Taking cash from the register and then entering a negative of the same amount so that the cash drawer balance agrees with the register tape balance. In the event that the register tape contains many (sometimes hundreds of) entries, the negative balance may be difficult to detect.
- Corporate executives working for lucrative companies that make "cash loans" and fail to pay them back.
- Failing to ring up a sale and taking the cash from the cash drawer for the same amount.
- Sales clerks charging more than the amount on the receipt and pocketing the difference, hoping customers won't notice the difference.

Manipulation of Accounts. Embezzlement cases in which accounts are manipulated typically involve employees of an accounting department. For example, a typical case would be an accountant who makes payments to a fictitious company for services never rendered or goods never received and then endorses the check for payment. A scheme such as this may result in insurmountable losses for the victim company. Another way to embezzle from records is to manipulate payroll accounts. Typically, this type of case involves entering a bogus employee on the records or failing to remove a former employee from the records. In either case, the suspect intercepts the payroll check, endorses it with the name of the person who is on the records, and cashes it.

Retail Theft. As indicated, one of the hallmarks of embezzlement is the stealing of merchandise by a company's employees, or **pilferage**. This form of crime is also extremely difficult to detect, and it is difficult to determine the value of goods taken by employees over a period. One estimate is that pilferage accounted for 30 to 75 percent of all shrinkage and amounts to losses of $5 billion to $10 billion annually. According to McCaghy, several different methods are commonly used to steal from employers:[7]

- Factory workers zip up completed garments and take them home.
- Cashiers ring up lower prices on single-item purchases and pocket the difference. Many work with accomplices.
- Clerks do not tag sale merchandise and then sell it at its original price, pocketing the difference.
- Receiving clerks obtain duplicate keys to storage facilities and return after hours to steal.
- Truck drivers make fictitious purchases of fuel and repairs and split the difference with truck-stop owners.
- Some employees simply hide items in garbage pails or incinerators or under trash heaps until they can be retrieved.

Another form of inventory theft is when an inventory clerk writes a receipt for "damaged" goods that are shipped to an accomplice's residence. The goods can then be sold for cash. Because the merchandise was never returned to the manufacturer, the company will probably not detect a problem. The receipt indicating "returned goods" indicates that the goods were damaged; therefore, they will not be included in the victim company's inventory. Many companies consider this type of loss as shrinkage, that is, an unexplained loss.

In a 1983 study of theft in the workplace, John Clark and Richard Hollinger found that 35 percent of employees reported involvement in pilferage.[8] The study indicates that most theft is a result of factors relating to the workplace, such as job dissatisfaction and a general feeling of worker exploitation by employees.

Credit Card Fraud

In September 1996, 36-year-old Nigerian-born Olushina Adekanbi was arrested on credit card fraud charges. What made this case unusual was the fact that Adekanbi, who also went by more than two dozen aliases, had earned the nickname "King of New York" because he ran the largest credit card fraud ring in the United States. The ring was wanted for obtaining at least $650,000 in goods and cash advances, as well as gaining illegal access to credit lines worth an estimated $8 million.[9]

Credit card fraud is a growing problem in the twenty-first century. The worldwide traffic in counterfeit cards costs issuers of plastic $1.6 billion a year in false charges.[10] Although credit cards were designed to provide consumers with convenience and increased purchasing power, the criminal has also identified ways to profit from this financial medium. Records from credit card transactions have provided law enforcement with a twofold benefit: the apprehension of the fraudulent credit card user and accurate records that often point to other crimes.

Millions of credit cards issued by both international and local banking institutions are negotiable instruments that can be used fraudulently to obtain goods and services. All credit cards have one thing in common: they can be used to obtain something of value simply by presenting the card. Therefore, the security of the card is of utmost importance. Many credit card companies go to great lengths to offer cardholders some type of security or "insurance" against unlawful use of the card.

Obtaining Credit Cards. Credit cards are acquired by criminals through a variety of methods, including burglaries, robberies, mailbox thefts, and falsified applications to issuing companies. In addition, pickpockets and muggers may seek credit cards as readily as they seek cash. Waiters and retail clerks have been known to retain credit cards that are forgotten by customers. Such cards are sometimes sold to professional **plastic workers** who have experience in dealing with stolen credit cards.

Using Stolen Credit Cards. Credit card thieves must act quickly to overcome protection systems offered by companies. Techniques used are designed to upset and confuse sales clerks while not attracting attention to the thief. The thief will typically stroll through a store as if he or she is shopping but is actually evaluating sales personnel. After he or she identifies a salesclerk who he or she feels is easily manipulatable, that person is selected as the target. It is the intent of the thief to manipulate the clerk so that he or she fails to follow the prescribed security measures established by the store.

The floor limit is one primary loophole that is easily exploitable. The conscientious plastic worker is careful to purchase items that are under the designated limit, typically $50 to $100. In the event that the thief is using a "hot" card, he or she must be careful that the clerk doesn't check the **hot list** or cancellation bulletin. Because these lists are so lengthy, clerks frequently fail to check them. This procedure is sometimes overlooked when the thief carefully plans his or her purchase at closing time when employees are rushed to balance their registers and go home.

Investigating Credit Card Theft. Police officers investigating lost or stolen credit cards should consult the credit card company for assistance because many companies employ professional investigators who can offer valuable help in the investigation. Certain types of information are necessary during the credit card investigation that can be acquired with the assistance of the card company's investigator. Such information includes:

- The victim store's name and address
- The names of the store manager and clerk who were victimized (the clerk may be an excellent witness if he or she observed the signing of the card slip)
- The name of the legitimate cardholder and his or her address and telephone number
- The facts and circumstances surrounding the theft or loss of the card
- A detailed description of the item(s) purchased and the amount of the sale

After being identified, the plastic worker will be charged with each purchase as a separate offense, each of which must be supported by documentation and evidence. Investigations should always include how the credit card was obtained in the first place. Depending on the circumstances, this can constitute a separate offense. For example, the card could have been purchased from a pickpocket. The investigator should learn how, when, and where the card was acquired from its lawful owner.

Decisions to prosecute are usually left up to the office of the prosecutor who functions in the jurisdiction of the victimized merchant. In the event the case does go to court, the lawful owner of the card and experts from the credit card company can testify on behalf of the state.

Shoplifting

Shoplifting is a common form of theft involving the taking of goods from retail stores. In fact, it has grown into one of the biggest concerns in the area of retail business. Statistics bear this out: Shoplifting incidents have grown dramatically in the past 20 years, and some retailers expect an annual increase of from 10 to 15 percent. Some studies have even suggested that one of every nine retail customers steals from department stores. Moreover, the increasingly popular discount stores such as Walmart, Kmart, and Target employ a minimum of retail sales help and rely heavily on highly visible merchandise displays to attract purchasers.

According to the *Economic Crime Digest*, shoplifting is the form of theft that occurs most frequently in business and accounts for some of the greatest losses: an estimated $16 billion a year. The FBI reports that shoplifting acts number some 1 million yearly and have increased 30 percent since 1985. Because shoplifting is a kind of larceny–theft, it has basically the same elements of larceny–theft as discussed earlier.

Modern retail stores market their wares by allowing potential customers to examine them while on display. Computers may be tinkered with, clothes may be tried on, and television sets may be adjusted to demonstrate the clarity of the picture and the function of other features. The list goes on. Because stores often provide carts for the transportation of goods that the customer may wish to purchase, the courts have held that they have a lawful right to possess those goods for limited purposes. Concealment of goods by customers, however, is not allowed by businesses or the courts. Accordingly, the merchandise is offered for sale, and if a customer chooses not to purchase the merchandise, it must be returned to the display shelves in good condition.

Generally speaking, the shoplifter can be characterized as either professional or amateur. Whereas a professional shoplifter will steal goods for resale or bartering, an amateur steals merchandise for his or her own use. Records show that the majority of shoplifters fall into the amateur category. The professional shoplifter, however, represents a much greater problem for investigators. The professional often works in groups of three or four and often victimizes several shopping areas at a time. They are commonly trained on what items to steal, how to conceal them (e.g., wearing special clothing to help them conceal merchandise), and where to take the merchandise for resale after the theft. Investigations have revealed women who appear to be pregnant but who are wearing a specially made receptacle for small items. In another case, a heavy-set woman had been stealing small television sets by concealing them in a prerigged harness that was located between her legs.

A classic study of shoplifting was conducted by Mary Owen Cameron, who found that about 10 percent of all shoplifters were professionals who derived the majority of their income from shoplifting.[11] Sometimes called *boosters* or *heels*, professional shoplifters resell stolen merchandise to pawnshops or fences at usually one-half to one-fourth the original price. According to Cameron's study, most shoplifters are amateur pilferers, called **snitches**.

FIGURE 14.11 The offense of shoplifting represents a significant percentage of larceny–theft crimes. Here a shoplifter conceals stolen merchandise. *Courtesy of Mike Himmel.*

Snitches are usually respectable persons who do not perceive themselves as thieves yet are systematic shoplifters who steal merchandise for their own use rather than for resale.

Investigating Shoplifting

One problem with shoplifting is that many customers who observe theft are reluctant to report it to managers or security personnel. Many store employees themselves don't want to get involved with apprehending a suspected shoplifter. In fact, an experiment by Hartmann and his associates found that customers observed only 28 percent of staged shoplifting acts that were designed to get their attention.[12] In addition, only 28 percent of people who said they had observed an incident reported it to store employees. Another study by Blankenburg showed that less than 10 percent of shoplifting was detected by store employees and that customers seemed unwilling to report even severe cases.[13] Even in stores with an announced policy of full reporting and prosecution, only 70 percent of the shoplifting detected by employees was actually reported to managers, and only 5 percent was prosecuted.

Shoplifting cases can be investigated in one of two ways: reactive or proactive. A reactive investigation will include interviews of witnesses, collection of physical evidence, and conducting of other follow-up functions. A proactive case will probably be handled by in-house security personnel and will focus on the shoplifter who is caught in the act. In the case of proactive investigation, investigators should follow several rules of thumb:

- Be sure that probable cause exists before restraining a suspect.
- Observe the person concealing store merchandise that has not been paid for, not simply concealing "something" that cannot be positively identified as store merchandise.

- Keep the person under observation.
- Before arresting the person, always ask first for a receipt.

Remember, if the person has not yet walked beyond the last pay station, an arrest may not be lawful or appropriate, but confronting the person may still result in reclaiming of the merchandise. Most shoplifting cases are handled through local police and sheriff's departments and are prosecuted locally as well. When a store is involved with cases such as these, store policy should be considered as well as the opinions of the local prosecuting attorney.

The Growing Problem of Retail Theft. Retail theft costs the industry more than $37 billion in 2005, up from $31 billion in 2003. Retail theft becomes especially problematic during the holiday season, when overcrowded stores make shoplifting more difficult to detect and fraudulent returns easier to conceal. In 2006, it was estimated that retailers expected to lose $3.5 billion due to just fraudulent returns after December's busy holiday season.

Retailers are particularly concerned about gangs that have established supply chains that make organized theft, known as "boosting," too profitable to give up without a fight. For example, a single **booster** operating as part of the gang can steal up to $200,000 worth of merchandise in a weekend. In August 2006, for example, in Ocala, Florida, Beall's cameras caught a gang of exotic dancers that stole approximately $170 worth of goods from the Bradenton store. Apparel from other retailers filled the women's rented SUV. Two of the three women, who worked for an exotic dancing and escort service called Black Xtasy, admitted that they were traveling the state to steal. The suspected leader of the gang had retail theft warrants against her in two other Florida counties.

In another case, Walgreens' Divisional Coordinator for Organized Retail Crime, Jerry Biggs, stated that one group shoplifted from 24 of the drugstores in seven hours. In a videotaped interview with police, shoplifter Jesus Hernandez said he could easily boost $10,000 worth of merchandise in four hours. Fernandez specialized in stealing diabetic test strip packages, which sell for up to $100.

During a typical boosting, one or more gang members distract store clerks while one or two others lift merchandise. Some members stand outside the store doors, ready to signal if police or security officials are coming. Still others are in parking lots ready with getaway cars. The gangs are often armed with knives, guns, and even brass knuckles for fighting off store security personnel.

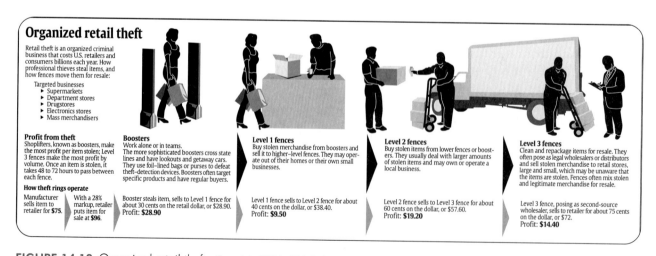

FIGURE 14.12 Organized retail theft. Copyright 2006, USA Today. Reprinted with permission.

The thieves typically seem to stay one step ahead of security devices. Even locked glass display cases can be cracked. For example, in 2006, 14 Target stores in California, Illinois, and Colorado were hit by thieves who broke open locked cases, filled carts with iPods, and pushed the carts out the doors. Professional shoplifters usually carry shopping bags lined with foil and duct tape to block the electric current that detects security tags. Some thieves remove security tags and hide merchandise under larger packages.

Some security analysts have suggested that antitheft systems seem to only work against people who don't know how to thwart them. Security personnel for retail stores must be cautious in making apprehensions. This is because retail companies must balance the importance of capturing thieves with possibly upsetting and frustrating paying customers.

Returns are one area where retailers have cracked down in recent years. Although some still give cash for a return without a receipt, many major retailers require receipts. In addition, many retailers use electronic receipts that track purchases made with a credit card or check. These receipts nearly eliminate the ability to use counterfeit receipts or to return stolen goods. They also use display devices that make it difficult to slide all the items on a hanging rack into a bag but that are not too difficult for legitimate customers to use.

The prosecution of retail crime is complicated in part because much of the merchandise stolen doesn't come with serial numbers. That makes it difficult for investigators to identify the merchandise as stolen. Unless merchandise is made under a retailer's private label and the store has alerted police of the theft, police who stop the driver of a car full of stolen items may have difficulty making an arrest and in many cases will not even seize merchandise as evidence.

As illustrated in Figure 14.12, retail theft has become more organized in recent years. Businesses such as supermarkets, department stores, drugstores, electronics stores, and mass merchandisers are frequently the targets for such theft rings. Thieves work closely with fences who act on numerous levels to quickly turn over their stolen merchandise and place layers of people between each stolen merchandise transfer.

In short, the criminal world has recognized retail theft is a much more profitable crime than burglary, with much less penalty. For example, although larceny overall was down 4.5 percent from 2000 to 2004, shoplifting increased nearly 12 percent, according to the 2005 UCR published by the FBI.[14]

Identity Theft

In 2000, golfer Tiger Woods discovered that his identity had been stolen and that credit cards taken out in his name had been used to steal $17,000 worth of merchandise, including a 70-inch TV, stereos, and a used luxury car. In 2001, the thief, 30-year-old Anthony Lemar Taylor, who looks nothing like Woods, was convicted of falsely obtaining a driver's license using the name Eldrick T. Woods (Tiger's given name), Wood's social security number, and his birth date. Because Taylor already had 20 previous convictions of all kinds on his record, he was sentenced to 200 years in prison under California's three strikes law. Like Woods, most victims of identity theft do not even know that their identities have been stolen until they receive bills for merchandise they haven't purchased.

Identity theft, which involves obtaining credit, merchandise, or services by fraudulent personal representation, is a special kind of larceny. According to a recent Federal Trade Commission (FTC) survey, identity theft directly impacts as many as 10 million victims annually, although most do not report the crime.

Identity theft became a federal crime in 1998 with the passage of the Identity Theft and Assumption Deterrence Act. The law makes it a crime whenever anyone "knowingly transfers or uses, without lawful authority, a means of identification of another person with the intent to commit, or to aid or abet, any unlawful activity that constitutes a violation of federal law, or that constitutes a felony under any applicable state or local law."[15]

Identity theft is the wrongful use of another's personal information, such as credit card numbers, social security number, and driver's license number, to commit fraud or another form of deception. This is usually done for monetary gain, although there may be other motives as well.

Identity theft has become a major problem in the United States. The target of identity theft is information that will enable the thief to assume another's identity for a criminal purpose. In the past few years, personal information has become one of the commodities most sought after by criminals in this country and elsewhere. Because it is usually part of a larger criminal enterprise, the theft of personal information is one of the most serious of all crimes. On May 31, 2001, the *Washington Post* reported:

> Some law enforcement officials and regulators say identity theft has become one of their most pressing problems. The federal Office of the Comptroller of the Currency recently estimated that there are half a million victims of identity theft per year in the United States. The Justice Department told Congress last week that Internet fraud, including identity theft, is one of the nation's fastest-growing white-collar crimes. And James G. Huse, Jr., the Social Security Administration's inspector general, testified that the misuse of Social Security numbers in fraudulent activity is "a national crisis."[16]

Although identity theft is in itself a criminal act under both federal and most state laws, the theft is almost always a stepping stone to the commission of other crimes. Typical crimes associated with identity theft include credit card fraud, bank fraud, computer fraud, Internet fraud, fraudulent obtaining of loans, and other schemes designed to enable the perpetrator to profit from the original theft. Often, there are several types of fraud involved in, or resulting from, the initial identity theft. Furthermore, funds obtained illegally as a result of the identity theft and its resultant frauds may be used to finance other types of criminal enterprises, including drug trafficking and other major forms of criminal activity.

The escalation of identity theft in the United States is due in large part to the technology revolution, which has brought the country into the so-called information age. The vastly expanded use of computers to store personal data and the growing use of the Internet have provided criminals with new incentives and new means to steal and misuse personal information. As the use of technology to store and transmit information increases, so too will identity theft. Consequently, identity theft will likely become an even greater problem in the future.

Financial Losses. Accurately defining the financial losses of the vast number of crimes committed by means of identity theft is not possible at this time. Many identity theft crimes are not reported to police, and there is no single source of information on this issue. The U.S. Secret Service, the U.S. Postal Inspection Service, and the FBI are among the principal federal enforcement agencies that share jurisdiction for investigation of these crimes. This does not include the thousands of reports and investigations that are handled by state and local authorities. It is fair to say, however, that the cumulative financial losses from identity theft and the various crimes that feed from it are staggering.

Financial loss statistics generated by investigations handled by the U.S. Secret Service's financial crimes division in fiscal year 2000 reveal total actual losses in closed identity theft cases totaled $248.1 million. However, the potential losses from identity theft cases discovered during the same period are estimated at nearly $1.5 billion. Furthermore, it is calculated that the average actual loss in each closed identity theft case in fiscal year 2000 was $46,119. These figures graphically illustrate the magnitude of the problem caused by identity theft in the United States today.

Personal Costs. Perhaps even more tragic than the monetary loss is the personal cost of identity theft. Because identity theft by definition involves the fraudulent obtaining of funds in the name of someone else, the victim of identity theft may sustain not only great financial loss but also severe damage to his or her credit standing, personal reputation, and other vital aspects of the victim's personal life. For example, the victim may suffer garnishments, attachments, civil lawsuits, and other traumatic consequences stemming from the identity theft. In some cases, the victim may be forced into bankruptcy, further damaging his or her reputation and credit. In other instances, the victim may become subject to criminal prosecution because of crimes committed by the perpetrator of the identity theft in the victim's name.

Even if the victim ultimately clears his or her credit records and avoids other personal and financial consequences of identity theft, the physical and mental toll on the victim can be significant. Typically, a victim of identity theft will spend months or years trying to clear his or her credit records. Many hours of difficult and stressful effort are often necessary because the merchants and institutions that have been defrauded in the victim's name are not easily persuaded that the victim is innocent of any wrongdoing. The frustration and distress engendered by this heavy burden often take a significant toll on the mental well-being and physical health of the victim. And, worst of all perhaps, the victim's efforts to clear him- or herself may be unsuccessful, leaving the victim under a cloud for the rest of his or her life.

Virtually anyone may become the victim of identity theft. Contrary to popular misconception, personal information is not stolen just from the affluent. Persons of even modest means may become victims of identity theft. In the majority of cases, all that is required is good credit, which is what identity thieves use to steal thousands upon thousands of dollars in the name of the victim.

No particular age group is immune from identity theft. FTC data indicate that although 6.2 percent of individuals reporting identity theft to the FTC during the period from November 1999 to March 2001 were age 65 years or older, the average age of victims was 42 years, and the most commonly reported age was 33 years. Younger Americans may be victimized at a higher rate because they are more likely to use the Internet, which is the primary tool in many identity theft crimes. However, elderly Americans are highly vulnerable to other types of identity theft schemes, particularly the various telephone scams used by perpetrators to acquire personal information.[17] Elderly people have always been targeted by perpetrators of fraud and will no doubt continue to be frequent victims.

The victims of identity theft may be residents of almost any geographical area. The FTC reports that between November 1999 and March 2001, complaints of identity theft were received from all 50 states and the District of Columbia. According to the same data, the greatest number of complaints came from California, New York, Texas, and Florida. The highest concentration of complaints per 100,000 people reportedly came from the District of Columbia, Nevada, Arizona, California, and Maryland. The FTC also reports that the cities with the largest number of complaints were New York City, Chicago, Los Angeles, Houston, and Miami, in that order. However, one should not conclude from this that identity theft is confined to any particular city, state, or region.

The problem is national in scope, and not even the residents of the smallest locality of the least populous states are safe from it.

Identity Theft Legislation

Identity theft was not a federal crime until Congress passed the Identity Theft and Assumption Deterrence Act of 1998.

> This statute makes it a federal offense when any person knowingly transfers or uses, without lawful authority, a means of identification of another person with the intent to commit, or to aid or abet, any unlawful activity that constitutes a felony under any applicable state or local law.

This crime carries a maximum penalty of 15 years' imprisonment, a fine, and criminal forfeiture of personal property used to commit the offense.

Although this provision specifically targets identity theft, identity theft usually is part of a larger criminal scheme and generally involves other federal statutes, such as statutory prohibitions against credit card fraud, computer fraud, mail fraud,[18] bank fraud, or wire fraud.[19]

In July 2006, the National Conference of State Legislatures reported that all 50 states had passed some form of identity theft legislation. These statutes impose varying penalties for identity theft. Typically, they base these penalties on the dollar amount of loss resulting from the theft: Whereas thefts involving small losses are treated as misdemeanors, larger monetary losses are usually considered felonies of varying degrees.[20]

Local law enforcement officials should check to determine whether their state has such a statute and what that statute provides. Online access to these statutes is available through the Internet.

The Role of the Federal Trade Commission

The FTC is the federal government's principal consumer protection agency, with broad jurisdiction extending over nearly the entire economy, including business and consumer transactions on the telephone, the Internet, and elsewhere. The FTC's mandate is to prohibit unfair or deceptive acts or practices and to promote vigorous competition in the marketplace. The FTC Act authorizes the commission to halt deception in several ways, including through civil actions filed by its own attorneys in federal district courts. Of particular importance in the realm of identity theft is the fact that the act also gives the FTC jurisdiction over cross-border consumer transactions. Many identity theft enterprises operate outside the borders of the United States.

Of particular importance here are the provisions of the federal Identity Theft and Assumption Deterrence Act of 1998 (18 U.S.C. §1028), which gives the FTC a substantial role in the campaign against identity theft. Under the Act, the FTC is empowered to act as a nationwide clearinghouse for information related to identity theft crimes. This is an important aspect of the effort to combat identity theft because in the past, one of the major factors that hampered detection, investigation, and prosecution of these cases was the lack of any central source of information about identity theft. Identity theft is widespread, and a single identity theft ring may operate over great distances and in many states. Consequently, the availability of a central database is essential to enable law enforcement agencies to identify organized or widespread identity theft operations and facilitate cooperation between appropriate federal and state agencies. Special agents from the federal enforcement branches previously mentioned work closely with the FTC in this regard.

In accordance with the mandate of the Identity Theft and Assumption Deterrence Act of 1998, the FTC has established a number of central resources to provide information to law enforcement agencies about identity theft crimes. The FTC also provides guidance to victims of identity theft to help them defend themselves against the effects of this crime.

Types of Identity Theft and Identity Theft Operations

We have already examined some of the national resources available for combating identity theft and alluded to the types of crimes that are committed as part of identity theft. In this section, we will take a closer look at the various types of identity theft schemes and the nature and modus operandi of the identity theft perpetrators.

As has been noted, the key target of identity theft perpetrators is personal and confidential information of individuals. There are so many methods by which identity thieves may acquire personal information that it is impossible to catalog them all here. However, the following methods are commonly used:

- Stealing wallets and purses containing personal identification, credit cards, and bank cards.

- Stealing mail, including mail containing bank and credit card statements, preapproved credit card offers, telephone calling cards, and tax information

- Completion of a false change-of-address form to divert the victim's mail to another location.

- Searching trash for personal data (a practice known as dumpster diving) found on such discarded documents as so-called preapproved credit card applications or credit card slips discarded by the victim. To thwart an identity thief who may pick through your trash to capture your personal information, tear or shred your charge receipts, copies of credit applications, insurance forms, bank checks and statements, expired charge cards, and credit offers you get in the mail.

- Obtaining credit reports, often by posing as a landlord, employer, or other person or entity that might have a legitimate need for and right to credit information.

- Obtaining personal information at the workplace or through employers of the victim.

- Discovering personal information during physical entries into the victim's home. Such entries may be unlawful, as in burglary, or initially lawful, as when friends, service personnel, or others are invited to enter the home.

- Obtaining personal information from the Internet. This may be information stolen by hackers or freely provided by the victim in the course of making purchases or other contacts. Many victims respond to unsolicited e-mail (spam) that requests personal information.

- Purchasing information from inside sources such as store employees, who may for a price provide identity thieves with information taken from applications for goods, services, or credit. At least one instance has been reported of an employee of a credit bureau collaborating with identity thieves to provide personal information from credit bureau records.

- Pretexting, in which a thief telephones the victim or contacts the victim via the Internet and requests that the victim provide personal information. For example, the thief may claim to be from a survey firm and ask for personal data. Another scheme is for the thief to claim that the victim has won a prize or been selected for some special honor or privilege that requires that the victim provide personal information. Still another means of theft is for the perpetrator to call the victim and pretend to have found something that the victim has lost and then demand that the victim provide personal information in order to obtain the return of the lost item.

- Shoulder surfing, a practice whereby the thief positions him- or herself near a victim to obtain personal information by overhearing the victim or seeing the victim's actions. For example, the thief may stand near a pay telephone in a public place and listen as the victim gives telephone credit card number information or other personal information in the course of making a call. Similarly, thieves may loiter near an ATM and visually observe the victim keying in password numbers on the machine.

- Skimming, which is the electronic lifting of the data encoded on a valid credit or ATM card and transferring that data to a counterfeit card. There are many variations of this practice. For example, an identity thief may recruit an employee of a retail store, restaurant, or other retail establishment. The employee is provided with a handheld electronic device that can read data from a person's credit card when the consumer presents it to the employee. The collusive employee then surreptitiously "swipes" the credit card through the handheld "reading" device, which records the electronic data from the card. The employee then returns the device to the thief, and the thief extracts the recorded data from the device.

- Identity thieves may also purchase personal information about potential victims from persons or entities that routinely collect such information. In some instances, these entities may be legitimate, but many times they are criminal enterprises formed for the specific purpose of selling information to thieves.

How Stolen Information Is Used

There are literally hundreds of ways in which identity thieves may use the information they have stolen. The following are just a few examples:

- After they have a victim's credit card number, thieves may call the victim's credit card issuer and, pretending to be the victim, ask that the mailing address on the account be changed. The thieves then run up high charges on the credit card and because credit card statements are no longer being sent to the victim's real address, the victim might be unaware of what is happening for weeks or even months.

- These same thieves who have obtained a victim's credit card information may also request that the credit card company send them credit card "checks," which are written for cash just as are bank checks. Again, the charges are unknown to the victim because the credit card statements are no longer coming to the victim's address.

- Having obtained personal information such as the victim's name, date of birth, social security number, and so on, the thieves open new credit card accounts in the victim's name and run up charges until the victim becomes aware of the fraud. Similarly, credit accounts may be opened at stores using the victim's identity.

- The thieves open bank accounts in the victim's name and write bad checks on the account.

- The thieves obtain loans, such as real estate, auto, or personal loans, using the victim's identity.

- The thieves counterfeit checks or debit cards and drain the victim's bank accounts of funds.

- The thieves establish services such as utility, telephone, or cell phone service in the victim's name.

- The thieves make long-distance calls using stolen credit card numbers.
- The thieves may obtain other goods and privileges by using the victim's identity and information, either in person, by telephone, or via the Internet.

These are only a few of the numerous schemes that an identity thief may use to obtain money, goods, or services at the expense of the unwitting victim.

Often a web of conspirators ties these individual criminal acts together. Investigation of one individual involved in identity theft therefore often leads to others working together, often in elaborate plots. The following actual case prosecuted in the western district of Washington State illustrates this point:

> Between January 27, 1999, and April 14, 2000, a woman and other persons conspired to execute a scheme to defraud several commercial businesses in western Washington and elsewhere, including financial institutions, investment companies, credit card companies, merchant banks, and merchants, and to obtain money and merchandise from these businesses by means of false and fraudulent pretenses.
>
> The conspirators assumed the identities of third persons and fraudulently utilized the social security account numbers and names of these persons. The conspirators then created false identity documents such as state identification cards, driver's licenses, and immigration cards. Using the identities and names of these third persons, the conspirators obtained credit cards and opened banking and investment accounts at numerous locations.
>
> The conspirators also prepared fraudulent and counterfeit checks using the account names and numbers for actual bank accounts. The perpetrators then deposited the counterfeit checks into accounts opened by them, using one of their assumed identities. Shortly thereafter, they would withdraw the funds fraudulently credited to their accounts at the time they deposited the counterfeit checks. Over an eight-month period, counterfeit checks totaling over $1 million were deposited at various banks and investment firms.
>
> In addition, the conspirators purchased legitimate cashier's checks with fraudulently obtained monies and then altered the checks to reflect much higher values than the amounts purchased. Over five months, these transactions accounted for more than $350,000.
>
> The scheme also included telefaxed "letters of authorization" using other identities authorizing wire transfer of funds to co-conspirators, altered credit cards, and related offenses.

Such involved criminal conspiracies begin with, and are perpetuated by, identity theft. The result of all of these schemes may be that bill collectors begin to pursue the victim, the victim's credit standing is ruined, and legal procedures may be instituted to collect the fraudulent debts from the victim. Identity thieves may even file for bankruptcy in the victim's name to avoid paying debts incurred while using the victim's personal information or for other reasons, such as to avoid eviction from the house or apartment they have obtained by using the victim's identity.

The Investigative Response

A police department's first step in combating identity theft is to ensure that its personnel have a comprehensive knowledge of what identity theft is, who commits it, and how it is committed. The department's members must be aware of federal, state, and local resources available to assist them in reporting, investigating, and prosecuting identity theft.

Because identity theft so often is a multi-jurisdictional crime, it is necessary for each department to cooperate closely with other agencies in identity theft cases. For example, investigation and prosecution of the illustrative case cited above could not have been successfully undertaken without coordination and cooperation with several federal agencies. The sharing of information about identity theft cases with other agencies is essential because it may lead to not only a successful prosecution of the case in one jurisdiction but also concurrent investigation in other areas of the country.

In this regard, it is essential for state and local law enforcement agencies to participate in the FTC's Identity Theft Clearing House. Such participation provides access to extensive information about identity theft activity, both nationwide and in the department's own region or state.

Reports of Identity Theft

In the past, police have been slow to respond to reports of identity theft. In some cases, local police departments refused to take complaints about identity theft because the crime was not well understood, a state statute was lacking, or the department could not identify the venue in which the theft occurred or the perpetrator was operating. This attitude by local police often creates great frustration among victims and generated considerable ill will among these victims toward the departments concerned.

Today, identity theft has been identified as a major crime problem in the United States, and most states now have statutes making it a specific crime. A relative wealth of information and assistance currently exists to deal with identity theft. These and other factors combined make it essential for police departments to respond properly to identity theft complaints, initiate investigations, and prosecute violators where possible. In addition, departments have an obligation to assist the victims through counseling, advice, and referral when reasonable and appropriate. A proper investigative response to identity theft will include the following:

1. *Develop a standardized procedure for taking identity theft reports.* Complaints should be taken by the police department in detail and in a manner consistent with the severity of the crime. Aspects of the online reporting form used by the FTC may be useful as a guide to local law enforcement agencies in their efforts to gather all pertinent information about the crime. Victims should not be brushed off or arbitrarily referred to other agencies as a standard course of action. Thus, departments should not merely refer victims to prosecutors' offices or to private attorneys for civil actions. It is the department's obligation to take the complaint and act on it.

2. *Initiate criminal investigations of identity theft reports.* Police should initiate investigation of identity theft reports. Again, identity theft is as much a crime as any other offense and should be treated as such. Unless and until it develops that the complaint is unfounded or for some other reason the department cannot proceed further, identity theft should be aggressively and fully investigated.

3. *Prosecute violators.* Identity thieves should be prosecuted. Identity theft is not just a prank; it is a serious crime and should be prosecuted to the fullest extent of the law. Unfortunately, the maximum penalties for these types of crimes in some states are not sufficient to garner the attention of prosecutors, whose caseloads may already be overloaded with other criminal activity. In these states, a long-term effort by local police and prosecutors needs to address this through calls for harsher criminal penalties for identity theft.

4. *Cooperate with other agencies.* Investigations of multi-jurisdictional identity theft schemes may involve a number of agencies. Each police department should cooperate fully with any agency participating in an identity theft case. If it proves impossible to prosecute the identity thief in the department's own jurisdiction, full cooperation should be given to departments in other

jurisdictions where there is a greater likelihood of successfully prosecuting the perpetrators.

5. *Assist victims by providing the victims with helpful information.* Victims of identity theft are often unaware of the proper steps to take to minimize the damage suffered because of the identity theft and protect themselves against further victimization. Each police department should provide every identity theft complainant with information as to the steps that the victim should take. Much of that information is available through counselors at the FTC. To summarize this and other information, police officers responding to victims of identity theft and taking crime reports on these matters should keep the following instructions in mind to deal most effectively with these crime victims:

- Contact the fraud departments of each of the three credit reporting agencies. Give the agency full details of the theft, including a case number as provided by local police, and request that a fraud alert be placed in your file.

- Request a copy of your credit report, review the report for errors or fraudulent entries, submit any changes necessary, and get a new copy at a later date to ensure that changes or problems have been corrected.

- Contact all credit card companies where you have an account and notify them of the fraud. Close existing accounts and open new accounts with new personal identification numbers (PINs) and passwords.

- Contact banks and financial institutions. To be safe, close accounts and open new accounts with new PINs and passwords. Major check verification companies should also be contacted and asked to notify retailers not to accept your stolen or misappropriated checks. The bank may be able and willing to do this for you. ATM cards that may have been compromised should be canceled and new ones obtained with new PINs and passwords.

- If there is reason to believe that investment or brokerage accounts have been tampered with or otherwise compromised, contact the broker or investment account manager as well as the Securities and Exchange Commission.

- If unauthorized new accounts have been opened through utility or telephone companies or if the victim's own service is being used to make unauthorized calls, contact the utility or service provider immediately. If the companies do not cooperate, contact the state's public utility commission, the Federal Communications Commission (FCC), or both.

- If there is reason to believe that the social security number is being misused, this should be reported to the Social Security Administration's fraud hotline. In addition, it is wise to contact the Social Security Administration to verify the accuracy of the earnings reported under the victim's social security number. Request a copy of your social security statement.

- If a driver's license or driver's license number is involved in the identity theft, contact the jurisdiction's department of motor vehicles. The same is true if a nondriver's identity card is involved. If the driver's license number is the same as the victim's social security number, a different number should be substituted.

- If someone has filed bankruptcy in the victim's name, the victim should contact the U.S. Bankruptcy Trustee in the region where the bankruptcy was filed.

- In some instances, the perpetrator of the identity theft may have committed a crime in the victim's name. When this becomes known, the appropriate agencies should be contacted for information as to how the victim's name may be cleared. The procedures for this vary widely among jurisdictions, and it may be necessary for the victim to hire an attorney to accomplish the name-clearing process.

- The victim should contact other police departments where the victim resides or where the identity theft may have taken place. The victim should obtain a copy of the police report regarding the theft from each department to whom the theft has been reported. This is essential because even if the police do not apprehend the perpetrators, the police report may assist the victim in dealing with creditors during efforts to avoid financial liability for fraudulent actions and to repair the damage done to the victim's credit. The fact that a victim has reported and personally attested to the truth of the allegations in a written police report helps other agencies verify the credibility of the victim and take measures on his or her behalf.

- The victim should contact the FTC via telephone or mail to report the identity theft.[21]

- Because the types of identity theft schemes are so varied, other agencies or entities may need to be contacted. If any agency or entity not otherwise discussed above is involved in some manner, it should be contacted immediately. For example, the Internal Revenue Service (IRS) should be notified if tax issues may be involved.

Many of the reports and requests discussed above may be made initially by telephone. However, all such requests should be followed up in writing because telephone reports are often insufficient to preserve the victim's legal rights, and written reports may be necessary to obtain the cooperation of the entity being contacted.

The telephone numbers, addresses, Web sites, and other appropriate data necessary to enable the victims to contact these various agencies should be kept on file in the police department and made available to them. These addresses, telephone numbers, Web sites, and related information can be found in several current guides for identity theft victims, such as the FTC publication *ID Theft—When Bad Things Happen to Your Good Name*. Police departments should consider maintaining a supply of copies of this or similar publications and distributing them to identity theft complainants for their information and assistance.

It is important that local police departments take a proactive role in the education of the public regarding identity theft and the means of preventing it. Even though no person in the information age can completely control the dissemination of his or her personal information, there are specific steps that everyone can take to minimize exposure to identity theft. Crime prevention units and community policing officers should take advantage of their roles within the community by providing citizens with information they can use to protect themselves against identity theft. There is considerable literature available, both in printed form and on the Internet, about preventive measures. Officers should be aware of these sources and provide them to citizens whenever possible.[22]

Motor Vehicle Theft

mycrimekit

Video: Larceny-theft

Carlos Ponce was one of the longtime leaders of an auto theft ring that operated throughout South Florida and sold stolen cars around the country. Ponce, also known as El Rey de los Carros (King of the Cars), ran an interstate auto theft ring that stole luxury cars in South Florida. The ring renumbered the cars using the **vehicle identification number (VIN)** identities of other identical "clone" vehicles and then shipped the vehicles to out-of-state buyers using fraudulent Florida titles. The ring was responsible for stealing hundreds of vehicles, worth an estimated $8 million, from South Florida and using an illicit pipeline—maintained in part from inside a federal prison—to ship the vehicles as far away as Massachusetts and California. In 2006, a Miami-Dade Police investigation known as Operation Road Runner arrested Ponce and 10 of his associates.[23] The Ponce operation illustrates the level of sophistication and organization of some automobile theft operations and reminds us that there are considerable profits for criminals involved in automobile theft.

Since the turn of the century, the advent of the automobile has either directly or indirectly changed the lives of all people. Its impact has inspired both positive and negative uses. Indeed, it has not only enhanced private lives, business, and public service organizations but has also offered criminals innovative ways of transportation to and from their crimes. The value and utility of the motor vehicle have, therefore, become deeply ingrained in today's society.

According to the UCR, the crime of motor vehicle theft includes trains, airplanes, bulldozers, most farm and construction machinery, ships, boats, and spacecraft. Vehicles that are temporarily taken by individuals who have lawful access to them are not thefts. Consequently, spouses who jointly own all property may drive the family car, even though one spouse may think of the vehicle as his or her exclusive personal property. Because most insurance companies require police reports before they will reimburse car owners for their losses, most occurrences of motor vehicle theft are reported to law enforcement agencies. Some of these reports, however, may be false. People who have damaged their own vehicles in solitary crashes or who have been unable to sell them may try to force insurance companies to "buy" them through reports of theft. Motor vehicle theft can turn violent, as in cases of carjacking—a crime in which offenders usually force the car's occupants into the street before stealing the vehicle.

According to the FBI, auto theft is an estimated $7 billion business and continues to grow despite a declining theft rate across the United States. For record-keeping purposes, the UCR defines a motor vehicle as a self-propelled vehicle that runs on the ground and not on rails. This definition includes automobiles, motorcycles, bicycles, trucks, motor scooters, buses, and snowmobiles. Motor vehicles that are taken temporarily by persons having legal access to them are not considered motor vehicle theft.

Trends

In 2008, the FBI reported that there were an estimated 1.1 million (1,095,769) thefts of motor vehicles during 2007. The national rate for motor vehicle thefts was 363.3 per 100,000 residents. This represents a decrease of 8.1 percent from the previous year. The majority of motor vehicle thefts, an estimated 93.1 percent, occurred in Metropolitan Areas.[24]

In 2007 the estimated value of motor vehicles stolen in 2007 was $7.4 billion, averaging $6,755 per stolen vehicle and among vehicle types, automobiles accounted for 73.4 percent of the motor vehicles reported stolen in 2007.[25]

Motor vehicle thefts are common throughout the United States and as a rule require a police report before insurance companies will act on claims. Both police and insurance investigators know that sometimes motor vehicle theft reports are false. Such cases involve persons who attempt to defraud the insurance company or dispose of a vehicle after using it to commit a crime while trying to claim insurance money for it.

TOP 10 U.S. METROPOLITAN AREAS WITH THE HIGHEST MOTOR VEHICLE THEFT RATES, 2008

Rank	Metropolitan Statistical Area	Vehicles stolen	Rate*
1	Modesto, CA	4,235	829.26
2	Laredo, TX	1,960	827.21
3	Yakima, WA	1,828	779.32
4	San Diego/Carlsbad/San Marcos, CA	22,554	751.53
5	Bakersfield, CA	5,918	739.33
6	Stockton, CA	4,963	738.12
7	Las Vegas/Paradise, NV	13,662	732.25
8	Albuquerque, NM	6,182	730.81
9	San Francisco/Oakland/Fremont, CA	30,735	719.03
10	Fresno, CA	6,533	718.58

*Ranked by the rate of vehicle thefts reported per 100,000 people based on the 2008 U.S. Census Population Estimates.
Source: National Insurance Crime Bureau, 2009.

Auto theft is big business. Investigations have shown that some large organized groups of car thieves fill orders for contract buyers. Some cars are stolen for shipment out of the country, typically to Mexico. Juveniles often steal cars as a lark or on a dare to joyride. Some thieves intend to keep the car for themselves, but others sell the stolen car to an associate after disguising the vehicle with new paint, plates, and wheels. Stolen vehicles may even be used in other crimes, such as armed robbery or drive-by shootings. Stolen cars are often involved in hit-and-run accidents with injuries, leaving the owners to explain their alibis and prove that they didn't cause the incident and then file a false auto theft report to cover it up.

MOTOR VEHICLE THEFT TREND

Year	Number of Offenses	Rate per 100,000 Inhabitants
2006	1,192,809	2,206.8
2007	1,095,769	2,177.8
Percent change	−8.1	−8.8

Source: Federal Bureau of Investigation. (2008). *Crime in the United States—2007*.

Experienced car thieves can steal an automobile in less than a minute. Many crude thieves simply smash the driver's-side window. A majority of stolen cars are taken for the value of their parts. Some of the most frequently stolen types of cars have remained constant over the years, suggesting that they are being stolen for parts. According to insurance companies, a $20,000 stolen vehicle can be stripped and sold into $30,000 worth of parts inventory to unscrupulous scrap and auto-body shops. Stolen cars, vans, trucks, and motorcycles cause economic hardship for victims and increase insurance premiums for law-abiding citizens.

Motor vehicles are stolen from a variety of sources, including shopping malls, streets, driveways, parking lots, garages, and car dealerships. Auto theft seems to occur with greater frequency where large groups of cars are parked together for extended periods, such as at airports, shopping centers, colleges, sporting events, fairgrounds, movie complexes, and large apartment complexes.

Motor vehicle thieves target a wide range of popular passenger vehicles, often seeking valuable parts from older model year vehicles for sale on the black market. Their preferred targets for theft vary from one year to the next, but many models remain a constant. For example, the Toyota Camry, Honda Accord, and Ford Taurus are particularly attractive targets, along with sport utility vehicles (SUVs), pickup trucks, and mini-vans, according to a recent study by the National Insurance Crime Bureau (NICB), a not-for-profit insurance organization committed to combating vehicle theft and insurance fraud.

The NICB reported that the 1995 Honda Civic was the most stolen vehicle in 2007, the same as in 2006. The 2007 report confirms that theft of older vehicles has remained constant for the past several years. Eight of the vehicles on the top 10 list shown below are 10 or more model years old. These vehicles have been consistent top sellers for many years, and some of their parts are interchangeable. Thieves dismantle them for their components.[26]

TOP 10 MOST FREQUENTLY STOLEN PASSENGER VEHICLES, 2007

Rank	Year, Make, Model
1	1995 Honda Civic
2	1991 Honda Accord
3	1989 Toyota Camry
4	1997 Ford F-150 Series Pickup
5	1994 Chevrolet C/K 1500 Pickup
6	1994 Acura Integra
7	2004 Dodge Ram Pickup
8	1994 Nissan Sentra
9	1988 Toyota Pickup
10	2007 Toyota Corolla

Source: National Insurance Crime Bureau, 2009.

Vehicles are typically taken for their parts, which are no longer manufactured and are too difficult or expensive to obtain. Individual car components in high demand are "tuners" or "street racers," which are often stolen for illegal export to Central and South America or Europe.

To help protect their vehicles, experts recommend that motorists always remove the keys from the ignition and vehicle, lock the doors, close the windows, hide valuable items, park in well-lit areas, and use a combination of antitheft devices. Motorists driving theft-prone vehicles need to take additional steps such as installing a visible deterrent such as a steering wheel lock, an alarm, a starter or fuel disabler, and a tracking device.

Historically, many vehicles have been stolen to remove major parts and sell them to salvage yards or repair shops. Today, another criminal goal has captured the attention of law enforcement authorities: vehicles that are stolen and stripped for valuable accessories, such as seats, expensive radios, custom wheels, and tires.

Motivations for Motor Vehicle Theft

Let us now take a closer look at the reasons for auto theft: joyriding, theft for resale, transportation for other crimes, and stripping and chop-shop operations. Understanding these motivations helps investigators understand motivations for the crime, which gives the investigator a handle on how to anticipate the instances of this crime as well as how to prevent such activity.

MOTOR VEHICLE THEFT IN THE UNITED STATES, 1998–2007

Year	Vehicles Stolen	Percent Change
1998	1,242,781	−8.2
1999	1,152,075	−7.3
2000	1,160,002	0.7
2001	1,228,391	5.9
2002	1,246,646	1.5
2003	1,261,226	1.2
2004	1,237,851	−1.9
2005	1,235,859	−0.2
2006	1,192,809	−3.5
2007	1,095,769	−8.1

Source: U.S. Department of Justice, Federal Bureau of Investigation. (2008). *Uniform Crime Reports.*

Joyriding. For years, **joyriding** has ranked as the premier criminal motivation for motor vehicle theft, committed primarily by juvenile offenders. Since the mid-1970s, however, the average age of the auto theft criminal has risen steadily. While typically in the company of friends, the juvenile auto thief steals a car for enjoyment for short periods. When the ride is over, the vehicle is sometimes stripped of certain "resalable" items, such as cellular telephones, radio equipment, and so on. Tracing personal effects left in a vehicle is difficult because frequently the identification numbers of the items have not been recorded by the victim.

Theft for Resale. Hard-core criminals have found motor vehicle theft for resale to be highly profitable, with minimal risk. Many methods are used to dispose of stolen vehicles. For example, many of these vehicles are transported to foreign countries for resale. Although this involves elaborate transportation schemes, after the vehicle makes it into the hands of the foreign car buyer, its chances of being recovered are minimal. Included in this category are luxury cars and heavy equipment, both of which frequently bring much higher illicit prices than the vehicle is actually worth.

Transportation for Other Crimes. In addition to the profit motive, automobiles have been stolen for use in the commission of other crimes. Here, the vehicle may be used either as transportation to and from various crimes or used in the crime itself. This helps insulate the criminal from detection by not having to use his or her own vehicle in the perpetration of the crime. The availability of potential target vehicles and the opportunity to steal them typically dictate which type of vehicle is chosen. One of the greatest problems in investigating stolen vehicles is the ability of the law enforcement officer to "read" a vehicle properly as one that has been stolen. These identification techniques are discussed in the following sections.

Stripping and Chop-Shop Operations. The high profitability of stolen motor vehicles has created a secondary market of sorts for auto thieves. This market's commodity is the parts of certain stolen autos. The terms **chop-shop** and **stripping operations** refer to locations where stolen vehicles are disposed of. In a typical stripping operation, a stolen vehicle is taken to a location, typically a private garage in an unpopulated residential area of town. Such garages are usually rented by people using fictitious names to avoid detection by authorities.

The strip location can sometimes be spotted as buildings with covered windows in areas of frequent deliveries. In addition, people who are seen loading large items into vans in residential garages would be worthy of further investigation. In contrast, chop-shop operations vary in size and represent a growing business in which market entry is fairly easy. Anyone with a truck, garage, backyard, or a piece of secluded land can get into the business.

Although similar to strip locations, chop shops usually involve larger garages and deal in larger quantities of goods. They are sometimes large enough to house both the stolen vehicle and the **tin truck** (the auto parts transport vehicle) inside the building, where detection is much more difficult. Another difference between strip and chop-shop locations is that chop shops usually remove any identifying numbers from remains of vehicles left behind after the valued parts have been removed. The unused parts are typically dumped in lakes or ponds or areas outside the location of the chop shop. Many salvage yards readily accept parts from auto thieves. Such parts are easily made part of the existing inventory.

Once inside the garage, the stolen vehicle is disassembled. It is here where the prime body parts are removed. These include bumpers, front-end assemblies, trunk lids, and doors. Interior parts, tires, and radios are also of great value to the thief.

Chop-shop operators use torches, power saws, or other tools to disassemble stolen vehicles. After thieves have stripped the stolen vehicle, the parts are transported in tin trucks, from which the parts are sold to repair shops and salvage yards that use them to repair damaged vehicles. After an auto has been stripped, the remaining parts are abandoned. Such vehicles are then typically driven or even pushed to a location away from the strip location.

Investigating officers should always remember that victims might be able to recall certain characteristic marks on their stolen vehicle. These markings, which include cigarette burns in the seat, dents on fenders, and so on, might be identifiable if they are shown to the victim.

The Preliminary Investigation

The investigation of a stolen auto typically begins with a report by the victim to the police. As a rule, it is the task of the patrol officer to respond to such complaints and determine the facts and circumstances surrounding the alleged theft. These inquiries should include:

- Where was the vehicle last seen?
- Who was the last person to use the vehicle?
- Were the keys left in the ignition?
- Was the vehicle left unlocked?
- Is the victim in arrears on payments?
- Are others allowed to drive the vehicle?
- Was the vehicle equipped with special equipment, such as special wheels, fog lights, or special sound system?

Answers to these questions allow the officer to determine if a crime has been committed or if another situation is at hand, such as a civil dispute (divorce) or vehicle repossession by a bank or finance company. Other explanations for the disappearance of a vehicle might also exist. For example, the driver might have been intoxicated and may have been involved in a hit-and-run accident. The motor vehicle theft claim might be an effort to cover up the details and avoid suspicion.

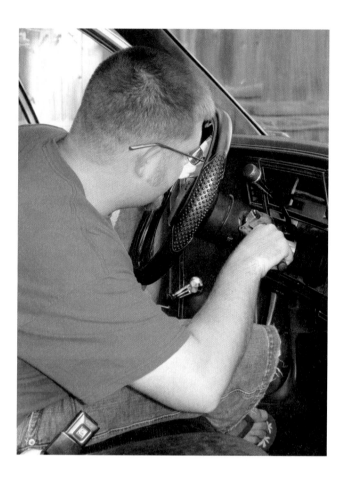

FIGURE 14.13 Car thief breaching the steering column of a vehicle.

True ownership of the vehicle must also be determined early in the investigation. This can be accomplished simply by requesting certain specific information from the victim, such as the title of the vehicle or a copy of the vehicle's insurance policy. Special characteristics of the vehicle should also be noted in the theft report. Details such as cigarette burns on the vehicle's seats, scratches or dents, rusted areas of the vehicle, decals or stickers, and so on will all distinguish the stolen vehicle from others like it on the street.

The Investigative Traffic Stop

Traffic stops are another way that motor vehicle theft investigations are commonly initiated. Again, the patrol officer is one of the primary players in this early stage of the investigation. After a motor vehicle has been observed as being in violation of the law, officers have legal authority to stop it. In most cases, law enforcement officers will focus their attention on the motor vehicle's license plates. These typically only provide officers with the information they are seeking regarding the registrant of the vehicle. In this situation, such limited information from the license plates includes the fact that the license plates are not stolen and that the owner's name and address match the registration.

It is here, however, that the motor vehicle thief may slip past the watchful eye of the patrol officer. Indeed, the officer making the stop should take time to record and check the validity of the VIN. In almost all cases, this will reveal whether or not the vehicle is properly registered or even stolen. Police officers must therefore have sufficient knowledge about the construction of the VIN to avoid common errors in recording and identifying it.

Professional motor vehicle thieves have practiced several methods of theft. Although complex to the inexperienced thief, these methods are commonly used

FIGURE 14.14 Photo of a typical vehicle identification number located on the dashboard of a vehicle. Courtesy of Mike Himmel.

in organized theft rings. Theft methods most commonly used include altering the VIN; **tagging,** or altering title documents; modifying body parts of a stolen vehicle; and dismantling the vehicle for sale or exchange of parts.

The Vehicle Identification Number

The VIN is as unique to a motor vehicle as a fingerprint is to a human being. It has no resemblance to other numbers commonly dealt with in criminal investigation, such as one's social security number or date of birth. Instead, it is

FIGURE 14.15 Photo of a vehicle identification number located on the doorjamb of a vehicle. Courtesy of Mike Himmel.

assigned to the vehicle by the manufacturer at the time of production and is designed to distinguish each vehicle from all others. The primary purpose of the VIN is for identification and registration.

History of the VIN. Before 1968, VIN locations varied from manufacturer to manufacturer depending on the make of the vehicle. Since then, however, all American-made automobiles are assembled with the VIN plate visible through the windshield on the driver's side of the automobile. It can also be found on a federal safety certification label located on the driver's door or the driver's doorpost.

Exceptions to typical VIN locations are those of certain luxury automobiles that have their VINs affixed to the left-side windshield post. Any alteration of the VIN should be grounds for a more complete inspection of the vehicle. Before 1981, manufacturers' VIN numbering systems varied. In fact, manufacturers used slightly different systems of VIN numbering. Since then, however, the standard 17-character VIN was adopted, requiring all vehicles manufactured in the United States to have the standardized VIN.

How the VIN Works. The VIN consists of a combination of letters and numbers. To the average car owner, these combinations would mean very little, but to the criminal investigator, they are invaluable in identifying a stolen motor vehicle. To understand the VIN better, let's look closer at the function of each digit of the 17 numbers. For illustration sake, we consider the following VIN:

1J3CJ45A0CR335521

The numbers and letters represent the following information:

1	Nation of origin
J	Name of the manufacturer (e.g., General Motors, Honda)
3	Specific make of the vehicle (e.g., Buick)
C	Type of restraint system
J45	Car line series and body type
A	Engine description
0	Check digit
C	Model year
R	Assembly plant location
3 3 5 5 2 1	Sequential production numbers

With the exception of the check digit, one can easily see the function of each of these characters. The ninth character is called the check digit. It may be a number or a letter; however, it is derived mathematically from the other characters in the VIN to reveal coding and recording errors. Beginning in 1968, U.S. automobile manufacturers have placed a portion of the VIN on other areas of the vehicle, such as the engine and the transmission.

The Altered VIN. Because many vehicles are stolen for the sole purpose of resale, many methods are used by the thief to disguise the true identity of the car. In fact, all outward appearances would indicate that the vehicle is legitimate, so after the VIN alteration has been accomplished, the stolen vehicle can then be sold to an unsuspecting customer.

Disguising the Stolen Vehicle

One common way of disguising a vehicle is to change the VIN and alter the documents that coincide with the VIN (i.e., tagging). Other ways that a vehicle's true identity can be altered include the salvage switch, a modified VIN, or a bogus VIN.

The Salvage Switch Method. The **salvage switch** involves the thief purchasing a wrecked vehicle that is unrepairable strictly for its certificate of title and for the VIN. The purchase can be made from an individual or an insurance company, but it is typically made from a wrecking or salvage yard. The vehicle must have both a VIN plate and documents to support ownership of the vehicle. Next, the thief steals a similar type of vehicle, removes its VIN tag, and replaces it with the salvaged vehicle's VIN. Any other numbers are either altered or removed from the vehicle. It is then sold either to an innocent buyer or to a person who may well suspect the validity of the transaction but participates anyway because of a favorable price.

The Modified VIN Technique. Another method of disguising a stolen vehicle is to replace the original VIN with a phony one. This can be done in several ways. One way is to use a simple label maker, which can easily be purchased at hardware stores. The VIN is then stamped on a label. Next, it is spray painted with flat black paint and placed over the original VIN. Other identifying numbers on the vehicle are either removed or altered. Vehicles tagged in this fashion should be fairly easily detected by observant investigators through observing the size, texture, and the size of the numbers of the tag. Another way that thieves have attempted to alter VINs is to remove the original VIN, alter it, and replace it on the vehicle. Again, this method is usually detected by the trained investigator but may appear legitimate to the untrained eye.

The Bogus VIN. Still another method is to construct a completely bogus VIN that closely resembles the original. Many criminals will attempt to steal blank VIN tags, which are then stamped with numbers and placed on vehicles. This is where the ninth digit of the VIN, the check digit, is beneficial in determining the authenticity of the tag.

Since 1970, American-made vehicles have also displayed a federal safety certification label on the driver's door or the driver's doorpost. This label also displays the VIN for the vehicle and should match the VIN tag on the vehicle's dash. To dispose of the vehicle after it has been tagged, the auto thief adopts several methods. For example, in the salvage operation, the title will typically be placed in the fictitious name before sale. In instances in which the VIN has been altered or manufactured by the thief, phony title documents can then be prepared to match the bogus VIN. In other cases, title documents may not even exist, only the registration of the vehicle. In such cases, buyers who might suspect that the car is of suspicious origin might continue with the transaction because of a low sale price. Such sales are typically conducted in cash at the thief's request.

The Rip-Off.

Typically, vehicles are stolen because of carelessness on the part of the owner—drivers who leave their keys in an unattended car or motorists who leave their cars running while they enter an establishment for a short period. Vehicle thieves commonly watch these locations to wait for the most opportune time to make their steal.

When the keys are not left in the ignition, many thieves have traditionally resorted to entry techniques ranging from the classic "smash-and-grab" technique to unobtrusive use of a screwdriver and flat iron. Today, entry into vehicles is becoming more innovative. One such innovation includes the use of porcelain chips broken from spark plugs. This technique involves attaching the chips to a wire, string, or other handle and simply hitting them against the vehicle glass for quick entry. This method reduces the time, noise, and chances of detection but may leave microscopic fragments of glass on the intruder's clothing.[27]

These fragments are excellent evidence and hopefully can be located shortly after the theft by seizing the suspect's clothing for examination.

Another technique commonly used by thieves is to observe, or "case," a parking lot where cars are parked while people are at work. In this case, the thief has several hours' leeway from the time the vehicle is stolen to the time the theft is discovered. Thus, the vehicle may be transported far from the theft location by the time of discovery.

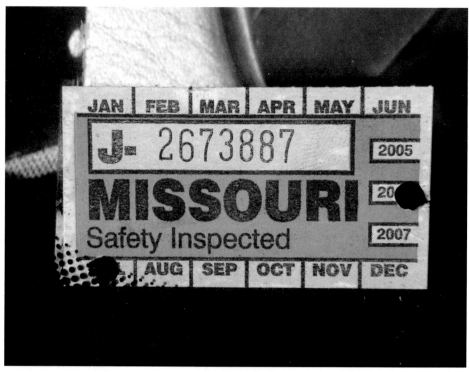

FIGURE 14.16 The vehicle safety inspection (**A**) and vehicle registration (**B**) stickers also provide identifying numbers and investigative leads. Courtesy of Mike Himmel.

FIGURE 14.17 Carjacking, depicted here, is also a form of robbery and is one method used by criminals to acquire a desired vehicle. Jack Star, Getty Images, Inc. PhotoDisc.

Many motorists invest in antitheft devices in their vehicles. Although many of these devices have proven to be effective, thieves have learned methods of defeating them in many cases. The level of expertise in disabling an antitheft device depends on several variables, including the thieves' degree of mechanical experience, the quality and effectiveness of the device, and the location of the vehicle when stolen.

Tools of the Trade

Vehicles are obtained by many different means by professional thieves. For example, tow trucks are often used to transport a vehicle desired by the vehicle thief. Other common methods are the use of public parking facilities, such as mall parking lots and car rental lots. In these instances, all vehicles are prime targets, especially if they are left with the keys in the ignition. Entry into a vehicle can be accomplished using several tools. Professional thieves become proficient in the use of these tools and use them in a manner in which little, if any, damage is done to the exterior of the vehicle, which could easily be noticed.

Many tools that thieves commonly use also have a legitimate function, which is, however, put to a sinister use by the criminal. When means are devised to counter or deter motor vehicle thefts, criminals inevitably devise methods with which to defeat these means.

Motor Vehicle Theft: Tools of the Trade

☑ *Slim jim.* This is a thin, easily obtainable piece of metal or aluminum that is notched at both ends. This tool enables easy entry by the thief, who slides the tool in the small crevice between the door and the door frame. After the lock is manipulated, the door is easily opened.

☑ *Slide hammer.* This tool is also referred to as a dent puller or slam puller. After the thief removes the lock cap of the ignition, the slam puller is inserted by screwing the tip into the keyway. Force is then applied to the slide mechanism, away from the steering column, and the lock is removed. The vehicle can then be started by inserting a screwdriver that is twisted just like a car key.

☑ *Ignition extractor.* The lock cap is removed upon getting into the vehicle. The extractor is attached and turned to remove the lock. The vehicle can then easily be started with a screwdriver.

☑ *Force tool.* The force tool is placed over the lock and tapped after removal of the lock cap. The ratchet is turned, thus destroying the locking mechanism.

☑ *Key cutter, codebook, and blank keys.* These tools enable entry into a single-key vehicle and are widely used. A door lock is pulled, and the code number from that lock can be obtained and a new key made. This gives the thief a new key that he or she can use at a time of his choosing.

Carjacking

In the early 1990s, a new form of auto theft began to emerge—carjacking. **Carjacking** is defined by the U.S. Department of Justice as "completed or attempted robbery of a motor vehicle by a stranger to the victim."[28] Carjackings occur most frequently in urban areas. They accounted for only 3 percent of all motor vehicle thefts, based on Department of Justice data from 1993 to 2002 (latest available).[29]

A carjacking typically consists of a single gunman placing a pistol to the head of an unsuspecting driver at locations such as stoplights, garages, fast food restaurants, gas stations, and parking lots. Another common technique is the so-called bump and run, in which the thief stages a minor rear-end collision. When the driver exits his or her vehicle to inspect the damage, one thief holds up the occupant(s) while, often, another person drives their vehicle.

The Anti-Car Theft Act, enacted in 1992, made armed auto theft ("carjacking") a federal offense. In 1994, the passage of the Violent Crime Control and Law Enforcement Act made carjacking resulting in death a federal crime punishable by death.[30]

According to the Bureau of Justice Statistics, an average of about 49,000 completed or attempted nonfatal carjackings took place each year in the United States between 1992 and 1996. In about half of those incidents, the offender was successful in taking the victim's vehicle. In addition, about 27 homicides by strangers each year involve automobile theft. Some of these may have been carjackings. Other statistics about carjackings include about seven of 10 completed carjackings involve firearms, most carjackings do not result in injury to the victims, and a majority of carjackings are committed at night.[31]

Motor Vehicle Fraud

The problem of motor vehicle fraud is also growing nationwide. For example, in 1989, the **National Auto Theft Bureau (NATB)** estimated that 15 percent of all vehicles reported stolen were fraudulent claims. The person who commits motor vehicle fraud does so with a clear profit motive and usually attempts to collect payment through her or his insurance company. The problem is compounded by the notion that many people have the attitude that fraud is only an insurance problem and doesn't really hurt anyone. Some believe that after paying

Red Flags to Indicate Motor Vehicle Fraud[32]

☑ Late-model vehicles are involved.

☑ There is a close relationship between the date of coverage and the date of the claim.

☑ The insured furnished the address and phone number of a bar, hotel, or motel as a place to be contacted by the claims adjuster.

☑ The insurance premium was paid in cash.

☑ The insured is unable to produce the title or proof of ownership.

☑ The vehicle has no lien noted, and the insured has no apparent means to have made a cash purchase.

☑ The previous owner cannot be located or is unknown to the claimant.

☑ The vehicle is reported stolen and is recovered a short time later, burned.

☑ The insured is unable to provide a sales invoice.

insurance premiums for years, they are entitled to get a return on their money. Indeed, many expenses are ultimately incurred in the detection, apprehension, prosecution, and incarceration of offenders.

Methods of Fraud

Although many methods of motor vehicle fraud exist, the most common is to alter the vehicle's identity by changing the VIN plate and reregistering the car. A second common method is the *owner give-up*. This term applies when the owner conspires with a third party, typically for a fee, to have the vehicle disposed of so that the owner can collect the insurance money. Reasons for motor vehicle fraud include:

- Desire for immediate cash
- End of costly repair bills
- Avoidance of the hassle of selling
- Breaking of the car lease

Many theft reports also include nonexistent vehicle contents such as camera equipment, furs, golf clubs, and so on. Here, the greedy thief attempts to "sweeten the pot" and increase her or his criminal profits.

The National Insurance Crime Bureau (NICB)

The NICB is a nonprofit private crime prevention agency underwritten by more than 600 property-casualty insurance companies.[33] The Chicago-based organization was established to aid law enforcement and insurance investigators in investigations and prosecutions of vehicle crimes such as vehicle theft, vehicle arson, and vehicle fraud. The NICB maintains district offices throughout the United States, Mexico, and Canada and publishes an annual manual for the identification of stolen automobiles. In addition, the NICB's role is to implement policies for the prevention of vehicle theft. To aid the investigator, the NICB publishes passenger identification manuals that interpret characters in the vehicle's VIN.

mycrimekit

Video: Motor vehicle theft

CASE IN POINT:

Possession of Burglary Tools

Ronald is standing in an alley behind a store late at night. A police car arrives, and the officers see Ronald. The officers also see a crowbar, a false key, a lock pick, and a force screw near the area where Ronald is standing. In addition, Ronald has no reasonable explanation for standing in the alley. Under these circumstances, Ronald has probably committed the crime of possession of burglary tools. Although many burglary tools can be purchased in hardware stores, investigators must show that the "intent" was present for the suspect to use them in a burglary. For example, the "reputation" or criminal history of the suspect can offer some evidence to show criminal intent to commit the crime.

Burglary tools may include:

- Explosives
- Slim jims
- Any instrument designed for cutting or burning or opening containers, such as torches or welders
- Portable key cutters
- Key blanks
- Pry bars
- Bolt cutters
- Explosives or chemicals
- Tension wrenches
- Lock picks

Summary Checklist

In this chapter, we consider the ways that information about crimes is documented by criminal investigators. A properly documented case is one that is more likely to succeed in court. See how well you are able to answer the following questions in your checklist.

1. **Do you know the various indicators of burglary?**

   The crime of burglary is generally considered a covert crime in which the criminal works during the nighttime outside the presence of witnesses.

   Burglary is considered a property crime in which the thief seeks to avoid direct contact with people during commission of the crime.

   Burglars may be amateur or professional. Indications of burglary include:

   - Open doors or windows
   - Entrance through a window after removing the glass
   - Debris on the floor from shelves or counters
   - Vehicles parked near the suspect location for no apparent reason or trucks parked close enough to a building to permit access to a roof or to conceal a window or door.
   - A person serving as a lookout

2. **Can you explain the steps in the preliminary investigation of burglary?**

   Most burglars are convicted on circumstantial evidence.

Evidence may include broken glass, tool marks, and fingerprints at the burglary crime scene.

Possession of burglary tools is considered a separate felony offense by most jurisdictions.

Preliminary investigative steps include:

- Determine the point of entry.
- Check to see if a window or door was forced open.
- What type of tool was used?
- Are there tool marks?
- Is there evidence of lock picks?
- Look for footprints, tire tracks, and so on.
- Look for other trace evidence such as cigarette butts, fibers, hair, pieces of broken tools, and so on.
- Sketch the scene.
- Interview victims and witnesses.
- Make a list of property taken (include serial numbers).
- Make a list of all persons on the crime scene.

3. Are you able to identify methods to trace stolen property?

After a successful burglary has occurred, the thief will probably seek to get rid of the stolen property as soon as possible. To this end, a fence is used.

- The fence is a person who buys and sells stolen property with criminal intent.

As a first rule of thumb, the property in question must be identified as stolen

To convict a thief for a property offense in this category, investigators must prove that the suspect received stolen property.

Investigators might need to rely on circumstantial evidence to prove receipt of stolen property. Such evidence is described as follows:

- Did the suspect pay for the merchandise with a check or cash?

- Was the property purchased for considerably lower than the normal retail price?
- Does the suspect have a receipt for the property?
- Were the stolen items isolated from other items in storage?
- Is there property from several different thefts present at the location?

4. Do you know the investigative considerations for the crime of embezzlement?

The investigator must show that the suspect first accepted the property in the scope of employment and then misappropriated it for his or her own use.

Embezzlers usually prefer to steal cash because it is both difficult to trace and easy to conceal. Investigators may, however, find this to be an advantage.

Categories of embezzlement include:

- Theft of currency
- Manipulation of accounts
- Retail theft
- Credit card fraud
- Shoplifting

5. Do you understand the extent of the problem of identity theft?

Identity theft, which involves obtaining credit, merchandise, or services by fraudulent personal representation, is a special kind of larceny.

Identity theft became a federal crime in 1998 with the passage of the Identity Theft and Assumption Deterrence Act.

- The law makes it a crime whenever anyone "knowingly transfers or uses, without lawful authority, a means of identification of another person with the intent to commit, or to aid or abet, any unlawful activity that constitutes a violation of federal law, or that constitutes a felony under any applicable state or local law."

(continued)

Summary Checklist (Continued)

Typical crimes resulting from identity theft include credit card fraud, bank fraud, computer fraud, Internet fraud, and fraudulently obtaining loans.

6. Are you able to explain the extent of the problem of auto theft and how the crime is investigated?

Auto theft includes the stealing of automobiles, trucks, buses, motorcycles, motor scooters, and snowmobiles, among others.

Motor vehicle theft can turn violent, as in cases of carjacking—a crime in which offenders usually force the car's occupants into the street before stealing the vehicle.

Motor vehicles are stolen from a variety of sources, including shopping malls, streets, driveways, parking lots, garages, and car dealerships.

The terms *chop shop* and *stripping operations* refer to locations where stolen vehicles are disposed of.

- Once inside the garage, the stolen vehicle is disassembled.
- Chop-shop operators use torches, power saws, or other tools to disassemble stolen vehicles.
- Parts are transported in tin trucks, from which the parts are sold to repair shops

and salvage yards that use them to repair damaged vehicles.

Most state laws dealing with auto theft address the act of unauthorized use rather than actual "theft" of the vehicle. The elements are typically as follows: A person commits the act of auto theft if he or she:

- Intentionally acquires, drives, or
- Transports a motor vehicle
- Without the consent of the lawful owner.

The investigation of a stolen auto typically begins with a report by the victim to the police.

An investigator's inquiries should include:

- Where was the vehicle last seen?
- Who was the last person to use the vehicle?
- Were the keys left in the ignition?
- Was the vehicle left unlocked?
- Is the victim in arrears on payments?
- Are others allowed to drive the vehicle?
- Was the vehicle equipped with special equipment, such as special wheels, fog lights, or a special sound system?

Key Terms

booster	hot list	shoplifting
burglary	identity theft	snitches
burglary tools	joyriding	stripping operations
carjacking	National Auto Theft Bureau (NATB)	tagging
check kiting		tin truck
chop shop	pilferage	vehicle identification number (VIN)
embezzlement	property crime	
fence	plastic workers	
fungible goods	salvage switch	

Discussion Questions

1. Discuss the distinction between robbery and burglary.
2. List and discuss the elements of the crime of burglary.
3. What physical evidence should be considered in investigating a burglary?
4. What role does a fence play in the crime of burglary?
5. What methods of forgery are considered most common?
6. What are the categories of embezzlement, and how are they best investigated?
7. Explain some of the methods most commonly used by criminals to avoid detection when using stolen credit cards.
8. Discuss the ways that stolen information is used by criminals.
9. Explain the VIN and its role in criminal investigation of motor vehicle theft.
10. What characteristics should the investigator look for in recognizing a stolen vehicle?
11. To what extent does the investigation of stolen motorcycles differ from the investigation of other motor vehicle thefts?

mycrimekit™

Go to MyCrimeKit.com to explore the following study tools and resources specific to this chapter:

- *Practice Quiz:* Multiple-choice, true/false, short-answer, and essay questions.
- *Flashcards:* There are 23 key terms in this chapter. Flashcards test your knowledge of the chapter's key terms.
- *Web Links:* Check out the hotlink to *The New York* Times criminology articles.

- *Career Center:* Check out the hot links to interesting careers in criminal justice, criminology, and juvenile justice.
- *The Research Center:* Check out the Cybrary and research navigator for even more resources.
- *Sample test items:* True/false questions and Essay/discussion questions

Notes

1. FEDERAL BUREAU OF INVESTIGATION. (2008). *Crime in the United States—2007.*
2. LOWRY, T. (1998). Cash machines provide new target for burglars. *USA Today,* March 16:1B.
3. FEDERAL BUREAU OF INVESTIGATION. (2008). *Crime in the United States—2007.*
4. AMERICAN BANKERS' ASSOCIATION (2007). Banker's Association Deposit Account Fraud Survey Report. See at: http://www.aba.com/Press+Room/112707Deposit+FraudSurvey.htm *Report.*
5. DUGAS, C. (1995). Check fraud costs banks, consumers. *USA Today,* November 14:4B.
6. BENNETT, W. AND K. HESS (2001). *Criminal investigation,* 6th ed. Belmont, CA: Wadsworth.
7. McCAGHY, C. (1976). *Deviant behavior.* New York: Macmillan:348–349.
8. CLARK, J. AND R. HOLLINGER (1983). Theft in the workplace. *Crime and Justice* October:117–118.
9. GREENWALD, J. (1996). Credit where none is due. *Time* February 19:50.
10. IBID.
11. CAMERON, M. O. (1983). The scourge of shoplifting. *Criminal Justice Ethics* Winter–Spring:3–15.
12. HARTMANN, D., D. GELFAND, B. PAGE, AND P. WALKER (1972). Rates of bystander observation and reporting of contrived shoplifting incidents. *Criminology* 10:248.
13. BLANKENBURG, E. (1976). The selectivity of legal sanctions: An empirical investigation of shoplifting. *Law and Society Review* 11:109–129.
14. O'DONNELL , J. (2006). Stores protect turf from gangs of thieves. *USA Today,* November 17:1B–2B; Federal Bureau of Investigation. (2008). *Crime in the United States—2007.*
15. FEDERAL BUREAU OF INVESTIGATION. (2008). *Crime in the United States—2007.*
16. Identity thieves thrive in information age. (2001). *Washington Post,* May 31:01. Available at http://www.washingtonpost.com.
17. FEDERAL TRADE COMMISSION REPORT. *Identity theft complaint data, figures and trends on identity theft, November 1999 through March 2001,* p. 3.

18. 18 U.S.C. § 1343.

19. 18 U.S.C. § 1344.

20. 18 U.S.C. § 1028.

21. These items are all listed in the FTC publication *ID Theft— When bad things happen to your good name* (2001)..

22. FTC online publications. (2001). *Pretexting: Your personal information revealed.* Available at http://www.ftc.gov/bep/conline/pubs/credit/pretext.htm.

23. State of Florida Attorney General. (August 14, 2006). Available at http://www.myfloridalegal.com.

24. Federal Bureau of Investigation. (2008). *Crime in the United States—2007.*

25. Ibid.

26. National Insurance Crime Bureau. Available at http://www.iii.org/media/hottopics/insurance/test4/.

27. Ferguson, B. E. (1990). Porcelain chips: An auto theft innovation. *Law and Order* September:154–155.

28. Klaus, P. (1999). *Carjacking in the United States, 1992–1996.* Washington, DC: U.S. Department of Justice, Bureau of Justice Statistics.

29. National Insurance Crime Bureau. Available at http://www.iii.org/media/hottopics/insurance/test4/ (accessed 4-28-2009).

30. Ibid.

31. Ibid.

32. Ibid.

33. National Insurance Crime Bureau. Available at https://www.nicb.org/cps/rde/xchg/nicb/hs.xsl/index.htm.

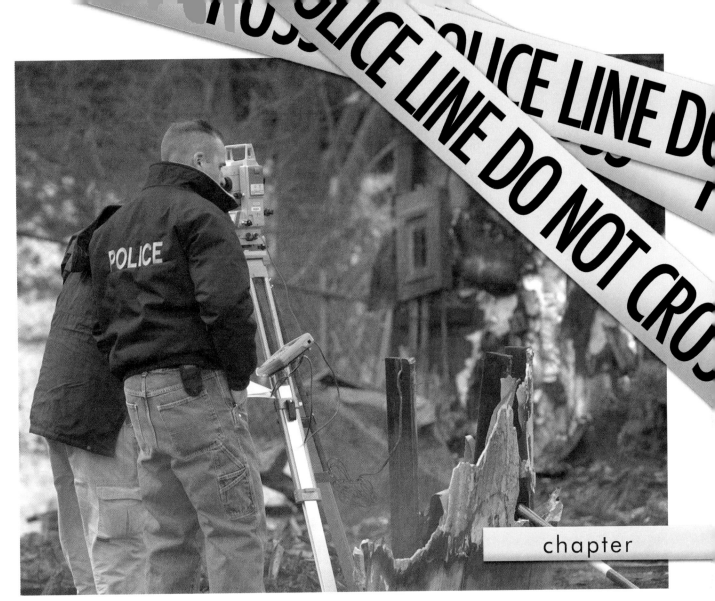

Arson, Bombings, and Terrorism

This chapter will enable you to:

- Understand the scope of the problem of arson.
- Learn the legal definitions and elements of the crime of arson.
- Appreciate the relationship between police and fire investigators.
- Explain the techniques of arson investigation.
- Learn how to investigate bombs and bombers.
- Understand the distinction between domestic and international terrorism.

Introduction

Perhaps one of the oldest known crimes is the act of arson. It creates a severe threat to human life and costs society billions of dollars per year. Although arson can be defined as the malicious or fraudulent burning of property, it can also be considered a crime against both persons and property. Furthermore, it receives little media attention and is difficult to investigate because evidence is difficult to locate and criminal intent is difficult to prove. Unlike other "sensational" media events such as murder cases and drug raids, arson is generally considered a low-priority crime even by law enforcement agencies. Several explanations can be cited for this:

- Arson is a time-consuming and difficult crime to investigate.
- There is much misunderstanding about the motives behind the crime of arson.
- Few arson cases lead to arrests, and fewer than 20 percent of arrests result in convictions.
- Arson used to be classified as a property crime rather than a crime of violence, as it is today.

Arson Offenses

The Uniform Crime Reporting (UCR) program defines arson as any willful or malicious burning or attempt to burn, with or without intent to defraud, a dwelling house, public building, motor vehicle or aircraft, personal property of another, and so on. Only fires determined through investigation to have been willfully or maliciously set are classified as arsons. Fires of suspicious or unknown origins are excluded from this category.

Trends

In 2008, the FBI reported that 64,332 arsons occurred during 2007.[1] These fires caused 3,430 civilian deaths and 17,675 civilian injuries.[2] Arsons involving structures (e.g., residential, storage, public) accounted for 42.9 percent of the total number of arson offenses. Mobile property was involved in 27.9 percent of arsons, and other types of property (e.g., crops, timber, fences) accounted for 29.2 percent of reported arsons. The average dollar loss due to arson was $17,289. Nationwide, the rate of arson was 24.7 offenses for every 100,000 inhabitants.[3]

The United States has one of the highest fire death rates in the industrialized world. According to a 1998 publication by the National Fire Protection Association, the U.S. fire death rate was 14.9 deaths per million population. Between 1994 and 1998, an average of 4,400 Americans lost their lives and another 25,100 were injured annually as the result of fire.[4] Furthermore, about 100 firefighters are killed each year in duty-related incidents. Each year, fire kills more Americans than all natural disasters combined.[5]

National statistics show that "when measured on a cost per incident basis, arson is the most expensive crime committed." The high cost and widespread misunderstanding associated with the crime of arson can be attributed to several factors, which include:

- A lack of public education concerning the problem of arson
- A reluctance on the part of prosecutors to file arson cases that rely on circumstantial evidence

- Quick payments on fire losses by insurance companies
- A lack of adequate training for investigators

Many arson crime scenes are not recognized or treated as such, and much evidence is destroyed. Despite the fact that many of the preceding considerations are no longer considered as great a problem as they used to be, arson still accounts for substantial losses to victims. For example, property losses alone are estimated at $5 billion annually.[6]

Because valuable evidence is sometimes destroyed during a blaze, it is often difficult to determine that arson was committed. Other complicating factors include the fact that there are few, if any, witnesses to the crime; physical evidence is difficult to locate; and if the crime is executed properly, it is difficult to determine the fire's point of origin. Finally, often the victim of the fire ends up being the perpetrator of the crime. For these reasons, arson investigation is one of the more difficult crimes to solve.

Elements of Arson

As with all crimes, the elements must be established before a criminal charge can be levied against the suspect. As with most other crimes, the elements of arson differ from one state to the next, but some commonalties do exist.

Legal Categories. Arson is also legally characterized by two distinct categories: aggravated arson and simple arson. *Aggravated arson* is the deliberate burning of property while creating an imminent danger to human life or risking great bodily harm. *Simple arson*, a lesser offense, is the burning of property that does not result in such a risk to human life. In addition to aggravated and simple arson, most states have recognized that attempted arson is also punishable under law.

The severity of the crime of arson can be seen in the case of Dr. Deborah Green. On the windy night of October 24, 1995, a raging fire demolished the Green home, a $400,000, six-bedroom home in Prairie Village, Kansas. Accelerants were poured in several areas of the house and fed the flames. Dr. Green escaped the fire through her back bedroom door on the first floor. One of her daughters, 10-year-old Kate, survived by climbing through her second-floor bedroom window onto the garage roof and jumping. The fire took the lives of 6-year-old Kelly Green and 13-year-old Tim Farrar. Green's husband, Dr. Michael Farrar, was not home when the fire broke out.

The investigation also included a closer look at a fire about 16 months earlier that damaged the family's previous home and the mysterious illness of the children's father, Dr. Michael Farrar, weeks before the October fire. Dr. Farrar was hospitalized again after the fire with apparent poisoning. The investigation revealed that Green had set the fire. As the investigation continued, evidence also showed that on at least three occasions, Green had poisoned her husband, Michael Farrar, with ricin, a derivative of castor beans.

Dr. Deborah Green was charged with aggravated arson and two counts of first-degree murder in the deaths of the children. Green was also charged with two counts of attempted first-degree murder of her husband and surviving daughter. She was held on $3 million bond.

The Deborah Green case demonstrates how arson can be a means to commit a crime or a means to cover one up. Despite the many underlying issues in the Deborah Green case, it is clear that investigators must have knowledge and resources to properly investigate this serious and violent criminal act to bring the perpetrators to justice.

FIGURE 15.1 Dr. Deborah Green views a police videotape in Johnson County District Court on Wednesday, January 31, 1996, during a hearing in Olathe, Kansas. The videotape was of her interview immediately after the fatal fire that killed two of her children. Courtesy of AP Wide World Photos.

The Police and Fire Alliance

After a fire has been determined to have a suspicious origin, investigators from the local fire and police departments as well as the victim's insurance company become involved with the case. Problems and confusion sometimes unfold if investigators from these agencies fail to understand differences in their roles. The traditional role of the fire department is to investigate every fire for cause and origin. Accordingly, 80 percent of the fire protection in the United States is provided by volunteer fire departments.[7] To this end, firefighters are usually trained in the suppression of fire rather than its investigation.

When a suspicious fire is discovered, however, it is generally while it is being extinguished. So what, then, is the role of the firefighter? As a rule, it is three-fold: (1) to extinguish the fire, (2) to investigate the origin of the fire, and (3) to "detect" the possibility of arson but not to investigate arson. Few fire departments have the legal authority to investigate arson fires, although their assistance in such an investigation is not disputed.

When the fire investigation becomes a question of who committed the crime, the matter then becomes a law enforcement concern. This is critical because after it has been determined that law enforcement should take over the investigation, fire investigators should yield the crime scene to the arson investigators and respond to them in an adjunct role. Immediate obeyance of this principle minimizes confusion and duplication of efforts at the crime scene.

The police investigator has a statutory role in investigating arson because it is a violation of state or federal law. The principal goal of the police investigation in an arson case is to identify the perpetrator(s) of the crime and to identify and secure sufficient evidence to prosecute and convict.

Finally, the role of the insurance investigator is to make a determination as to whether or not the insurance company owes payment for the fire loss. The insurance investigator is not a law enforcement officer. His or her authority to investigate is specified in the insured's contract. This contract refers to many of the provisions of the 1943 New York Standard Policy, which sets forth conditions subscribed to by the insured in the event of a loss.[8] In kind, most insurance companies state that coverage is void if the company's investigation proves arson or fraud.

Arson Investigative Techniques

The act of arson has been described as a stealthy, cowardly crime that, by its very nature, leaves very little direct evidence as to the identity of the arsonist. Many arsonists, however, fail to cover their tracks adequately and may therefore leave some type of evidence behind. For example, in many commercial arsons, the suspect leaves a **paper trail** that investigators can follow. This includes financial records, inflated insurance coverage, little or no inventory, and excessive debts. In an ideal situation, the arsonist will either be convicted, through the use of well-documented motives and opportunity, or might be willing to cooperate with authorities in identifying accomplices, motives, and prior victims.

The Preliminary Investigation of Arson

The preliminary investigation of arson begins basically like many other crimes, with a thorough examination of the crime scene. Arson does not have an immediate corpus delicti. It is, therefore, the responsibility of the investigator to prove that a specific fire did occur and that it was ignited deliberately. To accomplish this, both direct and circumstantial evidence can be used to show that the fire was ignited. Such evidence, however, may not reveal the opportunity or motive of the fire setter. As with most crimes, the motive is important, but the key responsibility of the arson investigator is to connect the suspect with the crime scene regardless of the motive.

Identify the Point of Origin. The first step in an arson investigation is to determine the fire's **point of origin.** This may be the most critical phase of the investigation because it includes the ruling out of natural or accidental causes. The materials used in the setting of the fire, along with the type of material being burned, may show a distinct burn pattern. Hence, it is important to identify the point at which the fire originated because it is here that most of the physical evidence can be located indicating a fire of incendiary nature. The fire's point of origin may be determined in several ways. The questioning of witnesses could reveal the necessary information. In addition, an inspection of the ruins at the fire scene might reveal valuable evidence.

Finding Accelerants in Arson Investigations. Arson investigators can prove that a fire was set intentionally by finding an accelerant at the scene of a fire. An accelerant is a chemical fuel that causes a fire to burn hotter, spread more quickly than usual, or be unusually difficult to extinguish. The presence of an accelerant in fire debris can be used as evidence of arson.[9]

The most commonly used accelerants are gasoline, kerosene, turpentine, and diesel fuel. These are all organic compounds containing mixtures of hydrocarbon molecules. As accelerants evaporate, the hydrocarbons more into the air above the fire debris, which is called the "headspace."[10]

Various techniques exist to detect accelerants at a fire scene. These range from an experienced fire investigator or a specially trained "sniffer" dog using its sense of smell to detect the characteristic odor of various accelerants in the surrounding air to more complex laboratory methods.

Elements of Arson

A person knowingly damages a building or property of another by

- ☑ Starting a fire or explosion, or
- ☑ Procuring or causing such property to be burned

One of the most advanced techniques for detecting accelerants in fire debris is called *headspace gas chromatography*. Gas chromatography involves separating mixtures of gases into their individual components based on the different boiling points of their hydrocarbons. Each gas in the mixture can then be identified because each one produces a distinct chemical fingerprint called a *chromatogram*.[11]

In headspace gas chromatography, solid debris taken from the suspected point of origin of the fire is placed in an airtight vial to prevent any accelerants from evaporating. The vial is then heated, releasing the accelerant's hydrocarbons into the trapped headspace above the debris. A needle is inserted through the cap of the vial to remove a sample of the hydrocarbons and inject them into an instrument called a *gas chromatogram* for separation and analysis.[12]

If an accelerant is used to start a fire, a small amount will likely still be present in the charred debris. Identification of the accelerant can serve as physical evidence to support a charge of arson.

Observe the Span of the Fire. Determining the time **span of the fire** is also of paramount importance. Although the majority of evidence collection is conducted at the crime scene, much can be learned simply by observing the fire. Specifically, physical characteristics of the fire, such as smoke, direction, flames, and distance of travel, are important. Immediately after the fire is extinguished, samples of debris should be collected that might have been the material used for starting the fire. When the rubble is being cleaned up, investigators should be present to observe any additional evidence that might be uncovered.

Photograph the Scene. Complete photographs of the structure should be taken to help preserve the crime scene for the courtroom. This makes a "record" of the condition of the scene at the time the fire was extinguished. When taking photos, the investigator should focus on the location of rags, large amounts of paper, cans, or empty receptacles that might have been used in setting the fire.

Identify Plants or Trailers. Finally, identifying the areas of **plants** (preparations used to set the fire) and **trailers** (materials used to spread the fire) can reveal important clues to the investigator.

- *Plants.* Preparations used to set the fire. These include newspapers, rags, and other flammable waste material.
- *Trailers.* Materials used in spreading the fire. These include gunpowder; rags soaked in flammable liquid; and flammable liquids such as gasoline, kerosene, and alcohol.

Some arsonists prefer to use delayed timing devices to allow a time lag between the setting up of the arson and the fire's outbreak. To this end, mechanical devices and chemicals are commonly used. Such devices may well be intact when probing the crime scene for evidence.

Question Witnesses. Witnesses also play an important role in determining causes of the fire and possible suspects. Questions to be asked of the witnesses include:

- Who are you and why were you present at the fire?
- What attracted your attention to the fire?

The witnesses' observations of the intensity, color, and direction of the fire may also prove to be of great value. Certainly, the observations of witnesses should only be viewed as information to give the investigator a lead as to where to begin looking for evidence. The actual point of origin, of course, must be determined by a thorough examination of the premises.

Observe Alligatoring. The term **alligatoring** refers to the pattern of crevices formed by the burning of a wooden structure. Resembling the skin of an alligator, this pattern reveals a minimum amount of charring, with alligatoring in large segments, when a fire is extinguished rapidly. As the fire continues to burn, the alligatoring will become smaller, with charring becoming deeper.

In a fire crime scene, liquids tend to flow downward and pool around fixed objects such as furniture. Their trails, however, are relatively easy to trace and provide the investigator with good evidence. An accelerant such as gasoline, kerosene, or alcohol can be traced from the point it was spilled to the lowest point of flow. At times, unburned amounts of these liquids may be found at low points, where the heat was not intense enough for ignition.

Other Clues. Many things may indicate that a fire of suspicious origin was arson. In one example, many fires were set at the scene, but evidence showed that each was set independently, with no proof of spontaneous combustion. Other clues include:

- *Flames.* The color of the flame is noteworthy in the early phases of a fire. For instance, a blue-orange flame represents burning alcohol. Certainly, if this material is not normally stored on the premises, one could assume that it was used as the accelerant in the fire. Information as to the description of the fire can be gained from witnesses who arrived on the scene before investigators.

- *Smoke.* As indicated earlier, smoke can also be of value in determining what substance was used to start a fire. If smoke can be observed at the beginning of a fire, before spreading to other parts of a structure, its color should be noted. For example, black smoke indicates that the material is made with a petroleum base. White smoke, conversely, indicates that vegetable matter is burning, such as straw or hay. If the structure is completely engulfed in flames, it will be difficult to make determinations as to what materials are being burned.

- *Size of the fire.* Depending on certain factors, such as the time element of the fire, the size of the fire might give investigators information to determine an act of arson. For example, structures that are engulfed in flames in a short period might indicate arson. Fire investigators recognize that fires of "natural" origin burn in a definable pattern. Therefore, fires burning

FIGURE 15.2 Photo of a burning house illustrates that the extent evidence of arson can be difficult, if not impossible, to recover.
Courtesy of Stock Connection.

quickly or in a direction that is not logical will indicate that an accelerant has been used. Factors to aid the investigator in determining the "normal" course or pattern for a fire should consider such variables as ventilation and contents of the structure.

- *Odors.* Distinguishable odors can be emitted from certain types of fires that might indicate a specific fire starter, such as kerosene, gasoline, and alcohol. These materials ensure that a fire will erupt, and arsonists expect any evidence of these accelerants to be destroyed in the fire. Investigators should, therefore, try to detect any odors by using their own **olfactory senses.**

mycrimekit

Video: Arson

Motivations of the Arsonist

As a defense attorney once said, "It is not a crime to have a motive." Indeed, when an investigator is successful in the collection of evidence to show the insured's participation in the crime, along with evidence of a motive showing arson as a reasonable alternative for the arsonist, a prosecutable case may have been developed. After it has been determined that the fire was of incendiary origin, possible motives must be examined to help identify the suspect. Motives for arson include profit, revenge, vandalism, crime concealment, and pyromania.

Arson for Profit. This category represents an estimated 50 percent of all fire-related property damage in the United States and the corresponding increase in the number of arsons reported to officials in recent years.[13] The typical arson-for-profit criminal is a businessperson who sets fire to his or her business or hires a professional arsonist to do the task. Traditionally, this category of arson has posed relatively low risk and high profit for the criminal and has virtually become a business in and of itself.

Economic gain from this type of arson may be either direct or indirect. For example, a home or business owner will see a direct financial gain when the insurance company pays the claim. In comparison, an employee in a warehouse who starts a fire and readily extinguishes it might benefit from a raise or promotion for his or her quick and "responsible" response and effort in saving the business. As indicated earlier, insurance fraud is a common motive for arson, perhaps one of the most frequent. A common method of insurance-related fraud is the purchasing of old, run-down buildings in inner-city areas. Over a period

---

Types of Evidence in Arson Cases

- ☑ *Evidence of incendiary origin.* The basic type of evidence in this category are physical evidence (e.g., laboratory analysis of fire debris), expert observation of burn patterns and fire characteristics, and negative corpus evidence (e.g., elimination of accidental causes).

- ☑ *Evidence of motive.* In fraud cases, evidence of motive may involve a complex analysis of financial and property records. Here, a distinction can be made between evidence of a general hostility (e.g., a previous argument) and specific hostility (e.g., threats to burn). In addition, the motive can be important in cases involving a pyromaniac and vandalism, which are frequently irrational acts.

- ☑ *Evidence linking a suspect to the commission of arson.* Direct linkage, such as eyewitness testimony or a confession, is clearly preferable to circumstantial linkage, which simply reflects opportunity.

of several months, shrewd businesspersons then sell and resell the property. Each of these transactions raises the value of the property, at least on paper. The properties are then insured for the highest possible dollar amount. Sometimes the target of the arsonist is not the building itself but what it contains. A computer dealer, for example, might remove any valuable computers and software from his or her business and leave behind computers and software that are outdated or in which he or she has invested too much money. After the fire destroys the building, the arsonist simply claims the insurance coverage that covered the burned stock and realizes a "market" return on the stock.

Not all arson-for-profit crimes focus on businesses or are perpetuated by people in big business. Indeed, high car payments or excessive mechanical difficulties with an automobile may compel the ordinary citizen to commit automobile arson to collect on the insurance. This type of criminal activity has resulted in an estimated 1,500 automobile arsons each year.[14]

Arson for profit can take many forms, so in all circumstances, the conditions surrounding suspicious fires must be investigated thoroughly for possible motives. These motives should include the possibility that arson was used to cover up another crime, such as homicide or burglary.

Arson for Revenge. A high percentage of arsons are attributed to revenge, jealousy, and spite. People committing such acts are usually adults who target both individuals and property. Offenders include jilted lovers in personal relationships, disgruntled employees, feuding neighbors, persons who were cheated in business and personal transactions, and persons motivated by racial prejudice. From an investigative standpoint, after revenge has been identified as a possible motive in a fire, the list of suspects can be narrowed greatly. From here, care should be exercised in interview and interrogation techniques to extract sufficient and pertinent information.

Arson for Vandalism. Not much planning or preparation is required for a fire designated as vandalism. In addition, readily available materials are commonly used by arsonists. As discussed later, about 95 percent of the arsons for vandalism are caused by juveniles, owing in large part to peer pressure. Statistics show that most violators in this category are youths from lower socioeconomic groups who choose to commit the crime in the morning or early afternoon.

Motives in this category differ from case to case but include vandalism and revenge. Typically, however, the motive is profit. Indeed, people who have been unable to contract a professional arsonist have been known to hire juveniles to commit such acts. Certainly, a juvenile fire starter will work for much less than a professional "torch."

Children of many ages have experimented with fire out of curiosity. Some, according to theorists, are abused children and set fires as a call for help. Juvenile fire-setter programs have sprung up across the country to identify these problem children and to deal with their underlying problems.

Arson for Crime Concealment. It is common for some criminals to try to cover up their crimes through the use of a fire. Murders, burglaries, and other crimes have been concealed through the use of this method. Fire investigators must consider this as an alternative motive for all fires.

Pyromania. A pyromaniac is a person who is a compulsive fire starter. This person is motivated by several aspects of the fire-setting experience. For example, some experts claim that pyromaniacs gain sexual stimulation by starting and viewing fires. In addition, excitation is achieved by the crowds that gather and the emergency vehicles that converge on the scene. Pyromaniacs are impulsive fire

Evidence of Planning or Pre-knowledge

- ☑ Removing items of value from the crime scene before a fire.
- ☑ Before the fire, making off-the-cuff remarks or jokes about burning the structure.
- ☑ Increasing insurance coverage or obtaining coverage for the first time before the fire.
- ☑ Making unusual changes in business practices just before the fire (e.g., closing earlier or later, having different people lock up).
- ☑ Taking obvious actions designed to avoid suspicion, such as booking for banquets that the insured has no intention of carrying out, filing for bankruptcy, and so on.

setters; their acts are seldom planned. Investigators can only examine the routes or paths that the fires seem to establish. Investigations have revealed that pyromaniacs may have a sordid past, which includes being abused as a child, bedwetting, and cruelty to animals.

Serial Fire Setters

Serial criminals of any type pose great concerns for communities and law enforcement officials alike. A serial arsonist can be defined as one who sets fires repeatedly. This criminal, however, is at somewhat of an advantage because expertise in fire investigations is not as common as in other crimes. The FBI's National Center for the Analysis of Violent Crime (NCAVC) has conducted research in this area and has concluded that compulsive fire setting can be classified as mass, spree, and serial.

A CLOSER LOOK

Arson for Revenge

Jane (not her real name) is a 27-year-old white woman, well-groomed and friendly. Her records indicate below-average intelligence. She was arrested in 1984 and charged with several counts of arson. This was her first incarceration. She set a fire to a vacant farmhouse in 1980, amounting to $30,000 in damages; a barn in 1984, resulting in a $150,000 loss; and a corncrib in 1984, worth $10,800. The fires were motivated by revenge, according to Jane, who claims that she set fire to the barn because she claimed the owner would not give her some kittens.

The corncrib fire was a result of a long-standing grudge against its owner, who years earlier had removed Jane from the school bus she was driving because of her bad language and behavior. Jane indicates that she was under medication for a heart ailment. While growing up, she had constant conflicts with her parents, who she claimed abused her emotionally and physically. Jane stated that she also had been raped at age 18 years by her father and brother. As with many arsonists, Jane reports problems establishing and maintaining relationships. While incarcerated, Jane had numerous run-ins with corrections officials for minor nuisance offenses. She is presently in a halfway facility, working on her high school equivalency diploma and holding down a part-time job. Her caseworker believes that Jane will be released sometime soon.

Source: O'CONNER, R. (1987). *Practical fire and arson investigation.* Boca Raton, FL: CRC Press.

- A *mass arsonist* sets three or more fires at the same location.
- A *spree arsonist* sets fires at three or more separate locations, with no cooling-off period between them.
- The *serial arsonist* sets three or more separate fires with a definite cooling-off period between them. This period may last for days, weeks, or months.

Profiling the Fire Starter

After identifying a possible motive, the investigator may wonder to what extent the fire starter shows a propensity for violence. Surprisingly, David Berkowitz, the "Son of Sam" mass murderer who terrorized New York in 1976 by killing five people and wounding seven others, reported to the police that he was personally responsible for setting more than 2,000 fires from 1974 to 1977.[15] Police reports also showed that Berkowitz set these fires in cars, dumpsters, brush, and vacant and unoccupied stores. In addition, police seized notepads bearing handprinted notes by Berkowitz that gave details on 1,411 fires for the years of 1974, 1975, and 1977, including the dates and times of the fires, the streets, the type of weather, and the fire department code, indicating the type of responding apparatus and property burned. The following questions are therefore raised:

- Does Berkowitz typify the fire starter?
- Are arsonists homicidal?
- Do they keep meticulous diaries of their fires?

According to James in his article "Psychological Motives for Arson," gender, age, education, intellectual level, and economic status do not in any way limit the possibility that a person will engage in arson.[16] On the other hand, from a study of large samples, it does appear that, statistically, persons of certain ages and with certain characteristics are more apt to set fires than are others.

The Role of the Insurance Industry

Because of the severe financial strain arson has placed on the insurance industry, insurance companies are becoming more involved with investigations

FIGURE 15.3 Arson investigator examining the scene to determine the origin of the fire. Courtesy of PhotoEdit, Inc.

Problems in Arson Investigation

- ☑ Locating witnesses
- ☑ Locating and preserving physical evidence
- ☑ Determining whether the victim is also the suspect
- ☑ Coordinating the investigation among police, fire, and insurance agents
- ☑ Determining if the fire was arson or had some other cause

involving arson. Insurance carriers are usually more than willing to assist local law enforcement and fire officials during the course of an investigation. In fact, independent information offered by an insurance company might prove to be highly valuable in discovering motives and suspects for a crime. Indeed, the crime of arson is one that permits the investigator to work hand in hand with the "victim." In addition, many insurance carriers might even offer financial assistance to fire investigators. This may come in the form of providing heavy machinery for aid in processing the crime scene or by bringing in experts in arson investigations to aid local investigators in the investigation.

Insurance company assistance may come in many other forms, such as providing local investigators with financial audits and income tax returns; such information may not be readily available to local investigators. To protect insurance companies from civil recourse in disclosing some of the information discussed previously, many states have passed laws granting limited civil immunity to insurance companies that assist local arson investigators during the course of an ongoing investigation. This contributes to an increased flow of information from insurance companies to local investigators, which increases the chance of an eventual prosecution of the arsonist and subsequent relief from civil claims liability for the insurance company.

Characteristics of the Fire Setter[17]

- ☑ *Age.* Typically around age 17 years
- ☑ *Gender.* Usually male
- ☑ *Race.* Predominantly white
- ☑ *Intelligence.* Research indicates that fire setters are often mentally deficient
- ☑ *Academic performance.* Most have a history of poor academic performance
- ☑ *Rearing environment.* Most appear to come from unstable home environments within lower socioeconomic groups
- ☑ *Social relationships.* Typically experience difficulties in relationships
- ☑ *Sexual disturbance.* Usually associated with sexual perversion; fire setting tends to serve as a sexual substitute
- ☑ *Motive.* Revenge most typically the underlying motive

Prosecution of Arson Cases

There exists an old adage: "Without the **fire triangle**—heat, fuel, and oxygen—there can be no fire." Similarly, the successful prosecution of an arson case must include a triangle consisting of police detectives, fire investigators, and a prosecutor. Sadly, in many parts of the United States, prosecution of arson crimes may never occur. Some reasons include:

1. There is no one qualified or trained to conduct the investigation.
2. The time required for a thorough arson investigation by police or fire authorities is not available.
3. Prosecuting attorneys are reluctant to file and pursue prosecution. This is the most prevalent reason because arson cases are difficult to prosecute.

Prosecution of an arson case is time consuming and requires expertise. Courts have ruled that circumstantial evidence, the most common type of evidence in an arson case, has the same probative value as direct evidence, but it is up to the prosecution to weave the web of circumstantiality.[18] Many prosecutors find this an intimidating and unrewarding task.

A good arson investigator begins with the notion that he or she must collect sufficient circumstantial evidence to convince a jury that the suspect committed the crime. Statistics reveal that most successful arson prosecutors rely on circumstantial evidence.

Proving the arson case "beyond a reasonable doubt" through the use of circumstantial evidence is difficult but not impossible. Prosecutors are frequently reluctant to proceed with charges in an arson case because evidence is fragmented and circumstantial. A trained investigator, however, knows what evidence to look for and is aware of the amount of evidence sufficient to remove reasonable doubt from the minds of prospective jurors.

Bombing Incidents

Even though this section addresses bomb investigations, a brief opening discussion about terrorism is prudent because a number of terrorist organizations in the twenty-first century have used bombs in various forms. The World Trade Center and Pentagon terrorist attacks of September 11, 2001, marked a dramatic escalation in a trend toward more destructive terrorist attacks that began in the

mycrimekit

Video: Career profile: Arson investigator

Evidence for Arson Prosecution

- ☑ *Evidence of participation.* This might be the disabling of a fire alarm or rearranging combustibles at a fire's location.

- ☑ *Exclusive access.* If firefighters are required to use force to gain entrance into a structure, the arsonist would have difficulty doing the same to set the fire. This indicates the complicity of the business owner in locking up the structure.

- ☑ *Motive.* Establishment of a motive is one critical element in showing jurors a suspect's criminal intent.

- ☑ *False statements.* A convincing element in an arson prosecution is the "victim's" false statements to the investigators.

1980s. Until the September 11 attack, the October 23, 1983 truck bombings of U.S. and French military barracks in Beirut, Lebanon, which claimed a total of 295 lives, stood as the most deadly act of terrorism. The attacks of September 11 produced casualty figures more than 10 times higher than those of the 1983 barracks attacks.

The September 11 attack also reflected a trend toward more indiscriminate targeting among international terrorists. The vast majority of the more than 3,000 victims of the attack were civilians. In addition, the attack represented the first known case of suicide attacks carried out by international terrorists in the United States. The September 11 attack also marked the first successful act of international terrorism in the United States since the vehicle bombing of the World Trade Center in February 1993.

Today, the most serious international terrorist threat to U.S. interests stems from Sunni Islamic extremists, such as Osama bin Laden and individuals affiliated with his Al-Qaeda organization. Al-Qaeda leaders, including Osama bin Laden, have been harbored in Afghanistan since 1996 by the extremist Islamic regime of the Taliban. Despite recent military setbacks suffered by the Taliban and the apparent death of Al-Qaeda operational commander Mohamed Atef resulting from a U.S. bombing raid, Al-Qaeda is still considered a capable terrorist network. The network's willingness and capability to inflict large-scale violence and destruction against U.S. persons and interests—as it demonstrated with the September 11 attack, the bombing of the *U.S.S. Cole* in October 2000, and the bombings of two U.S. embassies in east Africa in August 1998, among other plots—make it a clear and imminent threat to the United States and pose a number of unique challenges for criminal investigators.

Individuals who have been investigated for possible terrorist links include Richard Reid and Zacarias Moussaoui. Let's now consider investigative leads as well as evidence developed against these terrorist suspects to illustrate.

On December 22, 2001, Richard C. Reid was arrested after a flight attendant on American Airlines Flight 63 observed him attempting apparently to ignite an improvised explosive in his sneakers while on board a Paris-to-Miami flight. Aided by passengers, attendants overpowered and subdued Reid, and the flight was diverted to Logan International Airport in Boston. Evidence strongly suggests that Reid, who was traveling on a valid British passport, was affiliated with the Al-Qaeda network. Reid was indicted on nine counts, including placing an explosive device on an aircraft and attempted murder. The FBI investigation has determined that the explosives in Reid's shoes, if detonated in certain areas of the passenger cabin, could have blown a hole in the fuselage of the aircraft.

Investigators also learned that Reid and another subject, Zacarias Moussaoui, were known associates. Moussaoui came to the attention of the FBI while taking flight-training classes in Minnesota in August 2001. Moussaoui paid more than $8,000 in cash for flight simulator lessons on a 747-400, which far exceeded his training level as a pilot. Moussaoui showed unusual interest in the instructor's comment that airplane cabin doors could not be opened during flight. In addition, his flight instructor was concerned that Moussaoui expressed interest only in learning how to take off and not how to land the 747-400. In preparation for high-fidelity simulator training, he expressed strong interest in "piloting" a simulated flight from London's Heathrow Airport to John F. Kennedy Airport in New York. When the instructor took his concerns to the FBI, Moussaoui was interviewed by Special Agents from the FBI and the U.S. Immigration and Naturalization Service (INS). He was determined to be an INS overstay and was detained by the INS on August 16, 2001. After his detention, Moussaoui refused to allow a search to be conducted of his possessions, including a laptop computer and a computer disc. Attempts were made to obtain authority to conduct a search of

A CLOSER LOOK

Arson and Trace Evidence

In California in early 1989, a pipe bomb that had been placed on a vehicle exploded, killing the driver. An investigation by the ATF; the Rialto, California, Police Department; and the San Bernardino Sheriff's Department ensued. Evidence recovered at the scene was forwarded to the ATF laboratory for examination. Intact powder particles found at the end caps of the bomb enabled chemists to identify the type and brand of powder used. A subsequent search of the suspect's residence uncovered a can of smokeless powder identical to the powder identified. Additional evidence recovered during the search linked the suspect to the bombing, for which he was arrested and tried on state murder charges.

Sources: Harnett, D. M. (1990, Apr.). Bombing and arson investigations enhanced by advances in ATF labs. *Police Chief* 20, 24, 26, 28; James, J. (1965). Psychological motives for arson. *Popular Government March*

this computer. However, because of the lack of probable cause and lack of predication, neither a criminal nor intelligence search could be conducted. After the September 11 attack, a criminal search of the computer was conducted. Nothing was located that connected Moussaoui with the events of September 11; however, information about crop dusting was located on the computer. As a result, crop-dusting operations in the United States were grounded briefly on two occasions in September 2001. On December 11, 2001, the United States District Court for the Eastern District of Virginia indicted Moussaoui on six counts of conspiracy for his role in the events of September 11, 2001.

What Is a Bomb?

Bombs can be constructed to look like almost anything and can be placed or delivered in any number of ways. Bombs are often made out of common household items regularly found in the kitchen, garage, or under the sink. The easiest bomb to construct is the pipe bomb, which is often packed with screws and nails that act as projectiles, similar to a hand grenade. These are materials that the bomber relies on, partly to help conceal his or her identity. Because they are usually homemade, these bombs are limited in their design only by the imagination of the bomber. So when searching for a bomb, the investigator should simply look for anything that appears unusual.

Statistics show that the use of bombs by drug traffickers is becoming more common. In 1990, the ATF reported an increase of 1,000 percent between 1987 and 1989. These included 126 bombings across the country.

In addition to drug traffickers, in 1990, the ATF showed an increase in mail bombs. The mail bomber attempts to gain from violence and intimidation what he or she fails to attain peacefully. Such devices are typically sent by "hate" or special-interest groups representing a particular lifestyle or belief or protesting certain laws. During 1990, for example, mail bombs killed a federal judge and a city alderman.

Bombings by Teens

A disturbing trend across the nation is the growing number of teenagers who have been linked with bombing incidents. Many techniques of how to construct a bomb cheaply have been learned through the Internet. Experts theorize that well-publicized bombing incidents such as the Oklahoma City bombing and the

Unabomber saga have stimulated interest among teenagers in bomb making.[19] It is unclear whether teen bombers are really interested in hurting anyone or are just intrigued by their ability to manufacture a bomb. How-to information is also readily available in bomb-making manuals such as the *Anarchist's Cookbook* and the *Poor Man's James Bond*. These manuals have also been found online.

The Internet has given teens a way to communicate with like-minded youths who may also be curious about bomb building. In 1996, a Montgomery County, Maryland, neighbor who suspected that illegal drugs were being shipped to teenagers at a vacant house tipped off the police, who found bomb-making ingredients and plans for making a bomb. In a better known case, Harvey "Buddy" Waldron, a Washington State football player, was killed in an explosion in Pullman, Washington, in 1993 when he and a teammate assembled an 8-inch pipe bomb, wired to a clock, that they had planned to detonate in a wheat field. To combat the spread of bombings, in 1996, the state of Georgia enacted the first comprehensive antibomb law, which includes penalties for both teens and adults.

Investigating Bomb Threats

Bomb threats are delivered in a variety of ways, but most are telephoned in to the target. Occasionally, these calls are through a third party. Sometimes a threat is communicated through writing and recording. There are two general explanations as to why bombers communicate a bomb threat:

1. The caller has definite knowledge or believes that an explosive or incendiary bomb has been or will be placed, and he or she wants to minimize

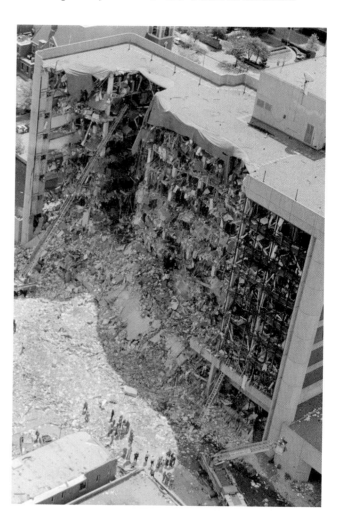

FIGURE 15.4 Rescue personnel converge on the scene of the 1995 bombing of the Murrah Federal Building.
AP Wide World Photos.

FIGURE 15.5 A graphic analysis of the 1995 bombing of the Murrah Building in Oklahoma City, Oklahoma. Copyright 1995 U.S. News & WorldReport, LP Reprinted with permission.

personal injury or property damage. The caller may be the person who placed the device or someone who has become aware of such information.

2. The caller wants to create an atmosphere of anxiety and panic that will, in turn, result in a disruption of normal activities at the facility where the device is supposedly placed.

Whatever the reason, there will certainly be a reaction to it. Through proper planning, however, the wide variety of uncontrollable reactions can be minimized. The bomb threat caller is the best source of information about a bomb. When a bomb threat is called in, the following steps should be implemented:

- Keep the caller on the line as long as possible.
- Ask him or her to repeat the message and record every word spoken by the person.
- Ask the caller the location of the bomb and the time of detonation of the device.
- Inform the caller that the building is occupied and the detonation of a bomb could kill or injure innocent people.
- Pay particular attention to background noise such as motors running, music playing, or any other noise that may give a clue as to the location of the caller.
- Listen closely to the voice (male or female), voice quality (calm or excited), accents, and speech impediments.
- Interview the person who received the call for the preceding information.

Written Bomb Threats. When a written threat is received, all materials should be saved, including envelopes and containers. Remember that paper is an excellent preservative of latent fingerprints. In addition, handwriting, typewriting, and postal markings can provide good investigative leads. Therefore, after the message has been recognized as a bomb threat, further handling of the material should be minimized, and it should be stored in a safe place.

Booby Traps. The use of bombs and **booby traps** has also become of particular concern to drug enforcement officials over the years. Many drug manufacturers have learned the skills of protecting their marijuana plots or chemical laboratories with such devices. The booby trap provides low-cost protection to the illegal drug operation and is designed to serve any of three purposes.

1. To warn the suspect of any intruders by the sound of explosive devices
2. To deny any intruder or police access to the inhabited area by injuring or killing them
3. To slow down police pursuit in a raid situation by injuring or killing officers

If explosives are located, officers should never attempt to dismantle or defuse them unless they have received technical training in bomb disposal. Instead, they should be sufficiently trained to identify such devices so that they can be avoided and properly trained personnel can be notified.

Explosive booby traps are activated by numerous methods, including remote control, manual control, or activation by the victim (usually, a trip wire or hidden pressure plates installed in the ground). Booby traps can be placed either outside or inside the suspect's residence, and their design is limited only by the imagination of the criminal. For example, one exterior trap is called the *mouse trap* because it literally uses a mouse trap that is used as a firing pin for a shotgun shell that is also attached to the trap. The trap can be affixed to trees or fence posts and can either maim or kill the intruder. An example of an indoor trap is the magazine bomb. This device consists of a magazine that has had a portion of the inner pages removed to conceal a hidden mouse trap. When the magazine is opened, the trap detonates a blasting cap.

Safety Precautions. In raid or search situations in which explosive devices are expected to be encountered, investigators should be accompanied by an explosives expert. This person can be used to inform officers of what type of device is at hand and how best to proceed safely with the raid. Other precautions include the following:

- Only one officer at a time should approach the suspected booby trap.
- When trip wires are located, both ends of the wire should be checked (some devices use more than one trip wire).
- Wires that appear to be electric should not be cut.
- Be aware of fuses or obvious means of detonation (e.g., mercury fuses).
- No containers should be opened without a thorough examination.

No single strategy exists to adequately safeguard officers from all hazards posed by booby traps and explosives. Each case is different and should be evaluated individually, with consideration given to the number of possible suspects (and their backgrounds) and the location of the raid. In any case, keen observation and prudent judgment are still the best investigative precautions.

Bomb Search Techniques

The following room search technique is based on the use of a two-person searching team. There are many minor variations possible in searching a room. The following contains only the basic techniques. When the two-person search team enters the room to be searched, they should first move to various parts of the room and stand quietly with their eyes closed and listen for a clockwork device. Frequently, a clockwork mechanism can be quickly detected without use of special equipment. Even if no clockwork mechanism is detected, the team is now aware of the background noise level within the room itself.

Background noise or transferred sound is always disturbing during a building search. If a ticking sound is heard but cannot be located, one might become unnerved. However, the ticking sound may come from an unbalanced air conditioner fan several floors away or from a dripping sink down the hall.

Sound transfers through air-conditioning ducts, along water pipes, and through walls. One of the most difficult buildings to search is one that has steam or hot water heat. This type of building constantly thumps, cracks, chatters, and ticks because of the movement of the steam or hot water through the pipes and the expansion and contraction of the pipes. Background noise may also include outside traffic sounds, rain, and wind.

The lead investigator of the room-searching team should look around the room and determine how the room is to be divided for searching and to what height the first searching sweep should extend. The first searching sweep should cover all items resting on the floor up to the selected height.

The room should be divided into two virtually equal parts. This equal division should be based on the number and type of objects in the room to be searched and not on the size of the room. An imaginary line is then drawn between two objects in the room (e.g., the edge of the window on the north wall to the floor lamp on the south wall).

First Room-Searching Sweep. Look at the furniture or objects in the room and determine the average height of the majority of items resting on the floor. In an average room, this height usually includes table or desktops and chair backs. The first searching height usually covers the items in the room up to hip height.

After the room has been divided and a searching height has been selected, both people should go to one end of the room division line and start from a back-to-back position. This is the starting point, and the same point will be used on each successive searching sweep. Each person now starts searching his or her

FIGURE 15.6 Graphic representation of fragmentation, blast pressure, and secondary forces produced by an explosion.

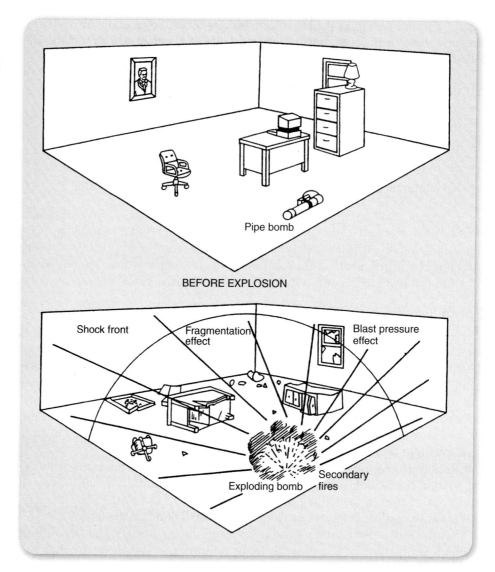

way around the room, working toward the other person, checking all items resting on the floor around the wall area of the room.

When the two people meet, they will have completed a wall sweep. They should then work together and check all items in the middle of the room up to the selected hip height, including the floor under the rugs. This first searching sweep should also include items that may be mounted on or in the walls, such as air-conditioning ducts, baseboard heaters, and built-in wall cupboards, if these fixtures are below hip height. The first searching sweep usually consumes the most time and effort. During all the searching sweeps, an electronic or medical stethoscope is used on walls, furniture items, and floors.

Second Room-Searching Sweep. The lead investigator again looks at the furniture or objects in the room and determines the height of the second searching sweep. This height is usually from the hip to the chin or the top of the head. The two persons return to the starting point and repeat the searching technique at the second selected searching height. This sweep usually covers pictures hanging on the walls, built-in bookcases, and tall table lamps.

Third Room-Searching Sweep. When the second searching sweep is completed, the lead investigator again determines the next searching height, usually from the chin or the top of the head up to the ceiling. The third sweep is then made. This sweep usually covers high-mounted air-conditioning ducts and hanging light fixtures.

Fourth Room-Searching Sweep. If the room has a false or suspended ceiling, the fourth sweep involves investigation of this area. Flush or ceiling-mounted light fixtures, air-conditioning or ventilation ducts, sound or speaker systems, electrical wiring, and structural frame members should all be checked. Have a sign or marker indicating "Search Completed" posted conspicuously in the area. Place a piece of colored cellophane tape across the door and doorjamb approximately two feet above floor level if the use of signs is not practical.

The room-searching technique can be expanded. The same basic technique can be applied to search any enclosed area. Encourage the use of common sense or logic in searching. For example, if a guest speaker at a convention has been threatened, common sense would indicate searching the speaker's platform and microphones first, but always return to the searching technique. Do not rely on random or spot checking of only logical target areas because the bomber may not be a logical person.

In conclusion, the following steps should be taken when searching a room:

1. Divide the area and select a search height.
2. Start from the bottom and work up.
3. Start back to back and work toward each other.
4. Go around the walls and proceed toward the center of the room.

When a Bomb Is Found

It is important to stress that personnel involved in a search be instructed that their only mission is to search for and report suspicious objects. Under no circumstances should officers attempt to move, jar, or touch a suspicious object or anything attached to it. The actual removal of the bomb should be left to professional bomb disposal personnel. After the suspected bomb has been located, the location and description of the object should be reported to the supervisor or command center. Fire department and rescue personnel should also be notified and placed on standby. If necessary, sandbags or mattresses (never metal shields) should be placed around the suspicious object. Do not attempt to cover the object. Instead, you should:

- Identify the danger area and block it off with a "clear zone" of at least 300 feet, including floors below and above the object.
- Be sure that all doors and windows are open to minimize primary damage from the blast and secondary damage from fragmentation.
- Evacuate the building.
- Do not permit reentry into the building until the device has been removed or disarmed and the building is declared safe for reentry.

Handling the Media

It is important that all inquiries from the news media be directed to one person who is designated as spokesperson. All other persons should be instructed not to discuss the situation with outsiders, especially the news media. The purpose of this provision is to furnish the news media with accurate information and to see that additional bomb threat calls are not precipitated by irresponsible statements from uninformed sources.

Terrorism

Never before in U.S. history have Americans been more aware of the threat of terrorism. The term *terrorism* is defined in a number of ways by a number of organizations. Simply stated, terrorism is policy intended to intimidate or cause terror.[20] The federal foreign relations authorization act defines *terrorism* in terms of four primary elements. The act says that terrorism is:

1. Premeditated
2. Politically motivated
3. Violent
4. Committed against noncombatant targets.[21]

Some definitions also include acts of unlawful violence or unconventional warfare, but at present, there is no internationally agreed upon definition of terrorism.[22] A person who practices terrorism is generally referred to as a *terrorist*. Acts of terrorism are criminal acts, according to United Nations Security Council Resolution 1373 and the domestic jurisprudence of almost all nations.

Regardless of the origin of its definition, the word *terrorism* is politically and emotionally charged,[23] and this greatly compounds the difficulty of providing a precise definition. A 1988 study by the United States Army found that more than 100 definitions of the word *terrorism* have been used.[24] The concept of terrorism is itself controversial because it is often used by states to delegitimize political or foreign opponents and potentially legitimize the state's own use of terror against them.

The history of terrorist organizations suggests that they do not practice terrorism only for its political effectiveness; individual terrorists are also motivated by a desire for social solidarity with other members.[25]

Terrorism has been practiced by a broad array of political organizations for furthering their objectives. It has been practiced by both right- and left-wing political parties, nationalistic groups, religious groups, revolutionaries, and ruling governments.[26]

Acts of terrorism can be carried out by individuals, groups, or states. According to some definitions, clandestine or semi-clandestine state actors may also carry out terrorist acts outside the framework of a state of war. However, the most common image of terrorism is that it is carried out by small and secretive cells that are highly motivated to serve a particular cause, and many of the most deadly operations in recent times, such as the September 11 attacks, the London underground bombing, and the 2002 Bali bombing were planned and carried out by close cliques composed of close friends, family members and other strong social networks.

These groups benefited from the free flow of information and efficient telecommunications to succeed where others had failed.[27] Over the years, many people have attempted to come up with a terrorist profile to attempt to explain these individuals' actions through their psychology and social circumstances. Others, such as Roderick Hindery, have sought to discern profiles in the propaganda tactics used by terrorists. Some security organizations designate these groups as violent non-state actors.[28]

Recent research and investigations into terrorist operations have shown that terrorists look, dress, and behave like "normal" people until they execute the assigned mission. Therefore, terrorist profiling based on personality or physical or sociological traits does not appear to be particularly useful. The physical and behavioral description of a terrorist could describe almost any average person.[29]

Criteria Describing Terrorists

Official definitions determine counterterrorism policy and are often developed to serve it. Most government definitions outline the following key criteria: target, objective, motive, perpetrator, and legitimacy or legality of the act. Terrorism is also often recognizable by a following statement from the perpetrators.

Violence. According to Walter Laqueur of the Center for Strategic and International Studies: "The only general characteristic of terrorism generally agreed upon is that terrorism involves violence and the threat of violence." However, the criterion of violence alone does not produce a useful definition because it includes many acts not usually considered terrorism such as war, riot, organized crime, and even a simple assault. Property destruction that does not endanger life is not usually considered a violent crime, but some have described property destruction by the Earth Liberation Front and Animal Liberation Front as violence and terrorism.

Psychological Impact and Fear. This means that the attack was carried out in such a way as to maximize the severity and length of the psychological impact. Each act of terrorism is a "performance" devised to have an impact on many large audiences. Terrorists also attack national symbols to show power and to attempt to shake the foundation of the country or society to which they are opposed. This may negatively affect a government while increasing the prestige of the given terrorist organization or the ideology behind a terrorist act.[30]

Perpetrated for a Political Goal. Something that many acts of terrorism have in common is a political purpose. Terrorism is a political tactic, such as letter writing or protesting, which is used by activists when they believe that no other means will effect the kind of change they desire. The change is desired so badly that failure to achieve change is seen as a worse outcome than the deaths of civilians. This is often where the inter-relationship between terrorism and religion occurs. When a political struggle is integrated into the framework of a religious or "cosmic" struggle, such as over the control of an ancestral homeland or holy site such as Israel and Jerusalem, failing in the political goal (nationalism) becomes equated with spiritual failure, which, for the highly committed, is worse than their own death or the deaths of innocent civilians.[31]

One definition that that combines the key elements was developed at the George C. Marshall Center for European Security Studies by Carsten Bockstette:

> Terrorism is defined as political violence in an asymmetrical conflict that is designed to induce terror and psychic fear (sometimes indiscriminate) through the violent victimization and destruction of noncombatant targets (sometimes iconic symbols). Such acts are meant to send a message from an illicit clandestine organization. The purpose of terrorism is to exploit the media in order to achieve maximum attainable publicity as an amplifying force multiplier in order to influence the targeted audience(s) in order to reach short- and midterm political goals and/or desired long-term end states.[32]

Deliberate Targeting of Noncombatants. It is commonly held that the distinctive nature of terrorism lies in its intentional and specific selection of civilians as direct targets. Specifically, the criminal intent is shown when babies, children, mothers, and elderly people are murdered or injured and put in harm's way. Much of the time, the victims of terrorism are targeted not because they are threats but because they are specific "symbols, tools, animals or corrupt beings" that tie into a specific view of the world that the terrorists possess. Their suffering accomplishes the terrorists' goals of instilling fear, getting their message out to an audience, or otherwise satisfying the demands of their often radical religious and political agendas.[33]

Disguise. Some terrorists pretend to be noncombatants, hide among such non-combatants, fight from vantage points in the midst of noncombatants, and (when they can) strive to mislead and provoke the government soldiers into attacking other people so that the government will be blamed.[34]

Unlawfulness or Illegitimacy. Some official (notably government) definitions of terrorism add a criterion of illegitimacy or unlawfulness to distinguish between actions authorized by a government (and thus "lawful") and those of other actors, including individuals and small groups.[35] Using this criterion, actions that would otherwise qualify as terrorism would not be considered terrorism if they were government sanctioned.

For example, firebombing a city, which is designed to affect civilian support for a cause, would not be considered terrorism if it were authorized by a government. This criterion is inherently problematic and is not universally accepted because it denies the existence of state terrorism; the same act may or may not be classed as terrorism, depending on whether its sponsorship is traced to a "legitimate" government; "legitimacy" and "lawfulness" are subjective, depending on the perspective of one government or another; and it diverges from the historically accepted meaning and origin of the term.[36] For these reasons, this criterion is not universally accepted; most dictionary definitions of the term do not include this criterion.

International Terrorism

The 1993 bombing of the World Trade Center in New York City and the 1995 conviction of Sheikh Omar Abdel-Rahman and eight other Islamic fundamentalists on charges of plotting to start a holy war and of conspiring to commit assassinations and bombing of the United Nations indicated to many that the threat of international terrorism could soon become a part of daily life for Americans. Some experts stated that the 1993 explosion at the World Trade Center, which killed four people and created a 100-foot hole through some floors of concrete, ushered in an era of international terrorist activity in the United States.[37]

In 2001, Islamic terrorist Osama bin Laden demonstrated to the world how terrorists can successfully strike American targets on U.S. soil when members of its organization attacked the World Trade Center and the Pentagon using commandeered airliners. As a result of these terrorist acts, approximately 3,000 people lost their lives. Earlier, in 1998, bin Laden's agents struck American embassies in Nairobi, Kenya and Dares Salaam, Tanzania, killing 257 people, including 12 Americans. In 2003, another coordinated attack by Islamic extremists on a residential compound for foreigners in Riyadh, Saudi Arabia, killed 34 people, including eight Americans, and wounded many more. As of the writing of this text, similar acts of terrorism are continuing in the Middle East and elsewhere.

Many believe that the wars in Afghanistan and Iraq, as well as a coordinated international effort against Al-Qaeda (discussed later in this chapter), may have substantially weakened that organization's ability to carry out future strikes outside the Middle East.[38] Experts in international terrorism, however, point out that *jihadism*, or the Islamic Holy War movement, survives independent of any one organization and appears to be gaining strength around the world. Jihadist principles continue to serve as the organizing rationale for extremist groups in much of the Muslim world. As such, Islamic fundamentalism continues to pose an ongoing global threat.

Islamic Terrorism. Islamic terrorism has its roots in **Islamism** (Islam+ism; Arabic: al-'islamiyya), a set of ideologies holding that Islam is not only a religion but

FIGURE 15.7 Second World Trade Center Attack occurring on September 11, 2001, in which the south tower burst into flames after being struck by hijacked United Airlines Flight 15. Corbis/Reuters America LLC.

also a political system and that modern Muslims must return to their roots of their religion and unite politically.

Islamism is a controversial term, and definitions of it sometimes vary. Leading Islamist thinkers emphasized the enforcement of sharia (Islamic law); of pan-Islamic political unity; and of the elimination of non-Muslim, particularly Western, military, economic, political, social, or cultural influences in the Muslim world, which they believe to be incompatible with Islam.[39]

Some observers suggest Islamism's tenets are less strict and can be defined as a form of identity politics or "support for [Muslim] identity, authenticity, broader regionalism, revivalism, [and] revitalization of the community."[40] Still others define *Islamism* as "an Islamic militant, anti-democratic movement, bearing a holistic vision of Islam whose final aim is the restoration of the caliphate."[41]

Many of those described as "Islamists" oppose the use of the term, maintaining that they are simply Muslims and that their political beliefs and goals are an expression of Islamic religious belief.[42] Similarly, some scholars instead favor the term *activist Islam* or *political Islam*.[43]

It is important to distinguish between Islamists and Islamist terrorists:

> While ignoring the overwhelming majority of Islamists who have little or nothing to do with terror and making them virtually irrelevant and stigmatized in Western political discourse. . . . To ignore the complexity of political Islam and tar all Islamists with the same brush of terrorism guarantees bin Laden's success.[44]

International Crisis Group warns that the tendency of "policy-makers . . . to lump all forms of Islamism together, brand them as radical and treat them as hostile . . . is fundamentally misconceived."[45] Furthermore, the International Crisis Group states:

> . . . the issues and grievances which have been grist to the mill of Sunni jihadism across the Muslim world have not been resolved or even appreciably attenuated since 2001, but, on the contrary, aggravated and intensified. The failure to address the Palestinian question and, above all, the decision to make war on Iraq and the even more extraordinary mishandling of the post-war situation there have unquestionably motivated and encouraged jihadi activism across the Muslim world. Unsophisticated Western understanding and rhetoric that tends to discredit all forms of political Islamism, coupled with the lumping together of the internal, irredentist and global jihadis. . . .[46]

Al-Qaeda. Al-Qaeda (also spelled al-Qaida and sometimes al-Qa'ida; Arabic translation: "the base") is perhaps the most widely known Islamist group. It was founded sometime between August 1988 and late 1989 or early 1990,[47] and it operates as a network composed of both a multinational arm and a fundamentalist Sunni movement.[48]

Al-Qaeda has attacked civilian and military targets in various countries, the most notable being the infamous September 11 attacks in 2001. These actions were followed by the U.S. government's launching the "war on terrorism." As of 2009, Al-Qaeda is believed to have between 200 and 300 members.[49]

Al-Qaeda's characteristic techniques include suicide attacks and simultaneous bombings of different targets.[50] Activities ascribed to it may involve members of the movement, who have taken a pledge of loyalty to Osama bin Laden or the much more numerous "Al-Qaeda–linked" individuals who have undergone training in one of its camps in Afghanistan or Sudan but not taken any pledge.[51]

Al-Qaeda's objectives include the end of foreign influence in Muslim countries and the creation of a new Islamic caliphate. Reported beliefs include that a Christian–Jewish alliance is conspiring to destroy Islam and that the killing of bystanders and civilians is Islamically justified in jihad.[52]

The management philosophy of Al-Qaeda has been described as "centralization of decision and decentralization of execution."[53] After the September 11 attacks and the beginning of the war on terrorism, it is thought that Al-Qaeda's leadership has become "geographically isolated," leading to the "emergence of decentralized leadership" of regional groups using the al-Qaeda "brand name."[54]

Domestic Terrorism

The term *domestic terrorism* was used commonly throughout the 1960s and 1970s. In a broad, general sense, acts of domestic terrorism in the United States are considered to be rare, but this has not always been the case. For example, according to the FBI, between 1980 and 2000, 250 of the 335 incidents confirmed as or suspected to be terrorist acts in the United States were carried out by American citizens.[55]

The statutory definition of *domestic terrorism* in the United States has changed many times over the years; also, it can be argued that acts of domestic terrorism have been occurring since long before any legal definition was set forth.

According to a memo produced by the FBI's Terrorist Research and Analytical Center in 1994, domestic terrorism was defined as "the unlawful use of force or violence, committed by a group(s) of two or more individuals, against persons or property to intimidate or coerce a government, the civilian population, or any segment thereof, in furtherance of political or social objectives."[56] Under current U.S. law, set forth in the USA PATRIOT Act, acts of domestic terrorism are those that:

1. "Involve acts dangerous to human life that are a violation of the criminal laws of the United States or of any State;

2. Appear to be intended—(a) to intimidate or coerce a civilian population; (b) to influence the policy of a government by intimidation or coercion; or (c) to affect the conduct of a government by mass destruction, assassination, or kidnapping; and

3. Occur primarily within the territorial jurisdiction of the United States."[57]

Domestic Terrorism Organizations in the United States

- ☑ *The Ku Klux Klan (KKK).* From Reconstruction at the end of the Civil War to the end of the civil rights movement, the KKK used threats, violence, arson, and murder to further its white supremacist, antisemitic, anti-Catholic agenda.

- ☑ *The Weathermen.* The Weathermen was a U.S. radical left organization active from 1969 to 1975. Its members referred to themselves as a "revolutionary organization of communist women and men." Their goal was the revolutionary overthrow of the U.S. government. Toward this end, and to change U.S. policy in Vietnam, they bombed a number of police and military targets. The group collapsed shortly after the U.S. withdrawal from Vietnam in 1975.

- ☑ *The Jewish Defense League (JDL).* The JDL was founded in 1969 by Rabbi Meir Kahane in New York City, with its declared purpose the protection of Jews from harassment and antisemitism.[58] FBI statistics show that from 1980 to 1985, 15 terrorist attacks were attempted in the United States by members of the JDL.[59] The FBI's Mary Doran described the JDL in 2004 Congressional testimony as "a proscribed terrorist group."[60] The National Consortium for the Study of Terror and Responses to Terrorism states that during the JDL's first two decades of activity, it was an "active terrorist organization."[61] Kahane later founded the far-right Israeli political party Kach. The group's present-day website condemns all forms of terrorism.[62]

- ☑ *The Symbionese Liberation Army (SLA).* The SLA was an American self-styled, radical-left "urban guerrilla warfare group" that considered itself a revolutionary vanguard army. The group committed bank robberies, two murders, and other acts of violence between 1973 and 1975. Among the SLA's most notorious acts was the kidnapping and brainwashing of newspaper heiress Patty Hearst.

- ☑ *Army of God (AOG).* The AOG is a loose network of individuals and groups connected by ideological affinity and the determination to use violence to end the legal practice of abortion in the United States. Its affiliates consist of right-wing Christian militants who have committed violent acts against abortion providers. Acts of anti-abortion violence increased in the mid-1990s, culminating in a series of bombings by Eric Rudolph, whose targets included two abortion clinics, a gay and lesbian nightclub, and the 1996 Olympics in Atlanta. Letters Rudolph sent to newspapers claiming responsibility in the name of the AOG focused attention on the issue of right-wing extremism.

- ☑ *Animal Liberation Front (ALF)* The ALF is a name used internationally by animal liberation activists who engage in direct action tactics on behalf of animals. This includes removing animals from laboratories and fur farms and sabotaging facilities involved in animal testing and other animal-based industries. According to ALF statements, any act that furthers the cause of animal liberation, in which all reasonable precautions are taken not to endanger life, may be claimed as an ALF action. The group is listed by the U.S. Department of Homeland Security as a domestic terrorist organization.

☑ *Earth Liberation Front (ELF).* The ELF is a group associated with environmental extremism and advocates direct action against alleged high polluters. Several fire bombings of SUV dealerships have been attributed to the ELF.

☑ *Black Liberation Army (BLA).* A splinter group made up of the more radical members of the Black Panther Party, the BLA sought to overthrow the U.S. government in the name of racial separatism and Marxist ideals. The Fraternal Order of Police blames the BLA for the murders of 13 police officers. According to a Justice Department report on BLA activity, the BLA was suspected of involvement in more than 60 incidents of violence between 1970 and 1981.

A current concern today regarding domestic terrorism is the existence of clandestine, survivalist, and separatist groups that are politically motivated and have their own vision for the future of America. For example, in 1993, a violent confrontation between David Koresh's Branch Davidian followers and U.S. federal agents left 72 Davidians (including Koresh) and former federal agents dead in Waco, Texas.

Occurring only two years after the Davidian standoff, a powerful truck bomb exploded outside the Federal building in downtown Oklahoma City (discussed earlier in this chapter). In this event, 168 people died, and hundreds more were wounded. The perpetrator, 29-year-old Timothy McVeigh, was found guilty of 11 criminal counts, including conspiracy to first-degree murder. As a result, McVeigh was sentenced to death and was executed by lethal injection at the United States penitentiary in Terre Haute, Indiana in 2001.

One year after the Oklahoma City bombing, 38-year-old Eric Robert Rudolph detonated a makeshift bomb during the 1996 Olympics in which one person died and 111 were injured. This explosion, known as the Atlanta's Centennial Park bombing, resulted from Rudolph's antiabortion and anti-gay visions of America's future. After eluding police for years, Rudolph was captured, prosecuted, and sentenced to life imprisonment without the possibility of parole.

Tactics to Destabilize Terrorist Organizations

The most visible and immediately effective tactic of U.S. terrorist financing strategy has been designating and blocking the accounts of terrorists and those associated with financing terrorist activity. Publicly designating terrorists, terrorist supporters, and facilitators and blocking their ability to receive and move funds through the world's financial system has been and is a crucial component in the fight against terrorism. On September 24, 2001, President Bush issued Executive Order 13244, Blocking Property and Prohibiting Transactions with Persons Who Commit, Threaten to Commit, or Support Terrorism.[63]

The Department of the Treasury's Office of Enforcement, in conjunction with the Treasury's Office of International Affairs and the Office of Foreign Assets Control, has helped lead U.S. efforts to identify and block the assets of terrorist-related individuals and entities within the United States and world-wide. Currently, 250 individuals and entities are publicly designated as terrorists or terrorist supporters by the United States, and since September 11, 2001, more than $113 million in assets of terrorists has been frozen around the world.[64] Beyond simply freezing assets, these U.S. and international actions to publicly identify terrorists and their supporters advance global interests in terrorist financing and combating terrorism by:

- Shutting down the pipeline by which designated parties moved money and operated financially in the mainstream financial sectors
- Informing third parties who may be unwittingly financing terrorist activity of their association with supporters of terrorism
- Providing leverage over those parties not designated who might otherwise be willing to finance terrorist activity
- Exposing terrorist financing "money trails" that may generate leads to previously unknown terrorist cells and financiers
- Forcing terrorists to use alternative and potentially more costly informal means of financing their activities
- Supporting diplomatic effort to strengthen other countries' capacities to combat terrorist financing through the adoption and implementation of legislation that allows states to comply with their obligations under U.N. Security Council Resolutions 1390 and 1373

Currently, more than 165 countries and jurisdictions have blocking orders in force. Alternative financial mechanisms to combat terrorist financing conducted through these mechanisms include the following measures:

- *Protecting charities from terrorist abuse.* Under the authority of Executive Order 13224, the United States has designated 12 charitable organizations as having ties to al-Qaeda or other terrorist groups.

  The Financial Action Task Force (FATF) Special Recommendation VIII on Terrorist Financing commits all member nations to ensure that nonprofit organizations cannot be misused by financiers of terrorism.

- *Regulating hawalas.* Informal value transfer systems. Terrorists have also used hawalas and other informal value transfer systems as a means of terrorist financing. The word *hawala* (meaning "trust") refers to a fast and cost-effective method for the worldwide remittance of money or value, particularly for persons who may be outside the reach of the traditional financial sector. In some nations, hawalas are illegal; in others, they are active but unregulated. It is, therefore, difficult to accurately measure the total volume of financial activity associated with the system; however, it is estimated that, at a minimum, tens of billions of dollars flow through hawalas and other informal value transfer systems on an annual basis.

- *Combating bulk cash smuggling.* Bulk cash smuggling has proven to be yet another means of financing adopted by terrorists and their financiers. Customs has executed 650 bulk cash seizures totaling $21 million, including $12.9 million with Middle East connections. Pursuing bulk cash smuggling from a domestic perspective, however, is not enough; disruption of this tactic requires a global approach.

- *Investigating trade-based terrorist financing.* With respect to trade-based financial systems, authorized enforcement agencies continue to investigate the use of licit and illicit international trade commodities (e.g., diamonds, gold, honey, and cigarettes, as well as narcotics) to fund terrorism. The U.S. Customs Service has developed a state-of-the-art database system to identify anomalous trade patterns for imports and exports to and from the United States. In the past, Customs has demonstrated this system to other nations, including Colombia, with excellent results.

- *Investigating terrorist cyberfundraising activities.* Terrorist groups now exploit the Internet to recruit supporters and raise terrorist funds. Developing a strategy to counter such cyberfundraising activities is a responsibility that the Treasury Department assumed in its 2002 Anti-Money Laundering Strategy.

U.S. Efforts in Combating Terrorism

In addition to the international impetus placed on combating terrorism, the United States has enacted numerous laws, strategies, and programs designed to protect Americans from international terrorism. However, laws designed to limit terrorist actions have not yet shown to be totally effective. The Federal Terrorist Firearms Detection Act of 1988 is an example. Designed to prevent the development of plastic firearms by requiring handguns to contain at least 3.7 oz of detectable metal, it applies only to weapons manufactured within U.S. borders. In 1996, The Antiterrorism and Effective Death Penalty Act became law. Included in its provisions are the following:

- It bans fundraising and financial support within the United States for international terrorist organizations.
- It provides $1 billion for enhanced terrorism fighting measures by federal and state authorities.
- It allows foreign terrorism suspects to be deported or to be kept out of the United States without the disclosure of classified evidence against them.
- It permits a death sentence to be imposed on anyone committing an international terrorist act in the United States in which a death occurs.
- It makes a federal crime to use the United States as a base for planning terrorist acts overseas.
- It orders identifying chemical markers known as taggits to be added to plastic explosives during manufacture.
- It orders the feasibility study on marketing other explosives (with the exception of gunpowder).[65]

After the September 11 attacks on the World Trade Center and the Pentagon, Congress enacted the USA PATRIOT Act. The act created a number of new crime categories, such as terrorist attacks against mass transportation and harboring or concealing terrorists. Those crimes were set forth in title VIII of the act titled "Strengthening the Criminal Laws Against Terrorism."

CASE IN POINT:

Understanding Fire Behavior

In one ATF (Alcohol, Tobacco, and Firearms) case, two eyewitnesses saw the two owners exiting the building while splashing liquid. One of the witnesses mentioned this to one of the firefighters during the fire, who suggested that she tell her story to one of the detectives. As sometimes happens, the witness chose not to bother and left the scene. Fortunately,

when the detectives went to reinterview the witnesses in the case, both of them were able to remember that they saw two men setting the fire. Therefore, it pays to reinterview witnesses.

Sources: Moenssens A. A., J. E. Starrs, C. E. Henderson, and F. E Inbau. (1995). Scientific evidence in civil and criminal Cases. Westbury, NY: The Foundation Press:16–417.

CASE IN POINT:

The Case Against the Unabomber

Ted Kaczynski, a math professor-turned-hermit, was charged with four of the 16 bombings linked to the Unabomber and faced the death penalty if convicted. After his arrest, he initially pleaded innocent of the charges and was remanded to the Sacramento, California, jail. After his arrest, Kaczynski's Montana cabin was searched by federal agents, who found, among other things, a bomb (which they exploded safely), the original antitechnology manuscript, and his secret identification number. Under law, the prosecution must also provide the defense with any evidence it has that might show that the accused is innocent. Here is what prosecutors filed in federal court:

- Investigators found a deposit credited to Kaczynski's account at Western Federal Savings in Helena, Montana, on December 11, 1985, the same day that he was alleged to have planted his first fatal bomb 900 miles away in Sacramento. But the deposit slip was actually dated December 9.
- The ATF determined that a bomb placed at the University of Utah in October 1981 was a hoax.

What prosecutors failed to say was that the FBI and postal inspectors disagreed. Also, in a letter to the *The New York Times*, the Unabomber described that bomb as a botched operation.

- Crime scene investigators found in excess of 20 latent fingerprints, some of which were identified and some which were not, and none of which were Kaczynski's fingerprints. But the Unabomber's letter boasted about using gloves to avoid leaving fingerprints.
- In earlier affidavits, FBI analysts had pointed to scores of similarities between Kaczynski's writings and the Unabomber's manifesto and letters, including similarly misspelled words. But in a later filing, prosecutors suggested that defense attorneys talk to a political science professor at Brigham Young University concerning his work on the Unabomber case.

In December 1997, Kaczynski admitted to the FBI that he was in fact the Unabomber and agreed to a plea bargain, pleading guilty to two counts of murder in exchange for a life sentence without the possibility of parole.

Summary Checklist

In this chapter, we consider the ways that information about crimes is documented by the criminal investigator. A properly documented case is one that is more likely to succeed in court. See how well you are able to answer the following questions in your checklist.

1. **Do you understand the crime of arson and the alliance between police and fire departments?**

   Arson is legally characterized by two distinct categories: aggravated arson and simple arson.

   - Aggravated arson is the deliberate burning of

property while creating an imminent danger to human life or risking great bodily harm.

   - Simple arson, a lesser offense, is the burning of property that does not result in such a risk to human life.

After a fire has been determined to have a suspicious origin, investigators from the local fire and police departments (as well as the victim's insurance company) will become involved with the case.

The role of the firefighter is threefold:

- To extinguish the fire
- To investigate the origin of the fire

(continued)

Summary Checklist (Continued)

- To "detect" the possibility of arson but not to actually investigate arson

When the fire investigation becomes a question of who committed the crime, the matter then becomes a law enforcement concern.

- This is critical because after it has been determined that law enforcement should take over the investigation, fire investigators should yield the crime scene to the arson investigators.

The police investigator has a statutory role in investigating the arson because it is a violation of state or federal law.

The role of the insurance investigator is to make a determination as to whether or not the insurance company owes payment for the fire loss.

Many arsonists, however, fail to adequately cover their tracks and may therefore leave some type of evidence behind.

- In many commercial arsons, the suspect leaves a paper trail that investigators can follow.

2. Do you understand the investigative steps of an arson investigation?

It is the responsibility of the investigator to prove that a specific fire did occur and that it was ignited deliberately.

- To accomplish this, both direct and circumstantial evidence can be used to show that the fire was ignited.

The first step in an arson investigation is to determine the fire's point of origin.

- This may be the most critical phase of the investigation, which includes the ruling out of natural or accidental causes.

A search for liquid accelerants should be conducted at all arson crime scenes.

Determining the time span of the fire is also of paramount importance.

- The majority of evidence collection is conducted at the crime scene; much can be learned simply by observing the fire.

- Specifically, physical characteristics of the fire, such as smoke, direction, flames, and distance of travel, are important.

Complete photographs of the structure should be taken to help preserve the crime scene for the courtroom.

Identifying the areas of plants (preparations used to set the fire) and trailers (materials used to spread the fire) can reveal important clues to the investigator.

Witnesses also play an important role in determining causes of the fire and possible suspects.

Observe "alligatoring," which is the pattern of crevices formed by the burning of a wooden structure.

3. Do you understand the motivations of arsonists?

After it has been determined that the fire was of incendiary origin, possible motives must be examined to help identify the suspect.

- Motives for arson include profit, revenge, vandalism, crime concealment, and pyromania.

4. Can you identify the elements of how to prosecute an arson case?

Implicit in the old adage "Without the fire triangle—heat, fuel, and oxygen—there can be no fire" is the evidence needed to prosecute an arson case.

The successful prosecution of an arson case must also include a triangle consisting of police detectives, fire investigators, and a prosecutor.

Evidence needed for prosecution includes:

- Evidence of participation. This might be the disabling of a fire alarm or rearranging combustibles at a fire's location.

- Exclusive access. If firefighters are required to use force to gain entrance into a structure, the arsonist would have difficulty doing the same to set the fire. This indicates the complicity of the business owner in locking up the structure.

- Motive. Establishment of a motive is one critical element in showing jurors a suspect's criminal intent.
- False statements. A convincing element in an arson prosecution is the "victim's" false statements to the investigators.

5. Do you understand the factors involved in investigating bombing incidents?

Bombs can be constructed to look like almost anything and can be placed or delivered in any number of ways.

Bomb threats are delivered in a variety of ways, but most are telephoned in to the target.

When a bomb threat is called in, the following steps should be implemented:

- Keep the caller on the line as long as possible.
- Ask him or her to repeat the message and record every word spoken by the person.
- Ask the caller the location of the bomb and the time of detonation of the device.
- Inform the caller that the building is occupied and the detonation of a bomb could kill or injure innocent people.
- Pay particular attention to background noise such as motors running, music playing, or any other noise that may give a clue as to the location of the caller.
- Listen closely to the voice (male or female), voice quality (calm or excited), accents, and speech impediments.
- Interview the person who received the call for the preceding information.

After the suspected bomb is located, the following procedures should be followed:

- Report the location and description of the object to the supervisor or command center.

- Fire department and rescue personnel should also be notified and placed on standby.
- Identify the danger area and block it off with a "clear zone" of at least 300 feet, including floors below and above the object.
- Be sure that all doors and windows are open to minimize primary damage from the blast and secondary damage from fragmentation.
- Evacuate the building.
- Do not permit reentry into the building until the device has been removed or disarmed and the building is declared safe for reentry.

6. Can you list the four elements that define terrorism?

Simply stated, terrorism is policy intended to intimidate or cause terror. The federal foreign relations authorization act defines terrorism in terms of four primary elements: premeditated, politically motivated, violent, and committed against noncombatant targets.

7. Are you able to distinguish between domestic and international terrorism?

No one definition of terrorism (international or domestic) has been universally accepted. *International terrorism* is generally defined as acts of violence against American targets by foreign nationalists. Jihadist principles continue to serve as the organizing rationale for many terrorist groups in much of the Muslim world. In comparison, *domestic terrorism* is defined as acts of violence by Americans against Americans or American institutions based on ideological, political, or radical visions of the United States.

Key Terms

alligatoring

booby traps

fire triangle

Islamism

olfactory senses

paper trail

plants

point of origin

span of the fire

trailers

Discussion Questions

1. Discuss the reasons why arson is considered a low-priority crime.

2. Discuss and compare the relationship between fire and police departments and the insurance companies that represent victims of arson.

3. Discuss the main things to remember in the preliminary investigation of suspected arson.

4. What significance does a fire's point of origin have regarding the investigation of a supected arson fire?

5. Explain the three sides of the fire triangle.

6. What types of evidence are necessary in the successful prosecution of an arson case?

7. Discuss the searching sweep methods that should be used when attempting to locate a bomb or booby trap.

8. Explain procedures to follow in the event that an explosive device is discovered.

mycrimekit™

Go to MyCrimeKit.com to explore the following study tools and resources specific to this chapter:

* *Practice Quiz:* Multiple-choice, true/false, short-answer, and essay questions.

* *Flashcards:* There are 10 key terms in this chapter. Flashcards test your knowledge of the chapter's key terms.

* *Web Links:* Check out the hotlink to *The New York Times* criminology articles.

* *Career Center:* Check out the hot links to interesting careers in criminal justice, criminology, and juvenile justice.

* *The Research Center:* Check out the "Cybrary" and research navigator for even more resources.

Notes

1. FEDERAL BUREAU OF INVESTIGATION. (2008). *Crime in the United States—2007.*
2. NATIONAL FIRE PROTECTION ASSOCIATION. (2008). *Fire loss in the United States.* Quincy, MA.
3. FEDERAL BUREAU OF INVESTIGATION. (2008). *Crime in the United States—2007.*
4. NATIONAL FIRE PROTECTION ASSOCIATION (1998). *Fire loss in the United States, 1987–1996,* 11th ed. Boston: National Fire Protection Association.
5. IBID.
6. WOODFORK, W. G. (1990). Not just a fire department problem. *Police Chief* December:28.
7. O'CONNER, J. J. (1987). *Practical fire and arson investigation.* New York: Elsevier.
8. GOODNIGHT, K. M. (1990). Arson for profit: The insurance investigation. *Police Chief* December:53.
9. SAFERSTEIN, R. (1998). *Criminalistics. An introduction to forensic science.* Upper Saddle River, NJ: Prentice Hall:265.
10. WHITE, P. (Ed.). (1998). *Crime scene to court. The essentials of forensic science.* Glasgow, UK: The Royal Society of Chemistry:133–138.
11. MOENSSENS, A. A., J. E. STARRS, C. E. HENDERSON, AND F. E INBAU. (1995) *Scientific evidence in civil and criminal cases.* Westbury, NY: The Foundation Press:416–417.
12. IBID.
13. O'CONNER, J. J. (1987). *Practical fire and arson investigation.* New York: Elsevier

14. IBID.
15. RIDER, A. O. (1980.). The firesetter: A psychological profile. *FBI Law Enforcement Bulletin* June–Aug:9.
16. JAMES, J. (1965). Psychological motives for arson. *Popular Government* March:24.
17. RIDER, A. O. (1980.). The firesetter: A psychological profile. *FBI Law Enforcement Bulletin* June–Aug:p. 9.
18. HART (1990). *The arson equation.*
19. FRANKEL and FIELDS (1996). New teen fad.
20. OXFORD ENGLISH DICTIONARY, 2nd ed. (1989). Second general definition of terrorism: "A policy intended to strike with terror those against whom it is adopted; the employment of methods of intimidation; the fact of terrorizing or condition of being terrorized."
21. Foreign Relations Authorization Act, US Code, Title 22, Section 2656 f (d)(2)
22. ANGUS, M. (2002). *The right of self-defence under international law—the response to the terrorist attacks of 11 September.* Australian Law and Bills Digest Group, Parliament of Australia, February 12; Thalif D. (2005). *Politics: U.N. member states struggle to define terrorism.* Inter Press Service, July 25.
23. HOFFMAN, B. *Inside terrorism* Columbia University Press:32. See review in *The New York Times.*
24. RECORD, J. *Bounding the global war on terrorism.* Available at http://www.carlisle.army.mil/.
25. ABRAHMS, M. (2008). *What terrorists really want: Terrorist motives and counterterrorism strategy.* Cambridge, MA: MIT

Press 32(4):86–89. Available at http://maxabrahms.com/pdfs/DC_250-1846.pdf.

26. TERRORISM. Encyclopædia Britannica. Available at http://www.britannica.com/eb/article-9071797.

27. SAGEMAN, M. (2004). Social networks and the jihad. Philadelphia: University of Pennsylvania Press:166–167.

28. WILLIAMS, P. (2008). Violent non-state actors and national and international security. Available at http://se2.isn.ch/serviceengine/FileContent?serviceID=ISFPub&fileid=8EEBA9FE-478E-EA2C-AA15-32FC9A59434A&lng=en..

29. LIBRARY OF CONGRESS. *The sociology and psychology of terrorism.* Washington, DC: Library of Congress Federal Research Division.

30. JUERGENSMEYER, M. (2000). *Terror in the mind of God.* University of California Press:125–135.

31. IBID.

32. BOCKSTETTE, C. (2008). *Jihadist terrorist use of strategic communication management techniques.* George C. Marshall Center Occasional Paper Series. Available at http://www.marshallcenter.org/mcpublicweb/MCDocs/files/College/F_ResearchProgram/occPapers/occ-paper_20-en.pdf.

33. JUERGENSMEYER, M. (2000). *Terror in the mind of God.* University of California Press:127–128.

34. BOCKSTETTE, C. (2008). *Jihadist terrorist use of strategic communication management techniques.* George C. Marshall Center Occasional Paper Series. Available at http://www.marshallcenter.org/mcpublicweb/MCDocs/files/College/F_ResearchProgram/occPapers/occ-paper_20-en.pdf.

35. FEDERAL BUREAU OF INVESTIGATION. *Terrorism in the United States 1999.* Available at http://www.fbi.gov/publications/terror/terror99.pdf.

36. UNITED NATIONS. *UN Reform* Available at http://web.archive.org/web/20070427012107/http://www.un.org/unifeed/script.asp?scriptId=73. The second part of the report, titled "Freedom from fear backs the definition of terrorism—an issue so divisive agreement on it has long eluded the world community" defines *terrorism* as any action "intended to cause death or serious bodily harm to civilians or non-combatants with the purpose of intimidating a population or compelling a government or an international organization to do or abstain from doing any act."

37. FRANKEL, B. (1995). Sheik guilty in terror plot. *USA Today,* October 2:1.

38. STEVENS, P. (2005). All nostalgia is futile at the beginning of history. *Financial Times,* May 27:13.

39. EIKMEIER D. C. (2007). Qutbism: An ideology of Islamic-fascism. *Parameters* Spring:85–98.

40. FULLER, G. E. (2003). *The future of political Islam.* New York: Palgrave MacMillan:21

41. Footnotes of 9/11 commission report Mehdi Mozaffari bin Laden and Islamist terrorism. *Militant Tidsskrift,* March 2002, 131:1.

42. KRAMER, M. (2003). Coming to terms, fundamentalists or Islamists? *Middle East Quarterly* Spring:65–77.

43. INTERNATIONAL CRISIS GROUP. (2005). *Understanding Islamism.* Available at http://merln.ndu.edu/archive/icg/Islamism2Mar05.pdf; Stanley, T. (2005). *Definition: Islamism, Islamist, Islamiste, Islamicist, perspectives on world history and current events.* Available at http://www.pwhce.org/islamism.html.

44. FULLER, G. E., (2003). *The future of political Islam.* New York: Palgrave MacMillan:21.

45. *Understanding Islamism Middle East/North Africa.* Report No. 37, March 2, 2005.

46. IBID.

47. UNITED STATES DISTRICT COURT, Southern District of New York, February 6, 2001. Testimony of Jamal Ahmad Al-Fadl. *United States* v. *Usama bin Laden* et al., defendants. James Martin Center for Nonproliferation Studies. Available at http://cns.miis.edu/pubs/reports/binladen.htm.

48. GUNARATNA. (2002). pp. 95–96. "Al Qaeda's global network, as we know it today, was created while it was based in Khartoum, from December 1991 till May 1996. To coordinate its overt and covert operations as Al Qaeda's ambitions and resources increased, it developed a de-centralised, regional structure. . . . As a global multinational, Al Qaeda makes its constituent nationalities and ethnic groups, of which there are several dozen, responsible for a particular geographic region. Although its modus operandi is cellular, familial relationships play a key role."

49. NOAH, T. (2009). The terrorists-are-dumb theory: Don't mistake these guys for criminal masterminds. Slate, February 25. Available at http://www.slate.com/id/2211994/.

50. WRIGHT, L. (2006). *The looming tower: Al-Qaeda and the road to 9/11.* New York: Knopf.

51. IBID.

52. FU'AD HUSAYN, A. Z. (2005). The second generation of al-Qa'ida, part 14. *Al-Quds al-Arabi,* July 13.

53. AL-HAMMADI, K. (2005). The inside story of al-Qa'ida, part 4. *Al-Quds al-Arabi,* March 22.

54. FEISER, J. (2004). Evolution of the al-Qaeda brand name. *Asia Times On-line.* Available at http://www.atimes.com/atimes/Middle_East/FH13Ak05.html.

55. COUNCIL ON FOREIGN RELATIONS. *Militant extremists in the United States.* Available at http://www.cfr.org/publication/9236/.

56. PRESLEY, S. M. (1996). *Rise of domestic terrorism and its relation to United States Armed Forces.* Available at http://www.fas.org/irp/eprint/presley.htm.

57. Available at http://frwebgate.access.gpo.gov/cgi-bin/getdoc.cgi?dbname=107_cong_public_laws&docid=f:publ056.107.pdf.

58. ANTI-DEFAMATION LEAGUE. (2009). *Backgrounder: The Jewish Defense League.* Available at http://www.adl.org/extremism/jdl_chron.asp.

59. BOHN, M. K. (2004). *The Achille Lauro hijacking: Lessons in the politics and prejudice of terrorism.* Brassey:67.

60. FEDERAL BUREAU OF INVESTIGATION. *Congressional testimony: Special Agent Mary Deborah (Debbie) Doran before the 9/11/2001 Commission,* June 16, 2004. Available at http://www.fbi.gov/congress/congress04/doran061604.htm.

61. National Consortium for the Study of Terror and Responses to Terrorism. (2007). Terrorist *Organization profile: Jewish Defense League (JDL).* Available at http://www.start.umd.edu/start/data/tops/terrorist_organization_profile.asp?id=183.

62. COUNCIL ON FOREIGN RELATIONS. *Militant extremists in the United States.* Available at http://www.cfr.org/publication/9236/.

63. INTERNATIONAL MONETARY FUND. (2003). *Enhancing contributions to combating money laundering: Policy paper.* Available at http://www.imf.org/external/np/ml/2001/eng/042601.htm.

64. U.S. TREASURY DEPARTMENT. (2003). *High intensity money laundering and related financial crimes areas (HIFCAs) designations.* Available at http://www.ustreas.gov/fincen/hifcadesignations.html.

65. White House. (2003). *National strategy for combating terrorism.*

Vice and Profit-Related Crime

PART

6

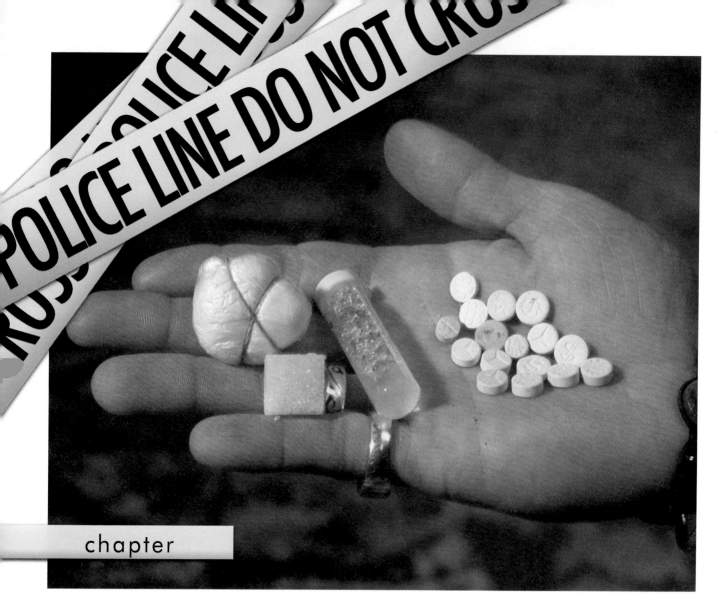

16 Gangs, Organized Crime, and Drugs

This chapter will enable you to:

- Understand the extent to which gangs exist in the United States.
- Explain the businesses of gangs and organized crime.
- Describe how criminal groups involve themselves in the illicit drug trade.
- List the categories of drug dependence.
- Describe the most common drugs of abuse.
- Learn the provisions of the federal Controlled Substances Act (CSA).
- Learn how drug and gang investigations are initiated.

Gangs

To a great extent, gangs and organized crime groups (discussed next) refer to the same thing. A subtle distinction can be made with regard to the size of the groups and the length of time they have been in existence. In a general sense, a gang is a group of people who, through the organization, formation, and establishment of an assemblage, share a common identity. In current usage, *gang* typically denotes a criminal organization or a criminal affiliation. In early usage, the word *gang* referred to a group of workmen. The word *gang* often carries a negative connotation; however, within a gang that defines itself in opposition to mainstream norms, members may adopt the phrase as a statement of identity or defiance.

The term *gangster* (or *mobster*) refers to a criminal who is a member of a crime organization, such as a gang. The terms are widely used in reference to members of gangs associated with American prohibition and the American offshoot of the Italian Mafia, such as the Chicago Outfit or the Five Families.

Gang Members

Los Angeles had been called the "gang capital of America," with an estimated 120,000 gang members.[1] There were at least 30,000 gangs and 800,000 gang members active across the United States in 2007.[2] About 900,000 gang members lived "within local communities across the country," and about 147,000 were in U.S. prisons or jails in 2009.[3] By 1999, Hispanics accounted for 47% of all gang members, blacks for 31%, whites for 13%, and Asians for 6%.[4]

There are between 25,000 and 50,000 gang members in Central America's El Salvador.[5] The Mexican drug cartels have as many as 100,000 foot soldiers.[6] The Yakuza is among the largest crime organizations in the world. In Japan, as of 2005, there are some 86,300 known members. Hong Kong's Triads includes up to 160,000 members. It was estimated that in the 1950s, there were 300,000 Triad members in Hong Kong.[7]

Gang Identifiers

Gangs often establish distinctive, characteristic identifiers, including graffiti tag colors, hand signals, clothing, jewelry, hairstyles, fingernails, slogans, and signs (e.g., the swastika, the noose, the cross, five-and six-pointed stars, crowns, and tridents).[8] Flags (e.g., the Confederate flag), secret greetings, slurs, code words, and other group-specific symbols associated with the gang's common beliefs, rituals, and mythologies are used to define and differentiate themselves from rival groups and gangs.[9] As an alternative language, hand signals, symbols, and slurs in speech, graffiti, print, music, or other media communicate specific informational cues used to threaten, disparage, taunt, harass, intimidate, alarm, influence, or exact specific responses including obedience, submission, fear, or terror.[10]

One study focused on terrorism and symbols states: ". . . Symbolism is important because it plays a part in impelling the terrorist to act and then in defining the targets of their actions."[11] Displaying a gang sign, such as the noose, as a symbolic act can be construed as:

> . . . a threat to commit violence communicated with the intent to terrorize another, to cause evacuation of a building, or to cause serious public inconvenience, in reckless disregard of the risk of causing such terror or inconvenience . . . an offense against property or involving danger to another person that may include but is not limited to recklessly endangering another person, harassment, stalking, ethnic intimidation, and criminal mischief.[12]

Rising Numbers of Gangs in the United States

Criminal gangs in the United States have grown to an estimated one million members that authorities say account for 80% of crimes in communities across the country. This number is up 200,000 members since 2005. According to a report by the United States Justice Department's National Gang Intelligence Center, anxiety, "primary retail level distributors of most illicit drugs" and several are "capable" of competing with major US-based Mexican drug trafficking organizations.[13]

As of the writing of this text, evidence suggests that a rising number of U.S.-based gangs have developed working relationships with U.S. and foreign drug trafficking organizations as well as other criminal groups to gain direct access to foreign sources of illegal drugs.

Despite the rising number of gang members in the United States, according to the Midwest Gang Investigator's Association, which monitors gang activity in 10 states, the number of gang members may be even higher than what is now estimated.[14] Specifically, there has been notable expansion in the number of gang members between 1999 and 2009. The report states that about 900,000 gang members live "within local communities across the country" at about 147,000 are in U.S. prisons or jails. The report also states that there is a rising number of gangs on the campuses of suburban and rural schools. According to the report, 58% of state and local law enforcement agencies reported the criminal gangs were active in their jurisdictions, up from 45% in 2004. Moreover, more gangs use the Internet, including encrypted e-mail, to recruit and communicate with associates throughout the nation and other countries. Some gangs, including outlaw motorcycle groups, still maintain a large presence along the US–Canadian border. These gangs are cooperating with Canadian gangs in various criminal enterprises focusing on drug smuggling.

The Rise of the MS-13. A relatively new group that continues to spread despite law enforcement efforts is the violent Salvadoran gang known as MS-13. This gang has established a reputation for extreme violence to protect its interests as well as extortion, prostitution, and other criminal enterprises. By all accounts, the MS-13's foothold in the United States is expanding. Specifically, recent statistics show that the MS-13 is now present in 42 states, up from 33 and 2005.[15]

MS-13 is the abbreviation for the gang known as **Mara Salvatrucha**. It gained national prominence in the 1980s in Los Angeles, where members were linked to incidents involving unprecedented brutality. It has since formed cells, or "cliques," across the United States.[16] In 2004, a national gang task force was established to target gang members similar to the way that previous investigations focused on organized crime groups from Russia and Italy. Investigative efforts have shown:

- *Omaha.* In 2009, a number of MS-13 members were arrested on federal firearms charges and conspiracy to distribute methamphetamine. The group emerged there in 2004.

- *Nashville.* Between 2007 and 2008, 14 MS-13 members pleaded guilty on charges of murder and obstruction of justice. The MS-13 started growing in 2004 by recruiting members from an influx of immigrant laborers. During April 2008, Davidson County investigators began checking the immigration status of all arrestees. An estimated 100 gang members, many of whom were MS-13 members, were turned over to U.S. immigration officials for deportation.

- *Maryland.* Between 2005 and 2008, 42 MS-13 members were convicted of criminal charges. The majority of these charges stemmed from a racketeering conspiracy in which members participated in robberies and beatings and arranged the murderers of other gang members. In one case, Maryland gang members allegedly discussed killing rivals within MS-13 while calling on a cell phone from a Salvadoran jail.[17]

Mexican Cartels in the United States.   In recent years, Mexican drug cartels have gained a foothold in some American cities. Of the 195 U.S. cities where Mexican drug trafficking organizations are now known to operate, Atlanta, Georgia, has emerged as the new gateway to the Southwest border.[18]

Based on the U.S. Department of Justice National Drug Intelligence Center, rival drug cartels—the same violent groups at war in Mexico for control of routes to markets in the United States—have established Atlanta as the principal distribution center for the entire eastern United States.[19]

Evidence of the presence of Mexican cartels in Atlanta is seen in seizures made in the area. For example, in 2008, FBI and **Drug Enforcement Administration (DEA)** agents seized more drug-related cash in Atlanta, an estimated $70 million, than any other region in the country. In 2009, more than $30 million has been seized in the Atlanta area. This exceeds the amount seized in Los Angeles ($19 million) and Chicago ($18 million).[20]

Despite the awareness of Mexican cartels in Atlanta and the knowledge that these same cartels have been known to be exceedingly violent in their home country, Mexico, the levels of violence thus far in Atlanta have been lower than expected. Is unknown, however, how long this trend will continue because of the unprecedented growth in Atlanta's Hispanic community. For example, its Hispanic population expanded from 8,470 in 1992 to 64,137 in 2000. In 2009, 17% of the county's 776,000 people are Hispanic.[21] Recent investigations have shown that Mexican drug traffickers assign representatives to hide within Hispanic communities within plain sight. Their job is to attempt to blend in to these communities alongside hard-working, law-abiding people.

Mexican cartel members in the United States work as drivers, packagers, and money counters and take orders from senior figures located in Mexico. From the southwest border, shipments of marijuana, cocaine, methamphetamine, and heroine are routed over land to Atlanta for storage in a network of stash houses. From there, they are moved to distribution operations in the Carolinas, Tennessee, and the mid-Atlantic (New York and New England). Cash is generally moved over the same routes back to the Atlanta area, where balance sheets are reconciled. Bundles of money are then turned over to transportation units for bulk shipments back to Mexico.[22]

Organized Crime

Organized crime or criminal organizations comprise groups or operations run by criminals, most commonly for the purpose of generating a monetary profit. The Organized Crime Control Act (U.S., 1970) defines organized crime as "the unlawful activities of . . . a highly organized, disciplined association . . ."

Mafia is a term used to describe a number of criminal organizations around world. The first organization to bear the label was the Sicilian Mafia, known to its members as Cosa Nostra. In the United States, "the Mafia" generally refers to the Italian-American Mafia. Other organizations described as mafias include the Russian Mafia, the Chinese Triads, the Albanian Mafia, the Japanese Yakuza, the Neapolitan Camorra, the Mexican Mafia, and the French "Milieu."

Some criminal organizations, such as terrorist organizations, are politically motivated. Gangs sometimes become "disciplined" enough to be considered "organized." An organized gang or criminal set can also be referred to as a *mob*. The act of engaging in criminal activity as a structured group is referred to in the United States as *racketeering*. In the United States, organized crime is often prosecuted federally under the Racketeer Influenced and Corrupt Organizations Act (RICO), Statute (18 U.S.C. Part I Chapter 96 § 1961–1968.

Dynamics of Organized Crime

For a criminal organization to prosper, some degree of support is required from the society in which it lives. Thus, it is often necessary to corrupt some of its respected members, most commonly achieved through bribery, blackmail, and the establishment of symbiotic relationships with legitimate businesses. Judicial and police officers and legislators are especially targeted for control by organized crime via bribes.

Organized crime most typically flourishes when legitimate government and civil society is disorganized, weak, absent, or untrusted. This may occur in a society facing periods of political, economic, or social turmoil or transition, such as a change of government or a period of rapid economic development, particularly if the society lacks strong and established institutions and the rule of law. Under these circumstances, criminal organizations can operate with less fear of interference from law enforcement and may serve to provide their "customers" with a semblance of order and predictability that would otherwise be unavailable. For similar reasons, organized crime also often takes root in many countries among ethnic minority communities or other socially marginalized groups whose members may not trust local governments or their agents. This lack of trust serves both to insulate the criminal organization from the risk that law enforcement will find cooperative witnesses, as well as to encourage community members to trust the criminal organizations rather than the police to handle disputes and protect the community. The existence of a black market, either because of market failure or to legal impediments, also tends to promote the formation of criminal organizations. An example of this is the rise in organized crime under Prohibition in the United States during the 1920s.

Lacking much of the paperwork that is common to legitimate organizations, criminal organizations can usually evolve and reorganize much more quickly when the need arises. They are quick to capitalize on newly opened markets and quick to rebuild themselves under another guise when caught by authorities. This is especially true of organized groups that engage in human trafficking.

The newest growth sectors for organized crime are identity theft and online extortion. These activities are troubling because they discourage consumers from using the Internet for e-commerce. E-commerce was supposed to level the playing ground between small and large businesses, but the growth of online organized crime is leading to the opposite effect; large businesses are able to afford more bandwidth (to resist denial-of-service attacks) and superior security. Furthermore, organized crime using the Internet is much harder to track down for the police (even though they increasingly deploy "cybercops") because most police forces and law enforcement agencies operate within a local or national jurisdiction while the Internet makes it easier for criminal organizations to operate across such boundaries without detection.

In the past, criminal organizations have naturally limited themselves by their need to expand. This has put them in competition with each other. This competition, often leading to violence, uses valuable resources such as manpower (either killed or sent to prison), equipment, and finances. In the United States, the Irish Mob boss of the Winter Hill Gang (in the 1980s) turned informant for the FBI. He used this position to eliminate competition and consolidate power within the city of Boston, which led to the imprisonment of several senior organized crime figures, including Gennaro "Jerry" Anguilo, underboss of the Patriarca crime family. Infighting sometimes occurs within an organization, such as the Castellamarese war of 1930 to 1931 and the Boston Irish Mob Wars of the 1960s and 1970s.

Today, criminal organizations are increasingly working together, realizing that it is better to work in cooperation rather than in competition with each other. This has led to the rise of global criminal organizations such as MS-13 discussed earlier in this chapter.

The Sicilian Mafia in the United States has had links with organized crime groups in Italy such as the Camorra, the 'Ndrangheta, and the Sacra Corona Unita. The Sicilian Mafia has also been known to work with the Irish Mob (John Gotti of the Gambino family and James Coonan of the Westies are known to have worked together, with the Westies operating as a contract hit squad for the Gambino family after they helped Coonan come to power), the Japanese Yakuza, and the Russian Mafia. The FBI estimates that global organized crime makes $1 trillion per year.

This rise in cooperation between criminal organizations has meant that law enforcement agencies are increasingly having to work together. The FBI operates an organized crime section from its headquarters in Washington and is known to work with other national (e.g., Polizia di Stato and the Royal Canadian Mounted Police), federal (e.g., DEA and the United States Coast Guard), state (e.g., Massachusetts State Police Special Investigation Unit and the New York State Police Bureau of Criminal Investigation) and city (e.g., New York Police Department Organized Crime Unit and the Los Angeles Police Department Special Operations Division) law enforcement agencies.

Well-known Organized Crime Organizations

Perhaps the best-known criminal organizations are the Sicilian and American Cosa Nostra, most commonly known as the Mafia. The Neopolitan Camorra, the Calabrian 'Ndrangheta, the Apulian Sacra Corona Unita, and Berlusconi's party Forza Italia are similar Italian organized crime groups. Other organized criminal enterprises include the Russian Mafia, the Israeli Mafia, the Albanian Mafia, Mexican and Colombian Drug Cartels, the Indian Mafia, the Chinese Triads, Irish Mob, the Japanese Yakuza, the Jamaican-British Yardies, the Turkish Mafia, and other crime syndicates. On a lower level in the criminal food chain are many street gangs, such as the Surenos, Nortenos, Latin Kings, Gangster Disciples, Vice Lords, Bloods, and Crips. As of December 2008, law enforcement reported an ongoing war between various Italian-American Mafia families in the United States and the U.S. Yakuza.[23]

Criminal organizations may function both inside and outside of prison, such as the Mexican Mafia, Folk Nation, and the Brazilian PCC. Biker gangs such as the Hells Angels are also involved in organized crime.

World leaders throughout history who have been accused of running their country like a criminal organization include Adolf Hitler of Germany, Idi Amin of Uganda, Mobutu Sese Seko of Zaire, Nicolae Ceausescu of Romania, Francisco Franco of Spain, Hugo Banzer of Bolivia, Kim Jong Il of North Korea, Slobodan Milosevic of Serbia and Yugoslavia, Alberto Fujimori of Peru (in league with his advisor Vladimiro Montesinos), Than Shwe of Burma (also known as Myanmar), and various other dictators and military juntas. Corrupt political leaders may have links to existing organized crime groups, either domestic or international, or they may simply exercise power in a manner that duplicates the functioning and purpose of organized crime.[24]

Businesses of Organized Crime

Organized crime often victimize businesses through the use of extortion or theft and fraud activities such as hijacking cargo trucks; robbing goods; committing bankruptcy fraud (also known as "bust-out"), insurance fraud, or stock fraud (inside trading); and white-collar crime. Organized crime groups also victimize individuals by car theft (either for dismantling at "chop shops" or for export), burglary, credit card fraud, identity theft, and stock fraud ("pump and dump" scams).[25]

Some organized crime groups defraud national, state, or local governments by bid rigging public projects; counterfeiting money along with counterfeiting of copyrighted, trademarked goods, and intellectual property; smuggling or manufacturing untaxed alcohol or cigarettes (also known as "bootlegging"); fencing (criminal); match fixing; point shaving; pornography; money laundering; and providing immigrant workers to avoid taxes.[26] Organized crime groups seek out corrupt public officials in executive, law enforcement, and judicial roles so their activities can avoid or at least receive early warnings about investigation and prosecution.

Organized crime groups also provide a range of illegal services and goods, such as loansharking of money at very high interest rates, bookmaking and gambling, prostitution, drug trafficking, gun running, providing murder for hire, illegal dumping of toxic waste, people smuggling, and trafficking in human beings. Organized crime groups also do a range of business and labor racketeering activities, such as casino skimming; insider trading; setting up monopolies in industries such as garbage collecting, construction, and cement pouring; bid rigging; getting "no-show" and "no-work" jobs; money laundering; political corruption; bullying; and ideological clamping.

Drug-Related Offenses

Without question, the common denominator between gangs and organized crime groups across the globe is illegal drugs. Over the years, the scope of the drug problem has expanded to the point where an estimated two of every three crimes committed are a result of some type of substance abuse. Drugs such as

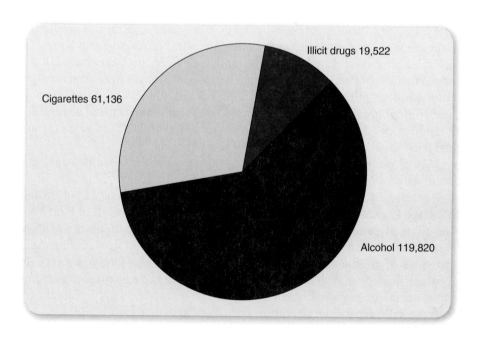

FIGURE 16.1 Treatment of illicit drugs, alcohol, and cigarettes. Current users by substance (in thousands). *From National Drug Council Strategy (2004). Washington, DC: The White House Office of National Drug Control Policy, March.*

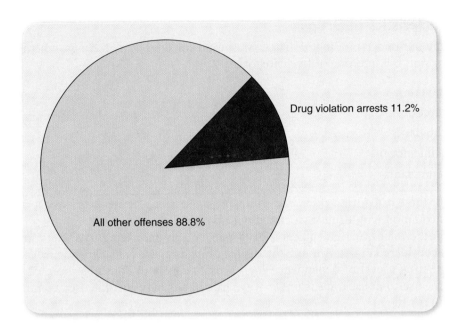

FIGURE 16.2 Drug violation arrests accounted for 11 percent of all arrests in 2002. *From National Drug Council Strategy (2004). Washington, DC: The White House Office of National Drug Control Policy, March.*

marijuana, cocaine, heroin, PCP (phencyclidine), LSD (lysergic acid diethylamide), methamphetamine, and designer drugs are representative of the most popular substances of abuse in the United States and, consequently, account for much of the nation's crime.

Because of the widespread nature of the problem in both the political and social arenas, policy makers are at a crossroads as to what to do about it. Drug crimes, for example, are generated from two general areas: drug users (both addicts and recreational users) and drug sellers (independent and organized factions). Therefore, the supply-and-demand argument is debated as police continue to concentrate on the arrest of dealers or users. In either case, police authorities are duty bound to enforce existing drug control laws vigorously on both local and national levels. Although much media attention has been given to drug control in recent years, law enforcement's drug control mission has been well underway since early in the twentieth century. It was during that period that one of the first major drug laws was passed by Congress: the 1914 Harrison Narcotic Act.[27]

Enforcement of this act required federal agents to arrest and interrogate suspects, search and seize contraband, and infiltrate criminal organizations through undercover techniques. Such duties represent only a few investigative responsibilities in this complex area. Many techniques have evolved since then, some more traditional and some controversial. In this chapter, we examine the many areas of concern for criminal investigators in investigating drug offenses.

Principal Drugs of Abuse

For the criminal investigator to be prepared best for his or her duties in drug enforcement, a certain understanding of the specific drugs of abuse is necessary. Because of the growing problem of drug abuse in the United States, much information about drug effects has surfaced in recent years. Accordingly, dealing with drug abuse requires a broad understanding of the most common drugs of abuse and how they affect public health and safety.

Characteristics of Drugs

To begin our understanding of drugs, we should consider that all drugs, whether legal or not, fall into one of five categories:

1. Cannabis
2. Narcotics
3. Stimulants
4. Hallucinogens
5. Depressants

Each of these categories, discussed in upcoming sections, represents the overall effects common with drugs associated within it.

Another element that makes a drug particularly menacing to society and that is considered in determining the degree of its legal use is its **dependence** factor. The drug's level of dependence fuels a user's desire to consume more of it. Once the use-to-abuse cycle is under way, drug habits may cost the user as much as $400 per day.

Dependence manifests itself in two distinct ways: physical and psychological. Drug users may experience only psychological dependence on drugs, but some drugs produce both physical and psychological dependence, making them more dangerous. Other danger factors should also be considered to understand drug abuse, such as withdrawal syndrome and drug synergism. These four terms are discussed next.

- *Physiological dependence.* This term basically refers to physical addiction to a particular drug. Physiological dependence on a drug creates an alteration of normal body functions, which necessitate continued presence of a drug to prevent the withdrawal syndrome.
- *Psychological dependence.* This usually precedes the physical dependence phase because it refers to one's "desire" to continue use of a drug. Physiological changes in the body do not occur with psychological dependence because the drug user merely "thinks" that he or she needs the drug.
- *Withdrawal syndrome.* This term is closely related to physiological dependence on a drug. The withdrawal syndrome is basically a series of adverse physical symptoms that appear when a drug to which a user is physically addicted is stopped abruptly or severely reduced. Withdrawal symptoms include vomiting, nausea, sweating, convulsions, and fever.
- *Drug synergism.* A synergy is a severe physical reaction that results when a user ingests more than one type of drug at a time. This typically occurs in a "party" situation when users experiment with more than one type of drug. This is a common cause of overdose that could result in coma, cardiac arrest, or even death.[28]

Cannabis

Although considered a mild hallucinogen, marijuana falls into its own category: cannabis (*Cannabis sativa*). It is the most commonly abused cannabis product and grows in almost all parts of the world. History has shown that this plant has been cultivated throughout time to make rope from its tough fiber. Cannabis products include:

- Marijuana
- Hashish
- Hashish oil

Each produces basically the same intoxicating effect, but hashish and hashish oil are more concentrated. Marijuana products are usually smoked in the form of loosely rolled cigarettes, or "joints," and are used in conjunction with other types of drugs. When smoked, the THC (tetrahydrocannabinol) is absorbed into the lining of the lungs and is passed into the bloodstream. Its effects are felt almost instantly and reach their peak in 10 to 30 minutes. Marijuana users remain under the influence of the drug for up to four hours.

Marijuana. Growers of marijuana cultivate the plant for the flowering tops, which produce high concentrations of the mind-altering substance THC. Accordingly, the high THC concentration in the plant is sought by marijuana consumers. Marijuana was first regulated in 1937 with the passage of the Marijuana Tax Act. Today, although some states have chosen to decriminalize the drug, it is still basically illegal to one extent or another. The effects of marijuana are somewhat difficult to articulate because different users are affected in different ways. Frequently, the effects of marijuana depend on the user's experience and expectations as well as on the activity of the drug itself. In low doses, restlessness and a sense of well-being are experienced. This is followed by a feeling of relaxation and sometimes hunger pangs, especially for sweets. High doses may result in image distortion, a loss of personal identity, and possible hallucinations.

Marijuana "Grow Houses." As of 2006, marijuana cultivators have increasingly begun to conceal their growing operation by making use of "grow houses." The grow house has proven to be a predominantly suburban phenomenon. For example, in December 2006, the DEA reported that more than 10,000 plants were seized in a four-bedroom house in Derry, New Hampshire. In California, such operations have grown considerably.

Growers have been known to pay as much as $750,000 in new subdivisions and typically obtain 100% financing and put no money down. Interiors are then gutted to make use of every available square foot for growing apparatuses and

Anatomy of a "Grow House"

Federal drug agents and local police across the country have raided dozens of "grow houses," where marijuana plants are cultivated. The houses are often outfitted with tens of thousands of dollars in equipment to grow and hide marijuana plants.

1,000-watt, high-intensity sodium lights shine on plants. The lights are attached to ballasts, which regulate voltage and current.

False walls and ceilings keep neighbors from seeing inside.

Holes in walls and ceilings vent into the attic to prevent neighbors from smelling marijuana. Charcoal air filters help soak up odor.

Added electrical wiring bypasses utility meter and taps into outside power line.

Mylar or foil window covering hides the interior and reflects light back into the plants.

Marijuana plants are cultivated in grow cubes made from molten rock. These provide nourishment without having to use soil. Irrigation systems on timers keep plants watered.

FIGURE 16.3 Home-grown marijuana can be a simple or complicated process. This figure depicts the complexities of a high-tech "grow house." *USA Today, February 7, 2007.* Reprinted with permission.

for the plants themselves. Irrigation systems with timing devices are also commonly installed and operated using water tanks, pumps, generators, and power packs. To avoid suspicion resulting from large power usage, growers have been known to bypass an electric company's utility meter and create their own circuit boxes. Grow houses are typically unoccupied.

As a rule, criminal investigators need a search warrant for entry into a grow house. Seizure of equipment, plants, and establishment of residency, however, can provide the basis for an arrest and prosecution under applicable state or federal law.

Narcotics

In medical parlance, narcotics are opium and opium derivatives or their synthetic substitutes. Narcotic drugs are essential in the practice of medicine because they are the most effective drugs for the relief of pain. For the most part, legally manufactured narcotics are administered orally or injected. Their illicit counterparts (e.g., heroin) may also be sniffed or smoked. Drugs in the narcotic category include:

- Opium
- Codeine
- Hydromorphone (Dilaudid)
- Diacetylmorphine(heroin)
- Meperidine (Demerol)

Those who use narcotics initially desire the euphoric dreamlike effects of the drug. Drugs falling into this category, however, are extremely physically addicting, and users may find dependency difficult to cure.

The withdrawal syndrome is also commonly associated with this class of drugs. In addition, continued use of narcotics produces tolerance. As **tolerance** develops, users find that they require greater and greater doses of the drug to feel its effects. This, of course, increases the user's propensity for overdose. Narcotic drugs produce pinpoint pupils, reduced vision, drowsiness, and decreased physical activity.

These drugs can be divided into two categories:

1. *Natural-origin narcotics.* Organic narcotics are derived from the opium poppy (*Papaver somniferum*), which is cultivated in such countries as Hungary, Turkey, India, Burma, China, Lebanon, Pakistan, Afghanistan,

Cannabis Products

☑ *Marijuana.* This is the most widely used of the cannabis family. It is a tobacco-like substance produced by the drying of leaves and the flowering tops of the plant.

☑ *Hashish.* Hashish, or "hash," consists of the drug-rich resinous secretions of the cannabis plant, which are collected, dried, and then compressed into cakes or cookie-like sheets that are usually smoked in pipes. The average THC content is 6 percent.

☑ *Hashish oil.* Hash oil is produced by a process of repeated extraction of cannabis plant material that yields a dark, syruplike liquid. The liquid is then placed in or on conventional cigarettes and smoked. The average THC content is 20 percent.

Laos, and Mexico. The milky fluid that is extracted from the poppy plant is raw opium gum base and is very addictive. This raw base is further refined to produce such drugs as opium, heroin, morphine, and codeine. Of these, heroin is the most widely abused narcotic of natural origin in the United States.[29]

2. *Synthetic narcotics.* In contrast to narcotics of natural origin, synthetic narcotics are produced entirely in the laboratory. Researchers have attempted to develop a narcotic drug that offers the analgesic properties of morphine without the dangerous side effects of tolerance and physical dependence. The most common types of synthetic narcotics include meperidine (Demerol), methadone, and hydromorphone (Dilaudid). Because these (and others) are produced by legitimate pharmaceutical manufacturers, diversion of them onto the street is a growing problem. This results from pharmacy robberies and burglaries as well as unscrupulous physicians, nurses, and other medical practitioners who either desire profit or have personal drug problems.

Heroin. The abuse of heroin (diacetylmorphine) occurs in virtually all parts of the world. It appears on American streets in both white and brown powder form and is most widely abused in the inner cities. First-time users of heroin are lured to the drug for its euphoric effects, but because of its addictive qualities, physical addiction develops rapidly after regular use.

Heroin is diluted by the addition of milk sugar or baking soda. Accordingly, pure heroin is rarely sold on the street. In some cases, the user sniffs heroin, but it is generally injected. Injection methods include skin popping (under the skin) and mainlining (intravenous [IV]). Because needles and syringes are commonly shared between IV drug users, the instance of infection with the AIDS virus is high among heroin addicts. Another form of heroin is called black tar heroin. Surfacing in the Western states in the mid-1980s, it is produced crudely in Mexico and resembles roofing tar or coal.

There are an estimated 500,000 drug addicts in the United States. Organized crime syndicates from the United States, Latin America, and southeastern and southwestern Asia strive for control of this lucrative illicit market.

Stimulants

Drugs falling in the stimulant category do so because they literally stimulate the central nervous system (CNS) and give the user a feeling of alertness. With this category of drugs, the use-to-abuse cycle often begins with users who work more than one job or need to stay alert for long periods. Such abusers may take "uppers" in the morning to get going and then take "downers" at night to sleep. Included in this category of abusers are over-the-road truck drivers, college students, entertainers, and so on. Stimulant drugs include nicotine, caffeine, amphetamine, methamphetamine, and cocaine.

Nicotine, found most commonly in tobacco, is the most prevalent stimulant, followed closely by caffeine, an active ingredient in coffee, tea, and many soft drinks. When used in moderation, these drugs relieve feelings of exhaustion and fatigue and have become an accepted part of our culture. The most dangerous stimulants, however, also possess a dependence-forming quality and are available only by prescription. These include cocaine, amphetamine, methamphetamine, methylphenidate (Ritalin), and phenmetrazine (Preludin).

Tolerance to stimulants develops rapidly, and users may ingest increasingly larger doses of the drug. Once the abuse cycle becomes chronic, users may become affected by the following displays of behavior: teeth grinding, touching and picking of the face, performing the same task over and over, suspiciousness, and even paranoia.

Commonly Abused Narcotics

☑ *Opium.* The raw milky liquid extract from the opium poppy plant. Raw opium is commonly abused in the areas of southeastern and southwestern Asia and is most commonly smoked in "gum" form.

☑ *Morphine.* The principal constituent of opium, considered one of the most effective drugs for the relief of pain. It is marketed in the form of white crystals, hypodermic tablets, and injectable preparations.

☑ *Heroin.* Available in brown or white powder and most commonly injected. Heroin is highly addictive and usually sold with a street purity of 5 percent.

☑ *Codeine.* An alkaloid found in raw opium but most commonly produced from morphine. Compared with morphine, codeine produces less analgesia, sedation, and respiratory depression. It is most typically found in prescription cough medicines.

☑ *Hydromorphone (Dilaudid).* A synthetic narcotic analgesic marketed in both tablet and injectable form. This drug is more sedating than morphine and is considered to be up to eight times as potent. It is most commonly obtained by addicts through fraudulent prescriptions.

Cocaine. Cocaine (*Erthroxylon coca*) is a stimulant that has achieved the highest degree of notoriety. Cocaine is the most potent stimulant of natural origin and is made from extracting coca base from coca leaves, which grow almost exclusively in South America. Cocaine, first isolated in 1844, was most commonly used as an anesthetic in eye surgery. Later, it became useful as an anesthetic in nose and throat surgery because of its ability to anesthetize tissue while restricting bleeding. Today, because of the dangers associated with cocaine, many other safer drugs are used for these purposes. Cocaine is distributed in both a white powder or a solid form called **crack**. Accordingly, the drug is administered by snorting, injection, or smoking in **freebase** form. It is commonly adulterated by adding lactose, baking soda, mannitol, or other anesthetics, such as lidocaine. In its freebase form, crack is converted to the form of small chips, resembling soap or paint chips, sometimes called *rocks*. After heating the drug in a pipe, the vapors are inhaled. The effects last only eight to 10 minutes and are usually followed by a sudden "crash," which leads to additional doses.

The process for conversion from powdered cocaine to crack is relatively simple. Cocaine hydrochloric acid (powder) is mixed with baking soda and water and is then heated. This produces a product that is "cracked" into small pieces that are ready to be sold. Other cocaine sensations include euphoria, increased alertness, and shortness of breath. Because of the intensity of its pleasurable effects, it has the potential for extraordinary psychic dependency. Those under the influence show signs of congestion, similar to those of the common cold.

Once dependency develops, users may experience anxiety, paranoia, restlessness, extreme irritability, and even tactile hallucinations. Extreme use of cocaine may result in seizures and death from respiratory failure, stroke, cardiac arrest, or cerebral hemorrhage. Complicating matters further, there is yet no treatment for cocaine overdose nor does tolerance develop to the toxic effects of cocaine. Indeed, studies in the late 1980s revealed that repeated use of cocaine actually lowers the dose at which toxicity occurs.

Methamphetamine. Methamphetamine, or "meth," is a dangerous, sometimes lethal, and unpredictable drug. Meth is also known as speed, ice, and crystal. Similar to cocaine, meth is a potent CNS stimulant. Meth represents the fastest-growing drug threat in the United States today. Meth can be smoked, snorted, injected, or taken orally, and its appearance varies depending on how it is used. Typically, it is a white, odorless, bitter-tasting powder that easily dissolves in water. Another common form of the drug is crystal meth, or ice, named for its appearance (that of clear, large chunky crystals resembling rock candy). **Crystal meth** is smoked in a manner similar to crack cocaine, and about 10 to 15 "hits" can be obtained from a single gram of the substance. Users have referred to smoking ice as a "cool" smoke, while the smoking of crack is a "hot" smoke. The euphoric effect of smoking ice lasts longer than that of smoking crack.[30]

Methamphetamine use increases the heart rate, blood pressure, body temperature, and rate of breathing, and it frequently results in violent behavior in users. Meth also dilates the pupils and produces temporary hyperactivity, euphoria, a sense of increased energy, and tremors. High doses and chronic use have been associated with increased nervousness, irritability, and paranoia. Withdrawal from high doses produces severe depression.

Chronic abuse produces a psychosis similar to schizophrenia and is characterized by paranoia, picking at the skin, self-absorption, and auditory and visual hallucinations. Violent and erratic behavior is frequently seen among chronic, high-dose methamphetamine abusers. The most dangerous stage of the binge cycle is known as *tweaking*. Typically, during this stage, the abuser has not slept in three to 15 days and is irritable and paranoid. The tweaker has an intense

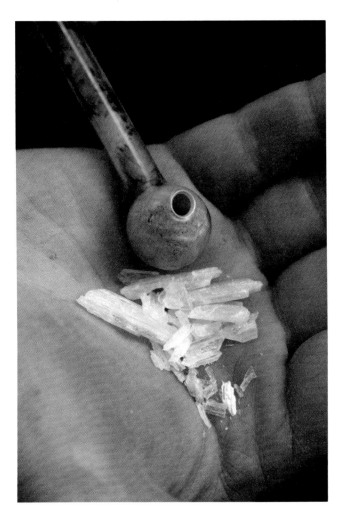

FIGURE 16.4 Close-up of methamphetamine crystals and pipe. Courtesy of Mike Himmel and the Missouri State Highway Patrol.

FIGURE 16.5 Photo of small "bindles" of cocaine. Packaging drugs in this fashion makes locating them a difficult task for officers. Courtesy of Mark Ide.

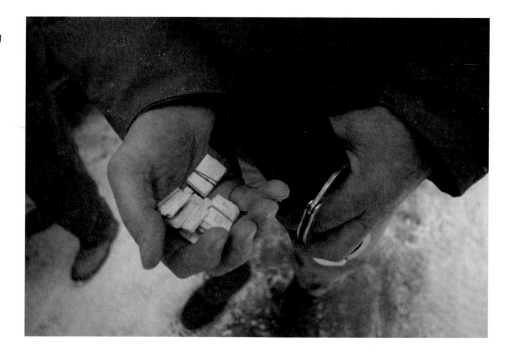

craving for more meth; however, no dose will help re-create the euphoric high. This causes frustration and leads to unpredictability and a potential for violence.

Hallucinogens

Hallucinogenic drugs, produced both organically and synthetically, create a sense of distorted perceptions in the user. Generally, they act on the CNS by creating sensations such as excitation, euphoric mood changes, and sometimes extreme depression. Of particular mention, those under the influence of hallucinogens experience an altered sense of direction, space, and time. Users sometimes claim to be able to "see" sounds and "hear" colors. Hallucinogens include LSD, Ecstasy (MDMA), peyote, and psilocybin mushrooms.

Hallucinogens are distinct from the other categories of drugs in that long after they are expelled from the body, the user may still experience flashbacks. A **flashback** is a temporary reoccurrence of a psychedelic experience. This could be described as the overintensification of a particular color, the perceived movement of a stationary object, or the mistaking of one object for another.

The abuse of hallucinogens has seen varied levels of popularity over the years. They reached their peak in the late 1960s and early 1970s but have become popular numerous times since then. The most popular forms of hallucinogens are LSD, PCP, psilocybin, and peyote.

LSD. LSD was developed in Germany in 1938 from the ergot fungus, a fungus that grows on rye. A chemist accidentally discovered its effects in 1943 and reported that he saw a stream of fantastic colors and extraordinary vividness. Since then, it has been used to study causes of mental illness because of its similarity to certain chemicals found in the brain. Today, LSD, or acid, is found in several street forms: tablets, thin squares of gelatin (also called windowpanes), or impregnated paper (also called blotter). Blotter acid is distinguishable by unique artwork, frequently depicting cartoon characters, printed on the paper.

PCP. PCP was developed in 1959 as a general anesthetic, but because of its adverse effects, its use in humans was discontinued. It later became commercially available for use as a veterinary medicine. In 1978, PCP was rescheduled from Schedule III to Schedule II because of public protests about its dangers. (See the section "The

FIGURE 16.6 LSD or "blotter acid." Courtesy of Mike Himmel and the Missouri State Highway Patrol.

1970 Controlled Substances Act" for more on classification of drugs.) PCP is also sold on the street by other names, such as angel dust, wack, water, juice, and rocket fuel. It is manufactured in illicit laboratories in both powder and liquid form and is usually ingested by smoking or inhalation. PCP produces varying effects on different users. For example, a moderate amount produces a sense of detachment, distance, and estrangement from surroundings. Heavier doses are associated with more severe reactions. Specifically, users experience a blank stare, rapid eye movements, acute anxiety, and extreme paranoia. Perhaps the most devastating effect is the user's sense of strength and invulnerability. Recent research has shown that such reactions may develop after only one dose of the drug, making PCP one of the most dangerous of the illicit substances.

Depressants

Drugs falling within the depressant category are potentially addictive in both the psychological and physical sense. Depressants act on the CNS, but when taken as prescribed, they may help to relieve anxiety, irritability, and tension and to induce sleep. When taken in excess, however, depressants affect the user much like alcohol. Specifically, when taken in smaller doses, they produce feelings of intoxication and euphoria. Depressant drugs include barbiturates and benzodiazepines (tranquilizers).

Commonly Abused Stimulants

☑ *Cocaine.* The most potent stimulant known. Primarily an illicit product coming from South America available on U.S. streets in both powder and freebase (crack) form. Cocaine is highly addictive and is ingested by smoking (freebasing), injection, or snorting.

☑ *Amphetamine.* Developed in 1887, used legally to treat narcolepsy and obesity. Amphetamines are produced both legitimately and clandestinely and may be found on the street in tablet, injectable, or powdered form.

☑ *Phenmetrazine (Preludin).* Synthetic stimulant similar to amphetamine that is commonly diverted from legal channels onto the street. Abuse generally involves the dissolving of tablets into a liquid solution and injection with syringes.

Tolerance with depressant drugs develops rapidly, thus closing the gap between an intoxicating and a lethal dose. Some depressant abusers have exceeded their prescribed doses up to 20 times, resulting in an increase in their dependence on the drug. In the drug abuse world, depressant abuse sometimes occurs because users are trying to counter or "come down" from the effects of stimulants. In addition, many overdoses are attributed to the deadly mixing of alcohol and depressants, or synergism.

Barbiturates. Barbiturates are the most frequently prescribed depressants and are used primarily as sedatives for their calming effects or to induce sleep. Of the hundreds of barbituric acid derivatives that have been synthesized over the years, only about 15 are currently in use.

Barbiturates are classified as ultrashort, short, intermediate, and long lasting. Of these, the most commonly abused are the short acting and intermediate acting, which include such drugs as phenobarbital (Nembutal), secobarbital (Seconal), and amobarbital (Amytal). Small doses of barbiturates tend to calm the nerves and even cause sleep. Commonly, a feeling of excitement preempts these more relaxed feelings. When doses increase, however, users risk more serious consequences, such as coma and death from respiratory arrest and cardiovascular complications.

Rohypnol. Rohypnol is a brand name for flunitrazepam and is commonly known as ruffies. Rohypnol has never been approved for medical use in the United States; therefore, doctors cannot prescribe it, and pharmacists cannot sell it. However, it is legally prescribed in more than 50 other countries and is widely available in Mexico, Colombia, and Europe, where it is used for the treatment of insomnia and as a preanesthetic. Therefore, it was placed into Schedule IV of the CSA in 1984 due to international treaty obligations.

Similar to similar drugs (e.g., Valium, Librium, Xanax, and Halcion), Rohypnol's pharmacological effects include sedation, muscle relaxation, reduction in anxiety, and prevention of convulsions. However, its sedative effects are approximately seven to 10 times more potent than those of diazepam (Valium). The effects of Rohypnol appear approximately 15 to 20 minutes after administration and last approximately four to six hours. Some residual effects can be found 12 hours or more after administration.

Rohypnol causes partial amnesia; users are unable to remember certain events that they experienced while under the influence of the drug. This effect is particularly dangerous when flunitrazepam is used to aid in the commission of sexual assault; victims may not be able to clearly recall the assault, the assailant, or the events surrounding the assault.

It is difficult to estimate just how many Rohypnol-facilitated rapes have occurred in the United States. Very often, biological samples are taken from the victim at a time when the effects of the drug have already passed, and only residual amounts remain in the bodily fluids. These residual amounts are difficult, if not impossible, to detect using standard screening assays available in the United States. If exposure to Rohypnol is to be detected at all, urine samples need to be collected within 72 hours and subjected to sensitive analytical tests. The problem is compounded by the onset of amnesia after ingestion of the drug, which causes the victim to be uncertain about the facts surrounding the rape. This uncertainty may lead to critical delays or even reluctance to report a rape and to provide appropriate biological samples for toxicology testing.

Although Rohypnol has become widely known for its use as a **date rape drug**, it is abused more frequently for other reasons. It is abused by high school students, college students, street gang members, rave party attendees, and heroin and cocaine abusers to produce profound intoxication, boost the high of

FIGURE 16.7 Photo of confiscated Rohypnol pills. Each pill contains one milligram of the benzodiazepine drug flunitrazepam. This has gained notoriety as the "date rape" drug. Courtesy of AP Wide World Photos.

heroin, and modulate the effects of cocaine. The drug is usually consumed orally, is often combined with alcohol, and is abused by crushing tablets and snorting the powder.

γ-Hydroxybutyrate (GHB). GHB, known as liquid X, Georgia home boy, goop, gamma-oh, and grievous bodily harm, is a CNS depressant abused for its ability to produce euphoric and hallucinatory states and its alleged ability to release a growth hormone and stimulate muscle growth.

Although GHB was originally considered a safe and "natural" food supplement and was sold in health food stores, the medical community soon became aware that it caused overdoses and other health problems. GHB can produce drowsiness, dizziness, nausea, unconsciousness, seizures, severe respiratory depression, and coma. GHB can be found in liquid form or as a white powder material. It is taken orally and is frequently combined with alcohol. Abusers include high school and college students and rave party attendees who use GHB for its intoxicating effects. Some bodybuilders also abuse GHB for its alleged anabolic effects.

Similar to Rohypnol, several cases have documented the use of GHB to incapacitate women for the commission of sexual assault. In 1990, the Food and Drug Administration (FDA) issued an advisory declaring GHB unsafe and illicit except under FDA-approved, physician-supervised protocols. In March 2000, GHB was placed in Schedule I of the CSA.

Designer Drugs

The term **designer drug** has been coined to refer to a class of drugs that are specifically designed to emulate controlled substances. Illegal chemists intent on circumventing drug regulations have become adept in creating such substances. Designer drugs include:

- Ecstasy (MDMA)
- China white (fentanyl)

One of the more infamous designer drugs is Ecstasy (also called Adam and Eve or XTC), a combination of synthetic mescaline and amphetamine that possesses a hallucinogenic effect. It is also called MDMA (for 3,4-methylene dioxymethamphetamine). Although controlled by the DEA in 1985, this drug still remains fairly popular on the illicit drug scene. Another successful designer drug is china white heroin. This drug, which is not actually heroin at all, may be thousands of times more powerful than heroin. But from a user's viewpoint, fentanyl and heroin are functionally interchangeable. Fentanyl can be packed like heroin and "cut" with the same diluents. The side effects, however, seem to be much more severe than with heroin. Indeed, Parkinson's disease is a common result of its use.

The General Structure of Drug Laws

As with all criminal violations, drug investigators must familiarize themselves with the law in order to make prosecutable cases. Laws governing illicit drugs appear in virtually all levels of government. Accordingly, drug penalties under different levels of government will also vary from one jurisdiction to the next. Generally, criminal law considers several categories of illegal behavior regarding drug abuse:

- *Possession.* Possession usually manifests itself in one of two ways: actual physical custody of the drugs or constructive possession. The latter requires the subject to have knowledge of the presence of the substance and the power and intent to control use of the drug.
- *Distribution.* The charge of drug distribution is of a more serious nature than possession and is most commonly imposed for any exchange of illegal drugs between two or more persons. Exchanges also include drug sales, passing drugs to another, or delivering an illicit drug whether or not for sale or profit.
- *Manufacturing.* Criminal charges can also be assessed for producing illicit drugs. Drugs such as LSD, methamphetamine, fentanyl, and PCP are more typically products of illicit drug labs. Most criminal laws also include as manufacturing the growing of cannabis (marijuana) or conversion of one drug to another, such as cocaine to crack. As drug distribution networks become larger and more sophisticated, more powerful laws may be needed for successful prosecution. Laws such as the RICO Act, the Continuing Criminal Enterprise (CCE) Act, and conspiracy statutes better enable prosecutors to attack the management figures of drug-dealing organizations.

The 1970 Controlled Substances Act

The CSA has been the legal foundation of the federal government's battle against illicit drug abuse since its implementation in 1970. This comprehensive law includes numerous laws dealing with the manufacture, distribution, and possession of dangerous drugs. The CSA basically took all drugs considered dangerous under existing federal law and placed them into one of five schedules. The placement of a drug under any particular category was based on its medical use, potential for abuse, and safety or propensity for dependence. Under this act, drugs can be added, removed, or rescheduled at the initiation of the Department of Health and Human Services, by the DEA, or by the petition of any interested person (i.e., a drug manufacturer, medical association, pharmacy association, public interest group, state or local agency, or individual citizen).

The point of concern in changing a drug's status is whether it has a potential for abuse. If a drug does not have a potential for abuse, it cannot be controlled. Unfortunately, the term *potential for abuse* is not clearly defined under the CSA and therefore has many different interpretations. Generally, however, the following items have determined whether or not a drug has a potential for abuse:

- There is evidence that people are taking the drug(s) containing such a substance in amounts sufficient to create a hazard to their health or to the safety of other people or the community.

- There is sufficient diversion of the drug(s) from legitimate drug channels.

- People are taking the drug(s) containing such a substance on their own initiative rather than on the basis of medical advice from a practitioner licensed by law to administer such drugs in the course of his or her professional practice.

- The drug(s) containing such a substance are new drugs so related in their action to the drug(s) already listed as having potential for abuse.

A CLOSER LOOK

Drug Abuse and AIDS

Needle Sharing

Among IV drug users, transmission of the AIDS virus most often occurs by sharing needles, syringes, or other "works." Small amounts of contaminated blood left in the equipment can carry the virus from user to user. IV drug users who frequent "shooting galleries"—where paraphernalia is passed among several people—are at especially high risk for AIDS. But needle sharing of any sort (at parties, for example) can transmit the virus, and National Institute of Drug Abuse (NIDA) experts note that almost all IV drug users share needles at one time or another. Because not every IV drug user will enter treatment and because some must wait to be treated, IV users in many cities are being taught to flush their "works" with bleach before they inject. Used correctly, bleach can destroy virus left in the equipment.

Sexual Transmission

IV drug users also get AIDS through unprotected sex with someone who is infected. In addition, the AIDS virus can be sexually transmitted from infected IV drug users to persons who do not use

drugs. Data from the Centers for Disease Control and Prevention (CDC) show that IV drug use is associated with the increased spread of AIDS in the heterosexual population. For example, of all women reported to have AIDS, 49 percent were IV drug users, and another 30 percent, non-IV drug users themselves, were sexual partners of IV drug users. Infected women who become pregnant can pass the AIDS virus to their babies. About 70 percent of all children born with AIDS have a mother or father who "shot" drugs.

Non-Intravenous Drug Use and AIDS

Sexual activity has also been reported as a means of AIDS transmission among those who use non-IV drugs such as crack or marijuana. Many people, especially women, addicted to crack (or other substances) go broke supporting their habit and turn to trading sex for drugs. Another link between substance abuse and AIDS is when people using alcohol and drugs relax their restraints and caution regarding sexual behavior. People who normally practice safe sex may neglect to do so while "under the influence."

Source: U.S. Drug Enforcement Administration. (1988). *Drugs of abuse.* Washington, DC: U.S. Government Printing Office.

Tools and Techniques in Drug Investigations

Because of ongoing public concern about drug abuse and violent crime, drug investigations have become a mainstay in many law enforcement agencies. Goals of drug investigation are to:

- Identify and locate known or suspected drug sellers.
- Understand the different types of drugs available on the street, their prices, and packaging methods.
- Identify locations of frequent drug abuse activity.
- Collect evidence on those involved in drug trafficking.
- Reduce the availability of drugs through the aggressive apprehension of drug users and sellers.

The planning and initiation phase of a drug case involves several steps that usually begin with the receipt and verification of information. In this early phase, investigators learn of suspected criminal activity through various sources of information. Great discretion is required here because not every source of information is reliable. Information sources include:

- Other law enforcement agencies (e.g., police departments, sheriff's departments, federal agencies)
- Other units within the police department (e.g., prostitution and vice divisions, the patrol division)

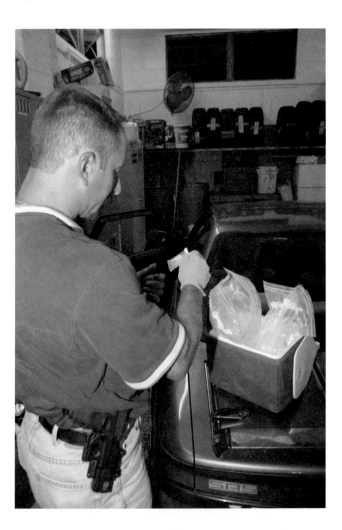

FIGURE 16.8 Photo of criminal investigator with the Kansas City, Missouri Police Gang Squad "field testing" suspected cocaine. If the tested substance turns blue, it indicates it is cocaine. The field test is typically used to provide probable cause for arrest or search until additional evidence can be identified. Courtesy of Arresting Images.

- "Unofficial" information from other officers within the department
- Other criminal justice agencies (e.g., probation and parole, the courts)
- Information provided by good citizens

Confidential Informants

Planning drug investigations through the use of informant information is one of the most common avenues in which drug cases are initiated. Ironically, such information may prove to be extremely valuable or extremely worthless, and investigators must determine its reliability early in the investigation so that costly time is not wasted. After information is received, the investigator must make an effort, independent of the initial source, to verify it. This is generally accomplished by one of three basic methods: surveillance, the development of an informant, and the use of specific sources outside the investigator's agency.

Case Planning

Drug cases frequently net suspects from all walks of society, from the old to the young, the very rich to the very poor, the meek to the violent. Over the years, thousands of drug cases have endured the scrutiny of many a prosecutor, defense attorney, and court of law. Therefore, investigative methods have been somewhat refined over the years, thus dictating that drug enforcement is not an area for trial-and-error tactics. Drug arrests and raids also typically draw media attention, and investigative methods and techniques might fall under close scrutiny. The drug case might also ultimately use sophisticated federal laws such as conspiracy, the RICO Act, and the CCE Act. Implementation of these laws may not be apparent early in the investigation because drug investigations typically gain momentum over time. Accordingly, investigators should plan their cases carefully and thoroughly in anticipation of the use of these laws.

The target of the investigation usually determines the level of involvement of the law enforcement agency. One important planning element is the extent of violations being committed by the target individual. The investigator should establish:

- Whether the person is a drug user or drug dealer
- If he or she is a dealer, whether the level is wholesale or retail
- Any other crimes that the target person is responsible for or involved in (e.g., assault, robbery, murder)
- Whether the target can be used to reach others in the drug organization

Other considerations are also determined by the level of involvement of the target individual. One of the most critical is the arrest strategy to be used. This consideration examines the use of a particular type of drug buy (buy-bust or buy-walk). This determination rests on whether or not the suspect is being considered for later use as an informant. Departmental factors also play a significant role in drug case planning. Obviously, some law enforcement agencies have more resources than others, but certain critical factors should be considered. Investigative resources to consider are:

- *Personnel.* Drug investigations require a sizable commitment of human resources, particularly sworn personnel. Multiple officers are required during **undercover** operations, raids, and surveillance operations.
- *Money.* As with many police operations, money is always an issue. Drug investigations, however, require large amounts of cash for drug transactions between undercover agents and suspects, as well as for overtime, investigative expenses, and equipment.

Drug Schedules Under the Controlled Substance Act

Schedule I

The drug or other substance has a high potential for abuse. The drug or other substance has no currently accepted medical use in treatment in the United States. There is a lack of accepted safety for use of the drug under medical supervision.

Examples: Heroin, LSD, marijuana, peyote, methaqualone

Schedule II

The drug or other substance has a high potential for abuse. The drug or other substance has a currently accepted medical use in treatment in the United States or a currently accepted medical use with severe restrictions. Abuse of the drug or other substance may lead to severe psychological or physical dependence.

Examples: Amphetamines, some morphine derivatives, cocaine, PCP

Schedule III

The drug or other substance has a potential for abuse less than the drugs or other substances in Schedules I and II. The drug or other substance has a currently accepted medical use in treatment in the United States. Abuse of the drug or other substance may lead to moderate or low physical dependence or high psychological dependence.

Examples: Some barbiturates, some opium derivatives, glutethimide

Schedule IV

The drug or other substance has a low potential for abuse relative to the drugs or other substances in Schedule III. The drug or other substance has a currently accepted medical use in treatment in the United States. Abuse of the drug or other substance may lead to limited physical dependence or psychological dependence relative to the drugs or other substances in Schedule III.

Examples: Chloral hydrate, tranquilizers, some stimulants and depressants

Schedule V

The drug or other substance has a low potential for abuse relative to the drugs or other substances in Schedule IV. The drug or other substance has a currently accepted medical use in treatment in the United States. Abuse of the drug or other substance may lead to limited physical dependence or psychological dependence relative to the drugs or other substances in Schedule IV.

Examples: Some extracts of opium, some extracts of morphine, some derivatives of codeine.

Since passing of the CSA, most states have adopted state versions of the law, which typically include a localized model of the five federal schedules. This allows prosecutors to file charges under either federal or state criminal justice systems, depending on the type of crime committed and the desired result of the criminal prosecution.

- *Equipment.* Drug investigations are becoming increasingly more technical with the introduction of high-technology equipment. Most equipment of this nature is typically used for surveillance operations, but investigators must be aware of what type of equipment is available and which is best suited for the agency's mission.

The resources cited earlier represent only a few of the most critical. Others include legal assistance, which should be a required ingredient in any drug investigation. Drug laws are becoming more complex in nature, thereby increasing the opportunities for investigators to make "technical" mistakes during their investigations. If there is any legal question in the mind of the investigator, he or she should always consult a knowledgeable prosecutor for advice before proceeding.

The list of potential informational resources is limited only by the investigator's imagination. The investigator should always keep in mind that information on just about everyone is available somewhere.

The Investigation of Illicit Drug Laboratories

The investigation of illicit drug laboratories usually begins with a base of criminal intelligence information. Such information can be acquired through many sources, including other law enforcement agencies or criminal informants. Other than the preceding sources of information, the drug laboratory can be discovered by other means. For example, an abundance of a drug such as methamphetamine or PCP that is selling at an unusually low price might indicate a laboratory nearby. When officers suspect an illicit drug lab, the following investigative steps should be considered:

- Check with the local utility companies to see if unusually large amounts of electricity are being used.
- Verify who is receiving mail at the suspect residence by checking with U.S. postal officials in the area.
- Conduct a criminal background investigation on each suspect.
- Survey the suspect location for evidence of exhaust fans used for ventilation.
- Be aware of any unusual odors in the area indicating the presence of a lab.
- Acquire a court order for the telephone tolls of the suspect's phone to reveal associates.

After the preliminary information has been acquired and verified, a second phase of the investigation should be conducted. This phase is designed to give information to the investigator of much greater depth to prepare for possible search warrants, undercover surveillance, or raids. The investigator should:

- Determine the number of inhabitants of the lab.
- Learn the identity of the inhabitants.
- Learn if any weapons are present at the lab location.
- Determine if any security measures have been taken by the suspects (e.g., use of guard dogs, booby traps).
- Attempt to determine the stage of the cooking process. (Is there any finished product available to seize?)
- Determine what chemicals are being used in the drug lab. These may serve as precursors, solvents, or reagents in the synthesis process. In addition, chemicals may be corrosive or even explosive in nature. For example, methamphetamine and PCP laboratories require large amounts of ether, which is extremely unstable and poses an imminent danger to anyone present on the scene.

A CLOSER LOOK

Becoming a DEA Diversion Investigator

A Diversion Investigator (DI) is a specialist responsible for addressing the problem of controlled pharmaceutical and regulated chemical diversion from their legitimate channels in which they are manufactured, distributed, and dispensed. DIs aid pharmaceutical and chemical industries in complying with the CSA and other pertinent acts, as well as international treaties and conventions. DIs investigate and uncover suspected sources of diversion and take appropriate criminal, civil, or administrative actions. To accomplish this mission, a wide range of work activities is used. One activity, for example, is the scheduled investigation of registered handlers of controlled substances. These investigations serve to deter diversion through evaluation of the registrants' record-keeping procedures, security safeguards, and general compliance with the CSA and implementing regulations. Legitimate handlers of controlled substances who are subject to investigation are drug manufacturers, distributors, importers and exporters, and narcotic treatment programs. Recently, there has been a push to investigate the diversion of controlled substances via the Internet. The rapidly changing environment and the increased diversion of controlled substances using the Internet have created the need for programs to target these sources of diversion.

Frequently, DIs are involved in investigations aimed at serious violators of controlled substance laws and regulations. These registrant violators have a documented or suspected history of drug and chemical diversion to illicit markets. DIs collect and analyze information developed during their investigations and consult with supervisory personnel to determine if criminal prosecution is warranted. DIs also work closely with DEA Special Agents and state and local law enforcement officers to provide assistance in making undercover purchases and executing search warrants. DIs work closely with attorneys for the DEA, the United States Attorneys Office, and state and local prosecutors. DIs are frequently required to testify about the results of their investigations in criminal trials, grand jury proceedings, and administrative hearings.

The job of a DEA DI involves maintaining contact with all levels of the drug and chemical registrant population. DIs often answer questions from registrants concerning their responsibilities under the CSA.

Qualifications

- *General.* Candidates must be U.S. citizens and possess a valid driver's license.

- *Physical.* Candidates are required to obtain a medical examination to determine their physical and mental fitness and must be free of any impairment that would interfere with normal work performance. Distant vision should be 20/40 (uncorrected or corrected with glasses or contact lenses). Near vision should be 20/25 and must be sufficient to read Jaegar Type #2 at 14 inches (glasses or contact lenses permitted). Depth perception and the ability to distinguish shades of color (color plate test) are essential. Candidates must be able to hear conversational voices at a distance of 20 feet with both ears. The use of a hearing aid is permissible.

- *Education.* Candidates must have a bachelor's degree (any major) and meet one of the following Superior Academic Achievement Provisions: a grade-point average (GPA) of "B" (2.95 or higher) for all completed undergraduate courses or a GPA of "B+" (3.5 or higher) for all courses in the major field of study or rank in the upper third of class in the college, university, or major subdivision.

- *Experience.* One year of specialized experience equivalent to the next lowest grade level or an equivalent combination of education and experience is required.

- *Special skills.* In addition to the minimal qualifications, credit may be given to individuals who possess one or more of the following special skills: investigative experience, proficiency in a foreign language, accounting experience or degree, chemistry experience or degree, pharmacology or pharmacist experience or degree, computer skills or experience, military service, or law enforcement experience or degree.

Reverse Drug Sting Operations

The reverse sting narcotic sale is one in which undercover investigators, posing as dealers, sell large quantities of narcotics to known traffickers (also see Chapter 7 on undercover operations and surveillance). These types of operations have proven successful in penetrating otherwise untouchable drug markets. The same reverse sting techniques can also be used against drug consumers on the street.

Street-level reverse sting operations can be used whenever any type of controlled substance is being sold in a high-traffic environment. However, police agencies have found it particularly effective in dealing with rock cocaine sales. Rock cocaine, or crack, has become the drug of choice and a serious crime problem on the streets of many American towns and cities.

Planning the Reverse Sting. The "rock reverse" is almost always set up on the street in an area generally occupied by large numbers of street dealers or directly in front of a known crack house.

The operation is dangerous for undercover officers and takedown officers, so it is important that personnel be selected carefully for this assignment. All weapons that may be used in the operation should be thoroughly inspected, and officers should wear soft body armor, as they should during all assignments.

Reverse sting operations are manpower intensive. The reverse sting operation discussed here requires between 20 and 25 officers to be conducted safely and efficiently. Although this is a considerable expenditure in manpower, the operation can be justified based on the large number of arrests that can be made and the positive impact this has on the community. Additionally, considerable amounts of property and assets may be forfeited to the jurisdiction as a result of these operations.

Manpower Considerations. Three undercover investigators should be designated to perform the principal street sales assignments. Each officer should be dressed in a manner characteristic of the local dealers. Primary undercover officer "A" is responsible for making the drug sale while undercover officers "B" and "C" position themselves within 200 feet of officer "A" on each side. Vehicle assignments are as follows:

- *Vehicle 1* is the principal vehicle used to accommodate officers making the arrest. Ideally, this vehicle should be an inconspicuous panel or step van without rear or side windows and with double folding side doors. Five officers should be assigned to this vehicle, three of whom should be uniformed and the remaining two wearing reflective raid jackets. Three of these officers should be designated to use weapons during the arrest, and the other two should be assigned to searching and handcuffing the arrestees.

- *Vehicles 2 and 3* are designated as blockade cars. These cars should be unmarked, inconspicuous sedans or other vehicles with two undercover officers assigned to each. Parked about 100 feet on each side of the van, these vehicles are pulled up to a position to block the suspect's vehicle at the time of the arrest or takedown.

- *Vehicle 4* should be a surveillance van with audio/video and night vision capabilities. The surveillance van is stationary and is placed undercover within 100 feet of the primary undercover officer (A).

mycrimekit

Video: Job profile: Dea agent

- *Vehicles 5 and 6* are marked units with two uniformed officers in each. These vehicles are assigned locations just outside the takedown area and are meant to provide additional coverage if the suspects flee the area.

In addition to these assignments, a prisoner transportation van should be stationed just outside the operations area to ensure expeditious handling of arrestees.

Conducting the Sting. The primary takedown vehicle must be in close proximity to the primary undercover officer because rapid response is essential in making the arrest. There must also be an appropriate place to locate the surveillance van so it will be inconspicuous and provide for good audiovisual coverage. In some cases, officers may choose to conduct surveillance from a building location directly opposite the takedown area rather than use a van.

After the operational area has been identified, diagrams of the neighborhood should be developed. These diagrams should include all relevant buildings and features and identify the positions of all police vehicles and personnel to be deployed in the operational area. The diagram should be used during the personnel briefings to walk through the entire operation. If feasible, it is preferred that the entire operation be practiced in a nonpublic area just before being used in the target area.

The reverse sting requires that a quantity of crack cocaine be packaged for sale. A court order may be required for use of this or other contraband from police property control. Preferably, the crack that is used in the sale should be laboratory tested.

Each cocaine rock should be sealed in clear plastic tape, a plastic bag, balloon, or other means. The method for sealing the rock should correspond with the method popularly used in a given area. The plastic bag or other method also allows the cocaine to be marked and discourages suspects from attempting to swallow the evidence.

Before sealing the crack, a piece may also be broken off from each rock and stored as evidence, a measure that helps in prosecuting buyers who manage to swallow or otherwise dispose of the evidence during their arrest. It should be noted that if the suspect swallows the cocaine, he or she should be immediately transported to an emergency medical facility. A potentially lethal overdose can thus be avoided.

Approximately 20 minutes before the operation begins, marked police vehicles with uniformed officers should be sent into the target area to disperse any actual drug dealers. While in the area, these officers should also make contact with the citizens and request that they and their children stay out of the operational area. Most citizens will comply, particularly in view of the fact that their neighborhood may have been overrun by the drug dealers for some time.

The primary undercover officer is responsible for selling the rocks while the two other undercover officers direct potential customers to him or her and provide backup protection. If the operation lasts for an extended period of time, these three officers should rotate assignments.

The primary undercover officer should be positioned directly opposite the takedown van so that takedown officers will be in position almost immediately after their exit from the vehicle. The primary undercover officer should also be wired with a body transmitter so that the transaction can be recorded verbatim.

A—Primary Undercover Officer
B & C—Undercover Officer
Vehicle 1—Takedown Van
Vehicles 2 & 3—Blockade Vehicles
Vehicle 4—Surveillance Van
Vehicles 5 & 6—Backup Officers

FIGURE 16.9 Locations of officers and police vehicles in a reverse sting operation.

The transmitter also serves as a backup safety device so problems that may develop can be overheard by the officer in the surveillance van.

The undercover officer who is responsible for the sale has the major responsibility for ensuring that an "entrapment" situation is not created by what he or she says or does. The guidelines for the operation developed with the local prosecutor must be specific in terms of the types of language and actions that can be used to establish contact and a dialogue with potential buyers.

Typical guidelines for reverse sting operations instruct undercover officers to stand alongside the street in the target area and act in a manner generally characteristic of local street dealers. Officers are told to ask (after first being approached by a suspect) general questions such as, "What do you want?" or "What are you looking for?" After the customer states that he or she is looking for crack, the officer is free to negotiate a price and conclude the sale.

Through the careful development of an acceptable dialogue between the undercover officer and customer, the danger of entrapment is virtually eliminated. Predisposition of the suspect to commit the crime can easily be shown through audio and video recordings of the incident. The suspect can be seen on videotape slowly driving into an area frequented by crack cocaine dealers. The suspect can be heard asking the undercover detective for cocaine. Predisposition can also generally be established by prior arrest records for drug offenses or by the presence of drug paraphernalia that may be found in the suspect's vehicle.

It should also be noted that in most cases, it is necessary that the suspect actually takes possession of the cocaine before he or she can be arrested and charged with possession. Examining the cocaine before purchase does not normally constitute possession.

Some agencies use prearranged signals between the undercover officer and the takedown team to initiate the arrest when the transaction is complete. A discrete signal, such as scratching one's face or another movement, is most useful if a body transmitter is not used by the undercover officer. If the transmitter is used in conjunction with visual surveillance, however, the officer conducting the surveillance should order the takedown. This latter approach is preferable for two reasons:

1. Police officers involved in undercover drug sales have been robbed of their drugs at gunpoint.
2. Some drug buyers, particularly those who have been arrested in stings on prior occasions, can readily detect commonly used police signals.

As soon as the takedown command is given, the officers from the van should exit the vehicle, announce that they are police, and establish a good field of fire that will not jeopardize the undercover officer or other police personnel. Speed in making the takedown is essential. It is far more likely that control and compliance of suspects can be established if officers deploy rapidly and thwart any attempts of the suspect to flee or otherwise react.

As officers exit the van for the takedown, the blocking vehicles should move into positions that will reduce the likelihood of an attempted escape. Officers in the blocking vehicles can also serve as backup for those in the van.

After all suspects are in custody, a prisoner van can be summoned, and other personnel can drive the suspect's vehicle to the impoundment area.

Pharmaceutical Diversion

As we see from our earlier discussion, many potent and addictive drugs are manufactured legally for legitimate medical treatment. The availability of these medications has created a relatively new type of criminality called **pharmaceutical diversion**. Criminal investigations into this type of activity, also called compliance investigations, have revealed widespread diversion of drugs by health care professionals and street criminals alike.

Diversion by Legal Registrants

Many restraints are in place under the CSA for those handling controlled substances. In addition to federal law, most states have adopted laws similar to the CSA to give a more localized means of controlling diversion activities. As the law is structured now, all medical professionals who are required to handle controlled substances must register with the DEA and obtain a registration number that is unique to them. Legal registrants of pharmaceutical drugs include:

- Importers
- Exporters
- Manufacturers
- Wholesalers
- Hospitals
- Pharmacies
- Physicians
- Nurses
- Drug researchers

Under law, any time that drugs are purchased by a registrant, the assigned number must be made available to the supplier. This creates an audit trail for investigators in the event that a registrant is suspected of diverting drugs.

Diversion Tactics

Since the passage of the CSA, both legitimate and illegal drug markets have become more sophisticated. Advancement in cancer treatment research has produced powerful painkillers that addicts have learned can substitute for heroin. Legitimate manufacturers now market popular "mood enhancement" drugs, which have potential for abuse.

Today's drug buyer has learned that it is safer to obtain brand-name drugs that have been diverted onto the street than it is to deal with a drug peddler who is dealing an unknown product from a clandestine laboratory. Drugs purchased from a clandestine laboratory cannot allow the buyer to know what kind of poison is before him or her if he or she will be ripped off with a no-impact placebo. On the other hand, when purchasing diverted drugs, the drug buyer has the assurance of a clearly identifiable, marked product coded by a manufacturer that prepared the dose under rigid guidelines enforced by U.S. government inspectors.

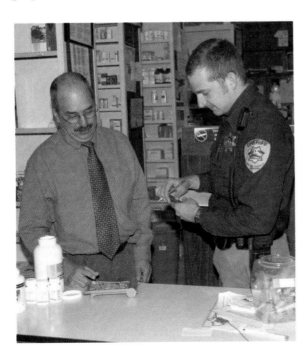

FIGURE 16.10 Sheriff's deputy conducting a pharmacy audit after suspected diversion activities by the pharmacist.

The availability of diverted drugs is also a factor in their increased usage. Unlike substances such as heroin and cocaine, diverted pharmaceuticals are produced within the United States and are not subject to the periodic shortages that affect smuggled products—the product is available at virtually every street-corner pharmacy in the country. The problem of the addict or the drug seller is reduced to how to divert the drug onto the street.

Drug diversion tactics may be classified under five general headings: wholesale-level diversions, illegal sales by medical practitioners, theft, fraud, and forgeries.

- *Wholesale-level diversion,* such as large-scale theft or fraud from the manufacturer or distributor, is minimal at the present time because of strict, enforceable controls that have been legislated for this level of the drug distribution system. The DEA reports few diversion incidents at this level, but a simple comparison of the number of incidents may be somewhat misleading because one diversion incident at the wholesale level—such as a hijacking of a major drug shipment—can place thousands of illegal doses on the streets. Nonetheless, wholesale-level distribution is believed to be adequately controlled by existing laws and investigative techniques.

- *Illegal sale by medical practitioners* accounts for the largest current volume of diverted drugs. Illegal sales may originate with doctors, pharmacists, or employees at hospitals. The person responsible for the diversion may attempt to cover his or her tracks with a fraudulent paper trail of some kind or may seek to confuse investigators by destroying part of the legitimate paper trail. The existence of required reports and records, however, constitutes an important part of any investigation of the medical practitioner.

- *Theft as a diversion tactic* is reported to be on the increase. This category includes burglary of storage facilities, armed robbery of pharmacies and doctors' offices, pilferage, and employee theft at both hospitals and pharmacies. According to DEA statistics, theft of legally manufactured pharmaceuticals accounts for nearly 300 million illegal doses reaching the streets per year. It should be noted that reports of theft or burglary are also used by doctors and pharmacists to account for inventory shortages or to explain missing reports and drugs that were dispensed illegally.

- *Fraudulent schemes* to fool a doctor or pharmacist into prescribing drugs produce an unknown quantity of diverted drugs that is presumed to be large. Frauds are perpetrated by persons who obtain drugs for their own use and persons who either sell the prescribed drugs or turn them over to a criminal employer who sells them elsewhere. The scale of such frauds varies from the individual addict who supplies him- or herself to well-organized activities that use paid "patients" to obtain prescriptions and paid "runners" to fill prescriptions at various pharmacies throughout a city.

- *Prescription forgery* includes consideration of counterfeit and altered and forged prescriptions. Many forgeries are carried out with the knowledge of either the physician or the dispensing pharmacist, although some forgeries have been shown to originate with the pharmacist to disguise the loss of drugs that were illegally sold. The exact volume of drugs diverted by prescription forgery is unknown but is presumed to be significant.

Drugs obtained with forged prescriptions can be sold on the street at inflated prices. For example, the painkiller Dilaudid, prescribed frequently for cancer patients, is known on the street as "drugstore heroin." The pharmacist pays about $0.30 per tablet for the substance and may market it at three times that for prescription sales to legitimate customers. A tablet of Dilaudid can be sold on the street to heroin addicts for $50, which explains the incentive for prescription forgery.

Physician Investigations

It is somewhat shocking to realize that doctors are as corruptible as any other human being. They prescribe drugs illegally for many reasons: They may want money, sex, security, or escape, just like everybody else does; the doctor may be an addict or an alcoholic; his or her practice may be slipping as he or she grows old or senile; or he or she may have become hardened and bitter because of personal failures. Doctors are people, and the DEA estimates that approximately 2 percent of them are engaged in illegal drug traffic. Such so-called "script doctors" write prescriptions for controlled substances for a fee without properly examining or diagnosing the patient.

Over the past decade, several investigative programs conducted by the DEA have confirmed that medical practitioners (doctors and pharmacists) are the major sources of diverted drugs.

Doctors Who Divert Drugs

Generally, four types of doctors are involved in the diversion of pharmaceutical drugs.

1. *Dishonest.* A dishonest doctor makes a profit from the illegal sale of pharmaceutical drugs or may be involved in cases in which prescriptions are given to suspects for the purpose of unlawfully distributing illicit drugs.

2. *Impaired.* Some physicians use drugs both on and off the job. Drug dependency may develop for a number of reasons, including marital problems, stress on the job, and recreational use. The recidivism rate, however, is generally low for those who are treated properly and on a timely basis.

3. *Dated.* A doctor who has been in practice for a number of years may be willing to indiscriminately hand out drugs to anyone who has an apparent legitimate need for medication. Doctors who fall into this category are not necessarily criminals but more likely are set in their ways and unwilling to conform to new rules and regulations.

4. *Gullible.* This physician is not cautious enough to recognize a scam. Although possibly an otherwise competent doctor, he or she easily falls victim to professional patients.

Examples of Drug Diversion by Doctors

1. A physician writes a prescription in a patient's name, picks up the drugs personally, and tells the pharmacist he or she will take it to the patient.

2. A physician sends a patient to the pharmacy to have a prescription filled but requires the patient to bring the drugs back to his or her office. Only part of the drug is administered, and the physician keeps the rest.

3. A physician writes a prescription in the name of a family member and then picks it up and uses the drugs.

4. A physician writes a prescription in his or her own name at various pharmacies at the same time.

5. A physician self-administers injectable drugs taken from nurses' stations, hospital emergency rooms, or hospital pharmacies.

6. A physician orders drugs from several pharmacies at the same time, using official DEA order forms, while also ordering the same drugs from a mail-order drug company.

7. A physician obtains drug samples and self-administers them.

A number of investigative responses have emerged over the years to deal with the diversion problem. The most effective response combines the strength of each investigative approach. Statistical data collected and analyzed by DEA identifies pharmacies and doctors who are prescribing or dispensing abnormally large quantities of drugs. DEA or other narcotics specialists in the state may provide guidance with respect to elements of proof required to convict under specific laws. Ultimately, however, the classic "doctor bust" is the result of one or more undercover drug buys, usually by a police officer who obtains controlled drugs.

For example, it became known (from a report made by a uniformed patrol officer) that a doctor who resided in an old hotel was prescribing drugs for a fee. An investigator visited the doctor and explained that he was a truck driver and wanted 100 Ritalin tablets, a stimulant that is sometimes prescribed for weight reduction. The prescription was written without a physical examination, although the detective was not overweight. Another investigator called on the doctor, again describing himself as a trucker, and received 200 tablets of Preludin, a stimulant that is also prescribed for the treatment of obesity. The investigator, who was in excellent physical condition, asked the physician if an examination was necessary. The doctor replied, "No. You look okay to me." The doctor was an alcoholic with a failed practice who supported himself by writing prescriptions for anyone who would pay the fee.

Doctors also provide drugs for sex. For example, a woman who wanted help kicking her addiction told police officers about a doctor who had been supplying her with drugs in return for sex. In this investigation, the officers decided to obtain evidence against the doctor by having the complainant record the transaction. The woman went to the doctor's office with a recording device. After a preliminary conversation about nonexistent medical symptoms, the woman offered to perform oral sex in return for 30 Preludin pills. The doctor agreed. The difficult problem with this technique is a claim of entrapment as a legal defense. This type of investigation must be carefully constructed.

A doctor who provides drugs for sex may take elaborate precautions, perhaps because he or she perceives discovery in this relationship more threatening to his or her family life than if he or she had taken money as payment. An investigation similar to the one described above involved a woman who attempted to acquire prescription drugs in return for sex, uncovered the following precautions: Acting as an informant for the police, the woman had to fill out a medical complaint form in the doctor's waiting room to see the doctor in his examination room. As soon as the woman was alone with the doctor, she offered to have sex with him in return for prescription drugs that she intended to sell. The doctor refused her request. As a result, the doctor made a notation on the woman's medical form, which was filed by his nurse. It read: "Patient has no illness. She offered to pay $50 for speed (amphetamine). Told her that it was impossible and discouraged her from returning to this office."

Actually, the doctor had told the woman to return to his office the next day, when his nurse would not be working. The woman returned, had sex with the doctor, and received her prescription.

A doctor who prescribes drugs may be an elderly practitioner who is losing his or her practice to younger competition. Responding to reports that one elderly doctor was providing drug prescriptions irresponsibly, an investigator visited the doctor's office, which was located in the doctor's home. During a preliminary conversation that remained largely social, the doctor appeared to be mentally confused, perhaps senile. The prescription for the requested drugs was then written by the doctor's wife without the benefit of physical examination or direction from the doctor.

It is not uncommon for a medical practice (at least the prescription-writing function) to be taken over by a family member, a nurse, or a paid assistant when the doctor becomes incompetent because of age or illness. Abuse of the pre-scription-writing power sometimes follows.

Nurses Who Divert Drugs

Diversion problems also involve nurses. A distinction needs to be made between diversion drugs for resale and diversion because of personal addiction. Both present unique problems and may require different solutions. Studies have shown that of nurses who are diverting drugs, more are physically addicted than are selling drugs for profit. This distinction may affect the manner in which an investigation is approached and how the suspect is dealt with.

Drug Theft

Most health care institutions experience some degree of diversion, and generally the employees are the culprits. The employees who are most likely involved with drugs are those who have access—physicians, nurses, pharmacists, and other employees. The most commonly diverted drugs are Valium, morphine, Demerol, Tylenol III with codeine, Percodan, Percocet, and Ritalin. The type of user and the opportunities available have a bearing on whether tablets, capsules, or injectable substances are preferred. Diversion may occur in many different areas of the health care facility, but it most commonly takes place at the hospital phar-macy, the nursing station, and the recovery floor.

Substituting Drugs

If outright theft is not considered safe by the violator, he or she may substitute a noncontrolled drug for a controlled drug. Drug substitution may be accom-plished, for instance, by appearing to inject a patient with a prescribed medica-tion while in fact a worthless substance may be used in its place. This may cause the patient to suffer and could result in medical setbacks.

Recognizing the Drug-Impaired Health Care Worker

Drug abusers often exhibit aberrant behavior. Certain signs and symptoms may indicate a drug addiction problem in a health care professional. Telltale signs include:

- ☑ Work absenteeism—absences without notification and an excessive number of sick days used

- ☑ Frequent disappearances from the work site, long unexplained absences, improbable excuses, and frequent or long trips to the bathroom or stockroom where drugs are kept

- ☑ Excessive amounts of time spent near where drugs are stored; volun-teering for overtime and being at work when not scheduled to be there

- ☑ Unreliability in keeping appointments and meeting deadlines

- ☑ Work performance that alternates between periods of high and low productivity and that may suffer from mistakes made because of inattention, poor judgment, and bad decisions

- ☑ Confusion, memory loss, and difficulty concentrating or recalling details and instructions; ordinary tasks require greater effort and consume more time

☑ Interpersonal relations with colleagues, staff, and patients suffer; rarely admits errors or accepts blame for errors or oversights

☑ Heavy "wastage" of drugs

☑ Sloppy recordkeeping, suspect ledger entries, and drug shortages

☑ Inappropriate prescriptions for large narcotic doses

☑ Insistence on personal administration of injected narcotics to patients

☑ Progressive deterioration in personal appearance and hygiene

☑ Uncharacteristic deterioration of handwriting and charting

☑ Wearing long sleeves when inappropriate

☑ Personality changes, including mood swings, anxiety, depression, lack of impulse control, suicidal thoughts or gestures

☑ Patient and staff complaints about health care provider's changing attitude or behavior

☑ Increasing personal and professional isolation

Substitutions are commonly carried out through "charting" (backdating patients' charts to show that drugs were administered, which were in fact stolen) or forging other nurses' names. To avoid the possibility of substitution, two nurses should be required to obtain drugs needed on the floor. This adds a check-and-balance system to prevent one of them diverting the drugs.

Diversion by Street Criminals

Finally, the scope of the diversion problem extends to the street, where criminals called **scammers** or professional patients fraudulently attempt to obtain prescriptions for controlled drugs. Physicians are the most likely target of the scammer because they can write prescriptions or literally give away certain drugs. The pharmacist is the second-most likely target of the scammer, who might attempt to "pass" a forged prescription. Hundreds of schemes have been revealed over the years in which scammers have tried to dupe medical care professionals out of drugs. Such cases include those who have a legitimate ailment (e.g., a toothache) and who travel from one doctor to another trying to obtain prescriptions for pain medication.

Another common scam involves the criminal who takes a legitimately written prescription and alters the quantity of the prescribed drug (provided that it is not written out in longhand). In this case, a quantity marked "10" might be altered to form a "40," and a quantity of "5" may be altered to form a "25." After they have been obtained, the drugs are usually sold on the street for many times their worth.

Extraordinary Drug Enforcement Techniques

The scourge of illicit drugs across the United States in the past two decades has resulted in vigorous enforcement of many drug control laws. Along with such aggressive enforcement of traditional drug laws (i.e., distribution, possession, and manufacturing of drugs) comes a wave of nontraditional drug control techniques. The use of nontraditional drug control measures has resulted from criminals who, through expensive attorneys, vast experience in drug trafficking, and common sense, have learned to avoid detection. Since the late 1980s, such control tactics have resulted in convictions of drug dealers, raids, curfews, random searches, and the forfeiture of property. Such measures have not only become increasingly more popular with the police and the general public but they also have enjoyed broad support from the courts. Proponents of unconventional enforcement techniques argue that such measures are necessary to combat the violence and social degradation that accompany drug abuse. Conversely, some civil libertarians claim that such techniques only tend to erode basic rights such as the safeguard against unreasonable search and seizure. Let's now take a look at a couple of the most commonly used nontraditional drug enforcement techniques.

Drug Courier Profiling

Since 1985, the DEA has used a tactic that has since been called a **drug courier profile** (known as Operation Pipeline). Basically, it involves agents observing suspected drug traffickers and developing a pattern of behavior typical of those who use commercial airlines or public highways for drug trafficking. The profiling technique originated with law enforcement officers stationed at airports looking for people paying for plane tickets with cash, using aliases, boarding long flights without checking luggage, and staying briefly in distant cities known to be drug-source cities.

Because these actions can also be innocent, the practice has drawn criticism from civil libertarians. They claim that profiling is a shortcut to establishing the level of suspicion required by the Constitution before the police can interfere with a person's liberty. Most lower courts have responded by upholding the practice because of earlier Supreme Court decisions that permit the use of a "totality of the circumstances" approach to brief detentions by police.

In a precedent-setting decision by the Supreme Court, the technique of drug courier profiling was upheld. The drug decision, *United States* v. *Sokolow* (1989), was written by Judge William H. Rehnquist, and it overruled an earlier decision by the U.S. Court of Appeals in California. In the earlier decision, the court ruled that a brief detention by drug agents of a passenger at Honolulu International Airport was unconstitutional. In his opinion, Chief Rehnquist described evidence available to the agents in what he called "a typical attempt to smuggle drugs through one of the nation's airports." Rehnquist added that "any one of these factors is not by itself proof of any illegal conduct and is quite consistent with innocent travel. But we think taken together they amount to reasonable suspicion."

The agents detained the man long enough to let a trained dog sniff his luggage, and then they found several pounds of cocaine in his shoulder bag. When they stopped him, the agents knew little about him except that he had paid $2,100 for tickets from a roll of $20 bills, had just made a round-trip flight from Honolulu to Miami, stayed in Miami less than 48 hours with no checked luggage, looked nervous, and had used a name that did not match the name under which his telephone number was listed. The man, Andrew Sokolow, was eventually convicted on federal drug charges. The issue was whether the factors matching Sokolow to a drug courier profile were sufficient to justify his stop and subsequent search without a warrant. The Court held that the stop was within the law.

In the Supreme Court's opinion, certain facts of the *Sokolow* case were pointed out, including Sokolow's attire of a black jumpsuit with gold jewelry and the roll of $20 bills appearing to contain a total of $4,000. Chief Justice Rehnquist also remarked "while the trip from Honolulu to Miami, standing alone, is not a cause of any sort of suspicion, there was more: Surely few residents of Honolulu travel from that city for 20 hours to spend only 48 hours in

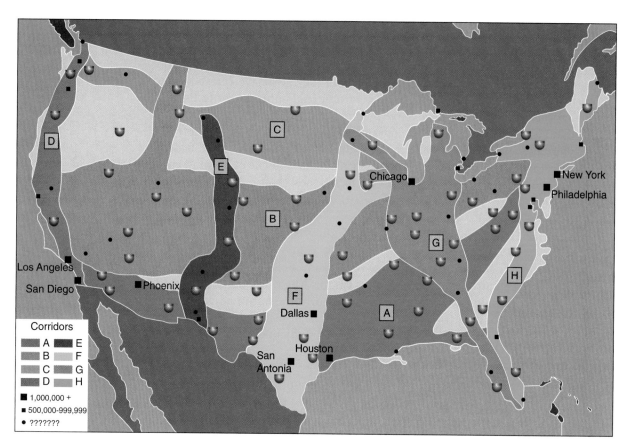

FIGURE 16.11 Major Domestic Drug Smuggling Corridors targeted by Drug Courier Profiling (Domestic Highway Enforcement Initiative). From National Drug Intelligence Center. (November 2006). National Drug Control Strategy: 2009 National Report.

Basic Principles of Drug Courier Profile Use

1. *Drug courier profiles may be used only as a basis for further investigation. Such profiles do not, standing alone, justify an arrest.*
   This principle has been made clear by the courts. Any attempt to arrest a drug courier based solely on the use of the courier profile will almost certainly result in all evidence being suppressed and the criminal charge being dismissed. In addition, the officers and agencies involved may face a very real threat of civil liability as a result of their actions.[31]

2. *The factors that make up the elements of a drug courier profile may, however, under certain circumstances justify an "investigative stop."*
   United States v. Sokolow and other court decisions have held that it is not the drug courier profile in itself but the facts and circumstances known to the officers at the time they decide to make an investigative stop that determine whether or not the stop was valid. If, under the totality of the circumstances, the officer's suspicion was reasonable, the stop is valid. The fact that the behavioral characteristics of the suspect that aroused the officer's suspicion happened to appear on a "profile" is irrelevant. It is the circumstances that determine a reasonable suspicion, not the existence or absence of a formal "profile."

   Therefore, the profile can be used only as a starting point: *All* of the circumstances of the case must be considered, not just the items appearing in the profile.

Even though the profile may certainly be used, it must not be applied in a mechanical, unthinking manner. The officer must consider the profile items in connection with the particular circumstances existing at the time and place. However, the officer may evaluate the circumstances in light of his or her own experience. Conduct seemingly innocent may, when viewed as a whole, reasonably appear suspicious to an officer who is familiar with the practices of drug smugglers and the methods used by them to avoid detection.[32]

3. *The officer must be able to articulate the factors that led him or her to form a reasonable suspicion of the person stopped.*
   Unless the involved officer can successfully explain to the court the factors that justified the stop, the stop will be held invalid, and any subsequent arrest, search, or seizure will likely be invalidated, too. It doesn't do any good to say to the court, "I just had a feeling that something was wrong." The officer must be able to list and explain the specific and particular observations that led him or her to conclude that the person in question might be a drug courier. The ability of the officer to state and explain his or her decision in clear, concrete terms can and often does make the difference between winning and losing a case of this type. Therefore:

4. *Know not only what factors are included in the profile but also why they are included.*
   Because the unthinking, mechanical use of a profile has been disapproved by the courts, the officer must be able to demonstrate to the court that the use of the profile was made intelligently and with an understanding of the meaning of the profile factors.[33]

5. *When possible, try to identify for the court factors in addition to those listed in the profile that contributed to the overall decision to detain the suspect.*
   This helps demonstrate to the court that the use of the profile was not mechanical and unthinking.

6. *Limit detention of the suspect to the minimum necessary to obtain further information.*
   Even if the initial detention is valid, if you hold the suspect for too long or otherwise exceed the balance of "reasonable" detention, the case may be thrown out by the courts. If the initial detention produces additional grounds for suspicion, the detention may be extended, but after a reasonable time, the officers must make the decision to arrest or release the suspect. This is particularly sensitive when the suspect has been removed to a private room for questioning.

7. *If the suspect has not yet been arrested, obtain either a valid consent or a search warrant before searching the suspect's luggage or automobile.*
   Because of the limitations imposed by *Terry* v. *Ohio*, do not permit a complete search of person, luggage, or automobile of the detained suspect unless an arrest has been made or probable cause for such a search has arisen. It will be necessary to have either the suspect's consent or a warrant before anything more than the *Terry* "frisk" can be conducted. Therefore, if the valid consent to search the suspect's

luggage or automobile cannot be obtained and there is not yet probable cause for an arrest or a complete search, get a search warrant
before searching luggage or vehicles. If the foregoing principles are
observed, the use of drug courier profiles will be both proper and
effective.

mycrimekit

Interactive: Gangs:
History and
development

Miami during the month of July." Airport detentions have now expanded to the
highways, where the DEA's Operation Pipeline identifies vehicles and their occupants who seem to "fit" a certain set of criteria common to those who transport
drugs or drug money across the country. Although practices such as drug
courier profiling remain controversial, there seems to be growing support in the
law enforcement community, the public sector, and the courts for innovative
drug control stratagems such as these.

Asset Forfeiture

Because of the increasingly high profits of the drug trade, the practice of asset
forfeiture has become an essential tool in drug control. Generally, the theory
behind asset forfeiture is to take the profit out of illicit drug sales by seizing
money or property that was either used to facilitate a drug crime or acquired
with illicit drug revenues. Today, in addition to federal forfeiture laws, most
state laws also provide for seizure of assets in drug cases. Although federal
seizure laws have been used effectively since the late 1960s, the locus for forfeiture on the federal level is now the 1984 Comprehensive Crime Control Act
(CCCA), which provides a revised civil provision for asset forfeiture. A unique
aspect of this act is that it specifically recognizes the important role played by
local and state law enforcement in drug control. Therefore, included in the act
is a provision that enables federal and local law enforcement agencies to work
together in facilitating the seizure of property. This can be accomplished on the
federal level even though a federal agency was not involved directly in the
investigation. The following types of property may be seized under federal forfeiture laws:

- All controlled substances
- Raw materials and equipment used to manufacture controlled substances
- Property used as a container for controlled substances
- Vehicles, boats, and aircraft to transport materials used in violation of the
  CSA
- All money, negotiable instruments, securities, or other things of value
  exchanged for controlled substances and all proceeds traceable to such an
  exchange
- Real property and any improvements thereon used or intended to be used
  to commit or facilitate a violation of the CSA

Under the 1984 act, the Attorney General or a designee can make an "equi-
table" transfer of the forfeited property so as to reflect the contribution of the
state or local agency that participated in any of the facts that led to the seizure
of the property. Under these circumstances, all agencies—federal, state, and
local—benefit.

CASE IN POINT:

Los Angeles Gangs: The Crips

The Crips is a primarily, but not exclusively, African American gang founded in Los Angeles, California, in 1971, mainly by Raymond Washington and Stanley Williams. What was once a single alliance between two autonomous gangs is now a loosely connected network of individual sets, often engaged in open warfare with each other.

The Crips are one of the largest and most violent associations of street gangs in the United States, with an estimated 30,000 to 35,000 members.[34] The gang is known to be involved in murders, robberies, and drug dealing, among many other criminal pursuits. The gang is known for its gang members' use of the color blue in their clothing. However, this practice has waned because of police crackdowns on gang members.

The Crips are publicly known to have an intense and bitter rivalry with the Bloods and lesser feuds with some Chicano gangs.[35] Crips have been documented in the U.S. military, found in bases in the United States and abroad.

Stanley "Tookie" Williams met Raymond Lee Washington in 1969, and the two decided to unite their local gang members from the west and east sides of South Central Los Angeles to battle neighboring street gangs. Most of the members were 17 years old.[36] Williams discounted the sometimes cited founding date of 1969 (or even the early 1950s) in his memoir, *Blue Rage, Black Redemption*. The original name for the alliance was "Cribs," a name narrowed down from a list of many options, and chosen unanimously from three final choices, which included the Black Overlords and the Assassins. "Cribs" was chosen to reflect the young age of the majority of the gang members. The name "Cribs" generated into the name "Crips" when gang members began carrying around canes to display their "pimp" status. People in

the neighborhood then began calling them cripples, or "Crips" for short. The name had no political, organizational, cryptic, or acronymic meaning. Williams, in his memoir, further discounted claims that the group was a spin-off of the Black Panther Party or formed for a community agenda, the name "depicted a fighting alliance against street gangs—nothing more, nothing less," Williams wrote.[37] Washington, who attended Freemont High School, was the leader of the East Side Crips, and Williams, who attended Washington High School, led the West Side Crips.

Williams recalled that a blue bandanna was first worn by Crips founding member Buddha, as a part of his color-coordinated clothing of blue Levi's, a blue shirt, and dark blue suspenders. A blue bandanna was worn in memoriam to Buddha after he was shot and killed on February 23, 1973, which eventually became the color of blue associated with the Crips.[38]

The Crips became popular throughout southern Los Angeles as more youth gangs joined; at one point, they outnumbered non-Crip gangs by three to one, sparking disputes with non-Crip gangs, including the L.A. Brims, the Athens Park Boys, the Bishops, The Drill Company, and the Denver Lanes. By 1971, the gang's notoriety had spread across Los Angeles. The gang became increasingly violent as they attempted to expand their turf. By the early 1980s, the gang was heavily involved with drug trade.

Sources: A. Vito Martinez Middle School. (2007). *Crips: Los Angeles and nationwide.* Available at http://avm.gangs.tripod.com/id28.html; Smiley, T. (2007). *Williams, Stanley Tookie. Blue rage, black redemption.* New York: Simon and Schuster:xvii–xix, 91–92, 136; Smith, D. and K. F. Whitmore. (2006). *Literacy and advocacy in adolescent family, gang, school, and juvenile court communities.* Lawrence Erlbaum Associates; SRA International; Fairfax, VA. Available at http://www.gangsacrossamerica.com/profiles_crips.php; Street Gangs. (2009). *Crip neighborhoods in Los Angeles County—a brief history.* < Available at http://www.streetgangs.com/crips/.

CASE IN POINT:

Operation Speedball

The "king of the road" in motorcycles is the world-renowned Harley-Davidson. It's the choice of many bikers, but apparently, owning a Harley-Davidson is also a requirement for membership in the infamous Outlaws Motorcycle Club of North Carolina, a

notorious motorcycle gang that originated nearly 30 years ago. Another requirement? Only white men need apply.

The Outlaws is one of the largest and most violent motorcycle gangs in the United States. It's

CASE IN POINT continued

composed of 36 chapters throughout the United States and has a following in Canada, Europe, and Australia. These bikers have done more than gone for Sunday afternoon rides on the interstate; their activities have included drug trafficking, racketeering, acts of violence, and property crimes. However, a successful local–state–federal investigation entitled Operation Speedball spiked the gang's activities and dismantled its entire operation.

Who Are These Guys?

The Outlaws gang based its operations in Charlotte and Lexington, North Carolina, where it controlled a major drug distribution network using the U.S. mail and Western Union. Its drug operations included cocaine, marijuana, and methamphetamines. Gang members also owned and controlled two motorcycle chop shops where dozens of bikes were illegally obtained, chopped (disassembled), and then sold as parts to other bikers for profit.

The gang's insignia is a skull crossed with two pistons, popularized by Marlon Brando in the film *The Wild One*. Its mottoes, "God forgives, Outlaws don't" and "Snitches are a dying breed," were big deterrents to getting witnesses to come forth and testify against members. From a law enforcement perspective, the Outlaws Motorcycle Club was not an easy group to infiltrate because its members were highly suspicious of any outsiders they met through business. In one instance, a couple of aspiring bikers wanted to be part of the gang's drug distribution operation run out of a topless nightclub. Unfortunately, the bikers' eagerness sent the wrong signal—the Outlaws suspected them of being "narcs" (they weren't). Gang members locked the doors to the club and beat the Outlaw wannabees into extended hospital stays.

Another instance involved two young African American men who wandered into an Outlaws motorcycle parts shop/tattoo parlor to get tattoos. One of the young men already had the word "Outlaw" tattooed on him. The letter-stenciled design was similar to the club's symbol. Gang members in the shop took offense at the tattoo and declared they would "beat" the tattoo off the guy. Both men were severely beaten.

Law enforcement, however, was finally able to infiltrate the group. The four-year investigation, which began in 1995, was spearheaded by the FBI's Charlotte office and the Charlotte–Mecklenburg Police Department. Many investigative techniques were used during this investigation. With all that hard evidence against the Outlaws, the efforts of the law enforcement joint task force culminated in Operation Speedball to put a halt to the gang's activities. The search warrants resulted in the recovery of more than 100 firearms, five pounds of methamphetamine, drug records, drug ledgers, several motorcycles, motorcycle parts, and other contraband. Then the arrests began.

To date, Operation Speedball has led to 33 arrests; 22 federal felony convictions on racketeering, firearms, and drug distribution charges; and seizures, forfeitures, and recoveries of stolen motorcycles, stolen parts, and property totaling in excess of $817,000. This case marked the first use of the RICO statute against a criminal enterprise in the Western District of North Carolina.

It was also the first time the Outlaws Motorcycle Club sent up the white flag in unison—most of them pleaded guilty. The investigation also led to the indictment and conviction of eight members of a Mexican drug trafficking organization that was supplying the Outlaws with methamphetamine.

Summary Checklist

In this chapter, we consider the ways information about crimes is documented by criminal investigators. A properly documented case is one that is more likely to succeed in court. See how well you are able to answer the following questions in your checklist.

1. **Can you explain the extent that gangs exist in the United States and nearby countries?**

   - Los Angeles has been called the "gang capital of America," with an estimated 120,000 gang members.

- In 2007, there were at least 30,000 gangs and 800,000 gang members active across the United States.
- By 1999, Hispanics accounted for 47% of all gang members, blacks for 31%, whites for 13%, and Asians for 6%.
- An estimated 25,000 and 50,000 gang members in Central America's El Salvador.
- The Mexican drug cartels have as many as 100,000 members.
- The Yakuza are among the largest crime organizations in the world, with 86,300 members in 2005.
- Hong Kong's Triads include up to 160,000 members.

2. Do you know the various businesses conducted by members of organized crime in the United States?

3. Do tou know the principles of the most commonly abused drugs?

All drugs, whether legal or not, fall into one of five categories:

- Cannabis
- Narcotics
- Stimulants
- Hallucinogens
- Depressants

Another element that makes a drug particularly menacing to society and that is considered in determining the degree of its legal use is its dependence factor.

Cannabis (*Cannabis sativa*) is the most commonly abused cannabis product and grows in almost all parts of the world.

- Cannabis products include marijuana, hashish, and hashish oil.
- Growers of marijuana cultivate the plant for the flowering tops, which produce high concentrations of the mind-altering substance THC.
- Marijuana cultivators have increasingly begun to conceal their growing operation by making use of "grow houses."

Narcotics are opium and opium derivatives or their synthetic substitutes and are the most effective drugs for the relief of pain.

- The withdrawal syndrome is also commonly associated with this class of drugs.
- Continued use of narcotics produces tolerance.
- As tolerance develops, users find that they require greater and greater doses of the drug to feel its effects.
- This increases the user's propensity for overdose.
- Heroin (diacetylmorphine) is a commonly abused narcotic that appears on American streets in both white and brown powder form.

Stimulants are a category of drug literally stimulates the CNS and gives the user a feeling of alertness.

- Stimulant drugs include nicotine, caffeine, amphetamine, methamphetamine, and cocaine.
- Cocaine is a commonly abused stimulant and is the most potent stimulant of natural origin.
- Cocaine is made from extracting coca base from coca leaves, which grow almost exclusively in South America.
- Methamphetamine, or "meth," is another dangerous stimulant.
- Methamphetamine is also known as speed, ice, and crystal. Like cocaine, meth is a potent CNS stimulant.

Hallucinogenic drugs are produced both organically and synthetically and create a sense of distorted perceptions in the user.

- Hallucinogens include LSD, Ecstasy (MDMA), peyote, PCP, and psilocybin mushrooms.

Depressants are potentially addictive in both the psychological and physical sense. They act on the CNS, but when taken as prescribed, they may help to relieve anxiety, irritability, and tension and to induce sleep.

- Depressant drugs include barbiturates and benzodiazepines (tranquilizers).
- Rohypnol is a brand name for flunitrazepam and is commonly known as "ruffies."

(*continued*)

Summary Checklist (Continued)

- Γ-Hydroxybutyrate (GHB) is a CNS depressant and is known as liquid X, Georgia home boy, goop, gamma-oh, and grievous bodily harm.

4. Can you explain the general structure of drug laws?

Laws governing illicit drugs appear in virtually all levels of government.

Drug penalties under different levels of government vary from one jurisdiction to the next.

Generally, criminal law considers several categories of illegal behavior regarding drug abuse:

- *Possession.* Possession usually manifests itself in one of two ways: actual physical custody of the drug, or constructive possession.

- *Distribution.* The charge of drug distribution is of a more serious nature than possession and is most commonly imposed for any exchange of illegal drugs between two or more persons.

- *Manufacturing.* Criminal charges can also be assessed for producing illicit drugs.

The Controlled Substances Act (CSA) has been the legal foundation of the federal government's battle against illicit drug abuse since its implementation in 1970.

The CSA basically took all drugs considered dangerous under existing federal law and placed them into one of five schedules.

5. Are you able to identify techniques in drug investigations?

Goals of drug investigation are to:

- Identify and locate known or suspected drug sellers.

- Understand the different types of drugs available on the street, their prices, and packaging methods.

- Identify locations of frequent drug abuse activity.

- Collect evidence on those involved in drug trafficking.

- Reduce the availability of drugs through the aggressive apprehension of drug users and sellers.

Investigators must be properly equipped with personnel, money for drug purchases, and equipment.

Legal assistance should be a required ingredient in any drug investigation.

The investigation of illicit drug laboratories is a high priority and typically begins with a base of criminal intelligence information.

Drug raids typically occur when search warrants are being served and have proven to be one of the most dangerous aspects in drug enforcement.

The reverse sting narcotic sale is one in which undercover investigators, posing as dealers, sell large quantities of narcotics to known traffickers.

6. Do you understand the problem of pharmaceutical diversion?

Pharmaceutical diversion is the diverting of legally manufactured drugs from hospitals and pharmacies to the street.

There are many restraints under the CSA for those legally handling controlled substances.

- All medical professionals who are required to handle controlled substances must register with the DEA and obtain a registration number that is unique to them.

- Drug diversion tactics may be classified under five general headings: wholesale-level diversions, illegal sales by medical practitioners, theft, fraud, and forgeries.

7. Can you identify special techniques in drug enforcement?

The DEA originated an investigative tactic called drug courier profiling.

- It involves agents observing suspected drug traffickers and developing a pattern of behavior typical of those who use commercial airlines or public highways for drug trafficking.

- The Supreme Court, in *United States* v. *Sokolow* (1989), upheld the technique of drug courier profiling.

Asset forfeiture has become an essential tool in drug control because of the increasingly high profits of the drug trade.

- The theory behind asset forfeiture is to take the profit out of illicit drug sales by seizing money or property that was either used to facilitate a drug crime or acquired with illicit drug revenues.
- On the federal level, the 1984 Comprehensive Crime Control Act (CCCA) provides civil provisions for asset forfeiture.

Key Terms

crack

crystal meth

date rape drug

dependence

designer drug

drug courier profile

flashback

freebase

Mara Salvatrucha

pharmaceutical diversion

scammers

tolerance

undercover

Discussion Questions

1. List and discuss the five categories of drugs and how the Controlled Substances Act differentiates between dangerous drugs of abuse.

2. Discuss the main drugs of abuse produced by the cannabis plant.

3. The term *narcotics* relates to a category of drugs that are distinguished in what fashion?

4. Compare and contrast characteristics of drugs in the stimulant and depressant categories.

5. Describe the hallucinogenic category of drugs. Give examples.

6. Explain how drug cases are initiated and developed.

7. Explain the various drug-buy operations most commonly used in undercover operations.

8. Explain the problem of pharmaceutical diversion.

mycrimekit™

Go to MyCrimeKit.com to explore the following study tools and resources specific to this chapter:

- *Practice Quiz:* Multiple-choice, true/false, short-answer, and essay questions.
- *Flashcards:* There are 13 key terms in this chapter. Flashcards test your knowledge of the chapter's key terms.

- *Web Links:* Check out the hotlink to *The New York Times* criminology articles.
- *Career Center:* Check out the hot links to interesting careers in criminal justice, criminology, and juvenile justice.
- *The Research Center:* Check out the Cybrary and research navigator for even more resources.

Notes

1. NATIONAL CRIMINAL JUSTICE REFERENCE SERVICE. (2001). *The growth of youth gang problems in the United States: 1970–98.* Available at http://www.ncjrs.gov/html/ojjdp/ojjdprpt_yth_gng_prob_2001/chap7.html#c.

2. Landesman, Peter (2007). L.A. gangs: Nine miles and spreading. *Law Weekly News*, December 13.

3. JOHNSON, K. (2009) Report: Gang membership on the rise across U.S. *USA Today*, January 30.

4. CARLIE, M. (200). Into the abyss: The racial and ethnic composition of gangs. *National Youth Gangs Survey 2000.* Available at http://www.faculty.missouristate.edu/m/MichaelCarlie/what_I_learned_about/gangs/racial_composition.htm.

5. JORDAN, S. (2002). El Salvador's teenage beauty queens live and die by gang law. *The Observer*, November 10.

6. CARTER, S. (2009). 100,000 foot soldiers in Mexican Cartels. *Washington Times*, March 3.

7. IBID.

8. DINGLEY, J. AND M. KIRK-SMITH (2002). Symbolism and sacrifice in terrorism. *Small Wars & Insurgencies* 13(1):102–128.

9. SCHAFER, J. R. (2003). The seven-stage hate model. *FBI Law Enforcement Bulletin.* Washington, DC: United States Department of Justice, Federal Bureau of Investigation.

10. IBID.

11. IBID.

12. U.S. LEGAL DEFINITIONS. Available at http://definitions.uslegal.com/t/terroristic-threat.

13. See http://www.usdoj.gov/criminal/ngic.

14. See http://www.nagia.org/MemberAssociations/MidwestGangInvestigatorsAssociation/tabid/62/Default.aspx

15. JOHNSON, K. (2009). FBI: Burgeoning gangs rival foreign drug cartels. *USA Today*, January 30:2A; United States Department of Justice, National Drug Intelligence Center (2009). Available at http://www.usdoj.gov/ndic/.

16. IBID.

17. MIDWEST GANG INVESTIGATORS ASSOCIATION. Available at http://members.tripod.com/~IN_MGIA/index.html.

18. UNITED STATES DEPARTMENT OF JUSTICE, National Drug Intelligence Center. (2009). Available at http://www.usdoj.gov/ndic/. Also see Copeland, L. (2009). Mexican cartels plague Atlanta. *USA Today*, March:3A.

19. IBID.

20. IBID.

21. U.S. DRUG ENFORCEMENT ADMINISTRATION. (2008). *Los Angeles International Chiefs of Police summit on transnational gangs to commence in Hollywood March 3rd–5th, 2008.* Available at http://www.usdoj.gov/dea/pubs/states/newsrel/la030308.html.

22. UNITED STATES DEPARTMENT OF JUSTICE, National Drug Intelligence Center. (2009). Available at http://www.usdoj.gov/ndic/.

23. "I remain convinced that there is no more important area in the fight against corruption than the challenge for us within the law enforcement and justice sectors to keep our own houses clean."—U.S. Attorney General John D. Ashcroft. Available at http://bvc.cgu.gov.br/bitstream/123456789/1619/1/Attorney+General+John+D.+Ashcroft%27s+Remarks+at+the+Second+Global+Forum+on+Fighting+Corruption.pdf.

24. LUNDE, P. (2007). *Organized crime an inside guide to the world's most successful industry.* DK Adult Publishers.

25. UNITED STATES DEPARTMENT OF JUSTICE, National Drug Intelligence Center. (2009). Available at http://www.usdoj.gov/ndic/.

26. IBID.

27. LYMAN, M. and G. POTTER. (2002). *Drugs in society: Causes, concepts and control,* 4th ed. Cincinnati, OH: Anderson.

28. IBID.

29. DRUG ENFORCEMENT ADMINISTRATION. Available at http://www.usdoj.gov/dea.

30. IBID.

31. IBID.

32. IBID.

33. IBID.

34. FLORIDA DEPARTMENT OF CORRECTIONS. (n.d.). *Los Angeles-based gangs—Bloods and Crips.* Available at http://www.dc.state.fl.us/pub/gangs/la.html.

35. IBID.

36. SMILEY, T. (2007). *Williams, Stanley Tookie. Blue rage, black redemption.* New York: Simon and Schuster:xvii–xix, 91–92, 136.

37. IBID.

38. IBID.

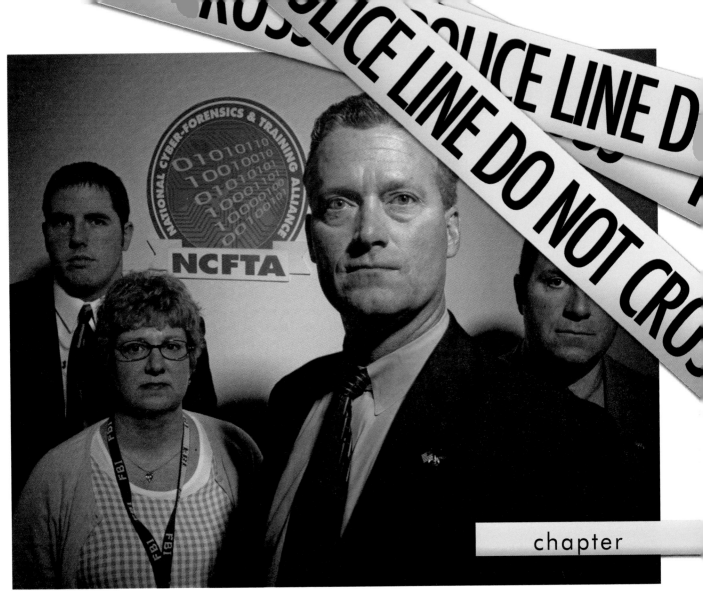

White-collar and Computer Crime

chapter

17

This chapter will enable you to:

- Understand the various types of white-collar crime.
- Understand the problem of money-laundering investigations.
- List the various techniques used by organized crime to hide or "launder" illicit financial proceeds.
- Learn the different types of confidence games and how they work.
- Describe the nature of computer crimes and the various types of computer offenses known today.
- Know what evidence to look for in the investigation of computer crimes.
- Understand the profile of the computer crime suspect.

Introduction

In the 1930s, criminologist Edwin Sutherland first coined the phrase *white-collar crime* to describe the criminal activities of the rich and powerful. He defined white-collar crime as "a crime committed by a person of respectability and high social status in the course of his occupation." Historically, law enforcement has paid little attention to the phenomenon of white-collar crime. In the past, even when a conviction did occur, offenders would typically get off with little more than a small fine and admonition by the court. Let's now consider the impact of white-collar crime by looking at the Martin Frankel embezzlement case.

Neighbors knew there was something strange going on in 44 year-old Martin Frankel's sprawling stone mansion well before firefighters found piles of documents burning in two fireplaces and the rest of the 12-room house ransacked and empty. There had been an all-day, late-night parade of limousines and leased Mercedes; armed guards, surveillance cameras, and spotlights; and the suicide of a young New York woman found hanged in a nearby house leased by Frankel. Then there was Frankel himself, a reclusive man who bought one, then another, $3 million estate on a secluded cul-de-sac in Greenwich, Connecticut's backcountry neighborhood, paying cash for both.

In May 1999, Frankel vanished along with hundreds of millions of dollars in insurance company money. He left behind a smoldering to-do list that included "launder money" and astrological charts asking, "Will I go to prison?" Among receipts found in the mansion was one for $10 million paid to a Los Angeles diamond broker.

The Frankel case was complicated to say the least. Upon his disappearance, police investigators began sorting out the clues that suggested billions of dollars in fraud. Those clues led to places such as the Vatican, a dozen Bible Belt insurance companies, and even past and present Justice Department officials.

Federal investigators uncovered an unlicensed brokerage operation on Frankel's Greenwich estates that siphoned investment money from a dozen insurance companies in Mississippi, Oklahoma, Tennessee, Missouri, and Arkansas. The companies were placed in state receivership because they could not account for the millions of dollars invested with Frankel's Liberty National Securities Inc., a firm not licensed by the Securities and Exchange Commission (SEC). Frankel systematically drained these assets through various financial accounts and transferred them into accounts outside the United States under his control. State regulators claimed that at least $218 million was missing; another estimate was as high as $915 million. Also missing was as much as $1.98 billion from the St. Francis of Assisi Foundation, a charitable organization that Frankel established in the Virgin Islands.

The scale of Frankel's operation was apparent by 1997, when Greenwich police went to interview him about the hanging of a 22-year-old woman living in a home Frankel rented for $15,000 a month. The interview took place in an office-type room with numerous computer monitors displaying information from various financial markets. The death was ruled a suicide, and the police went away. But when police returned one month later to investigate a fire, they found 80 computers, computer servers, and a sophisticated fiber-optic network tied to securities information services. It was a well thought out con.

But Frankel had even bigger plans. He established the Assisi Foundation in August 1998 and recruited the help of prominent people, including Thomas Bolan, a New York lawyer, and two priests, the Reverend Peter Jacobs and Monsignor Emilio Colagiovanni. But the operation began to crumble when Mississippi and Tennessee regulators became concerned about the money flow from local insurance companies to Frankel's unlicensed investment firm. After initial inquiries were made, Frankel's Greenwich neighbors saw moving vans at his mansion.[1]

The Frankel case was closed with his arrest on September 6, 1999, at a luxury hotel in Hamburg, Germany. Frankel's arrest stemmed from an anonymous tip.[2]

Defining White-Collar Crime

According to the Bureau of Journal Statistics (BJS), white-collar crime is not an official crime category, but it represents a unique area of criminality that differs from other categories of criminality, such as violence and property crime. *White-collar crime* is a somewhat generic term meaning different things to different people. Although white-collar offenses are less visible than crimes such as burglary and robbery, their overall economic impact may be considerably greater. The appropriate definition of white-collar crime has long been a matter of dispute among criminal justice practitioners. A particular point of contention is whether it is defined by the nature of the offense or by the status, profession, or skills of the offender.

In an effort to understand this criminal phenomenon better, the *Dictionary of Criminal Justice Data Terminology* offers the following definition of white-collar crime: "non-violent crime for financial gain committed by means of deception by persons whose occupational status is entrepreneurial, professional or semi-professional, and utilizing their special occupational skills and opportunities." Simply put, white-collar crime could be explained as "nonviolent crime committed for financial gain and accomplished by means of deception."[3] Some of the most notable white-collar crimes are insider trading, money laundering, confidence games, and computer crime.

Corporate Crime

Corporate crime is a form of white-collar crime whereby trusted executives working within a company mishandle funds or otherwise betray the trust of customers or other consumers. Motivations for corporate crime include gaining or increasing power or realizing personal wealth through mishandling funds. Corporate crime may also affect a small number of persons or millions depending on the extent of the actions of the players involved.

The 21st century is no stranger to corporate scandals. One of the best-known corporate scandals is the Enron scandal of 2001. Before its bankruptcy in 2001, Enron, the Houston-based Enron Creditors Recovery Corporation (formerly Enron Corporation; former NYSE ticker symbol ENE) employed approximately 22,000 people and was one of the world's leading electricity, natural gas, pulp and paper, and communications companies, with claimed revenues of nearly $101 billion in 2000.[4] *Fortune* named Enron "America's Most Innovative Company" for six consecutive years. At the end of 2001, it was revealed that Enron's reported financial condition was sustained substantially by institutionalized, systematic, and creatively planned accounting fraud, known as the "Enron scandal." Enron has since become a popular symbol of willful corporate fraud and corruption. The scandal was also considered a landmark case in the field of business fraud and brought into question the accounting practices of many corporations throughout the United States.[5]

Enron filed for bankruptcy protection in the Southern District of New York in late 2001. It emerged from bankruptcy in November 2004 after one of the

mycrimekit

Video: Definition of white-collar crime

biggest and most complex bankruptcy cases in U.S. history. On September 7, 2006, Enron sold Prisma Energy International, Inc., its last remaining business, to Ashmore Energy International, Ltd. After the scandal, lawsuits against Enron's directors were notable because the directors settled the suits by paying very significant sums of money personally. The scandal also caused the dissolution of the Arthur Andersen accounting firm, affecting the wider business world.[6]

After a series of revelations involving irregular accounting procedures bordering on fraud perpetrated throughout the 1990s involving Enron and its accounting firm Arthur Andersen, Enron stood on the verge of undergoing the largest bankruptcy in history by mid-November 2001 (the largest Chapter 11 bankruptcy until that of the investment bank Lehman Brothers on September 15, 2008). A white knight rescue attempt by a similar, smaller energy company, Dynegy, was not viable.[7]

As the scandal unraveled, Enron shares dropped from more than $90 to just pennies. Enron had been considered a *blue chip* stock, so this was an unprecedented and disastrous event in the financial world. Enron's plunge occurred after it was revealed that much of its profits and revenue were the result of deals with special purpose entities (limited partnerships that it controlled). The result was that many of Enron's debts and the losses it suffered were not reported in its financial statements.

Enron filed for bankruptcy on December 2, 2001. In addition, the scandal caused the dissolution of Arthur Andersen, which was one of the world's top accounting firms at the time. The firm was found guilty of obstruction of justice in 2002 for destroying documents related to the Enron audit and was forced to stop auditing public companies. Although the U.S. Supreme Court threw out the conviction in 2005, the damage to the Andersen name has prevented it from returning as a viable business.[8] Enron also withdrew a naming rights deal with the Houston Astros Major League Baseball club to have its name associated with its new stadium, which was formerly known as Enron Field (now known as Minute Maide Park).

Enron had created offshore entities, units that may be used for planning and avoidance of taxes, increasing the profitability of a business. This provided ownership and management with full freedom of currency movement and the anonymity that allowed the company to hide losses. These entities made Enron look more profitable than it actually was and created a dangerous spiral in which each quarter, corporate officers would have to perform more and more contorted financial deception to create the illusion of billions in profits while the company was actually losing money.[9] This practice drove up the company's stock price to new levels, at which point the executives began to work on insider information and trade millions of dollars worth of Enron stock. The executives and insiders at Enron knew about the offshore accounts that were hiding losses for the company; however, the investors knew nothing of this. Chief Financial Officer Andrew Fastow led the team that created the off-books companies, and he manipulated the deals to provide himself, his family, and his friends with hundreds of millions of dollars in guaranteed revenue at the expense of the corporation for which he worked and its stockholders.[10]

Other corruption cases have also gained national prominence. For example, Adelphia Communications Corporation, named after the Greek word "brothers," was the fifth largest cable company in the United States before filing for bankruptcy in 2002 as a result of internal corruption. Adelphia was founded in 1952 in the town of Coudersport, Pennsylvania by John Rigas, which remained the company's headquarters until it was moved to Greenwood Village, Colorado shortly after filing for bankruptcy. The majority of Adelphia's revenue-generating assets were officially acquired by Time Warner Cable and Comcast on July 31, 2006. LFC, an Internet-based real estate marketing firm, auctioned off the remaining Adelphia real estate assets.[11]

As a result of this acquisition, Adelphia no longer exists as a cable provider. Adelphia's long-distance telephone business, with 110,000 customers in 27 states (telephone and long-distance services), was sold to Pioneer Telephone for about $1.2 million. Had the 110,000 telephone customers been shut off versus being sold to Pioneer Telephone, those customers would have more than likely left Adelphia cable and high-speed Internet services. The potential financial damage to the creditors of Adelphia was more than $150 million dollars. Although the purchase price by Pioneer Telephone was relatively small ($1.2 million) the transaction was very significant.[12]

Upon divesting its cable assets, Adelphia retained a skeleton crew of 275 employees to handle its remaining bankruptcy issues. It still exists as a corporate entity, continuing largely to settle ongoing financial obligations and litigation claims, as well as to consummate settlements with the SEC and the U.S. Attorney.

Another case revolved around Metabolife International, Inc., an American corporation based in San Diego, California that manufactures dietary supplements. Metabolife's best-selling product, an ephedra-based supplement called Metabolife 356, once generated hundreds of millions of dollars in annual sales. However, Metabolife 356 and other ephedra-containing supplements were linked to thousands of serious adverse events, including deaths. These deaths caused the U.S. Food and Drug Administration (FDA) to ban the sale of ephedra-containing dietary supplements in 2004.

Subsequently, Metabolife's founder was convicted of lying to the FDA and concealing evidence of ephedra's dangers, and the company and its owner were both convicted of income tax evasion. A congressional investigation found that Metabolife had received thousands of reports of serious adverse events, many occurring in young and otherwise healthy people, and that Metabolife concealed the reports and acted with "indifference to the health of consumers."

In 2005, Former Tyco International chairman and chief executive Dennis Kozlowski and former chief financial officer Mark H. Swartz were accused of the theft of more than $150 million from the company. During their trial in March 2004, they contended the board of directors authorized it as compensation.[13]

FIGURE 17.1 Photo of Dennis Kozlowski (*center*), former CEO of Tyco International, leaving New York criminal court on September 12, 2002. Kozlowski was charged with fraud for allegedly pillaging millions of dollars from Tyco. Courtesy of AP Wide World Photos.

During jury deliberations, juror Ruth Jordan, while passing through the courtroom, appeared to make an "okay" sign with her fingers to the defense table. She later denied she had intended that gesture, but the incident received much publicity (including a caricature in the *Wall Street Journal*), and the juror received threats after her name became public. Judge Michael Obus declared a mistrial on April 2, 2004.

On June 17, 2005, after a retrial, Kozlowski and Swartz were convicted on all but one of the more than 30 counts against them. The verdicts carried potential jail terms of up to 25 years in state prison. Kozlowski himself was sentenced to no less than eight years and four months and no more than 25 years in prison. Then in December 2007, New Hampshire Federal District Court Judge Paul Barbadoro approved a class action settlement whereby Tyco agreed to pay $75 million to a class of defrauded shareholders.[14]

Money Laundering

Whether money has been derived through activities such as drug trafficking or corporate crime, the mere existence of large amounts of cash poses problems for those who possess it. This is because if the money is discovered, the government will seize the cash and those possessing it will be arrested and prosecuted. As such, criminals constantly search for methods to hide their financial rewards and make them appear to be legitimate. This process is known as *money laundering*. Investigations have revealed that such laundering activities commonly use the services of many Fortune 500 companies.

The History of Money Laundering

The practice of money laundering began in Switzerland during the 1930s as concerned Europeans began funneling their capital beyond the clutches of Hitler's Third Reich. In time, Switzerland's infamous numbered accounts became an enormously profitable business. Today, Swiss bank secrecy laws have been relaxed because of numerous criminal cases involving money laundering. Criminals are therefore seeking other financial havens in which to deposit their ill-gotten gains. The flooding of entire regions with drug money is one of the more sinister and surreptitious types of drug-related crime. The term *flooding*, tracked by the regional Federal Reserve Banks, seems to describe this phenomenon with great precision.

In 1985, another scandal surfaced involving the prestigious First National Bank of Boston. In this case, federal prosecutors charged that the bank was making unreported cash shipments of $1.2 million. It would receive $529,000 in small bills and send $690,000 in bills of $100 or more. The bank was fined $500,000 for violating federal reporting requirements under the **Bank Secrecy Act (BSA)**. In 1991, a New York State grand jury indicted the London-based Bank of Credit and Commerce International (BCCI) and its two principal officers for fraud, bribery, money laundering, and grand larceny after a two-year investigation. BCCI had looted depositors out of more than $5 billion, which was called "the largest bank fraud in history." In this case, bank officials knowingly made billions of dollars in loans to confederates who had no intention of repayment.

Combating the Money Laundering Problem

It's ironic that the very institutions that could do the most to stop money laundering seem to have the least incentive to do so. For example, whereas the basic fee for recycling money of a suspicious origin averages 4 percent, the rate for drug cash and other "hot" money may range from 7 to 10 percent. Perhaps one could inquire why the investment of drug money in legitimate businesses should be cause for concern. Considered very narrowly, the influx of large amounts of cash has provided some short-term financial benefits for Latin American debtor nations as well as domestic beneficiaries of illegal drug money.

It cannot be overemphasized, however, that this flood of money is not only a consequence of the drug problem but is also a major problem in its own right. For example, the money that enters the local economy is a primary cause of inflation. Even the banks that stand to gain from accommodating drug traffickers ultimately bear the costs of any losses that drug-related transactions generate. Part of the problem the United States has regarding money laundering activities is that U.S. drug users are primarily consumers rather than producers of drugs. Additionally, the United States is used as a repository for large amounts of drug proceeds.

Most drug profits are funneled to upper echelon members of drug cartels rather than the low-level producers and growers. Therefore, it is because of the tremendous profits of drug trafficking organizations that new members are constantly being lured into this illicit business. Unfortunately, profits are also so large that any losses, owing to forfeitures by the government, can usually be easily absorbed through future illicit dealings, making it unlikely that drug organizations will actually be put out of business.

Presumably, dealers consider that the risk of imprisonment or loss of assets is a mere risk of conducting business. Therefore, if we assume that the motivation behind the illicit drug trade is profit, we should conclude that government action against such a lucrative class of crime must include an attack against the proceeds of that criminal act. The success enjoyed by drug traffickers poses somewhat of a dilemma for them: how to reduce the likelihood of detection and subsequent asset seizure by law enforcement officials. This is accomplished by a criminal technique known as money laundering in which illegal cash proceeds are made to appear legitimate or the sources of illegal proceeds are disguised. As money laundering laws become increasingly more effective against the leaders of drug organizations, the risk of detection of such leaders is more likely.

The money laundering process can take many forms, including (1) simply merging illicit money with a legitimate cash source, which usually uses a business that generates large amounts of cash, and (2) using sophisticated international money laundering techniques (discussed next). The goal of the financial investigation is to reduce the rewards achieved through drug trafficking and therefore immobilize drug trafficking organizations.

Techniques of Money Laundering

On April 20, 2009, in Denver, Colorado, Edgar Diaz-Calderon was sentenced to prison for conspiracy to launder money and possession with intent to distribute cocaine. The investigation, which resulted in 53 arrests and the seizure of over $1 million in cash, showed that Diaz-Calderon was associated with organized gang activity that involved the distribution of more than 150 kilograms of cocaine in the Metro Denver area between 2005 and 2006. Using trusted runners and couriers, the cocaine was purchased in Mexico and transported to Denver. The cash proceeds of the illegal sales were then returned to Mexico to sustain the importation–distribution business cycle.[15] The Diaz-Calderon case is typical of money laundering efforts by drug traffickers and demonstrates how much money can go undetected if not properly investigated.

The amount of money earned by drug trafficking organizations and laundered through money laundering schemes is staggering. For example, a 2005 Drug Enforcement Administration (DEA) study determined that during 2003 and 2004, there were excess U.S. dollars present in Mexico that could not be accounted for from legitimate sources totaling at least $9.2 billion and $10.2 billion, respectively. It is estimated that the four major drugs that are smuggled into the United States from Mexico (methamphetamine, heroin, cocaine, and marijuana) generate as much as $22 billion per year for the sources of supply.[16]

Syndicates earn huge profits on the illegal goods and services they sell to the public and through their extortionary relations with the business world. Much of this profit is in the form of cash, and virtually all of it must be converted to legitimate forms before it can be invested or spent. Drug traffickers and other racketeers who accumulate large cash inventories face serious risks of confiscation and punishment if considerable unexplained hoards of cash are discovered. For these criminals to enjoy the fruits of their illegal enterprises, they must first convert those cash proceeds to a medium that is both easier than cash to use in everyday commerce and that avoids pointing, even indirectly, to the illegal activity that produced it.

Money laundering conceals the source of the illegal money and gives that money a legitimate history and paper trail. Despite extensive media saturation on the topic, our knowledge of the money laundering problem remains limited. Estimates of how much money is laundered are virtually impossible to make with any precision. The President's Commission on Organized Crime estimated that billions of dollars in illegal drug profits are laundered in the United States each year. The Commission further asserted that between $5 billion and $15 billion of those drug profits are laundered through international financial channels.[17]

Illegal drug transactions are usually cash transactions, commonly using large amounts of currency to pay off the various actors in each drug deal and to purchase sophisticated equipment. It is important for the trafficker to legitimize his or her cash proceeds in a fashion that permits the trafficker to spend it wherever and whenever he or she desires without attracting suspicion. Obviously, the trafficker could choose to store the cash in a strongbox or wall safe, but such methods would not be plausible for the trafficker who generates hundreds of thousands or even millions of dollars in illegal cash each year. To combat this

A CLOSER LOOK

Layering: A One-Man Smurfing Operation

A single suspect laundered more than $700,000 worth of drug proceeds for a money laundering group associated with Colombian narcotics traffickers. The suspect wired funds to bank accounts in Panama, Barbados, and Honduras. As part of the suspect's money laundering scheme, between November 1998 and June 2000, he made structured cash purchases of money orders totaling more than $600,000 without ever causing a Currency Transaction Report (CTR) report to be filed. On more than 50 occasions, the defendant made multiple small purchases of postal money orders at various post office locations, as many as 11 on a single day, keeping them below the $3,000 recordkeeping threshold. The suspect completed the money orders in his name, the name of his company, and the names of relatives and friends and then deposited the money orders into his company's business bank account. The suspect also exchanged more than $500,000 worth of what he understood was drug money for checks from various business accomplices, including numerous carpet dealers. This activity was determined to have been an intentional avoidance of federal reporting requirements.

Source: Office of National Drug Control Policy. (2008). *2007 money laundering strategy.*

technique, the Treasury Department implemented the CTR, requiring banks to report cash transactions of $10,000 or more. In 1989, the U.S. government processed an estimated 7,000,000 CTRs compared with an estimated 100,000 10 years earlier. Traffickers quickly circumvented this requirement by developing such activities as corrupting bank employees.

The many different techniques for laundering illicit proceeds are limited only by a trafficker's imagination and cunningness. An entire "wash cycle"—to transform small denominations of currency to businesses, money market deposits, or real estate—may take as little as 48 hours.

The method chosen by any given trafficker will no doubt reflect his or her own situation and any unique circumstances involved. Money laundering techniques illustrate the ingenuity of the drug trafficker in hiding millions (and even billions) of dollars of illicitly gained revenues. Money laundering techniques include bank methods, smurfing, currency exchanges, double invoicing, and acquisition of financial institutions.

Bank Methods. The most common method for laundering money is called *bank methods*. In this basic technique, the traffickers take their cash to a bank and conduct several transactions that usually involve trading currency of small denominations for larger ones. This is done for obvious portability purposes. It is also common for cash to be exchanged for Treasury bills, bank drafts, letters of credit, traveler's checks, or other monetary instruments.

During the early 1980s in Miami (considered the hub of the cocaine banking business in the United States), large daily shipments of currency would arrive and be deposited in numerous accounts, but they would then be disbursed immediately through the writing of checks payable to true or nominee names. Ultimately, these funds were deposited in other domestic accounts in the same or different banks or wire transferred to offshore bank accounts in foreign countries with strict bank secrecy laws.

Ironically, there is no requirement to report these transactions because the BSA's reporting requirements don't pertain to interbank transfers. Therefore, the biggest problem posed to the traffickers is the initial depositing of the currency into the banks. After funds are deposited, a trafficker can communicate with the bank through a fax machine or personal computer and literally route funds all over the world without ever coming face to face or even speaking with a banker. One method of conducting mass deposits, called **smurfing**, first appeared during the mid-1980s and is discussed next.

Smurfing. A trafficker provides several individuals, or "smurfs," with cash from drug sales. Each smurf goes to different banks and purchases cashier's checks in denominations of less than $10,000, thus bypassing the reporting requirement. The smurfs then turn the checks over to a second person, who facilitates their subsequent deposit into domestic banks or transports them physically to banks in Panama or Colombia. In some instances, the monetary instruments are premarked "for deposit only," making them nonnegotiable to the courier.

Currency Exchanges. Traffickers may also use either money exchanges or brokerage houses for facilitating movement of their money. Foreign currency exchanges are frequently set up as storefronts that deal regularly in large cash transactions. In using the exchange, the trafficker can avoid using traditional banking institutions and therefore avoid risky reporting requirements. Banks traditionally deal with exchange companies and customarily don't question large transactions from them. The currency exchange business can also move money in other ways for the trafficker. In particular, money sent to other jurisdictions in payment for foreign drug shipments is common. Using a dummy corporation, a

FIGURE 17.2 Smurfing chart.

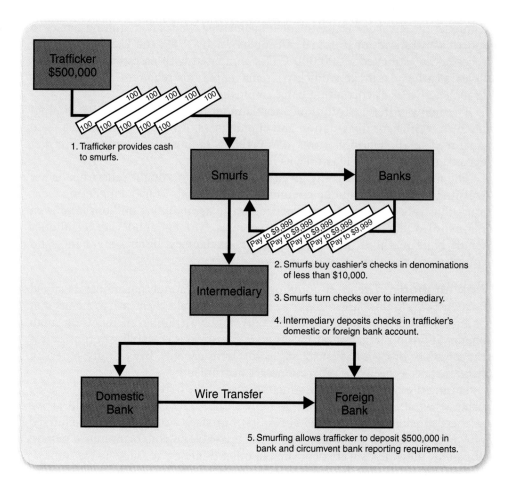

trafficker will sometimes contact his or her lawyer and request that the lawyer accept a huge deposit into the lawyer's foreign account. The lawyer will then wire the money directly into the dummy account, where it remains unsuspected.

Double Invoicing. Double invoicing is yet another popular method of hiding illicit financial gains. In this technique, a company orders merchandise from a foreign subsidiary at an inflated price. The difference between the inflated price and the actual price is deposited by the subsidiary in a special offshore account. Occasionally, the same technique is used in reverse: The company sells merchandise at an artificially low price, and the difference between the two prices is deposited in a secret foreign bank account maintained by the company.

Acquisition of Financial Institutions. This fifth money laundering method, possibly the most difficult to detect, simply involves acquiring a domestic or international financial institution. By controlling an entire institution, traffickers can go far beyond the immediate aim of concealing illicit earnings. They effectively take over part of the local banking system and divert it to their own needs. Such operations, which have been identified in South Florida and southern California, enable traffickers to manipulate correspondent banking relations, make overnight deposits, arrange Eurodollar loans, and take advantage of the abuse list (customers exempted from cash-reporting requirements).

These techniques represent only a few of the ways that traffickers hide their illicit revenues from drug sales. It is generally thought that traffickers, regardless of their national origin, make regular use of these techniques. The fact that so many different and unique mechanisms exist for money laundering makes investigation of these crimes difficult and presents many unique challenges to investigators. One great aid to law enforcement attempts was the passing of the Money Laundering

The Smurfing Process

1. The trafficker provides cash to smurfs
2. The smurfs buy cashier's checks in denominations under $10,000
3. The smurfs turn the checks over to an intermediary
4. The intermediary deposits checks in trafficker's domestic or foreign bank account

Smurfing allows trafficker to deposit $500,000 in bank and circumvent bank reporting requirements.

Control Act of 1986, which gave investigators more latitude in investigating this type of criminal activity and in uncovering these myriad techniques.

Although investigations of money laundering are routinely performed by such agencies as the Federal Bureau of Investigation (FBI), DEA, and the Internal Revenue Service (IRS), a recently established investigative unit housed under the Department of the Treasury called the Financial Crimes Enforcement Network (FinCEN) also conducts such investigations. FinCEN, established in 1990,

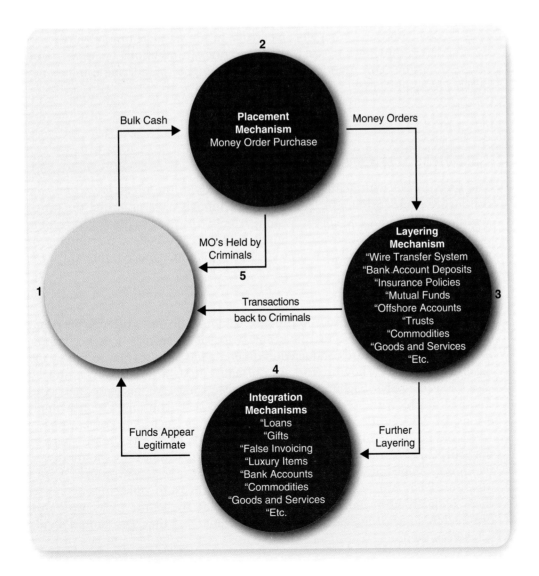

FIGURE 17.3 Typical cycle of money laundering through the use of money orders. *From Office of National Drug Control Policy. (2008). 2007 money laundering strategy.*

is a multiagency support unit that analyzes intelligence information that develops suspects in money laundering schemes. In addition to providing assistance to federal agencies, FinCEN also offers services to state and local police organizations investigating financial crimes, especially those associated with violations of the Bank Secrecy Act and the Money Laundering Control Act.

Money Laundering Using Money Orders

Money orders have proven to be a versatile vehicle for money laundering. Their use has been seen in crimes including narcotics trafficking, firearms trafficking, and depositing illicit proceeds from alien smuggling and corporate fraud.

In the legitimate world, money orders are used by approximately 30 million people annually to conduct business such as paying bills and sending money to families in foreign countries. It is estimated that more than 830 million money orders in excess of $100 billion are issued annually. The money order industry is small and easier to assess for criminals. Eighty percent of all money orders are issued by the U.S. Postal Service (USPS), Western Union, and Traveler's Express/MoneyGram. The remaining 20 percent are issued by smaller, regional companies scattered throughout the United States.

The greatest volume of money order activity is currently seen in New York/New Jersey, Los Angeles, El Paso, Dallas, Miami, Boston, and San Francisco. The extent that money orders are used is seen in national statistics. For example, the OCDETF has consistently reported that approximately 20 percent of its newly initiated money laundering investigations contains a money order component.[18] Law enforcement has documented a steady stream of money order use by launderers moving bulk cash from narcotics transactions to Mexico and other regions of Latin America. The process of money laundering using money orders is seen in Figure 17.3.

Confidence Games

The spectrum of white-collar crime also extends to the timeless scam of the **confidence game** (or "con"). For decades, criminals have practiced the art of getting something for nothing by stealing from a trusting person. When reading the following con-artist scams, it might be difficult to believe that intelligent people could actually fall victim to such manipulation. Indeed, they do. Let's examine some of the more common con games.

The Pigeon Drop

Probably the most practiced confidence game of all time, the **pigeon drop**, comes in many varieties. In this scam, a lot of losers pay a few winners. Although these scams are conducted in different ways, most seem to follow the basic pattern. Here's how it works: Con man 1 finds a wallet, purse, attaché case, or even a paper bag apparently filled with money. An unsuspecting victim standing nearby witnesses the discovery. At that time, con man 2 appears and claims that he is entitled to a share of the loot just as much as the other.

It should occur to the victim at this point that he or she should share in the proceeds. An argument then breaks out about whether they should divide the money immediately or check it out to see if it is stolen. Con man 1 says his "boss" has police "connections" and can check. A quick phone call is then made by con man 1 who then says that the money was probably dropped by some drug dealer or big-time gambler and that they should divide it between them.

The boss offers to hold the money until all three can produce a substantial amount of their own money to show that they are acting in good faith and can be trusted to keep the secret. Con man 2, apparently determined not to be cut out of the deal, produces a large sum of money on the spot to prove his reliability. Con man 1 and the victim then hurry off to get their part of the money. When the victim returns and hands over his share, it is the last he or she sees of the cons, the money or the boss.

The key to the success of this scam is the powerful acting between the cons—in particular, the bickering between the two men that makes the victim feel that he or she will be left out unless they abide by the conditions of the agreement. The reliability of the boss is the convincer (sometimes this character portrays a police detective). The amount of money in question is always so great that the victim wants to believe.

The Bank Examiner Scheme

In this scam, con artists pose as FBI agents, bank examiners, police officers, detectives, or bank officials. The victim is then contacted by them pretending to need help in conducting an investigation. The con asks the victim to verify their present balance, which is, say, $5,000. After doing so, the victim is advised that the bank's records reflect a lesser amount (e.g., $3,000), and it is suggested that someone might be tampering with the account.

Con man 1 instructs the victim to meet him at the bank, and con man 2 remains in the neighborhood and observes the victim leaving. After arriving at the bank, con man 1 meets the victim and accompanies him or her to the teller, where the money is withdrawn. During this process, the victim is told that one of the tellers might be the thief and not to act nervous. After the withdrawal, con man 1 advises the victim just to hang onto the money until the bank contacts him or her.

Later that day, con man 2 goes to the home of the victim and explains that a sting operation will occur to apprehend the suspect teller and that the victim should now give the money to con man 2 so that he can redeposit it at the "suspect" teller's window. Con man 2 then uses the victim's phone to call "the bank" and speak with con man 1. The victim is then allowed to speak to con man 1, who reassures the victim that the money will be kept safe. As a valued bank customer and upstanding citizen, the victim complies, and the money and the cons are never seen again.

The Pyramid "Get Rich Quick" Scheme

"Earn thousands the easy way. A small investment could earn you $100,000 in less than a year!" Among the oldest con games, pyramid rackets have been used to swindle millions of dollars annually, using everything from dollar bills to chain letters to more sophisticated schemes that sell franchises to unsuspecting persons who then must sell more franchises to more victims, and so on.

Theoretically, a **pyramid scheme** can continue indefinitely, but it actually "bubbles" and soon collapses because of the sheer numbers involved. A typical operation swept California during the 1970s. In the scheme, two players paid an entry fee of $1,000 apiece. Half this amount, $500, went to the top of the pyramid, while the remaining $500 from each of the two new players went to the player who recruited them. So the first player got his or her money back and then waited to move up another rung on the pyramid as each of the two new players each recruited two more players so that they could also recover their initial $1,000 investment. As each step of the pyramid was mounted, the initial player moved from rung 16, to rung 8, to rung 4, to rung 2, and finally to rung 1. After reaching the top rung, the player received the money that accumulated at the top for him or her: $16,000.

Although it may seem fairly easy for new players to induce two new players to the scheme, the numbers become astronomical. Essentially, each player on rung 16 creates two entirely new pyramids, and the progression gets bigger and bigger. For example, there are 16 players on the bottom rung, and it takes 32 new players to get them to advance to the next rung. Each of these 32 players must now recruit two new players, bringing the number to 64 total. Those 64 must now recruit two new players, each totaling 128 people. The total then jumps to 256, at which time the original 16 players have reached the top of the pyramid. However, for the players on the next rung, 512 players are needed for them to advance to the next rung. For the next group, the required number is 1,024, and so on. The California pyramid scam finally died out as cons were unable to attract enough gullible people to keep it alive.

Travel Scams

"Dear Consumer: You have just won a free vacation for five days and four nights in the Bahamas. Just call this 800 number for details." Postcards with messages such as this are becoming more common throughout the United States. The way this scam works is that when the victim calls the number, she is told that she will receive a package in the mail detailing the vacation offer. The operator then asks the victim for her credit card number, telling her that a small service charge will be made to her account if she accepts the vacation offer. The victim is assured, however, that she will have a review period to decide if she wants the package before her account is billed for the service charge. The company is slow in sending the vacation package materials, and when it does arrive, the review period, according to the company, has already expired. The company then quickly bills the victim's credit card for hundreds of dollars for its "service fee."

Home Repair Scams

The home repair scam begins with a worker who goes door to door offering repair services for a modest fee. Services include driveway repair, roof repair, and so on. Scammers accept money for repair jobs that they never finish or fail to honor warranties on home improvement projects. One such scam is the asphalt scam. Here, the worker offers to use the remaining asphalt from one job to repave a second driveway. More often than not, the worker either starts the job and then claims it will cost hundreds or thousands of dollars more to complete, or he will just lay black paint instead of asphalt on the driveway and leave town with the victim's money.

Elderly people are prime targets for such scams because many of them own their own homes, and many of those are older homes. Many such homes actually are in need of repairs, and the crafty con artist looks for this. The criminal will generally ask for a large downpayment before he or she begins the work, and there have been cases in which the worker will accompany the victim to the bank to withdraw the money. The con will sometimes use the obituaries to seek out elderly persons living alone. The con then claims to be a building or health inspector who is there to check out the furnace. Once in the basement, the con either causes damage or claims that a health or safety threat exists. Then they demand money from the victim for either repairs or reassembly.

Contest Cons

Contest cons usually begin by sending a computerized "personal" letter to the victim stating that he or she has just won a new car, a diamond necklace, a food processor, and so on. All the victim needs to do to collect the prize is visit a time-share resort. If the victim does so, however, he or she will be subjected to high-pressure sales tactics to buy one of the units. Then when prizes are given, they are usually cheap imitations of the real thing. Letters of this sort may appear urgent and may represent companies with names that resemble official organizations.

The Magazine Subscription Scam

The magazine subscription scam begins with a phone call asking the victim if he or she would like to receive five magazines for two years at no cost. The offer is that all the victim has to pay is a nominal fee, say $1.75 per week, as a service charge. The caller will then request the victim's credit card number. Victims may find that they are charged several hundred dollars of fees that are unwarranted. The scammers are so slick that consumers are unaware that they have purchased magazines until they receive the bill. Some salespeople avoid identifying themselves as magazine subscription salespeople or with the name of their company. Others encourage consumers to make purchases without giving the total costs or ask the consumer for a credit card number for "verification" purposes and then use the number to charge for unwanted subscriptions.

Because crime scenes are virtually nonexistent in cases involving fraud and confidence games, investigators should focus on learning as much as possible about the victim and those who are responsible for the crime. In addition, records and documents should be identified and examined for possible clues as to the identities of the perpetrators. Investigative efforts to identify suspects in the case are often stymied by the victim's inability to remember details about the swindler(s).

Computer Crime

Megan Meier was a teenager from Dardenne Prairie, Missouri. Soon after opening an account on MySpace, 13-year-old Meier received a message from Lori Drew, who had assumed a false identify of a 16-year-old boy, Josh Evans.[19] Meier and Josh became online friends but never met in person or spoke. Meier thought he was attractive and began to exchange messages with the fabricated Josh Evans. She was described by family as having had her "spirits lifted."[20] Allegedly, Evans claimed to have just moved to the nearby city of O'Fallon, was homeschooled, and did not yet have a phone number.

On October 15, 2006, the tone of the messages changed, with Drew saying (via the account), "I don't know if I want to be friends with you anymore because I've heard that you are not very nice to your friends."[21] Similar messages were sent; some of Megan's messages were shared with others; and bulletins were posted about her. After telling her mother, Tina Meier, about the increasing number of hurtful messages, the two got into an argument over the vulgar language Meier used in response to the messages and the fact that she did not log off when her mother told her to.[22]

After the argument, Meier ran upstairs to her room. According to Meier's father, Ronald Meier, and a neighbor who had discussed the hoax with Drew, the last message sent by the Evans account read: "Everybody in O'Fallon knows how you are. You are a bad person and everybody hates you. Have a shitty rest of your life. The world would be a better place without you."[23] Meier responded with a message reading: "You're the kind of boy a girl would kill herself over." The last few correspondences were made via AOL Messenger instead of MySpace. She was found 20 minutes later, hanging by the neck in a closet. Despite attempts to revive her, she was pronounced dead the next day.

The Megan Meier case is a sobering reminder that modern-day computer crime is not limited to criminals with a profit motive. Rather, it is evidence that cyber criminals out for revenge or other motives are keenly aware of potential victims who are young and impressionable. Worse yet, such criminals are often able to hide behind false identities while prowling the Internet and avoiding detection by the police.

With the personal computer now in many households and mainframe computers acting as the epicenter of almost all Fortune 500 companies, the problem of computer crime, or **cybercrime,** is now a mainstream social problem. According to one definition, cybercrime is "the destruction, theft or unauthorized use, modification, or copying of information, programs, services, equipment or communication networks."[24]

Some of the fastest-growing crimes in the country now are those labeled as cybercrimes, or crimes that take place over the Internet. Disturbingly, the Internet has become a popular hunting ground for child predators of all ages. It allows them to hide their identities and assume the roles of virtually anyone they choose. As a result, such criminals hide in chat rooms and sign up for popular social networking sites where children and teens socialize. Pretending to be teenagers, predators talk kids and teens into meeting with them, where they have been known to rape, molest, and sometimes murder them.

Perhaps one of the most frightening statistics about all of this is that in 100 percent of the cases, the victims met up willingly with their attacker, thinking they were meeting someone entirely different. The problem of Internet predators has become so great that many police departments have established dedicated units to investigate such crimes. In this capacity, undercover police also monitor chat rooms and try to attract predators by pretending to be teenage girls or other types of persons that might attract predators; they are then arrested. Investigators also discover Internet predators by acting on tips from parents or teens who have encountered or who believe they have come across an online predator.

For obvious reasons, cybercrime has had a relatively short history. Although electronic crime has been somewhat of a problem for the past three decades, it wasn't until the 1970s that a new term entered the public lexicon—**hacker.** Early hackers began using school computers for a number of misdeeds—the least of which was altering grades. By the end of the decade, modems (devices linking computers to telephone lines) and computerized bulletin board services emerged.

Although the first generation of hackers during the 1980s seemed more mischievous than criminal, their emergence was the predecessor for a far more insidious type of computer crime. Many large corporate computers are now "hacked" not as a prank but as a target of large-scale theft. Indeed, computers have provided opportunistic criminals with a new genre in which to ply their crimes, and many of today's criminals are quite computer literate. One early example of cybercrime involved the planting of an unauthorized program known as a Trojan horse, which automatically transferred money to an illegal account whenever a legal transaction was made. To many thieves and hackers, this was akin to striking pure gold.

Computer criminals today have posed as financial advisers or licensed brokers on the Internet and solicited investments in fictitious mutual funds.[25] In some cases, they have attempted to extort money from their victims. In one of the biggest cases of **cyber-extortion,** a computer hacker stole credit card numbers from an online music retailer, CD Universe, and released thousands of them on a Web site when the company refused to pay $100,000 ransom. In January 2000, *The New York Times* reported that the hacker claimed to have taken the numbers of 300,000 CD Universe customers. The hacker turned out to be a 19-year-old from Russia going by the name of Maxim.[26]

Defining Computer Crime

As indicated, many different types of crimes are committed through illegal use of the computer. Computer crime, however, is not well understood in the criminal justice community partially because of its newness on the criminal frontier and the level of competency required for many such offenses. Other factors also contribute to confusion about the crime, such as media sensationalizing of events involving computers. Because of this, a consensus of the definition of computer crime is difficult to obtain.

According to the National Institute of Justice (NIJ), state and federal criminal codes contain more than 50 different definitions of computer crime, each somewhat different from the other. For the sake of simplicity, let's define computer crimes as violations of criminal law that require a knowledge of computers for their perpetration.

Internal computer crimes are alterations to computer programs that result in the performance of unauthorized functions within a computer program. Such crimes have been around for years and have acquired names such as Trojan horses, logic bombs, and trap doors to indicate different programming techniques designed to carry out the unauthorized functions.

The Nature of the Crime

Computer crime is difficult, if not impossible, to detect. According to the FBI, it is believed to cost private and public businesses anywhere from $40 billion to $100 billion yearly. The gradual evolution of occupations in this field has created new opportunities for criminals, who benefit as computer programmers, operators, tape librarians, and electronic engineers. Here, criminality is removed from the street and resides in the privacy of the homes of computer criminals, many of which have raised flooring, lowered ceilings, flashing lights, and air-conditioning motors. Hence, methods of crime have changed. A new computer jargon has now developed that has identified automated criminal methods such as data diddling, Trojan horses, logic bombs, salami techniques, superzapping, scavenging, data leakage, and asynchronous attacks.

Targets or victims of computer crime have also taken on a nontypical effigy. For example, electronic transactions and money, as well as paper and plastic money (credit cards), are typical targets for automated loss. Financial transactions are typically conducted over telephone lines where money is debited and credited inside computers. In essence, the computer has become the vault for the business community. Physical assets such as warehouse inventories and materials leaving factories are also tracked through the use of computers.

The timing of computer crimes also differs greatly from traditional crimes. From a traditional standpoint, most crimes are measured in minutes, hours, or even days. In contrast, some computer crimes are measured in milliseconds (as little as 0.003 of a second).

Another atypical dimension to computer crime is that geographical constraints do not hinder the computer criminal, as with many other types of crime. A telephone with an attached computer terminal (modem) in one country can easily be used to engage in a crime in a different nation. All of these factors and more should be considered in dealing with the problem of computer crimes.

The extent that computer crime can result in violent crime is seen in the "Craigslist killer" case. In 2009, the Craigslist website came under intense scrutiny and criticism after Phillip Markoff, a 23 year-old Boston University medical student, was arrested as a suspect in the death of Julissa Brisman of New York City. Brisman advertised her erotic massage services on Craigslist. Phillip Markoff quickly became known in the popular media as the "Craigslist killer." Craigslist is a centralized network of online communities, featuring free online classified advertisements. It has sections for jobs, housing, personal ads, for sale ads, services, community, gigs, résumés, and discussion forums.

The investigation revealed that Markoff had not been sexually assaulting his victims but instead robbing them to pay off gambling debts and was keeping his victims' underwear as souvenirs of his crimes. Brisman is the only reported death in the alleged crime spree.

Craigslist defended the site, insisting that the murder is not the direct result of the erotic services ads and that without that section, those types of services would propagate all over the site in other sections. They argue that the erotic section was a good way to contain adult rated ads in one, avoidable place.[27]

Markoff's wasn't the only case that caused concern. After investigating for months, in the spring of 2009, Connecticut Police filed harassment and computer crimes charges against 38-year-old Jonathan Medina, a former CVS pharmacist who stole a woman's personal information from the pharmacy computer and posted it online in a fake Craigslist erotic services posting. The victim stated that the morning after visiting the pharmacy, she started receiving numerous phone calls from men looking for a "good time."

On May 13, 2009, Craigslist closed the "Erotic services" section of its site, replacing it with an "adult services" section where the postings would be reviewed by Craigslist employees.[28] The Craigslist cases are examples of how criminals can target victims by using legitimate computer networking businesses that offer dating or other personal services.

Computer Crime Investigations

Computer crime investigations are dynamic in nature. Therefore, their detection and investigation differ in several respects from the investigation of other more traditional crimes. These differences include:

- Physical evidence in computer crimes is different from that in traditional crimes.
- The volume of evidence encountered in computer crimes can be burdensome.
- Offenders can commit their crimes with ease.
- Offenders can destroy evidence with ease.

Such investigations require a greater amount of technical expertise by investigators and prosecutors. Despite the contrasts cited earlier, certain approaches of the computer crime investigation remain consistent. For example, such investigations generally require a considerable investment of time, sometimes taking from one month to a full year in duration. This is due, in part, to the fact that identification and analysis of data are necessary to organize information for complicated search warrants. In addition, the investigation of computer crime requires interaction between investigators and victims. Victims, because of their knowledge of computer systems, can aid the investigator in providing technical expertise.

Another commonality in computer crime investigations is that they are largely investigative in nature (i.e., standard investigative procedures can be used), using an estimated 90 percent traditional police work and 10 percent technical skill.[29]

Yet another distinguishing attribute of computer crime investigations is that they are typically proactive in nature. Proactive initiatives include the monitoring of electronic bulletin boards and regular contact with local schools and businesses to help prevent and detect possible crimes with computers.

Classification of Computer Crimes

Because computers have been used in almost all types of crimes, their classification extends beyond the simple category of white-collar crime. Computer crimes involve the use of both computer hardware and software. **Hardware** is generally considered the physical computer itself and any peripherals associated with it, such as printers, telephone modems, external disk drives, and so on. **Software,** conversely, refers to the media on which information is stored (e.g., computer tapes and floppy disks).

During the mid-1970s, the federal government attempted to amend the U.S. Criminal Code to make crimes of unauthorized acts in, around, and with the use of computers. In 1986, President Reagan authorized another law, outlawing the illegal use of computers: the Electronic Communications Privacy Act. This law basically prohibits eavesdropping on electronic mail, conversations on cellular phones, video conference calls, and computer-to-computer transactions.

In recent years, four main categories of computer crime have been identified:

1. The introduction of fraudulent records or data into a computer system
2. Unauthorized use of computer-related facilities
3. The alteration or destruction of information or files
4. The stealing, whether by electronic means or otherwise, of money, financial instruments, property, services, or valuable data

Computer crime has also been classified by the types of information loss, including modification, destruction, disclosure, and use or denial of use. These violations may involve changing information, prohibiting access to information, and removing or copying it wrongfully.

Typical Forms of Computer Crimes

Many computer crimes take the form of traditional crimes. They may, however, also concern special crimes in which the computer is the primary tool of the criminal of such crimes. These crimes have been labeled according to their criminal function and include computer hacking, scanning, masquerading, false data entry, Trojan horses, computer viruses, and others.

Computer Hacking. In its most favorable use, the term *computer hacker* signifies a compulsive computer programmer who explores, tests, and pushes the computer to its limits, regardless of its consequences. In reality, hacking may involve the destruction of valuable data, resulting in massive costs. According to a report issued by the NIJ, the typical computer hacker is a juvenile possessing a home computer with a telephone modem who uses electronic bulletin boards for a variety of illegal purposes. Such criminals may become involved in crimes such as credit card fraud and using unauthorized numbers to arrange mail-order purchases to vacant homes where the delivery can be intercepted and kept.

Scanning. Scanning is the process of presenting sequentially changing information to an automated system to identify those items receiving a positive response. The method is typically used to identify telephone numbers that access computers, user identifications, passwords that facilitate access to computers, and credit card numbers that are used illegally for purchasing merchandise or services through telemarketing. Many computer systems can deter scanners by limiting the number of access attempts and therefore create a long delay designed to discourage the scanning process.

Masquerading. **Masquerading** is the most common activity of computer system intruders. It is also one of the most difficult to prove after the case goes to trial.

It is the process of one person assuming the identity of an authorized computer user by acquiring items, knowledge, or characteristics. For one to have physical access to a computer terminal or system, many such systems require that the user enter a specified identifier such as a security code or password. Anyone possessing the correct security code or password can masquerade as another person.

An example of a clever masquerade occurred when a young man posed as a magazine writer and called a telephone company, indicating that he was writing an article on the computer system used by the phone company. The conversation revealed a detailed briefing on all of the computer facilities and applications systems. As a result, the perpetrator was able to steal more than $1 million worth of telephone equipment from the company.

Evidence showing the act of masquerading is difficult to obtain. When an intrusion occurs, the investigator must obtain evidence identifying the masquerader at a terminal as performing the acts producing the events in the computer. This task is especially difficult when network-weaving connections through several switched telephone systems interfere with tracing devices (e.g., pen registers and dialed number recorders).

False Data Entry (Data Diddling). The false data entry type of computer crime is usually the simplest, safest, and most commonly used method. It involves changing data before or during their input to computers. Generally, anybody associated with or having access to the process of recording, encoding, examining, checking, converting, updating, or transforming data that ultimately are entered in a computer can change these data.

A typical example of a false data entry, or **data diddling,** is the case of a timekeeping clerk who filled out data forms of hours worked by 300 employees in a railroad company department. He noticed that all data on the forms entered into the timekeeping and payroll system on the computer included both the name and employee number of each worker. However, the computer used only employee numbers for processing. He also noticed that outside the computer, all manual processing and control were based only on employee names because nobody identified people by their numbers.

He took advantage of this situation by filling out forms for overtime hours worked, using the names of employees who frequently worked overtime, but entering his own employee number. The scheme was successful for years until detected by an auditor examining W-2s, who noticed the clerk's unusually high annual income. A subsequent examination of the timekeeping computer files and data forms and a discussion with the clerk's supervisor revealed the source of the income.

Trojan Horses. The **Trojan horse** method is the secret placement or alteration of computer instructions so that the computer will tell a second computer how to perform illegal functions. It is unique in that it usually also allows the victim computer to perform most or all of the functions for its originally intended purposes. The Trojan horse program is also the primary method used for inserting instructions for other abusive acts, such as logic bombs, salami attacks, and viruses.

In 1981, one Trojan horse technique, the electronic letter bomb attack, received considerable news media attention because its use would have made most computers with terminal-to-terminal communication vulnerable to compromise. The attack method consisted of sending messages to other terminals with embedded control characters ending with the send-line or the block-mode control command. When the messages reach the intelligent terminals, the send-line or block-mode control command is sensed, and the entire message is sent back to the computer for execution of the embedded control character commands as though they came from the victim at the receiving terminal with all of his or her computer access authority.

Many local police computers are linked with state and national crime information networks. The Trojan horse technique can be prevented in two ways. First, send-line or block-mode types of commands can be removed from all terminals allowed access to the computer. Next, a logic filter can be placed in the computer to prevent all control character commands from being sent in terminal-to-terminal messages. Trojan horses can be detected by comparing a copy of the operational program under suspicion with a master or other copy known to be free of unauthorized changes. The suspect program can be tested with a wide range of data that might expose the purpose of the Trojan horse.

Computer Viruses. A **computer virus** is a set of computer instructions that reproduces itself in computer programs when they are executed within unauthorized programs. The program may be inserted through a special program designed for that purpose or through use of a Trojan horse—hidden instructions inserted into a computer program that the victim uses. Then the virus multiplies itself into other programs when they are executed, creating new viruses. Such programs can lie dormant in computer systems for weeks or even months and may infect entire computer networks, rendering them useless. Although the first three cases of computer viruses were reported in November 1987, hundreds of subsequent cases have since appeared in various academic and research cultures. Some cases have emerged as a result of disgruntled employees of computer program manufacturers who have contaminated products during delivery to customers.

Outlook

Viruses are easily concealed in e-mails which are spread primarily through applications such as Windows Outlook.

E-mail Attachments

The virus invades when the attachment to an e-mail is opened.

E-mail Addresses

The virus spreads by mailing itself to everyone in the user's e-mail address book. Internet chat software can also be a source for viruses.

PICT.JPG.VBS

Viruses do their damage by overwriting certain types of files, like pictures (jpg files) and music (mp3 files). They delete or move them and leave infected copies in their place.

Internet Home Page

Viruses can use Internet home pages to attempt to download programs that will copy the user's passwords and distribute them for illegal purposes.

FIGURE 17.5 The anatomy of a computer virus.

Investigators should first interview the victims to identify the nature of the suspected attack. They should then use the necessary tools (not resident system utilities) to examine the contents after a suspected event.

Superzapping. This superzapping technique stems from Superzapper, a macro or utility program used in most IBM mainframe computer centers as a systems tool. Most computer centers have a secure operating mode that requires a "break-glass-in-case-of-emergency" program that will bypass all controls to disclose any of the contents of the computer. Illegal use of the Superzapper program enables thieves, for example, to tinker with the program so that checks can be issued to their private accounts.

Salami Techniques. The salami technique is an automated form of the Trojan horse method where small amounts of assets (i.e., money) are taken from specified accounts or sources and where the whole appears to be unaffected. In this way, over time, a substantial amount of money can be diverted to the thief's personal account while going undetected.

Trap Doors. A trap door is a technique in which programmers insert debugging aids that break security codes in the computer and then insert an additional code of their own. This enables entry into the program for such purposes as false data entry.

Logic Bombs. A logic bomb is a set of instructions inserted in a computer program that looks for specific errors in a computer's normal functioning. After it has been identified, the logic bomb kicks into action and exploits the error identified. The end result is the victim computer reacting in certain ways that might result in crashing of the program.

Asynchronous Attacks. Many computer functions rely on the asynchronous functioning of a computer to complete certain functions, such as calling for the output of certain reports in a predesignated order. Frequently, many such functions are programmed into the computer at once. The asynchronous attack confuses the computer system, making it unable to differentiate one job from another.

Computer Program Piracy. Piracy is the unauthorized copying and use of computer programs in violation of copyright and trade secret laws.

Automatic Teller Machine Frauds

mycrimekit

Review: Internet-based crimes

Most states that have a computer crime statute include a provision for fraudulent use of automatic teller machines (ATMs). Typically, ATM fraud involves persons with legitimate bank accounts who made fraudulent deposits (e.g., depositing empty envelopes) and then withdrawing money from those accounts based on those deposits. Although most banks now use cameras to photograph customers, cases are difficult to make because suspects are difficult to locate. (Note: ATMs are also becoming targets of theft by criminals who simply steal the entire ATM machine. This decreases their risk of being shot while committing the crime and often enables them to steal more money than in other types of commercial robberies.)

The Preliminary Investigation of Computer Crimes

As with any preliminary investigation, each department's standard operating procedure should be followed regarding dealing with victims, evidence, and suspects. Investigators should remember that computer crimes involve persons who communicate in a language that may be difficult to understand. Because of this, a computer expert should be identified to assist the investigator in the course of the investigation. Indeed, it is imperative that every aspect of the investigation be fully understood throughout the inquiry.

The degree of cooperation by the victim will also vary from one investigation to the next. Precluding the possibility that the victim is also a suspect in the case, it is imperative that the victim understands that maximum cooperation is required to achieve both positive results and to avoid wasting much valuable time. Another problem encountered in computer crime cases is that often midway through the investigation, the victim will decide to settle for restitution and not pursue the prosecution further. Therefore, investigators should be assured by the victim that they will see the case through to the end and be willing to testify in court.

Jurisdiction is another important variable to consider early in the investigation of computer crimes. Often, a suspect computer will have been used in facilitating a crime in another jurisdiction because of complex computer networking. It is necessary, therefore, to determine what federal, state, or local laws might apply to the type of computer crime committed.

Evidence Considerations

As in the preparation of any case for criminal prosecution, the collection and preservation of evidence are critical elements. Experience has shown that the most typical defense ploy in a computer crime case is to attack the admissibility of evidence seized. Such attacks often result in the suppression of evidence that might otherwise easily incriminate the suspect.

Obtaining Computer Crime Evidence. It is fairly easy to obtain documents in computer crime cases because such documents are easily identified by noncomputer experts. These include computer manuals, program documentation, logs, data and program input forms, and computer-printed forms. Ascertaining whether they are complete, originals, or copies can be determined by document custodians.

Requesting specific program documentation may require assistance and knowledge of computer concepts to determine the extent and types of documentation required. In addition, taking possession of other computer media may be more complicated. Magnetic tapes and diskettes, for example, are usually labeled externally. Additionally, a large tape or disk file may reside on more than one reel or cartridge. In this case, assistance may be needed to check the contents of a tape or disk by using a comparable computer. The search for information inside a computer is usually highly complex and probably requires the aid of an expert. Preparing a search warrant for this task also requires expert advice. In both cases, expert advice can come from the following sources:

- Systems analysts
- Programmers who wrote the programs
- Staff who prepared the data in computer-readable form
- Tape librarians
- Electronic maintenance engineers who maintain the hardware

Advice and help from such people aid the investigator in his or her role in the investigation. When the case goes to court, the same people can offer expert testimony to establish the integrity and reliability of the evidence seized.

Examining Evidence for Criminal Content. Computers can maintain an extremely large amount of information in a small amount of space. A floppy disk is small enough to fit inside a pocket and can easily be hidden in books or taped to

FIGURE 17.6 Computer evidence. *From National Institute of Justice. (2004). Research in Brief: Computer Crime. Washington, DC: U.S. Government Printing Office.*

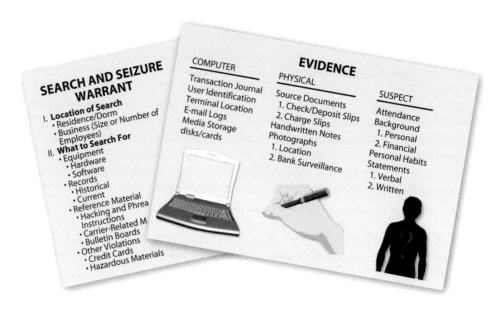

the bottom of a keyboard. The contents of a "flash drive" can hold more than enough information to make a case by providing direct evidence or direction to evidence.

If there is printer activity, this information can require a great deal of time to sort through. It is important not to blindly push this potential evidence aside; doing so may very well cost a case. Buried deep inside the amount of paper could be the secret bank account number where the suspects have hidden their assets or their list of past, present, and future victims for rape and murder.[30]

Preserving Computer Crime Evidence. Determining if the evidence can be collected and preserved for future analysis is not as easy as it sounds. Investigators must check their warrants constantly for what they can and cannot seize. If something is found that is needed but is not covered in a search warrant, the wording must be amended before seizure of that item can proceed. Seizing materials not included in a search warrant could cost an investigator the success of an entire investigation.

Some types of computer evidence require special care and attention. Because of this, storage areas must be controlled, and special care must be given to protect the evidence from physical damage. Certain care measures are required for the most common types of computer evidence:

- *Magnetic tape and disks.* These must be handled with care. This type of evidence is also easily destroyed by exposure to magnetic fields such as stereo speakers and printers.

- *Printed computer listings.* No restrictions on storage are required for paper printouts of computerized data except that they should not be stored in direct sunlight. This practice will reduce the chance of fading.

- *Computer.* All types of computers are sensitive—be careful. Even when a computer is turned off, disruption by moving it may occur. If there is a hard drive, it should be "parked" before being moved to avoid destroying information contained on the disk.

- *Additional computer hardware.* Investigators should document the configuration of a computer, what add-on equipment is involved, and how it should be disconnected. This equipment may include telephone modems, autodialers, and printers.

Investigators must also remember that the owners of computer-related evidence may have special problems when the evidence is removed from their possession. Such material may be necessary for continuing their legitimate business or other activities. One manner of dealing with this situation is to arrange for copying the material. After this is accomplished, the copy, not the original, is returned to the rightful owner.

Profile of the Computer Criminal

Computer crimes suspects can sometimes be identified on the basis of characteristics of known computer criminals who have been interviewed in computer abuse studies. Research shows that organizations are more vulnerable to people with the following described characteristics:

- *Age.* Most perpetrators are young and were educated in colleges and universities where computer attacks are common and sometimes condoned as "educational activity."
- *Skills and knowledge.* Most suspects are among the most skilled and higher-performing technologists. This is seen, in particular, in organizations in which a worker is overqualified for the work he or she is doing.
- *Positions of trust.* In most cases, perpetrators perform their acts while working at their jobs. Investigators should anticipate that vulnerabilities identified will usually result in the most qualified person taking advantage of them.
- *Assistance.* Perpetrators in many types of computer crime have been known to need assistance. This is because computer crimes require more knowledge and access than one person usually possesses.
- *Differential association.* Frequently, people working together may encourage each other to engage in unauthorized acts that escalate into serious crimes.
- *Robin Hood syndrome.* Most computer crime perpetrators interviewed in the study differentiated between harming people and organizations, the latter of which was easily condoned. In addition, they rationalized that they were only harming a computer and not causing any loss to people or organizations.

Interviewing the Computer Crime Suspect

To investigate computer crime, investigators should have a thorough understanding of the damage that a suspect can do in the computing facility. For example, if an employee believes that he or she is a suspect, the employee may have the means to go into the computer system and destroy valuable evidence, even after the crime has been committed. In addition, logic bombs could be inserted into the computer to render the system dysfunctional. In all cases, suspects should be restricted from access to the computer system after becoming a suspect except under strictly supervised conditions.

In addition, a criminal background check should be performed on both the suspect and victim. This is particularly important in computer crime cases because most employers fail to do this. Many suspects voluntarily talk with investigators because they may believe that their actions might be unethical or immoral but not criminal in nature.

CASE IN POINT:

A Ponzi Scheme[31]

The Ponzi scheme struck again, this time by a French businessman seeking fame and fortune in the United States. What made this case a little different, though, was the fact that the victims of the scam fought back—and to a certain extent succeeded—in getting back their hard-earned money.

What Is a Ponzi Scheme?

What are Ponzi schemes? They're an illegal investment named after Charles Ponzi, an Italian immigrant who settled in Boston and scammed thousands of victims in New England and others in a postage stamp speculation investment during the 1920s. According to the SEC, Ponzi said he made large profits by taking advantage of fluctuations in differences between U.S. and foreign currencies used to buy and sell international mail stamps. He raised millions of dollars from investors after claiming he could produce a 40 percent investment return within 90 days, far higher than the average 5 percent interest banks offered at the time for savings accounts.

As money poured in, Ponzi used funds from new customers to pay those who invested earlier. He ultimately took in an estimated $15 million, but the investment stream dried up as the government stopped paying cash for surrendered stamps shortly after Ponzi began his infamous scheme. He was never able to pay more than a fraction of the promised returns. Investors, hearing rumors that Ponzi had gone bankrupt, sought to get their money back. The redemption demands caused the scam to collapse.

The scams are also known as pyramid schemes, based on a geometric shape of a system in which money from large numbers of new investors at the base is funneled upward too small in numbers who invested earlier. Typically, pyramid scheme investors are offered to-good-to-be-true returns for simply investing your money and convincing others to do the same. The schemes ultimately grow too large and promoters can attract enough new investors to pay all the earlier ones. The scam then collapses.

Modern Example of a Ponzi Scheme

One of history's greatest Ponzi schemes was perpetrated by Bernard Madoff and uncovered in 2008. The Madoff investment scandal occurred after the discovery that former NASDAQ chairman Bernard Madoff's asset management business was actually a giant Ponzi scheme that generated an estimated $50 billion. Alerted by his sons, federal authorities arrested Madoff on December 11, 2008. On March 12, 2009, Madoff pled guilty to 11 felonies and admitted to operating the largest investor fraud ever committed by an individual. According to a federal criminal complaint, client statements showing $65 billion in stock holdings were fictitious, and no stocks were ever purchased since the scheme began in the 1980s.[32]

Madoff's sales pitch was an investment strategy consisting of purchasing blue-chip stocks and then taking options contracts on them, which is sometimes called a split-strike conversion or a collar.[33]

> Typically, a position will consist of the ownership of 30–35 S&P 100 stocks, most correlated to that index, the sale of out-of-the-money "calls" on the index and the purchase of out-of-the-money "puts" on the index. The sale of the "calls" is designed to increase the rate of return, while allowing upward movement of the stock portfolio to the strike price of the "calls." The "puts," funded in large part by the sales of the "calls," limit the portfolio's downside.[34]

Rather than offer high returns to all comers, Madoff offered modest but steady returns to an exclusive clientele. The investment method was marketed as "too complicated for outsiders to understand." He was secretive about the firm's business and kept his financial statements closely guarded.[35] Madoff "worked the so-called 'Jewish circuit' of well-heeled Jews he met at country clubs on Long Island and in Palm Beach." *The New York Times* reported that Madoff courted many prominent Jewish executives and organizations; according to the Associated Press, they "trusted [Madoff] because he is Jewish."[36] One of the most prominent promoters was J. Ezra Merkin, whose fund Ascot Partners steered $1.8 billion toward Madoff's firm. A scheme that targets members of a particular religious or ethnic community is a type of affinity fraud, and a *Newsweek* article identified Madoff's scheme as "an affinity Ponzi."[37]

The scheme began to unravel in December 2008 as the stock market continued to plunge. Subsequently, as the general market downturn accelerated, investors tried to withdraw $7 billion from the firm, and in the weeks before his arrest, Madoff struggled to keep the scheme afloat. To pay off those investors, Madoff needed new money from other investors.[38]

FIGURE 17.4 Photo of Bernie Madoff.

On December 10, 2008, he suggested to his sons, Mark and Andrew, that the firm pay out several million dollars in bonuses two months ahead of schedule, from $200 million in assets that the firm still had.[39] According to the complaint, Mark and Andrew, reportedly unaware of the firm's pending insolvency, confronted their father, asking him how the firm could pay bonuses to employees if it could not pay investors. Madoff then admitted that he was "finished" and that the asset management arm of the firm was in fact a Ponzi scheme. Mark and Andrew then reported him to the authorities.

Summary Checklist

In this chapter, we consider the ways information about crimes is documented by criminal investigators. A properly documented case is one that is more likely to succeed in court. See how well you are able to answer the following questions in your checklist.

1. **Do you understand the extent of white-collar and corporate crime?**

   White-collar crime is not an official crime category, but it represents a unique area of criminality that differs from other categories of criminality, such as violence and property crime.

   - White-collar crime can be defined as nonviolent crime for financial gain committed by means of deception by persons.

   - Some of the most notable white-collar crimes are insider trading, money laundering, confidence games, and computer crime.

2. **Do you know the means of money laundering and how it is investigated?**

   Money laundering is the process of taking money that was obtained illegally and making it appear to be legally acquired.

   - To combat money laundering, the Treasury Department implemented Currency Transaction Report (CTR) requirements that require banks to report cash transactions of $10,000 or more.

(continued)

Summary Checklist (Continued)

The most common methods for laundering money are called "bank methods."

- This technique is done when traffickers take their cash to a bank and conduct several transactions that usually involve trading currency of small denominations for larger ones.

"Smurfing" is done when a trafficker provides several individuals with cash from drug sales.

- Each smurf goes to different banks and purchases cashier's checks in denominations of less than $10,000, thus bypassing the reporting requirement.

Traffickers also use "currency exchanges" or brokerage houses for facilitating movement of their illegally earned profits.

- Foreign currency exchanges are frequently set up as storefronts that deal regularly in large cash transactions.

"Double invoicing" is yet another popular method of hiding illicit financial gains.

- In this technique, a company orders merchandise from a foreign subsidiary at an inflated price.

Acquiring a domestic or international financial institution is another technique.

- By controlling an entire institution, traffickers can go far beyond the immediate aim of concealing illicit earnings.

3. Do you know how confidence games work?

The confidence game (or "con") is the practice of getting something for nothing by betraying a trusting person.

The pigeon drop is a scam whereby a lot of losers pay a few winners.

The bank examiner scam occurs when con artists pose as FBI agents, bank examiners, police officers, detectives, or bank officials.

- The victim is then contacted by them pretending to need help in conducting an investigation.

The pyramid or "Ponzi" scheme is one of the oldest con games.

- Pyramid or Ponzi rackets have been used to swindle millions of dollars annually.
- These schemes use everything from chain letters to more sophisticated schemes that sell franchises to unsuspecting persons who then must sell more franchises to more victims, and so on.
- The schemes ultimately grow too large, and promoters can attract enough new investors to pay all the earlier ones. The scam then collapses.

4. Do you know about the ways computers are used by criminals to commit crimes?

The problem of computer crime, or cybercrime, is now a mainstream social problem.

Cybercrime is "the destruction, theft or unauthorized use, modification, or copying of information, programs, services, equipment or communication networks."

Computer crimes are defined as violations of criminal law that require a knowledge of computers for their perpetration.

- Electronic transactions and money, as well as paper and plastic money (credit cards), are typical targets for computer crime.
- Physical assets such as warehouse inventories and materials leaving factories are also tracked through the use of computers.

The investigation of computer crime requires a greater amount of technical expertise by investigators and prosecutors.

- The investigation of computer crime requires interaction between investigators and victims.
- Computer crime investigations are typically proactive in nature and include the monitoring of electronic bulletin boards and regular contact with local schools and businesses.

Typical forms of computer crime include computer hacking, scanning, masquerading, false data entry (data diddling); Trojan horses, and computer viruses.

5. **Do you know the steps in the computer crime preliminary investigation?**

Investigators should remember that computer crimes involve persons who communicate in a language that may be difficult to understand.

- Because of this, a computer expert should be identified to assist the investigator in the course of the investigation.

- Experience has shown that the most typical defense ploy in a computer crime case is to attack the admissibility of evidence seized.

- Evidence of computer crimes may include computer manuals, program documentation, logs, data and program input forms, and computer-printed forms.

- The search for information inside a computer is complex and probably requires the assistance of an expert.

Key Terms

Bank Secrecy Act (BSA)

computer virus

confidence game

cybercrime

cyber-extortion

data diddling

hacker

hardware

masquerading

pigeon drop

pyramid scheme

scanning

smurfing

software

Trojan horse

Discussion Questions

1. List and discuss the five most common techniques used by traffickers to launder illicitly gained drug currency.

2. What is meant by the term *confidence game*?

3. Explain the details of the pigeon drop scam and why it is used so widely.

4. List and discuss the types of crimes, both traditional and nontraditional, that are facilitated through the use of computers.

5. Discuss the crime and consequences of introducing a computer virus into a computer system.

6. Discuss the steps that investigators should consider during the preliminary investigation phase of the computer crime investigation.

7. List and discuss the primary types of computer crime evidence and how it should be collected and preserved.

8. In a computer crime, why is it important for investigators to move quickly in the investigation after a suspect has been developed?

mycrimekit™

Go to MyCrimeKit.com to explore the following study tools and resources specific to this chapter:

- *Practice Quiz:* Multiple-choice, true/false, short-answer, and essay questions.

- *Flashcards:* There are 15 key terms in this chapter. Flashcards test your knowledge of the chapter's key terms.

- *Web Links:* Check out the hotlink to *The New York Times* criminology articles.

- *Career Center:* Check out the hot links to interesting careers in criminal justice, criminology, and juvenile justice.

- *The Research Center:* Check out the Cybrary and research navigator for even more resources.

Notes

1. BAYLES, F. (1999). Man, millions vanish in Greenwich, Conn. *USA Today*, June 29:4A.
2. BLOCK, S. (1999). Fugitive goes from high life to prison cell. *USA Today*, September 7:3A.
3. U.S. BUREAU OF JUSTICE STATISTICS (1986). The impact of white collar crime in America. *Research in Brief*. Washington, DC: U.S. Department of Justice, National Institute of Justice.
4. MACLEAN, B. AND P. ELKIND (2003). *Smartest guys in the room: The amazing rise and scandalous fall of Enron.*
5. HEALY, P. AND K. PALEPU (2003). The fall of Enron. *Journal of Economics Perspectives* 17(2):3.
6. IBID.
7. NORRIS, F. (2001). Enron taps all its credit lines to buy back $3.3 billion of debt. *The New York Times*, Oct 27.
8. OPPEL, R. JR. AND A. BERENSON (2001). Enron's chief executive quits after only 6 months in job. (Jeffrey Skilling). *The New York Times*, August 15.
9. BERENSON, A. (2001). S.E.C. opens investigation into Enron; a company fails to explain dealings. *The New York Times*, Nov 1.
10. GILPIN, K. (2001). Enron reports $1 billion in charges and a loss. *The New York Times*, Oct 17; HEALY, P. AND K. PALEPU (2003). The fall of Enron. *Journal of Economics Perspectives* 17(2):3.
11. IBID.
12. HEALY, P. AND K. PALEPU (2003). The fall of Enron. *Journal of Economics Perspectives* 17(2):3.
13. Tyco International Securities class action settlement website. Available at http://www.tycoclasssettlement.com/faq.php3.
14. Shorn, D. (2007). Dennis Kozlowski: Prisoner 05A4820. *CBS News 60 Minutes.*, July 29. Available at http://www.cbsnews.com/stories/2007/03/22/60minutes/main2596123.shtml.
15. INTERNAL REVENUE SERVICE. http://www.irs.gov/compliance/enforcement/article/0,id=187285,00.html.
16. DRUG ENFORCEMENT ADMINISTRATION. (n.d.). *Money laundering.* http://www.usdoj.gov/dea/programs/money.htm.
17. PRESIDENT'S COMMISSION ON ORGANIZED CRIME (1984). *The impact.* Washington, DC: U.S. Government Printing Office.
18. U.S. MONEY LAUNDERING THREAT ASSESSMENT. *2007 national money laundering strategy.* Washington, DC: U.S. Government Printing Office (2008).
19. WOODARD, T. Prosecutor to review MySpace suicide. *Fox2News, St. Louis.* Available at http://www.myfoxstl.com/myfox/.
20. POKIN, S. (2007). "MySpace" hoax ends with suicide of Dardenne Prairie teen. *St. Louis Post-Dispatch*, November 11.
21. PARENTS SAY FAKE ONLINE "FRIEND" LED TO GIRL'S SUICIDE. *CNN*, November 17. Available at http://www.cnn.com/2007/US/11/17/internet.suicide.ap/index.html.
22. Anonymous. (2008). Annal of crime: The friend game. *The New Yorker*, January 21.
23. TAYLOR, B. (2007). Lawyer: Mother unaware of cruel messages. *Associated Press*, December 5.
24. PERRY, R. (1986). *Computer crime.* New York: Franklin Watts.
25. ROSNOFF, S. M., et al. (1998). *Profit without honor.* Upper Saddle River, NJ: Prentice Hall.
26. HACKER'S RANSOM. (2000). *USA Today*, January 11:3A.
27. JORDAN & SAMANTHA O&C. (2009). Craigslist to pull erotic services ads. Examiner, May 14. Available at http://www.examiner.com/x-2092-Sex-Scandal-Examiners~y2009m5d14-Craigslist-to-pull-erotic-services-ads.
28. STONE, B. (2009). Craigslist to remove category for erotic services. *The New York Times*, May 13. Available at http://www.nytimes.com/2009/05/14/technology/companies/14craigslist.html.
29. NATIONAL INSTITUTE OF JUSTICE. (1989). *Research in Brief.* Washington, DC: U.S. Department of Justice, National Institute of Justice, June.
30. CLARK, F. and K. DILIBERTO (1996). *Investigating computer crime.* Boca Raton, FL: CRC Press.
31. FEDERAL BUREAU OF INVESTIGATION. (2000). Available at http://www.fbi.gov.
32. REID, T. (2008). Wall Street legend Bernard Madoff arrested over $50 billion Ponzi scheme. *Times Online*, December 12. Available at http://www.timesonline.co.uk/tol/news/world/us_and_americas/article5331997.ece.
33. MOYER, L. (2008). Could SEC have stopped Madoff scam in 1992?. *Forbes*, December. Available at http://www.forbes.com/business/2008/12/23/madoff-fraud-sec-biz-wall-cx_lm_1223madoff.html.
34. See: http://www.reuters.com/article/topNews/idUSTRE52A5JK20090311?pageNumber=2&virtualBrandChannel=0&sp=true
35. BIGGS, B. (2009). The Affinity Ponzi scheme. *Newsweek*, January 3. Available at http://www.newsweek.com/id/177679.
36. ASSOCIATED PRESS. (2009). Tough task ahead to find Madoff money, co-schemers. March 13. Available at http://www.google.com/hostednews/ap/article/ALeqM5hnkPe640MG8WMCAvAwv5GqtqxsOAD96T6K8G0.
37. BIGGS, B. (2009). The Affinity Ponzi scheme. *Newsweek*, January 3. Available at http://www.newsweek.com/id/177679.
38. IBID.
39. CARUSO, D. (2009). A trusted man, $50B, a "giant Ponzi scheme." *Associated Press.* Available at http://seattletimes.nwsource.com/html/businesstechnology/2008508111_invest13.html.

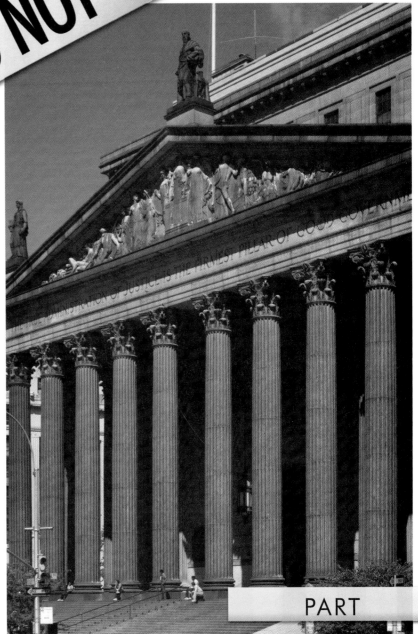

Prosecution

chapter 18   Preparation for Court

PART

7

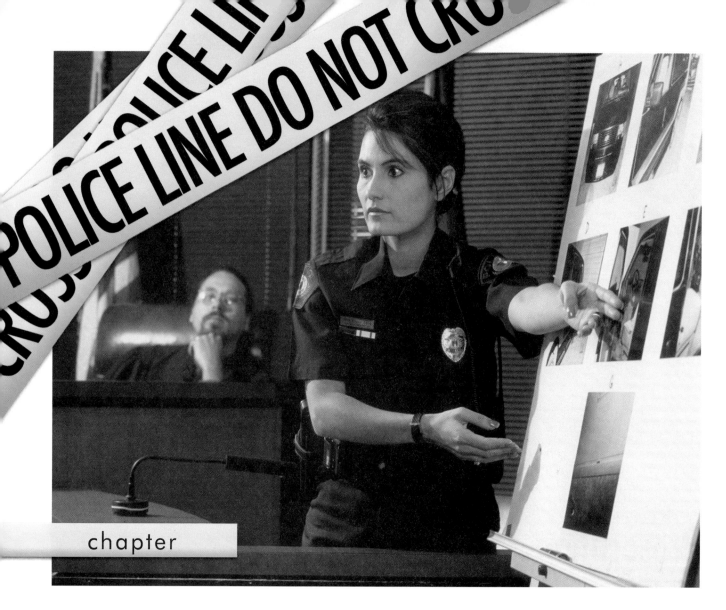

18

Preparation for Court

This chapter will enable you to:

- Learn the role of pretrial procedures in prosecution of the defendant.
- Understand how the criminal trial process operates.
- Evaluate the differences between direct and cross-examination.
- Learn how investigators prepare for court.
- Understand the techniques most commonly used by defense attorneys to discredit an investigator's testimony.
- Learn the importance of good courtroom demeanor when testifying in court.

Introduction

Not all criminal cases go to trial. In fact, most are settled outside the courtroom through the plea-bargaining process. For cases that make it to the trial stage, however, it is imperative that the evidence be well organized and that the investigator, who is essentially the "star witness," be prepared to give skilled courtroom testimony in the case. As we have discussed throughout the book, the admissibility of evidence in court is the compelling reason for investigators to follow closely the correct procedures in evidence collection. After investigators are satisfied that the evidence has been collected appropriately, the question of how best to present the evidence to the judge and jurors is addressed. For such a critical task, the role of the investigator in the courtroom is not always understood by all investigators. After all, police officers spend most of their time on the street and not in the courtroom. In this chapter, we examine several critical aspects of the courtroom process and how this important criminal justice function interacts with the duties of the criminal investigator.

Preparing for Trial

The importance of proper trial preparation cannot be overemphasized. In some instances, officers are overly casual about their prospective trial appearances. This often results in their appearing unprepared in court to testify effectively. The following principles should be understood and observed by officers in efforts to adequately prepare for court presentation.

First, officers should cooperate fully with prosecutors in the preparation of trial testimony and other evidence. Requests from the prosecutor's office should be complied with in all respects, when possible. If for some reason, a request cannot be fulfilled, the prosecutor's office should be made aware of the problem and alternate mutually agreed upon plans. Sometimes poor relations between the prosecutor's office and the police department cause a lack of communication or cooperation between these agencies. Such problems benefit no one but the criminals being brought to trial. Police agency managers must make it clear to all police officers that full and willing cooperation with prosecutors is expected by the department. Political feuds, "turf wars," personality conflicts, and the like cannot be tolerated. If a problem arises, it should be resolved quickly and without regard to who was right and who was wrong, and steps should be taken by the department to minimize the possibility of the same problem arising again in the future.

One of the typical areas of conflict between prosecutors and police revolves around the issue of when a case presented by the police will be brought to trial by the prosecutor's office. When the prosecutor declines to prosecute or a pretrial plea bargain is arranged that appears to be excessively favorable to the defendant, it is sometimes difficult for police officers who have labored on the case to understand why the matter is not being carried forward to trial. Police resentment toward the prosecutor's office is frequently the result. Officers must understand that the prosecutor's job is a difficult one and that sometimes hard decisions have to be made, decisions that may be unpopular with the police and others. For example, the heavy workload burdening the average prosecutor's office and the lack of adequate manpower to deal with that workload sometimes limit the number of cases that can be brought to trial. The result may be plea bargains or a decision not to go to trial on minor cases or on cases that appear to the prosecutor to be weak or to have technical problems that may make a successful trial result doubtful. The prosecutors are in the best position

FIGURE 18.1 Diagram of the relationship between police and prosecutors.

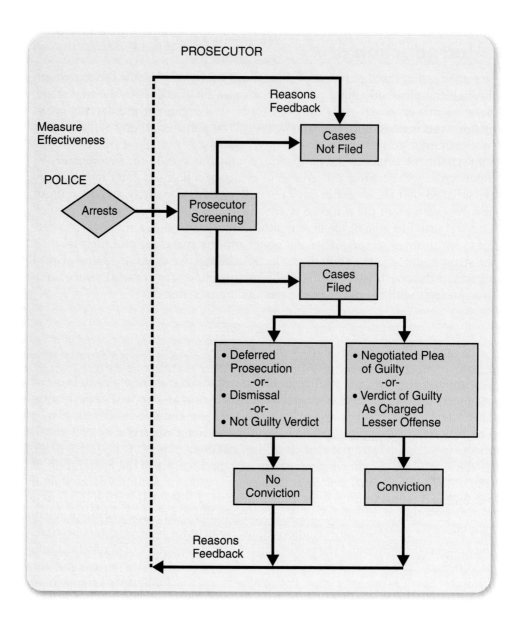

to judge the strength of the case and the probability of conviction, and officers should be sufficiently well-versed in the rules of evidence and the realities of the criminal justice system to accept the prosecutor's decision without resentment or recrimination. Blaming the prosecutor for the shortcomings of the judicial process is counterproductive and should be avoided.

This is not to say that all prosecutors are blameless when difficult working relationships develop between their office and the police. Prosecutors often share in the problem by not providing appropriate and timely feedback to police personnel on case progress and decisions, failing to brief officers adequately before trial, failing to work cooperatively with officers responsible for the evidence control aspects of criminal cases, and related matters. When poor prosecutor–police relations exist, there is generally sufficient blame to go around. The larger point to be made is that the police and the office of the prosecutor must come to understand that they are on the same team and each must take the steps necessary to maximize their collective efforts. Several steps can be taken to accomplish this.

For example, whenever possible, a **pretrial conference** should be held between the prosecutor and all officers testifying in a given case. Often this is difficult because of the busy schedules of both police and prosecutors, but it should be done in all cases when feasible and without fail in cases involving serious crimes or in those in which the testimony may be complicated.[1]

Regardless of the normal procedure, in any case in which police officers involved believe that a conference with prosecutors is needed, a request for such a conference should be made. If, after such a request, the prosecutor's office refuses or fails to hold the conference, this fact should be noted in the appropriate departmental records for the protection of the department and the officers concerned.

Officers should provide prosecutors with all information relevant to the case. No detail should be considered too minor because many cases turn upon minute factual or legal points, the significance of which may become apparent only in the full context of the trial. In particular, officers should disclose the following:

1. *Information beneficial to the defendant (disclosure of exculpatory evidence).* The prosecution's job is to convict the guilty, not the innocent. It is therefore the ethical as well as the legal obligation of every officer to disclose to the prosecution any information that may tend to establish the innocence of the defendant as well as guilt. From the purely legal standpoint, failure to disclose exculpatory matters may lead to a wrongful conviction, a mistrial, a reversal on appeal, or other unfavorable results.

2. *Information revealing flaws in the prosecution's case.* Full disclosure should be made by police to the prosecutor's office of any problems that may be associated with the evidence in the case. This is a frequent source of dissatisfaction with prosecutors, who may sometimes believe they have been misled into bringing a case to trial when some defect in the case, known to the police but unknown to the prosecutors, makes conviction unlikely. For example, if an officer knows or suspects that a search was or may have been unlawful or an arrest invalid, the problem should be disclosed to the prosecutor, either in the written report, during the pretrial conference, or by other means. This is not an easy thing for an officer to do, especially if the defect is due to some error on the part of the officer. But candor is vital, however painful or embarrassing it may be. In many instances, the prosecutor who is aware of such a problem may be able to deal with it effectively at the trial, avoiding adverse consequences from the defect. By contrast, when such a defect surfaces unexpectedly during the trial, the prosecutor is often powerless to save the situation, with resulting embarrassment for all concerned. Advance disclosure, however painful, greatly minimizes the potential ill effects of flaws in any case.

3. *Familiarity with the rules of evidence.* Officers should be familiar with the basic rules of evidence applicable to the court in which the trial is to be held. Although dealing with evidentiary questions at the trial is the province of the prosecutor and such questions will ultimately be decided by the trial judge, an understanding of the applicable rules of admissibility will assist police in several ways, including the following:

    • It will enable officers to identify and discuss with prosecutors possible flaws in the case before the trial date.

    • It will help officers prepare and give their testimony because fundamental errors (e.g., testifying in a forum that will render the testimony as inadmissible hearsay) can be avoided.

    • It will help officers to understand the reasons behind a prosecutor's strategy in the trial of a given case and will also help them to accept the decision without resentment when a prosecutor decides not to take a case to trial because of evidentiary problems.

Before the trial date, the officers should review carefully all reports and other documents relevant to the case to ensure that they are completely familiar with all of the pertinent facts. The more complex the case, the more important this step becomes. Nothing destroys the chances of a conviction more quickly than a police officer on the witness stand who is visibly unfamiliar with the facts and whose testimony is thus incomplete and generally lacking in credibility to the jury.

4. *Notes and reports in the courtroom.* In many instances, officers may wish to carry reports or other documents into the courtroom for reference while they are testifying. In some types of cases, particularly traffic cases, this is routine in many courts. However, in any case in which the use by police officers of notes, reports, or other items to refresh their memory is not automatic or routine in that particular court, the officer should discuss with the prosecutor in advance of the court date the necessity for and the desirability of carrying such aids to the witness stand. Although rules of evidence vary in different courts, in general, anything that the officer uses while on the witness stand to refresh his or her memory may be seen by the defense attorneys and may be used by them to cross-examine the officer or otherwise to attack the prosecution's case. Thus, the decision to take such items into the courtroom for use during testimony is not a matter to be taken lightly, and it should be discussed fully with the prosecutor before the trial whenever possible.

5. *Physical evidence.* Procedures for getting evidence and related materials to court vary among jurisdictions. In some cases, the prosecutor's office may take custody of evidence that is planned for introduction in court in a pending trial and make arrangements for its availability at trial. In other instances, it falls upon the police department to ensure that evidence requested by the prosecutor is available in court in accordance with established schedules provided by the prosecutor. Whatever the arrangement, the police should provide any assistance requested by, or necessary to, the prosecution to ensure that all of the physical evidence pertinent to the case will be available at the time of trial. This includes, for example, transporting exhibits to the courtroom and ensuring the availability of any supporting documentation (e.g., chain-of-evidence receipts) that may be needed. Laboratory certificates or other forensic reports that may be required in connection with the case should also be ready for presentation.

6. *Witnesses.* Failure of witnesses to appear at trial is a recurrent problem and one that often results in dismissal of criminal charges against defendants or failure of the prosecution's case. Officers should provide prosecutors with assistance as needed in ensuring that witnesses will be present and ready to testify on the day of the trial. The extent of this assistance should depend on local practice and any requests that may be made by the prosecutor's office in a specific case. In some jurisdictions, for example, victim and witness advocates are available to assist in this effort. Ideally, the prosecutor's office might fulfill most or all of these functions, but caseloads and lack of manpower often make it impossible for the prosecutor to interview witnesses adequately in advance of the trial. In addition, the police officer has usually dealt personally with the witnesses during the investigative stage of the case and may therefore be the person best able to work with the witnesses in the trial phase and to make certain they are ready, willing, and able to testify as planned. Therefore, unless local

practice or a specific request dictates otherwise, officers should be prepared to ensure that witnesses:

- Have been informed of the date, time, and place of trial
- Have transportation to the place of trial
- Have been adequately informed of what is expected of them during testimony
- Have been advised to respond truthfully to questions posed to them on the stand
- Have been advised to state facts and not to offer personal opinions or conjecture while on the stand unless requested to do so by the prosecutor
- Have been briefed on any other matters that will enable the witness to testify in a timely and effective manner[2]

Police officers should also ascertain whether the witnesses have any questions regarding the trial, whether regarding legal matters or other aspects of the witnesses' appearance in court. Questions that the officer cannot readily and fully answer should be referred to the prosecutor for clarification and the clarification transmitted to the witness.

7. *Communication with defense attorneys.* Defense attorneys frequently attempt to interview police officers about a case in the hope of developing information that will enable them to achieve a favorable result for their clients. There should be no communication between officers and defense attorneys regarding pending criminal cases without the express approval of the prosecutor's office.[3]

8. *Testifying for the defendant.* On some occasions, the defense attorney may summon a police officer as a witness on the defendant's behalf. This places the police officer in an extremely awkward position. The generally accepted practice is that officers shall not testify for a defendant in any criminal case without being legally summoned to appear, prior knowledge of the agency chief executive, and written authorization of the prosecutor's office. However, regardless of department policy or any other factor, if the officer is subpoenaed by the defense and the subpoena is not quashed, the officer is obligated to appear and testify. Any officer receiving such a subpoena should immediately notify the officer's supervisor (or other designated department official) and the prosecutor's office.

Going to Court

Before actually attending the criminal court proceeding, officers should ready themselves for the situation. One of the first steps is for the officer to prepare him- or herself psychologically by strengthening his or her feelings of confidence and self-assurance. Officers should also realize that as witnesses, they are also on display, as they are when on duty. It is a simple fact that the general public expects more stringent behavior from a law enforcement officer than from an average citizen. As a result, the following steps should be followed before entering a courtroom:

- *Know which courtroom you'll be testifying in.* If you are unfamiliar with the particular courthouse or courtroom, check it out before the trial so you will know your way around.
- *Do not discuss anything about the case in public or where your conversation might be overheard.* Anyone could be a juror or defense witness.
- *Treat people with respect, as if they were the judge or a juror.* Your professionalism, politeness, and courtesy will be noted and remembered, especially by those who see you in court in an official capacity.

mycrimekit
Review: Types of witnesses

- *Do not discuss your personal life, official business, biases, prejudices, likes and dislikes, or controversial subjects in public, for the same reasons as listed above.* You might impress a judge, juror, or witness the wrong way.
- *Be punctual.* Judges and attorneys have little patience with officers appearing in court late, so be on time. Know when you will be expected to testify.
- *Dress appropriately.* Look businesslike and official. If in uniform, it should be neat, clean, and complete. If not in uniform, a sport coat and slacks are as appropriate as a business suit.
- *Avoid contact with the defense counsel and any defense witnesses before the trial.* Assume that they will try to get you to say something about the case to their advantage.

These suggestions, in addition to the pretrial conference, will prepare an officer well for the courtroom experience. Above all, however, officers are expected to tell the truth.

The Investigator as a Professional Witness

The **testimony** given by the investigator is a crucial part of any criminal trial. An experienced and knowledgeable witness can make the job of the prosecutor and subsequent conviction of the defendant much easier. Conversely, a witness who is disorganized, unkempt, and unclear in thought can inadvertently sabotage even the best of criminal cases.

Preparing for Court

The best way for investigators to prepare for trial is not to wait for one or two days before trial to get organized but to keep the rules of evidence in mind from the beginning of the investigation through its closure (months or even years, in some cases). In addition, the investigator should be sure to meet with the prosecutor sometime before trial for the pretrial conference. The officer should check all personal reports and notes pertaining to the case and be sure that he or she has sufficient information to respond to the anticipated "who, what, when, where, why, and how" questions.

Reviewing Evidence and Reports

Before the trial, the investigator should go back over his or her list of evidence and be sure that all is accounted for and easily identifiable. The chain of custody should also be reexamined to be sure that all necessary persons who were

FIGURE 18.2 A model of a courtroom. Steve Gorton, ©Dorling Kindersley.

FIGURE 18.3 Prosecutor examining a criminal investigator. Courtesy of Mike Himmel.

involved with the evidence will be available if needed to testify in court. The investigator should also consider how the evidence will be transported to court and who will maintain possession of it after the court proceeding is underway. In the case of drug or forensic evidence, it is likely that the police chemist will already have custody and transport it to court. The investigator, however, might be required to locate and transport other items in evidence, such as written statements, cassettes or videotapes of transactions and statements, or photographs. All such evidence should be closely reviewed by the officer before the trial.

Because the investigator may not testify solely from notes and reports, they should be reviewed before the trial. Although lawful and appropriate to do so, the defense attorney may inquire of the officer on the witness stand whether this was done before trial and may even attempt to take custody of the report to place into evidence under the "past recollection recorded" exception to the hearsay rule. If the defense attorney gains access to the official report of the investigator, the report will be used to attack the **credibility** of the investigator. One typical defense ploy is to attack the credibility of the officer by highlighting any inconsistencies between the testimony given by the officer and what is reflected in the official report. An inconsistency can be just about anything but includes both facts testified to that differ from the report or a seemingly important fact in the report that the witness failed to mention in his or her testimony.

In the event that this occurs, it is usually a better idea to acknowledge the discrepancy and not become defensive about it. The prosecutor can then decide

Investigator's Courtroom Checklist[4]

- ☑ Elements of offense
- ☑ Probable cause for arrest
- ☑ Defendant's story
- ☑ Confession of suspect
- ☑ Prior statements and testimony of witnesses
- ☑ Reliability of witnesses
- ☑ Warrants and affidavits
- ☑ Physical evidence
- ☑ Exhibits, sketches, and diagrams

whether or not to "clean up" the problem through additional questioning if it appears to be of any consequence to the prosecution's strategy.

Credibility as a Witness

Other than the technique cited earlier, defense attorneys use other means to attack an officer's credibility. This is usually accomplished through attempting to demonstrate the officer's bias or that he or she is lying. Bias can be raised in many different circumstances. For example, the defense attorney can try to convince the jury that the officer is just trying to protect his or her conviction record by embellishing his or her answers to make the suspect look more guilty, thus resulting in a conviction.

In addition, racial bias can sometimes be argued if the defendant is a minority and is a different ethnic background from the officer. In this case, the officer must testify only to the facts of the case that indicate guilt of the defendant, not on stereotypic perceptions of the defendant's racial or ethnic group. Credibility can also be attacked on the basis of the officer's reputation for truthfulness. This is most typically used against undercover officers, who are required to work proactively and assume a false identity (e.g., a cover story and an assumed name). It is common for the attorney to have the officer affirm that he or she was required to "lie" while working undercover and then turn around and try to convince the jury that the officer is a liar by nature. If successful, the defense can argue that the investigator's testimony is not credible.

Appearance in Court

If for any reason it appears that the officer will be late in appearing for a court date or will be unable to appear at the specified time, he or she must notify the court as soon as possible. The notification should include the officer's name, the defendant's name, the court in which the appearance is scheduled (including the name of the presiding judge, if known), and the reason for the absence or tardiness. When absence or tardiness occurs, the matter should be reviewed by the officer's supervisor or other designated department official. If the reasons are inadequate, the matter may be referred for disciplinary action.

Some fail to appreciate the importance of the officer's physical appearance and personal conduct while the officer is testifying in court. In reality, these matters are of the greatest possible significance and literally can make or break a case. In this regard, there are several matters that officers should know when appearing in court.

Officers should dress appropriately when testifying in court. The International Association of Chiefs of Police (IACP) states that officers' personal appearance in court should "conform to the highest professional police standards." Uniformed personnel should wear the departmental uniform approved for such appearances; detectives and other plainclothes personnel should conform to their departmental dress standards for courtroom testimony.[5] Whether the officer is in uniform or in civilian dress, the clothing should be neat and clean, the shoes should be shined, and similar matters should be attended to. This is not just a matter of departmental pride; psychological studies reveal that jurors frequently give less credibility to the testimony of witnesses who are dressed sloppily. This is why exceptional care is taken by defense attorneys in dressing their clients (particularly in high-profile cases) in the most appropriate clothing. If the officer is in civilian clothes, conservative dress is normally appropriate. Extreme styles of clothing may prove distracting to the jurors, causing them to pay less attention to the substance of the officer's testimony and even in some cases arousing hostility toward the officer. Although the investigator may wear faded blue jeans when on duty, it is important for him or her to dress more formally for court. Some disagreement exists in this area because some think that the witness's choice of clothing should coincide with the atmosphere of the community. Others believe that a uniformed officer should wear plain clothes in court to avoid the authoritarian appearance depicted by the uniform.

The foregoing are general rules only; departmental guidelines regarding courtroom attire should be followed at all times. This includes specific courtroom regulations regarding the carrying of firearms in the courtroom.

Courtroom Demeanor

The investigator should also remember that a certain amount of theatrics plays a role in a trial. Both the judge and jury will be watching the investigator's **demeanor** closely as well as listening to what he or she has to say. First impressions can make a difference. Juries expect a certain type of person as a police witness. They expect that an organized, intelligent, serious, no-nonsense kind of person will be representing the government. There are times, however, when witnesses may reveal a sense of humor, and the jury can be impressed. Such displays of humor in the courtroom should not be directed toward anyone in particular and should be made with caution so as not to offend any member of the jury.

Testifying in Court

The manner in which an officer testifies may be as important as the content of the testimony. An officer's conduct on the stand often determines the degree of credibility that will be given to the officer's statements by the jury. Thus, the demeanor of the officer on the stand may be critical to the outcome of the case. Officers should remember that a trial is an adversarial proceeding and that defense attorneys will not hesitate to take advantage of any shortcomings displayed by the officer while on the witness stand. Therefore, officers must keep several principles in mind while testifying in court, including the following:

1. *Confine the testimony to known facts.* Officers should normally restrict their statements to those that are personally known by them to be the truth. If the officer is making a statement based on information or belief only, that should be made clear in the testimony. Defense attorneys are skilled at finding discrepancies in an officer's testimony and using those discrepancies to the detriment of the officer and the prosecution's case.

2. *Avoid expressing opinions or conclusions except when they are specifically authorized by the rules of evidence.* Police officers normally testify as "lay witnesses," meaning that they should state only facts and not express opinions or engage in conjecture or speculation. In some specific instances, lay witnesses are permitted to express opinions, and this applies to police officers as well as to any other witness. However, officers should not offer opinions or conclusions on **direct examination** unless an opinion or conclusion has been specifically solicited by the prosecutor. Officers should avoid expressing opinions during **cross-examination** by the defense attorney; when the defense attempts to get an officer to express an opinion, it is usually with the intent of using that opinion to embarrass the officer and discredit the officer's testimony. If the defense attorney on cross-examination asks the officer to express an opinion, the officer should delay answering to allow the prosecution an opportunity to object.

3. *Do not volunteer information.* Officers should respond only to the question asked. They should not volunteer information over and above the minimum required to answer the question posed. There are two reasons for this.

First, if the officer is testifying on direct examination, the prosecutor is intentionally attempting to place specific facts before the jury in a predetermined order. If the officer volunteers information that has not been requested, this may disrupt the prosecution's presentation of the case.[6] It may also provide the defense with an unexpected windfall that the defense can exploit to the benefit of the defendant and the detriment of the prosecution.

Secondly, if the officer is testifying on cross-examination, the defense attorney may be deliberately attempting to manipulate the officer to volunteer something that the defense can use to discredit the officer, the prosecution's case, or both. Defense attorneys are skilled in this technique. Therefore, on cross-examination, the officer should respond only to the question asked to avoid giving the defense an opening that may prove fatal to the prosecution.

4. *Speak calmly and audibly in a natural voice.* Always speak in a calm tone of voice. Keep the voice at its normal pitch; do not attempt to alter the natural voice because this causes stress and will be sensed by the jury.

   Speak in a tone of voice that is clearly audible to the jurors. Officers must remember that it is the jury that will decide the case, and jurors will not be persuaded by testimony they cannot hear. Studies indicate that when jurors have difficulty hearing or understanding the witnesses' testimony, their attention span becomes limited, they lose interest in the witness, and the witness's evidence is therefore wasted. This does not mean that the witness should shout when on the witness stand, but particularly in courtrooms where microphones are not used, testifying officers should make certain that they speak at a level that will make their words audible to the jury without requiring the jurors to strain to hear what is being said.

5. *Use plain, easily understood terms.* The officer must testify in plain, easily understood language. If the jury does not understand the words being used, the testimony will be unpersuasive. Officers should avoid using police terminology or slang; such terms confuse many jurors and may convey an adverse impression of the witness. This is a common error among police officers inexperienced in courtroom testimony, and it should be avoided.

   If technical terms are used, they should be explained in a straightforward manner, without any hint of condescension. Jurors, like anyone else, do not like to be patronized or talked down to.

6. *Maintain self-control.* During the stress of a courtroom appearance, it is often difficult for a witness to retain his or her composure. This is particularly true when a defense attorney is deliberately attempting to goad the witness, which is an all-too-common tactic. However, keeping one's self-control is vital on the witness stand, whatever the provocation.

   There is an old saying that "he who loses his temper loses the battle." This applies in the courtroom, too. The witness who loses his or her temper on the witness stand makes the defense attorney's whole day. Studies indicate that when any witness becomes visibly angry or otherwise loses composure, the jurors tend to lose respect for that witness and thereafter give that witness's testimony less weight. This is particularly true for police witnesses. Jurors apparently feel that a police officer who cannot retain self-control is not a credible witness—or a good police officer.

   One aspect of retaining self-control is remaining courteous on the stand. It is only human to feel the need to make a sharp or sarcastic retort to some insulting question or comment by the defense attorney, but to do so plays into the defense's hands. Courteous replies to discourteous questions enhance a police officer's status with the jury and defeat the defense attorney's goal of discrediting the officer.

The ability to maintain self-control and a courteous manner in difficult situations is an important tool for a police officer in any situation. It is the mark of a true law enforcement professional, and this is so regardless of whether the officer is in the courtroom or on the street. If the officer behaves in a professional manner on the witness stand, the prosecution's case is materially enhanced, and the chances of a conviction are increased accordingly.

The Role of the Expert Witness

Prosecutors may locate an officer with extensive experience in a given area and qualify him or her as an **expert witness.** This often strengthens the prosecution's case and paves the way for testimony by other witnesses. When an officer is designated by the court as an expert, conclusions may be drawn, and the officer may give his or her personal opinion as to the facts and circumstances surrounding the case. The expert witness is one whose knowledge exceeds the knowledge of anyone with a moderate education or experience in the field. Qualifications for the expert witness to establish when on the witness stand include the following:

mycrimekit

Simulation: Police testimony

- Name
- Occupation (and how long)

A CLOSER LOOK

How Reliable Is Eyewitness Testimony?[7]

One August night in Altoona, Iowa, the local McDonald's was filled with customers when a man with a gun in his pocket walked in, looking for cash. He slipped a note to the night manager, who led him to the office, opened the safe, pulled out money, and gave it to him. Before the police arrived, the gunman fled through a rear door, commandeered a car from a drive-through lane, ordered the driver out at gunpoint, and sped away.

Initial descriptions were contradictory, the defense lawyer would later argue, but with the help of McDonald's employees, the artist rendered a composite drawing, which led to a photographic lineup and eventually the arrest of Terry Eugene Schultz. Several eyewitnesses said Schultz was the gunman, and he was convicted and sentenced to 25 years in prison—based solely on eyewitness testimony. Powerful, indeed, but no physical evidence tied Schultz to the crime, and his girlfriend insisted that he'd been with her at the time. So, how accurate are eyewitness identifications?

Some experts say "not very." Now there's mounting evidence through DNA science that innocent people have been convicted as the result of faulty identifications. DNA evidence has already freed scores of convicts, and more could be in line if recommendations proposed in September 1999 by the National Commission on the Future of DNA Evidence become a reality. It's difficult to estimate just how many cases of mistaken identity occur, but in 2007, the Innocence Project concluded that over 75 percent of the more than 192 wrongful convictions in the United States involved mistaken identification.

Increasingly, courts are allowing experts to tell juries that eyewitness identifications are sometimes more convincing than they are reliable and that juries should be especially wary when certain problematic factors exist. Mistakes are more likely, for example, when the witness and suspect are of different races, especially when the witness is white and the suspect is black. We also now know that

A CLOSER LOOK CONTINUED

extreme stress, especially when violence or the threat of violence exists, interferes with recall.

Another problem that researchers found is that viewing a composite drawing or lineup can change witnesses' memories of an event. That is, a witness viewing a photo array may pick out a photo that resembles the culprit but isn't. But from that point, the photo becomes part of the witness's memory of the culprit. It is difficult, if not impossible, to quantify the overall reliability of stranger-to-stranger identifications, say experts. In some cases, experts estimate that the chance of faulty identification is as high as 20 percent.

As for Terry Schultz, his case—the McDonald's robbery in 1998—became the vehicle for the Iowa

Supreme Court to reverse its own precedent. Citing the wealth of new research on memory, the court reversed his conviction and said that Schultz should be allowed to present such evidence at retrial. However, at retrial, even with new expert testimony, the defense would have to overcome several eyewitnesses' testimony. Schultz, who had already spent two years in prison, didn't want to risk spending more time in jail. He pleaded guilty to lesser charges and received a probated sentence. But other Iowa defendants have used the experts that the Schultz case made possible. Des Moines prosecutors claim, however, that they have seen little difference in trial outcomes.

- Department (and how long)
- Specialized experience (e.g., drug enforcement and how long)
- Officer's training
- Number of training course hours
- Number of similar investigations in which the officer has participated
- Number of arrests made in this type of investigation
- Past experience as an expert witness (and how many court appearances)

At the end of the questioning, the judge will excuse the witness. Officers must remember that the eyes of the jury are still watching and making judgments; therefore, when exiting, witnesses should refrain from staring, smiling, or showing any emotion toward anyone in the courtroom.

Summary Checklist

In this chapter, we consider the ways information about crimes is documented by criminal investigators. A properly documented case is one that is more likely to succeed in court. See how well you are able to answer the following questions in your checklist.

1. Do you know how to prepare for an upcoming trial?

For cases that make it to the trial stage, it is imperative that the evidence be well organized and that the investigator be prepared to give

skilled courtroom testimony in the case.

- Officers should cooperate fully with prosecutors in the preparation of trial testimony and other evidence
- A pretrial conference should be held between the prosecutor and all officers testifying in a given case.
- Officers should provide prosecutors with all information relevant to the case.

- No detail should be considered too minor because many cases turn upon minute factual or legal points, the significance of which may become apparent only in the full context of the trial.

When preparing for court, one of the first steps is for the officer to prepare him- or herself psychologically by strengthening feelings of confidence and self-assurance.

Know which courtroom you'll be testifying in. If you are unfamiliar with the particular courthouse or courtroom, check it out before the trial so you will know your way around.

Investigators should observe the following steps:

- Do not discuss anything about the case in public or where your conversation might be overheard.
- Treat people with respect, as if they were the judge or a juror.
- Do not discuss your personal life, official business, biases, prejudices, likes and dislikes, or controversial subjects in public, for the same reasons as listed above.

- Be on time. Know when you will be expected to testify.
- Dress appropriately. Avoid contact with the defense counsel and any defense witnesses before the trial.

2. Do you know how to properly testify on the witness stand?

Investigators must keep several principles in mind while testifying in court, including:

- Confine the testimony to known facts.
- Avoid expressing opinions or conclusions except when they are specifically authorized by the rules of evidence.
- Do not volunteer information.
- Speak calmly and audibly in a natural voice.
- Use plain, easily understood terms.
- Maintain self-control.

Key Terms

credibility

cross-examination

demeanor

direct examination

expert witness

pretrial conference

testimony

Discussion Questions

1. By the time a case goes to trial, what pretrial procedures have already been concluded? Discuss the various phases of a criminal trial.

2. Explain the distinction between direct examination and cross-examination.

3. Discuss some of the most important things for a witness to remember before testifying at a jury trial.

4. What are the things that the investigator must do to best prepare for a jury trial?

5. In what ways can defense attorneys attack an officer's credibility in court?

6. Explain what is meant by an officer's courtroom demeanor and how the officer can leave the best positive impression.

7. Describe the procedure for qualifying an officer as an expert witness.

mycrimekit™

Go to MyCrimeKit.com to explore the following study tools and resources specific to this chapter:

- *Practice Quiz:* Multiple-choice, true/false, short-answer, and essay questions.
- *Flashcards:* There are seven key terms in this chapter. Flashcards test your knowledge of the chapter's key terms.

- *Web Links:* Check out the hotlink to *The New York Times* criminology articles.
- *Career Center:* Check out the hot links to interesting careers in criminal justice, criminology, and juvenile justice.
- *The Research Center:* Check out the Cybrary and research navigator for even more resources.

Notes

1. INTERNATIONAL ASSOCIATION OF CHIEFS OF POLICE (1998). *Court appearance.* Model Policy Center: Alexandria, VA.
2. IBID.
3. IBID.
4. WOOLNER, A. (1999). Courts eye the problems of eyewitness identifications. *USA Today*, September 29:15A.
5. INTERNATIONAL ASSOCIATION OF CHIEFS OF POLICE. (1996). *Testifying in court.* Model Policy Center: Alexandria, VA.
6. IBID.

appendix A

Collection and Preservation of Physical Evidence

The impact that a single piece of evidence can have in court is considerable. In maximizing the effectiveness of this evidence, correct collection and preservation techniques must be used by the investigator. By following the suggestions presented below, the investigator diminishes the possibility that his or her evidence will become contaminated or damaged, thus elevating its importance to the investigation.

Collection and Preservation

It is important that each item submitted as evidence be sealed with tamperproof evidence tape, dated, initialed, and labeled as to its contents and its association with the victim or suspect. Evidence stained with bodily fluids (e.g., blood, semen) must be air dried before packaging and submission to the laboratory. All items should be packaged and sealed separately in breathable, nonplastic (e.g., paper), loose-fitting containers. Packages should not be tightly bound; the criminalists must return items to containers, which must be resealed after examinations.

Tips for Packaging Evidence in the Proper Manner

1. Always submit a completed laboratory analysis request with each case. Use more than one if necessary.
2. Latent evidence submission envelopes should be used only with 10-print cards or latent-print cards. Other types of packaging should be used for nonprint evidence.
3. Do not package weapons with items of clothing or drug paraphernalia. (Firearms will probably be checked immediately to make certain that they are unloaded.)
4. Always package urine separately from blood. Leave expansion room in urine containers; they will be stored in a freezer.
5. Always package tubes of blood separately from clothing. Clothing will be stored in a freezer; whole blood is placed in a refrigerator.
6. Sexual assault kits should never be packaged with clothing. The kits contain whole blood and should be stored in a refrigerator.

(continued)

Tips for Packaging Evidence in the Proper Manner (Continued)

7. Whole blood should always be packaged separately from drug-related items.

8. Never package items for prints with items for serology, trace, firearms identification, and so on.

9. Do not submit open liquor containers to the lab. All containers should be capped and sealed.

10. Evidence stained with bodily fluids (e.g., blood, semen) must be air dried before packaging and submission to the laboratory.

11. Do not submit syringes with uncapped needles or knives or razor blades without protective coverings.

12. Do not submit wet or moist marijuana in plastic bags to the lab; air dry it before submitting.

13. Do not submit drug paraphernalia or miscellaneous items that do not need to be analyzed.

Serology/DNA Analysis

Bodily fluid stains are valuable evidence that can be used to associate a suspect with the crime or to eliminate him or her from consideration. For instance, the presence of seminal stains is confirmation that a sexual act has occurred.

Blood.   When materials stained with blood are to be sent to the laboratory:

- Air dry the stained material on a piece of clean paper placed in a ventilated area. Place the dried material in a paper bag; label it with your initials, the date, and an exhibit number; and seal the bag.

- Any debris that falls from the material onto the paper during the drying process should also be placed in a metal pillbox, labeled, and sealed. If you must fold the material, protect the stained area with a piece of paper.

- Wrap each bloodstained item separately after drying. Do not package items when they are still moist. Allow them to dry thoroughly. Package items from the victim(s) and suspect(s) into separate containers.

- Collect in a purple-capped Vacutainer a comparison blood standard from each person directly involved in the incident. Freeze or refrigerate dried specimens until ready for transport to the laboratory.

When items stained with blood cannot be sent to the laboratory:

- Always scrape dried blood from an object if possible. Using a clean knife or razor blade, scrape the dried blood into a paper fold and place in an envelope.

- If scraping is not possible, moisten a cotton swab with just enough water to make the tip damp. Do not saturate the swab completely with water. Rub the stained area with the swab to pick up the blood. Keep the blood as concentrated as possible on the tip of the swab. Air dry the swab and place it in an envelope or small paper bag.

- Large fabric items with bloodstains may be processed by cutting out the stained area and sending the cutting to the laboratory. Written notes, photographs, or both detailing the location and condition of the stain should be taken before the cutting(s) is removed. Place the cutting(s) in an envelope or paper bag.

- When a puddle of blood is available, soak up the moist blood with cotton swabs. Air dry the swabs before placing them in an envelope or small paper bag.
- Label all containers with your initials, the date, and the exhibit number and then seal them.
- If scrapings were taken, package and preserve the razor blade used.
- Collect a comparison blood standard from each person directly involved in the incident.
- Freeze or refrigerate dried specimens until ready for transport to the laboratory.

Comparison Standard for Blood. Obtain the standard by having a medical examiner or other qualified person collect at least 5 cubic centimeters of blood from the victim and all suspects. Use purple-capped Vacutainer tubes for the collection of whole blood. Label each tube with the donor's name, the physician's name, and other relevant information. Refrigerate the tubes until ready for transport to the laboratory. Do not freeze whole-blood samples.

Semen. Air dry the stained material on a piece of clean paper placed in a ventilated area. Condoms to be submitted should be frozen as soon as possible after collection. Stained areas on large items or items that cannot be sent to the laboratory may be cut out and submitted. Place the dried material in a paper bag, label it with your initials, the date, and an exhibit number and then seal the bag. If you must fold the material, protect the stained area with a piece of paper. Wrap each stained item separately.

Do not package items when they are still moist; allow them to dry thoroughly. Obtain a victim sexual assault kit and a suspect sexual assault kit (one per suspect) and follow the instructions provided with the kits. Label the kits with your initials, the date, and the exhibit number and then seal them. Refrigerate kits until ready for transport to the laboratory. Freeze or refrigerate dried specimens until ready for transport to the laboratory. Sexual assault kits can be obtained from your local crime laboratory.

Saliva. Air dry the stained material on a piece of clean paper placed in a ventilated area. Place the dried material in a paper bag; label it with your initials, the date, and an exhibit number; and seal the bag. If you must fold the material, protect the stained area with a piece of paper. Wrap each stained area separately. Do not package items when they are still moist; allow them to dry thoroughly. Collect a comparison standard. Freeze or refrigerate dried specimens until ready for transport to the laboratory.

Comparison Standard for Saliva. Obtain saliva samples from the victim and suspect, waiting 30 minutes if a person has eaten or been smoking. Have the person spit on a piece of clean cotton cloth about 1 square inch in size. Outline stain areas with a pencil, air dry them, and place the samples in separate envelopes. Freeze or refrigerate dried specimens until ready for transport to the laboratory. Obtain a comparison blood standard as described in the preceding section.

Accelerants and Explosives

Evidence in bomb and arson cases is difficult to find because of its small size, because of the presence of a large amount of debris, and because potentially useful evidence is often washed away when a fire is extinguished. For this reason, great care must be used in the collection and preservation of such evidence.

Arson Debris. Porous substances absorb liquid accelerants readily and therefore make good debris for laboratory testing. Consider carpeting, carpet padding, wood, and clothing or cloth products when collecting debris. Collect fire debris in unused metal paint cans or plastic bags approved for fire debris (e.g., nylon or Kapak bags). Submit liquids in their original containers if they can be sealed properly.

Explosive Debris. Collect any items that may have been part of the explosive device. Collect items that were impacted directly by fragments of the explosive device. If explosive residues are found on these items, the type of explosive used may be determined. Package the items in plastic bags or metal containers.

Explosive Substances and Devices. Any undetonated explosive device must be deactivated before it is submitted to the laboratory. If the device is to be processed for latent fingerprints, package and label it accordingly.

Fingerprints

Generally, latent fingerprints on nonporous materials deteriorate rapidly upon prolonged exposure to high temperature and humidity; consequently, items should be processed or forwarded to a laboratory as soon as possible. With the assistance of the Automated Fingerprint Identification System (AFIS), we are now able to search the entire fingerprint file; we do not need a suspect. A thorough file search can be made only if correct processing procedures are followed to obtain the best latent print evidence.

On Absorbent Materials. Place paper or other absorbent material in a plastic bag or cellophane protector. Do not handle the material with your fingers. Do not attempt to develop latent fingerprints on absorbent surfaces yourself. Label the bag or protector with your initials, the date, and an exhibit number. Collect a comparison standard.

On Hard Surfaces. Dust plastic cards, metal plates, glass bottles, or other hard-surfaced objects for latent fingerprints. Remove developed prints with lifting tape and place the tape on a 3" × 5"-inch card that contrasts in color with the dusting powder used. Mark the card with your initials, the date, and an exhibit number; place it in an envelope; and seal the envelope.

On Soft Surfaces. Carefully remove putty, caulking compound, or other soft material bearing visible fingerprint impressions. Leave as much excess material surrounding the fingerprint as possible. Glue the mass of material to a stiff section of cardboard that is marked with your initials, the date, and an exhibit number. Tape a protective cover over the specimen. A paper cup or baby food jar is useful for this purpose. Do not touch or otherwise distort the fingerprint. Collect a comparison standard.

Comparison Standard for Fingerprints. Collect and identify fingerprints of suspects and other persons under investigation who may have touched an object. Place fingerprint records in a stiff envelope to protect them from being bent. Seal the envelope and label it with your initials, the date, and an exhibit number.

Inked Prints. Enclose all inked prints for comparison and designate either on the print or in a cover letter whether prints are for elimination or are of the suspect. If latent prints are reported as palm prints, palm prints should also be submitted to the laboratory.

Packing of Evidence. Use ingenuity to construct special containers to protect latent print-bearing surfaces. Never place cotton or cloth next to latent impressions. Any amount of paper or cardboard specimens may be placed in one wrapper. Hard-surfaced latent print-bearing objects should never come in contact with another surface (e.g., paper sacks, plastic bags).

Identification. There is no set requirement of latent print size for a positive identification, and there is no specific number of characteristics required to effect an identification. As a general rule, if the investigator develops an area that appears to have several ridges, regardless of the size of the area, it should be lifted, marked, and submitted to the laboratory.

Firearms and Ammunition

Firearms leave unique markings on bullets and cartridge cases as well as detectable residues on shooters' hands.

Gunshot Residue Kits. The discharge of a firearm can deposit gunshot residues on any object in close proximity to the firearm and sometimes at a considerable distance downrange. Gunshot residue kits may be used to test the residue levels deposited on hands. Crime labs are usually capable of analyzing two different types of gunshot residue kits:

1. An A.A. kit consists of five cotton swabs with a bottle of dilute nitric acid and is analyzed using an atomic absorption spectrophotometer.
2. A SEM/EDX kit consists of two adhesive-coated aluminum stubs and is analyzed using a scanning electron microscope equipped with an x-ray dispersive detector.

Each kit contains specific instructions for its use as well as a request for certain information in regard to the shooting incident. Be sure to include the type of weapon, ammunition, and time interval until collection of the kit. Kits must be used as soon as possible after a shooting incident and before hands are cleaned or processed in any other way. An A.A. kit should not be used if the time interval until the collection of the kit exceeds six hours for an active person.

When shooting distance information is requested, submit the victim's clothing with the bullet hole along with the firearm and ammunition used. If the clothing is bloody, air dry it completely and package it in a paper bag. If the victim was not clothed over the area of the wound, take close-up photographs of the wound and remember to include a scale in the photographs. Gunshot residue kits can be obtained from the crime laboratory.

Handguns and Shoulder Arms. Never insert anything into the barrel of a firearm. All firearms should be unloaded before submission to the laboratory. Process the firearm for fingerprints if necessary. Take notes describing the position of any expended cartridge cases or live cartridges in the cylinder of the revolver. If pertinent to an investigation, make notes on a safety's position, hammer position, and so on. Remove the cartridge magazine from any semiautomatic firearm and process the exterior for fingerprints if necessary. Cartridge magazines can be placed in separate containers and submitted along with the firearms in a larger container. Attach an identification tag to the firearm that describes the item, serial number, case number, chain of custody, and other pertinent details.

Handguns should be submitted in plastic bags, paper bags, or boxes. If handguns are to be processed for fingerprints or serology, do not submit them in plastic bags. Shoulder arms are generally larger items and cannot always be submitted in containers.

Serial Number Restoration. If a firearm's serial number has been obliterated, make an identifying mark on it for future identification. The obliterated area can be restored in the laboratory using one of several methods.

Expended Bullets, Cartridge Cases, and Shotgun Shells. After recovering an expended ammunition component, it should be placed in a sturdy, unbreakable container such as a small box or metal canister. Bullets that are removed at an autopsy should be washed in warm running water (if not for trace or serology examinations), wrapped in tissue or similar material, and put in an appropriate container.

Do not scratch the sides or bearing surface of a bullet when it is being removed from an object. The base or nose of a bullet can be scribed for identification purposes. Do not scratch or scribe the headstamp area or primer of a cartridge case or shotgun shell. If a casing or shotgun shell must be marked for identification, do so on or near the open mouth area.

Expended ammunition components should be separated and packaged in separate containers. The component's location, case number, and related information can be labeled on the outside of the container. Each container should be sealed with tamperproof evidence tape before submission to the laboratory.

Food and Drug Specimens

Because food and drug specimens exhibit a wide variety of identifiable characteristics, they may corroborate other evidence or link a suspect with a crime scene. When handling this evidence, it is important to prevent contamination among the specimens or from other sources. Do not package too much evidence into a container because doing so could cause a break in the container, with a loss of integrity of the evidence. Also, do not completely cover the evidence container with evidence tape because doing so could prevent the container from being adequately sealed later.

Liquids. Try to collect a minimum of 4 ounces of a specimen using a leakproof container. Seal the container with adhesive tape and label it with your initials, the date, and an exhibit number. If the container used is glass or has a glass stopper, mark it as fragile. Collect a comparison standard of the same brand and concentration, especially when tampering of medical, food, or other commercial products is suspected. Submit unknown and comparison liquid samples to the laboratory.

Plant Material. Without heating, dry the sample thoroughly in a secure area by spreading it on clean paper for at least 24 hours. After the sample has dried, place it in a pillbox, vial, or other container and secure it with adhesive tape. Do not mix samples. Package each sample separately to avoid mixing during mailing. Label the outside of the container with your initials, the date, and an exhibit number. Collect a comparison standard. If wet plant material is collected in evidence containers (especially plastic bags), it will mold and degrade to the point where positive test results may not be obtained. These molds are also hazardous to your health.

When numerous plants, bales, or bundles of plant material are seized, submit to the laboratory only representative samples of plant material from these items. Photograph the entire number of original evidence items with a ruler as scale and weigh them. In a large drug seizure, do not submit the entire amount of evidence to the laboratory. A lab will not have sufficient evidence locker space for all drug seizures. Also, small amounts of drugs submitted to a laboratory allow for quicker testing.

Powders and Solids. Place powders and solids in a container such as a pillbox, plastic vial, or pharmacy fold. Seal the container and label it with your initials, the date, and an exhibit number. Refrigerate samples as needed. Do not add preservatives to solid food samples. Collect a comparison standard.

Tablets and Capsules. Place tablets and capsules in a container such as a pillbox or plastic vial. Seal the container and label it with your initials, the date, and an exhibit number. Collect a comparison standard.

Comparison Standard for Liquids, Powders, Solids, Plant Material, Tablets, and Capsules. Collect comparison standards for food, liquids, plant material, tablets, and capsules (in cases such as unattended deaths and suspected poisonings). When collecting standards, search the refrigerator, cupboards, and storage places for similar material, particularly that which is labeled. Do not remove these samples from their original containers; seal them in clean (sterile, if possible) second containers. Refrigerate samples as necessary to retard further growth of microorganisms and deterioration. Expedite their delivery to a forensic laboratory.

Comparison standards for drugs should be collected in the manner described above. When collecting standards, collect any containers displaying prescription labels. Do not remove pills, capsules, powders, or liquids from their original containers; seal them in clean second containers and label them. Never mix specimens regardless of the proximity to the scene or their similarity in appearance.

Glass

All glass except small fragments might contain latent fingerprints and should be handled accordingly. When glass fragments might be present on clothing, shoes, tools, or other objects, the articles should be submitted to the laboratory as soon as possible.

Large Fragments. Dust large fragments for latent fingerprints and submit the prints. Protect thin protruding edges of fragments against damage by embedding them in modeling clay, putty, or a similar substance. Avoid chipping the fragments. Use tweezers or similar tools to collect glass. Exercise care in protecting the edges and avoid scratching the surface. Place adhesive tape on each piece for identification. Place your initials and the date on the tape.

Wrap each piece separately in cotton; place it in a sturdy box with a tight-fitting lid; and seal and label each package with your initials, the date, and an exhibit number. Package questioned pieces of glass separately from known pieces. If you are submitting glass for the purpose of determining the direction of a bullet's impact or for other fracture analysis, mark surfaces with tape indicating whether the glass was found outside or inside the building. Similarly, mark glass taken from a window frame to indicate which side was facing out. Collect a comparison standard.

Small Fragments. Examine articles of clothing and shoes for the presence of small glass fragments. Use tweezers or similar tools to collect glass. Use care in protecting the edges and avoid scratching the surface. Wrap each article of clothing containing fragments separately in clean paper or plastic bags. Package any questioned pieces of glass separately from known pieces. Seal each bag and label each bag with your initials, the date, and specimen information.

Place shoes and other solid objects in separate containers such as shoeboxes. Tape each object to the bottom of containers to prevent rattling. Do not pack articles containing microscopic fragments in cotton or other soft protective materials. Seal each package completely, making sure that there are no holes through which glass fragments might be lost. Place loose glass fragments in pillboxes or plastic or glass vials and seal them tightly. Place cotton in the container to prevent rattling and chipping during transit. Do not use envelopes as containers. Label everything with your initials, the date, and specimen information. Collect a comparison standard.

Comparison Standard for Glass. Always collect glass standards from an area as near as possible to the point of impact. Collect samples that are at least the size of a quarter and wrap each comparison sample according to appropriate procedures.

Hairs and Fibers

In crimes involving physical contact, particles are often transferred among the victim, suspect, and weapon or other objects. Hairs and fibers are among the most common evidentiary items and can be extremely valuable to an investigation. When submitting hair and fiber evidence, be specific as to their source and association to the victim or suspect. Good evidence containers are a paper fold, pillbox, or tape lift. Each container used should be enclosed within an outside envelope.

Collection of Unknowns. If hairs or fibers are observed, remove them from the surface with clean tweezers. On suitable surfaces, a tape lift using wide transparent adhesive tape is an excellent procedure.

Collection of Knowns. Of the various hair regions on the human body, only head hair and pubic hair are considered suitable for comparison purposes.

Head Hair Standards. Pull 40 to 50 hairs from all over the head, taking approximately 10 hairs each from the top front, top back, back of head, right side, and left side.

Pubic Hair Standards. Pull approximately 25 hairs representative of the pubic region. Hair standards should be packaged in paper folds and enclosed in an outer envelope.

Impressions

Impressions made by footwear, tires, and tools can easily be destroyed during a preliminary crime scene search. To prevent inadvertent loss of such evidence, one of the earliest concerns of any crime scene investigation should be the security of the scene and the collection and preservation of impressions. Impressions should be photographed properly before attempting lifts or casting.

Footwear and Tire Impressions. Photograph each impression with a ruled scale next to it. Photograph the impression from directly above (use of a tripod is highly recommended). Photographs should be taken while a detached flash is held low and to the side of the impression. Each impression should be flashed from four different sides. Black-and-white film gives the best quality photographs for comparison purposes. Photographs of impressions for comparisons should be blown up to a 1:1 scale before submission to the laboratory.

After photographing an impression, a lift may be attempted if a residue impression is on a hard surface that cannot be submitted to the laboratory. Adhesive lifters, gelatin lifters, or electrostatic lifting techniques may be used. Residue impressions are delicate in nature and can easily be destroyed by improper handling.

Casting techniques should be practiced before crime scene utilization. Dental stone or die stone casting material is recommended for the casting of three-dimensional impressions. (The use of plaster of Paris for casting of impressions is discouraged.)

Approximately 12 ounces of water should be added to and mixed with 2 pounds of dental stone or die stone. This amount is generally sufficient to prepare casting material for a footwear impression. A 1-gallon plastic Ziploc bag containing premeasured casting material is ideal for the mixing and casting process. A 12-ounce beverage container can be used for measuring the water. Additional casting material will need to be mixed for larger impressions such as tire impressions. Prepare the dental or die stone materials into a pancake batter—like consistency in a plastic Ziploc bag.

Pour the solution off the side of the impression, not directly onto or into it. Allow the casting material to flow into the impression. A tongue depressor can be used gently to help the casting material flow over the entire impression. When the dental or die stone has set, place your initials, date, and case-identifying information into the back of the cast.

When submitting a cast to the laboratory, place it in a sturdy box or similar container with sufficient cushioning material (e.g., Styrofoam peanuts or scrap newspaper). If more than one cast is submitted, put each cast in its own box or container. Do not remove the dirt or debris adhering to a cast, footwear, or tire. Each container should be sealed with tamperproof evidence tape before submission to the laboratory.

Tool Marks. Do not insert a suspect tool into a tool mark. Whenever possible, preserve tool marks as you find them and submit the intact object bearing the questioned tool marks to the laboratory. If it is not possible to submit the object, remove the portion or section of the object bearing the tool mark. Before a portion or section of a large item is removed, photograph the entire item with the inclusion of a ruled scale. Also take close-up photographs of the questioned tool marks with the inclusion of a ruled scale for reference.

If an item cannot be submitted, a Mikrosil or silicon typecast of the tool mark(s) should be made and submitted to the laboratory for comparison. Tools, casts of tool marks, and so on should be submitted individually in separate containers. Information pertinent to an investigation should be labeled on the outside of the containers. Each container should be sealed with tamperproof evidence tape before submission to the laboratory.

Paint

Paint evidence can be in the form of liquid, chips, or smears. A dried paint specimen should be collected in a paper fold, placed in an outer envelope, and marked clearly as to its source. Any questioned paint specimen should also have a known paint standard submitted. Package specimens separately for comparison purposes.

Liquid Paints. Specimens of liquid paint should be submitted in original containers whenever possible.

Questioned Documents

Questioned documents contain a wide variety of identifiable characteristics that can be used to corroborate other evidence and associate a suspect with a crime. Similarly, these can be used by a laboratory to clear a suspect of a crime in certain instances.

Charred Documents. A thin but strong section of cardboard can be inserted gently under charred debris. Thick, firm cotton batting is then placed on a flat surface, with the charred paper deposited onto the batting. Place it in a crush-proof container; label it with your initials, the date, and an exhibit number; and seal it. Mark the container "Fragile" in a conspicuous spot.

Crumpled Documents. Do not unfold a crumpled document; rather, enclose it in a crushproof container. Label it with your initials, the date, and an exhibit number and then seal it. Mark the container "Fragile" in a conspicuous spot.

Intact Documents. Whenever possible, submit the original document rather than a photograph, photocopy, or other type of copy. Handle the document carefully; preserve latent fingerprints using tweezers or gloves as necessary. When identification is necessary, mark in a noncritical area of the document. Use a medium different from that used on the document (e.g., use pencil when the document is in ink). Do not use staples or pins on documents and do not fold documents. Place them in a protective covering such as an envelope or cover with plastic. Seal and label them with your initials, the date, and an exhibit number. Collect a comparison standard.

Comparison Standard for Questioned Documents. Standards for questioned documents are not the questioned documents themselves but facsimiles or replicas of handwriting, typewriter print, or ink visible on questioned document(s) that might have been made by the maker(s) of the original document.

Adequate Exemplars. Remember that unlike fingerprints, handwriting and hand printing will change over a period of time and can easily be disguised. Each of us has a normal range of variation in our writing. To make a proper comparison, the examiner must determine the range of variation in each suspect's writing. It is impossible to say whether this range will be shown in six, 16, or 60 samples. Handwriting (cursive) cannot be compared with hand printing. Age, gender, and writing hand cannot be determined conclusively. About the best that we can do in these areas is to make an educated guess.

Don't use a single sheet of paper or a single-page exemplar. To get an adequate sample of writing or printing from a person, it is much better to use several, perhaps 20 or 30, single pieces of paper as your exemplar. Using paper that is about the same size and texture as the document in question is suggested. Always try to duplicate the conditions under which the questioned items were prepared.

Guidelines for Obtaining Known Handwriting Exemplars. The following guidelines may be used to obtain known handwriting or hand printing exemplars from a person:

* Reproduce the original conditions as nearly as possible with respect to text speed, slant, size of paper, size of writing, type of writing instrument, and so on.
* Obtain samples from dictation until it is believed that normal writing has been produced. (The number of samples necessary cannot be determined in advance.)
* Do not allow the writer to see either the original document in question or a photograph thereof.
* Remove each sample from the sight of the writer as soon as it is completed.

- Do not give instructions in spelling, punctuation, or arrangement.
- Use the same writing media, such as type and size of paper, writing instruments, and printed forms such as checks or notes.
- Obtain the full text of the questioned writing in word-for-word order at least once, if possible. Signatures and less extensive writing should be prepared several times, each time on a different piece of paper. In hand-printing cases, both uppercase (capital) and lowercase samples should be obtained.
- In forgery cases, the laboratory should also be furnished with genuine signatures of the person whose name has been forged.
- Obtain samples of supplementary writings such as sketches, drawings, and manner of addressing an envelope.
- Have the writer sign and date each page.
- Witness each sample with date and initials (or name).
- Consider furnishing undictated specimens to supplement the dictated specimens.
- Obtain and submit original documents when possible.
- Familiarize yourself with all aspects of the questioned document involved in a case. Furnish copies of the documents to assist other officers when they are requested to obtain known writing.

Typewriter Examples. Collect specimens of typewriting from the typewriter believed to have been used and submit them to a document analyst. When obtaining these examples, use the typewriter in the condition in which it is found (i.e., the same ribbon). Type the text of the questioned material three times, once through carbon paper with the ribbon adjustment set on "stencil." On each specimen, record the brand name, model number, and serial number of the typewriter that was used.

Place specimens in a plastic or reinforced envelope. Do not fold them. Label them with your initials, the date, and an exhibit number. Film-type ribbon cartridges and correction tapes should also be collected and submitted for examination.

Ink Examples. Collect samples of unquestioned documents that contain the type of ink used in the questioned document. If you are unsure whether the ink on the standard is the same as that on the questioned document, submit samples of all available inks that might have been used. If samples of fluid ink are available, place the bottles containing the ink in a suitable container that is labeled with your initials, the date, and an exhibit number. Label the container as fragile and submit it to the laboratory.

Indented Writings. Loose papers and writing pads should be collected for possible writing and typing impression restoration.

Soil

The success of soil comparisons depends mainly on the quality of the samples collected. Soils located on the sides of suspect shoes are most suitable for soil comparisons. Consider the nature of the crime scene. Is it conducive to the transfer of soil onto a shoe (e.g., a paved parking lot compared with an open field)? Soil standards from the scene should consist of an area approximately

6 inches square by 1/4 inch deep. Plastic bags or metal cans are good containers for soil samples.

Toxicology

Blood Alcohol Determinations. Whole blood is the best body fluid for alcohol testing; urine is not a reliable specimen for accurate determination of a blood alcohol level. Blood should be collected in a sterile gray stopper blood collection tube that contains the additives sodium fluoride (NaF) and potassium oxalate (KOx). These additives are required to preserve a blood sample for alcohol testing. A new sterile needle must be used as well as a nonalcoholic skin cleanser. The needle cover or wrapper bearing the word "sterile" as well as the package from the skin cleanser should be preserved. These are needed in court to prove that legal collection requirements were followed. Do not preserve the needle itself.

After the blood is collected, mix the blood and the additives in the tube by gently inverting the tube at least 15 to 20 times. This prevents the blood from clotting. Mark the tube with the person's name and any other pertinent case information. One tube of blood (5 to 10 milliliters) is sufficient for alcohol testing. Do not freeze the blood sample. Protect the blood from extreme heat. Do not store the blood sample in a hot car during the summer.

Toluene or Solvent Abuse and Glue Sniffing. When glue sniffing or other solvent abuse is suspected, collect a blood sample as described above for alcohol testing. Toluene and other solvents cannot be detected reliably in urine samples.

Drug Testing. Urine is the specimen of choice for drug testing. Many more positive test results are found in urine than in blood. Drug tests on their own will not establish impairment at the time of arrest because different drugs take differing amounts of time to be excreted in the urine. The officer's observations relating to the person's degree of impairment is very important in establishing intoxication.

Urine collection must be observed to prevent the person from adulterating the sample. An officer of the same gender as the person should accompany the person into the bathroom stall and actually observe the urine flowing into the cup. At least 50 milliliters of urine should be collected if possible. If the person cannot provide sufficient urine, have the person drink some water and wait 15 minutes to try again. After the urine is collected, the sample should be marked with the person's name and sealed. The specimen cup should then be placed in a leakproof plastic bag. If the urine sample cannot be delivered to the laboratory within 24 hours of collection, the urine must be refrigerated. This is a legal requirement. For long-term storage (more than one day), the urine sample should be frozen.

Blood can also be tested for drugs. However, drugs do not remain in the bloodstream for long periods of time. Some drugs may be detectable in blood only for a couple of hours or less. Also, drugs have much lower concentrations in blood than in urine. For these reasons, urine is the preferred specimen for drug testing. If blood is submitted to the laboratory for drug testing, it should be collected in the same manner as for alcohol testing. At least two tubes of blood (20 milliliters) should be collected if a drug test is requested. When submitting evidence for drug testing, indicate which drugs are suspected.

Carbon Monoxide. If carbon monoxide poisoning is suspected, collect a blood sample in the same manner as for alcohol testing.

Safety Considerations. Assume that all samples are infected with something. Wash your hands after handling blood tubes or urine samples. Package all samples in a way that will contain leakage. Notify the laboratory if you believe that a suspect is infected with any disease.

Miscellaneous

Items such as cigarette butts, tobacco, jewelry, magnetic tape recordings, and writing instruments can all serve as evidence to connect a suspect to a crime. Each item, either through its use or basic structure, can provide a unique, identifiable characteristic. For instance, tape recordings of anonymous voices received as part of a threat before a bombing or extortion may be identified with known voices of a suspect through voiceprint analysis, provided that care is exercised during the recording of questions and known voices.

Cigarette Butts and Tobacco. Pick up the cigarette butt on a piece of paper or with tweezers and place in a pillbox. Do not handle the cigarette butt directly with your hands. Mark a label with your initials, the date, and an exhibit number as well as where the object was found. Place the label on the container and seal it. Empty tobacco material from pipes or clothes pockets into a pillbox. Mark and seal it as above.

Comparison Standard for Cigarette Butts and Tobacco. No comparison standard of the cigarette material need be collected. If serological testing is desired, however, saliva standards should be collected from both victims and suspects.

Jewelry. Handle with tweezers or cloth gloves. Dust for fingerprints and place in a suitable crushproof container. If the composition of precious metals such as gold, silver, or platinum must be determined to prove a common origin, send appropriate metal samples for comparison purposes. Label each sample container by writing on it in ink your initials, the date, and an exhibit number. Collect a comparison standard.

Comparison Standard for Jewelry. When possible, submit comparison samples of jewelry along with any questioned samples. The origin of some stolen jewelry may be traced to a particular jewelry store by analyzing the adhesive used to glue a precious stone to its setting. Known samples of the adhesive used by the jeweler should be submitted for comparison with questioned samples. Place samples in crushproof containers and seal them.

Small Objects. At each crime scene, search for small objects such as burned matches, fragments of glass, broken fingernails, and cigarette butts. Follow known procedures for each item. If you do not have specific directions for an item of evidence, place it in a crushproof container without touching it directly with your fingers. Seal and identify the container by writing on it in ink your initials, the date, and an exhibit number. Collect a comparison standard whenever possible.

Comparison Standard for Small Objects. Comparison samples of small objects or items found in the possession of a suspect or in his or her belongings should be submitted so that a comparison with items found at the crime scene can be made. Package and identify comparison samples.

Writing Instruments. Handle these with tweezers or cloth gloves, being careful not to smudge fingerprints. Dust for and collect fingerprints. Look for and submit instruments bearing teeth marks. Place the instrument in a suitable crushproof container and identify the container by writing on it in ink your initials, the date, and an exhibit number. Collect a comparison standard.

Collect any writing instruments found in the possession of a suspect or in his or her belongings in the manner described above. Package and identify comparison samples as described above.

appendix B

Cases

Aguilar v. Texas, 378 U.S. 108 (1964)

Alabama v. White, 496 U.S. 325 (1990)

Arizona v. Evans, 514 U.S. 1 (1995)

Arizona v. Hicks, 480 U.S. 321 (1987)

Arenson v. Jackson, 97 Misc. 606, 162 N.Y.S. (1916)

Ashcraft v. Tennessee, 322 U.S. 143 , 64 S.Ct. 921 (1944)

Barnett v. State, 104 Ohio St. 298, 135 N.E. (1922)

Berkemer v. McCarty, 486 U.S. 420 (1984)

Brinegar v. United States, 338 U.S. 160, 69 S.Ct. (1949)

Brown v. Mississippi, 297 U.S. 278 (1936)

Bumper v. North Carolina, 391 U.S. 543 (1968)

California v. Acevedo, 500 U.S. 565 (1991)

California v. Hodari, 499 U.S. 62 (1991)

California v. Prysock, 451 U.S. 1301 (1981)

Carroll v. United States, 267 U.S. 132 (1925)

Chambers v. Maroney, 399 U.S. 42 (1970)

Cheadle v. Barwell, 95 Mont. 299 (1933)

Chimel v. California, 395 U.S. 752 (1969)

Coolidge v. New Hampshire, 403 U.S. 443 (1971)

County of Riverside v. McLaughlin, 500 U.S. 413 (1991)

Cupp v. Murphy, 412 U.S. 291 93 S.Ct. 200 (1973)

Davis v. United States, 512 U.S. 452 (1994)

Department of Justice v. Landano, 508 U.S. 165 (1993)

Draper v. United States, 358 U.S. 307, 79 S.Ct. (1959)

Edwards v. Arizona, 451 U.S. 477 (1981)

Escobedo v. Illinois, 378 U.S. 478 (1964)

Florida v. Andrews, 1987

Florida v. Bostick, 501 U.S. 429 (1991)

Florida v. Jimeno, 499 U.S. 934 (1991)

Florida v. Royer, 460 U.S. 491 (1983)

Frye v. United States, 54 App. D.C. 46, 293 (1923)

Funk v. United States, 290 U.S. 371 (1933)

Gilbert v. California, 388 U.S. 263 (1967)

Graham v. Connor, 490 U.S. 396 (1989)

Hampton v. United States, 425 U.S. 484 (1976)

Harris v. United States, 390 U.S. 234 (1968)

Hayes v. Florida, 470 U.S. 811 (1985)

Horton v. California, 496 U.S. 128 (1990)

Illinois v. Gates, 462 U.S. 213 (1983)

Illinois v. Rodriguez, 497 U.S. 177 (1990)

Illinois v. Wardlow, 528 U.S. 119 (2000)

Katz v. United States, 389 U.S. 347 (1967)

Ker v. California, 374 U.S. 23 (1963)

Mallory v. United States, 354 U.S. 449 (1957)

Mapp v. Ohio, 367 U.S. 643 (1961)

Maryland v. Buie, 494 U.S. 325 (1990)

Massachusetts v. Sheppard, 468 U.S. 981 (1984)

McCray v. Illinois, 386 U.S. 300 (1967)

McNabb v. United States, 318 U.S. 332 (1943)

Michigan v. Tyler, 436 U.S. 499 (1978)

Minnesota v. Murphy, 405 U.S. 420, 104 S. Ct. (1984)

Mincey v. Arizona, 437 U.S. 385 (1978)

Minnesota v. Olson, 495 U.S. 91 (1989)

Minnick v. Mississippi, 498 U.S. 146 (1990)

Miranda v. Arizona, 384 U.S. 436 (1966)

Naler v. State, 148 So. 880, 25 (1933)

New York v. Belton, 453 U.S. 454 (1981)

New York v. Quarles, 467 U.S. 649 (1984)

Nix v. Williams, 467 U.S. 431 (1984)

Oliver v. United States, 466 U.S. 170 (1984)

Oregon v. Bradshaw, 462 U.S. 1039 (1983)

Oregon v. Elstad, 470 U.S. 298 (1985)

Payton v. New York, 455 U.S. 573 (1980)

Pennsylvania v. Labron, 518 U.S. 938 (1996)

People v. Forts, 18 N.C. [2nd] 31 (1933)

People v. Olivo, 52 N.Y.2d 309 (1981)

Petit v. Campbell, 149 S.W.2d 633, 635, 636 (1941)

Rhode Island v. Innis, 446 U.S. 291 (1980)

Roviaro v. United States, 353 U.S. 53 (1957)

Schmerber v. California, 384 U.S. 757 (1966)

Schneckloth v. Bustamonte, 412 U.S. 218 (1973)

Sherman v. United States, 356 U.S. 369 (1958)

Silverthorne Lumber Co. v. U.S., 251 U.S. 385 (1920)

Spinelli v. United States, 393 U.S. 410 (1969)

Stansbury v. *California*, 511 U.S. 318 (1994)

State v. *Bohner*, 210 Wis. 651, 246 N.W. 314 (1933)

State v. *Fournier*, 376 U.S. 575, 589 (1964)

Tennessee v. *Garner*, 471 U.S. 1 (1985)

Terry v. *Ohio*, 392 U.S. 1 (1968)

Texas v. *Brown*, 460 U.S. 730 (1983)

United States v. *Ash Jr.*, 413 U.S. 300 (1973)

United States v. *Chadwick*, 433 U.S. 1 (1977)

United States v. *Dunn*, 480 U.S. 294 (1987)

United States v. *Grubbs*, 547 U.S. __, __, (2006)

United States v. *Henry*, 259 F.2d 725 7th Cir. (1958)

United States v. *Irizarry*, 341 F.3d 273, 306 (2003)

United States v. *Leon*, 468, U.S. 897 (1984)

United States v. *Ross*, 456 U.S. 798 (1982)

United States v. *Sokolow*, 109 S. Ct. 1581 (1989)

United States v. *Wade*, 388 U.S. 218 (1967)

Warden v. *Hayden*, 387 U.S. 294 (1967)

Weeks v. *United States*, 232 U.S. 383 (1914)

Wilson v. *Arkansas*, 514 U.S. 927 (1995)

Wong Sun v. *United States*, 371 U.S. 471 (1963)

Wyoming v. *Houghton*, 526 U.S. 295 (1999)

glossary

A

Absolute judgment. When eyewitnesses compare each photograph or person in a lineup only with their memory of what the offender looked like.

Abductive reasoning. The process of proposing a likely explanation for an event that must be tested.

Acquaintance stalking. When a stalker and victim know each other casually.

Actus reus. Latin for "the criminal act itself."

Acute maltreatment. When a child's death is directly related to injuries suffered as a result of a specific incident or abuse or act of negligence.

Admission. A self-incriminating statement made by a suspect that falls short of an acknowledgment of guilt.

Affidavit. A legal document that presents facts that the officer believes constitute probable cause to justify the issuance of a warrant.

AFIS system. The automated fingerprint identification system.

Aggravated assault. A personal crime associated with a high probability of death; serious, permanent disfigurement; permanent or protracted loss or impairment of the function of any body member or organ; or other severe bodily harm.

Alligatoring. The pattern of crevices formed by the burning of a wooden structure.

Amber Alert. A system that quickly posts information about child abductions.

Analysis. A scientific examination.

Anger-retaliatory rapist. A person who vents his anger and frustration toward the opposite sex by punishing them.

Arrest. The act of a police officer taking a person into custody after making a determination that he or she has violated a law.

Arson. The malicious or fraudulent burning of property.

Assault. To intentionally put someone in fear of immediate battery or to threaten someone while having the apparent ability to carry out that threat.

Associative evidence. Evidence that links a suspect with a crime.

Autoerotic death. Death induced by solo sexual activity in which the participant incorporates the use of self-induced bondage and a ligature to reduce the flow of oxygen while attempting to achieve orgasm through masturbation.

B

Ballistics. The science of tracking the path of a bullet.

Bank robbery. The unlawful taking of money or other assets from a bank through the use of face-to-face contact between suspect and victims.

Bank Secrecy Act (BAS). A federal law passed in 1970 to require reporting of large-scale case transactions.

Baseline technique. Crime scene measuring technique in which a line is drawn between two known points.

Battered child syndrome. A clinical term referring to the collection of injuries sustained by a child as a result of repeated mistreatment or beating.

Battered children. Children who suffer from physical abuse.

Battery. An intentional nonconsensual bodily contact that a reasonable person would consider harmful.

Bertillon system. An early criminal identification or classification system based on the idea that certain aspects of the human body, such as skeletal size, ear shape, and eye color, remained the same after a person had reached full physical maturity. This system used a combination of photographs with standardized physical measurements.

Best evidence rule. A legal doctrine of evidence that says that no evidence will be admissible in court if it is secondary in nature.

Beyond a reasonable doubt. The standard of proof in a criminal case in which the deciders of fact are entirely satisfied that the defendant is guilty as charged.

Bill of Rights. A constitutional doctrine granting individual freedoms.

Binding material. Material used to incapacitate a victim during the course of a robbery.

Bobbies. The name of London Metropolitan Police Department officers; they were named this after the department's founder, Home Secretary Sir Robert Peel.

Booby traps. Deadly and dangerous devices used to warn the suspect of any intruders by the sound of explosive devices.

Bookmaking. A type of gambling that usually involves taking bets on sporting events.

Boosters. Professional shoplifters who resell stolen merchandise to pawn shops or fences at usually one-half to one-fourth the original price.

Bow Street Runners. A group of English crime fighters formed by Henry Fielding during the eighteenth century.

Burden of proof. The duty to establish the validity or factuality of the charge against a person.

Burglary. A covert crime in which the criminal works during the nighttime, outside the presence of witnesses.

Burglary tools. Any instrument designed for unlawfully entering a structure.

Burn. A term used in undercover operations when an undercover agent is identified by a criminal suspect.

Bootlegging. Smuggling or manufacturing untaxed alcohol or cigarettes.

Buy-bust. When an undercover agent makes a purchase of illicit narcotics and the suspect is immediately arrested.

Buy-walk. When an undercover agent makes a purchase of illicit narcotics and the suspect is allowed to leave for the purposes of continuing the investigation.

C

Carjacking. When an armed robber forces the driver of an automobile out of the vehicle before stealing it.

Carroll Doctrine. A legal principle that enables officers to search an automobile without a search warrant provided that they have probable cause to believe it contains contraband and that the vehicle is mobile.

Chain of custody. Documentation of all who handle evidence in a criminal case.

Check kiting. Drawing cash on accounts made up of uncollected funds.

Child abuse. The physical, sexual, or emotional abuse of children.

Child molester. One who engages in some form of child sexual exploitation.

Chop shop. A secret location where auto thieves dismantle stolen vehicles for the purpose of selling the parts.

Chronic maltreatment. Occurs when a child's death is directly related to injuries caused by maltreatment or neglect occurring over an extended period.

Churning. The practice of convincing insurance customers to use the cash value of old insurance policies to pay premiums on new, more expensive policies.

Circumstantial evidence. Evidence that tends to incriminate a person without offering positive proof.

Closed files. Intelligence files that are maintained apart from criminal investigation files to prevent unauthorized inspection of data.

Code Adam. An internationally recognized "missing child" safety program in the United States (and Canada) originally created by Walmart retail stores in 1994.

Coerced-compliant confessions. The use of fear tactics that include direct threats, intimidation or actual physical abuse.

Coerced internalization. When highly suggestible and confused suspects who actually begin to believe that they are guilty of the crime they didn't commit.

Coercion. The use or threat of illegal physical means to induce a suspect to make an admission or confession.

Collation. The process of comparing texts carefully to clarify or give meaning to information.

Commercial robbery. Robbery of stores and businesses located close to major thoroughfares such as main streets, highways, and interstates.

Composite. A freehand drawing of a suspected criminal.

Computer crime. A violation of criminal law that requires some knowledge of computers for perpetration.

Computer virus. A set of illegal computer instructions designed to ruin computer hardware or software while reproducing itself in the computer program when it is executed.

Confession. Direct acknowledgment by the suspect of his or her guilt in the commission of a specific crime or as an integral part of a specific crime.

Confidence game. The criminal practice of gaining the confidence of a would-be victim for the sole purpose of swindling money from them.

Consent search. When police gain permission to search without a warrant.

Conspiracy. An agreement between two or more persons to commit a criminal act, accompanied by the commission of at least one overt act in furtherance of the crime.

Constable. A term given to peace officers during the early formation of policing in England.

Contamination of evidence. The act of adversely affecting evidence by allowing it to be tampered with or by not protecting the chain of custody.

Coordinate method. Measuring an object from two fixed points of reference.

Corpus delicti evidence. Evidence that establishes that a crime has been committed.

Cover story. A fictitious story contrived by an undercover investigator to explain his or her presence as a drug buyer to criminal suspects.

Covert information collection. A clandestine process of data collection on criminal acts that have not yet occurred but for which the investigator must prepare.

Crack. A freebase form of cocaine.

Credibility. One's ability to be believed.

Crime. Any act prohibited under criminal law that is punishable by a fine, imprisonment, or death.

Crime scene. The location where the crime took place.

Criminal intelligence. Documented information regarding past, present, or future criminal activity.

Cross-examination. A legal line of questioning in a criminal trial designed to weaken or discredit any testimony given during direct examination.

Cross-projection method. Used in indoor crime scenes, it is basically a top-down view of the crime scene where the walls of the room have been "folded" down to reveal locations of bullet holes, blood-spatter evidence, and so on.

Crystal meth. A potent form of methamphetamine.

CSA. Controlled Substances Act of 1970.

Custodial interrogation. A process of questioning a suspect when his or her liberty has been restricted to a degree that is associated with arrest.

Cybercrime. The destruction, theft or unauthorized use, modification, or copying of information, programs, services, equipment, or communication networks.

Cyber-extortion. When a computer criminal extorts money from a victim.

Cyberstalking. Preying on a victim through his or her computer.

D

D.A.R.E. Drug Abuse Resistance Education prevention program.

Data diddling. False data entry.

Data mining. The process of generating computer models to predict a terrorist's actions.

Date rape. Rape that occurs when the victim and offender are acquainted before the crime is committed.

Date rape drug. Another term for the drug Rohypnol.

Deadly force. Actions of police officers that result in the killing of a person.

Deductive reasoning. The ability to draw conclusions based on critical thinking.

Deep cover. Working undercover for extended periods of time.

Demeanor. One's persona and how one is perceived.

Demonstrative evidence. Evidence used to clarify an issue rather than to prove something.

Deoxyribonucleic acid. DNA, the genetic material used in criminal investigations.

Dependence. The degree of an illegal and addicting drug's legal use.

Designer drugs. A class of illicit drugs that are specifically designed to emulate controlled substances.

Detention. Something less than an arrest but more than a consensual encounter.

Digital imaging. Generally referring to photographs taken with a digital camera and stored on digital media.

Direct examination. A courtroom procedure whereby a witness is asked what he or she knows about an alleged offense and asked to give a brief explanation as to how he or she personally observed or knew about the incident.

Dissemination. The phase of the intelligence process whereby information is shared with other law enforcement agencies.

Diversion. The trafficking of pharmaceutical drugs to the street from normal, legal channels.

DNA technology. The science of identifying the genetic facsimile, or "blueprint," of any particular organism in every cell within each human body.

Drug courier profile. The practice of observing suspected drug traffickers to develop a pattern of behavior that would constitute legal cause for a stop and search by police.

Drug Enforcement Administration (DEA). Established in 1973, the DEA is the only federal investigative body whose sole duty it is to enforce federal drug laws in the United States.

Due process. The essential elements of fairness under the law, ensuring that no person is deprived of life, liberty, or property without notice of charges, assistance from legal counsel, a hearing, and a chance to confront one's accusers.

Duress. The imposition of restrictions on physical behavior such as prolonged interrogation and deprivation of water, food, or sleep.

Dying declaration. A statement given by a dying person that implicates the killer. The legal requirements of a dying declaration are that the victim must be rational and competent and must ultimately die of the wounds.

E

Electronic evidence. Information and data of investigative value that is stored in or transmitted by an electronic device.

Elements of a crime. The legal characteristics of a crime.

Embezzlement. A low-profile crime consisting of employees who steal large amounts of money over long periods of time.

Entrapment. When an undercover officer convinces a criminal suspect to commit a crime he or she was not predisposed to commit.

Evidence. A statement, object, or other item bearing on or establishing the point in question in a court of law.

Exclusionary rule. The legal rule that excludes evidence that has been determined to have been obtained illegally.

Exemplars. Samples, as of a suspect's handwriting.

Exhibitionism. A sexual abnormality in which the offender receives sexual gratification through revealing his or her genitals to people of the opposite sex.

Exigent circumstances. Circumstances whereby a search may be legally conducted without a warrant.

Expert systems. A process of using artificial intelligence by computers to make inferences based on available information and to draw conclusions or make recommendations to the systems operators.

Expert witness. A witness whose knowledge exceeds the knowledge of anyone with a moderate education or experience in the field.

F

Family abduction. An abduction related to a domestic or custody dispute.

Federal Bureau of Investigation. Established in 1924, the primary federal investigative bureau within the U.S. Department of Justice.

Federal Bureau of Narcotics. One of the first federal investigative bureaus, established in 1930 to combat drug trafficking.

Felony. A category of crime that is of a more serious nature than a misdemeanor, usually punishable by more than one year in prison up to the death penalty.

Fence. A person who buys and sells stolen property with criminal intent.

Fetish. A psychological disorder in which a person has a sexual attraction to a nonsexual item.

Field interview. Interviewing technique used when patrol officers happen on people or circumstances that appear suspicious but when there is not sufficient cause for arrest.

Field notes. An investigator's most personal and readily available record of the crime scene search.

Field operations. The wide array of police patrol duties.

Finished sketches. A completed crime scene sketch drawn to scale.

Fire triangle. What a fire needs to burn: heat, fuel, and oxygen.

Fixated child molester. One whose primary sexual orientation is toward children and whose sociosexual maturation develops as a result of unresolved conflicts in his or her development.

Fixed surveillance. Observing from a stationary location.

Flashback. A temporary reoccurrence from a psychedelic experience.

Flash description. An emergency radio broadcast generally made by the first officer to reach a crime scene, to other officers in the area, in which descriptions of the suspect and his or her vehicle are communicated.

Fleeing-felon rule. A legal doctrine, no longer in effect, allowing police officers to shoot suspected felons.

Flowcharting. An informational tracking system that demonstrates a chain of events or activities over a period of time.

Follow-up investigation. A continuing phase of the investigation in which information that is learned in the preliminary investigation is added to or built on.

Forensic dentistry. Scientific examination of dental records.

Forward-looking infrared. A surveillance technology that measures radiant energy in the radiant heat portion and display readings as thermographs.

Freebase. A method of ingesting cocaine in a purified form.

Frye test. A legal standard used to determine the admissibility of scientific evidence.

Fungible goods. Items such as tools, liquor, and clothing that are indistinguishable from others like them.

G

Gambling. The wagering of money or other valuables on the outcome of a game or event.

GPS. Global Positioning Satellite.

H

Hacker. A computer programmer who explores, tests, and pushes the computer to its limits, regardless of the consequences.

Hardware. The physical computer and any peripherals associated with it, such as printers, telephone modems, and external disk drives.

Hearsay evidence. Second-party statements offered to the court by a person who did not originate the statement.

Herschel, William. A pioneer in the mid-nineteenth century in the use of fingerprinting for purposes of identification.

Homicide. The unlawful killing of one human being by another.

Hoover, J. Edgar. Director of the FBI for almost 50 years.

Hot list. A cancellation bulletin for stolen credit cards.

I

Identi-kit. A computer-generated composite of a suspected criminal.

Incest. Sexual relations between children and their parents.

Inevitable discovery doctrine. A legal doctrine stating that illegally seized evidence is admissible in court provided that eventually it would have been discovered anyway.

Informant. Anyone who provides information of an investigative nature to law enforcement authorities.

Inside team. A surveillance team responsible for briefing officers concerning their actions if a crime occurs.

Intelligence gathering. The covert process of gathering information on criminal activity.

Interrogation. The systematic questioning of a person suspected of involvement in a crime for the purpose of obtaining a confession.

Interview. A relatively formal conversation conducted for the purpose of obtaining information.

Intimate or former intimate stalking. When a stalker and victim were married or divorced, current or former lovers, serious or casual sexual partners, or former sexual partners.

J

Joyriding. When a juvenile auto thief steals a car for enjoyment for short periods of time.

Judicial notice. The admissibility of certain facts without the necessity of introducing evidence.

L

Labeling. Classifying a missing child case.

Latent evidence. Evidence that is not readily visible to the naked eye.

Latent fingerprints. Fingerprints that are nonvisible unless developed through a fingerprint-lifting process.

Lineup. The police practice of allowing witnesses or victims to view several suspects for identification purposes.

Link analysis. A charting technique designed to show relationships between individuals and organizations using a graphic visual design.

Lividity. A bloodstain on the body of a deceased person.

Loansharking. Usurious loans made to people for exorbitant interest rates, whose payment is enforced by the use of violence.

M

Manslaughter. The deliberate killing of another person, characterized by either voluntary or involuntary classifications.

Markers. Items placed in crime scene photos that call attention to specific objects or enable the viewer of the photo to get a sense of the size of the object or the distance between objects.

Masquerading. The process of one person assuming the identity of an authorized computer user by acquiring the victim's items, knowledge, or characteristics.

Mara Salvatrucha. A relatively new violent Salvadoran gang that continues to spread despite law enforcement efforts; also known as MS-13.

Mass murder. The commission of four or more murders in a single incident within a short span of time.

Material evidence. Evidence shown to be important enough to influence the outcome of a criminal case.

Maximization. The exaggeration of evidence available, telling the person that the interrogator knows he or she is guilty or stressing the consequences of the crime

Medical examiner. Public official who makes official determinations of the cause and time of death in wrongful death cases.

Mens rea. Latin term meaning "guilty mind," or criminal intent.

Method of operation (MO). The behavior of the criminal during the commission of the crime.

Miranda warning. The legal guidelines to protect the rights of the accused were defined further by the Supreme Court in such cases as *Miranda.*

Misdemeanor. A less serious crime than a felony, usually punishable by less than 1 year in the county jail, a fine, or both.

MO The method of operation used by a criminal to commit a crime.

Mobile surveillance. Observing a criminal suspect from a moving vehicle.

Money laundering. A process whereby illegally earned cash is made to appear legitimate or the sources of the cash are disguised.

Motion. A written request (also called a petition) or an oral request made to the court anytime before, during, or after court proceedings.

Motivations. Reasons why someone does something.

Münchhausen syndrome by proxy. A clinical term referring to when a parent or caretaker attempts to bring medical attention to him- or herself by inducing illness in his or her children.

Murder. The purposeful, premeditated, and unlawful taking of human life by another person.

N

NATB. National Auto Theft Bureau.

NCAVC. National Center for the Analysis of Violent Crime.

NCIC. National Crime Information Center.

NCMEC. National Center for Missing and Exploited Children.

Neighborhood canvass. A door-to-door search of the area of a crime to identify witnesses.

Neighborhood Watch. A program whereby merchants and residents are encouraged to take a more proactive role in detecting and reporting activity that might be criminal in nature.

NISMART. National Incidence Studies for Missing, Abducted, Runaway and Thrownaway Children.

Noncustodial parent. A parent who does not have legal custody of his or her child.

Nonfamily abduction. When a child is removed from his or her family through force or trickery.

O

Objection. A protest to the judge regarding the "form" of the question being asked of the witness.

Obsessive-compulsive behavior. A psychological disorder referring to a compulsion in certain people to involve themselves in specific types of behavior.

Off-road machinery. Machinery such as bulldozers, tractors, wheel loaders, and excavators.

Olfactory. Pertaining to smell. A distinguishable odor may indicate a specific type of crime.

Open files. Criminal information developed for the purpose of eventually making an arrest and gaining a conviction in a court of law.

Outside team. The arrest team in a surveillance.

Overt information collection. A method of collecting information involving personal interaction with individuals, many of whom are witnesses to crimes, victims of crimes, or the suspects themselves.

P

Paper trail. Evidence in an arson case that shows motive. This includes financial records, inflated insurance coverage, little or no inventory, and excessive debts.

Pedophilia. The basis of sexual misconduct with children.

Peel, Sir Robert. The founder of the London Metropolitan Police Department during the early nineteenth century.

Penal code. Each state's criminal statutes.

Personality profile. A means of identifying the type of person responsible for a particular crime. This is accomplished by identifying the psychological and social characteristics surrounding the crime as well as the manner in which it was committed.

Pharmaceutical diversion. The act of diverting controlled drugs from legitimate channels.

Physical evidence. Any type of evidence having shape, size, or dimension.

Physiological addiction. An alteration of normal body functions that necessitates the continued presence of a drug to prevent the withdrawal syndrome.

Pigeon drop. A commonly used confidence game.

Pilferage. The stealing of merchandise.

Pinkerton, Allan. The founder of the Pinkerton National Detective Agency in 1850.

Pinkerton National Detective Agency. Founded by Allan Pinkerton in 1850, this was one of the first criminal investigation bodies to exist in the United States.

Plain-view doctrine. A legal doctrine whereby police officers have the opportunity to confiscate evidence, without a warrant, based on what they find in plain view and open to public inspection.

Plants. Preparations used to set an arson fire.

Plastic fingerprints. A fingerprint impression left when a person presses against a plastic material such as putty, wax, or tar.

Plastic workers. White-collar criminals who have experience in dealing with stolen credit cards.

Point of origin. The location on an arson scene where the fire originated.

Polygraph. A mechanical device designed to aid investigators in obtaining information.

Polymerase chain reaction (PCR). A process in which DNA strips can be rapidly reproduced for scientific analysis.

Postmortem lividity. A purplish coloration of the skin of a deceased person.

Power-assertive rapist. A rapist who attempts to demonstrate his manhood to the victim through sexual assault.

Preferential molester. A child molester who has sexual desires focusing on children and typically has a more identifiable psychological disorder.

Preliminary investigation. A term referring to the early stages of crime scene processing, usually conducted by the first officer on the crime scene.

Premeditation. Planning beforehand that shows intent to commit a criminal act.

Preponderance of the evidence. The standard of proof used in a civil matter that says that the accused is at fault if he or she contributed more than 50 percent to the cause of the dispute.

Pretrial conference. A meeting between the prosecutor and the investigator at which the prosecution strategy to a criminal case is discussed.

Preventive response. Prevention through deterrence that sometimes achieved by arresting the criminal and by aggressive prosecution.

Prima facie evidence. Evidence established by law that proves a fact in dispute.

Primary physical aggressor. If the police have sufficient reason to believe that a person, within the preceding four hours, committed an active domestic violence or spousal battery, the officer is required to arrest a person. This person is known as the primary physical aggressor.

Private eye. A private investigator.

Privileged communications rule. A legal ruling that says that certain statements are inadmissible if stated by people in certain relationships (e.g., husband and wife).

Proactive patrol. An effective police patrol tool to prevent burglary as well as many other crimes.

Proactive response. An investigative approach to crime solving in which criminal activity is investigated before it occurs.

Probable cause. The minimum amount of information necessary to cause a reasonable person to believe that a crime has been or is being committed by a particular person.

Profile. A method used to identify an offender's motivations.

Prohibition. Lasting from 1920 to 1933, the period in which the manufacture, sale, and consumption of alcoholic beverages was outlawed in the United States.

Proof. The end or net result of the evidence collection process.

Property crime. A type of crime whereby the criminal is more concerned with financial gain and less prepared for a violent altercation with the victim.

Protection orders. A legal document that orders one person to stay away from another.

Psychological dependence. Feeling that a drug is necessary to one's well-being.

Pyramid scheme. A commonly used confidence game.

Pyromaniac. A person with a psychological disorder in which sexual gratification is obtained through the setting of fires.

R

Rape. Unlawful sexual intercourse, achieved through force and without consent.

Reactive response. An approach to crime solving that addresses crimes that have already occurred, such as murder, robbery, and burglary.

Reasonable force. The amount of force that is considered reasonable to capture or subdue a criminal suspect.

Reasonable grounds. Grounds for an arrest that usually depend on the facts and circumstances surrounding the specific case.

Regressed child molester. A child molester who views the victim as a substitute for an adult partner.

Relational databases. Databases that permit fast and easy sorting of large records.

Relative judgment. When eyewitnesses compare lineup photographs or members with each other rather than with their memory of the offender.

Relevancy test. Permits, in a court of law, the admission of relevant evidence that is helpful to the trier of fact.

Relevant evidence. Evidence that is considered logical or rational.

Res geste evidence. Unplanned and spontaneous statements made by persons present at a crime scene.

Residential robbery. Robbery when an armed intruder breaks into a home and holds the residents at gun- or knifepoint.

Resistance. Physical or psychological unwillingness to comply.

RICO Act. The 1970 Racketeering Influenced and Corrupt Organizations Act.

Rigor mortis. The process of stiffening or contraction of the muscles of a deceased person after the vital functions cease.

RISS projects. Programs of the federal Regional Information Sharing System.

Rogues' gallery. A compilation of descriptions, methods of operation, hiding places, and the names of associates of known criminals in the 1850s.

Rough sketch. The initial crime scene sketch drawn by officers on the crime scene.

Runaway or lost child. A category of missing children that is the most commonly encountered by law enforcement.

S

Salvage switch. When a car thief purchases a wrecked vehicle that is unrepairable, strictly for its certificate of title and for the vehicle identification number.

Scammers. Criminals who defraud; for example, attempt to obtain prescriptions for controlled drugs.

Scanning. A procedure used in computer crime whereby the criminal presents sequentially changing information to an automated system to identify those items receiving a positive response.

Scene-conscious. When the crime scene investigator becomes aware of the crime scene situation and is prepared to take certain immediate actions.

School robberies. Instances of petty extortion or "shakedowns" of students and teachers in public schools.

Scope of the search. An officer's authority to search incident to an arrest.

Scotland Yard. One of the first criminal investigative bodies originally formed in England in the mid-nineteenth century.

Search warrant. A legal document enabling a police officer to search.

Search warrant return. An itemized inventory of all property and material seized by officers at the location of the search.

Seed money. Money required to initiate an undercover drug transaction.

Self-defense. To protect oneself from harm.

Sensational murder. A series or group of murders that arouse the interest of the general public.

Serial murder. A sequence of murders in which there is a time break between victims of two days to several months.

Serology. The scientific analysis of blood.

Sequential lineup. A police lineup method whereby people or photographs are presented to a witness one at a time.

Shaken baby syndrome. A medical term for murder of infants who are violently shaken.

Shoplifting. A common form of theft involving the taking of goods from retail stores.

Simple assault. Threats by one person to cause bodily harm or death to another or purposely inflicting bodily harm on another.

Simultaneous lineup. A lineup procedure whereby the eyewitness views all the people or photos at the same time.

Situational molester. Child molester who commits such crimes because of one of several external factors. These include intoxication, drug abuse, mood or mental conditions, or other social conditions.

Smash-and-grab robbery. A type of robbery whereby the robbers approach a car, break the window, and hold up the driver at gunpoint.

Smurfing. When money launderers go to different banks and purchase cashier's checks in denominations of less than $10,000 for the purpose of bypassing the reporting requirement.

Snitches. Amateur pilferers who are usually respectable persons who do not perceive of themselves as thieves yet are systematic shoplifters who steal merchandise for their own use rather than for resale.

Software. The medium on which information is stored, such as computer tapes and floppy disks.

Span of the fire. Physical characteristics of an arson fire such as smoke, direction, flames, and distance of travel.

Spree. Numerous acts occurring in a short span of time.

Stakeout. Another term for stationary or fixed surveillance.

Stationary surveillance. Another term for fixed surveillance or stakeout.

Stranger stalking. When the stalker and victim do not know each other.

Strategic intelligence. Information that provides the investigator with information as to the capabilities and intentions of target subjects.

Street robbery. Robbery committed on public streets and alleyways.

Stripping operation. A criminal endeavor in which stolen vehicles are disposed of.

Stop and frisk. When an officer stops and searches a person for weapons.

Substantive due process. A concept of criminal law that determines whether a statute is fair and reasonable.

Sudden infant death syndrome (SIDS). A diagnosis made when there is no other medical explanation for the abrupt death of an apparently healthy infant.

Suicide. The deliberate taking of one's own life.

Support officer. A surveillance officer, sometimes called an intelligence, cover, or tactical officer, who works in plainclothes and who works with the undercover unit but not in an undercover capacity.

Surveillance. Surreptitious observation.

Synergism. A severe physical reaction that results when a user ingests more than one type of a drug at a time.

T

Tactical intelligence. Information that furnishes the police agency with specifics about individuals, organizations, and different types of criminal activity.

Tagging. A process of altering title documents for stolen automobiles.

***Terry* doctrine.** A legal principle that states that the police have the authority to detain a person even without probable cause if the person is believed to have committed a crime.

Testimony. A statement made in response to a question or a series of questions.

Texas Rangers. One of the earliest law enforcement and criminal investigative units; formed in Texas before Texas became a state.

Thermal imaging. Technology that is used to identify heat sources that might reveal criminal activity.

Thief catchers. People recruited from the riffraff of the streets to aid law enforcement officials in locating criminals during the European Industrial Revolution.

Tin trucks. A truck used to transport parts of a stolen vehicle.

Tolerance. A physical condition that develops when a person needs increasing doses of a drug to experience its initial effects.

Tort. A personal wrong committed by one person against another.

Trace evidence. A minute or even microscopic fragment of matter such as hair or fiber that is not immediately detectable by the naked eye.

Trailers. Materials used in spreading an arson fire.

Transfer of evidence theory. The theory that whenever two objects meet, some evidence, however microscopic, may remain to demonstrate that the encounter did occur.

Triangulation method. A bird's-eye view of the crime scene using fixed objects from which to measure.

Triggering condition. An anticipated future event giving rise to a probable cause to search.

Trojan horse. A criminal computer program that automatically transfers money to an illegal account whenever a legal transaction is made.

U

Undercover officer. When a police officer poses as a criminal to gain evidence for criminal prosecution.

V

Vehicle identification number (VIN). A 17-digit number assigned to each vehicle by the manufacturer at the time of production designed to distinguish each vehicle from all others.

Vertical integration. The ability of a criminal group to control both the manufacture and wholesale distribution of illicit drugs.

VI-CAP. Violent Criminal Apprehension Program; operated by the FBI.

Vice. Generally associated with organized crime, vice crimes supply illegal goods and services.

Victimless crime. Most typically, a vice crime in which all parties of the criminal act are willing participants.

Visible fingerprints. A type of fingerprint left at a crime scene that results from being adulterated with some foreign matter, such as blood, flour, or oil.

Voyeur. A person with a psychological abnormality whereby sexual gratification is obtained by secretly observing people who are engaged in sexual activity.

W

White-collar crime. A nonviolent crime committed for financial gain and accomplished by means of deception.

Withdrawal symptoms. A series of symptoms that appear when a drug to which a user is physically addicted is stopped abruptly or severely reduced.

WITSEC Program. The federal witness security program operated by the U.S. Marshals Service.

Z

Zone search method. A searching technique; also known as the quadrant method.

index